THE HOUSE THAT WASN'T THERE

      Stephen M. Roth

Published by Macabre Factory
ISBN (Paperback): *979-8-218-88047-7*
ISBN (eBook): *TBD*

Cover design: Radu Muresan
Printed in the United States of America.

Dedication

This book is dedicated to Avery, Abigail, Adelynn, and Wyatt, as proof to follow your dreams. Also, to Belinda, the mother of the four names above and the Queen of my heart.

The House

1.

Conner

"There's a darkness in you that is slowly consuming the light of your soul. It's like a solar eclipse, except instead of it happening over a few minutes, it's been years. When we first met that light could brighten the room. It took me a while to realize there was a shadow behind that light. What was once nearly imperceptible is now the majority. You should talk to someone."

Conner Keen frowned. "I am."

"Pastor Becky doesn't count. Besides, you're not even a believer. I'm talking about a psychiatrist, like—"

Don't say PJ. Don't say PJ. Don't say...

"PJ."

Discuss his thoughts and feelings with the man that was sleeping with his wife? No thanks.

Talking with someone with a Dr. before their name felt too clinical for Connor's liking. There would be notes scribbled rapidly on a page and judgements made about what was wrong with him. Pastor Becky didn't scribble notes while they talked. She discussed her own troubles freely enough to know there was no judgement behind her kind eyes. No, he wasn't a Christian, but his mother had been. Pastor Becky reminded him of his mother. That was enough for Conner.

"I thought you liked Pastor Becky."

Carlisle's mouth spread with a mischievous smile. "She's a surprisingly intelligent woman for someone who believes in a magical sky entity floating above our heads."

The comment summarized Carlisle in a nutshell. There weren't many compliments distributed without a side of criticism served alongside. A professor of women's history at Crestview College, she knew something about intelligence. He doubted there were many rooms that she had walked into where she wasn't the smartest person in it, especially in a small valley town like Crestview. It begged the question: why had she chosen to reside in such a place? Conner had pondered the question on many occasions, only to be faced with the humbling answer. Him.

Conner Keen was originally from a small town in Kansas, only choosing to leave when outside forces required such. It was no wonder he had found himself in a town similar to that of his youth. Large metropolitan cities left his skin itching, as if he was having an allergic reaction to the plentifulness of concrete. The buildings blocked out the sun during the daytime, making him wonder who could live in a world of shadow. No, Conner was a small-town man through and through. Carlisle hadn't complained.

They were polar opposites. He knew it was cliché, but he reckoned the one about opposites attracting was fitting in their case. She was outspoken and boisterous, while his nature was quieter and more melancholic. She craved the spotlight, while he would rather avoid it like the plague for various reasons. He was blue-collar to the core, while she was more of a white-collar as a professor. She had long blond hair and an hourglass figure, while he had started shaving his head five years ago when his forehead seemed to purchase all available real estate in his hair line.

"Conner! Get your head out of the clouds and get back to work!"

He tore his attention away from the setting sun and toward the diminutive figure with an overly compensated deep voice of his foreman. Hank Little stood with his arms crossed over his chest, resting atop his generous belly. Hank was the eldest son of Eli Little, owner of The Little Construction Company, and therefore could afford to stand around watching others work. Hank looked away from Conner's steely gaze.

Conner's employment history appeared as if he had lost a wager to be employed by all the major hard labor employers in the area before his back gave out.

Without a rich daddy around to cover expenses if he got canned, Conner tightened his grip on the jackhammer and continued breaking asphalt.

An hour later, he was behind the wheel of his twenty-year-old truck that was being held together by Conner's limited mechanical ability and a prayer. It was a pleasant autumn evening in the valley, so he had the windows down to take full advantage of nature's air conditioning. The real deal hadn't worked in years.

"Why don't you just get a new truck, Conny? We can afford it, especially with my salary," Carlisle had said on more than one occasion.

He shook his head. "Maybe someday, but today ain't that day, sweetheart."

The black Chevy Silverado had been his first purchase upon fleeing the disaster his life had become in Kansas. There were bridges burning in his rearview mirror and the old Silverado had been the getaway vehicle leaving plumes of dust in his wake. Conner had stuffed a wad of cash into the salesman's hand for no questions asked. It was the last of his life savings—paying for a new identity was expensive. Luckily, the used car salesman threw in a tank of gas with a wink. That tank ran out three miles outside of Crestview. He walked the rest of the way to town and hadn't left, except to retrieve the truck, of course.

There hadn't been a destination in mind when he left Prairieview, Kansas ten years ago, only a situation he wasn't sure he could outrun. Prairieview's population was officially three-hundred fifty-four, though he remembered it as little more than a collection of people huddled around highway 4 for companionship. Teens hung out at the Conoco on the edge of town trying to convince unsuspecting travelers to buy them booze.

Crestview had reminded Conner of Prairieview at first sight, and it was more than just the similarities in the names. Crestview was a sleepy little valley town that endured on fragmented sales as tourists made their way to or from exciting destinations. Crestview's population was deceiving. In August, when the semester started at Crestview College, the town boomed by several hundred. The raucous college students livened the streets until May, when they went home for a few months. With all the students away, it became what it had been when Conner walked into town. A place where a man was buried, and new man born.

Conner pulled up to the curb in front of the Slippery Whistle and cut the engine. He had every intention of going straight home when leaving the construction site, as he had yesterday and the day before. It was the daily habit of a man who was in denial about his constant state of inebriation. Instead of driving home to his beautiful, smart, and supportive wife, he found himself parked in front of his favorite watering hole—the only other option was a biker bar on the outskirts of town. The Slippery Whistle was a few blocks from his house, making it within walking distance. The convenience of a short walk to retrieve his truck the next morning inevitably made it his bar.

Situated at the southern end of the rapidly deteriorating downtown neighborhood, The Whistle stood out amongst the crowd. Of course, that wasn't hard when most of the surrounding buildings were closed down and boarded up. The neon lights in the bar's window reflected off the other storefronts that were still under occupation. The large glowing sign above the bar with a whistle perched on the edge of a mug of beer drew attention with the other darkened storefronts. That wasn't the most unique attribute to the bar. Instead, it was the radiant pink of the building's exterior.

It took Conner a few months of residency to work up the courage to ask Vic about the bar's color. With time he would come to know the retired trucker whose body couldn't handle the grind of the road anymore, like how cautious Vic was around newcomers. It was a wonder Conner got the story at all. As the story went, Vic and Lynell Dempsey, who owned a biker bar half a mile outside of town called The Kickstand, placed a bet on the '98 AFC Championship between their favorite teams, the New York Jets and Denver Broncos.

"There's no way in hell that old man stands a chance. No way!" Vic yelled at his only competitor and friend.

"You're doubting John Elway?"

"You care to prove you're as stupid as you are ugly, Dempsey?"

Thus, the wager was born, however, neither man had the inclination to part with any finances. It would strictly involve the single thing each man held nearest and dearest, especially since both had a slew of exes and no children they knew of. The bars. They traded outlandish ideas ranging from a wild bronco being let loose in the Slippery Whistle to Lynell replacing all Bronco's memorabilia with Jets. Lynell complained that would be too expensive, plus a Jets bar in the middle of Colorado didn't make sense. Finally, they decided the winner would get to paint the loser's bar the color of his choosing.

After a twenty-three to ten win by the Broncos, Lynell went straight to the hardware store to pick out the new exterior paint for the Slippery Whistle. Flamingo was the official name for the shade.

"Pink? You've got to be kidding me, Dempsey? I can't paint my bar pink. You were supposed to pick orange, like a normal Donkey's fan, you putz! Pink!" Vic yelled at Lynell from behind his bar.

"Ah, that's why I picked it, Vic. Ain't it great? A big, tough New York Italian man with a pink bar? What would the fam back home think? You'll be humiliated. It's beautiful."

So, Vic painted his bar flamingo pink and hated every minute of it. He noticed something over the next few weeks, however. There were more women in the bar than there had been with the sad, reddish-brown brick. With a shrug of the shoulders, he decided he could stand the new paintjob if it was good for business. Twenty-five years later, the pink exterior remained.

Upon entering Conner was greeted by the sound of country music playing on the jukebox in the back corner of the room. Vic hated country music, but he catered to the locals, so country played nonstop while occupied. A long, mahogany bar stretched along one wall with a mirror to match. The mirror made the already large room appear even larger. Booths lined the other three walls, upholstered in a mixture of faded black leather and duct tape colored with a sharpie. A dozen round tables filled the center of the room. Given the autumnal season, Connor wasn't surprised to see an equal mixture of Crestview citizens and college students.

He took up residence in his usual position at the end of the bar.

Before he even settled on the stool Vic was pouring a couple of fingers of bourbon. The bartender pushed the glass across the bar. Conner downed the shot and tapped the bar top. Vic refilled the shot glass. Conner downed the shot again and tapped the bar again. Vic refilled the shot glass. This time Conner nursed the bourbon.

"You know, Conner, you've got enough bourbon in you to open up your own bar and run me out of business! Fine taste in booze, too. Can't believe they make good booze in Kansas. I only keep it on hand for you. Everybody else's drinking IPAs or some mixed BS I have to google to find out how to make. Not you. You're simple. A fine bourbon and keep em coming."

"That's right, Vic."

"Yeah, and no small talk, I remember. You think I'm going to talk to all these college kids? Hell no. They pay the bills, but if I have to hear one more story about how unfair life is for them in a small town, well, I might just pull old Bertha out from underneath the bar and off one of em. Really, I might do it."

"Uh huh."

"A real conversationalist, you are, Conner. Tell me, how did you ever land a smoke show like Carlisle, anyway?"

Conner laughed. "Lucky, I guess. For once in my life."

"Lucky, that's for sure. She's a keeper, don't know if I can say the same for you though. No offense, of course."

Vic gave the counter a cursory wipe before sliding down the bar to check on another patron. Conner was glad to see the older man go, as he preferred to do his drinking alone. He was well aware of the oxymoronic qualities of his drinking preferences. He came to a bar filled with people during its busiest time of day, yet he didn't want to be around people. If Conrad had driven home, cracked open a sixpack of beer or poured a couple shots of bourbon, it wouldn't be much of a problem. If he did that every day whether his wife was home or not, well, things became complicated. People would start to use the word alcoholic, and staging interventions.

The front door swung open, yet no one stepped inside. The raucous laughter of hormone crazed youth carried into the Slippery Whistle. Broken glass shattering on asphalt was followed by more laughter. Eventually, three college age students stepped into the bar, their faces still buzzing with booze and laughter.

Don't come over here.

Naturally, God had a sense of humor. The three already drunken men walked along the bar, only stopping when they reached the stool beside Conner.

Thanks.

Over the next ten minutes the trio got rowdier, and Conner finished his third and fourth drinks. During that span, he lost what composure he had upon walking into the bar.

He didn't consider himself a confrontational man, though he didn't shy away from them either.

Vic watched with a knowing expression as Conner simultaneously cleared his throat and turned to the college kid that could have played for Crestview College's nonexistent football team.

"I'm glad you guys are having a good time, after all this is a great town and Vic is one hell of a bartender. That being said, would the three of you mind taking the party somewhere else? That booth in the corner is a hell of a spot, if you ask me. I'm trying to enjoy my drink in peace."

"Screw you, pops," the kid said, barely turning to acknowledge Conner.

"Screw me? Screw me?"

Vic shook his head and headed to the far end of the bar, away from the three college kids and his most cantankerous regular.

"Guys, I'm only trying to enjoy my bourbon. It's good, but it's hard with the three of you getting after it like you're at Randy's kegger instead of the Slippery Whistle. Do all of us a favor and go to Randy's or shut your mouth."

"Scr—"

Linebacker didn't get to finish the first word of his sentence before a stiff left hook landed on his cheek. Conner had a rule in bar fights when facing multiple people, always hurt the biggest of the group first, then worry about the others if they worked up the courage to jump in. Luckily for him, the two smaller guys seemed dumbstruck that someone dared punch their big friend. They had become bystanders, which was fine with him.

Linebacker stumbled backward off the stool while holding a hand to his face. The twenty-something kid had a few inches and twenty pounds on Conner, though his was in the form of muscle, while Conner's was more a paunch from too many bourbons and not enough exercise. Thus, Conner couldn't let this fight last long.

There was a darkness deep within him that had been festering for ten years, consuming parts of his soul if he allowed it, leaving nothing but blackness in its wake. Over the years he had sought the counsel of spiritual types inside of organized religion and beyond the mainstream, with little effect. It was the very reason he started counseling sessions with Pastor Becky. Of course, how effective could counselling sessions be when the subject refuses to speak about his past?

Pastor Becky didn't need to hear the story of his past to determine there was a darkness clinging to his soul. She claimed it was the devil trying to take hold in his life, and he needed to fight for his very soul by becoming a righteous man, lest he be damned to the fiery depths of hell for all eternity. Yeah, she could get dramatic. Conner wasn't a righteous man, was far from it. He wasn't lost but knew exactly what he was. Demons lurked both in his past and within his soul.

Despite the knowledge of the darkness within, Conner relished the opportunity to unleash that demon. Hell or not, it felt good. That was what Conner did. He unleashed his demon on that poor college kid, as blood poured from multiple wounds. When he walked out of the bar, Linebacker was lying in a heap on the barroom floor.

2.

Conner

A voice in his head told Conner that he was fine to drive. He squelched the voice immediately, having seen firsthand what happened when fine turned out to be not so fine, after all. The deciding factor was the altercation with the three college students. Plain sober, he wouldn't have laid a hand on petulant Linebacker, likely choosing to leave the bar out of sheer annoyance. It had taken that slight edge of a few drinks to change his behavior from passive to aggressive. Therefore, he decided to walk home. It had turned into a pleasantly cool evening, and the walk home would give time to calm down before he faced Carlisle.

Upon approaching the house, however, he realized the preparation was for nought. The one-story ranch was dark, and Carlisle's Audi sedan was absent from the driveway, where she parked nine months out of the year despite having an empty garage.

Then he remembered. She had an accelerated pace night class every night for the next three weeks. It must have started tonight.

The comforting buzz of liquor caused his autopilot to engage. Something fought through the filter. There was something off about his surroundings. Then he realized it had been in his peripheral vision as he walked down the street. The sun had fully set by then, and the moon was only a small crescent in the sky. As a result, it was a dark evening, with the stars doing their best to brighten the night sky. Still, it was enough to observe a strange and unnatural oddity across the street from his house.

The Keen's lived on a rural road just outside of the downtown area, where the burbs began. On one side of the street there were houses, mostly one-story ranches with a few two-story numbers thrown in to keep it from looking cookie-cutter. On the other side were the woods that surrounded Crestview. There were times it seemed as if the trees were slowly creeping towards the houses, as if nature was trying to take back what had once been pilfered without permission. Of course, it was only his imagination that the trees seemed closer under the cover of night.

He turned to look at the woods, for what he witnessed in his peripheral vision wasn't the trees themselves, but something hidden amongst them. It wasn't a good hiding place, however, due to the height of the object within the trees. As a child, his dad hid behind his mom while playing hide and seek to the immense pleasure of Conner. During her life Maribeth stood just over five feet tall, while her husband, Douglass, stood a foot taller. With dad behind mom, dad was visible from the chin up. That was what was happening with the object hiding just beyond the woods.

The tree line running mere feet from the road was comprised mostly of conifers, with a few tall cottonwoods mixed in for good measure. Conner had ventured into the woods on a few occasions in the eight years they had owned the house. It was easy to get turned around, losing all sense of direction with the thick concentration of trees. Luckily, in the modern era, a cellphone could double as a compass, and he eventually found his way out. Considering this thick tree line, it was impossible to see the base of the object. Yet, the top of the object protruded through the canopy of the woods, like a flower desperately searching for sunlight. He knew what the object was simply by the peak poking through the trees.

It was a house.

The stiff ridge of the roof contrasted with the swaying treetops surrounding it, though both were merely different shades of black in the darkness. Amongst the roof was a protrusion with a reflective surface that confounded Conner until he realized it was a dormer window. The full moon was reflected in the window. No, that wasn't right because the moon wasn't full. There was a light on in the house.

Conner didn't know much about trees, however, as a man who had worked various construction jobs over the years, he knew a thing or two about measurements. The wooded area was lined with the invasive boxelder tree, none of which were taller than fifty feet. The rooftop of the house peaked between two mature cottonwood trees. It stood nearly as tall as those trees at the peak of its roof. At 10-12 feet per floor, that would make the house seven or eight stories.

There wasn't supposed to be a house hidden in the woods across the street. There weren't any visible signs of construction in the area. Being a residential construction worker, Conner knew a construction site when there was one. There wasn't one. It was as if the house had appeared overnight.

Just like—

"Beautiful night, isn't it?"

He was still standing in his driveway, staring in befuddlement at the incomprehensibly tall house when the voice startled him. All of his surroundings had ceased to exist while he studied the house that wasn't supposed to be there. Conner turned in the direction of the voice.

It was his neighbor, Parker Wellington Jr., who was as pretentious as his name implied. Parker, to his credit, seemed aware of the connotations of snobbery associated with his name. To counteract this, he insisted on being referred to as PJ. An unfortunate choice considering PJ's profession. The thirty-something year old was a psychology professor at Crestview College, the same college where Carlisle taught.

According to her, the professor insisted the kids called him Professor PJ in class.

PJ was a constant presence on Crestview Way, the street where they resided. He was head of the homeowner's association, which he founded despite being told repeatedly by Conner and others on the street it wasn't necessary. It was also as if the man was the only member of the neighborhood watch. Stand outside your house for more than a couple of minutes, and PJ would manifest with a conversation, usually about what rule wasn't being followed according to the homeowner's association.

That was all fine with Conner. He could ignore the uptight prude. What he couldn't ignore was the constant presence around Conner's own home, most notably, his wife. On multiple occasions, he had come home to find PJ in his living room talking with Carlisle. The other man looked incredibly comfortable in a house that wasn't his own, with socked feet on the coffee table and a mug of herbal tea in his hand. The two would be deep in conversation upon Conner's arrival. Carlisle seemed disappointed by the sudden appearance of her husband, as if it meant the end of an intellectual conversation and back to living with a neanderthal. She had pointed out that he was threatened by PJ's intelligence. Sure, he was. The man could provide his wife with something he never would be able to, an intellectual conversation with someone on her level. Above all, Conner just didn't like the guy and was increasingly frustrated that his wife did.

"Do you see something in the trees, PJ?" he asked, turning back to look at the roof peeking through the treetops.

"Well, Conner, the woods in the Crestview Valley are teeming with things one might see. You have your predatory animals, of course, cougars, black bears, the gray wolf, bobcat, coyotes, just to name a few. Then you have your small mammals, such as the raccoon, North American porcupine, jackrabbit, ground squirrel. Now, we have been known to have some elk and even a moose or two, believe it or not. There are people, the uneducated variety, of course, claiming to have seen a bipedal ape in this area, commonly known as the sasquatch. The name sasquatch comes, of course, from the Salish word, meaning 'wild man.' If it was one of those, well, I know a *great* psychologist I can refer you to."

"No, it wasn't any of that. It's in the treetops. Look."

PJ turned to the woods and looked.

"I don't see anything unusual, Conner."

"You don't see it? It's poking out right above the treetops."

This time PJ came up directly beside Conner, so he had the same vantage point, and looked again. He shook his head.

"Nothing. What do you see?"

"Have there been any construction projects around here that you know about?" Conner asked, ignoring PJ's question.

"On this street? No, trust me, I'd know."

"Thanks, PJ," he said, patting the other man on the back and continued his walk up the driveway.

"Hey, what do you think you saw?" PJ called after him.

"It was probably nothing, my imagination, I guess."

PJ was standing in the driveway, looking at the tree line when Conner closed the front door.

The house was dark as he walked through, confirming what he already knew. Carlisle wasn't home. There was a white board hanging from a magnet on the fridge, usually it held either a grocery list or a to-do list belonging to his wife. Tonight, there was a note scrawled in Carlisle's neat handwriting. It read:

Night classes started tonight. I figured you'd forget and wouldn't pick anything up from the bar on your way home (that's right, I know about that). There's a salad I threw together and some leftover chicken breast from last night's dinner. Throw the chicken on the salad and voila, dinner is served. Don't drink your dinner, please.

Love,
Carlisle

Bear, a five-year-old Newfoundland, was staring up at Conner from the doorway when he finished reading the note. He fed Bear, then fed himself, taking care to follow Carlisle's instructions, though he did pour a tall glass of bourbon. She requested he not drink his dinner, but she hadn't said anything about drinking with dinner. He smiled at his cleverness, forgetting he was breaking his own rule. Drinking alone was something alcoholics did. Social drinking, now that was alright.

In the expansive kitchen it was hard to discern who was the louder eater, man or dog.

The master bedroom was dark and cold when Conner entered, much like the marriage of the couple sharing the room. It hadn't always been that way. Their relationship had been filled with heat and passion in the early stages. He had been a mysterious stranger in a new town, while Carlisle was in her third-year teaching at Crestview College. There had been no intention of staying in the small valley town for the rest of his life, let alone ten years. He was simply trying to raise the funds to fix the truck and move further west. The further from Kansas the better.

There was a large problem with raising funds. Crestview was a tightknit community that watched out for each other, and as a result was wary of strangers, especially if there was a darkness in the eyes of that stranger. He applied for everything from construction work to fast food and the consensus was the same. Nobody would hire him for a permanent job. Instead, Conner became a fixture around the downtown area where he was staying in a hotel he could barely afford doing odd handyman jobs. Paint over the graffiti on the exterior wall of The Donut Hut one day and unclog a sink at an elderly woman's house the next.

Then he received a call from a woman having a problem with her dryer. Conner hadn't ever worked on a dryer before, though with the power of YouTube, he could figure anything out. He had been taken aback by the woman's beauty. Long blond hair that reminded him of Kansas wheatfields, and piercing blue-gray eyes that seemed able to cut through steel. All those eyes did though was cut through his heart. She showed him the dryer then left him to work. Five minutes later, she was back asking him if he wanted anything to drink. The call had come in before he had his morning coffee, and he told her as much. She was back five minutes later with two cups of coffee. She stayed and talked while he worked on the dryer. They talked about their lives, with her being very open and him being rather vague. By the time he told her the good news—she needed a new heating coil, and he knew where to get it—he had realized she was far out of his league. That didn't stop her from calling him a week later.

She had been vague about what the problem was, which was fine. As a handyman, Conner had enough tools in his newly fixed truck to work on just about anything. Tools wouldn't be necessary that time around, however, as Carlisle kissed him as soon as the door opened. A haze of passion overtook him, as she had been the only thing on his mind since he left her house. When he left the bedroom an hour later, he realized they had left the front door open. He closed it, while giving the old lady across the street a good show.

Carlisle never had to call a handyman again. Instead, she called her boyfriend.

It had taken Conner six months to realize they spent more time having sex than anything else. Their conversations hadn't progressed past the superficial level that had been established on that first meeting. He knew her favorite color—black—but not her favorite aspect of teaching. He knew she had a younger sister, but not the reason she hadn't spoken to Kaitlyn in years. She wasn't stimulated by his mind. She didn't think of him as someone who could stimulate her brain, only her sexual appetite.

If she didn't think of him as an intellectual person, then he would have to prove himself worthy. With time Conner broached the subjects that seemed avoided or otherwise taboo. It was a risk, he knew. What if she was turned off by this new side of him that wasn't a walking penis existing only for her pleasure? What if he said something embarrassingly stupid while trying to prove his mental faculties were intact? It didn't matter. The conversations only brought them closer together, making love where once had been only lust.

In the early years, it seemed they were growing closer together every day. Soon they would encompass one body and be of one mind. It had seemed as if those days would never end. Then they did. It hadn't been a sudden occurrence, such as a house crumbling during an earthquake, but rather like the eventual withering of a house due to the strength of the wind. In the day-to-day grind of life, they had reverted back to their comfort level, which was simply a physical relationship.

Was it because someone else was stimulating her intellectual side? Or was it something more?

Bear pawed at something on the hardwood floor of the bedroom. The object glistened with slobber in the light of the lamp on the bedside table. Conner picked it up and looked at it for a long time.

It was a tie clip. He was concerned for two reasons. First, he didn't own a single tie. Second, it had the initials *PJ* engraved into the metal.

3.

Conner

The next morning, Conner was greeted by the pounding of a monumental headache. After finding the tie clip, he had been unable to face the tainted sanctity of their bedroom. He ended up in the living room finishing a bottle of bourbon too good to be drunk in such high volume. Yet he hadn't stopped, couldn't stop. He sat in the living room with the tie clip in his hands, staring at the initials, until the bottle was empty. When he went to bed that night Carlisle still wasn't home.

He felt her come to bed at some point in the night. He was too far into the dream world to look at a clock, though it felt later than on other such occasions. She didn't peck him on the cheek or cuddle, instead she curled up facing the opposite direction. The cold, callousness she exuded even while asleep was telling in more ways than one.

The other side of the bed was empty upon waking, making him wonder if the bitterly cold woman that joined him in his sleep was a figment of his imagination. The woman he fell in love with ten years ago wasn't cold, nor callous, but warm and blunt. He knew another woman hadn't traded places with his wife, of course. It had been the same woman he had slept with for the past six months to a year. Had he become so used to the lack of intimacy that he didn't recognize that there was a problem?

The smell of freshly brewed coffee finally brought Conner out of the bedroom. Carlisle was in the kitchen filling her thermos with hot coffee. Every morning, she brewed a large pot of coffee, which was enough to fill her thermos and give him a mug of coffee before leaving for work. That morning was different, however, the large pot Carlisle filled every morning without fail was empty.

"How was your class last night?" he asked, as he prepared another, smaller pot of coffee.

"Okay. One of the girls was having trouble with one of the guys in class, so I stayed late to talk with her. There's always a couple of guys that sign up that are only interested in meeting girls, or they think it's going to be an easy A. Obviously, they've never met me."

"Join the club."

She raised an eyebrow. "Someone's a little grumpy this morning. Funny, because it seemed like you were sleeping like a hibernating grizzly bear. I know you don't like these night classes; I don't like them either, but it's the only time I have free this semester. I also think it's important to give working women an opportunity to improve themselves. Just because you don't like it, don't take it out on me. It's juvenile."

"It's not that. It's just…"

"What? I can't stand around here waiting, my office hours start in ten minutes. You know how busy this time of year is."

Her bag was slung across her hip, thermos in hand. Carlisle wasn't physically in the car heading to work, but mentally, well, that was another story.

"Forget it. We'll talk about it later."

Conner looked down at the tie clip in the closed fist of his hand. *PJ.*

He could feel the tie clip burning a hole in his pocket as he walked to his truck. With the emotions of the morning, Conner had lost track of time and was now running late for work as a result. Carlisle had always been forthright in their relationship. The concept of her deceiving him wasn't computing in his head. Whether it was with words or with actions, he never had to wonder about her thoughts or emotions. That had changed.

A moderate breeze brought the scent of pine to his nostrils from the woods. Conner stopped in the empty driveway. His truck was still parked in the Slippery Whistle's parking lot. Now he was running really late.

The trees swayed under the strain of the wind. In the darkness the previous night, it had been hard to make out what he had been looking at. Luckily, he had spent ten years on and off working residential construction. He knew a house when he saw one. To an untrained eye, like PJ, it had only been different shades of black in the dark.

There was no mistaking it in the light of day, there was a house across the street, hidden in the woods. As the wind continued to blow the treetops back and forth, he was able to see more details of the house. The shingles were a normal flat black with little adornment. In the daylight, he could tell there wasn't a traditional ridge at the top of the roof. Instead, the roof appeared flat on the top, without the traditional peak. Two dormers were visible twenty feet apart, trimmed in what appeared to be wood that had been painted black. The base color of the house was white. A black and white house? It was a modern touch, and he instantly felt drawn to see the rest of the house.

He had taken two steps down the driveway when motion in his peripheral vision caught his attention. It was PJ. The other man looked briefly in the direction of the woods before getting in his Porsche Boxter and pulling out of his driveway.

Conner realized he also had to leave.

The house that wasn't there was at the forefront of Conner's mind during his day at the construction site. The construction company he worked for had regular safety briefings to comply with regulations. In those safety briefings they listened to the company's safety officer talk about how a distracted worker was a dangerous worker. It was important that all outside issued be kept off the jobsite, otherwise accidents would inevitably occur. When accidents occur, people get hurt. Despite his distracted state of mind, he managed to avoid injuring himself or anyone else.

What do you think you saw?

It was the wording of the question that bothered him. What do you think you saw, not what did you see? It was plain the psychology professor had been playing psychologist with him last night. It wasn't as if Conner had a habit of imagining things. He wasn't seeing houses everywhere he went where there shouldn't have been. It was a single house hidden in the woods. Why was that so hard for PJ to see?

The house was clearly visible in the light of day. Conner saw PJ looking directly at the house and not seeing it. Everything was as it should be in the mind of the psychologist that may or may not have been sleeping with his wife. Was this some kind of ploy to make him seem unstable? What would PJ have to gain from that?

Conner was well aware that his intellectual prowess wasn't sufficient to satisfy his wife's intellectual needs. It was his saving grace that she worked at a respected university where she was able to have conversations with others that were closer to her own IQ level. If his limited mental faculties were proven to be impaired to the point that he had started to imagine things, what would that do to their seemingly withering relationship?

Two things were clear by the time he left the jobsite for the day. He was putting too much stock into a man's point of view that he didn't even like, and he needed to have a conversation with Carlisle. He needed confirmation that the house was there. He needed to know she could see the house that wasn't there.

Conner paced the living room from the fireplace to the coffee table and back again. The time passed as if he was watching sand fall in an hourglass. It passed especially slowly because he had broken his routine of drinking at the Slippery Whistle. Despite desperately wanting a drink, he knew how it would make him look if Carlisle failed to see the house, as PJ had. He didn't want to look like a drunken fool who was seeing things. A regular fool would work fine.

A tremor went through his hands. It had started earlier in the evening, just after a dinner of leftover pot roast and veggies, washed down with a can of soda. His body had balked at the idea of a sugary drink instead of the caramel notes of bourbon. Tonight, several things were happening. He would come to grips with his sanity by confronting his wife about the house. In the meantime, the slow realization that he was an alcoholic was settling in, despite his attempts to define an alcoholic as something other than what he was.

He guzzled water from a large plastic cup from Bad Byron's BBQ that had a pig wearing an apron. Somewhere along the road he had heard alcohol withdrawal was due to dehydration. He hadn't bothered to look into the veracity of the claim, as he just needed something to do with his hands. Dealing with the reality of being an alcoholic was for another day. Today was about proving his eyes weren't deceiving him.

Headlights illuminated the front window of the house. Conner put the cup down on the coffee table and was out the front door before Carlisle was out of her vehicle. As he walked briskly to her car, he noticed PJ pulling into the driveway next door. *Forget about him, focus on not looking like a crazy person.*

"What's going on, Conny? Is something wrong?" Carlisle asked as she got out of the car.

"Nothing, Car, I just had a question for you is all."

"And it couldn't wait until I was inside? What is so important that you couldn't wait until I've put my bag and thermos down? Are you drunk?"

He tried to suppress a smile and failed.

"No, I knew you'd think that, so I haven't had anything to drink tonight, especially after what I'm going to ask you. PJ didn't see it last night, but I don't trust that guy. I trust you."

"Okay…" Carlisle said in a long, drawn-out voice.

"Turn around and face the woods."

She sighed but did as he asked. He could tell she realized how important this was to him, and he loved her even more for it.

"Look up at the trees right across from our house. Do you see it? Sticking up above the treetops? You see it, don't you?"

The moon was a tiny sliver just as it had been the night before, yet the stars were really luminescent. Overall, it was a much brighter night than last night. If there was a house across the street, Carlisle would see it. After all, Conner could see it from where he stood in the driveway. He knew she wouldn't let him down.

Then she let him down.

"Well, it's beautiful the way the moonlight is shining down on the canopy of the woods, especially with the mountains in the background. It looks like something they put on postcards for people that live in boring places, like Kansas," she said, laughing at the jab she had taken at his old home.

The smile faded from her face when she saw that he wasn't amused.

"What? You're serious? What is it?"

There were tears welling in Conner's eyes. His voice broke when he spoke.

"You don't see it, but for some reason, I see it."

She put a hand on his chest. "Conny, you're scaring me. What do you see?"

"In the woods, hidden by the trees so you can only see the rooftop above the canopy. I see a house. Carlisle, I see a house."

Carlisle turned to look at the woods again, then looked back at him. There was doubt in her eyes. Is this a joke? The question was written all over her face. The tears in his eyes answered the unspoken question.

She turned around, back to the woods. He could see her determination to see the house that wasn't there, the house that was only there for Conner. After five minutes, he took her by the arm and led her inside.

Tears moistened both of their cheeks, though for different reasons. Naturally, Carlisle was worried about her husband's sanity, while Conner's tears were rooted in fear. Fear that his past was coming back to haunt him.

4.

Conner

Conner exited the truck with a bottle of water in one hand and his phone in the other. A compass app was open on the phone's screen, just in case he got turned around in the woods. The house didn't appear to be deep in the woods, though looks could be deceiving. Deception seemed to be at the forefront of its game. If it was there. He needed to know if it was truly there, and that couldn't be accomplished by standing in his own driveway.

The decision had been made while pretending to work on the construction site. He needed to see the house, truly *see* the house. There would be no more staring into the trees, wondering if it was a figment of his imagination or a deception planned by the universe at his expense.

He crossed the street with deliberate steps, not bothering to look in either direction. His eyes were solely focused on the trees on the other side of the street. A car door slammed behind him. Somehow, he knew it was PJ before he heard the voice calling his name. Conner ignored the other man. If the subject came up later, say when PJ talked to Carlisle, he would feign ignorance. He had been focused on taking a hike and hadn't heard his neighbor calling his name. It was a simple lie, and far better than explaining the truth until he had answers.

I couldn't see it, but she saw a house. A house that wasn't there. A house that couldn't be there.

His mind was reaching to make connections that weren't there at this juncture. Jumping to conclusions without proper information was ill-advised. He wasn't even sure there was a house hidden in the woods. Conclusions could be drawn when he had laid eyes on the house. Only then would he come to grips with the meaning behind the house and the link to his past. A past thought buried far from view of his current life. A past left behind in another state that included another life his wife didn't know about.

Later.

Conner pushed the branches of two conifers out of his way and stepped into the woods. He let go of the branches, letting the trees overtake him. He stood there for a full minute taking in his surroundings. The darkness was like an unsuspecting force that sat atop his chest, causing his respiration to quicken in short, shallow breaths that did nothing to calm his nerves. In an instant he knew it had been a mistake to search for the house near the setting of the sun. Inside the Crestview woods it was as if night had already fallen, despite being an hour away from sunset. Yet, he wouldn't turn back despite only being a mere step away from the safety of the known. With another step, he confirmed that decision, forging a new path into the unknown.

Despite living in a state that seemed to be plagued by the "outdoorsy type" driving around in a Jeep while wearing plaid, Conner wasn't much of an outdoorsman. As a blue-collar worker, he spent most of his working life outdoors underneath the scorching sun in the summer and battling bitter windchills in the winter. It was for that reason he spent his leisure time doing activities that were leisurely, like sitting on the couch with a bourbon instead of wandering around in the woods, trying in vain not to get lost in the woods. Sure, he had a tan that fooled people into thinking he enjoyed the outdoors, but that was only a biproduct of his job.

TV and YouTube were filled with so-called survival experts inundating the web with their tips and experiences. His personal favorite was a southerner from an "undisclosed location" named Machete Mike. Conner had good reason to believe the undisclosed location was somewhere in the state of Alabama, considering Mike's affinity for wearing University of Alabama gear and yelling, "Roll Tide!" when a makeshift trap caught its prey. Conner watched the show purely for the entertainment value, knowing he would never be forced into a situation where the information would be deemed applicable. Despite having ventured only feet into the woods across from his house before tonight, he found himself in such a situation. It was a simple piece of advice spoken by Machete Man himself. "Now, when you done find yourself lost in woods, like these here. Boy, you'll think you're about to meet the big man, and I'm not talking about Nick Saban. Now, what you'll want to do is this. Find yourself a tree, say ten, maybe fifteen feet, down the way. Then walk to it. Simple as that. Then do it again. Now, it won't be as true as having a good old compass, but it'll get you going in a fairly straight line, I reckon."

Conner followed Machete Mike's advice, since he was trying to travel in a straight line anyway. Obviously, he wasn't in a self-rescue situation with his life in imminent danger, however, his psychological state of mind was very much in danger. Therefore, it was as close to a self-rescue situation as the middle-aged construction worker would come. He preferred to leave the danger in his past, where it belonged. Buried, like all his other sins.

The sound of a branch snapping somewhere around him brought his attention back to his surroundings.

His eyes darted from tree to tree, from shrub to shrub, looking for anything out of the ordinary. Nothing.

He shook his head as he started walking again. There weren't heavily wooded areas where he was from in Kansas. The sounds of the woodlands weren't ingrained into his auditory vocabulary as it was for someone who spent time surrounded by nature. The sound of a twig snapping might be as simple as a squirrel jumping down from a tree or as dangerous as a stranger following your backtrail from fifteen feet away.

While he didn't have experience with the outdoors, he did have experience in spotting a tail. There was definitely someone following him from a distance. They seemed to be voyeuristic in nature, otherwise they would have acted as soon as Conner stepped into the woodlands. No witnesses. No, this person was only interested in why he had ventured into the woods.

"Go away, PJ! I'm not in the mood," he said as he spun around.

No PJ. In fact, there wasn't anyone behind him.

Conner turned around and started walking again. A few minutes later, there was no sign of the house. Had he imagined the entire thing? Was his mind playing tricks on him? His mind was tired from the day-to-day grind of working construction five, sometimes six days a week. Perhaps that tired mind was trying to tell him it was time for a vacation. It had been a few years since he had gotten away with Carlisle. Then again, maybe it was something else, like suppressed guilt from his past.

No, don't go there.

Conner had been following Machete Mike's sage advice, while also taking the compass into account. He looked down at the compass again. The needle on the digital compass spun around in a circle, with startling rapidity. There was something wrong with the app, obviously. It didn't matter; he was sure he had been walking in a straight line. Yet, he was surprised he hadn't reached the house. It couldn't have been more than a few hundred feet into the woodland area. He should have reached it by now.

The air was moist. He could hear the rushing of water traveling at a high rate of speed.

He pushed the branches of two tall conifers aside and stepped between them. A clearing lay before him that he hadn't realized existed. Bear had a habit of chasing the local wildlife on occasion, forcing Conner to venture briefly into the woods. He had no recollection of encountering a clearing before, neither did he remember Carlisle—who enjoyed hiking on a regular basis—mentioning one either.

He stopped.

"It really does exist."

He shook his head.

Tree branches brushed the front exterior of the house. It was almost as if the house had been plucked from another location and placed there via a helicopter from the sky. Of course, that was impossible. There had to be a road somewhere around the house, or else the construction crew would have to haul all the tools and construction equipment through the woods. He couldn't imagine making the trek he had just made with his hands filled with all the materials he would need to build a house. No, there had to be a road.

Five minutes later, Conner returned to his starting point, having circled the house and finding no road of any kind, paved or unpaved. It was a confounding situation, yet he reminded himself that this wasn't about the road but the house itself.

The house was constructed of painted white brick, which was startling in contrast to the darkness provided by the canopy overhead. Each level of the house had four windows on the front side of the house, with two on the left side of the front door and two on the right side. All the trim work was done in black, giving the house a modern look that would please most buyers. He counted the stories. Seven stories, plus what appeared to be an attic of some kind on the top level. Eight stories in all.

Why would someone build an eight-story house in the middle of the woods? With no road access, no less.

You know the answer.

His attention was drawn to the front door. It was painted a crimson color that stood out in contrast to the white and black of the rest of the house. Blood red. It symbolized blood. Blood as penance for your sins, Conner.

I couldn't see it, but she saw a house. A house that wasn't there. A house that couldn't be there.

Conner backed up as far as he could. He switched his phone to the camara setting and snapped two quick pictures. Then he switched back to the compass app and retraced his steps.

Perplexingly, he was out of the woods in less than five minutes.

When he emerged from the woodlands night had fallen. It had taken no more than thirty minutes to find the house, plus ten minutes spent surveying the house, and another five minutes for the walk back. When he looked at the time on his phone as he crossed the street, however, three hours had elapsed. Had he been lost in the woods longer than he remembered? Did he hit his head on a tree branch causing him to black out? Where had the lost time gone? There weren't any answers to these questions, at least not yet.

Carlisle's Audi was in the driveway, proving that hours had passed instead of minutes. He drained the bottled water as he walked up the driveway. His throat was parched, though he didn't know why. There were voices coming from inside the house as he approached, both were familiar. One belonged to his wife, while the other was his neighbor, PJ. Absentmindedly, he squeezed the bottle in his hands, causing the cap to shoot off under the increased pressure. He discarded the bottle in the recycling bin next to the garage, deciding he would find the cap when there was sufficient light.

Conner kept the steps of his work boots light as he entered the house.

"Why would he go into the woods? That doesn't make any sense," Carlisle said from the living room.

"Maybe he wanted to take a hike? I've done it before, not when night is about to fall, but I've done it."

PJ.

"We're talking about Conner, PJ. He doesn't hike. All he wants to do after work is drink bourbon."

"He said he saw something Monday night, maybe he went investigating? I don't know, I just thought you should know. His behavior wasn't typical and with night looming, I figured you should know. Plus, I hadn't seen him return. Not that I was watching the neighborhood or anything."

"Thanks, PJ. You've been—"

Conner chose that moment to enter the living room. Carlisle and PJ turned to look at him as if they had been caught in a devious act of betrayal. Yet they were fully clothed and were ten feet apart. PJ stood in the middle of the room, as if he had entered the house only minutes prior. Carlisle sat in her usual spot on the sofa, with a blanket covering her lap, a bookmarked book in her lap, and a can of Dr. Pepper—her chosen guilty pleasure—on the end table. Clearly nothing nefarious had been going on.

"I'll leave you two alone. Good to see you again, Conner," PJ said, excusing himself.

Carlisle waited until they were alone. "Where were you? PJ said you went walking into the woods. That you ignored him when he called to you."

"I went looking for that house."

She raised an eyebrow. "You mean the house you could see in the woods, but I couldn't?"

"Yes. I found it."

"Okay…"

"I took a picture."

He pulled out his phone and opened up his photos. He handed Carlisle the phone without looking at the picture. She looked at it for a long time before speaking.

"What am I supposed to see, Conny? I only see trees."

It couldn't be.

He took the phone back and stared at the picture.

He had taken a picture of the house, he knew he had. But the image showed trees, shrubs, and the glowing eyes of an owl. Nothing more. No house.

He looked from the phone to Carlisle and back.

I couldn't see it, but she saw a house. A house that wasn't there. A house that couldn't be there.

"Maybe you should talk to PJ, Conny."
He stared at her.
"I'm scared for you."
Conner was too, but for a very different reason.

5.

Conner

"We're not going the right way. There's nothing back here, I'm telling you."

"It's here, trust me," Conner said, seeming to sound more confident than he felt.

The previous twenty-four hours had been filled with a myriad of emotions for him. Fear and trepidation had filled him upon realizing not only was his wife unable to see the house, but it hadn't appeared in the photo. He hadn't been faced with a situation where he was the one questioning his sanity, in the past he questioned everyone else's sanity except his own. Soon after, however, a stubborn determination settled upon him. Carlisle had only looked at the house from the driveway, where the exterior could be missed due to the heavy foliage. She needed to see the house, that was all.

It was obvious that his wife and PJ were keeping a secret. Conveniently, they were both gone in the evenings, arriving home at the same time. He had seen them together more times than he could count in the previous six months. Had they learned about his past and were now using it in a malicious manner? Perhaps getting him out of the way so they could be together?

He wasn't losing his sanity. He was losing his wife.

The thought turned fear into panic. That couldn't be allowed to happen.

He grabbed her by the wrist, with his body seeming to move on its own accord. Bear barked at his sudden movement, then watched him intently. Carlisle's eyes appeared as wide as flying saucers on a clear night as she turned to him in surprise. The fear pulsated through her body like a vibration inadvertently sent into his hand. She looked down at his hand digging into her wrist like it was the hand of a stranger. When she wrenched her arm free, he let her.

There were two different sides to Conner Keen, both competing for dominion over the host. One side had been mortified at the fear in Carlisle's face caused by his own hand, while the other side had been disturbingly pleased with her reaction. Fear was a deterrent, after all.

"Why don't we do it tomorrow, Conny? It's late and I'm tired. Aren't you tired?" she said softly as she put a hand on his chest.

After work he went about his normal routine. He stopped by the Slippery Whistle for a glass or two of bourbon. Then he came home and fed Bear his dinner, however, Conner was unable to eat because of the knot that had formed in the pit of his stomach. The trouble with a job that occupies the body but not the mind was that it allowed the mind to wonder. His mind had wondered across the state line to Kansas, to a past he thought he had left behind.

He knew that if there was something hidden in the woods across the street, Carlisle would know about it. Unlike Conner, she enjoyed the outdoors. She had been hiking through these very woods more times than he could count. Of course, she always invited him to come along, but it wasn't something he enjoyed. Plus, he knew somehow that it was time she spent inside her own mind, and he would get in the way of the tranquility she found with nature. Thanks to the night classes she had been teaching as of late, Carlisle hadn't been on a hike since the house appeared. Therefore, she might be surprised by the house's appearance.

"What's been going on with you recently, Conny? It's like I'm living with a stranger."

"Would you be acting like yourself if everyone around you thought you were seeing things? That you might be crazy? I don't think so."

She stopped walking and turned to look at him. "It's not that. This whole thing with the house is weird, sure, but that's not what I'm talking about. Recently, I've been getting the impression there's something you're not telling me, and I'm not talking about drinking. Actually, that has something to do with it, subconsciously, I think, but I'm not talking about the drinking itself. It's the reason for the drinking that I'm after. The reason you've never told me about your past, just vague details that could be from anyone's past. There's no personality to it, nothing that links you to any of it. You're lacking substance, is what I'm trying to say. In your past at least. There's something there that you're suppressing, something unimaginable that you went through.

"You know all about my past, Conny. You know how hard it was leaving an abusive marriage when I thought I was nothing. You know I never thought much of myself until I left Michael. Then I found myself here in the Colorado mountains, and I *found* myself. Then you found me. You know it all. What do I know about you? You're from Kansas, where something happened that you don't want to talk about, and you can be kind of a jerk at times. I have a feeling you were a good man once upon a time, instead of a guy going through the motions, and not valuing whether he's good or bad.

"If that's all I get, well, that's fine. I've lived this long with this version of Conner Keen; I could go a lifetime. I just wish you trusted me enough to let me in."

"Nothing happened in Kansas," he lied.

"See? There it is."

"What?"

"The jerk in you," she said and walked off into the trees.

"You really think I'm a jerk?" Conner said five minutes later, as they continued in the direction of the house.

"I know for a fact that this isn't the first time the subject has been brought to your attention, so don't act so surprised. Don't get me wrong, I think you're a good man at your heart, but you're too selfish. It never occurred to you that keeping your past from me would hurt me. You've isolated yourself inside our marriage. We're a team."

"I'm sorry, Carlisle. I—"

"No." She shook her head. "This isn't something that a simple 'I'm sorry, I love you,' will fix. Actions, Conner. I need actions. A change of heart. Proof. Give me something."

Hearing her call him by his given name had more effect than the rest of her speech. She didn't like his given name, found it too sophisticated for an unrefined, blue-collar worker such as himself. It was like punctuating a point with a kick to the testicles instead of an exclamation. Conner was reminded of one of the few competent phrases from an absurdly incompetent former boss of his, "Never start an argument with someone that's smarter than you, boy, and if you do, don't be dumb enough to stay in it." Carlisle was immeasurably smarter than him, and they both knew it. It was his fault for staying in the argument.

The sun was settling fast on the horizon outside of the woods, causing it to appear as if full night had already fallen underneath the canopy. An owl hooted overhead, signaling the beginning of its reign through the darkness. Carlisle had fallen back and was now walking in perfect harmonization with her husband. It was an irony he chose to keep to himself given his current status in the canine house.

They both had their phones in their hands with the flashlight function switched on. He also had the compass app open for reference. This time he was keeping an eye on the compass for any irregularities, such as the spinning needle that had happened when he neared the house. Next to him, Carlisle looked bored, as if she was ready to turn back and call off what seemed to be an ill-advised trek into the woods.

It was too soon, however, for such thoughts. On his previous venture into the woodland area, he had been ready to turn back, positive that the house that wasn't there surely wasn't there. Then there it was.

The sound of water rushing downstream, slapping against rocks in its wake carried to his ears.

The flashlight flickered in his hand. He glanced at his wife. She too was having trouble with the flashlight on her phone. She held it up to her face and stared at it. She turned the flashlight off and then on again. It continued to flicker.

Conner looked at his own phone. The needle of the compass was spinning rapidly in a circle. Meanwhile, the flashlight continued to flicker.

"We're almost there," he said, more to himself than to Carlisle.

"How do you know?"

"This happened last time."

"Maybe we should go back."

He shook his head and continued walking.

He pushed through the same two conifer trees, before coming into a clearing. There it was. The house.

It was even more majestic in the near darkness than it had been the previous evening with more light. Except that wasn't quite right, the house appeared to be emitting a light source of its own. Of course, that was aside from the faint glow of the porch light that barely seemed capable of illuminating the grass beyond the front porch. The white brick was reflecting light from the moon onto the woodlands that surrounded it. Conner looked at the sky for the moon and found that it wasn't visible. The house was radiating its own light as if it were a living creature.

No, that can't be right.

Conner had been around a construction site, thanks to an attitude that wasn't suitable for a cubicle and a resume so flimsy it would disintegrate if inspected thoroughly. He didn't know about every trick of the trade, yet he had seen a thing or two in his time. It was likely as simple as a glow in the dark paint, that charged during the daytime in the sun's rays, giving it the power it required to illuminate. It would take more than a cheap coat of gimmicky paint to fool him.

"What are you looking at?" Carlisle asked, pushing through the bushes to stand beside him.

"The house, it's glowing."

"Really? Like a ghost house? Creepy."

"No, It's really something. Like it created its own light source to brighten the darkness in the clearing. It's probably just a glow in the dark paint or something, but…"

"Clearing? We're in the middle of the woods, Conny, surrounded by trees, and you're talking about a glow in the dark house in a clearing. Honey, I love you, but you need help. Like, seriously, need help."

"You still don't see it?" he asked, turning to his wife.

She shook her head.

Conner picked up a small branch from the ground and threw it at the house. He wanted to prove a point, but the frustration that had been building for days was boiling over. The stick clattered against the blackened window, then fell into shrubs running alongside the house. He turned back to his wife.

"See?"

"What? You throwing a stick against a tree? "Yes, I saw that," she said, with the light from the house glowing in her eyes.

"Carlisle, tell me you can see it. I need you to see it."

"I can see it, okay? Is that what I'm supposed to say here? I can see it!" she yelled, throwing up her hands.

"Can we go home now?"

Conner nodded. He didn't trust his voice not to break with emotion. There were tears running down his face into his beard, which he wiped away with a shaky hand. He could see Carlisle's face was also damp with tears.

She didn't see it. He was the only one that saw the house that wasn't there. The knowledge was like a physical weight upon his shoulders, weighing him down to the degree that he stopped walking.

"No."

Carlisle sighed. "What?"

"There's a house there and I'm going to prove it."

Before she could answer he turned around and walked toward the house. His body tingled with electricity as he grew nearer, as if the house was giving off energy of some kind. His steps were slow and deliberate. His mind was made up.

He climbed the steps to the front porch and approached the front door. The crimson door was a barrier that called out to him, prime for the breaking. The golden doorknob was a beacon beckoning him to enter. A cold shock went through his body as he grasped the doorknob, causing goosebumps to break out on his body. A voice buried deep within cried out for him to stop, that this was a mistake. He squelched the voice and turned the knob.

He took a deep breath and stepped inside the White House.

6.

Conner

The door slammed behind Conner after he stepped inside the house. He turned and stared at it. The backside of the door had been painted black, contrasting with the bright crimson color on the other side. There was no need to try the door handle on the inside, because there wasn't one. In fact, there wasn't any decoration or adornment on the inside of the door. It was simply a slab of wood that had been painted black. There had to be some way of opening the door. He felt along the door, feeling the wood grains upon his hand as if his eyes were deceiving him. There was always a hole in the door where the handle was placed. That hole would do in this scenario. Yet he wasn't finding it. There wasn't anything along the inside of the door.

Filled with desperation, Conner pounded on the door with his fist. He called out to his wife, who was standing in the darkening woods, alone and waiting for him. The hope was Carlisle would hear his calls carried by the desperation in his voice and come to his rescue. There was a sizable problem with this decision. She couldn't see the house; therefore, would she be able to locate the house to rescue him? Would she be able to hear him now that he had stepped foot into a house that she couldn't see or were his words consumed by the primordial darkness within which the house seemed to exist?

After a few minutes of pounding, it became clear that either she couldn't hear him or couldn't find him. He turned away from the door, his shoulders slumping in disappointment.

He was just inside the entryway, at the center of a large open room that likely served as the house's living room. From the outside dimensions, he could tell the room took up most of the first floor of the house. Yet there had to be more.

The house was dimly lit, though where the diminutive light source was coming from, Conner couldn't tell. There didn't seem to be a light source. There simply was light. Perhaps it emitted from the walls itself or maybe there were hidden light sources in the ceiling. The more he investigated, however, the more questions he had instead of answers.

The flooring was a dark hardwood that he had seen countless times in older homes. Deep furrows were carved into the wood all across the surface of the floor. Were those from nails or claws? Either way, they were of little comfort. The dark wood continued halfway up the wall in wooden paneling, where it gave way to the same white paint that was found on the exterior. Most houses would have pictures, mirrors, or paintings hanging on the walls, something to reflect the owner's personality. There was nothing of the sort in this house, however. Instead, the walls were plain, as if a living soul hadn't stepped foot inside the house. Chunks of sheetrock were missing from the walls, exposing the innards of the neglected house. Entire planks of the wood paneling were missing from the wall, two of which he saw in the corner of the room having been fashioned together to form a makeshift cross for protection. But protection from what?

The ceiling was higher than he would have expected considering the exterior dimensions of the house. A seven-story house with twelve-foot ceilings should have towered above the trees in the Crestview woods, yet the house merely peaked above said trees. The white paint was wearing thin in several places, as if something extraordinarily tall had been rubbing against it on a regular basis. Just like with the walls, chunks of the sheetrock had fallen to the floor, where it lay in heaps. The exposed beams in the ceiling were blackened with rot. For the first time since he stepped foot inside the house, Conner worried about his safety.

As he looked at the ceiling, it started to groan with the stress of immense weight on the second story of the house. His pulse quickened. A cold sweat broke out on his brow despite the frigid temperature inside the house that caused plumes of mist to expel from his mouth.

He wasn't alone in the house. That thought was somehow more frightening than the rotten beams holding up the ceiling above from crashing down on him.

He scratched his beard covered chin as he looked around the room for answers. There were two windows in the large room, which he had seen from the outside. Feeling emboldened due to the thought of his life being in danger, he ventured away from the front door for the first time since stepping inside. From the outside, the window had appeared blacked out, giving him no hint at what was on the inside. From the inside, that didn't appear to be the case. While it was true that he couldn't see outside, there wasn't a layer of paint covering the window as expected. It definitely wasn't painted. The darkness had a depth that brought a shiver up his spine, as he was staring into an abyss, only to see it stare back.

Something moved in the abyss. It was as if different shades of black had shifted before his eyes. Conner leaped back from the window, unsure if he had truly seen anything or if his imagination was playing more tricks on his mind.

His index finger throbbed where he had touched the glass of the window when feeling for the paint. He studied his finger. The tip of the finger had turned a bright red.

Note to self: don't touch the windows.

Suddenly, he remembered the phone in his pocket. He grabbed it and held it up. The screen awakened with the motion of being taken from his pocket. The facial recognition technology unlocked the phone. He dialed Carlisle's number. It didn't ring. He looked at the signal on the bar at the top of the phone's screen. There wasn't a signal.

If he couldn't make a phone call, would a text message still be sent? There was only one way to find out. He opened the text thread he had with Carlisle and typed:

Help! I went inside the house and now I can't get out! Can't you hear me yelling?

He hit send. Then he shouted Carlisle's name, while staring at his phone. The icon on the screen continued to spin in a circle, signaling the phone was attempting to send the message. This continued for an agonizing minute before an error message popped up. *Unable to send message.*

The phone had a twenty-five percent battery charge. He had no way of knowing how long he would be trapped in the house. Hopefully, he will get a better signal later and could try again. With a sigh, he put the phone back in his pocket.

Unable to come up with another idea, he paced the large room. He came to a corner of the room, then turned right. He did this until his booted foot kicked the two wood planks from the wall that had been fashioned into a cross. He picked up the cross and walked to the nearest window. Once upon a time, in a land called Kansas, Conner Keen played Little League baseball. There was a collective groan when he stepped to plate every time. The reason was simple. He wasn't very good. Then one scorching July afternoon, he decided to close his eyes as he swung the heavy aluminum bat at the ball. There was a satisfying *ping* as bat found ball. It was ironic that chance had done something he had been unable to do on his own. He opened his eyes to see the ball sailing over the outfield fence. It was his one and only homerun.

Forty-year-old Conner Keen gripped the plank of wood, choking up a little as he had done on that day thirty years ago. He closed his eyes and swung at the window. Instead of the satisfying crack of the bat hitting ball, he expected to hear the sound of breaking glass. That didn't happen. He heard the sound of splintering wood as the plank broke on the window.

He opened his eyes. There wasn't a scratch or scuff on the window. Overflowing with frustration, he kicked the window with the toe of his steel-toed boots. The glass didn't shatter. In fact, it was as if his foot had encountered some kind of force field when it contacted the window. In that moment, he was thankful for the protection of the steel-toed boots.

With another escape attempt thwarted by the house, he continued pacing the large room. He was on his second lap around the room when he noticed a hallway had appeared along the front side of the house. The hallway hadn't been there on his first lap around the room. It hadn't been there at all until that moment.

Was he experiencing reality? Or was this a trick of the mind? The answer didn't matter. Reality was only his perception of the world around him, nothing more. The house wasn't a part of Carlisle and PJ's reality because they couldn't see it. Whether the house was a demented manifestation of a psychological disorder or as real as the trees in the woods that surrounded it didn't matter. His finger was bruised and sore from touching the window. There was a scuff mark on his boot from where he had kicked the window. Those things were real. The hallway that had appeared where there hadn't been one moment earlier was real. It was a house that shouldn't have been there. Nothing made sense.

I couldn't see it, but she saw a house. A house that wasn't there. A house that couldn't be there.

Conner gave into his delusion and walked down the hallway. There were two doors, both on the right side of the hallway.

He entered the first room.

Pride

7.

Conrad

The acidic, slightly burnt smell of fresh coffee permeated the one-bedroom apartment. Officer Conrad Cain stood with his arms crossed over the chest of his freshly pressed uniform, watching the coffee slowly drip into the pot. It was permanently stained from this very task performed three times per day. He brewed a pot before work to fill his thermos. Then made a pitstop around noon for a sandwich and a refill. A final pot usually accompanied his dinner.

He was aware it was an unusual habit for a single young man, such as himself. There was a simple explanation with a complicated history. His father had been an alcoholic, which was the simple explanation. The complicated part was the man himself, Douglass Cain. It had taken until Conrad was a high school freshman to realize his dad was a high functioning alcoholic. The man was an expert at masking the smell of alcohol on his breath with peppermints and menthol cigarettes, one of which was always in his mouth and sometimes both. Conrad had made the ill-advised decision to pull an all-nighter studying for a test in US History, a class he was failing. He had fallen asleep on his bed, with a book in his hand at one o'clock in the morning. The next morning, he had nearly slept through his alarm. US History was his first period. He needed to be awake for the test. His dad always had the same dented metal thermos with PPD stenciled on it filled with coffee. Whether it was day or night, the old man—a moniker that was instilled after what he thought of as "the incident"—always had that thermos. It was sitting on the counter in the kitchen while the old man had both of his arms wrapped around Conrad's mother, who was frying bacon in a pan. Conrad picked up the navy-blue thermos and put it to his mouth. He was expecting the bitter taste of coffee, which he got, however, there was a harshness that burned his throat on the way down, which he hadn't been expecting. Conrad was young but he wasn't stupid. The number of empty whiskey bottles in the dumpster was an indicator, but, of course, he had ignored them. This couldn't be ignored.

After that day everything about the old man came into focus. His father was an alcoholic but there wasn't anyone in town that had the balls to confront the man about it. Douglass Cain stood under six feet, but what he lacked in height, he made up for in sheer girth. The old man could bankrupt a buffet if he put his mind to it. The uniform pants had to be specially made, at least according to Conrad's mother after the divorce. It was the old man's deep bass voice that boomed whenever he spoke which commanded attention. The old man had a legendary temper around town. It also didn't hurt that Douglass Cain was the Chief of Police.

It wasn't the drinking that finally caught up with the elder Cain, causing his fall from grace, at least not directly. It wasn't the countless years he had spent drinking while on duty. It wasn't the drunken driving the entire town turned a blind eye to. It wasn't his liver, which should have been completely nonfunctional. Instead, it was a domestic violence incident at their home two years after Conrad's eyes had been opened. It had been a regular Friday night, just like any other in the Cain household. Conrad had gone to the Pirates football game with a couple of buddies, meanwhile, the old man was up to his usual Friday night shenanigans, which involved cheap whiskey and a lot of it. According to Conrad's mother, her husband had been feeling frisky. However, it was that time of the month and she wasn't in the mood to clean bloody sheets for a sexual encounter that started off as consensual but morphed into abuse when her husband was too drunk to get it up. Like many men in positions of power, the word "no" was a suggestion rather than a demand.

When Conrad arrived home from the game, his mother was naked on the floor with a bloody lip and a swollen eye. Meanwhile, the old man hovered above her in tighty-whities, with his massive belly heaving with each labored breath. His right hand was cocked, ready to strike again. Conrad grabbed his dad's arm and pulled the old man away. The old man's blood must have been fifty percent cheap whiskey at that point, because he stumbled backwards, only coming to a stop when the back of his legs hit the couch. The old man fell onto the couch and stared up at his son. Drunk as the old man was, Conrad was surprised when the old man popped immediately back up and was across the room, accompanied by a right hand that landed flush on the temple of his son. Conrad hit the ground. He sat there staring at his father, as if he was looking at a stranger. When the old man went to the kitchen to grab another bottle of whiskey—apparently, the thermos charade was over for the night—Conrad grabbed his mother and ran into his parent's bedroom. Inside, his mother pleaded with him, but he had no choice. He grabbed the pistol the old man kept in the nightstand. He held it tightly as he called the police from the phone on the nightstand. With help on the way, he helped his mother get dressed, protecting the little dignity the woman had left. Then he held her as they waited for the police to arrive. Five minutes later, there were raised voices as his father argued with one of his officers. Conrad didn't open the door until he was reassured by the officer that his father was no longer on the premises.

Douglass Cain avoided jailtime thanks to friends in high places, but the damage was done to his reputation. He was relieved of his duties because of his daytime drinking while on duty. Conrad expected his father to run away in shame, but the old man surprised him by sticking around. It was somehow worse seeing his father become an alcoholic hermit that only ventured out for booze and an occasional court date to his frequent drunk driving charges. Conrad still saw the man from time to time around town. Yet he had no words for the man that had taken his mother's dignity and pounded into the ground with a raised fist. Douglass Cain was as good as dead to his son, which was the reason Conrad had grabbed the gun in the first place. In the end, it was better for the authorities to handle it. The old man had deserved a bullet, but his son didn't deserve the torment of having to pull the trigger.

No, Conrad stuck to coffee.

He poured his coffee into a navy-blue thermos with PPD stenciled on it, and walked out the door, ready for another day as an officer of the Prairieview Police Department. The same police force the old man had been chief of fifteen years prior.

The streets of Prairieview were starting to awaken as Conrad drove the cruiser leisurely through the downtown area. Before his childhood innocence was shattered by a drunken father, he had viewed the town as an idyllic place to live seemingly straight out of a Norman Rockwell painting. After those Rockwellian tinted glasses had been shattered from his face, he realized it was nothing more than a façade. Instead of a Rockwell painting, the town was more akin to the false fronted towns that appeared in the Spaghetti Westerns the old man had been fond of watching half drunk on a Saturday afternoon.

After his awakening to the real world, he started to notice fallacies all around him. Everyone appeared to be smiling in those paintings, but those smiles were only painted on like a mask. Teresa Newhouse appeared to be a happily married woman who ran the Newhouse's Café. She ran the front counter, while her husband, Dale, worked the kitchen in the back. Then Conrad noticed every Thursday evening when her husband attended his weekly bowling night in Crimson Creek, Teresa would close for an hour despite having Weekend Willie manning the kitchen for the night. He also noticed the pharmacy closed for the same period of time. Conrad noticed because the pharmacy had an old-fashioned soda fountain in it, a rarity for the period. He became a regular when Fani Mickelson started working the soda fountain part-time, hoping to see her wearing the tight smock that Mr. Jacobs insisted on. He found that Fani wasn't there, in fact, there wasn't anyone there. Still with a hankering for something sweet, he strolled two blocks down Main Street to the café. He found it closed as well. Yet the parking lot wasn't empty. Both Mr. Jacobs and Teresa Newhouse were sitting in the front seat of a Volvo station wagon before they pulled out of the parking lot. Conrad knew what was about to go down.

That was peanuts compared to what he noticed in the midst of the old man's fall from grace. Milton Hightower served as the judge for the county, a well-respected position and a well-respected man. Judge Hightower had two nephews that served as deputies on the police force. Leonard Hightower spent a lot of time hanging around the high school, which wasn't unusual considering his son was in Conrad's graduating class. It was unusual that Deputy Hightower's son was nowhere in sight. The person who was in sight was Gerald Bunting, a well-known drug dealer in the area. It wasn't as if the deputy was investigating a crime, because the high school was outside of the city, making whatever crime happening on the premises a county matter. Nothing was ever confirmed, but rumor had it that Deputy Hightower supplied Bunting with drugs that disappeared from the evidence room at the police station. When Bunting and the deputy were caught, well, the judge simply threw out the case. The old man's constant inebriation had blinded him to the nefarious activity for years. Firing Leonard Hightower had been the old man's last act as Chief.

People lived with the assumption that nothing happened in a small town, however, there were dastardly deeds happening all the time, you only had to look closely enough to see them. Big city or small town, people were greedy and self-centered, and tended to do what best suited their interests. It was the human condition.

He parked the cruiser in front of the Newhouse Café with fifteen minutes remaining before his shift started. There were a couple of farm trucks parked out front, the usual clientele for that time of day. A familiar red Hyundai Veloster was also parked in front of the café. The sight put a smile on his face. He got out of the cruiser and went inside.

After the divorce Teresa Newhouse took over full ownership of the café. Meanwhile, Dale fled in humiliation with half his assets. Their daughter, Gabby, had come on board as a parttime waitress while still in high school. Now, she was there more than her mother, which was fine with Conrad.

The Newhouse café was a fifties themed diner, though Gabby refused to wear that awful poodle skirt her mother wore. Booths ran along the wall with a view of the parking lot. There were eight square tables positioned throughout the diner, though locals preferred to sit at the counter for quicker service. A stranger with slicked black hair sat in a booth. There was enough grease in the man's hair to lubricate a V8 engine. He was dressed in a long-sleeved black button-up shirt despite the nearly one-hundred-degree forecast. The man's eyes were locked on Conrad, with a thin smile spread across his face. Conrad nodded at the stranger before turning back to the counter.

Gabby was behind the counter pouring a cup of coffee into the mug of Owen Updike when Conrad walked through the door. A smile appeared in the corner of her mouth as she glanced in his direction. He took a seat at the counter and waited. When she was done with Owen, she grabbed a cinnamon roll sitting in the window on the warming rack and brought it over.

"Conrad, I know you've got a thermos full of coffee sitting in that cruiser out front. Your boots are always polished, and your uniform freshly pressed. That tells me you've got the time to fix yourself a good honest to goodness breakfast at home, but every morning you come in and spend $3.75 on a cinnamon roll. Now, you either want to have diabetes before you turn forty or there's some other reason for your visit."

Gabby smiled; a sight that made her face brighten. Her short red hair was in tight curls, as if little orphan Annie had grown up. Her blue eyes seemed as if they were picked out of the sky. Her crimson lips matched the roses growing in the flowerbed in the parking lot. Yes, Conrad knew exactly why he came in every morning. He had a feeling Gabby knew also.

"Well, these are the best cinnamon rolls in town, Gabby," he said, digging into the gooey goodness.

Gabby shook her head. "No, they're not. You and I both know that Hurts Donut makes the best cinnamon roll in town. Hell, probably in the county. Ivan's a good baker."

"Yeah, but he's not nearly the conversationalist that you are, Gabby. And I like a little bit of Gab with my breakfast."

"Oh, Ivan'll talk to you, Conrad, of course, it helps if you've got boobs to stare at while he does it."

"Now, Gabby, are you telling me that a happily married man enjoys looking at other women? I can't imagine."

"Are you kidding me? Have you seen his wife? If I were married to Loretta, I'd have a wondering eye too. Probably a damn sight more."

"No, I don't think you would, Gabby. You strike me as the loyal type."

"Oh, you can tell?" she said, laughing.

"Yep, it's in your eyes. I also noticed you remember my order every morning. What more does a man need?"

"Conrad, you've ordered the same thing every morning for five years. Who wouldn't remember that?"

"Ivan."

"Don't you have somewhere to be, Conrad?"

"I guess so. I'll see you tomorrow."

He could feel her eyes on him as he walked to the door.

The police station was a block away from the Newhouse café, which was a good thing because Conrad was cutting it close. Chief Nichols didn't need any added ammunition against his predecessor's son. The chief appeared to be under the impression that the apple didn't fall far from the tree. The old man, aside from his alcohol and domestic abuse, had a reputation for bending the law where he saw fit. Had a suspected drug dealer that wasn't carrying when you picked him up? No problem, a few ounces found mysteriously in the glove compartment would do the trick. Get a little aggressive with a perp? No problem, hadn't the guy been reaching for something in his waistband? Then, of course, there was the drug ring that had happened underneath the old man's nose. Rumor had it that the old man had taken bribes to look the other way. There were ways for Conrad to investigate his father's conduct while a member of the PPD, however, those channels were better left uninvestigated. He was aware of the man's character.

Unfortunately for Conrad, he had to live underneath the cloud the old man's reputation cast over the small town. He knew it wasn't fair, but that was life. Life was rarely fair or just, even to those that abided by the law. He believed that with time everything evened out. A sunny day was sure to follow a string of cloudy ones, where there had been nothing but torrential downpours. Chief Nichols was the catalyst for rain as of late, as if the man was standing on Main Street doing a rain dance. Conrad had a feeling that as long as Nichols was Chief of Police, there would be few sunny days.

The police station was a small brick building located on the corner of Main Street and 2nd Street. When Conrad had been a kid visiting the old man at work, the building had been in a severe state of disrepair. Leaky faucets, faded wood trim on the exterior of the building, and bubbled carpet that made him trip more than once as a rambunctious child. Nichols might have an axe to grind with him, but at least he was keeping up appearances.

Conrad entered the police station and waited inside the door for his eyes to adjust from the bright summer sun to the artificial fluorescent lighting. The bullpen wasn't like those seen on television. The PPD was a small department, and the size of the station reflected that. To his left was a tall reception counter, where civilians could talk to a uniformed officer without entering the station. There was a wooden gate that separated the reception area from the bullpen. He stepped through, allowing it to slam close behind him.

Officer Frank Hightower, brother of Leonard who had fallen from grace, was reclined at his desk with his feet on the desk. Frank's feet fell to the ground as the man straightened in his seat. The aging officer's hand reflectively reached for the pistol at his waist. The hand stopped when he saw Conrad standing on the other side of the desk.

"Hell, Conrad. You could have a bullet in you right about now."

"Shoot first and ask questions later, right, Hightower? Is that the way you Hightowers operate?"

"Are you kidding me? Is that a shot at my brother?" Frank said as he leapt to his feet, sending the desk chair rolling backwards.

Conrad held up his hands. "Hey, I'm just asking a question, Hightower. Now that you say it though, rumor has it your brother had a fondness for firing his weapon without cause. It could be a habit that runs in the family. And how did you avoid getting involved in that whole mess? The old man said the two of you were inseparable in those days."

"You're one to talk about shit running in the family, Conrad. Your old man was a joke of a cop. As far as I can see, you're following in his footsteps."

"Hightower, leave Cain alone. He's got a call," Nichols said from the open door of his office.

Hightower crossed his arms over his chest. "He started it. Besides, why can't I go on the call?"

Nichols looked at his watch. "I wouldn't trust you with anything other than the night shift, Hightower. Can't have you sleeping when there's actual work to be done. Anyway, your shift is over."

Hightower gave Conrad a long, hard look before storming out of the station.

8.

Conrad

The sun was high in the sky by the time Conrad parked the cruiser in front of a three-bedroom ranch just inside the town limits. A couple of blocks was the difference between the PPD getting the call or having to call in the county sheriff's office. The two department's officers were pooled from the same group of Prairieview citizens, yet they had had disputes in the past. Unseasoned officers had been known to cross over into the county jurisdiction, causing feathers to ruffle at the sheriff's office. Then a pissing contest would ensue. Luckily, he was well aware of where that imaginary line was drawn, and knew he was within the city's jurisdiction.

As he got out of the cruiser white puffballs of cotton from cottonwood trees floated through the air as if snowflakes in the summertime. The street was lined with ranch-style houses that looked as if they had been made with a giant cookie-cutter, with the only alterations being in the choice of trim color. Some of the houses had gone with a small garden in the front yard, while others had no landscaping to speak of. Then there was the eyesore of the neighborhood. The house across the street from where he was parked had burned down when Conrad was a rookie. Prairieview had a small volunteer fire department, with a single engine. They were ill-equipped to deal with a large-scale house fire. Reinforcements from Crimson Creek had to be called in, but by the time they arrived nothing could be done aside from ensuring the rest of the neighborhood didn't burn down as well. The house had reportedly been vacant at the time; the owner having gone bankrupt the year prior. The bank couldn't find a buyer in a town where everyone was wanting out, rather than in. An arson investigation had ensued regarding the prior owner taking his revenge against the bank that had foreclosed on the house. Nothing had been proven. Five years later, the pile of rubble sat as a reminder of the fire and broken dreams.

There was a Buick Enclave parked in the driveway, indicating the owner of the house was middle-aged. The lawn was well maintained, despite the recent heatwave and ban on watering aside from once a week. Appearances were important to the owner of the house, and they were willing to cut a few corners to maintain said appearances. There were twin Bradford Pears flanking the house on the front lawn. He was thankful the aromatic tree was long past its flowering stage, which he found smelled more like fish than any flower should.

There was a covered porch with a swing that hung from the roof. A short man with graying hair paced the small space. He stopped when he saw Conrad.

"David Nowitzki? I'm Officer Cain from the Prairieview PD."

"I know who you are, Conrad. She's missing, gone. I can't find Bianca," David said, running a hand through his hair.

"Mind if we sit down while we go over this?"

"Tell me what happened, David. Were you guys fighting?" Conrad said once they were seated on the porch swing.

"No, not really. I mean, every couple has a disagreement or two, right? That's normal, I guess. Last week, we argued about whether my mother liked her when I first introduced them. She said that mom hated her, but I disagreed. Mom loved Bianca, always has. That was last week. This week, it was about that house."

David nodded in the direction of the house across the street.

"You mean the house that burned down five years ago? Why would you argue about that?"

David shook his head. "No, that would make sense, Conrad. What we argued about didn't make sense. I couldn't see it, but she saw a house. A house that wasn't there. A house that couldn't be there."

"You mean across the street where the Comisky house used to be? How could she see a house there?"

"I don't know. At first, she was just staring across the street, as if in a trance. She would sit on this swing for hours, just swing and stare, swing and stare. Now, I enjoy sitting on the porch as much as the next guy, but this time of year? Forget about it. It's just too hot. Five minutes in the afternoon sun and I'm perspiring like a chicken in a fox den. But she was out here for three or four hours two nights in a row, even missed *the Bachelorette*. That's her favorite show, so I knew something was up. So, I finally asked her if she was okay. She sat there quietly for a long time. I figured she hadn't heard me, so I started to ask again. That's when she answered me. 'You see that house across the street, don't you, Davey?' She always called me Davey.

"I laughed, I didn't mean anything by it, but I did. I said, 'That's hardly a house, B. Just a pile of rubble the city should clean up before some kid goes playing around and gets hurt.' Sorry, Conrad, I know you work for the town, so I'm sorry, but it's true. She shook her head and muttered, 'You don't see it, I knew you wouldn't because it's not supposed to be there. My phone won't take a picture of it either.'"

"You're telling me that Bianca saw a house across the street? A different one than the burned façade that remains there now?"

David nodded. "She sure did. I couldn't see it, of course. She even described it to me. Tallest house she ever saw.

Seven, maybe eight stories tall, I think. It was a white brick house with black trim, said it was pretty but there was something she didn't like about the house. It had a hypnotizing quality to it, as if the more she stared at it the more she lost track of time. I guess that explains why she spent hours staring at the house. I was getting worried about her, real worried."

"I know this is a sensitive question, but did Bianca have a history of psychological problems? Any history in the family?"

"Her maternal uncle suffers from dementia. He lives in an assisted living community in Wichita. That's it as far as family. Now, Bianca has always been the sharpest person I know, she'd have to be, being a lawyer and all. Heck, I'm just a glorified secretary with a fancy title. Executive assistant is just a fancy secretary, Conrad. I've gotten depressed about that in the past, I'm not embarrassed to say. So, if this were the other way around, well, it would make a lot more sense. Bianca? This just isn't like her."

"When did you last see her?"

"Last night. She couldn't sleep, so she got out of bed. I—"

David's voice broke. Tears welled in his eyes.

"It's okay, David. Take your time."

"I just figured she was going to the living room or something, I guess. She would do that every now and then. Sometimes I snore, so she goes out to the living room and sleeps. We talked about getting me one of those CPAP machines but never got around to it. She never complains about it either, that's her way. She'd endure anything for me, like living in a small town even though she could be a hotshot lawyer in a bigger city.

"I figured she went to the living room, but I think she went out to the porch swing to sit and watch the house. God knows why, but I don't. I shouldn't have let her. I should have gone with her. She wasn't acting like herself. Maybe she went over there looking for the house, that's what I told myself."

"Have you been over there, David? To the house, I mean, to search for her?"

"Of course, I went over there. Didn't find anything."

"And she was gone when you got up this morning?"

David nodded. "I shouldn't have let her. I should have been with her."

Conrad left David Nowitzki on the porch swing while he went back to his cruiser to call for backup. The trouble was that Bianca was an adult, who hadn't been missing for twelve hours, let alone twenty-four. She could have gone into the office to get some work done when she couldn't sleep. She could have gone for a walk, got disoriented because of her lack of sleep in recent nights, and injured herself in some manner. Of course, she could have been out with a boyfriend, despite David's insistence that their marriage was strong. There were a thousand possibilities, Conrad's job was to find the right one and do it before it was too late.

While he waited for backup to arrive, he walked over to the empty lot, where the Comisky house once stood, now just a pile of rubble. An owl watched him from a nearby tree, despite the sun high in the sky indicating that it wasn't the proper time for the nocturnal animal to be out. Something moved in the rubble. His eyes followed the movement. A mouse scurried through the debris. The owl's presence made sense. It was searching for a meal.

He searched the debris pile for an hour, eventually being joined by the other members of the police force and sheriff's office. They walked the neighborhood and surrounding area for hours. They didn't find anything. Meanwhile, Tracy, who worked dispatch, made a few phone calls, including to Bianca's law firm. They hadn't seen her.

It was as if Bianca Nowitzki had vanished.

9.

Conrad

Like vultures to a carcass, the media descended upon the Nowitzki home to feed on the grief of a desperate man. Conrad knew it was inevitable; however, he had been hoping to delay his meeting with the media a few more hours. In a missing person's case, the media could be an ally, benefiting law enforcement in getting the word out to the general public. It was crucial if there was anyone with information about Bianca that they come forward. Just because something could be beneficial didn't mean its intentions were honorable.

Living in a small town meant the bad news that dominated the newscasts and filled social media was of a macabre variety. News of an uplifting nature didn't sell. It was the same reason people slowed down and stared when driving past a particularly devastating car wreck. People couldn't help themselves; they were drawn to the pain of others. Was it because they were secretly thankful it hadn't been them? Did that somehow make their lives seem better? Conrad didn't know. What he knew was there were always other towns in the spotlight when he turned on the evening news. It was unfamiliar people on camera discussing crimes and misdeeds that didn't happen in Prairieview. It was why he loved his hometown and would never live anywhere else, despite feeling like a large fish in a small bowl and dreaming of leaving most of his life.

Tonight, however, it would be his town on the evening news. It would be his face talking about the disappearance of someone he knew. This time he was the stranger to those other people.

As they swarmed the street, fighting for a prime position in front of the house, Conrad escaped to the comfort of the Nowitzki house.

After talking with David, it became clear that Bianca hadn't been in a good headspace in recent days. She had spoken of seeing a house that her husband wasn't able to see and had even gone as far as to describe it to him. David also spoke of dementia running in her family, though she had displayed no clear signs of suffering from any mental illness until recently. Was it possible for someone to suddenly develop mental illness, such as dementia, overnight? Shouldn't there have been symptoms pointing to it beforehand?

The questions were mounting, with no answers apparent.

The word of a husband was just that, the word of a husband. People lived under the assumption that we knew those we shared our lives with, when in reality there were times that we only showed them what we wanted them to see. At least that was the way it had been with his parents, which was the only relationship he had to base these thoughts on since his longest relationship hadn't lasted past the *I think I love you* stage. Conrad's father had more skeletons hidden in his closet than could be found in a graveyard, or so it seemed. A secret alcoholic, spousal abuse, and questionable practices as the Chief of Police. Conrad had been unaware of all of these allegations for years while living under the same roof as the old man.

That was what he found himself searching for as he looked around the Nowitzki home, a skeleton in the closet.

A secret boyfriend that she had been keeping from her husband, someone who she could disappear with. A drug problem that could explain the hallucinations in recent days. A gambling debt that would explain her disappearance. Clues that her mental state had been declining longer than her husband was aware. Anything.

What he found was a normal couple living an average, somewhat mundane life. There was a framed photo of the smiling couple standing underneath the purple water tower on the mantle above the fireplace. Instead of a television in the living room, there were stacks of books sitting on the coffee table. One stack consisted of several nonfiction books pertaining to law, while the other consisted of horror fiction books, including one by Stephen King. Conrad could guess which belonged to whom.

There was an empty mug with the remnants of coffee that had been laced with creamer by the sink in the kitchen. The mug had a trace of lipstick around the rim, indicating it had been used by Bianca at some point before her disappearance. It was an interesting find that gave insight into her state of mind, although it wasn't entirely out of the ordinary. David had said Bianca got out of bed because she couldn't sleep, however, the coffee indicated another possibility. She didn't want to sleep or was trying to keep herself awake for some reason. Why would a seemingly normal middle-aged woman force herself to stay awake in the middle of the night?

While riffling through magazines that were stacked in a woven basket next to the couch, he found a notebook with a Jayhawk on the cover. The Jayhawk was the mascot for the University of Kansas, the school where David and Bianca met twenty-five years ago. He flipped through the pages, finding much of what he expected: shopping lists, notes relating to law in some fashion, and some drawings. Whoever had sketched the drawings was quite talented. He recognized a sketch with the same image as the photo on the mantle, as if whomever had sketched it had been sitting on the couch, staring at it while working. There were even some sketches of David sitting in what appeared to be the same recliner that sat in the corner of the room. It appeared Bianca was the artist.

He continued to flip through the pages, telling himself he was conducting research into her state of mind, when in reality he had meandered into the realm of voyeur unintentionally. Yet, his curiosity paid off five minutes later when he stopped flipping pages and found himself staring at a familiar face. It was the man from the diner that very morning. Conrad had figured the stranger had been passing through town and stopped for a bite to eat at the Newhouse Café, as was typical.

Why was Bianca drawing a stranger in a notebook? Maybe he wasn't a stranger. Conrad flipped through the pages and found more sketches of the stranger. Each looked roughly the same as the previous, with a small change. It was as if she had been narrowing down the detail in the man's appearance over time. The final sketch of the man was a close up of his face. It was as if she had concluded that this was as close as she could to the real thing.

The next sketch was that of an unusually tall house, seven stories in all. David hadn't done the house justice in his description, but, of course, the man was unable to see the house and only knew what his wife had told him. It definitely wasn't the house that had burnt down years ago. It had looked much like the house he now stood in, a one-story ranch. The house in the sketch would stand out wherever it was located, as there weren't many seven-story houses.

Conrad located an evidence bag in the kit the responding officers had brought in and put the notebook inside. He wasn't sure it was actually evidence more than it was interesting. An abundance of caution was prudent in a situation such as this. What seemed merely interesting one minute could turn vital in the next.

One of the reasons Conrad had gone inside was to cool his nerves and gather his thoughts. As the officer in charge of Bianca's disappearance, it would be his task to talk to the media. It wasn't something he felt particularly comfortable with, but knew it was part of the job description in a missing person's case. He would have to talk with Chief Nichols and go over what exactly they wanted to say. A message from the husband was high on his list of possibilities.

He left the house and found the conversation wasn't necessary. Nichols had the members of the media gathered on the front lawn of the property. Conrad cringed, knowing the possibility that they were trampling on evidence was high. He would have delivered his statement from the driveway or even from the street, considering it was a neighborhood with light traffic.

Nichols held a sheet of paper in his hands as tremors of nervousness coursed through him. Next to the chief stood David Nowitzki. The man stared blankly at the cameras focused on himself, as if not quite understanding what was happening.

Nichols was mid-speech already.

"I will be handling this case personally, but we need your help. If you have any information about the whereabouts of Bianca Nowitzki, please contact the Prairieview Police Department. Can you put our number on the screen? Oh, well, they'll figure it out. She was last seen around two o'clock AM by her husband, David Nowitzki, and hasn't been seen since to our knowledge.

"The first twenty-four hours are crucial in a missing person's case. Therefore, it is crucial that if you have information, we hear from you as soon as possible. We've got law enforcement officials and volunteers searching for Bianca at this very moment. We haven't found anything yet, but we're hopeful that we can return her to her husband soon. Speaking of which, David has prepared a statement that he would like to read."

David continued scanning the faces of the media members, despite the cue from the chief. Nichols continued smiling, while giving the grieving husband a gentle nudge with his elbow. David turned to the chief in confusion. Nichols nodded to the cameras and whispered something to David that Conrad couldn't hear.

He stared at the cameras for another minute as the cameras appeared to zoom in on the man whose wife had gone missing in the middle of the night. Finally, he spoke.

"Bianca was the light of my world, like a beacon in the darkness. I'm afraid I'm already lost without her constant presence by my side, so you'll have to excuse my ramblings. I only wish to reiterate what Chief Nichols has already said. If you've got any information about where Bianca is or have seen her any time since two this morning, please come forward. If someone has taken her for some reason, please let her go. We've been saving up for retirement in a few years, that money is now yours if you choose to let her go. Bianca, if for some reason you've ran off with another man, as I've been asked by the officers, please simply let me know you're safe. If you've been worried about my reaction to the house that you could see but I couldn't, well, forget it. We can work through that. Just come home, Bianca. Come home.

"Thank you."

Conrad watched as the two men turned away from the cameras with reporters shouting questions in their direction. They walked toward the house, where he stood on the front porch, still stunned from the display.

Conrad was touched by the sacrifice in the man's statement. He had never known a love like the Nowitzki's shared. Someday, he prayed that changed.

Meanwhile, Chief Nichols had come across as the bumbling head of a smalltown police department that he was. Nichols was the type of man that liked to take control of a situation, despite his lack of experience in these types of situations. Nichols had been an officer who worked underneath the old man during his days as chief. Napping in a patrol car hidden behind the bank was Nichol's afternoon highlight as an officer. The man had his own comfort in mind, not the safety of others. It was the wrong type of man to head the investigation.

The investigation needed a man whose life would benefit from Bianca being brought home safely. Such an optimistic outcome wasn't necessarily in the cards, in fact, it wasn't likely. They needed a man with the determination to solve the case, even if it meant ruffling a few feathers in the process, including the powerful elite that controlled the mayor's attention. Someone who wasn't scared of ruining their reputation in the eyes of the town or the media, because his reputation wasn't squeaky clean to begin with, though not of his own accord. They needed someone with quick wits and nerve.

They needed Conrad Cain. He knew it. Now he would prove it.

Chief Nichols and Conrad exchanged a look as the chief led David Nowitzki inside the house. The look on his face told the chief what he couldn't with words. *You stole my thunder.* The chief huffed in return, as if to say, *what are you going to do about it?*

I'm going to solve the case, Conrad thought.

10.

Conrad

While the media members and police officials were still murmuring about the statement made by Chief Nichols and David Nowitzki, Conrad was starting the true work of solving Bianca's disappearance. He started by going back to the station and making a copy of the final sketch of the stranger from Bianca's notebook. He didn't want to take the actual sketch with him, as it could turn out to be important evidence if the stranger was linked to her disappearance. There was something unusual about this stranger. Conrad had seen him in the café the same morning as Bianca's disappearance. It could have been a coincidence, after all, why would the man stick around if he had done something to Bianca?

Ego. That was the answer. Perhaps the man was under the illusion that the police department didn't know he existed or was involved in the disappearance of Bianca. Pride. Conrad knew a thing or two about a false sense of self-worth, that you were untouchable. He had witnessed the downfall of the old man while he was a teenager. The man had been under the delusion that the Chief of Police could get away with whatever he wanted because no one would dare question his authority. The old man had been wrong about that. Conrad was hoping the stranger was just as wrong as the old man had been.

It was that same sense of false self-importance, defiance in the wake of a downfall that emboldened him. The old man hadn't been a good cop, as he had been led to believe for the first sixteen years or so of his life. Rumor had it that the old man had taken bribes to look the other way while members of his department were working with known drug dealers. There was no proof, of course, the whispers around Prairieview were loud enough that there had to be some amount of truth. As the old saying goes, where there's smoke, there's bound to be fire. After witnessing the old man's lack of respect for laws within his own home, Conrad knew anything was possible in regard to the old man's behavior.

On the contrary, Conrad knew himself to be a good police officer, despite carrying the same genes as a man who had been anything but. Conrad was the shining star of the department; Chief Nichols simply hadn't realized it yet. After all, it was a five-year officer that had been entrusted with the missing person's case in the first place, even if it had been ripped from his grasp at the last possible moment. He conducted himself with honor and a sense of pride in the badge that his father had disgraced. He worked every day to cleanse the tarnished name of the Cain family. Solving the Bianca Nowitzki disappearance would be a step in the right direction.

He returned to the Nowitzki house knowing he was the right man for the job, the chief be damned. There was vigor in his step as he walked to the first door and knocked.

It was his moment.

The Nowitzki's next-door neighbors on either side hadn't seen anything unusual, nor did they recognize the stranger from the sketch. Conard knew the likelihood of most people recognizing the man from the sketch was slim, they simply didn't pay close enough attention to notice. He needed to find the nosey neighbor that was always looking out the windows.

He approached a tired looking house that was next door to the burned down Comisky place. The lawn was in desperate need of trimming and looked parched from the hot summer sun. The white trim around the windows and garage was peeling. The remnants of a dying potted plant sat on the front step of the porch. There was a rocking chair on the porch in front of a large picture window. As he climbed the steps, he saw the blinds separate an inch as someone peered through.

Conrad smiled. He had found his nosey neighbor.

The front door opened before he had a chance to knock. An elderly woman opened the door and stepped onto the front porch. Conrad recognized the woman immediately. She frequently called the department about suspicious vehicles in the neighborhood and also had noise complaints about the house on the corner of the street that was rented by a couple of young men who worked at the fertilizer factory out near the county line.

"Good afternoon, Mrs. Lincoln. How are you doing today?"

"Oh, I'm fine, Conrad. Or should I call you Officer Cain, on account of you being here on official police business?" she asked with a mischievous smile on her face.

"Conrad is fine, ma'am, though you are right. I'm here on official police business. I'm sure you've heard about your neighbor, Bianca Nowitzki, right?"

"Hard to miss all those reporters hanging around in the middle of the street like they are. Some of them are still there, just waiting, as if she's going to just walk down the street and come home. God willing, I pray she does, honestly, I do, but I'm afraid it ain't likely. They seem like such a nice couple too. Good jobs. Nice and quiet. David mows my lawn from time to time, but I don't think he's had the time this week. A crying shame, if you ask me."

"It sure is, and we're doing everything in our power to find Bianca. In fact, that's why I'm here, Mrs. Lincoln. Have you noticed anything out of the ordinary in the past few days? Anybody hanging around that maybe shouldn't be? Anything at all would be helpful."

"Well, there was that man I called the station about yesterday and the day before. Did you guys ever find him?"

The trouble with frequent calls from one particular resident was that the department didn't know how seriously to take any of the calls. Therefore, all of the calls were treated in the same manner, which was a roll of the eyes and a promise that there would be an officer looking into it. It was the smalltown version of the boy that cried wolf. One day that boy would truly need help fighting off the big, bad wolf, only for no one to take the boy's calls seriously.

"I'm unaware of any calls, Mrs. Lincoln. When would this have been?"

"Yesterday and the day before, like I said. He would come around after dark, as if he didn't want anyone to see him, but you can't fool me. I saw him. I also saw one of your officers drive by and look around briefly, but it wasn't for long. I don't think he saw anything, of course, he didn't seem to be looking very hard either. It was that guy with the crooked brother, Hightower, is his name. Just between you and me, I'd put money on him being crooked too. I mean, his brother was as dirty as a pig in the pen, and you're telling me he didn't know anything about it? Hogwash, that's what I say. But that's just between you and me, I'm not one to gossip, Conrad. Just telling it like I see it is all.

"Anyway, the man would seem to come out of nowhere from the direction of the old Comisky place, which is weird as all get out because there ain't nothing there but a pile of rubble. Both nights, he would walk straight up to the Nowitzki place and just stand there on the front lawn. Didn't do nothing but stand there on the lawn. He was there for maybe an hour. Then he went back in the direction of the Comisky house and disappeared into the rubble. Never seen anything like it. A few minutes later, Hightower drove up and looked around. Didn't find anything, like I said. That's just like a crooked cop, arriving too late to find anything. Bet you would have found something, Conrad, of course, you ain't a dirty cop."

He suppressed a smile at the elderly woman's keen judge of character regarding Hightower. The woman was nosey, true, but she was still as sharp as anyone.

"Can you describe the man?"

"Well, it was dark, being late and all, but he was tall, I guess. Taller than you, Conrad. Maybe six foot three. Had a really stocky build to him, like he worked for a living. I mean, manual labor, not working out with weights like some people want to do these days. Dark hair from what I could see, but it *was* dark, like I said. The strange thing was, he didn't seem to be acting like he was doing anything out of the ordinary. Didn't look around or anything like that. You know how you can tell if someone is up to no good, right? Well, of course, you can, you're a cop. Well, he didn't seem nervous or anything. Wasn't looking around to see if someone noticed him, that's what I mean. He was acting like he was supposed to be doing what he was doing."

Conrad held up the photocopy of the sketch from Bianca's notebook. Mrs. Lincoln responded before he could ask the question.

"Well, I'll be a dog's uncle, that's him. That's the man. Tell me, Conrad, did he take Bianca?"

Conrad sent in a BOLO (be on the lookout) alert for the individual in the sketch to the station. He wasn't positive the stranger was involved; however, he still wanted to interview the man. It was the closest thing he had to a suspect and was their only lead in Bianca Nowitzki's disappearance.

After advising dispatch about the suspect wanted for questioning, he rejoined the search for Bianca. Prairieview wasn't a large city, however, the surrounding area was mostly open plains with a few scattered farms. All of those areas had already been canvased over the course of the day. Now, they were simply repeating the process in the hope that they had missed something the first time around.

By nightfall all the volunteers had departed for their homes, where warm beds awaited. The initial optimism of the group had begun to fade with the setting of the sun, as if all hope that she would be found alive disappeared with daylight. Conrad knew with each passing hour it was far more likely they were looking for a body instead of a missing person. That was something the average person couldn't handle. In his five years on duty as a police officer, he had never seen a dead body. He wasn't sure if he was prepared to find a dead body either, though he had no choice in the matter. If Bianca Nowitzki hadn't survived whatever trauma she had been through over the previous twenty-four hours, then he would be among the first to witness her body. It came with the job.

As the other police officials pulled away in their squad cars, he stayed in his. The media had all departed for the evening, some having gone home, while others had checked into the Prairieview Inn in the downtown area. The neighborhood was peaceful once again, as if the tears that had been shed during the day had evaporated away. Yet there was still a tension hanging in the air. Something was amiss. Porch lights were on, and front doors were locked.

He was parked two houses down from the old Comisky place, with a nice view of the neighborhood. It was time to see if Mrs. Lincoln's boogeyman came back.

Even with a thermos filled with coffee he had trouble keeping his heavy eyelids from closing. They would flutter closed, only to snap open a moment later. It was during one such instance he noticed movement near the old Comisky place.

A dark figure emerged from the pile of rubble walking toward the street. Conrad exited the cruiser quietly, shutting the door with care not to alert the stranger. He unsnapped the cover of his service pistol, though he didn't draw the weapon. Instead, he drew the flashlight on his belt. He pointed the flashlight at the figure without switching it on.

The figure was moving quickly across the lawn of the old Comisky place without looking around at their surroundings. Whoever it was, they knew where they were going and weren't concerned about being seen by the neighbors. It was as if they had made this trip before.

Conrad walked with urgency, however, there was caution in each step due to the boots he wore as part of his uniform. The boots tended to make a lot of noise with each step on asphalt.

With the figure having no regard for their whereabouts, he was able to get within twenty feet without being noticed. It was at that point he switched on the flashlight.

The figure turned in his direction.

It was the man from the sketch. The stranger from the Newhouse Café. He had dark hair, dark eyes, and ears that were slightly too big for his face. His skin looked pale in the glow of the flashlight.

The man smiled.

"Prairieview Police Department! Freeze!" Conrad shouted as he continued walking in the man's direction.

The stranger turned and ran back in the direction of the old Comisky place. Conrad cursed under his breath and gave chase.

The flashlight beam bounced with each jolt as he ran. Somehow, he was able to keep the beam trained on the running figure.

Mrs. Lincoln had been right about the man's height, Conrad believed. The stranger's gait was greater than Conrad's own, meaning he was pulling away.

The rubble from the Comisky's burned house was approaching. The playing field would be leveled on the unlevel ground.

Or so Conrad thought.

The man leapt onto the rubble pile, took a single step. Then disappeared.

Conrad searched the rubble pile for fifteen minutes, but the man was gone.

11.

Conner

Conner stumbled out of the room and fell to the hardwood floor of the hallway. He looked around in confusion. He was back in the house that shouldn't have been there. Whatever trip he had gone through to get from the past back to the present had made his head swim. He doubted there was pain reliever in the medicine cabinet. In fact, he hadn't seen a bathroom while walking through the hallway, only two doors that were too far apart for either to be a bathroom.

He leaned against the wall for a few minutes with his head in his hands. Was his head hurting because it had traveled through time or was it because he was losing his mind?

As soon as he stepped through the doorway into the room, it was as if he had been transported back in time ten years. It had been a time when he thought he knew what he wanted out of life, though he had been misguided by trying to outlive his father's reputation. In those days, all he had was his own ambition and the baggage of his father's complicated past. The coming days would only add to that baggage, and this time he didn't have his father to blame.

It had been as if he were trapped inside his own head, like a passenger taken hostage that was unable to speak, move, or act in any fashion. Yet he was able to feel and experience everything that his old self had felt back then. Inner thoughts that had seemed so personal in the moment were overheard by a version of himself that had been jaded by time. He felt both embarrassed for that version of himself ten years ago, and this version ten years later. Officer Cain would have been disgusted to know he had shared his body with a man that was more like his father than himself.

What was happening in this house? Why had he been taken back to a time that had been so significant to the person he had become?

The answer was obvious. The house. The house was the reason, of course. *I couldn't see it, but she saw a house. A house that wasn't there. A house that couldn't be there.* The words of David Nowitzki echoed in his mind. It was the link between his past and his present. Bianca Nowitzki had spoken with her husband about seeing a house that he couldn't see. Conner had dismissed the house at the time, thinking that it was only an indicator of her state of mind in the days leading to her disappearance. Now it was obvious to him that Bianca had truly seen the house she claimed to have seen. It had taken ten years and seeing the house with his own eyes to realize it truly existed.

In the coming days, he would dive deep into the dark world of the macabre in the search for the stranger and the man whom he now knew was linked to it. Even in the throes of a dangerous game, he wouldn't truly believe what they sought was an actuality. It had been nothing more than a mythical place that belonged in the pantheon of mythos with El Dorado and Atlantis. Places spoken about in hushed wonderment when overtaken by a deep fantasy.

After an unknown length of time, he lifted his head from his hands. Something had changed about his surroundings.

The second door at the far end of the hallway was now open.

At the opposite end of the hallway, whatever fantastical light the house was emitting was slowly being extinguished. A primordial darkness crept down the hallway toward

Conner, bringing a coldness he could feel in his bones. Heavy, plodding footsteps echoed in the hallway, coming from the darkness. The sight of the creeping darkness and whatever lurked within filled him with dread.

Desperate for help in some form, Conner pulled the phone from his pocket. It was at twenty-one percent battery. Still no signal.

Meanwhile, the heavy footsteps continued.

He got to his feet and ran for the door.

When he got there, he found a stairwell leading up. He climbed the steps.

On the second floor he found himself in a similar hallway to the one he had just left on the first floor. There were two doors in the hallway, both on the right side.

He turned and looked back down the stairwell. It was like looking into an abyss. Yet, this abyss stared back at him, because something lurked within.

Feeling as if there was no other alternative, Conner walked down the hallway in the direction of the two doors. Instead of opening the first door, he passed it, choosing the furthest door.

He grasped the doorknob and turned. It wouldn't open.

It was clear. He was supposed to enter the first door.

Conner sighed and trudged back to the first door. The doorknob turned easily in his hand.

He took a deep breath and stepped through, once again, into his past.

Greed

12.

Conrad

The next morning the weather matched Conrad's mood. A summer thunderstorm had come in after he left the Comisky house, dumping torrential downpours upon the parched earth. Eventually the thunder moved out of the area, leaving the rain behind. He didn't need the weather app on his phone to know that it was going to rain for most of the day. The sky had that rain all day look to it.

The twenty-four-hour mark of Bianca Nowitzki's disappearance had come and gone overnight with no sign of the middle-aged wife. After his run-in with the stranger, Conrad had returned to his apartment in the hopes of getting some much-needed rest. Sleep, however, had eluded him for much of the night. The stranger's appearance and disappearance played behind his closed eyelids as he lay in bed.

Despite his lack of sleep, it wasn't as if the case was static. His hunch to spend most of the night staking out the old Comisky place had paid off with the first real lead of the investigation. The stranger's actions had been peculiar to say the least. If the man had anything to do with Bianca's disappearance, then why return to the scene of the crime?

Conrad didn't work in a large city with a high crime rate, so he wasn't as seasoned in these matters as a concrete jungle detective, however, he watched a few true-crime documentaries on Netflix like everyone else. Suspects liked to revisit the scene of a crime because it reminded them of what had happened. Their senses relived every aspect of the encounter, and it was as if they were experiencing the feeling for the first time. He also knew suspects, especially murderers, were enamored by the investigation into the crimes they had committed. It was as if they couldn't keep away. Had the person responsible for Bianca's disappearance been a part of the search party? Had they been hanging around the neighborhood like the stranger had been?

Deep down he knew the stranger was linked to her disappearance in some fashion. He only had to prove it. That was why he found himself back at the old Comisky place scouring the rubble for any significant sign left behind by the stranger he had missed in the darkness. The stranger couldn't have disappeared into thin air. There had to be something left behind.

Wearing a rain slick over his uniform, he scoured the rubble for that overlooked clue. He found nothing. After an hour, Conrad was soaked to the bone, cold despite the humidity clinging to the air, and out of ideas.

As he was walking back to his cruiser to warm up with the coffee from his thermos, a flashy van pulled up in front of the Nowitzki house. The van itself was black with "Macabre Media" stenciled in red letters. The news vans were scattered around the neighborhood, with the crew escaping the rain inside, much like Conrad. Instinct told him to watch the van and its occupants.

A minute later, a heavy-set man with a bald head got out of the driver's seat of the van. He was joined by a young man with blond hair dressed in tight black denim jeans and a black T-shirt with Macabre Media written dripping red letters on it. The side door to the van slid open and a woman jumped to the asphalt. She was dressed in black leggings and a T-shirt that matched her companion. Her raven-black hair was pulled back into a sensible bun. Her eyes didn't go to the Nowitzki house, but to the pile of rubble that had once been the Comisky place.

While her eyes were locked on the pile of rubble, Baldy slid past her and reached into the van. He came out holding a camera. The three of them looked at each other, sharing some unspoken communication between them. Then they crossed the street and started filming the ruins.

Conrad sat in his cruiser and watched the documentary crew for a while. The rain was still falling at a steady pace, and he was in no hurry to brave it.

As he watched each crew member's role became clear. Baldy was the cameraman, which was made apparent by his wielding of the device as they shot what was likely B roll for whatever project they were filming. Raven hair appeared to be the on-air talent. She stepped in front of the camera on several occasions and spoke without a script. Mr. Macabre exuded an aura of authority—like when he shouted at Baldy, for instance—pegging him as the director/producer.

It seemed peculiar that the crew would be focusing so heavily on the ruins that had once been the old Comisky place. While true it was related to the disappearance of Bianca Nowitzki, it was only a small piece of a much larger puzzle, a puzzle he hadn't gotten far into putting together. The true story was across the street at the Nowitzki house, where David sat inside, likely praying for the safe return of his wife. It was in the people involved in the disappearance, not necessarily in the places surrounding those places. Conrad believed the stranger to be of importance to the investigation. That was where his focus was.

With that thought weighing heavily on his mind, he took a long swallow of his lukewarm coffee. He braced himself and stepped out of the cruiser.

Bianca had been missing for nearly thirty hours at that point. He aimed to find out where she had gone and, more importantly, why.

It was evident that Prairieview had gone indoors to escape the downpour. There was a small group of searchers looking for any sign related to Bianca Nowitzki, whether evidence or the woman herself. The group was almost entirely made up of law enforcement officers, with a few family members joining them. There was one notable person missing on the law enforcement side of the group of searchers. Chief Nichols.

It was important that the lead investigator in a missing person's case be present to give directions to the other officers. They needed to know what exactly constituted as evidence of importance, as what appeared to be mere garbage initially could turn out to be important to the investigation. If something of importance was found, it was crucial the lead investigator was present to ensure all protocols were followed to safeguard the evidence against being tainted. There was also the show of support for the family of the missing person. That investigator would often be the conduit to the department in all matters related to the case. All of these factors were an important reason for the lead investigator to be present, despite the constant rain.

As the self-professed lead investigator, Chief Nichols was that important person, at least in the man's own mind. Nichols was noticeably absent. Conrad also thought of himself as the lead investigator in the disappearance of Bianca Nowitzki. Nichols was all talk, while Conrad preferred actions.

He had been a constant presence at the Nowitzki home and in the neighborhood since he was handed the case by the Chief. Despite having that case ripped from his grasp, and in front of the media, no less, he still considered the case his. The only lead of the investigation was the result of his own investigatory skills and following up on a hunch, good police work in other words. It didn't matter who the lead investigator was at the moment, what mattered most was finding Bianca and what happened to her. Glory be damned, he just wanted to find her. Then the glory would come.

When the decision was made to break for lunch, thirty-four hours had elapsed since Bianca was last seen by her husband. David Nowitzki had joined the group as they searched for his wife. There was a knowing expression in each of the searcher's eyes. A knowledge that was becoming increasingly clear the longer they searched. They were looking for a body.

David seemed to wear that knowledge on his shoulders, as if being weighed down by it rather than the hours of rainfall gathered on his clothes. Yet there was a grim determination in the man's eyes. Defiance perhaps. An incessant need to prove everyone else wrong, that Bianca could be found alive.

David and Conrad walked to their vehicles in silence. They had spent much of the morning together. Reassuring words had been spoken. The moment didn't call for reassurance or empty words this time, however. He hoped his presence was sufficient.

When they arrived back on the Nowitzki's street, he noticed the documentary crew was still filming in front of the old Comisky place. Baldy was still filming, though this time it didn't appear to be B roll. Raven held a small device in her hand that looked like some kind of meter. She spoke to the camera in an excited tone. Mr. Macabre had his hands crossed over his chest, obviously unimpressed.

"Any idea what the documentary crew is doing at the Comisky place?" he asked David, nodding toward the crew.

"Documentary crew? Oh, them. That's a polite way of putting it, I guess. They knocked on the door this morning. I saw the camera and answered right away. I mean, I want to keep Bianca's name and picture in the news as much as possible. If we don't keep at it, then people will forget her. I won't, of course, but others will. So, I've done interviews with everyone that's knocked on my door.

"They were stranger than the rest, though. They kept focusing on the house Bianca saw across the street. Had me describe it in detail. I even looked for that sketch she drew of it, but I couldn't find it."

"Yeah, that's in evidence, David. There were other things she sketched that may be important."

David waved a dismissive hand. "That's fine, I just want her back. Whatever you need to find my wife."

"Why would they only be interested in the house? Did they say?"

"You don't recognize them?"

He shook his head.

"I don't blame you, neither did I. I was so thrown off by their focus on the house that I googled them after they left. Apparently, they're famous paranormal investigators. Their YouTube channel has millions of followers."

"Paranormal Investigators, huh?"

"A fancy word for ghost hunters, if you ask me. Of course, there isn't a ghost here. Just a missing wife that I want to come home." David's eyes welled with tears.

"Hey, we're going to find out what happened to Bianca. Okay?" Conrad said, breaking a promise to himself.

David nodded instinctively, as if he was too preoccupied with his own thoughts to listen to the empty reassurances. Conrad was thankful for that.

He watched as David trudged inside with slumped shoulders. He stood there for an unknown length of time watching the paranormal investigators. It was his penance for issuing empty words to a desperate man.

Conrad should have been driving back to his apartment for a sandwich and a refueling of coffee. It was going to be a long day if the rain continued to fall like it was. He should be getting out of the rain like a sensible person, however, that wasn't what he did, at least not yet.

He found himself crossing the street toward the old Comisky place and the crew that was still in the process of filming. It wasn't planned, so he didn't know what he was going to say, though a showing of police presence seemed warranted. The two men had their backs to him. Raven was facing him, though she was looking at the meter in her hand and speaking enthusiastically.

"The EMF meter shows a remarkable spike in the electromagnetic field the closer we get to the remnants of the burned house. As you can see, the meter is barely registering a reading at this particular point on the property. However, if I walk roughly twenty feet in the direction of the remnants, there's a clear spike in activity."

She turned and walked towards the pile of rubble as the cameraman filmed the meter from over her shoulder. Her steps were methodical, building the tension for the moment when the theoretical spike would happen.

"As you can see, there still isn't any noticeable change. Now, keep in mind that the small changes you currently see on the meter aren't enough to note any paranormal activity. Those are only minute changes that occur naturally in the atmosphere, of course, you've also got power lines and other electrical devices that could cause interference with a reading. Since this house hasn't had electricity in years, I think we're good. The neighboring houses are too far away to interfere with the reading too much.

"And... there it is!"

She turned toward the camera, while holding up the EMF meter to show the reading. A smile spread across her face. Conrad hadn't noticed her beauty until that moment.

Then the smile faded as her eyes fell upon him.

"It looks like we've got company, guys," Raven said to the men.

Then she turned to Conrad, with the smile returning to her face, though this seemed to be an artificial version of the previously genuine article.

"Officer, would you care to comment on the house Bianca Nowitzki claims to have seem in the days leading up to her disappearance?"

Conrad stood in silence as the camera turned in his direction. He was oddly aware of his sweaty hands in the pockets of his rain slick. He took them out, rubbed them on his pants, forgetting that he was covered in rain. Then put them back in his pockets.

"The Prairieview Police Department has no comment at this time," he said in a shaky voice.

"Look, we've found another department lemming. Can you believe our luck, Miriam?" Mr. Macabre said.

"I can only reiterate what David Nowitzki has already said at this time. Bianca claimed to have seen a house in the days leading to her disappearance. A house that her husband couldn't see. Now, what exactly that has to do with her disappearance is still under investigation."

This time he managed to control the nerves in his voice.

"Is there a suspect?" Raven said, crossing her arms over her chest.

"There is a person of interest, though we can't identify that person at this time."

"He's talking about the Thrall," Mr. Macabre said.

"That's all I can say at this time," Conrad reiterated.

Mr. Macabre sighed. "Well, if that's all he's got to say, then let's cut."

Conrad was walking back to the cruiser with his mind on the leftover lasagna he made last night—from frozen—when he heard footsteps approaching quickly in his direction. The encounter with the stranger the previous night was still fresh in his mind, despite it being daytime and having witnesses. His hand instinctively moved closer to his service pistol, without grasping it, as he turned around.

Raven stopped short when she saw his caution.

"Sorry, I guess I shouldn't sneak up on a cop, right? Especially considering the circumstances."

"Miriam Macabre on camera, Miriam Tanenbaum off. I host Macabre Media's Macabre Manor," she said, extending her hand.

They shook. "Officer Conrad Cain."

"Don't mind Gavin. He's a jerk to everyone, that's why we broke up. Plus, he cheated on me with some random towny in Poughkeepsie. Turns out he only cares about two things, money and his johnson. Worst thing? He thinks with both."

"No trouble, Ms. Tanenbaum. He was right, I wasn't much help."

"True, but a man in uniform always looks good," she said with a wink.

"Even a nervous officer shaking in his boots at the sight of a camera? I doubt that. Anyway…"

Conrad opened the door to his cruiser and started to climb inside. Miriam's words stopped him.

"What if we paid you?"

"Paid me for what?" he said after turning around.

"Paid you for appearing on the show, of course. Like I said, a man in uniform looks good, and not just to make all the naughty ladies want to be arrested. It lends credibility to the show, which we struggle with as I'm sure you can imagine. We've covered some cases like this before; it's going to be big. Especially our angle on it. Having an officer on the inside would be beneficial. It would also help spread the word on Bianca's disappearance, which I know you care about."

She ended by throwing out a figure that was more than his annual salary.

"Sorry, Mrs. Tanenbaum, but—"

"If you're going to turn me down the least you could do is call me Miriam."

"Okay. Sorry, Miriam, but it's against department regulations for me to accept payment for doing the media. Plus, I don't think I'd be any good at it."

Conrad started to close the door when Miriam grabbed his arm.

"Just think about it, Conrad. Think about the exposure. Could be your big break."

13.

Conrad

Ten minutes after his conversation with Miriam, Conrad was back at his apartment enjoying leftover lasagna reheated in the microwave and doing just as she had asked. He was contemplating her offer, despite having turned it down. Turning it down had been his instinct as a cop; it had been the job talking more than it been the man. Now, it was the man's turn to do his due diligence.

It was department policy that all media relations were to be vetted through the Chief. If an officer was approached by a member of the media, like the host of a YouTube show, that officer was to spout the line "the Prairieview Police Department has no comment at this time." Then the officer was to refer them to Chief Nichols through his personal line. It was usually a local reporter that was more than happy to get a sound bite from the Chief, however, this was the first time Conrad hadn't made the referral. After his initial refusal to comment was ridiculed, he decided to take the initiative. He was much more open-minded than the Chief, who would have scoffed at doing an interview with a ghosthunter show. Nichols was about as closed-minded as small-town police officials came. It simply wouldn't work.

It would benefit from having the *actual* investigating officer on-hand for the interview, instead of the Chief of Police that was only pretending to be in charge of the case. The media session the prior day had been the first time Conrad had seen the Chief outside of the department since the Bianca Nowitzki case had fallen into their laps. A missing person's case wasn't investigated from behind a desk, but by putting boots to the ground.

Of course, if Chief Nichols had been offered the sum of money that Conrad had been offered, there was little doubt the other man would have taken it. The man drove a brand-new Ford F-150 truck, while his wife drove to Wichita and back on a daily basis for shopping trips in a Range Rover. Conrad had seen what was affordable on the Chief of Police's salary and that was stretching it. The Chief definitely had his hand in a cookie jar.

If Chief Nichols was getting something on the side, why not get in on the action? Conrad considered himself an honorable man, but where had being honorable gotten him to this point? As an officer to an incompetent chief that cared more about lining his pockets than about investigating a missing person. Nichols became chief in the same manner that Conrad's father had, power and influence.

A positive and influential outcome could result from joining forces with the Macabre Media team. Obviously, there was the money to consider, which made the offer tempting. It was more money than he had ever had at one particular time in his life. It was more than his annual salary. It wasn't *quit my job and retire tomorrow* money, but it was enough to be a nest egg in case he wanted to start a family someday. It was the kind of money that meant he could afford to leave Prairieview without draining his lifesavings in the process. It meant he could finally afford to start dreaming.

The exposure it would bring to Bianca's disappearance couldn't be overlooked either. Despite uncovering a person of interest in the stranger, the case hadn't developed as quickly as he would have liked. Conrad hadn't heard of the

YouTube channel, but with millions of subscribers, the show obviously had an incredible reach. If just one of those viewers knew something that could aid in discovering what had happened to Bianca, it would be worth it.

There was also the exposure being on a popular YouTube channel would bring to Conrad. A solved case on a show like that could do wonders for his career. It would put him on the upward trajectory towards being Chief of Police, like his old man had been. Though he would do it better than the old man, of course. The exposure could also bring interest from other law enforcement agencies. Federal Agent Cain. Conrad liked the sound of that.

With all those pros swimming around in his mind, it was easy to forget about the cons. Chief among them being the Chief himself. Since all media relations were dealt with through the Chief, Nichols likely would be irate that one of his officers had taken things into his own hands. The ramifications varied from a suspension to being fired. In that case, he had better solve the case before word reached the Chief.

There was also the matter of what to tell the crew from Macabre Media. He knew the media got excited when they felt as if they were receiving inside information. The situation insinuated there would be some inside information shared, but how much was too much? At what point did sharing that inside information hinder the investigation? If he decided to team with the YouTube channel, only he would know where that line would be drawn. It wasn't something he could allow Gavin or Miriam to decide.

By the time he had finished the lasagna, he had nearly changed his mind. Yet he still wasn't sure what the crew was investigating. It was clear they weren't there to investigate the disappearance of Bianca Nowitzki, at least not directly. Instead, they had asked him about the claims that she had seen a house across the street, a house that her husband couldn't see. David had confirmed as much. Miriam had called the device in her hand an EMF meter, while talking about electromagnetic fields. The techno talk had been above his head, yet one thing was clear. They were investigating the plausibility of the house being real.

Conrad was getting back into his cruiser when his cellphone rang. He looked at the number on the screen and sighed. Chief Nichols.

"Hello, Chief."

"What are you doing? I've been trying to reach you all morning on the radio," Nichols shouted into the phone.

"Well, I was with the search party most of the day. We switched channels so we wouldn't interfere with an official line. Didn't think you guys back at the station would want to hear our chatter back and forth. I just finished lunch and am headed back rejoin the party now."

If you were with the search party then you'd know what channel to reach me, he thought but didn't say.

"Well, next time let the station know, so you can be reached," Nichols said in a huff.

"Will do, sir. So, why did you need to reach me?"

"What were you thinking last night?"

"Well, I thought about a lot of things last night, sir. You'll have to be more specific."

"Don't get smart with me, you know damn well what I'm talking about. I got a call from a resident in Nowitzki's neighborhood that said you were parked out there all night. Then you chased someone down that was just minding their own business. Tell me, why am I hearing that from an old lady and not my officer?"

Conrad took a deep breath and composed himself. "Well, sir, I was following a lead. You're aware of the BOLO I put out for the stranger that was seen in the neighborhood? A neighbor, probably the same one that called you, told me that he had been seen in the neighborhood late at night each of the past two nights. Came from the old Comisky place. So, I decided to have a stakeout. That person who was minding their own business appeared to be that same stranger. So, I approached him. When I did, he took off running. I gave chase."

"And... what happened?"

"That's just it. He disappeared into the pile of rubble at the old Comisky place. I spent fifteen minutes searching for him but didn't find him. I even went back this morning to double check the scene. Nothing."

"Disappeared? What do you mean he disappeared? People don't just disappear, Cain. There's always somewhere to go, like Bianca Nowitzki, we just need to find out where she went. Maybe you didn't look hard enough for this guy."

"I searched for him, sir. It was like he wasn't there at all."

"Now, you're talking mystical mumbo jumbo, Cain. You better be careful or I'll sit you behind a desk until the cows come home. What do you think you're doing anyway? Investigating this case?"

"Someone has to," Conrad said, fuming.

"I'll pretend like I didn't hear that, Cain. Next time, call it in. Don't approach a suspect without backup. Do I make myself clear?"

"Yessir."

When he ended the call, a decision had been made.

The rain had slowed to a trickle by the time Conrad parked the cruiser in Nowitzki's neighborhood. Maybe that would beckon the volunteers from the previous day that hadn't come back that morning. The police officials participating in the search were still filtering in from various locations—Conrad knew some of the Sheriff's deputies preferred the fast food in Crimson Creek over the choices in Prairieview, which didn't have fast food. They would be the last to arrive, then the search would resume in a different area.

There was a group of PPD talking with a Sherriff's deputy in the Nowitzki's driveway. Instead of joining them, Conrad crossed the street to the old Comisky place. Miriam, Gavin, and the nameless cameraman still on the premises. This time they weren't filming but were instead involved in a heated argument.

Miriam held up a hand to pause the argument when she saw him approaching.

"I'm in," he said without preamble.

"Great, meet us here at eight o'clock tonight. There'll be fewer eyes and ears around then," she said with a wink.

14.

Conrad

"The White House isn't new to residents of Macabre Manor—what we like to call our subscribers. If you aren't in the know, become a subscriber today and delve into all things Macabre as a member. You'll get access to all things Macabre Media, including Macabre Manor and the infamous White House Collection. For those of you that are new, I'll dive into the mythology of the White House in brief detail.

"We don't have confirmation on when the infamous White House first appeared, because of the house's wicked nature of making everyone that sees it disappear. Yet, thanks to eyewitness accounts, we can make an educated guess. In 1930, forty-three-year-old farmer, Hanz Bauman, was living a regular life in rural Nebraska. The work was hard, but Hanz enjoyed providing for his family and the surrounding area with the crops he grew. His wife, Ethel, was a homemaker and also sold items she knitted at the farmer's market where Hanz sold fruit and vegetables every weekend. His twin teenage sons, Albert and Karl, helped their father on the farm as often as possible. They were even known to miss school in the fall when crops needed to be harvested. The kids were often picked on for wearing ill-fitting clothing. Hanz and

Ethel tried their best to provide for their family, but sometimes, it just wasn't enough.

"According to legend, the couple was behind on their mortgage. Now, we know the great depression was hard on a lot of families. The Baumans were the same. They were an honest, hard-working family that was only trying to keep their farm afloat. Unfortunately for them, they weren't managing to keep their heads above the water line. The bank repossessed the Bauman's farm just a month after Hanz went missing. But what happened leading to his disappearance is where things begin to go macabre.

"There has been much speculation about Hanz Bauman's state of mind leading to his disappearance. The crops weren't performing well. The bank was threatening to repossess the house and land that he had worked so hard to attain. No small feat for a man that emigrated to America with his parents as a teenager. His parents had both passed away in the months leading up to his disappearance, though the causes of death have been lost to history. So, we have a grieving man who was on the verge of losing the house and farm that was the symbol of his American dream. More like an American nightmare, if you ask me.

"According to interviews with his wife and children, Hanz was a serious man, something instilled by his immigrant parents. Karl claimed his father didn't understand his tendency toward the fantastical world of make believe created by his own mind. Albert, on the other hand, was always rather quiet when his father was brought up after the disappearance. Let me explain.

"Hanz and Albert were working alone on the farm a week before the father would go missing. Usually, Karl would be with them, however, on this occasion the boy was nursing a broken arm. It was a consequence of the imagination that Hanz simply couldn't understand. On that day, something peculiar happened. Hanz claimed to see a house at the edge of their property. Obviously, this was strange, as the land in question belonged to the Bauman family and their house was in the opposite direction. The nearest neighbor's house was visible, though this was definitely not it. Albert later described the house according to his father's words. It was unusually tall, in fact, Hanz hadn't seen houses that tall in his lifetime. The house was constructed of brick that had been painted white, an oddity for the time. The wood trim had been painted black, very odd for the time, once again. The strangest thing, however, was that Albert couldn't see the house.

"According to Ethel, Hanz asked her a single time if she saw anything at the edge of their property, anything out of the ordinary. He didn't indicate that he had seen a house that shouldn't have been there. He simply asked her if she saw anything unusual. She didn't. It was the last time the presence of the house would be discussed in the Bauman household. One week later, Hanz Bauman would go missing while plowing the field."

Miriam paused, obviously letting the gravity of her words sink in with the viewer. She looked into the camera, as if locking eyes with each person watching. When she was ready, she continued.

"That was the first appearance of what has become known as the White House. Don't make any mistakes about the name. This isn't the stately manor in Washington, D.C. This manor has a much more Macabre nature. What happened to Hanz Bauman was tragic, but he would only be the first. The White House was hungry, and the Thrall was ready with more victims for the feeding.

"That hunger has brought us to Prairieview, Kansas, where Bianca Nowitzki has been missing for two days. A lawyer specializing in corporate law, Bianca lived in the quaint town with her husband David, who is an executive assistant for the local conglomerate, Langley Enterprises. The two met nearly thirty years ago when David's boss hired Bianca for advisement on a deal where he would be acquiring the now defunct Techno Town. There was instant chemistry, according to David. Six months later, they were married and lived happily ever after. The only problem is that happily ever after was interrupted.

"In the days leading up to her disappearance, Bianca Nowitzki would reveal to her husband that she could see a house across the street. David thought this very peculiar, as the house across the street had burned down years ago. All that was left was a burnt pile of rubble, a macabre symbol of what could happen if we let down our guard. She didn't have a flashback to a time when the Comisky house had stood. No, she saw a house that shouldn't be there, a house that, according to her husband, couldn't be there. He said she was transfixed on the house, as if it had hypnotized her in some fashion. Sound familiar, residence? She would sit on the porch staring at the house across the street that her husband couldn't see, despite the nearly one-hundred-degree weather this week in Kansas. The house had mesmerized her in such a fashion that it was disrupting her sleep patterns. Sound familiar?

"On the night of her disappearance, Bianca Nowitzki had gotten up in the middle of the night. David Nowitzki believes it to have been around two in the morning, though he could be mistaken. Our faithful viewers will remember the witching hour, otherwise known as three o'clock, to be the White House's favorite for taking its victims. Perhaps she sat on the porch for an hour before crossing the street and climbing those steps. We'll likely never know, as there isn't a soul that has seen the White House and lived longer than a week."

Conrad stood just out of the frame, waiting for Miriam's "brief" introduction to end. Then she would transition into an interview with "local law enforcement." Nerves had been coursing through his body as he waited for the camera to start rolling. Now, however, Miriam's monolog had captured his attention. He hadn't realized there was an entire mythology surrounding the house that Bianca Nowitzki claimed to have seen in the days leading up to her death. He still didn't believe it existed, but it was interesting.

"As we approach the forty-eight-hour mark of Bianca Nowitzki's disappearance, the town seems to have changed. Where once there was hope, now there is only despair. Police officials are short on both leads and hope on this dark summer night, where a grim outcome seems almost assured. To those of us that know about the White House, we can only pray for her family. Because if Bianca entered the White House, she wouldn't be getting out.

"We have Officer Conrad Cain of the Prairieview Police Department joining us for this very special episode, with more perspective on the case. Officer Cain, what can you tell us about Bianca's state of mind leading up to her disappearance?" Miriam asked, turning to Conrad.

He felt the camera turn in his direction. For the briefest of moments, he froze. Words left his mind. A moment later, they returned.

"Well, Miriam or Mistress of the Macabre, as I've heard your followers call you, Bianca's state of mind is something law enforcement has struggled with since the start of this case. On one hand, she was a successful lawyer, who was known for her level-headed thinking under the high-pressure environment of corporate law. She handled that pressure well. Enjoyed the occasional girl's night out for some margaritas to cut loose. Bianca and her husband, David, were in a place in their lives where they could get away for a weekend vacation on a whim. It seemed she was handling the pressure well. Then a week before she disappeared, things seemingly changed in her world. According to David, she started seeing a house across the street. As you said earlier, the house that stood across the street once upon a time, had burned to the ground in a tragic accident when I was a rookie on the force. I remember it well. Luckily, no one was hurt. The fact remains, there wasn't a house standing across the street, only a pile of burnt rubble.

"Now, as the week progressed, David grew increasingly worried about his wife's state of mind. She would stare at the ruins across the street for hours at a time, where she claimed to have seen a tall, white house. Her sleep was interrupted in the days leading to her disappearance. On the night she disappeared, David said she got out of bed in the middle of the night. He thought she was only going to the living room, because of his tendency to snore. Hours later, he realized that wasn't the case. He searched for her, but his wife was gone.

"It's fair to point out that there is a history of dementia in Bianca's family, which has to be factored into law enforcement's thinking when trying to find her. That being said, she got regular checkups with her healthcare provider and hadn't shown any signs of mental illness in the months leading up to her disappearance. Could she have been hiding the signs from everyone around her? It's possible, sure, but isn't likely. So, the question is what would cause a perfectly healthy forty-eight-year-old to suddenly see a house that wasn't there?"

Gavin nodded his approval from behind Stu, the cameraman.

"Are there any leads that law enforcement has discovered? What about evidence? If you can speak of it, of course."

"While searching the Nowitzki home, I found a notebook belonging to Bianca. There were sketches inside that gave a telling indication of her state of mind in the days leading up to her disappearance. The first one is a sketch of the house she told her husband she could see. A house that David, himself, couldn't see."

Conrad held up the sketch for the camera.

"This was only one of many that filled the pages of the notebook. It was as if she couldn't get her mind off the house, as if it encompassed every waking moment, every thought she had over the course of that week.

"The second sketch found in the notebook that I'd like to share also filled many pages. It's a man."

He held up the sketch of the stranger for the camera.

"That's the Thrall," Miriam whispered, excitedly.

"I don't know what a Thrall is, Miriam, but what I can tell you is this is a man she possibly saw before her disappearance. He has been seen by neighbors in the area, and by me."

Miriam gasped. "You've seen the Thrall?"

"Yes, ma'am, if that's who this man is."

"Tell us about your encounter with the Thrall, Officer Cain."

"It was last night. There were reports from a neighbor of a suspicious man seen leaving the Comisky property during the night. I decided to investigate by having an old-fashioned stakeout. Hours later, the man emerged from the pile of rubble just as reported. I approached the man with caution, not knowing if he was armed or knew anything about Bianca's disappearance. I flipped my flashlight on as I approached the man. He turned his dark eyes upon me. We both stared at each other for a moment. Then he bolted for the rubble pile, where he had come from. As an officer, I keep in fairly good shape, but I wasn't fast enough. He disappeared into the rubble pile. I mean, disappeared. He was just gone."

"There you have it, ladies and gentlemen, Officer Cain encountered the Thrall and lived to tell the tale. Others haven't been so lucky. Thanks for joining us, Officer Cain. Until next time, Macabre Manor residence. This is Miriam, Mistress of the Macabre, imploring you to keep an eye out, otherwise you might become the next resident of the house that wasn't there. Good night."

"And…cut. Conrad, I mean, Officer Cain, that was great. I tried to talk Miriam out of getting you involved. No offense, but you came across as a stick in the mud when we first met. You proved me wrong. A cop encountering Thrall? That'll really get people talking," Gavin said, barely containing his excitement.

Conrad left the old Comisky place feeling on top of the world. Chief Nichols had been wrong to take control of the investigation. Obviously, Conrad was the right person for the job. He had just proved it with an interview with an international YouTube channel. There was a strut in his step as he walked to his personal car, which he had taken to avoid prying eyes from seeing a department vehicle in the vicinity while the crew was filming. He didn't want word to get out that he was working with them yet. The longer he could put off another encounter with the chief, the better.

An hour later, he was back at his apartment enjoying a late dinner, when his phone pinged. It was a text message from Gabby.

Gabby: *Great interview! You look as sexy on TV as you do in person. Did he really disappear?*

He stared at the text for a full minute before responding.

Conrad: *How did you see the interview? I missed you there.*

Gabby: *Missed me? Lol. They didn't tell you?*

Conrad: *Tell me what?*

Gabby: *That you were live streaming. I missed the live version, but they uploaded the video to their social media page and tagged you. It's going viral.*

15.

Conner

Conner exited the room on the second floor of what he knew to be the White House. This time he was able to keep himself upright, though he *wanted* to fall to the floor and give up. The monologue delivered so eloquently by Miriam echoed in his thoughts. There wasn't a person who had seen the house and lived longer than a week. Obviously, meaning everyone who saw the house eventually went inside, and whomever went inside never came out.

The second room had been the same as the first, like a doorway to the past. A past he had wanted to forget so badly that he had moved out of the state and cleansed it from his memory. Both of the memories were linked to the same timeframe of his life, the same investigation into the disappearance of Bianca Nowitzki. The transition between the two memories had been nearly seamless, as if the house had been there. Of course, that was just it. The house had been there ten years ago; however, Bianca had been the only person able to see it because of the strange cloaking abilities the house possessed.

He knew it was the same house that Bianca had seen in the days leading to her disappearance. A house that had managed to move hundreds of miles seemingly by itself. Conner didn't know how that was possible. Was it a government experiment? While not a conspiracy theorist, he wasn't so naïve as to think the government wouldn't experiment on its own citizens. This experiment was conducted out in the open for the world to see, at least in the beginning stages. That didn't seem like the way the government liked to conduct its business. They preferred to conduct clandestine experiments outside of prying eyes, so they had plausible deniability.

This wasn't a government experiment. Then what was it? Who was responsible for the madness that he had experienced while trapped inside the White House?

Thrall.

Years later, Conner still didn't know much about the man who he would come to know as Thrall. When the word was spoken by Miriam ten years ago, he hadn't known what the word meant. According to the Mistress of the Macabre, Thrall was essentially a slave. A man that had been locked into servitude of whatever malevolent force controlled the White House. She hadn't known what that force or entity was in those days but had speculated that it was likely a demonic entity of some fashion.

If the government wasn't responsible for the White House, then it would have to be of supernatural origin. What was more supernatural than a demon?

A tear rolled down his cheek. He hadn't thought about Miriam in years; the pain was still more than he could stand. Suppressing the pain instead of dealing with it hadn't been the healthiest way of coping, yet it had been the only way he knew. The suppression had only caused the pain to fester deep within, growing in both size and intensity while going untreated, like an untreated battle wound. With time it had become infected. At least now he knew what the battle was over.

His soul.

Ten years ago, he fled Kansas a battered and beaten man, with his sins piling so high they could reach the heavens, rather than the depths of hell from which they came. Those sins started at a miniscule level compared to what they would become. He hadn't realized his actions fell under the wide blanket of sin until well after he had become established in Crestview. Such was the way with sin, we often don't know we are doing anything wrong until we have the benefit of hindsight. By that point it's often too late to rectify our actions, leaving us to deal with the consequences.

He was reaching into his pocket for the phone when a voice stopped him.

"It's at seventeen percent battery, not that it'll work in here."

Thrall stood at the far end of the hallway in front of the stairwell to the first floor.

"Conner Keen, huh? Now, if you're going to go and change your name, Conrad, why didn't you go with something that sounds different? Conner Keen. Conrad Cain. It's all the same man."

"I had no choice after what you did. People think I'm a murderer thanks to you."

"You and I both know there's blood on your hands, Conrad Cain. I did what you wanted to do but couldn't because you're weak."

"Why are you doing this to me?"

Thrall smiled. "All will be revealed in time, Conrad."

"I think the time is now."

"Ascend to the next level."

Conner crossed his arms over his chest to accentuate the fact that he didn't plan on moving from that spot.

Thrall's smile widened.

"My master awaits you at the final level. Words are more his forte. Me? I don't have much use for words, Conrad. I prefer pain. Much can be communicated through pain. Would you like me to communicate with you, Conrad?"

He tried to find the words for a clever response and failed. He stared at Thrall instead.

"I also prefer the dark."

The supernatural light that appeared to be emitting from the walls of the house started to fade. The phenomenon started where Thrall stood and slowly made its way in Conner's direction. After only a moment, the slave to the house was fully hidden under a cloak of darkness.

"Ah. The darkness envelopes me like a cold blanket, like a lullaby from the dark one himself. Why are so many people afraid of the dark, Conrad? Its comforting embrace is like the moment of death itself, only darkness lasts forever. It's as if that moment was extended for eternity. Do you wish to feel its embrace, Conrad? To join me in the darkness? Everyone says no, but it finds them in the end. It always finds them. Where can you run from darkness?"

As Thrall spoke, Conner was making his way to a third door that appeared after he exited the room. His choices were slim, either stay and face Thrall or ascend to the third floor as commanded. The choice was clear.

"I know the answer, Conrad. Why are people afraid of the dark?" Thrall said from the other end of the hallway.

"Because of things like me."

This time the voice was a whisper in his ear.

Conner opened the door and jumped inside. He took the steps two at a time, anything to keep distance between himself and Thrall. The darkness followed at his heels.

Upon exiting the stairwell, he didn't study his surroundings. He figured it would look the same as the two prior floors. He focused on the door halfway down the hallway. Once he was gripping the doorknob he gambled with a look into the darkness.

It was gone.

Thrall stood at the other side of the hallway as if nothing had happened, accept the smile on his face.

"See you soon, Conrad."

That smile was the last thing he saw before he stepped into the third room.

Gluttony

16.

Conrad

"What the hell were you thinking?" Chief Nichols yelled.

It was the next morning. Conrad had hoped word of the interview with Macabre Manor wouldn't reach the Chief. The man wasn't active on any social media platform that Conrad was aware of. He should have known that even a man as isolated as Nichols couldn't avoid hearing about how one of his officers had conducted an interview with a member of the media and that footage was quickly becoming national news. The mayor had brought the news to the Chief's attention.

If it had been the simple matter of an informative interview that would have been the end of the discussion, however, it was more nuanced than that. He had emphasized information regarding Bianca's state of mind that the department, meaning Chief Nichols, had wished to deemphasize in the hopes that she wouldn't be treated as a woman who had simply skipped town. Instead, Conrad had made the public question whether the woman had been of sound mind or had simply run off with the man she had sketched.

"I was thinking it would help the investigation. Macabre Manor is a popular YouTube channel that reaches millions of people across the world. We need to keep Bianca's name in the news. That means talking to media members even if they are less than conventional," Conrad said.

"Macabre? What the hell is that? Is that some kinky sex thing? Like a whorehouse?" Nichols said, looking disgusted.

"No, it's a YouTube show called Macabre Manor. It's a term the horror community throws out in spades. It's about death, I think. The show is about haunted houses."

"Why is a show about haunted houses interested in interviewing you in regard to the Bianca Nowitzki case?"

If you were more involved in the case or you'd watched the video yourself, then you wouldn't have to ask that question, Conrad thought.

"David Nowitzki told reporters Bianca was seeing a house across the street that he couldn't see. I believe you were there when he first mentioned it."

"Right. So? What does that have to do with a YouTube channel about a haunted house? Why would they be so interested?"

"You really should watch the video they made explaining the lore behind the house, but in the meantime, I'll give you the abridged version. Basically, there are other people that have claimed to see the White House, as they call it on the channel. It goes back nearly a hundred years. Always moving around from city to city, state to state, even across the world. Whoever sees the house goes missing. According to the show's lore, there isn't a single person that has survived seeing the house longer than a week, and no one has ever come out either."

Nichols raised an eyebrow. "Hold on, you're telling me that there are people all across the world who claim to see this house and don't survive? Then this podcast—"

"YouTube channel," Conrad interjected.

"—YouTube channel, right, comes in and covers the whole thing. Then…bam! Millions of followers? Sounds fishy if you ask me."

"Fishy? I mean, yeah, exploitive, sure, but it's no worse than what the rest of the media does for ratings. Their hook just happens to be a bit darker than the rest of the media. I don't think that's fishy."

"Oh, that? No, I don't mean exploiting the disappearance of Bianca and these other people," Nichols said, waving a dismissive hand.

"Okay? Then what?"

"Think about it. Wherever they show up there's already been a missing person that just so happens to align perfectly with the concept of their show. You already said they have a whole mythology around the, uh, house—"

"The White House."

"—the White House, right. Millions of viewers, you say. Imagine the endorsement deals and ad revenue they're doing. They might be worth millions of dollars, Conrad. I don't know about you, but I don't trust a millionaire. What if that guy you saw is working for them? Like an accomplice. He comes into town in the days leading to the disappearance and sets everything up. Kills whatever person they've picked out, gets rid of the body in such a way that no one has ever found the body. Then they're all setup for the big YouTube show."

"Wait, you think Miriam and the crew are in on this? As in they've plotted to kill all these people, including Bianca Nowitzki?"

"First name basis? What you got feelings for this broad?"

"No, Miriam is her name. We've talked a couple of times since they came into town. They offered me a spot on their team as the inside man to the investigation, which I turned down. I did the interview to bring awareness to the case."

He omitted the part where it was a paid gig, and he had actually accepted it.

"So, you've got an in? That's perfect! I want you to get in touch with Mary and—"

"Miriam."

"—Miriam and accept that job. We can't trust that YouTube show. There's something strange going on there, I just know it. Keep an eye on them and keep me informed!"

"Sure thing, Chief."

"Now, what is this I hear about you seeing a man disappear into thin air? Is this guy that's working for Sexy Manor some kind of magician or something? Tell me what happened."

Conrad explained his encounter with the Thrall in as much detail as he could remember. Nichols raised an eyebrow when he had finished.

"Sounds like either you need to see a psychologist or that Sexy Manor is playing with your head if you ask me."

He nodded. "It had occurred to me."

"Alright, well, keep me informed, Cain. Get out of here."

"Oh, and let me know if you're going on the TV next time," Nichols said as Conrad was getting out of his chair.

"Yessir."

He was closing the door when Nichols spoke again.

"Cain!"

"Yeah?" he said, poking his head back in the office.

Chief Nichols was polishing his nameplate with a handkerchief and averting his eyes. "That, uh, gig, did it pay anything?"

"Nah, they didn't mention anything."

"Too bad, the department really could have used it."

As he left the Chief's office, Conrad's mind instinctively turned to Miriam and the Macabre Manor crew. He had the urge to warn her, let her know in some fashion that Chief Nichols suspected them, as absurd as it was. Yet he resisted that urge, knowing such actions belonged in the realm of the foolish. While it was true he knew the Chief's intentions were usually anything but honorable, he knew next to nothing about the Macabre Manor crew. Could they be trusted?

Prairieview was a tightknit community, as was common with small towns. They didn't trust people from "the outside." Even people that weren't born there but had lived in town for years weren't as trustworthy as original townies. The outside was a powerful place that was filled with ideals that had been skewed by a world much larger than their own. The outsiders didn't know what it took to survive in a town where everyone seemed to know your business, let alone your name. They might as well have been from another planet, that was how much they had in common. The question was which planet was the crew from? It would take a longer amount of time to know whether he could trust them or not.

In the meantime, the Chief had brought up an interesting point. It was feasible for the crew and the stranger they had dubbed the Thrall to be working together. Conrad had concerns about that theory, however. This wasn't the first time the Macabre Manor crew had invaded a town with their investigation into the White House. If they were somehow behind the disappearances in some nefarious way, why hadn't it been discovered? He found it hard to believe the PPD was the first law enforcement agency to investigate the YouTube channel. Then again, there was always the first time for everything. Maybe they would be the department that would uncover a diabolical ploy to boost their ratings by executing an unspeakable crime.

There was video evidence just waiting on the Macabre Media YouTube channel to be watched, for research, of course. It appeared he would be binge watching Macabre Manor in the few hours he had in the evenings. The videos needed to be vetted for evidence of their involvement in the other disappearances. A link between the crew and the disappearances would give them a fighting chance of bringing charges. That was putting the cart before the horse, as their involvement was unclear, both in reality and in his mind.

While he was at the station, Conrad made a list of all the disappearances the Macabre crew had covered of the five-year span of their YouTube show. This list was daunting until he realized he only needed the shows relating to the

White House. That sliced the list in half but was still a large number. Thirteen. Thirteen people had disappeared after claiming to see the White House in a five-year span. If the mythology was true, how many people had disappeared in the nearly one-hundred-year span of the house's macabre history?

Locating all the departments that had been involved in each investigation took longer than anticipated. It was midmorning before he dropped an email to each department regarding information about the Macabre Manor crew. He didn't anticipate hearing anything out of the ordinary, but he didn't want to leave a stone left unturned. Bianca Nowitzki was still missing. Conrad intended to find out what had happened to her.

As an officer, Conrad had come to trust his instincts. It had been on instinct that he had searched the living room, finding Bianca's notebook and the sketches. It had also been on instinct that he had stayed in the Nowitzki's neighborhood on the night he had an encounter with Thrall. It was instinct that told him Chief Nichols was the wrong man to lead the investigation, which was proving to be right thus far. Those same instincts were telling him the Macabre Manor crew wasn't directly involved in any of the disappearances they investigated. They were simply taking advantage of the situation for views. It was exploitive, sure, but wasn't illegal.

Those instincts had let him down in the past. Those same instincts hadn't yet developed as a teenager when he thought the old man had been nothing more than a clean cop and a father that enjoyed a drink from time to time. It was those same instincts that told him Hightower was as dirty as his brother had been. It had even led to him following the other officer around town, while Conrad was off duty and Hightower was on duty. The results were disappointing to say the least. The only thing he had uncovered was a lazy cop that would rather cut a few corners instead of following official police procedures. Nothing groundbreaking there.

There were a lot of things happening in the department that didn't sit well with him. A Chief that would rather nap in his office instead of conducting the duties of his office. The department had been riddled with corruption during the old man's reign as Chief of Police. Those same hints of corruption still lingered despite the fact that most of the officers were either new to the department since the cleansing or had been deemed clean by an internal investigation. When it came to the Prairieview Police Department, Conrad knew he was the only one trustworthy. That was fine with him, as that had been the case ever since he witnessed the old man's brutal beating of his mother. He was a lone wolf, and he liked it that way.

Conrad exited the station knowing his days there were numbered. He was moving on to bigger and better things. The small fishbowl that was the PPD couldn't contain him any longer.

It was the beginning of the third day of Bianca Nowitzki's disappearance. The forty-eight-hour mark and come and gone overnight with no indication that the case would be solved soon. The first twenty-four hours had been a media blitz that Conrad hadn't encountered in his life as an officer. Reality had set in on the second day, with the media losing interest that was facilitated by the dreary rain. He had been prepared for a continuation of the media presence from day two. There were other cases happening around the country; the world would move on whether they found out what had happened to Bianca Nowitzki or not.

Conrad had been wrong; however, the media presence was similar to the first day of the case. Were there more photographers and journalists than there had been on day one? He thought so. It seemed as though there had been an increase in the nontraditional media presence covering the case. But why?

He got his answer when he stepped out of the cruiser.

"Officer Cain! Officer Cain! Is it true that you were suspended when your boss found out about the interview with Macabre Media?" a journalist with hair straight out of the eighties asked as she approached with a hoard of her compatriots.

"Officer Cain! What did you say to the suspect? Did you fire your weapon?" another shouted.

"Is it true that the department is making you see a psychologist before you return to work?"

"Well, I'm here and in uniform, so that wouldn't be the case, now, is it?" he said with a wink.

"Can you show us where the man disappeared? Where did he go?"

Conrad pushed through the throng of media. "Now, if I'd known that, then he wouldn't have disappeared, right? If you'll excuse me."

He left the media blitz despite feeling a yearning to stick around and give an interview for a sustained amount of time. There was a smile on his face. He had enjoyed the attention; despite thinking he was the type of person that shied away from the limelight.

There was more for him to learn about himself yet to come.

17.

Conrad

After leaving the media circus that he helped create, Conrad decided he needed to speak with Miriam and the Macabre Manor crew. He had his doubts about their involvement in the disappearance of Bianca Nowitzki and the other people that had reportedly seen the White House, however, that wasn't a reason to leave them uninvestigated. After all, they had been around these types of cases before, meaning they likely had valuable information to share with him. It was time he found out.

He found the Macabre Manor crew in front of the old Comisky place. It was as if they never left the site where the supposed White House stood. That was probably sound journalism, he figured. They were from out of town, so they likely had a room at the Prairieview Inn, but the rest of their time was spent there. If the White House truly existed and was on the premises of the old Comisky place, then would it be smart to let it out of your sight?

Miriam was standing next to the Macabre Media van, using the side mirror to do her makeup. Her hair was up in a bun that seemed to be her trademark. Gavin was talking into his cellphone on the front lawn of the old Comisky place. Stu was standing next to the open door of the van, where his camera sat. There was a cinnamon roll in his sticky hands. Conrad noticed a takeout container next to the man's camera.

"Are those cinnamon rolls from the Newhouse café? Because I'm starving," he said as he approached the van.

"Well, if it isn't the man of the hour. Tell me, did you get laid last night?" Stu said around a mouthful of cinnamon roll.

"Not that it's any of your business, Stu, but no, I didn't get laid last night."

"Well, I bet it'll be the last time that happens. You're practically a celebrity now."

Stu opened the takeout container and offered a cinnamon roll to Conrad, who gladly accepted.

"Stu, I think our resident law enforcement expert is too much of a gentleman to go around kissing and telling, especially with the likes of you. Besides, the man probably already has a lady at home," Miriam said, as she applied lipstick in the mirror.

"I try to be a gentleman, Miriam, really, I do. It hasn't gotten me very far, though."

"No girlfriend, Miriam. That was subtle," Gavin said, as he joined the group now that his call was over.

"Well, a lady needs to know her options. A good guy is hard to find, especially while hanging around with the likes of you two."

"Hey, you can have some of this any time you want, Miriam," Stu said, grabbing a second cinnamon roll.

"Thanks, Stu. I'll let you know when I want to become a future ex-wife."

"Tell me about the Thrall," Conrad asked.

He could feel the change in atmosphere as if he had broached a subject they hadn't been prepared for.

Miriam stopped applying makeup and turned to look at him.

"Why the sudden interest in the Thrall?" she asked.

"He's our lead suspect, for one. In fact, he's the only lead we've had in this case so far. Secondly, you guys have been around the White House disappearances before. Miriam, you made it sound as if he's been involved in a number of those cases. Obviously, you know something about him."

"The man we've come to call the Thrall has been around almost from the beginning, although not quite. The first eyewitness to claim to have seen the Thrall was back in the forties when a housewife went missing in Chicago. The White House had appeared across the street from her apartment in the downtown neighborhood, where there was an empty parking lot. The doorman for the apartment complex claimed to have seen a man fitting the Thrall's description. Dark hair, dark eyes, ears that were too big for his face. The whole nine yards.

"Now, I know what you're thinking. How could this same man be alive in the forties and look the exact same today, right? Well, that is one of the mysteries of the White House. It's one of the reasons our viewers can't seem to get enough of these stories. Hey, I know they're real people, but the viewers don't think of them as real people. It's only a story for most of them. I guess it's how they sleep at night. Me? I prefer whiskey.

"Any who, the Thrall is a mysterious man. We've done a lot of research into who he could be but have come up empty in all regards. For the longest time, I thought it might have been Hanz Bauman, but it's not. The resemblance is uncanny, but not quite right. We've got lots of pictures of Hanz and we've even got a few supposed photos of the Thrall. True, they're similar, but that's it. It's not the same man.

"I think the Thrall is fed in some fashion by whatever entity or force is inside the White House. I don't know if he's immortal, but he's close to it. Maybe it has slowed down his aging process or something. Of course, that's implying that the Thrall is a man, which I think he was, at least at one point. Whatever happened to him over the years inside that house, whatever process he goes through to renew, has changed him. Not for the better either. I've heard his eyes are unhinged, as if he's suffering from psychopathy. Of course, that's just a guess. I wouldn't mess with him, Conrad. I don't think he's human, and he's dangerous to those that are."

I wouldn't mess with him.

Those words echoed in Conrad's head. It was the clue he had been hunting for. Miriam didn't want him to get too close to Thrall. Was it because it would jeopardize the scheme they had going with the White House? Criminals got desperate when you were close to the truth. Yet her words didn't reek of desperation, but instead they were words of true concern for his wellbeing. At least, that was what he wanted to hear.

"Have you seen him?"

Miriam shook her head. "You'd think all the time we've spent covering the White House that we would have, right? No, we haven't seen him. I think he's aware of us, like he knows that we're aware of him. He doesn't like the spotlight, as you've learned. He prefers it in the shadows. Monsters lurk in the shadows."

"Enough about that creepy guy. Conrad, how did the Chief handle the video going viral? Did you get in trouble?" Gavin asked, smiling.

"Well, he wasn't happy. By the way, next time you guys' livestream, let me know, okay?" he said, crossing his arms over his chest.

"Oh, you've got it. Now, how about an update on the fallout of the video? How is the attention affecting you?"

"I don't know, I've got to get to work."

"Oh, come on. It'll be quick," Miriam said with a pouty look.

"Alright, as long as it's quick."

After a long day of searching for Bianca Nowitzki, the Chief had made the difficult decision to call off the search. Despite his feelings toward Chief Nichols, Conrad knew it was the right decision. It wouldn't be popular with the public, media, or the Nowitzki family—although David had been understanding in person—but the reality of the case had changed. They were no longer looking for a person, but a body. It was a harsh reality, but it was the reality they had to face all the same.

Of course, if the Macabre Manor crew was correct about the White House being real, and Bianca having gone inside, there wouldn't be a body. He was in awe of people that could believe in something they couldn't see. His mother was a devote Christian despite the difficulties she had faced in her marriage. When he was a child, the three of them would go to church on Sunday mornings at the Prairieview Church of Christ. Bible class was first, where Conrad would be in a classroom with three other kids his age making puppet whales that would swallow Jonah and singing songs about the wise man that built his house upon a rock. The affection and support he felt while in that building had been different than what he received at home. It became one of his favorite places, much like it had for his mother. That feeling was ripped from his heart when he was a teenager by a father that betrayed his trust. How could God allow his father to beat his mother in such a manner in front of their own son? Why hadn't God filled her with the strength to leave the husband that had abused her and her son for years? If there was a God, then why did such things happen?

A decision had been made while he sat waiting for the police, with his father's pistol in his hand and his hysterical mother crying against his shoulder. There wasn't a God; there couldn't be a God. He couldn't go on living in a world where an almighty deity with the power to rid the world of such evils as Douglass Cain. Therefore, that deity didn't exist.

"It's a matter of faith, Conny," his mother often said, as if that answered everything. It didn't, but it told him all he needed to know about Maribeth Cain and why she had stayed with her abusive husband for so many years. Faith. Faith her prayers would be answered. Faith that her husband could change. Faith in the impossible.

Maribeth Cain and Miriam Tanenbaum had their blind faith to fall back on. His mother's faith in God, and Miriam's faith in the White House. Conrad understood neither but was envious of both.

Conrad's phone chimed as he sat down on the couch after a long and fruitless day of searching. It was his mother with a text message, as if he had manifested the contact by thinking of her.

Maribeth: *Thought you could go viral and not tell your mother?*

Conrad smiled.

Conrad: *lol It was impromptu, Mom. Didn't think it would be a big deal.*

Maribeth: *Seemed like an intense encounter with that guy. You okay?*

Conrad: Yep.

Maribeth: *K You know I hate texting. Call me.*

Conrad smiled and called his mom.

After a conversation with his mother that lasted an hour, Conrad switched on the television in the living room. He pulled up YouTube and searched for Macabre Manor, the White House. The first search result was the interview he had conducted with Miriam the previous night. It already had two million views. Gabby had been right; it was going viral. He selected the second search result, simply titled Pete Downing.

The video was an hour long, consisting of various live updates on the case from Miriam that were filmed on location at the supposed site of the White House that were compiled together. The story was much the same as the others Conrad had heard revolving around the house. Pete mentioned the house to a family member; this time it was his mother. Pete's mother came across on the program as your typical over-parenting single mother, which family members said drove the nineteen-year-old crazy—a poor choice of words on the family member's part. Pete didn't have the grades to go to college, so after high school ended, he simply kept working as a delivery driver for Papa John's. He had been fired from the job when his boss caught him smoking weed while out making deliveries. Instead of finding a new job, his mother said he stayed in the basement smoking weed and playing video games. The basement's small window looked out on the front yard. It was from that basement window where Pete Downing first saw the White House. The house across the street was a ranch-style home constructed of red brick, just like the others in the suburbs of the small North Carolina town. Yet he didn't see the house that had been across the street since the day he moved into the house with his mother ten years ago when his parents divorced. Pete saw the White House. He mentioned the house to his mother, who dismissed it as the imagination of a kid that was perpetually stoned. Pete went missing four days later. The video doorbell his mother installed for security purposes caught Pete leaving through the front door around 3:00 AM. His body was never found.

It was an intriguing story, and Conrad sympathized with the mother for losing her son in such an unusual manner, however, there wasn't anything groundbreaking in the episode. He had already familiarized himself with the show and how each episode was formulated. What he needed was an episode dedicated to the Thrall. So, he added Thrall to his initial search.

He got more than he bargained for.

Once again, his interview was at the top of the list. Underneath that, however, was a video with a thumbnail of the Thrall staring back at him from his television screen. It was unsettling. He started the video just to get those creepy eyes off the screen.

It was obvious the Macabre Manor crew had a formula for their show. Each episode started with Miriam on screen giving a brief overview of the victim and how the White House had come into their lives. That was followed by any interviews from locals they could muster. In the case of Bianca Nowitzki, that had been Conrad, a bonus because he was a law enforcement officer. At some point, they conducted their own investigation of some kind. In this episode, it centered around a strange man whom a neighbor with insomnia had seen prowling around in the early morning hours the night the victim had gone missing. The neighbor had even managed to snap a photo with their smartphone.

It was that image that became the thumbnail for the episode.

The photo was taken from a distance, due to the neighbor standing on his own front porch. Thrall had been walking down the center of the street, towards the neighbor's house, which gave him the perfect view of the stranger's face. The image was grainy due to the low quality of the camera and having to be amplified to get a better look at Thrall's face. This was where the Macabre Manor's investigatory skills came into play.

Gavin, who Conrad was surprised to learn wasn't just the guy giving directions, used his computer skills to remove the graininess from the photo. There was a lot of technical terminology used in this segment that went above his head. According to Miriam, this gave them the first true look at the man known simply as Thrall.

He had simple features that wouldn't stand out, and that was likely by design if the man truly was the White House's surrogate in the outside world. His eyes were dark, almost black, and were deeply set on his face. His mouth was little more than a thin line on his face. His complexion was pale, as if he spent his entire existence hiding from the sun. His ears were the defining feature of his face, otherwise he was nondescript. They were much too big for his face, making it the feature that bullies would have been drawn to in school.

Conrad found himself staring at Thrall for far too long. As time passed, it was almost as if the man's thin lips were curling upward into a smile. Miriam's voice had faded away, leaving only Conrad and Thrall staring at each other. How could that be? He hadn't paused the video.

Thrall winked at him.

Conrad pressed the back button on the remote that was still in his hand. The image of Thrall disappeared from the screen. It was replaced with the results from his most recent search. In desperate need of a palate cleanser, he selected the viral video of his interview with Miriam.

When it was finished, he found more coverage of his video from other sources. He gluttonously fed his ego with each video, unable to stop himself.

18.

Conrad

The next morning Conrad awoke on his couch, having fallen asleep while watching videos of himself late into the night. He poured a steaming cup of coffee down his throat while he got around. The coffee usually waited until it was in his thermos as he was heading out the door. Today wasn't one of those days. The extra fuel was needed to trudge through what would likely be another monotonous day in the Bianca disappearance case. The case needed a break in the worst way. As he got dressed, he prayed that today would be that day.

His prayers were answered.

The days working from the field were nearing an end in the case. There were only so many leads to be followed up on. Many of these leads suffered from what Conrad liked to call the Elvis effect. Elvis Presley died in August of 1977, whether that was truly on a toilet while eating a cheeseburger, Conrad neither knew nor cared. After his death, there were reports of eyewitnesses claiming to have seen the King of Rock and Roll. These reports continue to this very day, despite the simple fact that Elvis would be nearly ninety years old. It was the same situation in a missing person's case. People, being the helpful species they like to believe they are, come forward with eyewitness sightings of said missing person. There have been local cases in which a missing person was sighted in the days after the initial disappearance, only for the body to be found weeks later, having been slain in the hours after going missing.

Bianca Nowitzki had been sighted at Shop N Save in Crimson Creek, buying milk and bread. This turned out to be a woman in her thirties that only had a passing resemblance to the missing woman. She had also been spotted in Wichita buying a bus ticket to Omaha. This woman wasn't found, though CCTV footage from the Greyhound station in Wichita showed it wasn't Bianca.

All of these eyewitness accounts had to be verified for the miniscule occasion that one turned out to be accurate. Tracy in dispatch had plenty of time on her hands with the crime in Prairieview reflecting the small town that it was. As a result, she handled all the verifications before they made their way to Conrad and Chief Nichols, who were both being treated as the lead investigators, Nichols in title alone, and Conrad in every other meaningful fashion.

The lead that morning had nothing to do with the Elvis effect but rather was a result of the emails he sent to other departments regarding their information about the Macabre Manor crew. Several departments had replied that they hadn't investigated the crew, despite their involvement in similar incidents. Then he opened an email from the Eureka Springs Police Department in Arkansas.

So, you're interested in the Macabre Manor crew, huh? Good for you. We didn't start looking into them until after they had flown the coop, so to speak. There isn't much to share regarding our own case, as it is still unsolved and is about as cold as a polar bear at the North Pole. We did uncover some interesting information about that YouTube show that you might find interesting. Take it if you want.

We've been blessed with a hell of a researcher in our department, named Sergeant Peabody. He's the one that looked into the crew when one of our officers remarked that this case sounded a lot like something he had seen on an episode of a YouTube show. You can guess which one. Peabody got things rolling from there.

Gavin Huxley seems to be an interesting character. He's the producer/director for the Macabre Manor show and is the creator of Macabre Media. The guy is probably a millionaire if Peabody's research is any good, and it usually is. By now I'm sure you know about the White House, right? Those are the most popular on their channel. Well, they've done other things on that channel, such as investigations of supposedly haunted houses. Peabody talked to a few sources that confirmed a good number of the occurrences during those hauntings were faked. "If nothing happened, then they made something happen," to quote a source. We're talking about faking voices and objects moving, things of that nature. I get it, they need ratings. If nothing happens, then people don't watch.

That sounds innocent enough. Hell, I bet a lot of ghost hunter shows do the same thing. Well, what those other shows don't do is hire someone to lurk around neighborhoods where someone has gone missing, scaring people half to death. Have you heard about the Thrall? Well, I won't get into the lore of what he is, but it's a part of their show. Huxley is being sued by the family of a missing person in Oregon for misleading an investigation and causing emotional distress. Seems as though Huxley paid an actor to impersonate this Thrall guy or maybe the guy was the Thrall all along, I don't know. Anyway, they settled out of court. Probably paid them off.

Hope this helps. Good luck with your investigation.

Detective Mike Leonard

Conrad was taken aback by the email. He reread it to make sure he understood correctly. It was a glaring admonishment of the practices of the Macabre Manor crew, most importantly, Gavin. The producer/director was the person giving orders on the set, and as it turned out, he was also the financier of the show. That gave the man an enormous amount of power over Stu and Miriam, who he could fire on a whim if they didn't listen to his direction.

It wasn't surprising to read that a ghost hunting show was suspected of faking a number of their occurrences of paranormal oddities. Most of those shows had a hokey quality that Conrad had never been able to get passed. There were paranormal occurrences in every episode. What were the odds of that happening? Slim, if you asked him. A ghostly voice could simply be a crew member whispering in the darkness. Spikes in readings on an EMF meter—like the one Miriam had used—could be explained as the presence of a spirit rather than the buildings power supply, as it likely was. These buildings were often abandoned, without sufficient heating or insulation against the outside elements, which caused the cold spots often associated with these programs. It was common practice. He had been under the impression Macabre Manor was a different type of show. He had been wrong.

The question was what to do with the information? There was what he wanted to do and what he should do having an internal battle within him. He wanted to sit on the information and do nothing, giving Miriam and the crew the benefit of the doubt that they had been innocent of the alleged charges. As an officer, this wasn't the best choice, although now that he was aware of the situation, he would watch with a keen eye. See how they handled things now that he was aware. He should start investigating the crew to prove whether they were involved in Bianca's disappearance. Treat them as if they were involved, then let the pieces fall where they may. It was the biggest lead the case had since his encounter with Thrall.

Conrad decided on a toned-down version of what he should do. He would watch them with a vigilant eye while he proceeded with his investigation. If Gavin had hired an actor to play Thrall, it would have been inexcusable and made him a person of interest in Bianca's disappearance by association. Conrad didn't have a good read on the producer just yet, but Gavin struck him as the type of guy that would do just about anything for the show. It was a quick read based mostly on instinct, but it felt right.

Meanwhile, he needed to investigate the allegations put forth by the Eureka Springs detective. The producer of the show would be able to spin a believable yarn to ensure he looked as innocent as possible. That wasn't what Conrad was interested in, at least not yet. There were two other people involved that might be willing to talk without implicating themselves directly in any illegal activity. It was a save your own skin type of situation.

He would talk to Miriam. The Mistress of the Macabre had quickly endeared herself to the smalltown police officer. She was smart and witty, not to mention was a beautiful woman. She was the face of the show and had a lot to lose if the show was implicated, however, with the presence she had on camera and a catalogue of episodes of Macabre Manor, she would do well if forced to go on her own.

There was one thing playing in Conrad's favor in talking with Miriam instead of Gavin. She had been burned by her ex-boyfriend and producer, Gavin, in the past. There might be an axe to grind if he played his cards right.

It was still early, but he wanted to speak with Miriam as soon as possible. He preferred to do it without Gavin knowing; the less the producer knew about Conrad's suspicions the better. Through a series of text messages, he found out she was still at the Prairieview Inn, where the crew rented two rooms. *So, they weren't sleeping in the van,* he thought.

Ten minutes later, his hand paused as it hovered an inch from the door to room thirteen. The movies had given him the impression that hotels removed all traces of the number thirteen from their premises. A bad omen? Or a silly superstition?

Conrad shook his head and knocked lightly on the door.

Miriam opened the door wide enough for him to slip inside. Strands from her trademark bun came loose as she slammed the door closed behind him. She was wearing an oversized black Macabre Media T-shirt and white cotton panties. Nothing else. Despite being forewarned that he was coming over. It was a frivolous attitude, and he liked it.

"The boys are in the other room, so keep your voice down. Stu insisted I have my own room because he's a gentleman. Gavin grumbled but gave in. If they hear you, I'll just pretend you came over for a quicky," she said with a wink.

"They'd believe that?"

She nodded. "Hey, it's happened before. Guys think they're the only ones that like sex. Well, Conrad, women like it too. I don't make it a habit of sleeping with people I work with, but I might make an exception."

Conrad could feel his face flush.

"I'm on duty, Miriam," he said, his voice thick and gruff.

"That wasn't a no, officer."

"Observant."

Her hand was on his chest, fiddling with the top button of his uniform. She looked up into his eyes; he looked down into hers. Seconds passed without either able to break the connection that had formed in an instant. Then she bumped the pistol holster on his right hip. It was another reminder of what he had already stated. He was on duty.

He wanted to kiss her. Instead, he said, "I came to talk to you about Gavin."

Miriam's hand dropped from his chest. She turned and plopped down on the bed.

She sighed. "Well, if there's any way to kill a mood, bringing up a girl's ex-boyfriend sure is a way to do it. What about him?"

"Is Gavin working with the Thrall? Did he hire someone to play the Thrall for the show?"

"So, you've heard about the Eugene case." It was a statement, not a question. "I knew you were too smart not to be suspicious of us."

"I checked around, if that's what you're wondering. I'm a police officer. Now, Gavin and Thrall…"

Miriam sighed. "I didn't know anything about it at the time, honest, but, yeah, Gavin hired a local actor to play Thrall. Things were a little off in Eugene from the start. We weren't even sure if the person had seen the White House or not. It was more of a rumor that was circulating in the hours after Victoria Vanguard's disappearance. She lived alone, which made things complicated. Her possibly obsessive, and definitely creepy neighbor, who spent most of his retired existence watching her, said she had been spending a lot of time staring at the house across the street in the days before she disappeared. There wasn't much there for us to go on, I told Gavin as much. He didn't listen; said it didn't matter if there wasn't anything there because we controlled the narrative of our show. People would believe whatever we told them to believe.

"I objected as the face of this show. I'm the person the public wants to attack and demonize when he makes decisions like this. They don't understand that an arrogant jerk like Gavin is making questionable decisions and insulting their intelligence. Most of them just see me and think it ends there—not all of them, we've got some great fans that know all about Gavin.

"Anyway, it didn't matter, as I'm sure you've deduced, when Gavin has his mind set on something, he isn't easily swayed. I took away the only power I had over him when we broke up. The guy thinks with his third leg more than his brain sometimes, but that's most men.

"Things didn't go as planned. We had to manufacture the readings around the house, which Gavin is an expert at thanks to his background with ghost hunting shows. Yeah, those shows aren't real, including most on our channels. There wasn't any sign the White House had been there, was there, and there wasn't any sign of Thrall either. At that point, we only had eyewitness accounts of Thrall, but there hadn't been any photos of him yet. We had descriptions of what he looked like and a local college with hungry thespians. Gavin decided for the benefit of our show. It was the wrong one, but he made it.

"The family thinks we took advantage of the situation, which we did. We had to pay the price for that, and Gavin had the money to settle it out of court."

"So, you admit that Gavin and Thrall are working together?"

"Wow, that's not what I said, Conrad. Gavin paid a guy one time to impersonate Thrall because we didn't have anything for that episode. That's it. That was the only time he did it as far as I know. The rest of the time, well, that was the real deal. The Thrall is real, Conrad. You know, you met him."

"That was the only time Gavin has hired someone to play Thrall that you know of? What about the other times you guys have faked hauntings?"

"Well, sure, we've faked some things here and there. I mean, that's good for ratings. We've got to keep the viewers interested. It was only small stuff, though. Triggering the EMF meter. Rigging objects to move on their own. Things like that. That was all in the other episodes, none of the White House episodes have been faked, aside from that one in Eugene. Those episodes are sacred to the fans, and they're sacred to me, too."

"Would Gavin fake things without telling you or Stu about it? Would he hire someone to play Thrall and keep it a secret? Knowing where you stand ethically?"

"No."

"But—"

"What is this? I thought you were on our side. That's why Gavin's paying you, after all," Miriam said, throwing up her hands in frustration.

"I'm on Bianca's side, Miriam. The only thing that matters is finding out what happened to her. The money is just a bonus."

She raised an eyebrow. "Is that right? Because it seems to me like you're enjoying yourself. Small town cop goes viral. It's a big deal and you know it. It's all over your face."

"It's a distraction, plain and simple. I'm just after the truth. I'll get it one way or another."

Miriam stood up and crossed the room to him. She put a hand to his cheek.

"Just don't go thinking Thrall is someone we hired, Conrad. He's dangerous. You don't want to meet him again. He has killed before. He'll do it again."

19.

Conrad

An hour later, Conrad was standing on the front lawn of the old Comisky place with the pile of rubble as a backdrop. Miriam stood at his side, Stu was behind the camera, and Gavin stood behind the cameraman, likely so he could whisper directions into the man's ear. Conrad hadn't had the opportunity to speak with either man about the allegations leveled by the Eureka Springs detective. It was awkward enough being in Gavin's presence when he had just discussed the allegations with Miriam.

Miriam thought it was a good idea to give the viewers an update on the case, despite an absence of new developments. Conrad agreed due mostly because it would keep Bianca's name in the media for a day longer.

"Hello, residence of Macabre Manor. It's Miriam and I'm back with an update on the disappearance of Bianca Nowitzki. Joining me once again is Officer Cain of the Prairieview Police Department. Officer Cain, what can you tell us about the case since we last talked to you?"

"Hi, Miriam. I'd first like to thank you for inviting me back. Things have been a little crazy for me personally since we last talked, unfortunately, that has little to do with the case."

"Things aren't developing as quickly as you'd like, huh?"

"I'm afraid not, however, we've got a few leads that we're following up on," Conrad said, locking eyes with Gavin.

"Care to tell us about those leads, Officer?"

He shook his head. "I'm afraid I'll have to play those close to the vest for now, Miriam. What I can tell you is we're being diligent in our pursuit of the truth. Deciphering truth from rumor can be difficult at times, but it's what we do in law enforcement. We'll follow the truth, no matter where it leads us. Even if it leads us to an unsuspecting place, like in front of what is believed to be a house that no one can see, aside from a handful of people, obviously."

"Are you telling me that you're investigating the house and its purported reality? Or are you referring to something else?"

"Well, we are looking into the house, that much is true. It's an unlikely probability, but a probability none the same. What I'm actually referring to is the man known as Thrall and whether he truly exists or not."

"Ah, still not a believer in Thrall, huh? That's interesting considering you've seen the entity with your own eyes, officer. Care to explain?"

"All I can say for the time being is we have it under good authority that the man known as Thrall is just that, a man, nothing more. You referred to Thrall as an entity. I'm guessing you believe he is some kind of supernatural being, right? Well, that makes one of us. I believe Thrall is a man. A man that knows something about this case. We would still like to question Thrall about Bianca's disappearance. If anyone knows the whereabouts of Thrall, please contact the Prairieview Police Department."

Conrad made eye contact with Gavin when delivering the last line. The man knew something; he had to.

"Got that, residence? Officer Cain needs your help. If you've seen Thrall recently, get in touch with Prairieview

PD and you can help find out what happened to Bianca Nowitzki. Speaking of Bianca, is there any progress with finding her?"

He shook his head. "No, Miriam, there hasn't been any progress in locating Bianca Nowitzki. At this point, we've resigned ourselves to the fact that we may very well be looking for a body. It's a harsh reality, but it's the one we live with."

"Thank you, Officer Cain."

As the filming wrapped, Conrad's eyes fell on David Nowitzki, who was standing at the edge of the property watching them. He had been listening to the interview.

Might as well face this head on.

Conrad could feel the confidence that had been building wither away as he crossed the street to speak with the man who was likely a widower. Doing the interviews and seeing how the media talked about him had inflated his ego, which had already been healthy to begin with. When he was speaking with the media, it was like he controlled the narrative of the story, as if whatever he said would be that day's news. It was a powerful feeling and made him feel as if he was capable of anything.

Except finding what happened to Bianca Nowitzki.

There was no other way around it, the case had gone cold. Bianca wasn't walking through the door today or tomorrow to inform the police what had happened to her. At this point he was certain she was dead, and they were searching for a body. The simple question that wasn't so simple to answer was how she had become that way? What had happened to her after David witnessed her leaving the bedroom at two in the morning? Had she even left the bed? Or had her husband brutally murdered her while she slept and was Conrad was making a catastrophic mistake by not investigating him further? There was no indication that such an incident had taken place. The little evidence there was pointed at an outside source. Plus, the house hadn't looked spotless or staged, as was often the case after a violent crime has taken place and the spouse is the culprit. The sheets on the bed had been free of blood yet hadn't been spotless by any stretch of the imagination. Bianca's bra had been hanging from the bedroom door. Her cellphone was sitting on the nightstand. There was a pan soaking in the kitchen sink from dinner that evening. David said she had planned to clean it in the morning. Who does that and then walks out the door forever?

David Nowitzki was the poster boy for grieving husbands. He said the right thing at the right time, while managing to pull off a despondent in an aloof manner. The guy was a wreck, and it showed. Conrad had accepted David's version of the events that night without much doubt. Was that fair? Wasn't Bianca owed more? Bianca had been missing for three days and counting. He had trusted David Nowitzki. That trust forced Conrad to look beyond the home's front door, when he should have closed the front door and looked at the man that shared Bianca's bed.

In a small town where everyone seemed to know everything about everyone else, how much did he truly know about David Nowitzki? People put up a façade in public, a mask of sorts, for the world to look at. This façade included everything that you wanted people to see. Loving husband. Good friend. Devoted employee. Hidden beneath that mask were the things we didn't want other people to see. A cheater. A drunk. A man that beats his wife. Conrad had glimpsed the mask and taken it as David's real face. What if there were dark secrets hidden underneath?

Conrad's own father had hidden enough dark secrets underneath the mask that he hadn't recognized the man once those secrets were revealed. The two men had rarely spoken since he left the house at eighteen, despite living in the same town. The horrors beneath Douglass Cain's mask had embarrassed the man both publicly and privately. What if there were similar secrets hidden in David Nowitzki's closet?

"Seems like you're enjoying yourself in front of the camera, Officer Cain," David said as Conrad approached.

He noticed the official title the other man used but decided to ignore it.

"I wouldn't say that. It comes with the territory, though," he said, shrugging.

"You think Bianca is dead."

It wasn't a question. David had been listening to the interview. It had to be a blow to the man knowing that the lead investigator thought his missing wife was dead. Still, Conrad tried to soften the blow.

"You know what they say, pray for the best, prepare for the worst. Unfortunately, if she had simply gone missing, got lost while out for a hike or was in an accident, then I think we would have found her by now. Three days later, and all we have are rumors and eyewitness accounts of seeing someone that kinda, sorta matches her description. It doesn't look good, David. I'm truly sorry, I am, but, yeah, I think we're looking for a body."

"So, you think she's dead. You think she's dead because you can't find her? Why did you call off the search? Maybe you could have found her if you were still looking for her. Maybe she's still out there in need. We won't find her if we aren't looking."

There were tears welling in David's eyes. Conrad felt for the other man. Yet he had to remain a neutral party.

"Three days in the elements wouldn't be good for her, you know that. There are wild animals in the woods. What if one of those found her? It's hot this time of year, could she survive without a proper source of water? Look, I don't mean to be callous, David, I don't, but we have to face reality here. We need to find out what happened to her. There are a few leads that I'm looking into. They may turn out to be fruitless, but we have to try.

"It's good that you have hope, David, it is. It may be the one thing that brings Bianca back."

"Because you won't. You've made that clear."

"David, don't be like that. We're trying the best we can."

"You better go, wouldn't want you to miss another interview. I hear there's a dangerous man out there, wouldn't want you to meet him in the middle of the street. He might disappear."

Conrad locked eyes with the older man, as if challenging him to say more. Then he realized who the other man was. A grieving husband. Conrad turned away in shame.

The summer heat had given way to a humid evening that wasn't much cooler. Rumbles of thunder whispered their promises in the distance, foreshadowing what was to come. Given the ominous sky, Conrad was enjoying the evening before he eventually had to run for shelter. He was leaning against the Macabre Media van, while the crew filmed on the lawn of the old Comisky place.

He was officially off duty but was hanging around anyway. Miriam had occupied his mind since seeing her that morning when he had interviewed her about Gavin's involvement with Thrall. He hadn't liked what she had to say, yet he *had* enjoyed the company. For the first time he looked at her in a manner that wouldn't be considered professional. In his opinion there were fewer things sexier than a confident woman. Her demeanor in the hotel room changed his view of her, opening the possibility of something happening between them. There was a problem, however.

Miriam was from Chicago, not Kansas. Eventually she would have to return. As far as he was concerned, there wasn't anything holding the crew in town any longer. There hadn't been any new developments in the Bianca Nowitzki case in two days, despite Conrad's frequent updates. He understood the situation with the Macabre Media crew. There was always another small town with an old, haunted house, another town where the White House had appeared.

He was hardening his heart in preparation for the goodbye with Miriam.

"Who should I call about you stalking me?" Miriam said, after they had finished filming.

"I know a guy. In fact, he's a cop. Handsome, charismatic, good guy. Maybe I'll give you his number."

Gavin and Stu were talking animatedly on the front lawn of the old Comisky place. The normally mild-mannered cameraman was upset about something, as he was inches from Gavin's face. Gavin looked remarkably calm considering he was outmatched in both height and weight. The director simply shook his head, reiterating a point that had already been made.

"What's that about?" Conrad asked, nodding in their direction.

She waved a dismissive hand. "Eh, boys being boys. Stu's son has a birthday tomorrow and he's going to miss it. Gavin doesn't want to leave."

"I mean, I enjoy your company, but why not leave? This is privileged information, but the case isn't going anywhere right now. How long do you guys normally stick around after someone goes missing?"

She looked at him long and hard before responding.

"You don't know, do you?"

"Know what?"

"Sometimes we stay for two or three weeks at a location. Just depends on how long it takes."

"How long it takes for what?"

"For the second person to go missing."

20.

Conrad

"Excuse me? What are you talking about? The second person to go missing," Conrad said, after a moment of silence.

"How many episodes of the show have you watched, Conrad?"

"Two or three, I guess."

"Well, you should watch more, and I'm not just saying that to increase our views. Then you'd understand. On Macabre Manor we give each victim of the White House the respect they deserve. The respect the house took from them when it ripped them from this world and into whatever Macabre world that exists within its walls. That means it can be hard to discern the fact that some of the episodes are linked, but they are.

"We don't understand why it happens this way, only that it does. Thrall tends to show up when the White House does, their existences are intertwined. It takes a week or so for the first person to go missing. Then there's a lull. That's where we're at now, the lull. Yet as we speak there is someone else in the vicinity that is either seeing the house or is about to see the house for the first time. That'll be the house's next victim. We've never been able to distinguish who that person was before it was too late."

"Why does it need more than one victim?"

Miriam shrugged. "That's another thing we've never been able to figure out, but I've got a theory. We don't know what's inside the house, but it can't be empty, right? Does Thrall serve the house? In some form, sure, but I think there's more to it than that. I think there's an entity inside, possibly demonic in origin, that Thrall serves. Thrall is the conduit for the demon in our world. He's basically a slave that fulfills every want and need of the demon. Mostly what it wants is human souls. It must have a gluttonous appetite. We go from city to city without much rest in between. It doesn't stop feeding."

"How many more people are going to go missing in Prairieview?"

"Two maybe three more, I'd guess. It varies. Sometimes it was a single person, which is rare, but it does happen. The most I've ever seen was five. That was only once."

"What can we do to stop it?"

"Warn people. That's what the show's about. That's all we can do. Oh, and don't go in the house."

"Obviously."

Conrad was meeting Miriam in front of the old Comisky place later that night. There still wasn't much to go on in the Bianca Nowitzki investigation, aside from Macabre Manor, of course. With the revelation that there could be more victims, he had suggested an old-fashioned stakeout. In his five years as an officer Conrad hadn't done any stakeouts. Now, in the span of a week, he was doing two. Desperate times, as they say.

Miriam had appeared excited about the possibility of being involved in official police business and quickly agreed. He informed her that he would be off duty, so it was more like unofficial police business. That appealed even more to the host of the macabre show.

"Sounds clandestine! Count me in!"

Miriam and the crew had driven off in the van on a mission to film some night scenery of Prairieview for the episode before it started to storm. The distant rumbles of thunder weren't as distant any longer. He wasn't sure if they would make it back before the heavens were unleashed.

He had an hour free before they were meeting. With nothing to do, he pulled out his phone and started scrolling through social media. He landed upon a post about his recent update and started reading the comments.

DachshundLover666: He's kinda cute or is it just me?

CraigNotGreg: Meh. It's the uniform. It adds 2 points on a scale of 1-10. I'm far better looking than that guy.

ReelGirl316: Did U hear he saw a guy disappear? Psych eval?

RockNRoll4Eva: My cousin works with him, and she says he's totally bonkers. Been suspended 4 times this year. Probably 5 after this.

ReelGirl316: I bet he did it.

RockNRoll4Eva: DUH! Probably knows where the body is. That's why they can't find it.

*PoPoHater: F*ck the police!*

DachshundLover666: Still cute lol.

The coming storm brought a cool breeze that was refreshing. Conrad had the window down and the engine off so he could enjoy it before the storm. Then someone grabbed his elbow that was resting on the window.

"I remember a time when you wouldn't have cared what those people said about you. Of course, I remember a time when you'd come to the café every morning for a cinnamon roll and conversation. Two days later, and you haven't been in. No hello or anything. What the hell has gotten into you, Conrad Cain?" Gabby said from beside Conrad's personal vehicle.

"So, you had to track me down? Is that it?"

"I'm serious, Conny. I don't like this big shot investigator you're trying to be. It isn't you, at least I don't think so. You've never let me get close enough to figure that out for sure. Always pushing people away when they get too close. I thought we were different. I thought we *could* be different."

"I'm not a big shot investigator, Gabby. I'm just trying to find Bianca, despite what everyone thinks."

Just then the heavens unleashed a torrent of rain upon Prairieview, as if trying to cleanse the town of the many misdeeds that had come to pass in recent days. If that were the case, there would be more rain to come.

"Get in, Gabby, or you'll get washed away!" he said, motioning to the passenger's seat.

Gabby ran around to the other side of the car and got into the passenger's seat. Once she was in the car, he noticed the plastic bag she was holding.

"What's that?"

She looked down at the bag, as if she had forgotten she was holding it. "Oh, like I said, you've not been in the café for a few days, so I brought the café to you."

She opened the bag. Inside were two takeout containers. The first held a double smashburger with extra fried onions and a side of tater tots. The second held four cinnamon rolls.

"I figured you missed breakfast the past two days, so I might as well double it up."

"You know I don't come in for the cinnamon rolls, right?"

"I said the same thing the other day, and you said, 'These are the best cinnamon rolls in town, Gabby.' And I argued because Hurts Donut *are* better. Then you said, 'I like a little bit of gab with my breakfast.' What was that? You lying to me, Conny?"

Conrad didn't wait to start eating. He started with the burger and tots.

"Of course, Hurts Donut cinnamon rolls are better than yours. They're better than any I've ever had. I meant what I said, though. I like a little bit of Gab with my breakfast. Get it, Gab?"

"Lord have mercy, are you telling me that was a pun on my name, and I didn't get it? What are you a forty-year-old dad or something?" she said, laughing.

"Apparently, it wasn't a good one, because you didn't get it."

They both laughed.

"See? This is what I'm talking about. This is you, not that guy I saw giving interviews with a black clad broad with too much eyeliner and scrolling through social media posts to see if people like him. You don't care about that. You don't need to. People around here like you. I like you."

He dropped the burger into the Styrofoam container in his lap. Gabby met him at the center console, where their lips took control. Five years of flirting with a diner counter between them, four years of eyeing one another in the hallways of Prairieview High School, suddenly was released in one simple action. Years of wondering why he hadn't made a move or whether she was that nice to all the customers were forgotten.

It was also forgotten that they were on a public street for everyone to see. The rain pelted the windshield, giving some cover to the lustful actions that took place inside. Rumbles of thunder echoed the cries of passion from the reclined passenger seat, where Gabby straddled him. All was forgotten in their world, except two people in a Jeep Grand Cherokee.

The outside world, however, had not forgotten about them. Two figures, independent of each other, stood some distance away, watching as the two bodies coupling together created enough steam to fog the interior glass. One of these people was Miriam Tanenbaum, who shouldn't have been hurt but was. She didn't have any claim to the man inside the SUV, only an emotional connection she thought had been reciprocated.

The other wasn't even a man, not really.

Thrall stood in the shadows, watching as lustful action took place, knowing his demonically touched powers had a hand in bringing it to fruition.

The fervent nature of the passion that unfolded inside the SUV aided in ensuring it was a hasty endeavor. Ten minutes later, Gabby and Conrad were getting dressed in the front seat of the car. Neither had the ability to look at the other, as if suddenly filled with shame at the spontaneous nature of the actions, despite the feelings having been authentic. Because of their inability to meet each other's eyes, Gabby noticed the woman standing in the street, holding an umbrella.

"Um…Conrad? That woman is staring at us," she said in a shaky voice.

"Miriam?"

"Wait, is that the woman from the show? You know, the one that interviewed you?"

"Yeah."

"What the hell is she doing here?"

Waiting for me, Conrad thought but didn't say. Instead, he exited the SUV. He heard the passenger's side door slam a moment after his.

"Hey, Miriam, you're early."

He hadn't known what to say, therefore, had chosen poorly.

"Yeah, well, the boys are fast eaters. That café has some tasty treats, but I guess you know all about that, don't you, Officer Cain?" she said, eyeing Gabby.

Gabby flushed but returned fire. "Excuse me, Mistress Mary or whatever the hell people call you, but I don't get why it's any business of yours."

Miriam looked at Conrad. "I guess it's not. Shame on me, right?"

"Miriam, wait!"

She fled through the rain in the direction of the van. Conrad called out to her, but she didn't turn around.

"When did they build a house where the old Comisky place used to be?"

He turned to look at Gabby. Then at the pile of rubble that had once been the Comisky place.

"No."

21.

Conner

The world was out of focus as Conner exited the third-floor room. It took him a few moments to realize two things. First, his vision was cloudy because there were tears in his eyes. Old memories he thought he had suppressed were coming back to the forefront of his mind, a mind that wasn't prepared to deal with those memories and the knowledge of where things would lead. Second, he wasn't alone in the hallway.

Thrall stood leaning against the wall of the hallway opposite the door, as if waiting for an old friend. It was an unsettling sight for a mind that was already exhausted and overstimulated. Conner wiped away the tears with the back of his hand. Then he faced the entity that took the form of a man.

"Have you figured it out yet?" Thrall said through a flurry of laughter.

"What? That you're as sick and twisted as whatever boss of yours that is waiting for me on the top floor?"

The smile faded. "No. Who I am, Conrad Cain. Have you figured out who I am?"

"Wait, you were human? Before you became whatever it is that you are now, I mean."

"Oh, yes. I was a human. Technically, I still am, in some form, anyway."

"That figures. I should have known. I mean, it makes sense that the house would take a human for a slave. That way it can feed on you, while it feeds on me. It does feed on you, doesn't it Thrall?"

Thrall's face went dark. "I don't like that name."

"Too close to the truth, is it?"

Thrall took a step towards Conner.

"Okay, okay. I was only joking," he said, holding up his hands in what he hoped was a reassuring manner.

"What should I call you then?"

Thrall laughed long and hard, ending with what sounded like a sob.

"So, you want me to figure it out, right?"

Thrall nodded.

"Have we met before?"

"Directly? No. My time as a human came much earlier than yours. But you know my story."

"Okay, that would mean—"

"No! No more clues. You have to figure it out for yourself. You can do that, can't you Officer Cain? Just like you solved Bianca's disappearance. Oh, wait…"

"That's a low blow. Plus, I'm not a cop anymore."

"You know what they say, once a cop, always a cop."

"Cops don't do what I did, not good ones, anyway."

"Enough with the pity party, Cain. You must ascend. The master is waiting. He's hungry."

Conrad didn't move. The purpose of the White House was coming into focus. He was reliving some of his worst sins, with each floor devoted to a different one. Pride. Greed. Gluttony? He wasn't sure the third sin was right. It would have to be a loose definition of gluttony or a warped version from a warped mind that wanted it to fit in any way possible. His worst sins happened to have taken place in the span of a week in Prairieview, Kansas ten years ago. That week had changed him as a person forever, into someone that Miriam and Gabby wouldn't recognize today.

He knew what was ahead on the above floors and where it would lead. Pain. There would be lots of pain.

"I'm sorry, Officer Cain, but did you think it was a request? Or have you forgotten what happened the last time we met?" Thrall said, with a smile that revealed sparkling white teeth.

"Is she here?"

"Run!"

Conrad didn't need any more warnings. He ascended the steps as directed and stepped through the door on the fourth floor.

Here lies pain.

Lust

22.

Conrad

Conrad stared straight ahead through the windshield with his insides as combustible as the weather outside the SUV. His heartrate was only now returning to normal after the excitement. The cotton PPD T-shirt he had changed into after his shift was sticking to his skin, so he peeled it off and draped it across the passenger's seat to dry. He did the same with his pants, this time draping them across the dashboard. There he sat in his skivvies, shivering and embarrassed.

It was ironic that he felt embarrassed being in his underwear in the car, when minutes earlier he had been naked and having sex in the front seat of a car while someone watched. In the moment, he hadn't thought anything. He was simply overcome with lust for Gabby. It had been the only thing on his mind, even during the act there had been nothing else.

To combat the lack of clothing on his body he switched on the seat warmer. Then he set about the business of the evening. He scanned the street for any sign of Thrall. Alone.

Gabby had fled shortly after Miriam in embarrassment at having been discovered. He had tried to stop her, as he had with Miriam, but neither stopped. She wasn't to blame for what had happened, no one was. It had been an act of passion from years of flirting. The only regret he had was that it had taken place in a vehicle, instead of somewhere more comfortable. As for Miriam, that was another matter.

There was no denying he had feelings for Miriam, it was obvious to him and had apparently been obvious to her as well, due to her reaction of seeing him with another woman. Yet he owed nothing to her. They had only just met. She was a stranger in a small town. There was likely nothing there that would last beyond a fling. Of course, that was him trying to validate his actions after seeing the hurt in her eyes. Yes, there had been hurt in her eyes, he couldn't deny that.

They had been meant to do the stakeout together, however, because of his actions he was forced into solo action. He sat in his SUV, cold and alone as penance.

Conrad hadn't ever watched paint dry, but he thought he knew what it felt like after sitting alone in the car for two hours during a stakeout. With his sexual appetite satisfied, the lustful side had abated, taking the frisky member it controlled with it. The rest of his body was left to deal with the consequences of his actions.

He had watched as the storm's ferocity diminished, slowly fading into the distant sky. Soon, all signs of the storm had vanished, leaving behind only a saturated Earth that drank the water greedily. Even the storm had left him.

As the rumbles of thunder became distant, people emerged from their houses, despite the late hour. The storm hadn't been particularly fierce, simply another thunderstorm rolling through the Midwest. The people of this city had seen fierce storms before, had had their lives altered by them. High winds knocking down tree limbs, taking power lines with them, thus causing power outages. A lightning strike hitting a secondhand clothing store in the downtown area, causing a fire to spread to multiple buildings. Flooded streets because the drainage system wasn't properly maintained. It only got worse if there was tornadic activity. The citizens of Prairieview needed to see the outside world. They needed reassurance that it was still standing despite what they had heard and seen transpiring from the relative safety of their homes.

He watched as Mrs. Lincoln stepped out onto her front porch and fiddled with the rosebushes that lined her front porch. Brian Robinson emerged from the gate of his backyard holding a flashlight and proceeded to check the fence line and yard for damage. David stepped out onto his front porch, looked around his front lawn for a few seconds, then stared at Conrad's SUV for an uncomfortable length of time.

Did he recognize the SUV? It was Conrad's personal vehicle, rather than the police cruiser he drove during the daytime. It didn't matter. The man was likely only being cautious with a reported stranger lurking in the neighborhood and his wife missing and presumed dead. That or David Nowitzki was mad as hell. His wife had been missing for nearly four days without a break in the case. The police had theories in spades, yet nothing had come to fruition. Then he sees a young, hotshot officer taking over the investigation from the Chief of Police and putting himself in the spotlight, instead of Bianca. David had a right to be upset with Conrad. The only way he knew how to fix that was by finding Bianca or what had happened to her. Anything else simply wasn't good enough.

Eventually, David went inside, likely to escape the mosquitoes that were coming out after the rain. Conrad was forced into rolling up the window after several feasted on his flesh. He kept an eye on the Nowitzki house, as he did every house. The blinds shifted a few times, as if someone was peering through to look out at the street.

Then someone knocked on his window.

"I thought you could use some company," Miriam said.

"Listen, about earlier. I—" he started to say, thankful he had gotten dressed minutes before.

"Don't. You don't have to make excuses for yourself. So, you had a quicky with the hottie from the café? Okay, good for you. Don't trivialize that on my account, okay? Obviously, you two have something going. I'm happy for you. I wish you had said something about it earlier, but I'm happy for you."

Conrad sighed. "I don't even know what we have, to be honest. I go into the diner every day for a cinnamon roll, and we flirt. We went to high school together, so there's history. I mean, we didn't date or anything, but we always talked, you know? We were friends. She's one of those people who I could see myself settling down with if I ever thought about settling down and being a townie, you know? It's stupid, but I've never thought about myself as a townie. I'm thirty, and I still live in Prairieview. I've thought about leaving, but where would I go? What would I do? I like the smalltown life, so I guess this small town is as good as any other. Anyway, I don't even know how that happened. Something came over me. I can't really explain it."

"That has a way of happening when the White House is around. My theory is that Thrall has some kind of magical power that enables him to influence others, causing chaos. Maybe lower their inhibition, I guess. He can't force them to do anything they wouldn't normally do, or at least I don't think so. Like with you and diner girl—"

"Gabby."

"Gabby, right. Like with you and Gabby, for instance. It sounds like the two of you genuinely like each other. You've got some kind of feelings for her, you've said so yourself. I would venture to guess that Gabby feels the same way about you. That's how he works. There was something holding the two of you back from acting on those feelings. For instance, your desire to someday leave Prairieview, and probably her willingness to stay and run that diner of hers. Thrall threw those blockages out the window. Boom. Now you're screwing in a car."

"It is funny."

"What? A police officer getting caught screwing someone in a car?"

"Yeah. It's the type of thing I've caught teenagers doing for years. Now, it's me that's getting caught."

They both laughed.

"It sounds like you've been on the receiving end of Thrall's touch. Care to share?"

"Now who sounds like they're in the media? Sure, I'll bite." She smiled. "Yeah, there's one time that I know Thrall influenced me. There may have been other times. Hell, as much as I've been around him, I'm almost sure there are. It was when I first joined the show. I was new and just trying to make a good impression. Gavin flirted with me, and I liked that. Made me feel special. Well, one night Stu was off shooting some B roll for the show, so it was just Gavin and me. Like I said, we flirted, and I liked it. I liked him. Well, I kissed him. Stu comes back and the van is rocking, if you know what I mean. It's why we started dating, though why I dated him for so long I don't know."

"So, do you believe in all this?"

"You mean, the paranormal stuff?"

"Yeah. Hauntings, the White House, Thrall. All of it. You really believe, don't you?"

Miriam nodded.

"Why? There's got to be a reason."

She took a deep breath.

"When I was a little girl, my family lived in a small town about an hour outside of Chicago. It was my parents, my older sister, and me crammed into a two-bedroom house. My dad worked the nightshift at a factory making boots in Chicago. My mom was a registered nurse, so she worked twelve hours a day, three or four days a week. There were times when we were little that it was just me and Samantha until late at night. Sam made a killer grilled cheese sandwich, at least that's how I remember it, but you know how your mind makes everything better when you're a kid, right? That's probably true. Anyway, money was tight, and that was okay. We loved each other, that was the important thing. That's what Mom always said, 'all we need is love.' I was an adult before I realized she was quoting a Beatle's song.

"Sam and I shared a room in those days. Later on, Mom got a promotion and a raise, so we moved into a bigger place where we both had our own rooms, but in those days, it was me and Sam together. She was three years older, and I worshipped the ground that girl walked on. I mean, she was like a second mom to me, because my own mom was gone so much working, you know? So, we shared a room.

"Well, despite being older than me, Sam wasn't much of a night owl. In fact, she liked to go to bed early. I think it was because she had to get up earlier than I did on account of middle school starting earlier. So, she was always fast asleep, while I sat there staring at the ceiling and waiting for Mom to get home from work. You see, Mom would always open the bedroom door a crack, poke her head inside and blow me a kiss. Somehow, she always knew I was awake. It was a while before I told her, but there was a reason I was awake.

"Every night, the closet door would open on its own. Not much, mind you. Only a few inches; just wide enough for someone to peer out into the bedroom. I would lay awake in bed just staring at that door and waiting for it to happen. It always did. One night, I even put the folding chair against the door handle to wedge it closed. I did this after Sam fell asleep, so she wouldn't ask me any questions. It didn't matter. The chair fell over, and the door swung open just like it always had.

"After that happened, I finally told Sam what was going on. She turned white. Then she asked, 'Have you seen the white lady?' Well, of course, I hadn't seen anyone, not yet. Turns out, Sam had seen a pale lady, dressed all in white when she was about my age. Scared her so badly that she didn't want to stay awake. That's why she didn't like staying awake late.

"I wanted to tell Mom about it, but Sam shook her head. Said that she tried talking to her about it back then but wouldn't listen. 'It was just a dream, Sammy.' A dream? It was a ghost, not a dream, same with the door. I didn't listen to her. I told Mom anyway, and you know what? Sam was right. Mom said it was my imagination.

"So, I decided that I wanted to see the white lady, not realizing that it was a ghost and that a kid ought to be afraid of a ghost. I was going to prove that it wasn't my imagination, right? Prove my mom wrong. It was just after Halloween, so we had a lot of candy from trick or treating. I ate a whole bunch of candy to get a sugar high, not realizing that it really didn't work. Then I lay in bed and waited. It seemed like that door was never going to open. Just my luck, I'd decided to stay awake and see the white lady on the one night that she wasn't going to come. Well, eventually, she did come. Mom had just checked on me when that door creaked open. Most nights, I turned over and faced the wall because I was so scared of that door opening on its own. That night I didn't turn away. Instead, I kept watching. Nothing happened for the longest time. An hour later, the door opened wider. Wide enough for someone to just slip through. Ever so slowly, a pale lady dressed in an old-fashioned white nightgown came out of the closet. Her eyes glowed in the dark. Don't ask me how, but they did. She stopped a few feet into the bedroom and just stood there, staring at me. We stayed that way for a long time, her staring at me, and me staring back at her. I started to panic. What if the white lady never went away? What if she stood there all night? I'd never get to sleep. Mom was probably already asleep. I didn't want to wake her because I knew she had a long day at work, and she was supposed to work again the next day. So, I lay there, staring at that ghost.

"After a while, the white lady started walking towards my bed. Well, that was when I'd had enough. I'd thought I was brave, and I was wrong. I was nine years old and scared and wanted my mom, so I called for her. Mom came running into the room and flipped the light switch on. Nothing was there. The room was empty. The closet door was closed. I started to tell her what had happened, but then I saw Sam shaking her head. So, I told Mom I had a bad dream. She gave me a hug and told me it would be okay. Then she left the room. I didn't sleep the rest of the night.

"The next night, I went to sleep early, just like Sam. I never saw the white lady again."

"That's why you got into this."

"Yeah, I guess you could say that. I spent most of my life wondering whether the white lady was real or if it was something my sister made up and I just saw what she wanted me to see. Eventually, I got tired of wondering and started looking for answers. I started trying to validate that scared little girl. Prove there had been something in that closet, and maybe it wasn't so scary. Well, I've proven to myself that there was something in the closet, and while scary at the time, the white lady wasn't as scary as she seemed. The trouble was that I discovered other things in this world that are worth being scared of. Like Thrall and the White House."

As if being summoned by speaking his name, Thrall appeared in the glow of the streetlight mere feet from the SUV.

23.

Conrad

Conrad sat rigidly in his seat, unable to move. He didn't know if this was Thrall's supernatural powers working on him or if terror was working its dark magic on his body. Either way he was motionless. Out of the corner of his eye, he could see that Miriam had also spotted the paranormal entity that was the conduit for the house. She seemed equally frozen in the passenger's seat. Neither of them moved as Thrall stared back at them, smiling.

The glow from the streetlight cast an eerie glow over Thrall's face, illuminating his sinister smile, while casting his eyes into shadow. Conrad knew the entity's eyes were locked on them, as if studying them as part of some deranged science experiment. He could feel the power of Thrall's eyes upon him. Perhaps it was that gaze that glued him to the leather seat.

Time seemed to stand still as they stared at each other, as if the world existed without them for the time being. If someone were to glance out their window, they wouldn't see a strange man standing in the glow of a streetlight, staring at two frightened occupants of an SUV. They wouldn't see anything at all. In fact, Conrad thought they would be compelled *not* to look in their direction. As if their brain was telling them there wasn't anything to see out of the corner of their eyes.

As he pondered the compulsions of others, a compulsion of his own had started to form at the forefront of his thoughts. The pain inflicted upon Miriam had been evident in her eyes. She had feelings for him, and he had feelings for her. Why were they sitting in the car talking? They should be acting upon their feelings. It wasn't wise to let feelings go unexplored. He should lean over and kiss her. No, he should grab her and pull her into the backseat and do things that would make Gabby blush.

There was a devilish grin on her face.

They met at the center console.

His hot breath met her trembling lower lip.

A long, ravenous kiss later, she held a finger to his lips.

"We can't. It's him, not us."

Conrad responded by kissing her mouth with her finger between their lips. She dropped her finger and returned the kiss. Her lips tasted like coffee with a hint of cinnamon. He knew instantly that she had gone to the Newhouse Café after leaving him standing in the rain. It was a brief thought that was of his own, which was quickly replaced with an invasive one.

Undo your seatbelt, so you can feel her body pressed against yours.

He followed the thought without thinking about whether the thought had originated from his own mind or was planted there with nefarious intentions. Their bodies were pressed together. His chest against her bosom, where he felt each intense and labored breath.

"It's Thrall," she said as she kissed him.

His ears heard her words, though they didn't process in his mind. In that moment, Thrall didn't exist, only Miriam and him. The rest of the world was a gray cloud outside of his vision. The backseat existed. Yes, they should climb into the backseat.

He climbed onto the center console, intending to use the narrow space to enter the backseat, where they could be more comfortable. Miriam pushed him back into his seat. When he turned to her, she slapped him across the face. Pain ignited in his cheek. The fog over his thoughts lifted, as he looked at her like a wounded dog.

"It's Thrall. He's putting thoughts into our heads. Remember, the story I told you?"

"I remember."

His breathing was labored. With each thought he wondered if it was his own or if it had been planted there by Thrall.

"He removed our inhibitions, so we act on our feelings. Now, we know there's something between us, Conny. That should make me feel better, but it doesn't."

"I don't know where my head is right now. I've had feelings for Gabby for a long time. Eventually, I figured we'd get together. If I stayed, that is. It never happened. Since you've come to town, well, I've been confused."

"Is this you talking or is this more of Thrall's powers lowering your inhibitions? I can never tell and I'm an expert on him."

Conrad laughed. "I think it's a bit of both. The words are mine, but I can feel that I'm more open to things that I wouldn't normally do. Like professing my true feelings to someone I've known for three days, for instance."

"Sorry I screwed up your boring existence in this sleepy little burg."

"It wasn't a complaint. Simply an observation. I'm definitely not complaining about having the balls to kiss a beautiful woman and having her kiss me back. Plus, you're right. There's something here. We both feel it."

Miriam reached over and grabbed a handful of his T-shirt. She pulled him close to her, as his body started to tingle. Their hot breath over the last few minutes had caused the windows to fog, giving the illusion of privacy, unable to see the voyeur that lurked nearby. Their lips met again. This time it was soft and sensual, lacking the ferocity from before, yet retaining the same passion. The softness of her lips. The strength of her hands as she grasped his shirt. The uneven breathing as she struggled to control her composure. He took it all in.

He sat back in his seat when she pulled away, suddenly out of breath.

"Was that you or Thrall?" he finally asked.

"That was me."

"Speaking of our friend…"

Conrad swiped a hand across the inside of the windshield to clear the condensation. They both leaned forward and looked into the night.

Thrall's smile was as wide as ever. As they watched, he turned and walked in the opposite direction. Appearing to head to the old Comisky place.

A car door slammed shut. He looked in the passenger's seat and found it empty. Miriam waved a hand at him as she chased after Thrall.

Conrad cursed under his breath and exited the SUV.

He had time to wish he had grabbed the pistol in the glove compartment of the SUV. Despite being off-duty, Conrad liked to be prepared for anything. There was a Glock 21 for such an occasion as these. It was the same gun he carried as his duty weapon, so it had a familiar feeling. It would do him no good in the glove compartment.

By the time Conrad was out of the SUV, Thrall was already across the street on the Comisky lawn. Thrall was still walking at a leisurely pace, as if he hadn't noticed that he was being chased. Miriam was running across the street in pursuit. Conrad took off after them.

The road was still wet from the rain earlier in the evening, leaving a slick layer of water on the asphalt. He had lost track of the number of traffic accidents he had responded to that happened just after it rained, even in a small town. Luckily, he was able to keep his footing as he crossed the street. Miriam wasn't so lucky. She was sprawled on her backside in the middle of the street. He stopped to help her.

"Leave me behind," she shouted, trying to wave him off.

Conrad helped her up. "You've seen too many movies."

"I knew these boots were a mistake tonight."

She bent down and slid out of the black leather boots that were equipped with a two-inch heel. They were sexy as hell, but running wasn't their intended use. She was right to ditch them. Miriam threw the shoes onto the lawn of the old Comisky place.

Thrall reached the rubble pile that had once been the old Comisky place and turned to look at them. That same twisted smile was still spread across his demented face.

This was the moment. Conrad knew he was about to see where Thrall had disappeared during their first encounter. It had dominated his thoughts ever since, calling into question the merits of his sanity. Was it the entrance to the White House? Were Thrall's dark powers strong enough to perform some kind of a cloaking spell? The only things he knew about magic were from Harry Potter. That wasn't exactly practical under the circumstances.

The torrential downpour earlier had been soaked up by the parched ground, but it had left the grass covered in rainwater. It was like stepping onto an ice-skating rink without any skates on. He had managed to keep his footing on the asphalt. He couldn't say the same thing about the grass. His feet slid out from underneath him with the first step. Miriam was a step behind him. She reached out and grabbed his arm, thus keeping him from falling to the ground.

As he went down, he managed to keep his eyes on Thrall. The caretaker of the White House leapt high into the air. It was as if the man had replaced his legs with springs. Thrall soared over their heads. Conrad spun around in time to see him land in the street behind them.

Thrall smiled again.

Conrad was beginning to hate that smile.

Thrall turned away from Conrad, as if he was about to take off running. Conrad was already preparing himself for another chase. Before his eyes could register what was happening, Thrall ran towards him. Miriam still had a hold of his arm. Instinctively—there wasn't enough time for conscious thought—he shrugged her off, sending her falling to the wet ground. Conrad had never seen a human run as fast as Thrall had, of course, Miriam claimed the man wasn't human. Perhaps she was right.

Growing up, Conrad hadn't been much of an athlete. However, when he was twelve years old, he had played football in a desperate attempt to gain much wanted approval from the old man. It didn't work as planned. Prairieview's Jr. Pioneers were horrendous that year, not only because of Conrad but the entire team. Undersized and with a bit of speed, the coach had the brilliant idea that he should be a running back. The problem was that he didn't possess two of the key features that make a good running back. Vision and patience. He lacked the patience to wait for a hole to open up. Then lacked the vision to see the opening, if one did happen to open. After two games as a running back, Coach Hayes realized his error, and relegated young Conrad to defense. He became a defensive back, and a decent one at that. He had the speed to keep up with fast wide receivers. Since he wasn't a wide receiver, he didn't have to worry about catching the ball or finding an opening to run through. It was simple, make a play on the ball, and if the receiver caught the ball, tackle him. That was on passing plays, which he liked. Running plays were a different matter. Defending the run required one of the traits he had been lacking at running back. Vision. The ability to see the run wasn't something that could be taught. Conrad struggled at identifying running plays.

The Jr. Pioneers were winless going into the fourth game of the season. They were playing their archrival, the Crimson Creek Cougars. The Cougars had the best running back in the state of Kansas, Dionte MacIntosh, who would go on to star at Crimson Creek High School and even play some collegiate ball. Big Mac, a fitting nickname for the six foot, two hundred pound twelve-year-old, was having his way with the Pioneer defense. He was bigger, faster, and stronger than all the other kids on the field. All game long Conrad counted his blessings that he hadn't been forced into an attempted tackle of the man-sized child. That changed in the fourth quarter, when his vision chose the worst possible time to have an unfortunate change in ability. The wide receiver he was matched up against was a foot taller than Conrad, but the Cougars were having so much success running the ball that they hadn't looked his way. At the snap, the receiver started blocking him. This had been happening all game long, he knew it was a sign the Cougars were running the football. His eyes scanned the field and found Big Mac taking a toss from the quarterback in the backfield. The running play was coming in his direction. He took a step backward and threw both hands up, connecting with the receiver's hands. That caused the receiver to disengage his hands and lose balance at the same time. Now free, Conrad looked for Big Mac. As it turned out, Big Mac enjoyed hitting people, therefore, he was also looking for Conrad. Conrad squared his hips to the runner, stretched out his arms in preparation for a tackle. Big Mac lowered his shoulder and bulldozed right over him. Conrad landed on his tailbone, which was sore for a week afterward.

Big Mac had nothing on Thrall.

Thrall lowered his shoulder as he approached Conrad without slowing. There was no time to prepare for the pain he knew was coming. Thrall's shoulder impacted his ribcage, where several ribs were cracked in the process. Big Mac had sent him falling back onto his butt. Thrall sent him catapulting backwards into the yard of old Comisky place. He landed flat on his back, knocking all the air out of his lungs. His head connected with the ground, which was still hard despite having been softened by the rain.

Miriam rushed to his side.

Upside down and in blurred vision, he watched as Thrall disappeared into the rubble pile again.

Then everything went black.

Conrad was only unconscious for thirty seconds, but it was enough for Miriam to insist on a trip to the emergency room. Prairieview Hospital wasn't equipped for more than scrapes and bruises. He hoped a visit there would be good enough, otherwise, there was a trip to Crimson Creek in the immediate future.

Miriam was helping him to the SUV, which she insisted on driving, when she stopped suddenly. His attention was solely on the pain in his head and ribs, thus didn't realize why she had stopped. When he asked, she pointed to a figure standing in the middle of the street, staring at the spot where the old Comisky place had once stood.

It was Gabby.

"Gabby, what are you doing here?" Miriam asked.

Her voice was soft and comforting, which he found endearing for two reasons. It was obvious she had seen such behavior before, likely in her journey as the on-air talent for Macabre Manor. Secondly was her ability to forget the recent events that had pitted these two women against each other, with Conrad as the responsible party, in the middle.

Gabby didn't respond. In fact, she seemed as if she hadn't heard Miriam at all.

Miriam ushered him to the SUV, where he leaned against the front bumper. Meanwhile, she approached Gabby. She did so with the same caution one would use if approaching a dangerous and unpredictable wild animal. She put a hand on Gabby's shoulder with the lightest of touches, barely perceptible. When she spoke, it was in the same soft and comforting voice as before.

"Gabby, what are doing standing in the middle of the street? That's dangerous, sweetheart."

"I had to see it. It's so beautiful. I can't stop thinking about it."

Gabby spoke without taking her eyes off the pile of rubble.

"Had to see what, Gabby? Tell me what you see."

"The White House, silly. It's so beautiful."

"Did you drive here?"

"No. Drive? No. I walked, I think. I don't remember how I got here," she said, turning to Miriam as if seeing her for the first time.

"Let's get you home."

She ushered Gabby to the SUV, where they rode in silence.

24.

Conrad

As it turned out, the Prairieview Hospital was equipped to treat Conrad, which meant he would avoid a needless one-hour drive to Crimson Creek to confirm what he already knew. He had a concussion and broken ribs. Technically, they were waiting for the results of the X-ray, but he knew they were broken. The question was how many? Each breath expanded his ribcage, causing pain to ignite in his midsection. They gave him something for the pain while he waited.

Miriam stayed with him the entire time. He figured it would be awkward considering how the night had gone, but it was pleasant. She regaled him with a story about her one and only trip to the ER when she was a college student at Northwestern University, involving a bowling ball and a sorority house hazing gone wrong.

"Just a reminder that alcohol and heavy objects don't go well together," she finished with a laugh.

"At least not on a pool table, right? I'll try to keep it to the bowling alley."

The Prairieview Hospital's *ER*—a term that was used very loosely in this case—wasn't equipped with rooms for patients that weren't being admitted. Rather, it was a small square room with two examinations tables, a few medical posters on the wall, and not much else. It made Conrad thankful that the injury hadn't been worse or else he would have had to take that drive to Crimson Creek. It also made him weary of getting injured in such a small town, working a job that could be dangerous.

Another reason you should have blown this joint years ago, he thought.

One of the two doors leading into the room opened, and in walked Dr. Hazel Jenkins. She held the X-ray in her hand that had been delivered to her by the nurse. No doubt, Hazel had seen the name of the patient and decided to deliver the news in person. Just his luck.

"Well, Officer Conrad Cain, it's been a while, hasn't it? But I'm sure that's fine by you, the way we left things," Hazel said, locking intense eyes with Conrad.

"Two years, right? That's a long time considering how small this town is. Of course, you're usually trapped in this small excuse for a hospital, and I'm usually on duty. We've managed to avoid each other. Probably a good thing."

"We were hot and heavy there for a while, right? You almost got me fired that one time…"

Hazel was biting her lower lip as she looked back on the memory. Then her eyes widened as she looked at Miriam, as if noticing the other woman for the first time. They smiled at each other.

"Sorry, I don't think we've met. Of course, like Conrad said, I don't get out of this little office much. I'm Dr. Hazel Jenkins."

"Miriam Tannenbaum."

The two women shook hands.

"So, how long have you two been together?" Hazel asked.

Conrad and Miriam looked at each other.

"Oh, we're not together," Miriam said.

"We're not together," Conrad said at the same time.

Hazel raised an eyebrow. "Okay, but you could've fooled me. The two of you looked pretty cozy in here when I opened the door, that's all I'm saying."

"Friends. We're just friends," Miriam said.

"Look, I don't know you, Miriam, but I know him. He's a good guy, despite being screwed over by a selfish prick of a dad. He's never used that as an excuse. In fact, he's overcome it. He's hard working as they come, doesn't make excuses for not getting things done. Not to mention, he's easy on the eyes."

"Then how come you're not still dating him?"

"Well, he's also a stubborn child that never knew how to back down from a fight. With me or with a perp, as they call them. He may be a nice guy, but he's not good at saying I'm sorry. He's also crummy at accepting an apology or forgiving someone else. He pushes people away until they run into the arms of someone else."

"How many times do I have to tell you? It wasn't that you cheated. Hell, I've done that to people before. It was who with. A highway patrolman?" Conrad said, crossing his arms over his chest.

Hazel shrugged. "I'm a sucker for a man in uniform, what can I say?"

"But Dick Sandburg? Talk about a meathead."

"That meathead is my husband, Conny. But you're right, he's a meathead. You should be happy. I cheated with the man I eventually married. It was fate. Did you want to stand in the way of fate?"

"Fate? So, it was fate that you fell into bed with him after a night out with the girls?"

"Yeah, that's right. And it was fate that you acted like a jerk and decked him when you found out. Damn sucker punch."

"Okay, you two. Let's cool it." Miriam stood between the two exes. "How are the ribs, Doc?"

"You've got two broken ribs. You're going to be in some pain for a while, I'll prescribe something if you want. The best thing you can do is get some rest."

"Wait, I've got a concussion too. I'm not supposed to sleep, right?"

"That's just a myth. As long as you've got someone around to make sure you wake up then you'll be fine. So, again, rest. Nothing physical for a few weeks. In fact, I'd talk to the chief about taking some time off if I were you. That or you'll have to do some desk duty. Either way, I wouldn't go chasing after perps..."

She narrowed her eyes at Miriam.

"Or having sex."

"We're not together," Conrad said.

"Yeah, I heard both of you the first time, but there's definitely a vibe here."

The two women locked eyes for an uncomfortable amount of time, at least for Conrad. It was some kind of unspoken feminine language that he didn't speak. Or maybe it was more of a territorial standoff between two women who were interested in the same man, despite Hazel being married. Either way, it was awkward.

He stood up. "Okay, this was fun. Whatever this was."

"Yes, it was," Miriam said, with what was obviously a fake smile directed at Hazel.

The other woman matched the smile in intensity and authenticity.

The sunrise was only a mere thought in the morning sky, foreshadowing what would likely be a beautiful Kansas sunrise. Conrad wanted to put off the call to the chief informing him of the incident with Thrall. Chief Nichols didn't like talking about anything before his morning coffee. At this hour of the morning, the chief wasn't likely to be out of bed, let alone satisfied his caffeine addiction. Conrad's ribs hurt. His head hurt. All he wanted to do was go to bed. Miriam had a good point, however.

"How would the chief react if a neighbor saw the incident with Thrall, which is likely, and you didn't report it to him? Add your injury on top of that? You've got a combination for a pissed off chief. Call him."

Conrad did.

"Hello?" Chief Nichols said in a voice that was half growl.

"Chief? It's Cain. I've got some information for you."

He filled the chief in as briefly as he could. It didn't take long.

"Take the day off, Cain. Rest, whatever, but I want you in my office day after tomorrow. We've got to talk, and not in the middle of the night."

"See you tomorrow, Chief."

Miriam insisted on accompanying him back to his apartment, and on staying with him for the next twenty-four hours. He insisted that he would be fine on his own. This wasn't his first concussion in the line of duty—she pointed out that he wasn't technically working when it happened—and that nothing bad had happened the other time when he had been alone. She wouldn't hear anything about it. She would stay, so he needed to drop the subject. He did.

Back at his apartment, she helped him undress and climb into bed. He was certain she sneaked a peak while he was naked, but he didn't mind. His body felt as if it had been run over by a train, there would be no intimacy for the foreseeable future. Once he was in bed, she disappeared into the bathroom, where he knew she was looking through his medicine cabinet.

A few minutes later, he heard the shower turn on. Images of her naked body covered in suds were the last thoughts he remembered before his heavy eyelids closed.

At some point, he felt a warm body pressed against his own. Firm breasts against his broken ribs, as if their supple touch could heal their fractured nature.

He dreamed about making love to her.

When he awoke a few hours later, Miriam was wearing an oversized T-shirt, likely pulled from one of his drawers. He must have imagined her nude body next to his or it had been part of the dream. She had propped herself up with a pillow against the headboard and was engrossed in her phone.

"Were you naked earlier?"

She looked over at him with a smile, surprised to see him awake.

"I was. That was about two hours ago, and you didn't seem to notice. Plus, I got cold, so I stole one of your shirts."

"Oh, I noticed."

"Did you? You were supposed to be asleep!"

"I was. Still, I felt them. I'm not asleep now."

"What about Dr. Ex-girlfriend? No sex, remember?"

"I guess we won't tell her then."

Miriam smiled. Then tossed the shirt across the room.

25.

Conrad

The job monopolized his time to such a degree that Conrad rarely got enough free time to focus on himself. Now, he was forced into it, thanks to the injuries sustained in his encounter with Thrall. He couldn't remember the last time he had spent a day doing absolutely nothing. Even the weekends were filled with tasks that needed his attention. Visits with his mom were a common weekend task. There was always something to do.

This was different. With Miriam willing to fulfill his every need, in more ways than one, there was no reason to leave the bedroom. The doctor had ordered him to rest, and that was exactly what he was doing.

She took the time to move the television into the bedroom for the day. Being a single bachelor, Conrad didn't see much use in having more than one television in the apartment. Connecting it was a snap since he didn't own a DVD player or DVR. Thanks to smart television technology, Miriam was able to log into his Netflix account. The biggest trouble of the day was deciding what to watch. Ultimately, they settled on some horror show he knew nothing about, figuring she could watch it while he slept.

They both fell asleep while zombies munched on brains.

The next morning, he awoke naturally as the sun's bright rays shined through the bedroom window. It had been a long time since he had allowed himself to wake up without an alarm on a weekday. It was a good feeling, made better by having someone he cared about lying in bed with him.

He had a meeting with the chief that morning. There wasn't a set time, but he knew the chief would be anxious to learn the details about the encounter with their one and only suspect. Considering how the chief would react to the news, Conrad didn't want to keep the man waiting. His ribs ignited with fresh pain at the first movement in twenty-four hours.

Miriam was still sleeping as he entered the bathroom. He took a quick shower. There were places on his body the pain wouldn't allow him to reach. Maybe she could help with that later.

He came out of the bathroom with a towel wrapped around his waist. It was his habit from years of living alone. Miriam sat on the bed watching him.

"Where do you think you're going?" she asked.

"I've got to talk to the chief this morning. He wants to talk about what happened the other night. I imagine he'll want to talk about how we're going to handle my injury."

"What time is your appointment?"

"There isn't an appointment, but I figured I'd get it over with."

A devilish grin crossed her face. "So, you've got time."

She lifted the oversized T-shirt over her head. The nipples of her small breasts were erect with anticipation. Goosebumps were visible on her bare skin. Raven-black hair cascaded down her shoulders, covering her breasts, as she pulled the shirt over her head. It was the first time he had seen her with her hair down. She threw the shirt at him playfully. Instinctively, he took his hands away from the towel to catch the shirt. The towel fell to the floor as a result, exposing his penis that was ready for what awaited.

"I'll be gentle."

She was.

Miriam and Conrad left the apartment at the same time. Apparently, she sent Gavin a cryptic text message yesterday saying she wouldn't be around that day. Her producer/ex-boyfriend was patient with her because the fans loved her, but she couldn't push it too far. "As an ex, I have to watch it. I can't give him an excuse to fire me. He'd enjoy that too much." The boys likely spent their time shooting B roll, which they already had a mountain of, according to Miriam. They needed her genius to direct their focus.

The brightness of the early morning sun hurt his eyes. Relief flooded over him as he put the sunglasses on in the SUV that were stashed in his center console.

As he drove toward the downtown neighborhood where the station was located, questions seemed to inundate his brain. It felt good to have a day to relax and recover his physical strength. Obviously, one day wasn't going to heal broken ribs and a concussion, however, it had done wonders for his mental state to put aside the stressful situation he found himself in at work. Now that his mind had returned to the world of police investigation, those same worries came back.

Day four of Bianca Nowitzki's disappearance had come and gone while Conrad healed in bed. It was now day five, and still there had been no sign of her or her body. Truth was closer than ever regarding what happened to Bianca. The encounter with Thrall had been painful but revealing at the same time. It had long been established that perpetrators of violent crimes enjoyed watching the police investigation, basking in the chaos that was their creation. They inserted themselves into the investigation. Thrall fit that description. If that were the case, then so did every member of the Macabre Manor crew, including Miriam.

Her presence had been unexpected, both in the investigation and in his life. The monotony simply trying to exist had blinded him to the world around him. Miriam was like a slap to the face, an awakening in the form of a woman. He was enjoying every moment now that his eyes were open.

But what happens when she leaves?

Was it a fling or was it something with substance? Dating had never been his strong suit, as the encounter with Hazel had reminded him. She had been right; he tended to push people away. More than one woman had said he needed therapy. He had thought they were simply being funny and cruel. Maybe they had a point. Maybe there was something wrong with him, and it was best to let Miriam leave before he hurt her.

He arrived at the station before his mind had answers to any of the questions.

"Well, did you learn anything about this guy? What did you call him? Thrall?" Chief Nichols asked.

Conrad had just gone over the events of the other night in greater detail than he had over the phone. The chief wasn't happy, but then again, he never was.

"Yes, sir. I learned that this guy, Thrall, is unusually strong. When he hit me, it was like being hit by an offensive lineman, only he's faster. He was watching me. That's why I got out of the car. So, he obviously has an interest in the investigation. Like I said, there are ties to Macabre Media, more specifically, to Gavin Huxley. I've been unable to prove that it's the same person as in previous cities, but that's only a matter of time. I think he's our guy. Proving it is another matter."

"That or he's a demented psychopath that gets his jollies from attacking plain clothed police. That's a sicko, either way. Let's take this guy down before he hurts someone else."

"Yes, sir."

"Now, there's the business of your injuries."

"It's not that bad, Chief."

"Oh, I know that, Cain. You're a tough kid, but even tough kids need some rest and recoup time. That's why I want you to take two weeks off. Let those ribs heal. How's the head? Didn't you say that you had a concussion?"

"It's not bad," he said, hoping the Chief didn't notice the sunglasses in his breast pocket.

It was true, at least for the moment.

"Still, I want you to take a week off, maybe two. I want that doctor to give you a clean bill of health before you return to active duty. You might have to pull some desk duty."

"Chief, it's only a few broken ribs and a concussion. I'll be fine. I don't need to work at the desk. I'm not Hightower. You can trust me."

"Oh, I know that, Cain. That being said, I think you've become like some kind of maverick cop, like in the movies. Trying to do everything yourself and forgetting there's an entire department to back you up. That's what we're here for, Cain. To provide backup so one person doesn't screw things up for the rest of us."

Ouch.

"Who's going to work the Bianca Nowitzki case while I'm gone?" he asked, knowing the answer.

"Oh, I'll probably do it. Hightower might do some leg work, too. He deserves a shot; he's a good cop."

"The hell he is!"

"I'm going to ignore that. Chalk it up to the pain medication making you delirious. Now, get out of here. Get some rest."

Conrad left the station feeling dejected. A dirty cop was helping with his investigation. It couldn't get worse.

To boost his spirit, Conrad decided to stop at the Newhouse Café for a cinnamon roll. As he parked, however, he noticed something strange. Gabby's car wasn't in the parking lot. This saved him the embarrassing conversation that would inevitably happen following their tryst. While relieved that he wouldn't be having such an awkward conversation with her, her absence from the café was unsettling.

I had to see it. It's so beautiful. I can't stop thinking about it.

Those words chilled him to the bone. Gabby had seen the house. Everyone that had seen the house had disappeared. He didn't want that to happen to Gabby.

Then he remembered she hadn't been in the right state of mind to drive the other night and walked to the White House instead. There was a remote chance that had been the case today, after all, everywhere in Prairieview was within walking distance. He climbed out of the SUV with renewed hope that Gabby might be inside.

His shoulders dropped when he stepped through the front door. Twila was behind the counter working at a frenzied pace. The forty-year-old single mother was one of the café's two waitresses. The counter was Gabby's domain, and Twila was definitely out of her element.

Conrad took a seat at his usual spot and patiently waited for Twila to make his way over. Five minutes later, she appeared across from him with a scowl on her face.

"Your girlfriend needs to get her can in here, now! It's her café and she doesn't even call off? Doesn't show up. Are you kidding me? Don't get it twisted, she's the owner, not mommy."

"Hello to you too, Twila. I take it Gabby isn't here?" he said, trying in vain to suppress a smile.

"No, didn't you listen to me? She didn't show up. As if you didn't know."

"Look, I don't know what you think, but Gabby and I aren't an item. We're just friends."

"Sure, and I work this job for my health. Honey, you don't fool me. I've seen the way the two of you look at each other. You might not have made it official, but don't fool yourself, that's your woman."

"Have you tried calling her?"

"Oh, great work, Officer Cain! Why didn't I think of that!"

"Okay, so you've called. No answer, huh?"

"No. It went straight to voicemail, as if the phone had been turned off or the battery went dead. I had to pull Teresa out of the office and hand her an apron. This ain't like Gabby, even when she was a teenager she cared for this place. She's always been such a good kid. I mean, this is practically her place. Teresa says as much. It's her life. So, if she ain't here then I'm concerned."

"Tell you what, I'm off duty. In fact, I'm going to take a week or two off. I've got broken ribs, nothing serious. But I can stop by her place after this. We'll call it an unofficial welfare checkup. How does that sound?"

"That sounds great, Conrad. And if she ain't hurt, I'll hurt her!"

Gabby lived in a quaint, two-bedroom ranch-style house on the outskirts of town. Despite being on the outskirts of town, it was still within walking distance of the café, of course everything in Prairieview was within walking distance. Conrad had known Gabby his entire life. His parents took him to the café when he was a kid. Gabby would be sitting at the counter after school, drawing in a notebook while her parents worked. He had also stopped in the café for a cinnamon roll every day for the past five years. He couldn't remember her ever walking to work or anywhere else for that matter.

The house was dark when he pulled into the driveway, which wasn't unusual considering it was daytime, and Gabby should have been at work. But it didn't look as if someone was playing hooky from work inside. Most people turned lights on or had curtains open while they were home to let in light. Gabby's house had neither.

He paused long enough to grab the pistol in the glove compartment and stuck it in the waistband of his jeans. If there were surprises inside, he would be ready.

With a woman having already disappeared in Prairieview, and not sold on the White House theory, Conrad used extreme caution when approaching the house. The pistol remained in his waistband; however, his hand never strayed from the butt of the weapon. The front door was ajar as he approached. Instinct and training took over as he drew his pistol.

"This is Officer Cain of the Prairieview Police Department. I'm entering the premises to perform a welfare check on Gabriela Newhouse. I'm armed. If anyone is present, please make yourself known now."

The house was silent.

The foyer was nearly nonexistent. It gave way almost immediately to the living room. His eyes scanned the room, taking in everything in quick fashion. A half empty mug of coffee and a familiar cinnamon roll sat forgotten on the end table. A singular bite had been taken out of the sugary goodness. There was a well-worn sofa with floral upholstery in front of the window and a leather recliner in the corner. Spread across the floor of the room was white printer paper. Each sheet of paper contained a sketch done in charcoal pencil. Conrad had long known of Gabby's affinity for drawing. In fact, while in for his daily dose of sugar, he had often asked her directly why she hadn't applied to art school and never looked back. "Mom needs me. Dad left her, I can't," she had said. Loyal as ever.

Twila was right. This wasn't like her.

Each sketch contained either the White House or the man known as Thrall. It was as if the pages of Bianca Nowitzki's notebook had been ripped out and scattered across the floor. There was a difference, though. Bianca's sketches were good, especially for a non-artist, while Gabby's sketches looked as if they had been done by a professional artist. She had managed to capture the darkness of Thrall's eyes perfectly. Conrad's skin broke out in goosebumps.

He kept moving throughout the house. Five minutes later, the house was cleared. It was empty.

He tucked the pistol back in his waistband as he left the house. If Gabby wasn't at home or at the café, he knew where he was likely to find her. The White House.

Thrall stood on the front lawn.

Conrad stopped. His hand instinctively went to the butt of the pistol, but he didn't draw the weapon.

"Where is she?" he yelled at the man.

Thrall only smiled in response.

Then he turned and ran.

Conrad was off duty, but that didn't stop him from giving chase. Instead of pursuing on foot, he opted for the SUV. The pistol jabbed into his ribs as he got behind the wheel. He wanted the weapon within reach. The passenger seat wouldn't work, as it was unsafe to have the weapon unsecured. His ribs would have to deal with the pain.

Thrall was already a block away when Conrad started the engine. He backed out of the driveway and floored it. The engine roared as he pulled up alongside Thrall. The caretaker for the White House looked over at him and smiled. Then the man found another gear and disappeared into the distance.

Conrad looked down at the speedometer. Forty miles per hour. How could a man run that fast?

26.

Conrad

Thrall was still troubling Conrad's mind when he parked in front of the old Comisky place a few minutes later. It was the first time he had seen the unusual man in the daytime, refuting the possibility that Thrall was a kind of vampire feeding on the souls of those that entered the house.

If Thrall wasn't a vampire, then what was he?

His strength was superior to that of a typical adult male. He also had superior speed, proven by having escaped a car while on foot. Then there was the charming technique he had used on Miriam and Conrad. They had acted upon the impulses they normally suppressed. Once acted upon, it had taken great effort to further suppress those impulses again. Had Conrad seen the full potential of Thrall's powers? It was a frightening notion that Thrall could be capable of more.

First Thrall was seen in Bianca Nowitzki's neighborhood. Now, he was outside of Gabby's house. Obviously, Thrall was stalking the White House's victim. Possibly using his charming technique into doing the house's bidding.

Without Gabby home, it became clear Thrall was watching Conrad. Multiple encounters in the span of a week, including one that had become physical. He was an unrelenting force that wouldn't be stopped until he had learned the truth about what had happened to Bianca. He was growing closer to the truth. Unfortunately, growing closer to the truth had garnered Thrall's attention. Garnering the attention of a dangerous man wasn't advised, law enforcement officer or not. Dangerous people did dangerous things when backed into a corner.

He was pulled from his thoughts by a figure standing in the shade of a Bradford Pear on the Nowitzki's front lawn.

Gabby.

"Gabby? What are you doing here?" he asked, approaching her with caution.

She didn't answer.

"Gabby? Aren't you supposed to be at work? Your mom is worried about you."

"She was standing there when we got here this morning. I've tried talking to her, but she won't answer. It's like she's in some kind of trance."

Miriam had approached while he had been talking with Gabby. The Macabre Media van was parked a few houses down, so it would be out of the shot when they started filming. He couldn't help but smile when he looked at her.

"I went to the café after my meeting with the chief. They said she didn't show up for work today, so I did a welfare check at her house. When I left, Thrall was waiting for me. The guy outran me in my Jeep. Can you believe that? Outrunning a car. Who is this guy?"

"If we only knew," Miriam said, shaking her head.

"How did the meeting go?"

Conrad updated her on the meeting with the chief, including his leave of absence to heal from injury. She was happier about the situation than he had been.

"That gives us more time to spend together. Can't be mad at that."

"Yeah, but there's an investigation to run. I can't trust the chief or Hightower to make a break in this case. I'm the only one that can."

"But you said it yourself, you're taking a medical leave. What can you do?"

"I can still work the case as an adviser for Macabre Manor. He didn't say I couldn't do that. I'd like to continue by interviewing Stu."

Miriam looked apprehensive. "I don't know."

"Why not. He's worked for Gavin twice as long as you have. He's the perfect guy."

"Yeah, but I don't know if he'll talk. He's loyal to Gavin, maybe even afraid of him."

"Afraid? Why?"

She shrugged. "That I don't know, other than the usual 'he's my boss and can fire me' stuff, I mean."

"Mind playing decoy with Gavin while I talk to him?"

"Play decoy with my ex-boyfriend, so my new boyfriend can interview a coworker about my ex-boyfriend? Man, you owe me."

Gabby was still standing under the Bradford Pear as their plan went into action.

Miriam convinced Gavin the tapes needed reviewed for a social media post to boost their ratings, which had dipped without any new developments in the Bianca Nowitzki case. It was an easy sell because it was something the two of them normally did together without Stu's input. That left Stu and Conrad standing on the lawn of the old Comisky place. They would talk about Stu's boss with the van containing the boss inside, within view.

The big cameraman had a knowing expression on his face, as if he had known this conversation would be happening at some point.

"I knew when you came on board that we'd be having this conversation," Stu said, as if reading Conrad's mind. "You're too smart not to have done your homework on us. I know, it's too convenient that wherever we show up, people go missing. It doesn't take a great investigator to realize that something fishy is going on. Not to say that you're a bad cop, of course, actually the opposite. You're too damn smart not to have noticed."

"Thanks for the compliment, Stu. You're right, I've done some checking around about you guys. For instance, I know that you guys, mainly Gavin from the sounds of it, have faked hauntings in the past."

"Everyone in our industry does that."

"Sure. You've got to keep eyeballs on the show, right? That's not my concern. My interest is in whether Gavin and the guy known as Thrall are working together. I know Gavin hired him in the past. Tell me how that went down."

"I don't remember where we were, seems like we go everywhere. Things weren't going that well. We weren't even sure if this was a real White House case or not, so Gavin decided to make it one. He found an actor that looked a lot like Thrall. His hair was going gray, so we had to dye it black, but other than that, the guy was a good match. Especially in the dark. When it's dark, people see what they want to see. If they want to see Thrall, then by God, they see Thrall. That's what Gavin gave them. He gave them Thrall. Now, I knew not to capture him up close. There were two reasons for that. One being obvious, it wasn't the same guy. Eagle eyed viewers might have been able to pick up on the subtle differences in the two guys' features. I kept the shot wide to avoid that. And two, well, Thrall hadn't ever been photographed up close at all. He's too elusive. He seems to know when you're trying to film him and just slips away. That's the shot we were going for, and that's the shot we got."

"And Gavin has kept that guy on, I'm assuming."

Stu shook his head. "That was a one-time thing. Plus, the spouse of the missing person found out what we had done and sued Gavin and the company. He's willing to pull the wool over the eyes of the viewers, when necessary, but not at the expense of his pocketbook. Don't be fooled, he's got some green, but not enough to spend it stupidly. That was the one and only time we hired someone to play Thrall. Miriam didn't like it. Thought we shouldn't deceive the viewers, which I understood. I mean, she's got a real connection with the viewers, being the face of the show. She'd get attacked online when word got out about what we had done. Luckily, it didn't end the show. I still don't know how we survived."

"Do you think Gavin would do anything for ratings? Would he arrange for someone to go missing?"

Stu's eyes twitched towards the van, as if trying to look inside.

"Look, Gavin's morals are flexible if given the right opportunity. Anything for a dollar, right? You know that he was willing to fake a haunting. You know that he was willing to hire someone to play Thrall. Well, those are the things that you know about. What about the things that you don't know about? There are things I can't speak about."

"Like what?"

Stu's eyes switched back to Conrad. His gaze was firm.

"Like I said, I can't speak of those things."

"Hold on, are you afraid of Gavin?"

"Problems have a way of disappearing for him. I can't explain it, and that's all I'll say about it. You're a cop, right? So, investigate."

That's what I'm trying to do, Conrad thought but didn't say.

"Fair enough. So, you guys aren't working together with Thrall, and you know nothing about the disappearance of Bianca Nowitzki."

"Of course not," a voice said from behind them.

Conrad whirled around. Gavin stood behind him, smiling.

27.

Conrad

"Gavin, it's not what it looks like," Stu said, holding his hands up in protest.

Conrad noted the fear, genuine fear, in Stu's face. It wasn't the healthy type of fear one has for the person that controls their job security. Conrad had seen that often in his line of work, had been able to discern the difference between the two from interviews regarding theft at various employers. Being a cop in a society that vilified law enforcement to the degree that public perception of police was that of mistrust and skepticism, he had been on the receiving end of fearful gazes. The look on Stu's face was the latter.

Most of Gavin's face was smiling, though his eyes hadn't gotten the memo. His eyes were hard and firm, locked onto his cameraman as if he had decided the longtime employee was a trader.

Gavin raised an eyebrow. "What it looks like is a police officer I have paid to be under my employ is questioning my employees about the happenings of my company. It looks like my paid law enforcement officer is trying to turn my employees against me, without having all the proper information. Didn't your mom ever teach you that it isn't nice to talk about other people behind their backs? Or was your mom too busy running from your dad to teach you anything?"

"Well, I see you've lifted the mask, Gavin," Conrad said.

"Mask? I'll admit that I have to refrain from losing my temper while handling business. I'll also admit to keeping a business persona that most people get to see, including Stu here. Few have ever glimpsed it. That being said, the accusations that you've leveled are false, Officer Cain. Now, I'll admit to bending the law sometimes and breaking it blatantly at others. That comes with the territory of our business. I've committed fraud by faking hauntings and deceiving my clients. I gave them what they wanted to see. It's not my fault that they weren't intelligent enough to know when the wool was being pulled over their eyes. As a businessman you've got to make the best of a situation. Losses hurt the company and take money out of my pocket. If I can mitigate a loss or even turn it into a win, isn't that a good thing? That's good for business. And if my media blitz brings attention to a case, then a grieving spouse ought to have the nerve to endure that, instead of suing me to make themselves feel better."

"That was a long way of saying it's not your fault, Gavin. What I didn't hear you say was whether you have business with the man known as Thrall. The man that attacked me. Did you hire him?"

"I'd enjoy nothing more than to take credit for injuring you, Officer Cain, but I am in no way working with Thrall. It was a one-time thing, as I believe both of my employees have already told you."

"How do you know what I've talked about with Miriam and Stu, Gavin?"

"You have your ways of learning things, Officer Cain, and I have mine. Mine aren't as tactical as yours, but they work just the same."

It was at that moment that Conrad saw Miriam standing next to the company van. Tears were streaming down her face.

"What the hell did you do?" he asked, turning back to Gavin.

"I will not have my employees turned against me by some two-bit lawman who thinks he's Magnum P.I. all of a sudden. Especially when he's inventing things in his own mind."

"What the hell did you do?"

His voice had risen in volume. He took a step closer to Gavin.

"What had to be done."

Conrad prided himself on always being prepared. It was hard to catch him off guard. In this scenario, however, he wasn't ready.

The punch to the ribs came quick and hard, doubling him over. The second punch landed flush to his temple. It sent him to the ground on his back. He looked up at Gavin, stunned.

"I believe our working relationship has come to an end, Officer Cain. You're fired."

Gavin smiled down at him. Then he turned and walked to the van. He passed Miriam as he walked. There weren't words exchanged, only a fearful look from her to him.

"Are you afraid of Gavin?"

They were back at his apartment, lying in bed after making love. His ribs were sore, but he was content.

"I guess, I mean, I haven't really thought about it before. He can get really angry. That's usually reserved for Stu, like when the shot isn't exactly how Gavin wants it. Or sometimes Stu has ideas for what we can do on the channel. Gavin has a problem taking direction from others, especially other men. I've been able to make suggestions in the past, but I don't think he's threatened by me, being a woman and all. In Gavin's mind, Stu is only there to hold the camera and take direction, that's it."

"Stu's afraid of Gavin. 'Problems have a way of disappearing for him.' That's what Stu said about Gavin. Is there something I don't know about Gavin?"

Miriam shrugged her shoulders, jostling Conrad's head that was resting against her bare chest. His groin tightened.

"Gavin's backstory is a mystery to me. Sure, we dated for a while, but I never met any family or close friends. It's as if the channel is the only thing he has, which is strange considering how much money he has."

"Are you saying he's rich?"

"He runs a YouTube channel with multiple successful shows on it. Sure, we're the most successful, but there's also Tales of the Macabre and Macabre Memoirs. There's some crossover with all three shows, by the way. The guys that run those shows usually do a deeper dive into the individual stories, like in a narrative form. Anyway, the ad revenue for those shows is lucrative from what I hear. So, yeah, Gavin is a rich man."

"There's crossover with those shows? Have they covered Thrall before?"

"Aren't you a detective?" she asked with a laugh.

"I'm a small-town cop. Wait, are you making fun of me?"

He rolled over and started tickling her. She stopped him with a kiss. That ended the discussion and started something else.

28.

Conner

There was a broad smile on Conner's face as he exited the room on the fourth floor of the White House. The taste of Miriam was still on his lips, which brought him a moment of guilt as a married man, no matter her level of faithfulness. The reenactment of his memory confirmed what he remembered; he had been truly happy simply lying in bed with Miriam. It was the last time he had been truly happy without the addition of survivor's guilt sprinkled in. The following day everything would change, both for him and for Prairieview.

The smile disappeared from his face suddenly, as if it had never existed. The three floors below him represented the past, his past, while those memories were meaningful and worth remembering, it was only because of what lay ahead on the floors above his head. The reason for following his father into alcoholism—at some point during this strange journey Conner had accepted this term applied to him—lay in the memories behind the doors yet to come. The reason he had trouble meeting his own gaze when he looked in the mirror lay ahead.

Up ahead there was darkness, and in that darkness, there were monsters. The biggest monster was himself, and the darkness came from within.

Suddenly there were tears pouring from his eyes. He let them come.

Instead of moving upward to the next floor, to the next door, to the inevitable, Conner collapsed to the floor. He lay on the ground with his head in his hands.

He wouldn't move on. Thrall couldn't make him.

Time had a funny way of passing inside the White House. When Conner took his head out of his hands, he wasn't sure if five minutes had passed or five years. He had heard it said that time was an illusion, that it was simply the way our primitive minds experience reality. Since he wasn't a theoretical physicist, the subject was more complex than he could comprehend. Yet, he thought he was smart enough to figure out how this place worked.

While he was crying softly into his hands, he realized that he should have been gasping for breath. He wasn't. Carlisle didn't cry often, she was far too resilient for such things, however, there had been one occasion. She had been raised by a strong-willed single mother, who had also been raised by a strong-willed single mother that couldn't get enough free love during the sixties. Both her mother and grandmother had been too strong for the meek men in their lives and had eventually left them to forge their own path. At times it was as if he was fighting against all three generations when arguing with Carlisle. It was a wonder she hadn't left him considering how similar to her mother and grandmother she was. The one-time Conner had seen her cry was the passing of her mother two years ago. Her shoulders had heaved as she gasped for breath.

His shoulders were doing no such thing. In fact, he wasn't breathing at all. A fact that was confirmed as *time* passed. He wasn't breathing at all.

"I thought you deserved some time to prepare for what is to come. You've had that time, now it is time to move upward."

Thrall stood at the far end of the hallway, as if he had just climbed the stairs from the fourth floor. Conner stared at him for a long time before responding.

"Did you know I would enter the house? Back then, I mean. Did you know ten years ago that I would be walking these hallways, reliving these events now? Did you know?"

"You give me too much credit, Conrad Cain. My master only shares with me what is necessary. I only know who enters the house when I am preparing them for their entrance. Did he know then? I think he did, yes. He has a plan, that much I can assure you, however, he doesn't share that plan with me. Yet, when I think back, which I don't do often, hindsight is for the weak, I did have an inclination that you would eventually find your way into these halls. As you have noticed, time works differently here. For you, it has been ten years since the house appeared in your life. For me, it seemed like an eternity and like five minutes at the same time. Both are true, and yet, both are wrong. Either way, you are here now."

"What is about to happen on the fifth floor, the events that unfold in the coming days, how much of that was you? How much would have happened had you not been involved? Would it have changed things if your master hadn't decided to take three people in Prairieview, Kansas?"

Thrall cringed. It was an ugly sight.

"Retrospection and second-guessing the hands of fate. Another tool of the weak minded, Conrad Cain. It doesn't matter. What I will say is my master is fate. He was always destined to come to that sleepy Kansas town and capture three souls. Do you really think it was only three? Oh, how foolish you are. You are only aware of three. There were more. There are always those that the eyes of the self-righteous deem unworthy of their attention, thus unworthy of their gaze. No one notices them when they enter the house.

No one notices when they go missing. Where is their episode of Macabre Manor?"

"Wait, there were others? Who?" he asked, coming to his feet.

"I've grown tired of our dialogue, Conrad Cain. It is time for you to ascend to the next level. I've told you, talking isn't my forte, save all your questions for my master, for he will be able and relish in answering them for you. Me? I want to watch you suffer."

"But—"

"Ascend!"

The lights that had no origin went out. Thrall had been on the other side of the hallway. In the next moment Conner could feel the paranormal entities' presence near him.

"Ascend," Thrall whispered.

The sound of the voice whispering in his ear forced Conner into motion. He turned and ran in the direction of the door to the fifth floor of the White House. He did this despite the darkness, feeling his way as one does in a space that has become familiar. He found a doorknob with his outstretched hand. He opened the door and ascended the stairs.

The fifth floor hadn't been touched by Thrall's magic. It was bright with the unnatural light of the house. Conner didn't waste any time making his way to the door. He had learned pain was best dealt with quickly, like a band aid. There was only pain from here on.

Sloth

29.

Conrad

"Grandma, this is Little Red Riding Hood. I'm all done on the trail and headed back to Grandma's house."

"Hightower, that radio is not a toy, and you don't have to use code names. Your patrol vehicle number will work fine. Plus, I'm not anyone's grandma, especially not yours, Frank Hightower. If I was, there certainly wouldn't be any cookies waiting when you got here."

"Wait, you've got cookies?"

"No! I meant… Oh, never mind. Cruiser 13, on its way back to homebase, heard loud and clear."

"Aren't you going to call me Little Red Riding Hood? Come on, Grandma."

Conrad was lying on the couch in the living room with an icepack on his ribs. Without anything to do, and uninterested in watching television, he had turned both the police scanner and his radio on. It had only been a few hours since he had been placed on medical leave, and he was missing the action of the job already. He had done so with the hope of overhearing an update on the Bianca Nowitzki case. Instead, what he heard was the back-and-forth banter of Frank Hightower, who had taken his place on the day shift, and Tracy, who worked dispatch.

Hightower hadn't ever taken the job seriously, which had also been the case for his older brother, Leonard. The older brother had been relieved of his duties after the drug scandal when Conrad was in high school, while the younger brother had managed to keep his job, somehow. Conrad had waited for the other shoe to drop on Frank, so far it hadn't happened. The two brothers had been as thick as thieves, which he also suspected they were, as close as brothers could be without being twins. It was for that reason that he had a hard time believing Frank hadn't been involved in the drug scandal with Gerald Bunting and their uncle, Judge Milton Hightower. Someone had to pay the price for what had happened, and it certainly wasn't going to be the judge. Gerald Bunting had managed to get away without doing any jail time. Leonard had also managed to avoid jail time, which the middle-aged man had to be happy about. Conrad had heard horror stories about what happened to former lawmen who found themselves in prison. Some didn't make it out alive. The cost had been Leonard Hightower's job as an officer of the Prairieview Police Department. Rumor had it that he had gone fulltime with Bunting running drugs. This time they kept their product away from the high school, having learned their lesson. In fact, despite keeping a careful watch over the town and the surrounding area, Conrad didn't know how they were distributing their product. The only thing he knew for certain was that Frank Hightower was keeping a watchful eye on the PPD as their inside man.

It was that flippant attitude about his job that emboldened Frank to pollute the radio waves with nonsense, rather than keeping it free for official business. Of course, Conrad knew he was only annoyed by the banter because of who was involved. Had it been Don Lee gabbing with Tracy, as he often did, Conrad wouldn't have had a problem with it. Then again, Lee was a good man and a good cop. The same couldn't be said for Frank Hightower.

The radio was on the coffee table in front of the couch, just out of reach. Switching the radio off would involve manipulating his torso in a manner that would assuredly cause pain in his ribs. He stared at the radio for five minutes, debating whether it was worth the pain. Ultimately, Frank's shift ended, and Conrad was blessed with silence.

At some point, while listening to the silence of his home, Conrad dozed off. It had been a long day, despite not having logged any hours on the clock. He had been put on medical leave by the chief, had done a welfare check, had an encounter with Thrall, interviewed two people regarding the Bianca Nowitzki case, and been beaten up by one of those people. His days on the clock were rarely that eventful.

He couldn't get comfortable on the couch, thanks to his ribs, which had worsened due to Gavin using them as a punching bag. It caused him to toss and turn on the couch. Every few minutes, his eyes would flutter open as he adjusted. He knew it would be more comfortable in the bed; however, he couldn't muster up the energy in his half-asleep state to move. Plus, he knew the pain of rising from the couch would reignite the pain in his ribs. So, he endured.

A dark shadow had fallen over the corner of the room, where there was a bookshelf filled with DVDs, since he wasn't much of a reader. With the rise of Netflix, it had been a while since he had pulled a movie from the shelf to watch.

Something in the shadow moved.

It was hard to discern the varying shades of black from each other, thus, he wasn't sure what had moved.

His eyes fluttered closed as he stared into the shadowy corner.

When his eyes opened again—he wasn't sure how long, it could have been five seconds or five minutes—the shadows had shifted again.

Now there was a dark figure that looked as if it had just emerged from the darkened corner of the room. The figure was cloaked in darkness, despite having stepped out of the darkened corner. Whoever the figure was should have been standing in the light of the lamp, which was next to the couch where Conrad lay, motionless.

In his sleep fogged brain, he tried to recall what was in the corner of the room other than the bookshelf lined with DVDs. Wasn't there a coat rack in that corner of the room? No, he didn't own a coatrack. There were two hooks by the front door where he hung his jacket and hat. That was on the adjacent wall.

This was a man.

A man in his home.

"Are you done poking around in my business, Officer Cain? I sure do hope so. So does your girlfriend."

Conrad sat up quickly. Too quickly, in fact. His ribs cried out in pain as he looked around the room.

It was empty.

After fifteen minutes of checking his one-bedroom apartment for an intruder, in which he checked every room multiple times, Conrad resigned himself to the fact that he had been dreaming. It was more comforting than the alternative, which was Thrall had managed to sneak into his locked apartment without him noticing, taunting him while he slept, then disappearing without a trace. It was as horrifying as the man himself, so Conrad dismissed it.

There had to be an explanation for the mystifying abilities of the man known as Thrall. He was able to influence other people's actions without saying a word, causing them to do things they had thought about but had always resisted. He was able to disappear seeming at will, though Conrad had only seen this on the property of the old Comisky place, which was where the supposed White House was located. There was also the superhuman strength and speed, which had been on full display when Thrall had broken his ribs and caused a concussion. Thrall wasn't a large man, in fact, he was rather unassuming in size and stature. Yet, the man—Miriam didn't think he was a man, Conrad disagreed—was a physical specimen hidden beneath the veneer of an average middle-aged man. Conrad knew it was the unassuming type that you had to watch out for.

Gavin and the rest of the Macabre Manor crew had insisted they weren't working with the man known as Thrall, despite the simple fact that the producer had hired someone to play Thrall in the past. He needed to locate the actor that was hired to play Thrall. There were channels Conrad could go through to find such a thing out. Those channels, however, were for active members of the Prairieview Police Department. Since he was on medical leave, that didn't include him. Yet, he was sure that rules could be bent in the pursuit of justice. Especially if Thrall turned out to be working with Gavin, and together they were responsible for the disappearance of Bianca Nowitzki.

That wasn't a task for the present. His ribs were aching from the battering they had taken from Gavin and the sudden movement searching for a man that had been a figment of his imagination. Instead, Conrad replenished his icepack and laid back down on the couch.

His nap was over. The fear of having an intruder in his home had awoken him fully, whether that intruder had been real or imagined. Instead, he searched for the remote to the television—which he found buried in the cushions of the couch—and turned on YouTube. Miriam had taken the time to move the television back into the living room before leaving for work.

"I don't like it in the bedroom anyway. It ruins the intimacy," she said as she fiddled with the wiring.

Conrad hadn't protested. To him, intimacy was a fancy word for sex. He wasn't going to argue about something that would get him laid.

Earlier in the day, Miriam mentioned the other shows Gavin produced. He had figured he wouldn't have an opportunity to watch either show due to lack of time. Since he had the house to himself and nothing better to do, there was no better time than the present.

He started with Macabre Memoirs. Among the episodes to choose from was a name that sounded familiar. The Bauman survivors. Then he remembered. Hanz Bauman had been the first known victim of the White House in the

1930's. It was about Ethel Bauman and her twin sons, Albert and Karl.

Conrad selected the episode and sunk deeper into the cushions of the couch.

The episode started with a tall, slender man in his mid-twenties standing on the edges of a cornfield. It was obviously supposed to be rural Nebraska, though it could have been in any corn field in middle America. He had a John Krasinski with glasses vibe that the camera found oddly appealing. When he spoke with the bass voice and cadence of someone that had taken narration lessons, and found he had a knack for it.

"On August 13, of 1930, Hanz Bauman went missing from his farm, here in rural Nebraska. According to legend, Hanz entered the fabled White House, never to be seen again. For more on his story, I invite you to watch the episode of Macabre Manor, our sister channel. There's a link in the description.

"Today, however, isn't about Hanz Bauman. He has an entire episode dedicated to him. Instead, I'd like to tell you the story of those that survived him. Ethel, Albert, and Karl Bauman. What happened to the thirteen-year-old twin boys and their mother after the peculiar events that fateful autumn week that took their father and husband from them? How was a single mother to survive in an era where women were only a decade removed from having the respected honor to vote for President of the United States? How would a housemaker cope with suddenly being the sole provider of two teenage boys? Let's find out."

The show was interesting enough to keep Conrad's eyelids from fluttering further. It was fairly typical of the times. Ethel was forced to find a job doing the only thing women had been deemed capable of in those times, secretarial work. They lost the house to the bank and were forced to move to the city, where Karl flourished. Albert became increasingly isolated, holding onto the hope that his father was still alive. At the age of eighteen, Albert ran away from home. Never to return. Karl went on to put his imagination to good use as a writer, something his father wouldn't have understood. He kept looking for his twin brother throughout his life. Once saying, "I know he's out there somewhere. Alive. I can feel it. We've always had a special connection that way. He's out there. Someday I'll find him."

At the age of forty, the same age as his father, Karl Bauman went out for a pack of cigarettes and never returned. His wife, Martha, was left to raise five-year-old daughter, Ethel, named after Karl's mother, alone.

"Two brothers disappeared twenty-two years apart, both under equally mysterious circumstances. One had been traumatized by a father that had disappeared seemingly before his very eyes, while the other hadn't been able to forget the unspeakable connection that can occur between twins. What happened to them? Did they survive when they left their families? Or was there a certain house waiting for them? Let us know in the comments what you think. As for me, I like to believe Karl found Albert, who had also managed to find their father, Hanz. The three Bauman men reunited. It doesn't quite fit the usual narrative of Macabre Memoirs, and that's okay with me. In fact, it brings some brightness to the dark side. Let's end on that bright note this week. I've been Rich Stanfield, see you next time."

Conrad was reaching for the remote, thinking about whether he wanted to watch another episode or not, when his phone chimed. It was a text message from Miriam.

Guess who's back? She's been staring at the house for an hour. Help! She won't talk 2 me.

Gabby.

30.

Conrad

The sun was setting on what had been a very long day off for Conrad. He wanted nothing more than to end it on a relaxing note. The only trouble he had five minutes ago was whether he should wait for Miriam or eat without her. Then she texted. He stared at the text, wanting to not answer it, yet knowing that he would. If not for Miriam, then for Gabby.

Gabby had been a friend—or whatever their relationship had turned into since they had sex in the front seat of his SUV—for a long time. He wasn't sure what sleeping together would do for their relationship, but he *did* know that he didn't want it to end. If they were going to remain friends, that meant making a commitment to the relationship.

He sighed and picked up the phone.

On my way.

Conrad could see Gabby standing underneath the Bradford Pear tree in the Nowitzki's front yard when he pulled up. Her eyes were locked on the ruins that had once been the old Comisky place. For a moment, he wondered what she saw where that pile of rubble had once been a house. Did she see a seven-story white house? Or was she simply trying to manifest the old Comisky house from a pile of rubble into the house that it had once been?

Realization washed over him. Never before had an investigator been able to get into the mind of a deceased victim without at least a modicum of doubt. There was a lot of hypothesizing, which was a fancy word for guessing in Conrad's book, that went on during the course of an investigation. There wasn't anything wrong with it, after all, that was what investigating was all about, studying the facts and the clues, then forming your judgement for a better understanding of what had happened. This was also true with the mindset of the victim of a crime. Bianca Nowitzki had seen the house in the days leading to her disappearance, that much had been made exceedingly clear by David Nowitzki and the notebook Conrad had found in her house. She had been unable to get the White House and the man known as Thrall out of her mind. It seemed as if every waking moment had been spent obsessing over those two. The White House and Thrall. The White House and Thrall. Nothing else. Now, there was someone who appeared to be suffering from the same symptoms as Bianca had before her disappearance. Gabby was obviously obsessed with the house. He had discovered similar drawings of the White House and Thrall in her house. Now, she was displaying obsessive behavior by abandoning her job, a job that was as important as anything else.

He had the opportunity to study Gabby in order to gain a better understanding of Bianca's mindset in the days leading to her disappearance. While it was true that they weren't the same person, it was the closest he could come. Plus, watching Gabby would hopefully keep her safe from whatever happened to Bianca. He wasn't convinced by the lore of the White House just yet. It sure made for an interesting plotline for a show, one that he might watch under other circumstances, but this was real life. This was reality. Ghostly houses only seen by a select few were a thing of fantasy. What had happened to Bianca had been frighteningly real. His job was to figure out what had happened to her, despite the fact that he wasn't on the job. His old man had always carried a handgun somewhere on his person, even when off-duty. His favorite place to hide a handgun during off hours was a small holster around his ankle. When Conrad was a little boy, he had asked his father about this seemingly strange habit. His old man had ruffled his hair and said, "A cop is never off-duty, even when they are. You've always got to be prepared. Even when I'm not physically working, my mind is working." He hated to admit when the old man was right, but this was one of those situations.

Conrad exited the SUV and slammed the door. Gabby remained rigged, eyes locked on the alleged White House. It seemed as if the rest of the world didn't exist for Gabby, a fact that was confirmed as he approached in the darkness. He purposefully trod heavily upon the asphalt, making as much sound as possible so he wouldn't sneak up on the mesmerized woman. Gabby didn't turn her head or so much as blink as he approached.

"How are you doing, Gabby?"

She didn't answer. He let the question hang around in the air for a few minutes to percolate. The great thing about being on medical leave was that he had all the time in the world and nowhere in particular to be.

"Okay. I'm okay, Conrad."

She had spoken without turning her head, her focus remained on the White House that Conrad couldn't see. Her voice was soft, just above a whisper.

"You know, you forgot to go to work this morning. Twila and your mom are worried about you. I'm worried about you."

"Why? You fucked me then fucked someone else."

He was taken aback at her bluntness. "How did you know that?"

"The Caretaker told me. You guys call him Thrall, but he doesn't like that. He says it's another word for slave, which is what he is, but doesn't want reminded of it. He likes Caretaker, because he takes care of the house and those that are inside. It gives him a sense of control. Of course, it's a false sense of control, but I didn't tell him that. He's scary. I can't stop thinking about him."

The cadence of her voice was monotone. It sent a shiver down his spine.

"Gabby, you talked to Thrall. The Caretaker?"

"Yes, Conrad Cain. I've talked to the Caretaker of the White House. He watches me. He watches you. He watches all of us. He'll come for me. He'll come for you."

"Why would he come for me? What have I done?"

"You're too close. Caretaker didn't say he would come for you, but I think he will. The house must eat. The master must eat. More souls. All the time he needs more souls. Why not yours? Why not the soul of a promiscuous man that screws whoever he pleases without regard for anyone else's feeling but that thing hanging between his legs?"

"Gabby, I'm sorry you're hurt. Thrall, I mean Caretaker, he can control people's actions, make them lose their inhibitions. He can't make you do anything that you haven't at least thought about doing, it's not mind control, per se, but he can override that part of your brain that causes you to have self-doubt about the whole ordeal. I take it you've thought about me sexually? Well, I have thought about you that way, Gabby. In hindsight, we should have acted upon those feelings a long time ago. I should have acted on those feelings. Now, I think it's too late."

"Oh, yes, I've thought about it a lot, Conrad Cain. Too late? Because I'm going into the house? Yeah, I'm going in the White House."

"Don't go in the house, Gabby. Whatever you do, don't go in that house."

"Don't tell me what to do, you made your choice, Conrad Cain."

"I just don't want to see something bad happen to you, Gabby."

"You made your choice. I know what type of man you are now, Conrad Cain."

She took one last look at the ruins where she saw the White House, then took off running down the street. Shame and regret cemented his feet to the ground.

The Macabre Manor crew was filming on the front lawn of the old Comisky place. He wondered what content they were creating for the show. There were no new developments in the Bianca Nowitzki case that he knew about. Could they be sharing the information that there was another Prairieview citizen that had seen the White House? That seemed like an underhanded tactic, but Conrad didn't think it was beyond Gavin's capabilities. According to authorities, Gavin had tried some underhanded tactics in the past.

Conrad wanted to walk over to the crew and watch them film so he would know what they were doing. It didn't sit well with him that they would take advantage of Gabby like that, hopefully they would keep her name out of the report. He remained near his SUV and watched from a distance. After what had transpired with Gavin, he knew his presence was no longer wanted by the film producer.

The sun had fully set on day five of Bianca Nowitzki's disappearance without further knowledge coming forth as to what had happened to her. It was beginning to seem as if they would never learn the truth. Yet, he held out hope there was someone out there with information regarding her disappearance that would help the investigation. It was that hope that kept him from going home, where a warm bed awaited.

Fifteen minutes later, however, he realized that hope could wait until tomorrow. He was hungry and tired after a long day. It was time to go home. Hopefully, Miriam would join him as soon as the crew finished filming.

He was walking back to his SUV, reluctantly prepared to spend the rest of the night alone if Gavin kept them filming much longer. As he turned toward the SUV and reached his hand for the handle, he noticed a dark figure watching him from the shadows. They were standing underneath the canopy of the Bradford Pear, where Gabby had stood twenty minutes earlier. This figure wasn't a woman, however. The broad shoulders indicated it was a man.

Thrall.

He likes Caretaker, because he takes care of the house and those that are inside.

Conrad thought about getting in the SUV and fleeing. In that moment, where he knew he was being watched all that seemed to matter was getting away from those eyes.

He watches me. He watches you. He watches all of us. He'll come for me. He'll come for you.

Gabby's words sent a chill down his spine, but was Caretaker really watching him? If that were the case, Conrad didn't want the strange man to know where he lived. Of course, if Caretaker was a paranormal entity, then there wasn't anything Conrad could do to keep him from learning the information. Still, it was better safe than sorry.

Conrad patted the pockets of his jacket and blue jeans, feigning losing his keys. The keys were safely in the pocket of his blue jeans, but Caretaker didn't know that. He sighed and slumped his shoulders, as if resigning himself to walking.

He stuffed his hands into his jeans and started walking down the street. The route he took purposefully put the shadowy figure into his line of sight as he passed the spot where the figure was hiding.

The figure was still there, hiding in the shadows of the Bradford Pear. Conrad could feel eyes upon him as he passed. It was difficult not to look directly at the hiding spot that wasn't really hidden. Instead, he used his peripheral vision to watch the shadowy figure. At first, the figure remained motionless, as if only turning his head to watch Conrad as he passed.

Doubt settled into his mind as the figure went out of his field of vision. Had he been wrong that the figure had been watching him? What if it wasn't Thrall or Caretaker at all? What if it was simply someone out for a walk, who happened to see a stranger lurking around the neighborhood and decided to watch them to see if they were up to anything nefarious.

Grass crunched on a lawn somewhere behind him.

Conrad kept walking.

Footsteps echoed off the asphalt into the night.

Conrad kept walking.

He kept his eyes forward and his head down as he walked around the block, away from the location where the Macabre Manor crew filmed. Away from help. Once again, he had been unprepared when he exited his vehicle. He hadn't any idea that a short conversation with Gabby would turn into a situation where he would want the comfort of the pistol tucked away in the glove compartment of the SUV.

Was he overreacting? Could this simply be a person out for a walk that happened to be going in the same direction as him? He decided to put that theory to the test. Conrad increased his speed to a fast walk, as if he was in a hurry to get home. After half a block, he glanced behind him. The shadowy figure had also increased their speed, managing to maintain the same distance between them.

He stopped suddenly and bent down to tie his shoe. Of course, his shoe wasn't untied, but he went through the motions of tying the shoe. As he pantomimed tying, he glanced back once more. The shadowy figure had stopped in the middle of the street, waiting for Conrad to begin walking again.

Conrad stood up, straightened his jacket and began walking again. This time he walked slower than before, as if he didn't have any destination in mind, but was only out for an evening stroll enjoying the night. The shadowy figure matched his pace.

Why was Thrall playing these games with him? It didn't seem like his style. Each time they had met, Thrall's actions had been deliberate and perceptible. Thrall was also stealthier than this shadowy figure was turning out to be. Doubt was creeping into Conrad's mind. Was this Thrall?

Conrad stopped. He had had enough of this charade. He turned around and faced his stalker.

He was surprised by two things when he turned around. The first thing was that the shadowy figure had managed to close the distance without making any noise. The second thing was that it wasn't Thrall.

It was David Nowitzki.

"David, what are you doing?" he asked in a surprised voice.

David didn't answer with words. Instead, the grieving husband punched Conrad in the nose.

Stunned but not hurt, he stepped back in surprise. He braced himself for another punch, but none came.

"What are you doing, Mr. Policeman? Huh? The case is going cold and you're out here taking a walk? Talking to your girlfriend? You had something to do with it, didn't you? That's why you're not doing anything. That's why you haven't found my wife. You had something to do with it, didn't you?"

David's voice grew louder as he continued talking. By the time he finished, he was yelling at the top of his lungs. This attracted the attention of the Macabre Manor crew that was still filming down the street. Miriam came running in their direction.

"Hey, David. Remember me? I'm Miriam from Macabre Manor. We spoke to you about Bianca a few days ago."

David's fists unclenched as he turned to look at Miriam. A brief look of incomprehension passed briefly over his face before being replaced with recognition.

"I remember you. You're doing that show about the house my wife saw. Your show was weird, but good."

"Thanks," Miriam said, taking the backhanded compliment in stride.

"He had something to do with my wife's disappearance. This town is full of dirty cops. He must be one of them. I used to think he was a good one. Not anymore."

"Well, that's too bad, David. Why don't you tell me about it, okay?"

Miriam put her arm around David's shoulder and gently turned him away from Conrad. He watched as she ushered the angry man away.

In his peripheral vision, Conrad thought he saw a tall, shadowy figure slip into the darkness of shrubbery along the street.

He kept his eyes on that spot for a long time, but nothing emerged.

31.

Conrad

The wind howled outside of Conrad's apartment, a common occurrence in the sunflower state. It managed to find a crack in the front door and squeezed through, creating a whistling sound that made him wish he had been cleared for active duty. Instead, he sat silently in the house, with only his thoughts and the wind to keep him company.

Miriam had spent the night in her hotel room the previous evening, so he had been flying solo. He hadn't realized until now just how much time he had been spending with her, and how effortless being in her company was. When he wasn't with her, he was thinking about her. Of course, every new relationship was like that, what people called the honeymoon period, when everything was great, and you couldn't get enough of each other. In his experience, it was safer to get out of the relationship before that period came to an end.

He wasn't thinking about that when it came to Miriam. It was actually quite the opposite. They had started their relationship without expectations of where it would lead, if anywhere at all. It had been a long time since he had been in a relationship where neither person had expectations about where things would go. Did he want to get married? Have children? Did he want to stay in Prairieview forever? There was always something, usually those had to do with his shortcomings or inadequacies. Sometimes, he self-sabotaged the relationship so it would end before he could get hurt. *Thirty years old and still acting like a child.*

Not with Miriam. They both knew the relationship wouldn't last after she left town with the crew. That could be in two weeks, or it could be tomorrow. She wouldn't know until that moment when Gavin decided the Macabre Manor vampire had drained all it could from the town of Prairieview. They hadn't talked about what would happen then, but Conrad imagined it would be a clean break. For the first time in his adult life, he wasn't looking forward to it.

He hadn't been able to find anything worthy of treasuring with someone in Prairieview. Had he found that something in the arms of what had been a virtual stranger until a week ago? Maybe, but it didn't matter. He shouldn't dwell on what wasn't meant to be. Remember the good times and move on. It had served him well in the past. It would again.

Miriam said that things between the three members of the Macabre Manor crew were strained. Gavin complained that she was spending too much time away from the rest of the crew, meaning too much time with Conrad. Without her calming presence to act as a mediator, the two men had started arguing nonstop. It was something that happened from time to time but had reached a nuclear level in recent days. She blamed herself.

Conrad tried not to be wounded by her decision to stay with the rest of the crew. He tried not to see it for what it was, her choosing them over him. He told himself that it wasn't like that. He failed. It was like that. It had to be like that if she was going to leave town with the crew when all of this was over. Miriam wasn't going to stay.

Have you thought about asking her to stay?

Conrad couldn't do such a thing. It was far too early in the relationship to ask someone to make a significant life change in order to stay together. That was the sort of action that led to marriage, something he wasn't ready for now, possibly ever. The thought of being shackled to someone for the rest of his life had always caused his heart rate to increase, leading to him saying bye-bye to whomever he was dating at the time. Yet, the thought of spending the rest of his life with Miriam didn't sound bad. In fact, he would welcome it, but he wouldn't ask her to stay. He would accept it willingly if she decided to stay, of course. As a career woman, he doubted the thought had occurred to her.

Let her know that whatever it was that they had together didn't have to end when she left town. Talk to her.

He had made up his mind. He would talk to Miriam about their relationship and what would happen when the Macabre Manor crew eventually leaves town. There would be no ultimatum involved. If she was open to keeping things going after the crew left town, then great. If she wanted to stay and make Prairieview her homebase when she wasn't traveling with the crew, even greater. If she wanted to make a clean break, then, well, not so great, but he would survive.

He had seen the witty and insightful side of Miriam, which was the side he had fallen for. Last night, she had shown him the softer side, a side he hadn't been aware existed. Her ability to talk David Nowitzki down from his attack had endeared her to him even more.

Had he fallen in love with Miriam?

Conrad hadn't spoken that four letter word to a woman since high school, when he had confused lust with love. He wasn't ready to speak those words until he was absolutely ready.

Speaking of the man that was likely a widower and just didn't know it, David's attack on Conrad the previous night had been out of character for the middle-aged man. Conrad had been under the belief he was being stalked by Thrall/Caretaker. It was an action that went along with the paranormal entity's stealthy habits, if not too passive-aggressive. Caretaker was more of the straight-forward aggressive type. Conrad had been fooled into thinking it was Caretaker instead of the grieving husband. The sight of

David had taken him off guard, which had left him vulnerable to the attack.

David wasn't to blame for what he had done to Conrad. It had been the man's inability to deal with grief that had led him to act against the person of authority he felt was closest to the case involving his missing wife. That person being Conrad, obviously. Grief was a vampiric entity sapping joy from every aspect of life if you let it. If ignored, that vampire would drain you completely, leaving only an empty husk of the person you once were. The trick was in learning to deal with that vampire, using therapy and support instead of garlic and holy water. While he had never suffered through anything remotely like what David Nowitzki currently was, the department had recommended therapy to deal with his unresolved issues stemming from years of abuse at the hands of his father.

Conrad still held hope that Bianca was out there somewhere alive and could be found, though that hope was diminishing by the day. As that hope was diminished, with it a stronger belief that she had been lost forever, whether inside the White House or not, grew. As an officer, he knew the chances of her being found alive at this point were slim, yet there were cases of such things happening. She could have been taken by someone involved in human trafficking and sold to the highest bidder. She could have been taken hostage by someone who had her locked away in a basement. Those were remote possibilities, possibilities that usually left clues behind, but they were still at the back of his mind.

Until evidence proved that she was alive somewhere, he would act under the assumption that Bianca Nowitzki had perished in the elements due to a wide range of factors. Therefore, they were looking for a body. That was a hard realization to come to for him. He couldn't imagine how hard that was for David to accept.

You had something to do with it, didn't you? That's why you're not doing anything.

David's words echoed in his mind. The grieving husband obviously didn't know what he was talking about. If Conrad had something to do with Bianca's disappearance, then he wouldn't be lost as to what had happened to her. He would be leading the police in the opposite direction, instead of leading them nowhere at all. It was true that he had worked with Gavin and the Macabre Manor crew for a short time, whom he still thought might have something to do with her disappearance. That working relationship had ended without him ever truly being in the know about what Gavin's underhanded tactics truly were. Conrad didn't trust the producer, mostly due to his past that dealt with manipulating both the public and grieving families. The pummeling he had taken at Gavin's hand hadn't helped those beliefs diminish.

As far as the latter part of that accusation goes, well, it was true that Conrad wasn't currently investigating the disappearance of Bianca. There were good reasons for that. He had been placed on a medical leave of absence from the police department. Hopefully, in time he would be able to be cleared for desk work that would allow him to resume the investigation. Until then, he would be forced to sit on the sidelines or do some unofficial investigating and risk a possible suspension. He had already been caught doing some unofficial investigating during the case. Anything further would risk his reputation as a cop and put his job in serious jeopardy.

He had done his due diligence while he was able to investigate, including looking into the marital relationship between David and Bianca. According to everyone he had spoken with, the couple had been as happy as ever. There wasn't any trouble with any of their neighbors or anyone else in the surrounding area. The only question mark had been the mysterious Macabre Manor crew, which he had investigated. Their involvement was still under investigation, including Miriam. He had already cleared him in his mind, though he had yet to do that in any official compacity. There was always the remote possibility that she had lied to him.

Conrad sipped his morning coffee, listened to the radio that he had switched on again, while feeling righteous about the decisions he had made.

The chatter was slow on the radio as the morning progressed. As a result, Conrad's eyelids grew heavy as his morning cup of coffee wore off. Those eyelids snapped open as the radio came to life.

"All units we have a B&E with a possible hostage. Two confirmed suspects spotted by neighbors, reportedly armed and dangerous," Tracy said over the radio.

Conrad snickered at the terminology of all units, which consisted of two vehicles that were currently on duty during the dayshift. If they needed backup, it would likely come from the state police or the KBI. Such events rarely called for such actions. In some cases, the chief had been known to call upon off duty officers to aid if the situation became dire enough. Again, such events were rare, but he kept his phone nearby just in case.

There was a smattering of responses from the officers around the area as they headed to the scene. Frank Hightower, Conrad's replacement on the dayshift, being one that was headed to the scene of the B&E. Tracy came back on the line shortly after with more information.

"We had a call come in from Judith Hightower, Judge Milton Hightower's wife. Apparently, the B&E is at their residence. She locked herself in the bathroom, but the suspects have the judge cornered in his home office. She said they pistol whipped her husband and it was gushing blood. She was going to get some towels for all the blood, then locked herself in the bathroom instead. She was able to identify the suspects."

"Well, who the hell broke into my uncle's house and pistol whipped him, Tracy?" Frank asked.

"You know, Frank, maybe you should sit this one out."

"The hell I will. Now, who is it?" Frank yelled.

"Gerald Bunting and your brother."

There was silence on the radio for a full minute. Conrad could feel Frank processing the impossible information that he had just been given.

"Gerald Bunting?"

"Yes, Frank."

"And Leonard?"

"Yes, Frank."

"Aunt Judith has to be off her rocker. Leonard wouldn't do such a thing. He's a cop!"

Used to be a cop, Conrad corrected in his mind. *And a dirty one at that.*

"Frank, this is Chief Nichols. You should sit this one out and let us handle it. We can handle Gerald and Leonard without you. You're too close to the situation."

Fat chance of that happening.

"I'm here. There's no chance in hell that I'm going to let my brother make a further mockery of our good name. What the hell was the bastard thinking?"

"What good name?" Conrad asked the empty apartment.

"I was thinking that I'd like to make everyone else pay for what we all did, that's what I was thinking. Gerald is a free man. Well, he was before I freed him of the time he had left on this Earth. How come he didn't even get any jail time? How is that? The guy's a known drug dealer. Dealing to kids and whatnot. Did he go to jail for that? No. Did anything happen to the judge for looking the other way all that time? No. Just gets to keep on keeping on, making his crooked deals with criminals. Chief Cain got what was coming to him, I guess, though he wasn't directly involved. Is being completely blind involved, Frank? I guess not. Then there's you, Frank. You were as guilty as me, but here we are. You with the job that I helped you get, and me shooting our uncle that covered our tracks. We had a good run, didn't we, Frank?"

"Leonard, what the hell are you doing? You can't shoot Gerry and Uncle Milton. You were a cop, remember? That's hard time, especially for killing a judge. Hard time as a former cop, Leonard. How many guys have we double crossed that are behind bars? You want to be behind bars with those guys? You won't make it past breakfast. Just let them go. Walk out of there, and maybe Uncle Milton will make this all go away. What do you say?"

"Nice speech, Frankie. Didn't know you had something like that in you. Only problem is, I already shot both of them before I got on the horn with you. Stupid, huh?"

"Dadgummit, Leonard. Don't shoot, I'm coming in."

32.

Conrad

You get time off and don't even come to see your momma?
That was the text message he received from his mother as the chatter was winding down regarding the shooting of Judge Hightower. His eyelids were once again growing heavy. A nap before or after lunch was the most complex thought going through his mind until that text. He thought about ignoring the message but knew it would only increase the guilt he felt the next time he saw her. The guilt he felt regarding his mother was ever increasing for various reasons, built on top of being the reason she stayed in a loveless marriage for years after she should have left.

The next layer of guilt was far less complex and wouldn't require years of therapy to alter. It was the guilt he felt for how little he saw his mother despite living in the same town—there was no guilty conscience for infrequent visits to the old man. His parents had been divorced for nearly ten years yet had remained living in the same small Kansas town. How they had managed to not kill each other in those ten years, Conrad had no idea.

He managed to visit his mother at least once a month, which was more often than most adults he knew saw their parents, but still not often enough considering they lived in the same town. It would usually happen in the same manner every time, with a complaint from his mother accusing him of ignoring or mistreating her. She had a victim mentality, which he had tried unsuccessfully to convince her to seek treatment for. He withheld his judgement, knowing that the victim mentality had been instilled in her by an abusive husband, yet they remained within his head all the same. Phones worked two ways.

The visits with his mother usually revolved around food, which had always been her way of communicating love and affection. When he started noticing the bruises appearing all over his mother's body and connecting them to his father, another realization had happened. Her slumped shoulders and battered body belied her body's true need. Looking as if she belonged in bed, he would instead find her in the kitchen. It was usually something sweet, which in hindsight was purposeful. Douglass Cain despised sweet treats, calling them the sins of the weak-willed. A humorous statement considering the man weighed in at well over three-hundred pounds at his heaviest. Conrad, on the other hand, had a sweet tooth that was after his mother's heart. It was their bonding time, a time when both of them knew the old man wouldn't be bothering them.

The previous month, his mother had made lasagna, salad, and homemade peanut brittle for a Sunday lunch. There was so much food that he had been forced to bring some home with him. There was still leftover lasagna in his freezer.

With the Bianca Nowitzki case monopolizing most of his time for nearly a week, he hadn't thought much about their monthly tradition. It was time for Sunday lunch with his mom, only this time it wouldn't wait until Sunday.

You want to do lunch today?

I thought you'd never ask.

"So, are you seeing anyone?" his mother asked.

She had just set down a plate of hamburger steak, mashed potatoes, both smothered in gravy, and a side of green beans coated in bacon grease in front of him. There was a big glass of sweet, iced tea to wash it all down. He was already eyeing the pecan pie sitting on the counter. It was as if she had known he would be coming over today. Mother's intuition, he guessed.

At every meal since he had moved out of the house at the age of eighteen, his mother had asked the same question at the same time. She had been upfront about her desire to become a grandmother someday. As they both grew older, him having reached the milestone of thirty, the likelihood seemed more remote. It wasn't her fault that she was forced to ask this question every month, after all, he was the only opportunity she had to become a grandparent, therefore, all the weight rested on his shoulders.

"Actually, I am."

His mother raised an eyebrow in surprise. "Really? Don't tell me, you and Gabby finally decided to stop beating around the bush and make it official. I always liked her."

"I like Gabby, Mom, but no, it's not Gabby. We've had a bit of a falling out recently. She's been acting strangely the past few days, probably because of the Bianca Nowitzki case. In fact, I had to do a welfare check on her the other day. Hasn't shown up for work in a few days. Her mother is getting worried."

"That doesn't sound like Gabby. That café has always been important to her, even when she was a kid. She was always there when we would go in when you were little. I remember the two of you flirting back then. Always thought the two of you would end up together. So did Teresa. We'd talk about it when you guys weren't around. I guess you guys didn't get the memo. That's fine, it's your life after all." She paused. "So, who's the girl if it isn't Gabby?"

"Did you watch that YouTube show that I appeared on?"

"Oh, you know I don't like those horror shows, Conrad. Gives me the heebie jeebies. But, yes, I did watch the segment with you in it, not the rest. I just couldn't stomach it."

"It's Miriam, the host. We've started seeing each other. It's still pretty new."

"Well, where is she from? How is that going to work? Is she going to move here?"

"She's based out of Chicago. As far as moving here, well, we haven't talked about it. Like I said, it's new. I'm just trying not to scare her off. That kind of talk definitely would."

"Well, will you two keep dating when she goes back to Chicago or onto another one of those cases? Long distance relationships are hard you know. It was hard for us when your father was in the Air Force and would leave for months on end. Just about killed our marriage. Of course, now I wish it had. But then I wouldn't have you."

"Thanks, Mom."

"I don't know if we'll try long distance or not, Mom. It's new, and I like her, but I don't want to scare her or run her off like I normally do."

"Why do you do that, Conny?"

"Why do I push people away from me? Why don't you ask my therapist, but in order to do that you'd have to go to therapy yourself. Don't worry, I'll give you the abridged version. It starts with my old man, who was an abusive prick. After that day when I found out he was abusing you and stood up to him, well, the true Dougie-boy came out. He had no trouble knocking me around after that. I never thought in a million years that you'd stay, especially after he started taking out the frustration from losing his job on the both of us. You stayed. Damn you, you stayed, Mom. You stayed until I was an adult, then you quietly filed for divorce, without telling me. As if I didn't have a right to know that my parents were getting a divorce or that my mom, who had been abused for most of my life, was finally breaking free from the abuser that I called dad.

"You want to know why I push people away? I push people away before they can hurt me, because the two most important people in my life hurt me. The old man in a direct way, and through you. Don't get it twisted, Mom, you hurt me too. By staying, you hurt me by staying and believing that you could pray away his abuse. That's not how it works. Sure, prayer is great, but you still have to use the tools God gives you to help yourself. Instead, you stayed and put your child's life in danger. My life, you put my life in danger.

"Plus, what if I'm like him, Mom? What if I ended up hurting someone I vowed to love and cherished above all? How could I live with myself?"

There were tears in his eyes that he hadn't planned on shedding. This wasn't a therapy session; it was lunch with his mother. These were thoughts and feelings he had addressed with his therapist in the past, though he had to admit they remained unresolved.

His mother squeezed his hand.

"You're not your father, Conrad. Your dad put up a façade because of his insecurities and wouldn't let us see passed it, no matter what. He was always sensitive about his weight, being a heavier guy. He could have dieted; lord knows I tried to convince him to lose some weight. Always thought people were secretly talking about him behind his back, or they were staring at him because he was a bigger guy. He also wasn't bringing a lot to the table in the brains department, but he made to Chief of Police with hard work and the connections he made around town. I'd taken some college classes when we started dating, just some intro level classes, but I liked it. I wanted to keep going when we got married. He was threatened, I guess. Wanted me to stay home and raise a family.

"Anyway, that's not you, Connie. You're not insecure like your father was and still is. You're a strong young man that just needs to get out of his own head and start living."

"Now, you definitely sound like me therapist."

"You don't have to be a genius to figure you out, Conrad. I just wish you could figure yourself out."

He was about to respond when he was interrupted by his phone ringing in his pocket. He gave his mother an apologetic look as he reached into his pocket.

"It's Dad. I'll call him later," Conrad said, sending the call to voicemail.

"Why do you do that to us? Why is it such a burden to speak with your parents?"

"We've already covered this subject earlier, only it was under the question: Why do I push people away? I should have had lunch with my therapist at this rate, Mom."

"How long has it been since you saw your dad? You see me once a month, and you like me a hell of a lot more than him."

"I haven't seen dad in, I don't know, six months, I guess. If it were up to me, I'd never see the old man again."

His mother fixed him with a disapproving gaze. "He may have hurt you and me, but that doesn't mean he isn't your father. You should see him. Six months? You live in Prairieview, how have you managed that? I saw him last week at the grocery store."

"Fine, I'll call him."

"We're almost done with lunch, and he lives five minutes away. That's the beauty of living in a small town; everything is five minutes away. Go see him after lunch."

"I'll go see him after lunch."

"Great idea, Conny," she said, smiling.

Thirty minutes later, he pulled up in front of his father's double-wide trailer. For some unknown reason, the old man still lived in the same town as Conrad's mother. It was a strange situation considering what had transpired between his parents. He figured one or both of them would want to flee the town where their life had been ruined, at least so they wouldn't risk running into the ex that was a constant reminder of their failures.

For a brief moment, he was saddened at how far his father had fallen since the days when the old man was Chief of Police. He had a beautiful, two-story home in the heart of Prairieview, a good job, a dedicated wife, and a son that loved him. Looking around, all of that had disappeared, as if it had only been a mirage. Conrad's mother had gotten the house, which she had promptly sold, and bought a smaller, more convenient home for a middle-aged woman that had recently become an empty nester. The job had been taken away a few years before the divorce, replaced by rent-a-cop work at the mall in Crimson Creek. Apparently, there wasn't anyone that would hire the disgraced chief in Prairieview. The dedicated wife withered away with every blow to her face and body, until all that was left was a woman trying to survive on her own. The loving son, well, that love had ripped from his heart with the realization that his own father was a monster.

The only thing the old man had left was himself. Alone, Douglass buried himself in the only thing that had never left him or let him down. Food. Always a big man that was made even bigger by the sheer boisterousness of his personality, he became even bigger after everything he loved was taken away by his own actions. Conrad knew all the old man did when home was eat and watch television. The sight of what his father had become saddened him. Then he remembered it was the only penance received for the sins the old man had committed against the wife and son that had their love taken advantage of.

Accompanying the memory of the old man's sins was the knowledge that the state of his life was penance for what he had done. The pain in the elder Cain's life was deserved.

There was always one house on the block where the owner didn't take as much pride in the upkeep of their property. During the few visits he had made to the Peaceful Prairie Mobile Home Park, it had become evident that the same was the case for these communities. That designation was firmly held by the old man. Parched weeds in desperate need of mowing surrounded the lot. There was a black 1977 Pontiac Trans Am parked in the single spot allocated to the resident, which had seen better days. There were rust patches on the vehicle, and it was currently driving on a spare wheel. Every mobile home had bushes planted at the base for some added curb appeal, all of which were alive except for the ones in front of the old man's place. There were boards missing from the small deck that served as a front porch.

Conrad watched his step as he knocked on the front door.

"Yeah, it's open," came a booming voice from inside.

He took a deep breath. He did this for two reasons. First, to prepare himself for the encounter that was about to take place. Second, the old man wasn't a housekeeper. There were dirty dishes and takeout containers everywhere. The previous time he had seen a cat in the mobile home, which explained the overwhelming aroma of excrement. It wasn't a pleasant experience.

The inside of the mobile home matched the unkempt nature of the outside. It was as if the old man hadn't cleaned since Conrad was last inside six months earlier. The front entrance opened into the living room, which was cluttered with furniture, piles of magazines stacked waist high, and what looked like garbage. There was a small kitchen that the old man likely never used off to the right. At the back end of the living room was a hallway that led to the bathroom and the one bedroom. A large, flat screen television showing highlights from the previous night's sporting events blared in the corner of the room. The old man sat reclining in a La-Z-Boy chair that was held together with duct tape and broken promises.

Douglass Cain looked up from the television as his son entered the mobile home.

"Well, he can't answer his phone, but he can show up unannounced."

"How have you been doing, Doug?" he asked.

"How about you start calling me dad again. Can you do that, Conrad?"

"How about you travel back in time and stop yourself from beating my mother? How about you travel back in time and stop yourself from beating your teenage son? Both are just as impossible as me calling you dad again."

"Did you come over to pick a fight with me? Or did you actually want something?"

"Actually, I was with mom when I ignored your call. She convinced me that I ought to come see you, since I never do. For some reason I think she feels you deserve a chance at redemption."

"Ah, she's a good woman."

"She is, despite what you put her through."

"I deserve that. Lord knows, I deserve more."

Conrad sighed. "I don't want to do this with you. You can wallow in self-pity all you want, because, yes, you deserve it, but I won't pity you."

Silence hung in the air for a moment.

"Now that that is out of your system, how about you tell me what happened with the judge."

"Oh, I should have known that was why you called me. I thought for a minute that you were concerned about my life."

The old man leaned forward in his seat. "When you come in here, you don't tell me about your life, Conrad. Sure, I've asked, but you've made it clear as glass that you don't care about me and aren't going to share what's going on with you. Would I like to know? Sure, you bet you, but until you decide to start sharing? I'm just going to wait. Now, what happened with the judge?"

"Thanks for that. I've been on medical leave because I broke some ribs and got a concussion, you have to take what I say with a grain of salt. I wasn't there, just heard what happened on the radio. Plus, you can't go repeating any of it or I might get in trouble."

"Look around, Conrad. Who am I going to tell?"

"Still, I've got to say it. Apparently, the judge's neighbor initially called in a B&E taking place at the judge's house. Two armed men. A few minutes later, the judge's wife called in herself. Leonard Hightower and Gerald Bunting broke into the house, and pistol whipped the judge. She locked herself in the bathroom and called police."

"She always was a smart woman. Did Frank hear about it?"

"Yep. In fact, Frank is my replacement on the day shift while I'm out on medical leave. He was one of the responding officers. The Chief tried to talk him out of it but couldn't. Leonard found a radio somewhere and got involved in the conversation."

"I bet that didn't go over well."

Conrad told the old man what he could remember about the brother's conversation.

"Leonard Hightower killed the judge and Bunting? That doesn't make a lot of sense. He's been living with it all these years. Why wait until now? Why not do it fifteen years ago when I fired him? Why not go after me? I'm the one that canned him. Should have fired Frank too. There just wasn't any evidence against him. Has he cleaned up any?"

"What do you think?"

"I think he's just smart enough to have learned a lesson so he's more careful and less likely to get caught, but too stupid to have actually gone clean. That is if I know Frank, like I think I know Frank."

"Sounds like you know Frank, alright. Yeah, I've had inclinations about him since I joined the force but haven't been able to prove anything. He never does things by the book, but that's not enough. I'm starting to think that I was wrong about him."

The old man shook his head. "Oh, no. I'd put money on you being right, Conrad. You're a good cop. Plus, you're observant, like I was in my youth before I got fat and lazy. Just keep your eyes open, he'll screw up eventually."

"Yeah, you're probably right, Doug. Thanks."

"Hey, listen, I know that you hold a grudge against me for what happened with me and your mom. Could you find it in yourself to forgive me? I'm sorry, Conrad."

Conrad ignored the emotion he heard in the old man's voice.

"Someday maybe, but that day isn't today."

Then he left.

33.

Conrad

There were no regrets in Conrad's mind when he left the old man's mobile home. The old man didn't deserve forgiveness, despite his mother having already forgiven the old man for what he had done to both of them. In Conrad's mind, there were things that couldn't be forgiven, no matter how much it was wanted by both parties. Irreversible damage done to a child's psyche and abuse of those that are weaker than you fell into that category.

There were still no regrets an hour later, as he sat on the couch in his apartment.

Then the phone rang.

It was the old man.

"Not today, sunshine. Try again tomorrow," he said to the empty apartment.

Instead of answering the phone, he pushed the ignore button on the screen. Then he put his feet up on the couch and decided to take a nap.

Ten minutes later, his phone rang again. He ignored the call, knowing it was the old man trying desperately to reach out for forgiveness.

A few minutes later, it rang again. This time he looked at the screen. It wasn't the old man. The number was withheld. That usually meant it was the PPD calling. He was on medical leave for the next two weeks, minimum. Why would they be calling?

"Hello?" he said, hoping his voice didn't sound groggy from sleep in the middle of the day.

"There you are! What on earth are you doing in the middle of the afternoon? Never mind. We've got a situation at your dad's house," Tracy said.

Conrad wished he was in his patrol car as he made the five-minute drive to the old man's mobile home. A siren would have helped the urgency that was causing his breathing to quicken. Since he wasn't in the patrol car, he made sure to obey all traffic laws, including stopping at both red lights he hit as he drove through the downtown neighborhood.

An hour earlier, the mobile home park had been enjoying a quiet weekday afternoon. As he entered the park, the place was bustling with activity. It appeared that every mobile home had emptied, and the residents had all congregated at the old man's mobile home. They were being held back by a line of tape cordoning off the front yard of the mobile home. There were three PPD patrol cars and several highway patrol cars that had responded to the call.

Sitting on the same front steps he walked on an hour earlier was his mother. Frank Hightower and a Sheriff's deputy stood on each side of her, seemingly guarding her in case she decided to take off. There was a gray blanket wrapped around her shoulders, yet she appeared to be shivering. A confused expression was plastered on her face, as if she didn't understand what was happening.

Frank had a smug expression on his face, despite the events earlier in the day. It was as if the man was grateful to learn that he wasn't the only member of the PPD that had complicated family members. Conrad wanted to remove that expression from his fellow officer's face with a stiff right hook. He had even taken several steps toward his fellow PPD officer out of instinct but was stopped by Holly Dupree. Holly was a part-timer that usually worked the weekends. Given the excitement of the day, Conrad guessed she had been called in for extra support with the Judge Hightower shooting and was still on when they receive the call from the old man.

"You don't want to go in there, Conrad. You don't want to see him like that," she said, putting a gentle hand on his chest.

"My mom. Can I see my mom?"

"Of course, maybe you can talk some sense into her. She hasn't talked to Hightower, of course, I can't blame her. The chief is on his way. He wants to talk to her."

Holly lifted the tape so he could duck under.

"Mom? Are you okay? What happened?"

Her eyes were in a haze as she looked at him. She looked confused, as if it took her a second to recognize his face. Recognition came for a brief moment, only to be replaced with confusion again.

He looked to Frank for approval as he sat down next to his mother. Frank gave a curt nod.

"What happened? Why would you do that to dad?"

In that moment, he had forgotten his vow to never refer to Douglass Cain as dad again.

"I've always thought about doing it, you know? It's just been thoughts. That's it, just thoughts. When thinking about what he did to you, and the resentment he's filled your heart with. I've thought about it. I mean, sure, there's me too, I guess. All the punches to the stomach. He liked a good gut punch because it didn't show when I was out in public. I used to wear a two-piece bathing suit before we got married, did you know that? Well, I quickly realized that wasn't going to happen anymore. I switched to a one-piece shortly after we got married. The girls at the pool would always say, 'Maribeth, you got married and all of a sudden, you're a prude! You've got a great body, show it off!' Well, they didn't know I couldn't show it off. Not if I wanted to keep people from finding out. And I did, but he had to punch me in the face. Then you found out, and it was all over. He started in on you after that. I could forgive him for punching me, after all, all relationships have their hard times. I always gave him something to complain about. 'Maribeth, why isn't dinner ready.' Or 'Damnit, Maribeth, you know I like my uniform starched.' But not you. I couldn't forgive that. All you did was try to protect your mom. That's commendable if you ask me. I always thought about it, not for me, but for you. I never forgave him for laying his hands on you."

"Mom, why now? Why would you shoot dad now? Why wait until now? You were doing so well alone, without that monster in your life."

She looked at him with tears in her eyes. "I don't know, Conrad. Honestly, I don't. I don't even remember how I got here."

"Tell me what happened. Start with when I left your house after lunch."

"Well, after you left, I went to drop off a slice of pie with Barb. You know her as Mrs. Lincoln? She lives across the street from the missing woman, next to that house that burned down years ago. She loves pecan pie, and doesn't get many visitors, so I figured what the heck? We talked for a bit while she ate the pie, just two old ladies gabbing away. There was this man standing in the burnt remains of that old house. He looked like he was staring at me, watching me. It was creepy, so I got in the car and started driving home.

"I didn't go home. I came here instead. I mean, you brought up your dad earlier, so I guess he was on my mind."

"Mom, where did you get a gun?"

"Oh, I got that after the divorce. It's dangerous out there for a single woman, even at my age. Did you know there are people out there that get their jollies by raping old ladies? I won't be one of them. I keep it in my purse when I leave the house, and in the top drawer of the nightstand when I'm asleep. Don't worry, I've had lessons, and I've even got a concealed carry license.

"Anyway, I drove here instead, without realizing I was doing it. I don't know what I was doing. It was kind of like an out of body experience, like I was a passenger in my own body. I stormed into the house, pulled the gun from my purse, and shot your dad."

"When you were at Mrs. Lincoln's house, you said you saw a man at the old Comisky place, right? Can you describe him?"

"Ordinary enough, I guess. White gentleman with dark hair and eyes, brown, think, but could've easily been black. Slicked back hair. He was tall, of course that could have been the rubble pile playing tricks on my eyes. There was an intensity to him that gave me the creeps. That's why I left in a hurry."

Thrall had visited his mother.

"Cain, sorry to hear about your dad. He was a good cop," Chief Nichols said as he ducked under the tape line.

Conrad wondered how hard that lie had been for the chief to tell, after all, Nichols had benefited from the old man's firing. He took it in stride, however.

"You're going to take care of her, right? She's still a little confused. Doesn't seem to know why she did it. Just doesn't make sense."

"We'll take good care of her, don't you worry. Hightower is going to take good care of her, right, Hightower?"

"Oh, sure, Chief," Hightower said, as he placed handcuffs on Conrad's mother.

The smug smile returned to Frank's face. Once again Conrad had to fight for control of his emotions. He clenched and unclenched his fists. Then the moment passed.

Seeing his mother put in the back of a patrol car was a surreal sight. Their eyes locked for a moment as the car drove away. His eyes filled with tears.

34.

Conrad

The world seemed to be moving quickly around him, meanwhile Conrad felt as if he was moving in slow motion. The realization that his mother had killed his father had him in a daze. He had just come from seeing his mother, who had seemed to be in great spirits. A woman who was known to suppress her anger towards others, that type of display was completely out of character. It was as if the woman he had known all his life had been replaced in the hour they had been apart.

Maribeth Cain had taken years of abuse from her husband and bottled it up within her, repressing the anger Conrad knew she felt. There were studies that showed how dangerous unresolved anger can be for your health. Of course, he figured the mental health experts were talking about high blood pressure or a weakened immune system. In his mother's case, it appeared that anger could overwhelm someone when suppressed for too long, leading to bursts of rage-filled fits. She had said it herself, talking about her ex-husband caused her to think about the past. Had their conversation brought up unresolved feelings that had triggered her to take vengeance on her ex?

It didn't make sense to Conrad. His parents had been divorced for ten years. The three members of the Cain family had moved on to live separate lives in Prairieview. With the town being the size that it was, they were bound to encounter each other from time to time. During lunch, his mother had commented that she had seen her ex-husband at the grocery store a few weeks ago. It was a common occurrence for the divorced couple, and according to his mother, they remained cordial. In fact, she had been unimpressed with his inability to forgive his father for past misdeeds. An hour later, she was shooting that same ex for the misdeeds she had already forgiven him for. It didn't make sense.

This was Caretaker. His mother had seen someone fitting Caretaker's description while leaving Mrs. Lincoln's house. Then she had gotten in the car, and instead of driving home, she drove to her ex-husband's house, shooting him three times in the chest. According to Miriam, Caretaker had the ability to remove the inhibitions of people, making them do things they had always wanted to do but had thought better of it for some reason or another. It was quite natural for his mother to have fantasized about killing her ex-husband as revenge for the years of abuse she had endured during their marriage. Ten years after their marriage ended was an unusual amount of time to elapse, waiting for the perfect time to follow through on murder.

Conrad had been driving without a clear destination in his mind. Still in a daze, he realized he didn't want to go home to an empty apartment. Being alone with his feelings didn't sound like something he wanted to do at the moment. He didn't want to be alone period. Miriam was likely filming with the crew at the old Comisky place. Wherever she was, that was where he wanted to be.

Now that he knew where he was going, getting there would be easier.

His thoughts momentarily went to Gabby as the Newhouse Café came into sight. According to a text message from Twila, she hadn't been seen since the previous day. In fact, if the timeline was correct, Conrad was the last person to see Gabby. This was the first time she had crossed his mind due to the eventfulness of the previous twenty-four hours. He knew she hadn't been in her proper state of mind in recent days, much like Bianca Nowitzki before her disappearance. He was supposed to be keeping an eye on her as a case study to gain a better understanding of what Bianca had experienced. If Miriam and the residence of the Macabre Manor were to be believed, Gabby had been selected as the next victim of the White House. Twenty-four hours was more than enough time to open a door and step inside.

Enough had transpired in the six days since Bianca went missing that Conrad wasn't sure what he believed and if his doubts about the paranormal were the same. That being said, he still didn't believe a house had anything to do with her disappearance. He didn't believe Bianca had vanished inside the White House and was currently wandering its halls, lost somewhere in time and space. He didn't believe the man known as Thrall had paranormal powers that included mind control.

The man known as Thrall—Conrad believed he *was* a human man—had something to do with Bianca's disappearance, that much was certain. The mind control angle, which he had just heard witness testimony from his mother, could be explained. It might be as simple as the power of suggestion. In a documentary that had taken the viewers behind the scenes of magic tricks, he had seen that the key to a trick could be as simple as planting a certain card in someone's mind without them realizing it. This wasn't a card trick, of course. Thrall had convinced Conrad's mother to shoot her ex-husband that she had seemingly forgiven. Assuming a woman that had been the recipient of abuse for years would fantasize about murdering her abuser wasn't a great leap to make. Getting her to pull the trigger was another matter. Planting imagery in her path throughout the day would be a start, which could be easily arranged. His mother was paranoid enough to carry a handgun around with her. It wasn't farfetched, but it definitely was a leap.

His mind would make any leap possible to excuse the behavior of his mother, even though that leap meant believing in something as absurd as the White House and Thrall.

These thoughts came in a whirlwind as he desperately tried to deal with what was happening around him. He was pulled from these thoughts as he got closer to the Newhouse Café. His troubled mind had trouble processing what he was looking at. He stopped the SUV in front of the café and got out.

The front of the café was constructed of large glass windows that faced the street, letting in sunlight in the morning when the café was at its busiest. A white van had driven through the front of the building and was parked in the dining room of the café. As Conrad got closer, he saw that Hurts Donut was emblazoned on the side of the van. Teresa Newhouse stood in the parking lot taking in the damage with visible tears in her eyes. There was a commotion coming from inside the café.

"What in the hell are you doing, Ivan? You almost killed me!" Twila yelled at the man behind the wheel of the van.

"What's going on? How did I get here?" Ivan said from inside the van.

Conrad knew there wouldn't be anyone available to respond for a while due to the investigation still ongoing at his father's mobile home. He pulled out his phone and called Tracy in dispatch to report the incident. When that was done, he stepped inside the newly remodeled café and started defusing the tension.

Conrad was back in the SUV after a thirty-minute detour that involved Ivan trying to drive away in the van when Twila threatened him with a piece of broken wood from a chair. Fortunately, the van's rear tires were punctured from the broken glass, so Ivan didn't get out of the parking lot before Holly showed up to take over. The owner of Hurts Donut would be taking a ride to the station, likely facing charges from the incident.

He found Miriam on the front lawn of the old Comisky place, as he knew he would. It was as if the crew lived in the van parked in front of the house, despite having two hotel rooms in town. Everything didn't seem copasetic between the crew, however. The sound of angry shouts reached him inside the SUV. Stu was in Gavin's face, yelling.

Conrad got out of the SUV and crossed the street, ready to defuse another confrontation. What was happening in Prairieview today? Was it simply something in the air? Or was this Thrall and his meddling ways?

"How about I take this camera and shove it down your throat?" Stu yelled.

"What the hell is your problem, Stu? All of a sudden you can't follow simple directions? You know, I don't really need you, right? Miriam and I could do this job by ourselves. I just keep you around because I pity you and the child support," Gavin retorted.

"Oh, really? Then who would you yell at, huh? Who is the big shot producer and owner of a small YouTube channel going to boss around? We both know Miriam won't take your BS, that's why she broke up with you. Plus, you cheated on her. Yeah, I know about that. She's too good for you anyway. No, you need me around. I've seen your camerawork. It's worse than a PBS documentary."

Miriam pushed her way between the two men. "Now, boys. Let's get ahold of ourselves. We're practically family. We can't fight like this. I need both of you."

"We only need him because he signs the paychecks."

"Don't get mad at me because you're a loser that can't keep a job or a wife."

Stu punched Gavin in the face, bumping into Miriam with his shoulder as he did so. Gavin stumbled backward as Stu followed, going for the knockout. Meanwhile, Miriam fell to the ground. Stu followed up the right hook with a stiff left to the stomach that doubled Gavin over. As Stu went for a haymaker of an uppercut, Conrad stepped in. He was afraid Miriam would be trampled in the scuffle.

"Hey, what's going on here? You two get ahold of yourselves! You've knocked Miriam down," he said as he got between the two men.

Both men turned to look at Miriam, who was getting to her feet. She brushed herself off, while giving her two coworkers the evil eye.

"What started this? You guys usually work so well together."

"I don't remember. The last thing I remember is Gavin going on and on about getting the shot right, as if I'm not a professional cameraman. I was just thinking, I ought to pop him one and show him who he's talking to. I mean, I was thinking it, like I've done a thousand times. I've never done it before. This time, I guess, I lost my cool," Stu said, rubbing his bald head with his hand.

"Is that really what goes through your head when I'm talking to you, Stu? You want to hit me? Maybe I should get another cameraman."

"Maybe you should."

Conrad held up his hands. "Wow. Now, guys, that's a little rash, don't you think? The two of you have been a little stressed, I think. It's natural. I mean, Bianca has been missing for nearly a week, and the case has gone cold. Miriam has said that the White House normally takes multiple victims at the same location, if the house is truly responsible for what's happening here. I guess you're waiting for the next victim. I hadn't thought of it like that, but I think that's what you three are doing. Just waiting for someone else to go missing. That's really morbid if you ask me. It can get you down, maybe build up the tension. Plus, Miriam has also said that Thrall can influence your behavior, make you lose your inhibition and overcome your better judgement. Don't you think that's what could have happened here? Stu, you said it yourself, you've thought about punching Gavin before. Don't you think that Thrall could be working his magic on you?"

"Yeah, I suppose so," Stu said, sheepishly.

Miriam stepped forward with a grateful look in Conrad's direction. "I think we've been working really hard this last week. Spending a lot of time together. Why don't we take the rest of the day off, and everyone goes their separate ways until tomorrow. How does that sound?"

"Yeah, sounds good to me. Boss?" Stu said, looking at Gavin.

Gavin nodded while rubbing his chin that was turning red.

Motion caught Conrad's attention out of the corner of his eye. He turned his head away from the argument to see a dark figure step out of the shadow cast by the Bradford Pear in the Nowitzki's front yard.

Gabby.

He sighed in relief.

She hadn't been seen for twenty-four hours by friends or family. Teresa Newhouse was likely ready to declare her daughter missing. Conrad feared that she had been taken by whomever had taken Bianca. Obviously, that wasn't the case.

"Gabby! Your mother is worried sick about you," he called out to her.

Her head didn't turn or give any indication she heard him.

Gabby hadn't stopped walking as she emerged from the darkness. Instead, she stepped out into the street without looking in either direction. Conrad checked for her. Luckily, there wasn't any traffic coming in either direction.

"Stu! Get your camera," Gavin whispered behind him.

"Luckily, I never leave the van without it these days."

Conrad had started walking toward Gabby, intent on getting her attention.

"Gabby! Hey, I'm talking to you!"

"He's ruining the shot."

"No, it's great. His yelling gives it some reality, some drama. It's perfect."

Gabby stepped seamlessly up onto the curb with her eyes focused straight ahead, as if in a trance.

"Gabby!"

"It's beautiful. Goodbye, Conrad."

She spoke as she crossed the front lawn of the old Comisky place. One foot in front of the other. Her eyes didn't leave the old burnt pile of rubble.

"Gabby! You don't know what's in that house! You can't go inside."

"Goodbye, Conrad," she repeated.

She stepped onto the rubble pile as he broke out into a sprint. Thrall had been in that exact spot when he had disappeared during their first encounter.

I don't believe in the White House. I don't believe in the White House.

Then why are you running?

He reached out to her as he leapt onto the rubble pile. His hand grasped air.

She was gone.

35.

Conner

Thrall was waiting for Conner when he exited the room on the fifth floor of the White House. There was a smile on that smug face. Conner's anger boiled over at the sight of the man, while not solely responsible, had a large hand in what transpired ten years ago. Forgotten was the brief physical encounter he had with Thrall on the lawn of the old Comisky place that had left him concussed and with broken ribs. The only thing on his mind was Gabby entering that house, vanishing forever.

He landed a clean left jab to Thrall's nose and followed it up with a right hook to the chin. If Thrall was expecting the punches, he gave no indication. His hands were down. The smile still plastered to his face, even as Conner landed a second jab to the nose. Conner kept his hands up, expecting retaliation from the man who wasn't really a man at all. None came, so he kept punching. Left jab. Right hook. Right hook. Left jab. Right hook. Right uppercut. And on it went, while Thrall smiled back at him.

Black liquid started to seep from the nose and mouth of Thrall. He should have known the caretaker for the White House wouldn't have normal blood, after all, Thrall wasn't a man. He was a fiend, a puppet for the house and whatever demon or entity dwelled in it.

The black blood covered Conner's fists. The assault on Thrall had opened up wounds on his knuckles. He had a brief thought about what would happen if the tainted blood got into his bloodstream, infecting him whatever disease had corrupted the once human man known as Thrall.

Yet he kept punching.

Thrall kept smiling.

Eventually, Conner grew tired. He was unaware of how much time had elapsed since he had started punching Thrall. It could have been five minutes or five hours. Time didn't seem to work the same way inside the White House. It seemed to exist outside of the realm of time and space. How much time had elapsed in the outside world since he had stepped foot in the White House? Had Carlisle realized he was gone? Was she an old lady, remarried and happy without him? Or had no time elapsed at all. If he walked out the front door now, would it be as if he hadn't left at all?

Conner dropped his hands to his side.

"My turn," Thrall said, still smiling as blood trickled down his chin.

Conner didn't see Thrall's arms move. Instead, he felt pain explode throughout his body as dozens of punches landed within a fraction of a second of each other. Blood exploded from freshly opened wounds on his face. He could feel his nose break. A tooth flew from his mouth. He staggered backward as his knees started to buckle, unable to remain standing. An unseen hand kept him upright, kept him absorbing the punishment.

The final blow from Thrall was more powerful than any blow he had ever felt, including the shoulder tackle ten years in the past. The invisible hand that kept him upright released its grip. Conner felt himself flying through the air. Confusion erupted in his fractured mind. I'm not supposed to be able to fly. Then he hit the wall of the hallway and fell to a heap on the ground.

There he laid for an unknown length of time. It didn't matter. Time didn't matter. He could lay there forever, taking mental inventory of his injuries. Broken nose. Missing tooth. Broken ribs—the same two ribs Thrall had broken ten years prior. It didn't matter. Nothing mattered.

He had failed them. He had failed Bianca. He had failed Gabby. He had failed Miriam. He had failed everyone.

He would lay there and die. That wouldn't matter either.

At some point, Thrall went away. Conner wasn't sure if the White House's caretaker had walked away or simply vanished into thin air. The heaviness in his chest that accompanied Thrall had ceased either way. After a long time, he opened an eye to confirm what he already knew. Thrall was gone, for now.

The remnants of his phone, which had fallen out of his pocket during the fight, lay in pieces on the floor.

The pain was immense, exquisite in its ability to encompass his entire body. He hadn't known pain like that in his life. Was this life? Or had he died the moment he crossed the threshold of the White House's front door? It didn't matter. He welcomed the pain. It was his penance for his inability to act when those that counted on him needed him most. If he had acted sooner, had acted at all, maybe he could have saved his father, his mother, and maybe even Gabby. Maybe he could have saved all that would come later, including the third person that went missing in Prairieview. The person that left a hole in his heart that had never truly healed. Doing so might even have saved himself whatever fate the White House had in store for him.

Was this purgatory? Had he died when he entered the house, only to undergo a purification process brought on by experiencing his past misdeeds? Conner wasn't a theologian. He wasn't even a Christian any longer, mostly due to witnessing the sins of his father, a man who had been a professed Christian. Thus, he couldn't speak on the matter. If the experience in the White House was a punishment, well, it was a damn good one.

Thrall had spoken of the entity that had dominion over the White House in an excitable tone. That meant whatever the entity was, it likely hadn't come from heaven, as Thrall didn't appear to be a servant of God. Was it a demon? Conner thought that was the closest thing to the truth he would get until he came face to face with whatever controlled the White House. If it was a demon in charge what fate would be dealt to him when he exited the last room? Was he bound for the fiery reaches of hell? Could this be hell? Reliving the mistakes that you made that had likely cost people their lives was hellish in its own way.

Conner didn't know. It didn't matter.

"Conrad."

He was awoken from sleep at the sound of someone speaking his name. Conner hadn't thought rest had been possible in a place such as this. As it turned out, beat a man hard enough and even his tired and weary mind will need a break.

"Conrad."

The voice sounded as if the speaker had swallowed a mixture of sandpaper and marbles. It had a deep, base tone that was deeper than he had ever heard before. There was also a warbling quality to it that sent a shiver down his spine. It wasn't Thrall. Conner knew who the voice belonged to.

"Aren't you going to come see me? Thrall, as you call him, tells me that you're a fighter. I see he is wrong. Pity. I was looking forward to our endeavor together."

Conrad looked around but couldn't locate the owner of the voice.

"You think I would bother coming to the lower levels, Conrad? That is why I employ Thrall. He will deal with you. Now, come to me!"

It did matter. The length of time he had been in the White House. Time itself. All the broken bones and broken teeth suffered at the hands of Thrall. Redeeming Bianca, Gabby, Miriam. Ensuring his father hadn't died in vain. That his mother hadn't been controlled by a bondsman to a demon for nothing. That all of those people back in Prairieview hadn't suffered for nothing. Dying mattered. Whether this was heaven or hell. Whether he was trapped in purgatory. It did matter. It all mattered.

He pushed himself to his feet with muscles that ached. It was a good thing. It reminded him that he *was* alive, at least for the moment. Dead people don't feel physical pain.

"Good boy."

The demon thought he was rising to his feet to climb to the next level. It thought he was listening. It thought he had finally given up hope of escaping this madhouse.

A twitch of a sneering smile gave a momentary indication of his next move. Luckily, the demon didn't notice.

Conner should have started walking straight ahead, toward the door that led to the next floor, where more sins from his past waited for his viewing displeasure. Instead, he made an about-face, facing the way he had come. The trials and tribulations of his past lay both above and below where he stood. If he stopped ascending, it would end. The pain would end. There wouldn't be any more pain. He could hide away in one of the rooms with the lesser sins, forever. Then he wouldn't have to experience the pain over again. Then he wouldn't have to lose her again. Once had been hard enough. It was still hard after all this time. He wouldn't do it again.

"What are you doing, Conrad?"

He didn't answer with words. Instead, he sprinted down the hallway, away from the stairwell to the sixth level, and towards the stairwell descending to the fourth level.

The demon sighed. "Ah, very well. Have fun in the dark, Conrad."

All the lights went off in the hallway, as if on voice activation from the entity living on the top floor of the White House. Of course, that was exactly what it was, since the house belonged to the demon. It could control it like the house was an extension of its physical being. It was as if the demon had told its eyes to blink. How was he supposed to escape a demon that controlled the very environment he was trapped in?

Conner descended into the darkness, taking the steps one at a time. He did this despite the desperation he felt urging him onward. His body was broken and battered. If he fell down the stairs, he might not be able to get back up again.

He had grown accustomed to the darkness thanks to Thrall switching the lights off while chasing him. Each of the floors was the same, exactly the same as the previous, making it easier to navigate in the darkness. Still, there was a small voice at the back of his mind that implored him to be cautious.

He listened to the voice until the sound of laughter started. It echoed off the walls. Maniacal laughter, filled with madness. Conner knew that laughter belonged to Thrall, not the demon who had been speaking only seconds prior. It seemed to be coming from both in front of him and behind him at the same time. It was at that point that all sense of caution left him.

The hallway seemed longer in the darkness, causing him to doubt whether he had passed the door. He put his hand against the wall, so he could feel for the door as he ran. He ignored the feelings of anger and rage that were exuded from the surface of the wall. These were the feelings straight from the demon himself. At last, he came to an opening. A moment later, his fingers brushed something hard and cold. The door handle.

He grasped the handle and prepared himself.

The room on the fourth floor wasn't too bad. His relationship with Miriam had been hot and heavy, meanwhile, the case had grown cold because of his preoccupation. Yes, Miriam. He would go inside this room, instead of facing what lay ahead. Anything was better than that.

He turned the handle. It wouldn't move.

Locked.

Conner screamed in frustration.

The laughter continued.

Spurred by the laughter, he continued walking until he found the stairwell descending to the third level of the White

House. Inside that room he watched while he fed his ego in a gluttonous manner.

That door was also locked.

The laughter continued.

He descended to the second level of the White House. Inside that room he had greedily taken the money to work with the Macabre Manor crew, then lied to Chief Nichols about it later.

That door was also locked.

The laughter continued.

He descended to the first floor of the White House. Inside that room he had pridefully taken on the case of Bianca Nowitzki, accepting no help from anyone, including Chief Nichols.

That door was also locked.

The laughter continued.

Left without anywhere else to go, Conner exited the hallway into the large front room. His mind was exhausted. He just wanted out of the house.

After several minutes of searching in the dark, he found the front door. He reached for the doorknob. He didn't find one. In his panic fleeing the house, he had forgotten that when he first entered the house, there hadn't been a doorknob on the inside of the door.

He tried to pry the door open with his fingers. He banged on the door with his fists. He rammed the door with his shoulder.

Nothing worked.

Conner collapsed in despair.

36.

Conner

Conner lay on the floor in front of what he believed to be the only exit of the White House for an unknown length of time. Light might have helped the situation, possibly giving a reason to get up and move around, probably not. It would have at least given him some comfort in what he already knew that he was utterly and completely alone. There was a positive aspect of not being able to see. It made him unable to see the extent of the damage Thrall had caused during the retaliatory attack.

The events of that had unfolded inside the room on the fifth floor played back over and over again behind his closed eyelids. His eyes snapped open in the darkness as a realization came over him. He knew who Thrall was. Or, rather, who Thrall had been in life.

He should have known ten years ago, but he had been so distracted by his injuries that he had been blinded to the truth when it presented itself. The truth had been hidden in the documentary he watched about the surviving Bauman family members. Being a factual documentary series, Macabre Memoirs hadn't used actors to reenact the events that had taken place during the 1930's. Instead, they had used photographs taken of both the family and the area from the time period. Most of the photographs of the twin boys had been from their early years, prior to and immediately after their father's disappearance. There had been a single photograph of a forty-year-old Karl Bauman that had a striking resemblance to Thrall. Shed thirty pounds of a paunch from years spent sitting behind the desk as a writer, deprive him of sunlight for a while, and you've got yourself Thrall.

Karl Bauman should have been an old man by now, if not dead. He had been a teenager when his father had disappeared in 1939, making Karl nearly a hundred years old. With the advancement of modern medicine people were living longer and longer, therefore, it was possible, though unlikely, that Karl would still be alive. How then had the son of the first known victim survived this long only to appear that of a middle-aged man?

The demon—if that was what it was—must have something to do with it, after all, it had bestowed Thrall with tremendous powers of the likes Conner had never seen. It likely had the power to slow down the aging process of Karl, if not completely stopping it altogether. Karl had found a way to slow down the aging process, all it had cost him was his eternal soul.

"Thrall! I know who you are! Come out here and face me!" he stood up and yelled.

Silence clung to the darkness that surrounded him. He knew Thrall had heard him despite the silence. He had learned that not much happened in the White House that Thrall was unaware of, whether that was a knowledge gifted to him by the demon that was his master or simply an inherited trait he didn't know.

"Thrall! Face me!"

The lights flickered on.

Thrall stood in the middle of the room with an amused smile on his face. Despite the rough exterior, he seemed to be enjoying himself. Conner wished he could say the same for himself.

"I know who you are, Karl. I can't believe I didn't notice it before. I guess I was too preoccupied with myself. You're Karl Bauman, son of the White House's first victim, Hanz Bauman."

The smile disappeared from Thrall's face. "How do you know about my father?"

"Are you kidding? Everyone knows about Hanz Bauman, the incredible buffoon that was the first person to step inside the White House. It's a cautionary tale, really. Parents tell their kids about your father at bedtime, so they won't ever do anything as stupid as he did. It was my grandpa that first told me about your dear old dad. Why in God's name would you step foot inside of a house that suddenly appeared out of the blue? There can't be anything good waiting inside."

"You mock my father?"

Conner shrugged. "No, I mock you. Just testing my theory on who you are."

"You have a point, Conrad. Really, you do."

"Oh? Do tell."

"Why in God's name would you step foot inside of a house that suddenly appeared out of the blue? But you did, didn't you. Did you know that I would be waiting for you inside? I don't think so. If you had, I don't think you'd be here right now."

Conner couldn't argue with that.

"Enough of this, ascend."

"I don't think so, Karl."

"You don't have a choice. Ascend."

Conner sat down cross legged on the floor in front of the door.

"I see. You want to do things the difficult way. Okay."

Thrall snapped his finger. A sly smile spread across his face. Then he turned and walked toward the hallway at the back of the room.

A deep, guttural growl caused Conner to jump to his feet instinctively. In the corner of the room, a black dog appeared. At its shoulders the dog stood nearly as tall as him. Its ear brushed the ceiling of the large room. Its mouth was pulled back in a snarl, showing yellow teeth that appeared to be able to crush bone. Its eyes glowed a menacing red. Eyes that were locked on him.

"Good boy."

The dog barked. It took a step toward him.

"No."

It growled deep in its throat.

It took another step towards him. Conner compensated by taking a step backward. The front door hit him in the back. The dog barked menacingly. He was going in the wrong direction.

"Okay, I'm going. I'm going."

He stepped toward the hallway. There was one problem with that move. It took him in the same direction as the dog. It growled as it stepped closer to him.

"Okay, Conrad. Thrall and the demon want you to go inside the next room. That means the dog won't actually attack, right?" he said aloud to himself.

The dog sprung forward, as if rebuking his silly theory about not attacking. Conner responded by sprinting for the hallway. With the dog's long legs, he knew that he stood little chance of outrunning it. Yet, he thought his theory remained sound.

That theory was in doubt when he felt teeth nipping at the tail of his shirt as he climbed the first set of stairs to the second floor.

He glanced back, noticing that the lights had gone out on the first floor. In fact, the lights seemed to go out as he passed. That meant the dog remained in the darkness. It was only a glowing set of red eyes in the blackness.

He continued to climb, always with the enormous black dog nipping at his heels. Several times, the dog's teeth scraped his flesh, or its paws scratched his legs. Conner continued running. Continued ascending.

When he got to the sixth level, he glanced back a final time. The dog had stopped on the stairwell. Conner could hear the deep, guttural growl echoing in the darkness.

Without another thought, he opened the door to the sixth room and stepped inside.

Envy

37.

Conrad

The sun shone through the window onto Conrad's face, despite the curtains being drawn. It was midmorning and the sun had been up for hours. Usually, that meant he would be up as well, he was a habitual morning person and had been since his teenage years. Even during his medical leave, he had gotten out of bed with the rising of the sun. That morning, however, was different. He couldn't bring himself to get out of bed.

She just disappeared.

There had been something chaotic in the air the previous day, as if a spell had been put on the entire town. Having learned about the powers that Thrall wielded, that was likely the case. His entire universe had been unraveled in the course of a few hours. His mother, who had seemed perfectly rational and sane less than an hour previously, had murdered her ex-husband. His father was dead, and his mother would be going to jail. No jury would buy a mind-control defense no matter the skill of the defense attorney. A long-time friend, and frequent subject of "what if" questions pondered late at night, Gabby had…

She just disappeared.

No. I won't go there.

Gabby had disappeared before his very eyes, and in broad daylight, no less. It had been just like his first encounter with Thrall, except daylight had shed light upon his doubts regarding the encounter itself. Our minds often question what we see in the darkness. It's not only that our minds don't trust what we do not see, but we are untrusting of what *lurks* in the darkness. Thrall himself was proof enough that strange things lurked in the darkness if only we took a closer look. In daylight, the disappearance had been as astonishing and revelatory as the first. It wasn't simply Thrall's mystical powers that caused him to vanish. Gabby had no such powers, obviously. It was the location, not Thrall's powers.

Was the White House real?

Conrad wasn't ready to declare the mythological White House a reality yet, but his mind was starting to open up to the idea. There were things happening in Prairieview that couldn't be explained by nature; therefore, the natural leap was to something unnatural. He didn't have a lot of experience in that realm, what could only be described as paranormal. What was to be done with a house that no one could see?

In a horror movie where a couple is residing in a haunted house, the first step would be to bless the house. Of course, in those movies something always went wrong with said blessing, be it the priest suffering a heart attack or the spirits being unreceptive to the powers of God. This wasn't a movie, and Conrad didn't know a priest well enough to ask such a question. Could a priest even bless a house that wasn't truly there? Perhaps blessing the lot where the invisible house stood would have to be sufficient.

That was a problem for another time. For the time being, he had better things to do with his time, like trying to forget about his mere existence.

Despite his vow to not get out of bed for the rest of the day, Miriam had other ideas. She came into the bedroom and drew the comforter back from his covered face. There was a scowl on her face, thoroughly unimpressed by his reaction to his entire life being thrown into the shredded at the hands of an alleged paranormal entity. He wished he could be more for her in that moment, yet all he could manage was a raised eyebrow.

"You've got to get up and get to the station," she said with her hands on her hips.

"My mom just killed my dad because a paranormal entity got inside her head. The girl I've flirted with since high school and slept with once has gone missing after I saw her vanish before my eyes. I couldn't solve the Bianca Nowitzki case, and now the chief has handed the case to my arch enemy. The whole town has decided to commit every sin they've ever repressed. Plus, I'm on medical leave, so pardon me if I'm wallowing in my own misery."

"Arch enemy? This isn't a comic book, Conny. So, you had a bad day. Big deal. My dad always said, 'You can't have a good day while sleeping the day away.' Or something like that. I don't know, the point is, you've got to get up and get to the station."

"Why? Is something going on?"

"Hightower made an arrest in the Bianca Nowitzki case."

"You're kidding. Who?" he asked, sitting up in bed.

"Remember that actor that Gavin hired to play Thrall?"

"Sure, I was going to try and track him down when I got injured. Thought he might have some dirt on Gavin. Wait. You mean?"

She nodded. "Hightower arrested him."

It felt odd walking into the police station in civilian clothing, especially since Conrad was on medical leave. From the outside the station appeared to be perfectly normal. It was a different situation on the inside, however. The station was buzzing with activity, which was a rarity for a small town where the crime was nearly nonexistent. The activity centered around the bullpen, where the rest of the officers of the PPD were gathered around Frank Hightower. Some were on duty, like Chief Nichols, Holly, and Frank, while the rest were dressed similarly to Conrad, in street clothes. Apparently, he hadn't gotten the message about a gathering of station staff.

Chief Nichols cleared his throat. A speech was coming.

"Now, let's not get ahead of ourselves, we've still got some work to do to prove that this is the SOB that killed Bianca Nowitzki. This is an all hands on deck kind of affair. We'll need people to check with eyewitnesses, like Mrs. Lincoln, to prove that this is the guy that was seen lurking in the neighborhood. We'll need someone to corroborate the connection between our guy and Mr. Luxley, who we still need to prove has something to do with this. The work isn't done, but my oh my, does it feel good to have the guy in custody. How about a hand for Frank!"

Cheers and applause rang out through the station, with everyone but Conrad taking part in the affair.

He couldn't believe what he was hearing. They thought they had the right guy in custody. Was it Thrall or was the actor that had been hired to play Thrall? He knew the answer without stepping into the holding area, but he would do it all the same. He had to be sure that they hadn't locked up the paranormal man that had laid a beating on him. If Thrall was in custody, then the entire station was at risk.

"Now, let's get back to work!" Chief Nichols said.

The bullpen slowly cleared out, leaving Conrad alone with one man he didn't want to speak with but felt obligated by duty to do just that. Frank Hightower.

Frank's eyes turned to him, as if seeing him for the first time.

"Well, look what the cat drug in. Did you come down here to congratulate me? Or did you come to find out how I solved the case in one day that you've let slide for a week?"

"Didn't you hear the chief? The work isn't done; you've still got to prove that he did it. And that he was in town when Bianca went missing. Hell, I'd doubt that the guy was in the same state a week ago. But, sure, congratulations for bringing someone in."

Frank laughed. "It's more than you did with the case."

"It is, because I like to make sure I have enough evidence for it to stick when I make an arrest. I've already been down the Gavin Luxley road, by the way, it looks like a dead end. I'm not telling you how to do your job, Frank, but I don't think you'll get anything to stick to that guy."

"Ah, don't tell me that your undercover work has made you soft on him too. I know that sweet little piece of tail that works for him as gotten a hold of you, but now the guy too. It's a crying shame."

"I wouldn't talk about her in that manner if you know what's good for you, Frank."

"Is that a threat, Cain?"

"It's a promise."

Silence hung in the air as the two men stared at each other. Frank finally broke the silence.

"Did you actually need something, Cain?"

"As you may recall, I'm on medical leave because of an incident that took place with the man they call Thrall. The same man that you're holding for questioning. I'd like to see him for myself, make sure it's the same guy."

"Why should I let you back there? What's in it for me?"

"If it's the right guy, then I'll say as much. That gives you another witness, an officer, no less, that puts this guy in the area around the time of the disappearances. That work for you?"

Frank thought it over for a moment. Then nodded.

"I'm sure it wouldn't hurt to let you see the guy. Come on."

"You know, Frank, I was wondering, how did you find this guy? I mean, the guy is from Oregon," Conrad said as they walked to the holding area.

Frank chuckled. "You wouldn't believe it. Now, this guy, Russel 'Rusty' Pendergast is his name, he *is* from Oregon originally. Chief told me about your lead with Huxley hiring Rusty to play this Thrall guy. So, I called up the Eugene department and asked around. This guy has a rap sheet a mile long, burglary, possession, possession with intent to sell, you know, the usual junky stuff. They know the guy, sure, but haven't seen him in over a year, figured he must have skipped town. Probably right, because a guy with his kind of rap sheet ain't going clean, that's for sure."

"It's believable so far, Frank."

"I'm getting there, keep your pants on. Anyway, I figured that was the end of that, right? That was until he was delivered to me by God himself, literally. It was the end of the day, and I was tired and headed back to the station to punch out. That was when this junky stumbled out into the middle of the street into traffic. Then falls over on his face in front of my cruiser. Guess who?"

"Our friend Rusty."

"Bingo. Turns out he's in town with that Huxley fella. Been following him and that show around for fourteen, fifteen months."

There were four cells in the holding area of the police station. They were used mostly for drunken and disorderly conduct on the weekends. When they did get a bigger criminal in, they were held for a period of time while awaiting transfer to the county jail for trial. The stations holding area was equipped with enough room to separate men from women, therefore, he knew his mother was in one of these cells. He looked into the first cell, hoping to get a glimpse of the woman that had protected him all those years as a child. He didn't know if he could handle seeing her behind bars. It would be too much. It wasn't his mother behind the bars of the first cell.

Instead, it was a middle-aged man with long, lean limbs sitting on the cot that served as a bed. His hair was dark and had been combed backward at some point but had become disheveled. His eyes were deep set and dark. There were dark patches under his eyes, as if he hadn't had a good night's sleep in a long time. The man scratched his arm, the telltale sign of a junkie in need of a hit.

It wasn't Thrall.

"Are you Rusty?" he asked the man.

"What's it to you? You ain't in uniform, so you're either a detective or a nobody. My guess is that you're a nobody.

So, screw you," Rusty said, staring Conrad down with those dark eyes.

"Hey, show some respect. This is Officer Cain. If he asks you a question, you better answer," Frank said, then turned and left the holding area.

It went against protocol to leave an off-duty officer alone in the holding area with a suspect, but he wasn't going to complain. It would give him an opportunity to question the man that Gavin had hired to play Thrall. He didn't think Gavin had anything to do with Bianca or Gabby's disappearances, but he wanted to know what Hightower had on Rusty. He didn't think it would hold up in a court of law, if it even got that far, which he doubted. Hightower no longer had a crooked uncle overseeing cases locally, which meant the longtime officer was screwed and didn't know it.

"How do you know Gavin Huxley?"

"Man, I already went over this with that prick that just left."

"Humor me."

Rusty sighed. "So, I was living in Eugene a couple of years ago. Grew up there, left town with my band, thinking we were going to hit it big. We'd go on the road, trying to get enough green so we could record a demo. Those things aren't cheap, especially if you want a good studio. We recorded one, but didn't have any bites. Few nibbles, but no bites. That's whatever, man. I was just in it for the chicks anyway. Along the way, I developed a problem. Guess what problem, right? Well, it got pretty bad, I'll admit. Now, if you're sick on the ax or got killer vocals, the band'll let that slide, right? Guess I wasn't as good as I thought, but whatever. It's like I said, I was in for the chicks, anyway. So, they kicked me out of the band.

"You think things are bad when you're in a band, right? Well, how about when you don't have anything to do but sit around and get high, right? Did some pretty stupid stuff around that time, most of which I don't remember. Things got bad enough that I was living with my parents. Can you imagine that? A thirty-eight-year-old man living with his parents. I mean, they were preparing for retirement, then their middle-aged drug addict son that hasn't been home in five years shows up and wants to move back in. I don't blame them for kicking me out. I don't. They were willing to pay for rehab, put off retirement a few more years. Can you believe that? For a junky son. Couldn't let them do that. Plus, I was enjoying myself. I mean, if I got clean then I'd have to be responsible. That's a bummer.

"So, they got tired of me after a couple of years of that. Kicked me out. After that, I went from couch to couch, staying with friends and former band mates. Wearing out my welcome faster and faster. I mean, how long would you put up with someone eating all your food, doing drugs in the bathroom, and not pitching in for rent? Not long, trust me. Eventually, I ended up on the streets.

"That's where Gavin found me. He stared at me for a long time before approaching. Thought he was gay or something. Hey, whatever, I mean, I'll do anything for that next hit. It wasn't like that. Told me a weird story that you probably know about since you're asking about him. Said I looked just like that weird dude, if I got a haircut and shaved. I thought he was joking when he told me the price. Then he handed me a thousand dollars cash. I was camping out behind a gas station next to a busy off ramp by the highway in those days. Do some panhandling, you know? So, I told Gavin to wait while I went inside. Grabbed a sandwich and a bottle of cheap whiskey. I watched as the cashier ran a counterfeit marker across the twenty I gave him. There was doubt in his eyes, I mean, hell, I was doubtful too, but it worked. Ran back outside and shook Gavin's hand. Been with him ever since."

"That's the extent of the deal? A thousand dollars?"

Rusty shook his head. "Nah, man. That was just that first gig. I mean, I thought I was done after that. I mean, it was a sweet gig. All I had to do was walk around this neighborhood late at night, make sure someone saw me, but don't get caught. Weird gig, but it was easy money. A week later, Gavin leaves town. He gave me a cell phone. I had to sell mine for…well, you know. Told him I couldn't afford to pay a phone bill. He told me not to worry about it, that he'd cover it. There was only one condition. When he calls, answer.

"He called three weeks later, by that time I'd nearly gone through that money he gave me. A thousand dollars seems like a lot of money, especially when you've got nothing, right? Well, when you give a drug addict money, guess what they're going to spend it on? Stuffs expensive. So, when Gavin called, I was eager. Told me he had another gig for me. Only this time the deal was different. Got me a car, cash, and some clothes—the kind this other guy would wear, nothing I liked. Now, he's a smart guy, so he only gave me enough money to get me through one gig at a time. Told me to stay close, but act like we didn't know each other. I got the feeling that the rest of the crew didn't know about me, which was a shame because that girl is hot. Seemed like Gavin had dibs on her, if you know what I mean.

"It's been like that ever since. Don't even know how long I've been doing it. I mean, it's a good gig, but I'm getting bored. He hasn't even used me this trip. I guess the other guy, you know the guy I'm pretending to be? He showed up this time. I mean, why would you need an Elvis impersonator if you've got Elvis, right?"

"Let me get this straight, Rusty. You've been following Gavin and the crew around all over the country, pretending to be Thrall. He gave you money and a car. It's been over a year, why are you still doing it?"

Rusty shrugged. "I mean, it gets boring sometimes, sure, but it beats getting a real job. Especially one where I can't get high whenever I want. I mean, it ain't hurting anyone, right?"

"That's where you're wrong."

38.

Conrad

There was no sign of Frank after he finished talking with Rusty, so Conrad decided to venture further into the holding area. He hadn't seen his mother since she was taken into custody the previous day. There was no telling how she had reacted to the realization that she had murdered her ex-husband and wasn't responsible for her own actions. It was the sort of thing that could fracture the mind if dwelt upon for too long. He hoped she wouldn't do that, hadn't done that already.

He also wasn't sure how he would react to seeing her behind bars for the first time. His mother and prison were two things that had no correlation and didn't belong together. The only true connection had been her ex-husband's job and now her son's job, which was an indirect connection at best. She was the best person he knew, despite what had happened to her. She could have shunned the world, turning her back on a community that had watched knowingly and done nothing to help her. Yet she hadn't. Volunteering at the soup kitchen once a week, teaching bible classes at church, hosting other victims of spousal abuse in the area. These were all the things she had started doing after her life had undergone a well overdue change. He admired her. Now, Thrall had made her a murderer.

Maribeth Cain, ex-wife to the now deceased former Chief of Police, Douglass Cain, was lying on the poor excuse for a bed, facing the wall. The steady intake of breath seemed to indicate that she was asleep. Conrad thought about leaving her alone, letting her sleep considering the despondency that she was obviously feeling. He thought better of it, after all, a visit from her son could raise her spirits.

He cleared his throat.

She stirred but didn't turn.

"Mom."

She turned her head at the sound of his voice. A smile appeared on her face at the sight of him. It was quickly replaced by a look of apprehension. Why was she nervous? Was she really that worried about his reaction to seeing her inside of a cell? Surely, she thought he was strong enough to withstand it.

Be calm. You don't want to get her worked up, then leave her to sit alone in a jail cell for the rest of her life.

"How are you doing?"

His mother looked as if she had aged ten years in the twenty-four hours they had been apart. With curious reluctancy, she got up from the bed and crossed the cell to the bars where Conrad stood. There were noticeable tears in her eyes as she looked at him. Meanwhile, his eyes were on her. The PPD didn't have the orange jumpsuits that were seen on so many television shows. Those were mostly reserved for penitentiaries, as were the white and black striped garb that was also common. Instead, she wore a tan colored top with a pair of burgundy elastic waist pants with the drawstring removed for safety reasons. There was a bruise on her right forearm, near her wrist. It was as if she had been grabbed roughly. There was a bandage on her left cheekbone, the perfect placement for someone delivering a right hook.

"What the hell happened to you?" he asked, his tone going ice cold.

"Calm down, Conrad. It's nothing. I just got a little out of hand when they were bringing me in, didn't listen. I was confused with what was going on. I don't remember hurting your dad, so I acted out. Don't worry," she said, averting her eyes.

"When someone says don't worry, that's the first thing you should do."

"Look at you being the detective. I'm fine. I just wish I knew why I did it. I've wanted to, Lord knows, I've wanted to. Had fantasies about it for years, especially after that incident with you. I even held the gun in my hand a few times. His gun. Wouldn't that be something? Killing a man with his own gun? Of course, I never did it. It was just a fantasy. I even fantasized about it after I purchased my own gun. I got it for safety reasons, that's what I told myself, of course. I did get it for safety reasons, but I still thought about it. Never would I do something like that. It's the devil in my ear, whispering sweet nothings as he does. I resisted. Yet he persisted. Testing my forgiveness for your father. I was weak."

"It's not your fault, Mom."

"Oh, did someone else pull that trigger? Did someone else drive to your father's place and shoot him? I don't think so. Just because I don't remember making the clear decision to commit murder doesn't mean I'm not guilty of it."

"You deserve better than this. I should have pulled the trigger when I was a teenager. Then you wouldn't be here. You wouldn't be facing charges because someone else eliminated your inhibitions."

"Conrad, you were a child. That wasn't your fault. None of this is your fault. If you had shot your dad then, you wouldn't be standing here today. It would have sent you down a path where there is no turning back. I wouldn't have that. It's better me in here, than you."

Silence hung in the air for a moment.

"Have they provided you with a lawyer?" he finally asked.

"And take one of their public defenders? I've got my own lawyer, thank you very much. Brenda Halloway is her name. She specializes in battered women from what I gathered on the phone. Derek Thompson, who handled the divorce for me, recommended her. They went to law school together. Said she's as sharp as they come and a real ballbuster."

"There's definitely some balls that need busting around here," he said laughing.

"Oh, I could name a few."

He could tell it was meant as a joke, however, there seemed to be some truth to her words. Had she told him the truth about her bruises?

"Well, I leave you alone for five minutes, and look what you're doing," Frank said, as he entered the holding area.

Conrad took a deep breath before turning around to face his fellow officer. His fists were clenched into fists. His face was a tight line.

There was a smirk on Hightower's face that begged to be punched.

"Take care of her, Frank. Take good care of her," he said instead.

"Oh, I will."

There was still a smirk on his face.

"I'll hold you to that. If you don't, you deal with me."

The bruise on his mother's arm was behind his eyelids every time he blinked. The bandage on her cheekbone was emblazoned onto his mind. The way she averted her eyes when she told him about what happened had been the clue. She was lying, that much had been obvious. What was the truth? Was it something that he could handle? Or was it something that would cause him to act in a manner that would alter his life forever? If it came to choosing between his badge and the mother that had protected him from an abusive father his entire life, there was no contest.

He kept seeing her slumped shoulders, kept hearing the confusion in her voice when trying to justify her actions, despite her actions not being justifiable to the person she had become with Douglass Cain in her life. She had been a battered and broken woman when Conrad had been a child. A woman that didn't believe she could survive without the man she had married, despite his ever-present abuse. After the divorce, she became stronger than ever. He had been proud of her, was still proud of her. It wasn't right that Thrall had taken that strength from her and returned her to the broken woman she had once been, all with one simple and monumental action.

Seeing the confusion in his mother's eyes, both immediately after the murder and minutes ago, cemented it in his head. Thrall was responsible for what was happening in Prairieview. Thrall was responsible for what his mother was going through, and the fact that she would likely spend the rest of her life in jail. It was time for the paranormal entity known as Thrall to pay for what he had done.

How? That was the question that plagued him. How could a man that served a paranormal house be affected?

An idea struck him. Instead of driving home, where he had instinctively headed, Conrad drove to the old Comisky place. He needed to see Miriam.

"You want to bless the White House?" Miriam said with a raised eyebrow.

"I want a priest to do a blessing where the house is supposed to sit. Look, I know we can't see the house, but we've got to try something. What if this is an entity from hell? What if Thrall is a demon? If this were a haunted house movie or a movie where a house is plagued by a demon, the obvious answer would be to bless the house. Well, why not do that? We've been too defensive in our actions. I think it's time to go on the offensive."

Miriam shrugged. "I mean, sure. It couldn't hurt. I think it would make for a great visual for the channel. I'll run it by

Gavin. If he thinks it's good for the channel, then he'll do it."

He started to protest, but she was already speaking excitedly to Gavin. This wasn't about the channel. It was about Bianca. It was about Gabby. It was about saving someone else the fate they had been dealt. Yet, if teaming with Gavin and the crew on this increased the chances of it being successful, then Conrad was on board.

Gavin had shooed Stu away when Miriam came over, so the two could talk more privately. It was as if the cameraman wasn't part of the team in the producer's eyes. The man shooting the shots would have a more than fair idea of what would be visually appealing to the audience. As Conrad watched, however, Gavin's motivation became clear. He wanted time alone with Miriam.

Gavin's eyes flickered to Conrad as they talked.

Stu ventured over to where Conrad was standing. Together they watched Miriam and Gavin talk.

"The boss is getting mighty close to your girl. They dated, you know."

"Yeah, I know."

They watched the rest of the conversation in silence, two men that had been withheld from a conversation that would be better served by having them in it. Stu so he could give his opinion on how they would shoot the blessing, and Conrad so he keep Gavin's roaming hands away from Miriam.

He watched as Gavin brushed a stray hair away from Miriam's face, as if he had been prompted by Conrad's thoughts. The sight of the producer glancing at him afterward cemented that it had been a purposeful action. Miriam was none the wiser to her boss's actions, as she talked excitedly about blessing that seemed to be getting bigger and bigger as the conversation continued.

Conrad reminded himself that Miriam had dated Gavin and hadn't enjoyed the experience. He had cheated on several occasions with other women while they were dating, something that a lot of women found unforgiveable. Yet, it hadn't been enough of a betrayal to cause her to leave the job, despite being hurt. The closeness of their relationship could go a long way in improving the former couple's relationship. As they say, time heals all wounds. He also knew that money was a good convincer when things were in doubt.

Nonsense.

She hugged Gavin before running excitedly back to Conrad. His eyes locked with Gavin. The other man winked at him.

39.

Conrad

The burning ball of hydrogen in the sky had finally disappeared from sight, bringing forth an evening that was only slightly less hot. Conrad stood on the curb as he watched Miriam interview Frank Hightower about the recent disappearance of Gabby and the suspect that was in custody. The seasoned officer was enjoying the limelight, likely a welcome change from the ridicule he normally received.

"Officer Hightower, what can you tell us about the suspect and his connection to the White House?" Miriam asked.

"You'll have to forgive me, Miriam, but I haven't watched your little program. What exactly is the White House?"

"Officer Cain, our former correspondent with the Prairieview Police Department, has drawings from both missing persons of a white house. Bianca's husband reported that in the days leading to her disappearance she saw a white house. Officer Cain himself reported that Gabby Newhouse saw the house in the days leading up to her disappearance. While we do have certain mythos revolving around the White House on this show, you should be familiar with it because it's a part of the case."

"Well, Miriam, I believe you're trying to make me look foolish on television. Shameful."

"Just safeguarding the integrity of our show by ensuring you're doing your research, after all when you're in front of our camera, the viewers will assume that you represent our show. That's not the case, however, unlike Officer Cain, who was a well-respected member of the Prairieview Police Department, you don't represent our show because we're not paying you a dime. You saw the bright, shining lights and came running. Plus, I've heard rumors that you're not well-respected either."

"Mmmm. You're a feisty one. I like that," Hightower said, with a sneering smile.

"Alright, Officer Hightower, we'll withdraw all the questions about the White House due to your lack of knowledge and preparation. What can you tell us about the suspect?"

"Are you kidding me? I should be asking you the same questions, little missy. After all, your show hired the guy to pretend to be some creepy guy that doesn't really exist. I don't know. The point is that you're complicit in this. I just need to prove it. That's why I'm here."

"Let's cut. This guy's an imbecile," Gavin said, stepping in front of the camera.

Gavin pulled Miriam aside to talk about the upcoming blessing by the priest, who stood smoking a pipe by his car. Hightower noticed Conrad standing on the curb. He tried to avoid making eye contact, but the other man came over anyway. Conrad braced himself for the gloating that was about to take place at his expense.

"Came to watch them interview the hero, huh?"

"If by hero, you mean the guy that arrested the wrong man, then yes. Rusty isn't innocent in this. His ethics are definitely warped. The guy would do anything for money, it seems, but I don't think he murdered anyone. He also isn't the man I had a confrontation with. He isn't the man that steamrolled me."

"You still can't admit when you're wrong, just like your old man. This was good old-fashioned police work, Cain. You should try it some time."

He watched as Gavin leaned in close to Miriam, who was oblivious to the attention she was receiving from her boss. Conrad tried to ignore it.

"I can admit when I'm wrong, Hightower. The problem is that I'm not wrong, not now. You've got the wrong guy. Don't worry, the truth will come out eventually."

"You know, I saw how much you enjoyed being the center of attention when you were getting interviewed by all those reporters. You were glowing, Cain, glowing! Sure, the attention is nice, but that's not why I'm here. I'm here to make sure you're wrong, then shove it in your face for the world to see."

"I'll be there, watching, when this blows up in yours."

Hightower muttered under his breath as he walked back to his vehicle. Apparently, he had no intention of watching the blessing for the White House that he knew nothing about.

Conrad had grown up attending church with his parents. His mother was a devout Christian woman, who married a man that adopted her faith despite not having any of his own. To a young child church was a place where he was meant to behave and there were consequences when he didn't. As a result, convincing her husband and son to attend church every Sunday had been a chore the saintly woman didn't deserve.

The old man stopped attending around that same point, though for very different reasons. After Conrad called the police on his father, the police chief, for beater his mother, the entire town was forced to look at Douglass Cain in a whole new light. There were judgmental gazes everywhere he went, which Conrad enjoyed but his father didn't. After a sermon where he was all but called out by name at the pulpit, the old man called it quits on God.

Conrad stopped attending when he discovered the old man was a liar and a wife beater. What kind of God would allow that to happen to his mother? How was that just? There had been the occasional Christmas or Easter service to appease his mother, but Conrad hadn't been inside a church of his own volition since that day. Today, he believed there was a God, but didn't understand the decisions that were made on the world's behalf. His mother had repeatedly told him that reading the bible would help him understand God's will. That wasn't something he was prepared to do anytime soon.

When it came to religious questions, the first person he would normally turn to would be his mother. Facing charges of murdering her ex-husband, his mother had more important things to occupy her time. That left him without someone to turn to for help in finding someone that would help with the blessing.

His mother's congregation was the Prairieview Church of Christ. He doubted the traditional Christian church did house blessings. Pastor Gabriel would scoff at his request to bless a house that wasn't there. That was the last thing he needed. What he needed was someone with an old-school mindset for an ancient evil. He needed a Catholic priest.

There was exactly one Catholic church in Prairieview, St. Mary's Catholic Church. Father Harrington was the head of St. Mary's, whom Conrad only knew through reputation. The priest was in his late seventies and had been in charge of the church for nearly forty years. He had a pension for consuming the communion wine during the late-night hours, which everyone including the nuns at the church ignored. He had a slow, methodical way of speaking that let everyone know he wouldn't be rushed, especially through the sermon. Conrad had attended mass with a girlfriend years earlier, the elderly priest had reminded him of the old farmers that were around town, and how they could talk for hours without really saying much.

Father Harrington arrived while Miriam was interviewing Hightower, driving a non-descript Ford sedan that looked nearly as old as the priest. Conrad had been glancing at his watch, wondering if the segment for Macabre Manor would have to be postponed. He exited the vehicle with the methodical nature of someone accustomed to taking their time. Rather than walk the block that separated the priest's car from the old Comisky place, the priest leaned against the car and pulled a pipe from his pocket.

That was where the priest stood until he was summoned by Miriam, who approached the smoking priest with surprising timidity. Father Harrington's behavior appeared unchanged from before she approached him. She could have been having a conversation with herself. After a full minute, he blew a plume of smoke in her face, dumped the tobacco from his pipe onto the street, placed it in his pocket, and nodded. He followed Miriam to the awaiting crew.

"I'm joined by Officer Cain of the Prairieview Police Department. In a few minutes, we'll be joined by Father Harrington of St. Mary's Catholic Church. Father Harrington will be conducting a blessing of the property locally known as the old Comisky place. It's the location where both Bianca Nowitzki and Gabby Newhouse have reportedly seen the White House.

"Officer Cain, what do you hope is the result of this blessing?"

Conrad cleared his throat. "Well, Miriam, first I'd like to thank you for having me on the program again. It's been a trying week for the Prairieview Police Department, and we thank the public for their cooperation and understanding during these difficult times. To answer your question, it's a leap of faith, quite honestly. I won't pretend to be a believer in the White House phenomenon, but my eyes have been opened to the possibility over the previous days. I came into this case as a staunch skeptic on the matter. Now, I'm open to the possibility, whatever possibility that is, that there is something unexplained going on in our small town. There have been unexplained phenomena that have occurred during the previous week. Phenomena that I, nor science can convincingly explain away. Two people have gone missing after seeing a house at this location. People I know and respect. People that seemed to have all their mental capacities in order in the days leading up to seeing the house.

"I honestly don't know what we'll achieve here tonight, that's the honest truth, however, if it is a demon or a spirit that dwells within that house, we'll know a little more about it afterward. When I became an officer, I took an oath to protect and serve. That's what I'm doing today."

"Father Harrington, can I have a word with you before you begin the blessing?" Miriam asked the priest, who was standing just off camera.

The priest had been watching the interview with a puzzled expression on his face. That look remained on his face as the camera moved from Miriam and Conrad to Father Harrington. The elderly priest reluctantly joined Conrad's side. The puzzled expression was replaced by a bemused smile, as if the entire ordeal was humorous.

"Father Harrington, have you ever done a blessing quite as unique as this one?"

Father Harrington laughed. "No, miss, I have not. When Officer Cain contacted me about doing the blessing, I asked for the address, as I often do, especially when it's not one of our parishioners. I was confused when he gave me the address. You see, the house that once stood here once belonged to Joseph Comisky, a member of my flock. It was a very unfortunate situation; I remember it well. It's been a few years since I've been in this neighborhood, so I assumed that someone had bought the property and rebuilt the house. I wasn't expecting this. Officer Cain explained the situation upon my confusion. I fear you might need someone with knowledge of the occult, which I do not have. I shall do my best, however."

A few minutes later, the priest was ready for the blessing. In one hand he held a bible, from which he repeatedly recited a prayer as he walked amongst the rubble that had once been the old Comisky place. In the other hand, he held a bottle filled with holy water. As he recited the prayer, he sprinkled the holy water and made the sign of the cross. Miriam followed closely to his side; in case he needed a hand navigating the rubble. Surprisingly, he didn't need assistance.

Conrad watched from the grass just outside of the rubble pile, standing next to Stu, whose girth and sound-mindedness prevented him from stepping foot where there might be a demon.

Father Harrington made several passes around the rubble pile while he recited the prayer, sprinkling holy water all the while. With each pass the priest's voice became increasingly strained, and his breathing labored. Conrad feared the elderly man would have a heart attack.

"Father Harrington, are you okay?" Miriam asked, placing a soothing hand on his shoulder.

"Of course, dear."

Father Harrington resumed his blessing. A few minutes later, he was forced to stop again. A noticeable sweat had broken out on his brow. Miriam helped him down from the ruins. The elderly priest looked as if he had aged twenty years while performing the blessing.

"Are you sure you're feeling alright, father?" Miriam asked.

"Yes, a warm cup of tea in front of the fire and I'll be right as rain tomorrow. I'm sorry I can't continue. There's a presence here, a dark one. I can feel it in my soul. Hopefully, the blessing does some good."

"I'll walk you back to your car, father."

"It's so dark. It's almost like a physical presence sitting on my chest. Did you feel it, child?"

"I felt something, yes."

Miriam escorted Father Harrington to his vehicle. She paused upon her return. Her eyes were fixed on the ruins.

"No."

"What?" Conrad asked her, looking from her to the old Comisky place.

"I see it."

40.

Conrad

"It's beautiful. Majestic, even. It's constructed of brick that appears to have been painted white. Of course, I doubt it's been painted, after all, why would a supernatural house need to be painted? There are two windows flanking the front door on each floor. All of the trim is black, the darkest black I've ever seen. If I stare too closely, it's like I'm staring into a void. The front door is bright, crimson red. It's as if whatever entity that dwells here has cut itself, bleeding onto the door. There isn't a front porch to speak of, the house simply starts at the façade. Oh, it's so tall. I don't know why I haven't been able to see it until now. How could I miss it? There are seven floors, plus what looks like an attic at the top. I could be wrong. The seventh floor could just be exceptionally tall, but that doesn't make sense.

"Oh, it's so beautiful. I wish you guys at home could see it."

Miriam stood in the middle of the old Comisky place's lawn, staring up at the house. After first seeing the White House, she walked over in a trance-like state. Her eyes hadn't moved from the house, nor had she blinked the entire time. Several minutes went by without her saying a word, despite Gavin and Conrad speaking to her the entire time. Stu had simply watched with his camera in his hand, ready if called upon. When she started speaking, Stu started filming without being prompted.

The three men watched silently as she spoke, not wanting to interrupt the conversation Miriam had entered with her viewing audience. It was a special relationship they shared. Conrad realized it could be the last time she coherently spoke to them. He wouldn't interrupt.

He waited for her to continue. To possibly go into detail about the way the house was making her feel. For more precise details about the White House's appearance. For a monologue about how she had always known the house to be real, and not a delusion of the mentally ill. Something. Anything.

She remained silent. In the short time he had come to know Miriam, he had never experienced a moment where words failed her. Words were her livelihood. Communicating with the audience sitting at home on their couch watching on a laptop or watching a video on their phone while on break from the job they hated. That was who she was. It was what she did. Words wouldn't fail her.

That wasn't the situation. Words hadn't failed her at the most important moment of her life—for the last two years, her life had revolved around the White House, therefore seeing it would definitely be that moment. Rather, the house's hypnotic hold tightened its grasp upon her mind, squeezing until all that remained was the house. Conrad, Gavin, Stu, the viewing audience, and even her sense of self, all disappeared in the presence of the White House.

He watched unblinking, hypnotized by the woman that had stolen his heart in a matter of days. Her back was straight as a post. Tears poured from her eyes, whether that was from the prolonged strain of remaining open without blinking or from the magnitude of the moment, Conrad couldn't fathom. Her hands remained at her side, making no move to wipe away the moisture, despite it obviously blurring her vision.

He turned to the location where the White House supposedly resided, willing himself to see it. The white brick façade with black trim and a crimson red front door. The lawn led straight to the front door, without a front porch. Seven levels into the sky, towering above all things that surrounded the suburban neighborhood. With every fiber of his being, he willed himself to see it. Willed himself to see it so he could experience what Miriam was experiencing, to know how she felt. Willed himself to see it so he could join her when she entered the White House in the coming days. Willed himself to see it so the emptiness that he had felt until she came into his life wouldn't return when she went missing, when the White House claimed her as its next victim.

He willed himself to see the White House.

He saw the old Comisky place.

His vision blurred with tears.

He didn't wipe them away.

"Do an ending," Stu whispered into his ear.

The three men were still watching Miriam as she stared at the White House. She hadn't moved or said anything since her description ended five minutes earlier. Stu was still filming her.

"I can't do that."

"Man, you're good on camera. You can do it. We just need a conclusion for the end of the episode. Boss will cut out most of this standing around in the edit, but we got to get the fans some sort of an ending."

"Is that alright with you, Gavin?"

Gavin was still staring at Miriam. There were tears in the man's eyes. For the first time, Conrad realized how much Miriam meant to him.

"Huh? Oh, yeah. Give it a shot. I can always do a voice over if necessary."

"Let me know when you're ready," Stu said.

Conrad breathed deeply and nodded.

Stu pointed the camera at him and gave him a thumbs up.

"The White House. At the beginning of the Bianca Nowitzki investigation, I wasn't a believer in the White House. It seemed as if a perfectly healthy woman had suddenly had a mental breakdown, nothing more than that. You'll have to forgive me, but I believed that you guys watching this had the wool pulled over your eyes by the Macabre Manor crew. It's an interesting narrative, I'll give you that, but that's all I thought it was. A narrative spun by a film crew that was willing and ready to take advantage of the situation. Their show, this show, directly benefited from the myth of the White House, whether it was real or not.

"When I had an encounter with Thrall, which you guys know about, I'm sure. I found every excuse I could to make him a normal man. He was a supreme athlete with a background in football. I even found excuses for his mind controlling powers, which could have been the power of suggestion.

"I know now that he is not a normal man. I know now that the White House is not a normal house. It's not a figment of the imagination or a product of mass hysteria. My mind changed when Gabby Newhouse first saw the White House. I've known her my entire life. She's a dear friend, maybe even closer. She was the most down-to-Earth person I know. Mental illness didn't run in her family. No, the White House did this to her.

"I've spent most of my adult life watching people live their lives, while I went to work and earned a paycheck. All the while, I was wasting away, pushing people away at every turn because I wasn't good enough for them. Or I thought they'd eventually hurt me, so I hurt them first. So, I watched as the world went on around me. I could have had something special with Gabby. That possibility is likely over, now that she is a victim of the White House.

"Recently, a beautiful, smart, and witty young woman came into my life. She wooed me with her intellect and willingness to help others. In short, she made me rethink this unrealized vow I seemed to have taken to abstain from happiness. I found the woman of my dreams in the form of your Mistress of the Macabre."

Conrad turned to look at Miriam, who was still gazing at the house.

"Pray for her, if that's your thing. Send positive thoughts and vibes if it isn't. Because she has a long road ahead, down a road where no one returns. A road to nowhere, I guess. A road to a house that isn't there.

"For Miriam, Mistress of the Macabre, I'm officer Conrad Cain, imploring you to keep an eye out, otherwise you might become the next resident of the house that wasn't there. Good night."

Miriam was still looking at the space where she saw the White House. Conrad couldn't leave her alone to stand on the lawn of the old Comisky place. Stu had gone back to the van, where he was packing his equipment. Gavin was leaning against the van, watching both Miriam and Conrad. He approached her with the intention of taking her back to his place where he could supervise her state. Gabby was on his mind in that decision. He didn't want the same thing to happen to Miriam.

"Miriam? Can you hear me? You can't stay out here all night. Let's get you back to my place. Maybe you can draw the house. How does that sound?"

She didn't respond or give any indication that she heard him.

He put his arm around her waist and gently guided her to turn around. She resisted him, trying to keep her eyes on the White House.

"Miriam, we can come back to look at the house tomorrow. Would you like that? Miriam, it's Conrad. Can you hear me?"

No response. Her eyes didn't waver from the house, as if in a trance. The White House's power over her was already incredibly strong.

"Get your hands off her, Cain. She's not going anywhere with you."

Before he could turn, a strong hand pulled his arm away from Miriam.

Gavin.

"Look, I'm just trying to take care of her. She can't stay out here all night."

"She's not going anywhere with you. You think I'm going to let her leave in the care of some small-town fling? I don't think so. The Macabre Manor crew is like a family. She should be with family during her last days, not some guy who got her into the sack a few days before she saw the house," Gavin said, sneering.

Gavin put his arms around Miriam, pushing Conrad out of the way in the process. He wanted to punch the producer; however, he knew that Miriam's well-being was the most important thing at the moment. Gavin may have been a dirtbag, but he truly cared about Miriam. He would take care of her, Conrad hoped.

"Miriam, sweetie? It's Gavin, remember me?"

"Gavin. Yes."

"See? She didn't even recognize your voice," Gavin said to Conrad with a smug smile.

"Just take care of her, okay?"

Gavin turned away without responding.

He watched as Gavin led Miriam to the van, where he helped her into the passenger seat. Stu was relegated to the back of the van, while Gavin drove.

Conrad watched them pull away as his heart fell into his stomach.

The neon sign of the Prairieview Motel illuminated a corner of the parking lot. The rest of the parking lot was bathed in darkness, aside from the parking spaces directly in front of the walkway where the rooms were located. The Macabre Media van was parked at the far end of the motel. Gavin had taken her back to the motel to keep an eye on her.

He parked the SUV in the darkest corner of the parking lot and cut the engine. Luckily, the parking spot gave him a direct line to the adjoined rooms where the crews were staying.

Conrad sipped from the large thermos of coffee he had packed for the occasion. There were lights on in both rooms. He knew instantly what had happened. Gavin had taken Miriam into the room the guys were sharing, giving Stu the boot in the process. Stu had been forced to stay in Miriam's room.

Gavin was alone with Miriam.

Conrad watched and waited. He wouldn't sleep. He wouldn't leave her.

41.

Conrad

The sound of a ringing phone awoke Conrad from an unpleasant sleep. The early rays of morning sun were beginning to appear on the horizon. A few more minutes and it would have been shining directly in his face. His bearings weren't there in that first second after opening his eyes. At first, he had the disastrous thought that he had fallen asleep while on duty. Then his eyes fell upon the Macabre Manor van sitting in front of the Prairieview Motel, and it all fell into place. The blessing. Mirriam seeing the house. Gavin refusing to let her go with Conrad.

The phone continued to ring.

"Hello?" he said, hoping his voice didn't sound sleep riddled.

"Yeah, I wish I could have slept in. Sounds nice," Holly said in her familiar high pitch voice.

"I was awake. I'm just not out of bed yet."

"Right. And I'm not eating a jelly donut. The chief doesn't like us fulfilling the stereotype."

"Alright. I was asleep. I've got another week, minimum until I'm cleared. I've got to take it while I can get it."

"I hear you. Listen…" Holly paused, as if she didn't know how to precede.

"Just spit it out. I'm well aware that you didn't call to chat. Whatever it is, let's get out with it."

"Have you had breakfast? I need to do this in person, for both our sakes."

Conrad agreed to meet Holly at Hurts Donut in ten minutes. He was about to pull out of the parking lot when the door to the motel room opened. Gavin exited the room and locked eyes with him. Conrad put the car in park and walked over to meet the producer of Macabre Manor.

"What are you doing here, Cain?"

"Just keeping an eye on Miriam, same as you."

"Stalking, huh? Isn't that illegal? I might have to inform the police."

"Look, I'm just making sure she doesn't go anywhere near that house. I don't want to lose someone else I care about."

"No, that's what I'm doing. You don't need to be here. Besides, we're leaving town soon. The best way to avoid having Miriam go in the house, is to get her as far away from it as we can. I don't need some small-town cop that thinks he's a hero getting in the way."

"I'm just trying to help."

"We don't need your help, Cain. Go home. You'll just make it harder for her to leave, give her a reason to stay. You've got to admit that the best thing for her is to be as far away from the White House as she can get."

Gavin had a good point, but Conrad wasn't going to give him the satisfaction.

"Take care of her. Keep her here. I want to say goodbye."

"Sure," Gavin said, noncommittally.

Conrad would have preferred to meet at the Newhouse café, but it was closed until further notice for repairs. According to Ivan, it had been an accident that caused him to drive into the Newhouse Café. Conrad didn't buy it, but he didn't have a say in the matter. After all, it was Ivan's business that stood to gain the most from the café shutting its doors for the time being.

He looked around the packed dining room of Hurts Donut and knew that it had worked. The small donut shop had never been so busy. The town was split into two factions, people that ate at Newhouse Café and those that ate at Hurts Donut. The former group was larger than the latter, but that morning everyone fell into the latter category.

Holly began her shift with the sun, as Conrad had while on active duty. As a result, she was in uniform, and breakfast would have to be quick so she could get back to her beat. They ordered coffee and cinnamon rolls. It was time to see if the Hurts Donut cinnamon roll was truly better than the ones at Newhouse Café, as Gabby said.

"You made it sound pretty important on the phone. So, what's going on?" he asked as they dug into warm cinnamon rolls.

"You could say that. Now, I know that your relationship with Hightower hasn't always been the best, but I think all of us on the force can say the same. I mean, the guy's a jerk. Worse yet, he's probably dirty. His brother damn sure was. What kind of brother does illegal stuff like that and doesn't at least make sure his brother has his back, right? So, yeah, I think Frank's at least guilty of helping his brother clean up."

"Holly, why are you telling things I already know about Frank Hightower?"

"I'm just letting you know that I don't trust him is all, and I already know that you don't. I just want you to know that we've got that in common. Anyway, I've been on the force a lot longer than you, Cain. Worked with your dad for a year or two. Didn't know him that well, to be honest. I mean, your dad had his favorite officers, and a twenty-five-year-old female rookie officer wasn't one of them. He might have been a lazy alcoholic most of the time, but the man was incorruptible. Always admired that about your dad. There was one time I walked into his office without knocking, being the stupid rookie that I was in those days. Well, Judge Hightower was in your dad's office. Hightower was practically begging him to do some deal, but your dad wouldn't have any of it. Didn't know what it was about at the time. When Leonard went down in the drug ring, well, I figured it out.

"I tell you that so you know I cared about your dad. Had I known what he had been doing to your mom, well, I would have done a number on him, that's for sure. I'm sorry to hear about what happened to him. You planning the funeral?"

"I hadn't given it a thought, honestly. I guess I should make some calls," he said.

"Eh, he's a former cop. The department will help," Holly said, waving a dismissive hand.

"Out with it, you old hag."

"What?" Holly said, smiling.

"We both know that you didn't bring me here to talk about my dad. We both know what kind of man he was. I appreciate the sentiment, really, I do, but I'd also appreciate it if you stopped jerking me around."

Holly laughed. "Don't beat around the bush, huh? I've always liked your mom. Real nice lady. Always asked how my mom was back when she was dealing with cancer. I still can't believe what she did. It's unreal. Anyway, I know that you and Hightower haven't ever seen eye to eye. It's like you've known all along that he's dirty, and he knows you know. With that in mind, I've been keeping an eye on your mom and how he treats her."

"How has he been treating her, Holly?"

"Well, it's not good, Cain. It's not good at all."

"How not good."

"Now, keep in mind that I've never caught him in the act, but she's got bruises. Bruises that I don't remember being there before she was arrested. Hightower has been handling that investigation, despite also taking on the Bianca Nowitzki and Gabby Newhouse cases. He's got a full plate. In fact, I asked the Chief if I needed to take some of the load off, you know, because I don't have much going on. The Chief didn't want that. Said Hightower was going to handle it, period. Hightower is the only person that has gone back to see her, except you that one time. He spends a lot of time back there, more so than you'd think considering there isn't much to investigate. He's the only person that could have given her those bruises."

Conrad pulled a twenty from his wallet and tossed it on the table.

"Thanks, Holly. You've always been a good friend," he said as he got up from the booth.

"What are you going to do?"

"Handle it."

The Prairieview Police Department was quieter than it had been on Conrad's previous visit. Tracy was pouring a cup of coffee while wearing her headset to communicate with the officers out on patrol. He could see Chief Nichols sitting in his office through the window to the bullpen. The Chief's eyes were seemingly closed.

Less than ten seconds after he entered the department, Holly pushed through the front door. He wasn't surprised to find that his fellow officer had followed him. He would have done the same. It was an unpredictable situation.

"Cain, Hightower isn't here. He's out on patrol. Your mother shouldn't be here either. She was scheduled to get picked out by the county first thing this morning. They're transporting her to county for holding until the trial. You know we're not equipped to hold anyone long term."

He heard the words that were spoken but couldn't bring himself to take them as truth. Instead, he pushed through the swinging gate that separated reception from the bullpen area. His eyes scanned the large room, desperately trying to manifest Hightower into the building. The small kitchen equipped with a stove that no one used and a microwave that only reheated TV dinners and leftovers was empty. The holding area only held Rusty, the Thrall doppelganger.

No sign of Hightower.

"Cain, what the hell are you doing here?"

Conrad found Chief Nichols standing with Holly as he exited the holding area. She shrugged, as if to say that he had given her no other choice.

"I'm looking for Hightower. I hear he's been roughing up my mom."

"I'd watch it if I were you. Those are some mighty heavy accusations you're throwing around. You got proof?"

He nodded at Holly.

"Hey, don't look at me. I already told you; I don't have proof."

Conrad gave her a pleading look.

She sighed. With obvious reluctance, Holly relayed what she had told Conrad, leaving out both Conrad and her own disdain for Hightower.

"Bruises? We're standing here because of a few bruises and a scrape? Are you kidding me, Cain? Look, your mother was arrested for murder. Not just any murder, but murder of a former cop. That's going to ruffle some feathers around here, if that bothers you, I guess you'll just have to change into your big boy pants. Your father would be ashamed."

"My father was a wife beating, child abusing, alcoholic, Chief. The only one ashamed is me. I don't condone what my mom did, but I understand it. Hell, if the roles were reversed, I don't know if I could have waited so long."

"I'm going to pretend this entire conversation didn't happen, Cain. Dupree, the next time you have concerns about a fellow officer, please take them to me, instead of spreading gossip around the station. This isn't high school."

"Right, sir. Sorry, sir."

"Cain, have you talked with a therapist since your father died? I think it would be tremendously beneficial."

"No."

Conrad walked out of the station without another word.

If Conrad had been in his patrol car, he would have turned on the lights as he drove the five minutes to the Prairieview Motel. Since he was in his personal vehicle, he settled for speeding at a forgivable rate. He had been gone for just under an hour, which wasn't that long. Yet, he knew what to expect when he pulled into the parking lot.

The Macabre Media van was gone from the parking lot.

He banged on both motel room doors but got no answer.

Miriam and the crew were gone.

42.

Conner

The events that had taken place in the six rooms, ten years in the past, weighed heavily on Conner as he emerged from the room. His shoulders slumped. It was as if he was feeling every loss over again for the first time. The gravity of it all made him want to lay down and give up. Instead, he pressed on.

Thrall was nowhere in sight. That was good. It gave him time to think. A plan started to develop in his mind as he walked methodically down the hallway toward the stairwell to the seventh and possibly final level of the White House.

He ascended the stairs with heavy, deliberate footsteps, as if he was carrying everything that had happened on the previous six floors with him on his shoulders.

The seventh floor looked identical to the previous six floors. He had been expecting something different, after all, he was told he would meet Thrall's master after he exited the room he was about to enter.

There was an eagerness to have all this behind him, despite what lay behind the door of the seventh room. Everything until now he could have come back from. It was the events that transpired in that room which had altered his life forever. The choices that were made weren't ones that could be forgiven. It was the reason he had been forced to flee Kansas, changing his name and his life forever. Conner wasn't a believer in holding onto regret, because if he did, he would never have been able to look at himself in the mirror. It had also led him to meeting Carlisle. Their marriage had troubles—he still suspected she was cheating on him with PJ—but she had given him a reason to move on, given him something to hold onto when all hope was lost.

Conner opened the door to the seventh and final room but didn't step inside. He stood there, staring into the darkness beyond the threshold.

He waited. Eventually, what he had been waiting for came.

"What are you waiting for? Go inside. The master is waiting," Thrall said as he approached.

Conner didn't respond.

"Do you remember what happened last time you didn't listen? Would you like a reminder?"

Thrall was mere feet behind him now.

"Go inside!"

A little closer.

"Go!"

He could feel Thrall's hot, putrid breath on the back of his neck. Still, he didn't move.

"Go!"

Thrall pushed Conner in the back. He had been counting on the overly aggressive caretaker to use brute force. He hadn't been disappointed.

With speed that his middle-aged body shouldn't have been able to produce considering its damaged state, Conner whirled around. He grabbed the outstretched arm of Thrall and allowed himself to fall backward into the room.

Together Thrall and Conner tumbled into the seventh and final room.

Wrath

43.

Conner

Thrall: What did you do? Where am I?

Conner: What's wrong, Karl? Don't like having someone pull one over on you? You know, this is the second time I've gotten one over on you, if you think about it.

Thrall: What did you hope to accomplish with this desperate act of rebellion, Conrad Cain? It doesn't change your fate. You will still meet the master when all is done. You shall reside with the others that have visited our sanctuary. You will fall. All fall in the end.

Conrad Cain, do you really think you pulled one over on me, as you put it, before? What if I told you it was all part of the plan?

Conner: What was the big plan, Karl? Tell me how that was part of the plan.

Thrall: The master doesn't tell me about the ends and outs of the plan; all I know is that it was part of the plan. You are here, Conrad Cain. That means the plan was effective.

Conner: Was waiting ten years part of the plan? Oh, right, you don't know what the plan is.

Thrall: I trust that you're aware of what happened after you left me, correct?

Thrall: Correct?

Conner: Sorry, I nodded. I forgot that we're stuck inside the head of thirty-year-old me and you can't see me. Yes, I'm aware of what you did. That was part of the plan?

Thrall: No. That was simply fun.

Conner: You're sick.

Thrall: If you only knew.

Conner: I know enough.

Hope filled Conrad as he pulled out of the Prairieview Motel parking lot driving in the direction of the old Comisky place. He had been gone for an hour. Was that long enough to pack up two motel rooms and leave town? The three members of the Macabre Manor crew had been staying in those rooms for over a week. That was enough time for them to get comfortably situated. Packing it all up wouldn't be an easy task. Yet, he reminded himself that they traveled for a living. They likely had moving down to a science.

Would they leave town immediately? Or would they make one last stop on the way out of town? They could film a final scene of sorts at the location where the White House stood before Miriam was lost entirely to the incessant ramblings it filled her head with. Gavin was a producer by trade. Conrad was counting on the man's producer card trumping the ex-boyfriend, despite his obvious lingering feelings for Miriam.

That hope was dashed as he parked the SUV in front of the old Comisky place. The street was empty. There was no sign of the van.

Instead of wallowing in self-pity, Conrad turned his attention to another problem. According to Holly, Frank Hightower was responsible for the cuts and bruises he had seen on his mother. While she hadn't seen it with her own eyes, Holly suspected that Hightower had been abusing Conrad's mother while she was in the department's holding cell awaiting transfer to the county jail. His mother hadn't wanted to discuss her physical condition when he saw her previously. It was time that changed.

The county jail was in Crimson Creek, a forty-five-minute drive from Prairieview. The Crimson Creek Police Department had recently undergone an administrative change due to unexpected developments that had come to light. Conrad knew that was HR talk for a dirty cop without airing the dirty laundry. According to a friend who worked for the CCPD, the department was in inexperienced hands that had survived the vetting but likely shouldn't have. Luckily, his mother wouldn't be under the questionable care of the CCPD but instead was being held at the Crimson Creek County jail, under the care of the Crimson Creek Sheriff's Department. He knew them to be a trustworthy department.

When he arrived, they told him that it would be a while before he was able to see her, as she was still getting checked in and settled in her cell after arriving earlier in the morning. He should have known better but had forgotten in his hasty attempt to avoid dealing with the pain of Miriam. For the next hour Conrad sat in a waiting room with his face buried in his phone in a desperate attempt to avoid dealing with his pain again.

"Sorry to keep you waiting, Officer Cain. You showed up right as she was getting checked in. You know she was in your neck of the woods just this morning, right?" a sheriff's deputy said as he entered the waiting room.

"Yeah, I know. I just wanted to see how she was doing, but she was already gone by the time I got to the station."

"Well, right this way."

The deputy escorted him to the visiting room, which was a large room with cafeteria style tables set up a respectable distance apart. When most people visited an inmate, they expected to see something like they had seen on television, such as a seat at a table with a length of plexiglass separating them from their loved ones. Those were only in the higher security prisons, while this was mainly a holding area for those that were awaiting trial.

Conrad took a seat at a table in the empty room and waited for his mother. He didn't have to wait long. Two minutes later, she entered escorted by a guard.

She was wearing the trademark orange jumpsuit that was most associated with prisoners. Seeing her in the prisoner garb made him seethe. He took a couple of deep breaths, calming his anger. He didn't want to let her see that side of him, instead he wanted to leave her with a good memory of him. There was no telling when he would have another chance to see her.

The scrape on her forehead was healing, which was good. It was the only good thing he saw, however. Her left eye was black, and there was a fresh scratch underneath that same eye. She was hunched over as she walked. Her gait was slow and shuffling, as though it was taking great effort just to walk. Again, he seethed. This time he didn't hide it.

"How are you doing, Mom? You don't look well."

"Oh, I'm fine. Don't worry about me," she said as she sat down next to him.

"Mom, you're in jail for murdering dad, and you've got a black eye. You're limping and you're finally looking your age. Sorry, but I'm worried about you. What happened. For real this time."

"What are you going to do?" she asked, looking him in the eyes.

"Depends on what you tell me. Not nothing, that's for sure."

"Conrad, I murdered a cop. It shouldn't surprise you that I was roughed up a little. It didn't surprise me, that's for sure. Your dad might have fallen from grace after the incident with you, but he's still held in pretty high regard around the department."

"I understand that, Mom, but I'm not hearing names."

"You want a name? Fine, Frank Hightower. He's the one with the dirty brother, you know. Your dad always suspected Frank was dirty, too. Never could prove it, though."

"What happened?"

"You think that man needs a reason? You're old enough to know that people don't always need a reason to carry out bad deeds. Evil is evil, Conrad. I learned that from your dad. No, your dad wasn't evil, but he did bad things, evil things. It's easier to give into that inner demon, to let it break down your resolve. Sinning feels good, makes you ugly on the inside, but it dang it, it feels good. Have you ever heard the saying that the higher road is the road less traveled? Well, that's a saying for a reason, Conrad. It's harder to be a better person, to say no to that demon. To resist. That's what I've done with your dad until now, until all this."

"What if I told you that it wasn't your fault? Would that help?"

"Hogwash. It's me, and I don't want to hear any outlandish conspiracies otherwise. I take responsibility for my actions, Conrad. I'll live with my sin. Besides, I don't have that long left anyway."

"You're not that old, Mom. You could be in here a long time."

"Conrad, I've got cancer. Doc says I've got less than a year left. That's probably why I did it, I guess. A moment of weakness, despite having forgiven your father," she said with a shrug.

"Mom?"

"I'm dying, Conrad."

With the sun setting on both the day and his entire world, Conrad Cain drove back to Prairieview with only one thought on his mind. Find Frank Hightower and make him pay.

44.

Conrad/Conner

Thrall: That was really sad, Conrad Cain. Did you ever see your dear mother again?

Conner: No.

Thrall: Too bad.

Conner: Shut up.

Thrall: There's more sadness ahead. Just wait.

The sun had fully set by the time Conrad entered Prairieview. That meant Frank's shift as a member of the PPD would be coming to an end. It would be easier to spot an officer in a police cruiser, but assaulting an officer in the line of duty was a good way to get shot. It was likely better this way. He kept alert as he made his way through town, scanning the streets for Frank's red truck.

Instead, he found the Macabre Media van parked in front of the gas station on the far side of town. With his thoughts returning to Miriam, Conrad pulled into the parking lot.

Gavin exited the gas station as Conrad got out of his SUV. They met at the van.

"I thought you were leaving town."

"That was the plan. I went to use the bathroom, and when I came out Miriam was gone. The door to the motel room was wide open. She couldn't have gone far, but I haven't been able to find her."

"Did you check the White House?"

Gavin rolled his eyes. "Of course, that's the first place I went. She wasn't there. I keep checking back every thirty minutes hoping to see her. I haven't."

"You should have called me."

"Sorry that I didn't think about calling the guy she's been screwing for three days when there was an emergency. It won't happen again."

"Alright, easy. I know a thing or two about looking for missing people is all I'm saying."

"Yeah, because you've done a real bang-up job with Bianca."

"Would you like my help or not? Either way, I'm looking for her."

Gavin nodded.

"Good. She's bound to go back to the White House sooner or later. It's got a pull on her. I'll wait there, stake the place out. You and Stu keep making the rounds around town. Call me if you find anything."

"You'll call me if she shows up?"

"Sure."

Hemingway Road was as quiet as he had ever seen it. Conrad didn't blame the residents, after all, two people had gone missing in the previous week. They didn't want to be next. Other than the occasional splitting of blinds as someone peered out at him, he hadn't seen anyone. Fear had Prairieview in its clutches. Conrad aimed to free it, but didn't know how to go about doing that just yet.

Frank Hightower thought he had the perpetrator behind bars. Conrad knew he was wrong. The closed blinds and glances out the window as he sat in his SUV indicated the neighborhood wasn't positive either. With Prairieview being the small town it was, they were all aware of Frank's reputation for sketchy police work. Their doors would remain locked, and their nerves still on edge.

The man responsible for both Bianca and Gabby's disappearances was still on the loose. Thrall, while obviously a subservient of a higher power of some kind, was responsible for their disappearance. He roamed the nights, coming and going as he pleased, seemingly taking whomever the White House desired, disappearing as quickly as Gabby had, as if by magic. It was time for the mythical man to atone for the sins that had been committed against the town of Prairieview. Conrad was watching for Miriam, who would likely show up here at some point, but there was a part of him that was desperate for Thrall to manifest onto Hemingway Road that evening.

There was an innocent man in prison. As a police officer, that went against everything Conrad stood for. Rusty had made a deal with Gavin to pull the wool over the eyes of the viewing public, which wasn't altogether innocent, but had played no part in the disappearances of anyone related to the White House. It was simply a case of being in the wrong place at the wrong time.

Conrad sat in the SUV for an hour but couldn't sit anymore, so he got out to stretch his legs. Moving helped him expend some of the energy caused by the agitation that had remained festering inside of him. He circled the block, while keeping the old Comisky place in his sights. He noticed an increased number of stares from the windows he passed as he walked the neighborhood. Eventually, he escaped their eyes by retreating to the SUV.

With plenty of rage and no coffee, he sat, waiting.

Hours passed with nothing to do but seethe at his current situation. His mother was in prison for a crime she had resisted for years, thanks to Thrall. He had been unable to solve the case of Bianca Nowitzki's disappearance. The wound from Gabby entering the house before his eyes had yet to heal. Fresh still was the wound of seeing his mother's beaten body at the hands of a man that wore the same uniform as him. He was on the verge of losing Miriam, if he hadn't lost her already.

Then a glimmer of hope appeared before him, walking across the middle of Hemingway Road.

Thrall.

Conrad started the engine without thinking. He kept the headlights off. He put the engine in gear. The engine revved as he pushed the gas pedal to the floor. Thrall filled the windshield as he switched on the headlights. Surprisingly, Thrall smiled. The smile was the last thing Conrad saw before the SUV's front bumper collided with the seemingly indestructible man.

Thrall: You saw the smile, right?

Conner: Yeah, I saw it. Why did you smile?

Thrall: You thought you pulled one over on me, but it was part of the plan. What happened next was fun. I enjoyed myself. I don't get to enjoy my work as often as I'd like.

Conner: You're sick.

Thrall: I know.

45.

Conrad/Conner

The police station was empty, which was strange considering they had a prisoner in the holding area. Cade Warren took over full-time night duties when Frank was moved to the daytime. There was a rumor that while Cade worked the weekend night shift he would sneak over to the gas station, where his girlfriend worked, for a quickie in the bathroom. It appeared the rumors were true. It was lucky for Conrad.

After unlocking the front door, he went back to the SUV to retrieve Thrall's body. The sight of the unbreathing man worried him at first sight. Then Conrad remembered that Thrall wasn't a living man, therefore, had no use for oxygen. That fact was confirmed when Thrall shifted his body while unconscious.

Thrall was a solidly built nonhuman in a human-like husk, so Conrad hadn't expected him to be light. He wasn't. In fact, Conrad was surprised at the density of the man's weight. It took all his strength to move Thrall from the backseat of the SUV to the lobby of the station, and out of sight.

Once in the comfort of the station, he retrieved an office chair with rollers and deposited Thrall onto the seat. Moving him to the holding area was much easier at that point.

The lights were off in the holding area. He switched them on as he entered.

"Morning already? Or is it another visit from officer sunshine?" Rusty called from his cell.

"Is that your nickname for Officer Hightower?"

"Oh, it's you."

"Hightower visits you? Puts his hands on you?"

Rusty looked at the ground. "Yeah. Keeps asking questions about where we take the girls, get rid of the bodies, you know? I keep telling him I'm not involved, that I'm just an actor. He doesn't want to hear it."

"Luckily, I believe you."

"Who's that?" Rusty asked, acknowledging the body in the chair for the first time.

"Meet the man you were impersonating, Rusty. This is Thrall, just Thrall. Kind of like Madonna but more dangerous."

"So that's the guy. He doesn't look so dangerous to me."

"Oh, he is. In fact, he's so dangerous that I'm going to put him in that cell so he can't hurt anyone else."

"Not with me. Please, not with me."

"How about I let you out then?"

Rusty wasted no time running out of the holding area and out of the station. Meanwhile, Conrad dropped Thrall onto the cot in the corner of the cell.

"Nighty night," he said as he switched off the light.

He was putting the office chair back in its place when there was movement at the front door. Rusty had been gone for five minutes. Conrad doubted the man would be coming back for any reason. The front door opened, revealing a familiar figure.

"Cade, is that your ride parked in front? The front fender is smashed all to hell."

Frank Hightower.

"It must be Christmas morning."

"Cain? What the hell are you doing here?"

"I could ask you the same thing."

It was the middle of the night and Hightower was dressed in all black. Whatever the officer was doing, it wasn't legal.

"You don't have any authority here, Cain. You're not even medically cleared for duty. I ought to arrest you for trespassing."

"I ought to arrest you for assault. My mom told me what you did to her, made her think it was her own fault."

"She killed a cop, Cain. She's a cop killer. She got what she deserved."

"Relax, Hightower. I'm not going to arrest you."

Hightower's shoulders relaxed.

A sinister smile spread across Conrad's face.

Sixty seconds later, Conrad had to force himself to stop punching the unconscious body of Frank Hightower. He thought unleashing his fury on the man would alleviate the tension that coursed through his body. Yet, it remained.

He deposited Hightower in the cell with Thrall, who was stirring in time to welcome his new cellmate. Conrad switched off the light in the holding area, and on his career as an officer.

The street was still lifeless as he drove down Hemingway Road. That was until he spotted the unmistakable black and red van of the Macabre Manor crew. The van looked empty, however, there was a commotion happening beside the van. Conrad slammed on the brakes, put the laboring SUV into park, and sprinted to the van.

"Stop! Miriam, Stop!"

He found an unexpected scene as he approached the van. Gavin was on the ground, half in and half out of the van's open sliding door. There were deep scratch wounds on his cheekbones, as if someone had tried to gouge out his eyes and missed. The producer held his hands up to block off another attack from Miriam. It wasn't necessary, however, as she had moved onto Stu, who had apparently pulled her off Gavin. With a hand that appeared more like a claw as it dripped fresh blood, Miriam eviscerated Stu's face. The cameraman's screams pierced the darkness, waking up the entire neighborhood.

Gavin sat in stunned silence, unable or unwilling to help his friend. Then his eyes fell upon Conrad for the first time.

"Where were you? You were supposed to be here waiting for her."

Conrad ignored him. "Miriam. I know you want to go in there, but—"

He was cut off as a knee found his groin. Pain exploded between his legs as he fell to the ground. He stared at Miriam's bare feet, the red and black alternating painted toenails filling his vision. Then they were gone.

In his peripheral vision he noticed two things. First, that Gavin wouldn't be any help. Second, the camera was still rolling. Amazingly, pointed at the altercation.

"Miriam," Conrad tried to scream, but it came out a whisper.

He pushed himself to his knees while turning toward the old Comisky place, where the White House supposedly stood. Miriam was already on the threshold of the rubble pile.

He forced himself to his feet, despite the excruciating pain.

A siren wrang out in the distance, whether it was intended for the police station or his current location, Conrad didn't know.

Look back.

Conner: Look back.

Thrall: She didn't look back.

She didn't look back.

Instead, she took another step and disappeared, becoming the White House's next victim.

46.

Conrad

There were tears in his eyes as Conrad stumbled out of the seventh and final room. Thrall came running out of the room immediately after him, as if the room had been on fire. The two men collided in the doorway and fell to the floor. The emotions of what happened behind the door were overwhelming, sapping the strength from his body, and leaving him without the ability to stand. So, he lay there on the ground, even as Thrall stood over him.

It was over. He had been forced to relive the sins committed ten years prior, when the White House first came into his life. He knew he had relived the seven deadly sins of lore, but why these specific sins? From his recollection there had been other times when he had been guilty of committing those sins, yet they remained free from whatever list the so-called demon, Thrall's master, had compiled. Was the power of the memories that accompanied those sins? Did the demon feed on the emotions that were evoked from Conrad reliving it?

What lay ahead? According to Thrall, Conrad was to meet the master upon exiting the seventh and final room. Yet, he was lying on the floor in the hallway on the seventh floor.

Was there even a master? Or was Thrall, aka Karl Bauman, truly in charge of the house? He didn't think so. Thrall was what he had always appeared to be, what his title implied, a slave to the White House and the demon that lurked somewhere in its midst.

Pain exploded in his ribs as Thrall kicked him. Conrad cried out in pain, while protecting himself as best he could. The powerful entity was undaunted by the maneuver and kept kicking. Instead of deflecting the pain, agony cried out in both his arms and his ribs. He knew he should get to his feet, and fight. The events of the day, however, had sapped all the fight out of him.

He was content to accept his fate, whatever that may have been.

"Did you really think I was Karl? I thought you were paying attention, Conrad Cain," Thrall said as he continued to kick.

He wasn't Karl Bauman? Then who was this man known as Thrall?

"Flummoxed, are you?"

"Yes!" Conrad screamed.

"I'm Albert," Thrall said, landing a kick that sent Conrad flying into the wall.

He spat blood on the floor and waited for the assault to continue.

"Stop! Albert Bauman, your fun is done. He is not yours to finish, but mine. Bring Conrad Cain to me."

The voice seemed to be coming from all around them, as if emitting from the house itself.

"Yessir," Albert said with reluctance in his voice.

A staircase appeared at the end of the hallway. Conrad's eyes were tear-filled, so he couldn't be sure, but he didn't think it had been there upon exiting the seventh room. He took it in stride. It was just another oddity among many that the White House displayed. He shuffled toward the staircase on feet that seemed to know what lay at the top of the staircase and were reluctant to expediate the trip.

"Let's go," Albert said, giving him a forceful shove in the back.

"What made you this way, Albert? How did you end up as the servant to a demon?"

"I suppose this is the time when the bad guy reveals his past, giving motivation for his misdeeds. Sure, I'll take the bait. I always blamed myself for my father's disappearance. My mother and brother told me that it wasn't my fault. That's what their words said, but their eyes said differently. They blamed me for not doing more to stop my father from going inside the house, this house. Truth be told, I blamed myself for a long time, but what could I have done? I was a teenager, little more than a child. My father was strong, both in body and in mind. As an immigrant farmer, he had to be or else he wouldn't have survived. People don't trust those that are different from themselves, even if all that is different is the way we look or the way we speak. The ignorance of others made him a stubborn man, holding his convictions above all else. No, I couldn't stop him. I know that now, but back then I didn't.

"The guilt kept mounting on my soul, until it became more than I could stand. You see, I knew my father to be a rational and sane man. If he had seen a house, then there was a house there. At the age of eighteen, when I became a man, I decided that I could stand it no more. I would go in search of my father and the house that had stolen him from me.

"You see, while I was at home, I had done research into a house of white that only certain people were able to see. While it was true that my father was the first that we know of, there were many others after. Stories and legends were written about those people, as was done with my father. I read them with great fervency, for my father wasn't crazy, as he had been made out to be. He had seen the White House, and maybe, just maybe, he was still alive.

"I spent years traveling around the country searching for the White House of lore, always one step behind. I talked to the loved ones of those that had fallen victim to the house. You see, they were like me, except they weren't. They wallowed in their despair, saturated in a disgusting display of self-pity. I could barely stand it. Then, I thought I could stand it no more, the White House appeared to me.

"It didn't appear to me because I was to be a victim. No, I had been chosen. The master had witnessed my tenacity and decided to show me favor. He is glorious, my master. I have served ever since."

"What about your father?" Conrad asked.

They were at the top of the stairs and had been for some time. Perhaps it was a stalling tactic, but Conrad wanted to hear the story.

"What about him?"

"Did you find him?"

"Yes. He is with the others that have been chosen by the master to serve as sustenance."

"Where is that?"

Albert smiled. "You'll find out."

Finally, Conrad pushed the door open to the attic. He was unsure what to expect as the door slowly swung open on rusty hinges. The room was large, spanning the entire length of the topmost level. As with most attics, the ceiling was lower than the floors below, just over six feet, meaning the top of his head grazed the rafters. It was empty, void of any of the usual junk that most people threw in their attic and forgot about. There weren't any high school yearbooks or photo albums, nor were there Christmas decorations that would only see the light of day for a month out of the year.

There was only a solitary statue on a black pedestal in the center of the room. The statue was simple; however, intricate details caught the eye the closer he walked. A jet-black snake with its body coiled as if resting. The head of the snake stood at attention, looking in the direction of the door to the attic, as if watching him.

Conrad stopped ten yards from the statue, not daring to go any closer. He circled the statue, feeling its eyes follow him around the room.

Albert dropped to his knees, prostrating himself before the idol.

"Creepy, but I thought I was going to meet the master, not some idol a crazy man worships."

"You will show the master respect, Conrad Cain!" Albert said, jumping to his feet.

"Albert Bauman, I will handle this. Hold your tongue."

"Yes, master. Sorry, master."

"Conrad Cain, you are not impressed with me in this form?"

"I went through hell reliving the memories of my past. I watched the lives of people I loved die while in those rooms. My mother died of breast cancer in prison because of a deed Albert convinced her to commit. I relived the most devastating moments of my life, moments I'll never get over. I think I deserve to see the quote unquote 'master' in all his blasphemous glory. So, no, I'm not impressed, Beelzebub."

"Oh, you flatter me, Conrad Cain, but I am not the dark one. This is not the fiery pits of Hades, and you are not in hell. I am simply one of those that serves the dark one, just as Albert serves me. This is simply a house, nothing more. Oh, I shouldn't say nothing more, for it is so much more than that. It exists outside the normal realm of time and space."

"Blah blah blah. Just show yourself."

"Be careful what you wish for, Conrad Cain."

The voice came out as more of a hiss than an actual voice, which was disturbing enough. Yet, even more disturbing was that the voice was no longer coming from the statue, but from directly behind him.

Conrad whirled around. A living embodiment of the statue was behind him. An enormous black snake was coiled as if ready to strike. The head of the snake was as big as his own head, and it brushed against the rafters holding the roof. The eyes of the snake glowed red and seemed to have hypnotic qualities. Once he looked into them, he couldn't look away.

"Not so tough now, are we?" the snake hissed.

Run, you idiot, run!

Despite the desperate call from his brain to flee, Conrad found that he couldn't. It was as if his entire body was frozen in place. His body broke out in a cold sweat. Tremors coursed through his body. The only movement he seemed capable of at the moment.

"Oh, your fear is so delicious. Mmmm. Perhaps I won't need to feed for a while."

Feed? What did that mean?

"How would you like to have Gabby back? Or Miriam? How does that sound?" it hissed.

Luckily, his voice seemed to be the only part of his anatomy capable of working. "What would it cost me?"

"What makes you think it would cost you anything?"

"Because you're a demon, not exactly a righteous creature. Also, that wasn't an answer."

The snake's black tongue flicked out of its mouth, tasting the air. "Your soul."

"Not a chance."

"I don't need it now. Just give it to me when you die. That way you can enjoy your time with Miriam. You would pick Miriam, right?"

Toby spit on the serpent in response.

"Fine. Albert, put our newest guest in the basement with the others."

"Yes, master."

Once the snake—he never did hear a name for the demon—had removed its gaze from him, Conrad found himself able to move again. That, however, didn't stop Albert from dragging him down eight levels to the basement.

Albert opened the door to the basement, revealing a staircase descending into darkness. Without warning, he hurled Conrad down the steps. He tumbled head over heels down the steps; thankful he had the wherewithal to tuck to his chin into his chest. It was a wonder he didn't suffer serious injury in the fall.

He landed on the dirt floor on his stomach. He thought about getting up but didn't. Until a voice from the past spoke to him.

"Are you going to lay there forever? Or are you going to get up and say hello?"

His head whirled around so fast that it gave him a headache. The puzzlement at the woman standing over him didn't help either.

Miriam stood with her hands on her hips, looking as beautiful as the day she had disappeared into the White House.

47.

Conrad

Conrad embraced Miriam. Tears filled his eyes as the memory of her disappearance washed over him. As they parted, she leaned in for a kiss. He turned awkwardly away. The last time they had seen each other, which was the last moment she had been outside of the house, they had been an item. He saw the confusion on her face. Then she looked down at his left hand and saw the ring on his finger.

"Married, huh? Well, that figures."

"I'm sorry, Miriam. It's been ten years. It was hard, but I moved on."

"Okay, fine. Well, tell me about your life now."

And so, he did. His eyes scanned the crowded basement as he spoke. There had to be more than a hundred people in the basement. All victims of the White House and the demon that controlled it.

He was finishing his story when Gabby approached. They hugged. Then he retold his story for her.

"So, do we call you Conrad or Conner?" Gabby asked when he finished.

"Conrad, I guess. I've got paperwork with Conner Keen on it, but it's fake. That's always felt like a lie because it was."

"Does your wife know?" Miriam asked.

Conrad shook his head while averting his eyes. His eyes locked on a middle-aged man in the corner of the basement.

Miriam saw him eyeing the man.

"Hanz Bauman. I've spent a long time trying to talk with him. He doesn't say much, other than that he blames himself. He knows his son is partly responsible."

Without saying a word to Miriam or Gabby, Conrad walked over to the man.

"It's not your fault, Hanz. What happened to Albert, I mean. His mind was corrupted by the demon that controls this house. Until your disappearance, Albert appears to have been a good kid, turning into a fine young man. You did a good job raising him. Don't let the sins of others weigh heavily on your soul."

There were tears in Hanz' eyes as he looked up at Conrad. "Thank you for the kind words, sir, but you're wrong. It is my fault. I know that the demon corrupted my boy. I don't blame myself for that. I blame myself for going into the house, for giving in to temptation. Knowing what I know now, I'd strike myself down before stepping foot in this hell. It would have saved Albert from becoming what he is now."

Conrad searched deep in his mind for words of wisdom to share with the mournful man and found himself empty. There were times when words weren't sufficient. This was one of those times. Instead, he patted the man on the shoulder and retreated across the basement.

Time was a peculiar thing inside the White House. Conrad had no way of knowing how long he had been within its walls or how long he had been in the basement. Therefore, he had no way of knowing how much time had elapsed from his retreat in his pursuit of comforting the heart of Hanz Bauman to the first twinge of smoke that touched his nostrils.

"Is this normal? The smell of smoke? We are dealing with a demon, after all," he asked both Gabby and Miriam.

Gabby shook her head. "No, it's not normal."

"Everyone, stick to the walls in case the floor above caves in," Miriam announced to the basement.

It was obvious that Miriam had been in the basement long enough to gain the respect of the other basement dwellers, because they moved without word to the walls of the basement. As if by premonition, the ceiling started to buckle. Then it collapsed.

A pile of burning rubble littered the basement floor, along with what looked like an ATV. As Conrad stared up at the hole in the ceiling, a rope fell from above, as if falling from the heavens.

"Climb this rope if you want to live," a familiar male voice said from above.

"Gavin?" Miriam asked.

Conrad grabbed the bottom of the rope and held it as the basement dwellers climbed one by one. Gabby and Miriam stood by his side the entire time, until finally it was their turn.

He emerged from the basement into a fiery hell that had once been the first floor of the White House. Gavin helped him to his feet, then turned to Miriam, who was lurking nearby. She stared at Gavin in disbelief, as if he were a new man. Perhaps he was. The Gavin Conrad had known ten years ago wasn't heroic, nor was he selfless. Time can do wonders, especially if that time was spent reliving a mistake over and over in your head.

"I'm sorry I wasn't more for you, Miriam, that I wasn't better. I don't know what will happen to you when we escape these walls, but I want you to know that I'm sorry," Gavin said.

"Thanks, but let's get out of here. We can talk about it later."

"I needed to say it, that's all. Again, I don't know what will happen to you outside of the White House."

"What do you mean, Gavin?"

"The demon feeds off the people that enter the house, I'm sure that much you've deduced by now. Food for a demon, that's what you are. The problem is that you've been trapped in purgatory for ten years, with it feeding off your soul, and leaving your body nothing more than a husk."

"Are you saying I'll die if I leave the house, Gavin?"

"I'm saying you might already be dead, Miriam."

"No, that can't be."

"It's not certain, but I've done a lot of research. It's what I'm afraid is true."

"Then why save me at all?"

"To save your soul. Plus, his wife made me," Gavin said, nodding toward Conrad.

"Carlisle? She's here?"

Conrad didn't wait for the answer but took off running in the direction he had seen the others. He came to a hole in the exterior wall.

Peering through the hole and into the White House was Carlisle.

Carlisle

48.

Carlisle

"There's a house there and I'm going to prove it."

The determination in Conner's voice was sexy as hell, and for a second she forgot what they were trying to accomplish by venturing further into the woods than they should have. She wanted to throw him down on the overturned tree that he had climbed onto, rip off his shirt and have her way with him. She liked to take control, and Conner seemed to enjoy it as well. There hadn't ever been complaints spoken aloud.

Her mind set, Carlisle gripped the hem of her blouse and started to disrobe as she walked toward the overturned tree where Conner stood. The cold air caressed the bare skin of her stomach. The blouse was up over her breasts, still covered by the bra, when she let it fall back into place.

Conner was gone.

Panic threatened to overwhelm Carlisle as time seemed to stand still. Her heart rate increased, and her breathing accelerated. She scanned the clearing for any sign of the husband that had gone from lucky enough to get screwed in public to just plain screwed in a matter of seconds. He had been standing on the overturned tree trunk, pretending he was about to enter a house. What had happened to him?

It was her fault. The realization flooded over her like a wave. He had been acting strangely for the past several days, practically crying out for her attention. She had been so caught up with the daunting schedule of the accelerated pace night class that she hadn't paid attention to how it was affecting her husband. It must have been hard for him to come home to an empty house every night. Was the house that obviously wasn't there simply a ploy to gain her attention? Conner wasn't that conniving or thoughtful. He was a simple man. It was one of the things she liked most about him, what you see was what you got with Conner Keen.

Or so it had seemed for a while. Carlisle was more and more aware that there was something in his past he wasn't telling her. Ten years into their relationship and she still knew next to nothing about his past before they met, aside from the fact that he was from Kansas and that all his family was dead. There were unresolved issues there for him to deal with, yet how could she help him deal with those issues if she didn't know what they were?

A therapist had been the obvious answer. Conner wouldn't hear anything about it. Being the resourceful woman that she was, Carlisle decided that she would be the mediator between Conner and the best therapist she knew, PJ. A few times per week, they would meet to discuss Conner and what she knew about his past. PJ would then give her a list of questions and tactics she could use to help draw the truth out of her husband. This had been occurring for over a month with no true results.

A large problem had arisen in the process, however. Carlisle realized PJ was only involved in the mock therapy sessions in an attempt to sleep with her, while Conner thought they were already sleeping together. Part of her wanted to see her husband fight for her, even if it meant PJ would be collateral damage. Yet, something worse happened. Conner didn't seem to care. He didn't fight for her.

Now, he had left her alone in the woods.

Fifteen minutes and a search of the surrounding area later, Carlisle came to the realization that he had truly vanished into thin air. He wouldn't have left her. They were both aware he had married above his level. Something had happened to him. Instead of panicking, she sprang into action.

She pulled her phone out of the pocket of her slacks and dialed a familiar number. Five minutes later, a flashlight fumbling through the woods signaled the arrival of PJ.

"So, you wanted a romp in the woods, huh?" he said when he saw her standing in the clearing.

"Will you give it a rest, PJ? I'm not going to have sex with you. I'm married."

"That didn't stop Leslie Harding."

"Well, that's because Leslie Harding married for money, while I married for love."

"Love? You've got to be kidding me."

"Have you ever thought about self-diagnosing your perpetual womanizing, PJ? Perhaps you're sleeping with your mother over and over."

"Freudian, really? Actually, I happen to have a fear of commitment that is derived from a heartbreak that happened in high school. Every time I sleep with a new woman, it's as if I'm proving to Samantha that I'm worth a damn. Yes, I have self-diagnosed."

"Enough about your woman problems, PJ. I need help finding Conner."

"Finding Conner? What happened?"

She explained what had happened between them over the course of the previous few days as quickly as she could.

"Well, Let's find Conner," PJ said when she was finished.

An hour later, it was obvious that Conner was nowhere to be found. She had even gone back to the house to make sure he hadn't stormed off in a huff and was waiting for her back home.

"So, what next?" PJ asked, looking at his watch.

"It's not like him to just take off like that. I mean, sure, we've had some arguments. He just goes to the bar and drinks."

"That's probably where he is. Check the bars. Give it some time."

"I don't know."

"Carlisle, you've said yourself, he's an alcoholic. Alcoholics drink. It's what they do. He has a pattern of behavior established. Give him until morning. If he's not back, then it's time to worry."

She didn't like it, but she knew PJ was right. Reluctantly, she walked home. PJ wanted to come inside. She shut the door in his face.

"He just disappeared. As in, he was there one second and gone the next?" Deputy Dwight Adcock asked with a skeptical raise of the eyebrow.

"I know how it sounds, Dwight. You don't have to raise that eyebrow and use the skeptical cop tone with me. I remember when you were taking my class to pick up chicks, and as I recall, that's where you met Jainy."

"Mrs. Keen, I'm just doing my job. You're in charge in the classroom, but right now I'm in charge. Got it?"

"Does Jainy like it when you get forceful? I bet she does."

"Mrs. Keen, let's focus on your husband. Why were you out here?"

Carlisle hesitated, fearing how Conner would be perceived. Then she decided to go for it, holding nothing back that might help the Sheriff's Department deputy.

"He had been seeing something in the woods across the street from our house. I didn't see it. He couldn't believe I couldn't see it, so we came out to investigate. I thought he was just trying to get me alone in the woods for a quickie or something."

"Right. What was it that he saw?"

"A house."

Deputy Dwight raised an eyebrow. "Your husband thought he saw a house in the woods across the street from your house? I've lived in this town all my life, Mrs. Keen, and I don't remember there ever being a house back here."

"I know, I know. That's why I didn't take him seriously at first. He knows as well as I do that there's never been a house here, but he was convinced. I finally decided to humor him. He disappeared while we were out here."

Deputy Dwight looked skeptical.

"That was last night, correct?"

Carlisle nodded.

"And you waited until this morning to call?"

"Yes. Look, Conner has a drinking problem. He doesn't think he has a problem, but he does. We came out here, like I said. He was adamant the house was here. I didn't see the house, which upset him. When he's upset, he drinks. I checked the bars last night after leaving here. They hadn't seen him. After multiple rounds around the local bars, I came home. I couldn't sleep, so I came back out and looked around some more. No sign of him. At first light, I realized there was definitely something wrong, so I called you guys."

"Given his history, Mrs. Keen, I think it's best that we give him some more time. You said it yourself; he's an alcoholic. He's probably out drinking somewhere. I'm sure he'll be home when he sobers up."

Carlisle glared at her former student. "No, Dwight. That's not good enough. He's a functioning alcoholic. He's got a routine. Sure, he drinks when we have a fight, but he usually does that at home. He doesn't like to worry me. We are going to get a search party organized, either your department can be involved in that and be helpful or I'll do it on my own. Either way, I'm going to find my husband."

As it turned out, Deputy Dwight and the Sheriff's department decided that it wanted to be helpful, rather than face the alternative. The alternative being made a mockery of in the media as Carlisle formed and led a search party without their help. She didn't care whether they helped or not, in her mind, she was the only one with the willpower to find Conner.

Within an hour, a group fifty strong was combing the woods for any sign of Conner. They comprised mostly of law enforcement officers from various agencies, with some colleagues and students from Crestview College mixed in. The woods were dense, surrounding the town of Crestview in its entirety. It would take all the manpower they could gather to locate her missing husband.

She spotted Pastor Becky in the group of searchers and ensured they would be next to each other. Carlisle had some questions for her husband's "therapist."

"Have you noticed anything peculiar about Conner recently?" she asked, struggling to match the long strides of her partner.

With her faded denim jeans, red flannel shirt, and brown hair that had only just started to show signs of gray, Pastor Becky looked just at home in the woods as she did at the pulpit. The older woman turned those kind eyes upon her—Conner was right, she really did have kind eyes—and smiled.

"Other than the fact that he doesn't like to talk about his past?" Pastor Becky waited for Carlisle to nod. "I texted him two, maybe three days ago, about getting together for our usual monthly coffee. I didn't get a reply, which isn't like him. The trouble with men like Conner is you can't push them. If I push too hard or if they realize you're trying to save their soul, well, they'll run as quick as they can. So, I didn't push. Now, I wish I had."

Silence hung in the air as they continued walking in the woods.

"You're right. I tried to probe into what was troubling him and he only pushed me away. Now, he's the one that's away."

Pastor Becky laid a hand on her shoulder. "Lost is what he is, dear. What was lost can be found. With God anything is possible."

The sun was going down when they finished searching for the day. Carlisle wanted to keep going, but logic overruled her. Searching in the dark wasn't safe. It would do no good if someone else got lost while searching in the dark. With resignation, she followed the group out of the woods.

A dozen cameras were awaiting her as she stepped onto the street. They sniffed out the grieving spouse, like vultures to a rotting carcass.

She took a deep breath and addressed the media throng.

"My husband, Conner Keen, is missing. He was last seen in these woods directly behind me, just last night. If anyone has seen him, please contact the Sheriff's Office. Here's a recent picture," she said, holding up a photo of them together taken at Christmas the previous year.

Questions rang out from the group of reporters. A local reporter was the loudest, however.

"Mrs. Keen, what was your husband doing in the woods last night?"

"My husband saw something in the woods over the course of the last few days. We were investigating what he saw when he disappeared."

"What did he see?" a young reporter with enough gel in his hair to withstand a gale force wind asked.

"He saw a house, a white house. Now, if you'll excuse me, it's been a long day."

A hot shower and crawling into bed were the only things on Carlisle's mind as she opened the front door. Her body was exhausted from a day spent trekking through the woods with no sleep. Bear had other ideas, however. The large dog had been confined to the house the entire day. Seeing the open door as she entered, Bear, who was waiting at the door, sprang through the opening, and into the front yard.

This had happened before, usually when they had been away from the house for the day. Bear would run into the front yard with a full bladder, relieve himself at the tree in their yard, then romp back to the house with his tail wagging.

Unfortunately, that wasn't what happened this time.

Bear bypassed the tree in the front yard and entered the street. Carlisle watched from the front porch, fearing the dog was headed for the throng of reporters that were camping out in the street outside of the house. Bear, however, bypassed the reporters as well.

"No, not the woods. Anything but the woods, Bear."

That was exactly where the Newfy went.

Carlisle sighed as she gave chase.

Five minutes later, she found Bear whining in the clearing where Conner had gone missing. The dog's eyes were staring at the overturned tree where Carlisle had last seen her husband.

"Come on, Bear."

The dog didn't move. Instead, he whimpered louder.

"Bear, Let's go!"

Bear turned to look at her. There was a pleading quality to his eyes, as if imploring her to see what he saw.

"What is it, boy? Do you smell Dad?"

Bear whimpered as he turned back to the tree. An obvious yes.

Carlisle remembered a bag of beef jerky a fellow searcher had thrust into her hands midafternoon, imploring her to eat, that she needed her energy. She had eaten a few pieces to placate the motherly woman but hadn't finished the bag. It would work in the place of a dog treat.

It took the rest of the bag, but she managed to get Bear back home. Now, if she could only do something similar to Conner.

At first light the next morning, Carlisle was dressed and ready for another day of searching. She was preparing a thermos of coffee—the caffeine was needed, despite her dislike of the bitter brew—when the doorbell rang.

She looked at the clock on the wall with surprise. Who could it be at this hour? Thinking it could have been a detective with information about Conner, Carlisle ran to the front door.

The man she found standing on the front porch obviously wasn't a detective. He had the five o'clock shadow of a man that had forgone shaving that morning in favor of getting things done. There were bags underneath his eyes. Those eyes had the haunting quality of a man that had seen some things and would rather not talk about it. The most obvious indication that he wasn't a cop was the van parked in front of her house. It was black with Macabre Media written in red letters on the side.

"Good morning, Mrs. Keen. I'm sorry to bother you this early, but I thought you'd be awake given your current situation. My name is Gavin Huxley. I'm the producer and host of a YouTube show called Macabre Manor."

"That's wonderful, Mr. Huxley, but I'm very busy this morning. I've got to search for my husband," she said, starting to shut the door.

"You won't find him."

"Excuse me?"

"You won't find him, not without me."

"Do you know something that I don't, Mr. Huxley?"

Huxley smiled. "Yes, ma'am, I do. Your husband saw a house, a white house, to be more precise. Your husband is trapped in that house. We can save him, but we're running out of time."

49.

Carlisle

"So, let me get this straight. You think my husband is trapped in this White House with Thrall, who is a slave to the house, and possibly to a demon, but you're not sure if there is a demon or if it's just the house that is in control of him. No one has ever gotten out of the White House, and you can't prove any of this because everyone that has ever seen it has disappeared. The demon or the house feeds on them, sapping all of their life force until they die. You can't prove any of it, but I should believe you because you were abusive to your ex-girlfriend, and you feel really bad about it. Does that seem about right, Mr. Huxley?"

"I wouldn't have put it quite that way, but, yeah, that about sums it up," Huxley said.

"You know, I know a very good psychologist. In fact, he lives next door. Perhaps you'd like a word with him."

"Funny. Look, Mrs. Keen—"

"Carlisle, please."

"Look, Carlisle, I don't know how much time your husband has. I've been chasing this house for ten years, if I can get the truth out, then maybe I can keep someone else from going inside that house. If we're lucky, maybe we save your husband."

"Why should I trust you?" Carlisle asked as she watched the group of searchers gathering at the edge of the woods.

"Because I know your husband. I know that Conner Keen isn't his real name. I know he's from Kansas, where…"

Huxley must have noticed the perplexed expression on her face, because he stopped.

"Wait. You don't know what happened in Kansas, do you?"

She shook her head, reluctant to admit how little she knew about her husband's backstory.

Gavin pulled a newspaper clipping out of the pocket of his jacket. "Oh, have I got a story for you. In those days he went by Conrad Cain. Officer Conrad Cain."

Police Have Suspect in Triple Murder

In a shocking turn of events, two officers were found dead at the Prairieview Police Department last week. The deceased officers are twenty-six-year-old Cade Warren and fifty-two-year-old Frank Hightower. Warren was a rookie paying his dues by working weekend and night shifts. At the time of this writing there wasn't word on what Hightower was doing at the station overnight. Complicating matters is the identity of the third victim, fifty-five-year-old Leonard Hightower. The disgraced former PPD officer was in custody following the double murder of Gerald Bunting and Judge Milton Hightower.

Rusty Pendergast, who was in custody for the murder of Bianca Nowitzki, was locked in one of the four cells in the small prison. Rusty, who goes by the alias Thrall, is believed to be armed and dangerous.

Former PPD officer, Conrad Cain, is a person of interest wanted for questioning in the incident.

"We've reviewed the footage. Unfortunately, it was damaged, and we were unable to confirm what happened inside the station that night. What we do know is Conrad Cain showed up with what appeared to be either an

unconscious man or a dead body. That much we can see from the security footage on the bank across the street. Why?"

The whereabouts of Conrad Cain are unknown at this time. The five-year officer hasn't reported for duty since the incident and is believed to have skipped town. Possibly with Pendergast.

"That's a lot to take in, Gavin. I'd love to believe you, but I really need to find my husband."

"I'll make you a deal, Carlisle. I'm going to stick around, film a few episodes for the show. While I'm not doing that, I'll help with the search. We had our differences back then, your husband and myself, but I liked him. I only ask that you show me where the house is, maybe do an interview for the show if you feel so inclined. Deal?"

"Deal. Let me grab Bear. He's in need of a walk. Then I can show you."

"Bear?"

"Don't worry, he's not a real bear. He's a dog that's as big as a bear."

"Splendid."

While it was true that Bear needed a walk, it wasn't why she brought the dog along. She still didn't trust Gavin, therefore, didn't want to be alone with him. Bear had a protective streak when it came to Carlisle. Her hope was that the one-hundred-and-fifty-pound dog would give the man second thoughts about pulling anything on her. If that didn't work, there was always the mace that was attached to her keychain. Taking precautions was something she taught the young ladies in her class; she followed her own advice.

It didn't take long to trek through the woods to the spot where Conner had gone missing. She had taken the same route multiple times in the thirty-six hours since he had gone missing. Remembering the way proved to be unnecessary, because Bear knew the way and was uncharacteristically pulling hard on the leash. Once they were safe in the woods, she unhooked the leash, letting Bear run.

They caught up with Bear in the clearing, where he was sitting in front of the overturned tree. The dog's eyes stared intently up at the sky, as if seeing something that neither Huxley nor Carlisle could see.

"This is the spot where Conner went missing. Bear got out last night and ran straight here. I don't know why. It's like he sees something that we don't," she said as they watched the dog.

"The White House. Bear can see the White House. I've seen this type of behavior before with the pet of a missing person. It's like they sense their owner is nearby. Other animals go out of their way to avoid it. Did you notice the lack of animals nearby? Besides the creepy owl that always seems to lurk near the house."

"Yeah, it's creepy. These woods are usually teeming with wildlife. Tell me, has this always been a solo gig for you?"

Huxley was silent for a long time. She didn't think he was going to answer when he finally spoke.

"No. Back when I met your husband there were two others working with me. It's funny. They thought I was mysterious and dangerous when in reality I just paid people off. Anyway, Miriam was the host of the show, and a brilliant one at that. She became a victim of the White House, mostly due to my lack of action and ineptitude. I've been the host since that day. Stu, our cameraman, left shortly after it became apparent we weren't going to be able to bring her back. He resented me for my actions that led to her going inside the house. I don't blame him for it, because I resent myself."

"Was it your fault?"

"It's more complicated than a simple yes or no. Directly, no. But I exposed her to the house, brought her along all across the country. I put her in danger, despite caring for her deeply. The moment she saw the house I should have left. I didn't. She hooked up with Conner upon coming to town. I was jealous of their relationship and wanted to see him in pain. So, I stuck around, grinding salt into the fresh wound. It was stupid, but I was a stupid man back then."

"We all make mistakes, Gavin. That's part of life. It's how we respond to those mistakes that matter. You've traveled the country trying to inform the public about the White House. That's something."

"I wish it were enough."

"If it helps me find my husband, maybe it is enough."

"Are you saying that you believe in the White House?"

"No. I don't believe in things that I don't see. It's the reason I've never been very religious. I'm going to continue to look for my husband, while keeping our agreement in mind, like an insurance policy. I hope I don't have to use it, but it'll be nice to have if we aren't able to find him."

"Would you care to invest in your insurance policy by participating in an interview for the channel?" Huxley asked, pulling out a camera from his backpack.

"I'll do anything to find Conner. I'd walk through hell for that man."

"Funny you should say that, because if the house is what I think it is, you may have to."

50.

Carlisle

The next two days were a whirlwind of searching and helping Gavin with aspects of the Macabre Manor program. It all seemed futile as she trekked through the woods to the spot where Conner had gone missing, a routine she had gotten into the habit of. The search had been fruitless, with the hope of finding him being sapped from the group with each passing day. She had overheard some of the volunteers discussing whether it was worth coming out for another day. She knew few would be back for another day without being paid to do so.

Despite the rest of the community losing hope of finding Conner, Carlisle was still hopeful. That hope wasn't as high as it had been on day one, and she wondered how long it would last until she was resigned to the fact that her husband wasn't coming back. That wasn't now, however. She still felt it in her heart that Conner was alive. Wouldn't she know it in her heart if he were dead? Wouldn't there be a void left in her heart? A lost connection? She thought so yet still felt that same connection they had possessed since the day they met.

Gavin kept his word, helping with the search for Conner while also filming content for the YouTube channel. He was an intriguing character. She still didn't believe in the White House but believed that he believed in it. With each passing hour, the insurance policy became more appealing, and the hope that was lost was transferred to the White House that Gavin so desperately needed to be real.

No, she didn't believe in the White House. A fact that changed when she entered the clearing and found herself staring at a seven-story tall Victorian style house hidden in the woods.

"What brought on this change of mind, if I may ask?" Gavin asked.

They were standing in the clearing. Carlisle's gaze was locked on the White House. It beckoned to her without words. Yearning for her to enter, to explore its halls.

Gavin seemed to notice her gaze and silence.

"You see it, don't you?"

She didn't answer.

He snapped a finger in front of her face.

"You see the White House."

It was a statement, not a question.

"Yes."

Carlisle took a lighter out of her pocket and flicked it with her thumb, creating a flame. Gavin watched her with disinterest, likely thinking it was the habit of a smoker. She didn't smoke.

He turned his head, staring at the place he knew the house to be.

"What do you want to do? You should probably get far a—"

His words were cut off by the sound of glass shattering against a solid wall. Flames ignited in the bushes nearby. He turned to Carlisle with a puzzled expression.

"A Molotov cocktail, Gavin. I won't let a house keep me from rescuing my husband. My neighbor with the Corvette in the driveway has an ATV in the garage. The door is usually open. Go get it. The keys are in the ignition. If he gives you trouble, tell him it's for me. That should do the trick."

"Why do we need an ATV?"

"I'm going to drive it through the wall of the house."

"Why don't you go get it?"

"I can't move. The house. It's making me stay here. Can't think clearly."

Carlisle didn't see Gavin leave. Her attention was on the White House that was now engulfed in flames.

An unknown amount of time later, she heard the high throttle whine of an approaching engine. She was so mesmerized by the house that was being engulfed in flames that she completely forgot about the man that had gone to retrieve the ATV.

Sweat glistened on her forehead. She knew that she should step away from the house, yet her feet refused to cooperate. Instead, she watched the flames dance up the exterior wall transforming the White House into the house of orange.

A bee buzzed nearby, which was strange considering both the late hour and the time of year. She was allergic, hopefully it wouldn't sting her. Absentmindedly, she swatted at the bee with a hand, while keeping her attention on the house.

"Get out of the way!"

The shout came from behind her. It was the man that had left to get…something. What was his name? Carlisle couldn't remember. Why was he yelling at her? All she wanted to do was stare at the house. It was beautiful. She wished the flames would go away so she could see it more clearly, they were starting to obscure the house.

"Carlisle! Move!"

It was the man again. Still yelling.

She glanced back at him. He was riding an ATV of some kind, weaving through the trees. In fact, he was heading straight for her. That wouldn't do. If he ran into her, then she wouldn't be able to watch the house. That wouldn't do at all.

At the last second, she took two steps to her right. The man on the ATV drove right through the spot she had vacated.

Good, she thought, *now I can watch the house uninterrupted.*

There were more bees now. In fact, a hole swarm of them, though she couldn't see them. Was that infernal racket coming from the machine the man was riding. She turned her head in its direction, wishing it would stop. As she watched, the ATV accelerated up a slight embankment. At the top of the embankment, the ATV caught air.

"No!" she screamed.

She could do nothing about it. The man riding the ATV collided with the side of the house. He disappeared inside; a hole left in his wake.

At that moment, it was as if the fog had been lifted from Carlisle's mind.

"Gavin!"

There was a cacophony of bangs as the ATV landed somewhere in the White House.

She stood in the woods watching the burning house, afraid to enter in case it triggered whatever trance it had put on her.

Five minutes later, people started escaping the White House. Lots of people. None of them made it very far before they collapsed onto the ground. Carlisle was staring at a young woman, who had collapsed at her feet, when the woman disappeared.

She took a step back from the woman and looked around in shock. They were all disappearing, as if they were spirits that weren't meant for this realm.

Her eyes darted across the crowd of vanishing people for Conner. He had to be among them. He wasn't.

"Carlisle!"

It was Conner, emerging from the house. He was battered and bloody, but he was alive. She ran to him.

He took two steps out of the White House and into the clearing, then collapsed at her feet.

Epilogue

Conrad awoke in a hospital bed the next morning, groggy and unsure about what had happened. Carlisle was sitting in a chair beside the bed, holding his hand despite being asleep. He watched her sleep, thankful for the ability to do so. Memories of the White House and what had happened slowly came back to him over the course of the next five minutes. It hadn't been a dream, that much was clear, but he was still unsure of what exactly had happened within its walls.

What had happened to the rest of the White House's occupants that had been trapped in the basement with him? He had seen them escape the house, though there had been doubt about their ability to survive in the outside world considering the demon had feasted on their souls. The demon had feasted on Conrad's soul, yet he was alive. Hopefully, the same was the case for them.

In all the madness, there had been no sign of Thrall as the group made their escape. Conrad would have thought the demon's slave would have tried to prevent them from escaping. In a way, Albert Bauman had been a prisoner of the White House, just like everyone that had escaped the basement. The only difference was that he had entered into the contract with the demon willingly, though likely without all of the information on the cost to his soul. Conrad hoped that with the demon weakened with the fire to the house that fed it, Albert had taken the opportunity to free himself from its shackles.

"Good morning, Conrad," Carlisle said.

"You called me Conrad."

"I did."

"There are some things I need to tell you. About my past, I mean."

"Later. Gavin filled in some of the information, but I'd like to hear it from you. For now, I just want to be with you."

Conrad was in the hospital for two days recovering from smoke inhalation and exhaustion. Carlisle took the liberty of filling him with some information he had missed. Three days had elapsed while he was inside of the White House, which explained the exhaustion. During that span, he had nothing to eat or drink, causing serious fatigue to his body in the process. Any longer and he wouldn't have survived.

Sadly, he was the only person that had made it out of the White House. Carlisle witnessed the previous victims of the house escape, though it had only been their spirits freed from purgatory. Yet, he took comfort in the fact that their souls would no longer suffer but would be able to rest in peace.

His identity had yet to be revealed, however, Conrad's appearance hadn't changed much over the previous ten years. Authorities would soon seek answers to what had happened in Kansas. Rusty overdosed on heroin shortly after escaping from jail. That made Conrad the only remaining person who knew what had happened. They would come. He would go willingly when they did.

Carlisle had seen the White House with her own eyes, having been claimed as its next victim. The combination of the fire she started and the breach of the house by the outside world had broken the demon's grip on her, causing whatever spell it had under her to break. Within minutes, the house disappeared, leaving her to explain the bushfire she had started to the authorities that were beginning to respond.

Somehow, she managed to deflect blame, avoiding jailtime. Conrad figured her aloofness caused by the White House's spell had worked in her favor.

Gavin also could have pulled the right strings in the form of opening his wallet. It was hard to tell; the man disappeared before Conrad was out of the hospital. The grief of seeing Miriam again only to lose her was the likely culprit.

They walked out of the Crestview hospital hand in hand.

Upon arriving home, they both sighed as PJ started walking to the SUV before they had even exited the vehicle. Neither was in the mood. Conrad had confronted his wife with his worries, taking advantage of the newfound openness they were experiencing with their emotions. Carlisle hadn't been cheating, of course. Instead, she had been consorting with PJ over Conrad's deception and withholding of his past. She admitted it had been underhanded, but both agreed he had given her no other choice considering his refusal to have a conversation about his past.

"Get rid of him. I've been spending so much time with him that he wants to screw me. Worse, he might think I want to screw him," she said as they got out of the car.

"Can I screw him?" he said, fidgeting with the tie clip that was still in his pocket.

"Be my guest. I'll see you inside."

Carlisle hurried inside as PJ approached. Conrad thought the man looked a little disappointed to see her go.

He flipped the tie clip at PJ without warning. Annoyingly, the psychologist caught it deftly in his left hand.

"PJ, I've been thinking. I'd like to speak to someone about starting therapy."

PJ raised an eyebrow. "Therapy, really? Well, I'd be happy to handle the matter myself. I'll have to look at my schedule."

"There are some unresolved issues in my past. Things that I thought I'd worked through resurfaced recently. How often do you usually have sessions?"

PJ was silent.

"PJ? Are you okay?" Conrad asked.

No answer. The psychologist's eyes were locked on the treetops across the street.

Conrad snapped a finger in front of PJ's face.

"Are you alright?"

"Do you see a house across the street? I can just make out the crest of the roof from here."

"A house? What color is it? White?"

PJ shook his head. "No. It's black, as if it's been damaged by a fire."

There was movement in the peripheral of Conrad's vision. A dark, shadowy figure slipped into the trees a few houses down. It almost looked like Albert Bauman.

A Note from the Author

Thank you for entrusting me with the responsibility of directing the movie of your mind. If you enjoyed this book, do me a favor and leave a review wherever this book was purchased. As an independent author, reviews are invaluable in helping others discover this book.

Thanks again,
Stephen Roth

About the Author

Stephen Roth lives in Wichita, Kansas with his wife and four children. He is also the author of Reel Ghosts, available on Amazon. Visit Stephenmichaelroth.com for more information about Stephen.

Selected Letters of Hamlin Garland

Hamlin Garland

Edited by Keith Newlin and

Joseph B. McCullough

University of Nebraska Press

Lincoln and London

Publication of this book was assisted by a grant
from the University of Nevada, Las Vegas, and from
the University of North Carolina at Wilmington.

∞ The paper in this book meets the minimum
requirements of American National Standard for
Information Sciences – Permanence of Paper
for Printed Library Materials, ANSI Z39.48-1984.

Library of Congress Cataloging in Publication Data
Garland, Hamlin, 1860–1940.
[Correspondence. Selections]
Selected letters of Hamlin Garland / edited by Keith
Newlin and Joseph B. McCullough.
p.   cm.
Includes bibliographical references and index.
ISBN 0-8032-2160-6 (cloth: alkaline paper)
1. Garland, Hamlin, 1860–1940 – Correspondence.
2. Authors, American – 19th century – Correspon-
dence. 3. Authors, American – 20th century – Cor-
respondence. I. Newlin, Keith. II. McCullough,
Joseph B. III. Title.
PS1733.A44 1998 813′.52–dc21 [B] 97-15356 CIP

CONTENTS

ILLUSTRATIONS

Acknowledgments

I N THE PREPARATION of this volume we have incurred many debts. We wish especially to thank Hamlin Garland's daughters, Isabel Garland Lord and Constance Garland Doyle, for their permission to publish Garland's letters and, after their deaths, Garland's granddaughter, Victoria Doyle-Jones, for reaffirming that permission.

We are enormously grateful to the following libraries, which gave us access to their collections and granted permission to publish Garland's letters: the American Academy of Arts and Letters; Bancroft Library, University of California, Berkeley; the Boston Public Library; Special Collections and Manuscripts, Brigham Young University; Rare Book and Manuscript Library, Columbia University; Manuscript Division, Library of Congress; Special Collections Library, Duke University; Hampden-Booth Theatre Library, the Players Club, New York; Houghton Library, Harvard University; the Huntington Library, San Marino, California; the Indiana Historical Society; the Lilly Library, Indiana University; Seymour Library, Knox College; Walter Havighurst Special Collections, Miami University; Starr Library, Middlebury College; National Archives and Records Administration; the Newberry Library; Northwestern University Library; Rare Books and Manuscripts Division, the New York Public Library; Division of Rare Books and Manuscripts, Ohio State University Libraries; the Historical Society of Pennsylvania; Special Collections, the Pennsylvania State University Libraries; the Pierpont Morgan Library; the Pulitzer Prize Office, Columbia University; Southwest Museum, Los Angeles; Special Collections, Syracuse University Library; Manuscripts Department, Howard-Tilton Memorial Library, Tulane University; Special Collections, Shields Library, University of California, Davis; Special Collections, University of Chicago Library; University of Delaware Library, Newark; Rare Book and Special Collections Library, University of Illinois at Champaign-Urbana; University of Illinois Archives; University of Iowa Libraries, Iowa City; Western History Collections, University of Oklahoma; Special Collections, University of Pennsylvania Library; Special Collections, University of Southern California Libraries; Harry Ransom Humanities Research Center, University of Texas at Austin; Special Collections, University of Virginia Library; Wagner College Library, Staten Island; the State Historical Society of Wisconsin; Yale Collection of American Literature, Beinecke Rare Book and Manuscript Library, Yale University. For permission to publish photographs held in their collections, we are grateful to Special Collections, Miami University Library; and to the Hamlin Garland Collection, University of Southern California Library.

In annotating and transcribing the letters we have been greatly aided by Janice McIntire and Pamela Cantrell, graduate research assistants for Joseph McCullough, and by J. Trent Leonard, undergraduate assistant for Keith Newlin. For their prompt answers to many queries, general encouragement, and assistance we are especially grateful to John Ahouse, Curator of Special Collections, University of Southern California; and C. Martin Miller, Head of Special Collections, Miami University. The reference and interlibrary loan staff of the University of North Carolina at Wilmington Library have been extraordinarily helpful, in particular Madeleine Bombeld, Mary Corcoran, Donna Gunter, M. Louise Jackson, and Sophie Williams.

We are indebted to Kenneth M. Price and Robert C. Leitz III for allowing us to publish their annotations to Garland's letters to Walt Whitman, which originally appeared as "The Uncollected Letters of Hamlin Garland to Walt Whitman," *Walt Whitman Quarterly Review* 5 (1988): 1–13. Errol Kindschy of the West Salem Historical Society patiently answered questions about Garland's family history. Our deep gratitude too to Donald Pizer, James Nagel, Jackson Bryer, Don L. Cook, James Justus, Christoph Lohmann, Joseph McElrath, and Lee Schweninger for their encouragement, helpful suggestions, and assistance at various stages of this project.

The preparation of this volume was made possible in part by generous grants to Newlin from the National Endowment for the Humanities, Summer Stipends Program; and from the University of North Carolina at Wilmington, Charles Cahill Faculty Research and Development Fund and the College of Arts and Sciences Summer Initiative program, and other generous support. We are also indebted to the University of Nevada, Las Vegas, for generous assistance to McCullough for travel to research collections over the years and other support. Keith Newlin would like to thank Robin, Michael, and Sarah Holowaty for their cheerful support and steady enthusiasm. Finally, Joe McCullough would like to thank Judy, again, for her usual patience and good humor and Jessica for being his best buddy ever.

General Introduction

As he neared the end of a long and varied literary life, Hamlin Garland mused in a letter to the critic Van Wyck Brooks: "I have gone beyond any illusions about my career. Few are interested in me now and no one will be interested in me tomorrow" (31 August 1939, letter 394). Despite his pessimism about the value of his contribution to American literature, Garland has continued to attract a steady and growing body of critical work. Born on a farm near West Salem, Wisconsin, on 14 September 1860, Garland took a modest first step in launching his literary career in March 1885 with the publication of his first story, the Hawthornesque "Ten Years Dead." Within six years a flood of stories, verse, and essays arguing for a native realism attracted the epithet, "That radical Garland," and inaugurated what was to become the earliest of several controversies surrounding his career, for the energetic writer was an outspoken advocate of the realistic depiction of speech, setting, and character, as well as a vigorous campaigner for "veritism" and realistic drama, painstakingly lobbying on its behalf in letters to magazine editors, critics, and other writers. Later, however, as writers such as Sinclair Lewis, Theodore Dreiser, and Eugene O'Neill were gaining ascendancy, he came to condemn their work as "pornographic" after the manner of the French naturalists, notably Émile Zola, and as pandering to prurient interests.

What these letters share in common is Garland's earnest proselytizing for his beliefs, and they lament the loss of a genteel tradition in American life, reflecting the gradual shift in his standards as a new generation built upon the path he helped to blaze. Moreover, his rancor reflects his growing discomfort with current literature and his shock at the portrayal of sexuality in novels and movies about which he often lectured with his daughter at his side. Ironically, some of Garland's own early works, such as *Rose of Dutcher's Coolly* (1895), were similarly condemned as unwholesome by many contemporary readers and reviewers. After his death on 4 March 1940, some forty books and fifty-five years after his first publication, Garland's career was no less controversial, for critics would debate whether Garland compromised the standards of his youth as he gained increased fame and influence.

Yet Garland's prophecy about his marginal place in literary history is not far off. Most people remember him today chiefly for his earliest work, especially the innovative collection of short stories, *Main-Travelled Roads* (1891), and his memoir, *A Son of the Middle Border* (1917). In these volumes Garland demonstrated that it had at last become possible to deal realistically with the American farmer in literature instead of seeing him simply through the veil of literary convention. By creating new types of characters, Garland hoped not only to inform readers about the realities of Midwestern farm life but to touch the deeper feelings of the nation.

As one of America's foremost local-colorists, Garland graphically depicted the countryside of his native Middle West in fiction, verse, plays, and compelling autobiographical narratives. Among Garland's best stories are those found in *Main-Travelled Roads*, for they portray more vividly than any other work of its time the conditions that led to the Populist revolt. The book has not only become an important historical document, but its poignant portrayal of man's struggle against overwhelming forces in nature and social injustices led William Dean Howells to observe that "these stories are full of the bitter and burning dust, the foul and trampled slush of the common avenues of life: the life of the men who hopelessly and cheerlessly make the wealth that enriches the alien and the idler, and impoverishes the producer."[1]

But in addition to Garland's historical importance as a purveyor of realism, he is significant for another reason. During his long life, he was intimately involved with the major literary, social, and artistic movements in American culture, responding as a zealous reformer to issues that still engage us today, such as agrarian populism, the inequities of the tax system, the necessity for a more humane treatment of Native Americans, and the struggle for women's rights. Pulitzer Prize-winning author, proponent of local-color, regionalism, and realism in literature and impressionism in art, unabashed advocate of literary and cultural elitism, dabbler in research on psychic phenomena: the range of Garland's interests extended to nearly all aspects of American literary culture.

Garland was an exceedingly gregarious man, and his many letters to such literary figures as Walt Whitman, William Dean Howells, James Whitcomb Riley, and George Washington Cable reveal him to be a vigorous literary nationalist and proponent of realism in literature. Applying this advocacy to Garland's own work is problematic, however, for a man whose early writings are now considered by many to be quintessentially Naturalistic, who eventually wrote a book advocating "veritism" (*Crum-*

bling Idols, 1894), who wrote about Impressionism and even described himself as an Impressionist late in his life, and who wrote a series of conventional romances extolling the virtues of the Rocky Mountain West. After some initial skirmishes over the future of American letters conducted through the press, Garland achieved some prominence as a man of letters. He began an extensive correspondence with the intellectual leaders of American culture, and his letters demonstrate his role in the formation of such cultural institutions as the American Academy of Arts and Letters and other organizations devoted to propagating a national literature, and they illustrate his influence in the administration of the Pulitzer Prize awards and in the development of avant-garde drama.

Garland's letters are not only interesting to students and scholars of American literature, but also to literary and cultural historians and others who wish to further understand the political, social, and cultural issues in American life during the late nineteenth and early to mid-twentieth centuries. His letters to Theodore Roosevelt and other government officials, for example, testify to his concern for our nation's appalling treatment of Native Americans and of the necessity for an enlightened conservation policy. He also maintained an influential correspondence with such early literary historians and critics as Brander Matthews, Edmund Clarence Stedman, Fred Lewis Pattee, Stuart Pratt Sherman, and Van Wyck Brooks who, with Garland, are largely responsible for the shape of academic study of American literature and culture today. And still other letters reflect Garland's gradual awareness that he himself represented the last of his generation of literary pioneers; his correspondence with Ph.D. students, themselves engaged in writing the first biographies of his peers, suggests a bemused Garland, wryly observing history being written, aware of his own recollections shaping that history.

That Garland eventually became friendly with the literary and cultural leaders in the country could not have been anticipated by his early farming years in which his family progressively moved westward from Wisconsin to Iowa, and then to the Dakotas. His early years on the farm were difficult, as he was expected to do a man's work—plowing, sowing, threshing, cornhusking, haying, caring for animals, and cleaning the stables. He gradually developed an intense dislike for farm work and yearned for a better life away from the middle border.

Garland made the most crucial decision in both his personal life and his artistic career in the fall of 1884: possessing approximately one hun-

dred dollars and letters of introduction, he journeyed to Boston to prepare himself for a career as a teacher of literature. But though he had
abandoned the life of farming, his early experiences influenced his later
and best fiction, for they provided him with an intimate knowledge of the
actual details of farm life. As Donald Pizer has observed, the two actions
of leaving his father and mother and making his way to Boston constitute
the emotional and literary center of his personal and literary life for over
a decade: "On the one hand, he had successfully rebelled against the life
of the farm and had escaped to the richer world of the East. On the other,
escape meant desertion—desertion not only of his family, particularly of
his overworked and rapidly aging mother, but also of his region and its
needs. When Garland came to write his early stories of the middle border,
he discovered that the themes of joyous escape and guilty return were
intimately associated with his response to his area."[2]

Garland's best fiction can be found during his early years—years in
which he also spent considerable time lecturing about Henry George's
theories of economic reform and campaigning for populist candidates. In
addition to *Main-Travelled Roads*, he produced a number of other social
and economic documents during the early 1890s. But while Garland was
appearing often in print by 1892, his work was not selling as well as he had
hoped. At the same time, much of his middle border material was being
criticized in both the East and the West. As he later recalled:

> I had the foolish notion that the literary folk of the west would take
> local pride in the color of my work, and to find myself execrated by
> nearly every critic as "a bird willing to foul his own nest" was an
> amazement. Editorials and criticisms poured into the office, all writ-
> ten to prove that my pictures of the middle border were utterly false.
>   Statistics were employed to show that pianos and Brussels carpets
> adorned almost every Iowa farmhouse. Tilling the prairie soil was
> declared to be "the noblest vocation in the world, not in the least
> like the pictures this eastern author has drawn of it."[3]

After completing *Rose of Dutcher's Coolly* in 1895, Garland turned to
"the high country" of the Mountain West for material, which signaled a
change in those subjects with which he had been occupied in his middle
border fiction. Even while working on *Rose*, however, he felt the lure of
the Far West and began to exploit the new region as a source of local-
color material. Garland had always considered himself a Western writer,
and as early as 1892 had extolled the West in an article entitled "The West

in Literature" written for the *Arena*. Garland was convinced not only of the need to delineate the West in literature, but that a truthful study of Western life must involve the actual speech of the common people and must be rendered in native dialects so that each character would have his individual accent, as he has his individual thought. In assessing the success of contemporary Western regionalists and looking to the future development of Western writers, he concluded:

> That this Americanism, this truth to local conditions, is the certain road to success for young Western writers, is evident already in the success of James Whitcomb Riley, Opie Read, Joseph Kirkland, Octave Thanet, James Lane Allen, and others who have written of Western people. We are certain soon to have a group of Western novelists (Will they be women?) to represent the West, as Mrs. Cooke, Miss Wilkins, and Miss Jewett represent New England. But they must be born of the soil. They must be products of the environment. They must stand among the people, not above them, and then they can be true, and being true they will certainly succeed.[4]

In his new material Garland attempted to deal with a variety of facets of Western life and to create a multiplicity of types, but he usually focused on mountaineers, miners, foresters, and Native Americans. With few exceptions, most of his works during this period contain common elements: mild social themes, a sense of the glory of mountain scenery, and a conventional love plot. These elements were usually combined with one or more themes that dominate his Western writings: the life in the mining camps, the displacement of the American Indian, and the importance of conservation and controlled management of Western lands. Most of his works were derived from his travels during this period, whether his gold mining expedition to the Yukon (recounted in *Trail of the Goldseekers* [1898]), his journey to England (recorded in *Her Mountain Lover* [1901]), or his many trips to Indian reservations (in *The Captain of the Gray-Horse Troop* [1902] and *The Book of the American Indian* [1923]).

Despite the popular appeal of many of Garland's Rocky Mountain romances, critics have consistently disparaged most of his writings during this period.[5] Part of Garland's difficulties in his Western fiction, especially that dealing with mountaineers and miners, stemmed from the fact that he did not have as intimate a familiarity with his subject as he had, for example, with the middle border. To be sure, Garland had spent much time touring the West, and he attempted to transmit the exhilaration, freedom, and emotional quality that he had experienced into his fiction. But since he was usually not emotionally involved in the social issues which serve as backgrounds for this material, these themes are often presented almost perfunctorily. Such problems, however, did not exist in Garland's treatment of the American Indian.

Garland had the opportunity to travel extensively and to live for extended periods among the Indians from 1895 to 1905. His firsthand knowledge of American Indians and his awareness of the effects of giving up the modified lifestyles of the reservation and adopting those of the dominant white culture resulted in many sensitive portrayals of these painful transitions. From the start his treatment of the Indian was sympathetic, and his moral indignation at their mistreatment at the hands of government officials was as sincere as his earlier concern for the beaten-down farmer and the farm wife in his middle border fiction. His sympathy caused him not only to expend much of his energy on numerous writings, both fictional and nonfictional, about the American Indian, but to lend his hand at various reform movements concerning the Indian.[6]

Garland closed his Western phase by pursuing his passion for conservation policy. He had become interested in forestry as early as the 1890s, but his interest was especially encouraged when he met with President Theodore Roosevelt and Gifford Pinchot, chief of the Forest Service, in 1902 concerning the conservation of the nation's forests. In addition to writing a number of short stories and two novels on the subject—*Cavanagh, Forest Ranger* (1910) and *The Forester's Daughter* (1914)—his notebooks between 1902 and 1913 are filled with forestry matters. As guardian of America's natural resources and as an example of enlightened government, the forest ranger, the hero of both novels, represented the future of the West for Garland. Garland believed that the pioneer ethic of the exploitation of the Western forests was no longer valid, and he modeled his own conservation ethic on that of Roosevelt's combative forester, Pinchot.

Unfortunately, despite Garland's passionate interest in the subjects of conservation and forestry, his two novels were obtrusively melodramatic and overall embarrassing failures. By this time Garland had completed his picture of "the high country," continued to indulge his interest in psychic experimentation that was the subject of *Tyranny of the Dark* (1905), *The Shadow World* (1908), and *Victor Ollnee's Discipline* (1911), and began again casting about for new subjects.

Shortly after the appearance of *Cavanagh*, Howells wrote to Garland on 27 March 1910: "One day, I hope you will revert to the temper of your first work, and give us a picture of the wild life you know so well, on the lines of 'Main-Travelled Roads.' You have in you greater things than you have done, and you owe the world which has welcomed you the best you have in you. 'Be true to the dream of thy youth'—the dream of an absolute and unsparing 'veritism'; the word is yours." Garland's response on 29 March 1910 recognized what should be done, but also acknowledged his own limitations: "Your letter came this morning and I gratefully acknowledge and welcome your criticism. I have *not* measured up to my opportunity but perhaps waiting would have been to no avail. The plain truth is I watched the Forestry Service develop for sixteen years and it was only last summer that the motive to use it came. I'm running low on motives. I don't care to write love-stories or stories of adventure and I can not revert to the prairie life without falling into the reminiscent sadness of the man of fifty" (letter 172). Discouraged by the artistic success that had eluded him but too tired to attempt another major romantic work, Garland amplified his feelings in another letter to Howells on 3 April 1910: "I do not see another book (even of this quality) when I look into my mind. Writing is coming to be a weariness and a plodding. What is the use when all the themes are old and one has grown old with them?" (letter 173).

As his interest in fiction began to decline after 1910, Garland felt the need to deal more directly and fully with the major events of his own life. Although his fiction was, from the beginning, never without strong autobiographical elements, he was determined by 1911 to give his career new direction by turning to autobiography as his chief, and final, literary form. With this new resolve Garland undertook *A Son of the Middle Border*. After a long and complicated process of creation, revision, and numerous rejections, it was finally published in book form in 1917. Encouraged by its almost instantaneous success, which not only brought about his election to the American Academy of Arts and Letters in 1918, but was also the significant reason that he was awarded the Pulitzer Prize in 1922 (ostensibly given for his next autobiographical volume), Garland was able to rescue his artistic reputation as well as remain in the public's eye. He proceeded to write three more family autobiographical volumes, though none could match the strength or poignancy of the first: *A Daughter of the Middle Border* (1921), *Trail-Makers of the Middle Border* (1926), and *Back-Trailers from the Middle Border* (1928).

Garland had long supplemented his royalties through lecturing. Early in his career, in the 1890s, he had travelled widely and lectured on American authors and the various social causes that caught his interest. In 1899 he made his first trip to England and met and formed friendships with such authors as Israel Zangwill, George Bernard Shaw, James Barrie, Thomas Hardy, and Arthur Conan Doyle. Upon his return Garland incorporated his impressions of British authors into his lectures, and he made subsequent trips in 1906, 1922, 1923, 1924, and 1925, each time returning with a new harvest of literary anecdotes that provided him with a steady livelihood as lecturer. Tiring of the lecture circuit, he began to explore other ways of mining what was now a considerable store of memories. In 1930 he published *Roadside Meetings*, the first of his literary "logbooks," a blend of autobiography and recollections of authors, based on his notebooks, diaries, and letters received from various luminaries. Despite the lukewarm reception of the book, Garland plodded away on three subsequent volumes, studiously transcribing the diaries he had begun keeping in 1898 into *Companions on the Trail* (1931), *My Friendly Contemporaries* (1932), and *Afternoon Neighbors* (1934). Thus through autobiography, Garland had discovered his final literary voice, which he used until his death in 1940.

Within a year after he had arrived in Boston in 1884, Garland became an avid letter writer who made a point of initiating a correspondence with the authors of the books he read during his frequent travels, whose first reaction to any new cause was to start a letter-writing campaign, and whose many interests demanded an unceasing flow of letters. As an eminent man-of-letters, Garland produced an extensive body of correspondence, a good part of which has fortunately survived. Because the recipients of his letters were themselves equally prominent, their papers have tended to be preserved in libraries across the country. During the fifty-five years of his professional life, Garland received letters from over three thousand correspondents. More than 5,325 of Garland's letters, to approximately seven hundred correspondents, survive in some eighty-eight archives.[7]

Because Garland's letters are so widely distributed among libraries, scholars have been unable to examine them in any systematic way. To cite only one example, Garland's letters to Herbert S. Stone, his important publisher of the mid-1890s, are held by the Newberry Library, the New York Public Library, and the libraries at eight different universities. Given the problems posed by such distribution, few of these letters have previously appeared in print. Much of this correspondence, as would be expected, is routine chit-chat: acceptances to dinners, hurried scrawls proposing meetings, almost daily letters to his wife, Zulime, and to his daughters, Mary Isabel and Constance, written while on his many lecture tours, and the like. But many of his letters to his family are personally revealing, while a significant number of letters to other correspondents offer informative and interesting insights about Garland's varied career and contemporary cultural events.

With so many letters available, selecting those to include in this edition has not always been easy. Because of the importance of William Dean Howells and Walt Whitman to Garland's career, we have included all extant letters to these correspondents. It is especially regrettable that the majority of Garland's letters to Howells have not survived; although he received some one hundred thirty letters from Howells, only twelve of Garland's have been located. Garland's letters to Whitman have previously been published as "The Uncollected Letters of Hamlin Garland to Walt Whitman," edited by Kenneth M. Price and Robert C. Leitz III.[8] We are indebted to Professors Price and Leitz for graciously allowing us to incorporate their annotations of Garland's letters to Whitman in this edition, which we have, on occasion, modified slightly for consistency. We have excluded all letters written specifically for publication, believing that a published letter is more a small essay than a private document, and we have included only a sampling of the many letters Garland wrote on behalf of the American Academy of Arts and Letters and other organizations that engaged his interest. But the letters chosen for this edition, arranged chronologically, do represent the full range of Garland's life and career, as well as provide insight into the major cultural and literary issues of the day.

Much of Garland's involvement in these causes and movements has been only haphazardly understood. Literary critics and historians have been chiefly concerned with his early fiction, decrying his later forays into Rocky Mountain romances, and readers interested in Garland's cultural activities have tended to rely upon Garland's account of his career in his two series of four-volume autobiographies. Understandably, Garland presents himself in a favorable light in these volumes, but his letters reveal, particularly as he aged, a less favorable perspective as his growing antipathy to the emergence of modern literature led him to campaign against it. One of the reasons, therefore, for making available this selection from

Garland's extensive correspondence is both to correct some prevalent misapprehensions concerning Garland's career as a writer and to demonstrate his influence in the formation of American literary culture.

Critical studies of Garland and his works abound, the most important of which are documented, when applicable, in the notes to various letters. Not only did Garland receive a considerable amount of critical attention during his lifetime, but assessments of his work began to appear regularly after his death, and they have continued at a slower but steady pace ever since. Following Eldon C. Hill's "A Biographical Study of Hamlin Garland from 1860–1895" (Ph.D. dissertation, Ohio State University, 1940), four book-length studies have appeared that deal exclusively with Garland's life and works: Jean Holloway's *Hamlin Garland: A Biography* (Austin: University of Texas Press, 1960), Donald Pizer's *Hamlin Garland's Early Work and Career* (Berkeley: University of California Press, 1960), Robert Mane's *Hamlin Garland: L'homme et l'oeuvre (1860–1940)* (Paris: Didier, 1968), and Joseph B. McCullough's *Hamlin Garland* (Boston: G. K. Hall, 1978). Jackson Bryer and Eugene Harding's *Hamlin Garland and the Critics: An Annotated Bibliography* (Troy NY: Whitston, 1973) provides a useful index to Garland criticism. Garland's own writings have been listed in Donald Pizer, "Hamlin Garland: A Bibliography of Newspaper and Periodical Publications (1885–1895)," *Bulletin of Bibliography* 22 (1957): 41–44; and Keith Newlin, "Hamlin Garland, A Bibliography (1896–1940)," *Bulletin of Bibliography* 54 (1997): 11–20. Finally, two collections provide valuable access to a variety of essays, from early reviews to contemporary scholarship: *Critical Essays on Hamlin Garland*, edited by James Nagel (Boston: G. K. Hall, 1982); and *The Critical Reception of Hamlin Garland*, edited by Richard Boudreau, Charles Silet, and Robert Welch (Troy NY: Whitston, 1985).

Garland's long literary career has been typically divided into three principal phases, which has privileged his writing career at the expense of his no-less significant career as a cultural gatekeeper: an early period of involvement in reform movements and middle border fiction (1888–1895); a period of Rocky Mountain romance (1896–1916); and a final period of literary autobiography (1917–1940). To aid the reader in recognizing his wider influence, we have divided Garland's correspondence into four manageable sections, each with its own introduction detailing the main issues contained in the correspondence during that period: The Tyro (1885–1899), The Activist (1900–1918), The Advocate (1919–1929), and The Memoirist (1930–1940). We have also supplied routine identifications as well as provided ample annotations for each letter so that readers will be able to understand the cultural or artistic context of issues being discussed.

NOTES

1. William Dean Howells, "Editor's Study," *Harper's Monthly* 83 (September 1891): 639.

2. Donald Pizer, introduction to *Main-Travelled Roads* (Columbus OH: Charles E. Merrill, 1970), p. vi.

3. *A Son of the Middle Border* (New York: Macmillan, 1917), p. 415.

4. "The West in Literature," *Arena* 6 (November 1892): 675–76.

5. See, for instance, Charles T. Miller, "Hamlin Garland's Retreat from Realism," *Western American Literature* 1 (summer 1966): 119–29; Frances W. Kaye, "Hamlin Garland: A Closer Look at the Later Fiction," *North Dakota Quarterly* 43, no. 3 (1975): 45–56; Robert Gish, *Hamlin Garland: The Far West* (Boise: Boise State University Press, 1976); and Joseph B. McCullough, "Hamlin Garland's Romantic Fiction," in *Critical Essays on Hamlin Garland*, ed. James Nagel (Boston: G. K. Hall, 1982), pp. 349–62.

6. In addition to the novel *The Captain of the Gray-Horse Troop* (1902), Garland published some twenty-five stories concerning the Indian between 1896 and 1905, half of which were later collected in *The Book of the American Indian* (1923). He lobbied on behalf of the Indian in such articles as "The Red Man's Present Needs," *North American Review* 174 (April 1902): 476–88; and "The Red Man as Material," *Booklover's Magazine* 2 (August 1903): 196–98.

7. For a list of correspondents, and the number of letters by each, see Lloyd A. Arvidson, *Hamlin Garland: Centennial Tributes and a Checklist of the Hamlin Garland Papers in the University of Southern California Library*, USC Library Bulletin no. 9 (Los Angeles: University of Southern California Press, 1962). See also the list of principal locations of Garland's letters in the section on editorial practice.

8. Kenneth M. Price and Robert C. Leitz III, "The Uncollected Letters of Hamlin Garland to Walt Whitman," *Walt Whitman Quarterly Review* 5 (1988): 1–13.

Editorial Practice

THE INFORMING purpose behind this edition of Garland's letters is to reproduce as fully and as accurately as possible the contents of each selected letter, with minimal editorial emendation. The letters are, with few exceptions, generally presented as clear text, without the use of "*sic*" or bracketed insertions. Garland was a fair speller (although he nearly always misspelled "necessary" as "nescessary") but he was erratic with punctuation, displaying a pronounced fondness for the dash and an habitual aversion to the apostrophe in non-pronoun contractions (*dont* for *don't*; *cant* for *can't*). Because our desire is to reflect Garland's habits as a writer, eccentricities of spelling, punctuation, and phrasing have been preserved, but we have made no effort to indicate Garland's cancellations or corrections. The text printed here is the finished letter, after Garland revised it, with whatever misspellings or errors he left. We have limited our corrections to obvious typographical errors or slips of the pen, and to those emendations required for clarity, as outlined below.

Idiosyncracies

In his early letters especially, Garland frequently used a dash of various lengths in place of commas or periods, in addition to the appositive dash within the sentence and the transitional dash between sentences. On other occasions, he would follow a period, question mark, or exclamation point with a dash. Our transcriptions uniformly reproduce the appositive, transitional, and comma-replacing dashes, as well as dashes following punctuation, as an em dash (—).

Some early letters use a plus sign (+) in place of a period; we have silently emended this use of the plus sign as a period.

Garland often wrote the colon after the salutation as an equals sign (=); we have uniformly emended this equals sign as a colon.

Commas and periods used with quotation marks have been placed in the order in which they appear; where aligned, commas and periods are printed within quotion marks.

In early holograph letters, Garland occasionally indicated unindented paragraph breaks by leaving space of various lengths between sentences. Because we cannot always determine Garland's intent, we have chosen not to speculate about whether such space indicates a new paragraph or a change of emphasis or something else. We have therefore not indicated eccentricities of spacing.

Emendations

The letters comprising the copy texts for this edition exist in four states, which have required different protocols for the emendation of error: mailed holograph letters; mailed typed letters; and typed carbon copies and holograph drafts, written mostly in the 1930s after Garland had moved to Hollywood, all of the latter housed in the Hamlin Garland Papers, Doheny Library, the University of Southern California. In general, we have restricted editorial emendation to correction of manifest error required for clarity. When it has been necessary to insert words or to supply missing punctuation, we have enclosed our insertions in brackets, with two exceptions. Particularly in holograph letters, Garland habitually dropped periods when the sentence's end coincided with the end of the line. We have silently supplied missing periods. On occasion Garland failed to supply a closing quotation mark, especially when he revised a letter; these marks we have also silently supplied.

On some occasions Garland did not finish revising a phrase (such as failing to strike out all the words when he inserted a revision); since the apparatus required to signal the resulting syntactic tangle would have proved too cumbersome for this edition, we have silently adopted Garland's intention in the revision. For those instances where we have not been able to decipher Garland's handwriting, we have indicated each illegible word as [illeg.]. Silent correction of obvious error is as follows:

Mailed holograph letters: We have faithfully preserved Garland's errors in spelling and his inconsistencies in punctuation. We have silently emended only obvious slips of the pen (inadvertent duplication of letters or words, unintentional word substitution [e.g., "the" for "to"], and the like).

Mailed typed letters: Garland was a careless typist, and he invariably corrected errors and revised for clarity before he mailed the letter. Yet he was also careless in his corrections, frequently failing to correct transpositions, double-strikes, missed keys, and dropped letters. In mailed typed letters, we have silently emended obvious typographical errors that, had Garland been more alert, he would have corrected as his usual practice indicates. We have not, however, corrected errors in spelling or punctuation.

Typed carbons: Many of the carbons contain egregious typographical errors, obvious misspellings, duplicated punctuation caused by misalignment of the platen and paper, and the like. And since Garland normally corrected these errors before he mailed his letters, preserving these errors would prove only that Garland was a poor typist. We have therefore silently emended typographical errors, supplied or corrected punctuation necessary for clarity, and corrected misspelled proper names or misspellings that diverge from Garland's normal practice.

Holograph drafts: Because holograph drafts do not exhibit the sort of error created by poor typing skills, we regard them as more reliable reflections of Garland's intention. Our emendations are therefore more conservative than they are for carbons, which are clearly earmarked by errors of haste. We have silently emended misspelled proper names when they diverge from Garland's habitual practice. For example, in a letter to Barrett C. Clark (letter 322), Garland twice spells Eugene O'Neill's name as "O'Neil" and once correctly. But we have preserved other misspellings as well as punctuation and grammatical errors.

Garland wrote on a wide variety of stationery throughout the fifty-five years represented in this edition. While the letterheads are often an accurate indication of the letter's point of origin, they are not always reliable since Garland often carried stationery with him on his travels. To distinguish printed letterhead from addresses which Garland supplied, we have regularized the placement of inside addresses as follows.

Letterhead is uniformly centered. When the letterhead contains a mix of large and small capitals, or upper and lower case, we have regularized our transcriptions to follow standard practice. For printed letterhead, we have retained the name, address, and city but have silently omitted telephone numbers, the names of hotel proprietors, and the like. For letters with extensive letterhead (e.g., The Joint Committee on Literary Arts), we have included only enough to indicate the organization and place. When Garland has added to the printed material—occasionally the name of a town or other detail—we have indicated the addition by placing it flush left.

Holograph addresses are placed flush left and transcribed in their entirety. We have not retained Garland's inconsistent underlining, which can exist as double, single, or ornamental underlining. When Garland has duplicated the address—both heading and closing the letter, for example—we have ignored the duplication. Where the second address differs from the first, we have included both in their respective places. Finally, we have treated cancelled letterhead as holograph, since in such cases the letterhead becomes merely a sheet of paper.

The placement of dates, closings, and marginalia have been regularized as follows: all dates are placed flush right, following the address; as with the duplication of addresses, we have also ignored the duplication of dates. Ornamental underlining has been omitted. We have, however, retained Garland's eccentricities of format: e.g., "Dec. 12."; "Dec./12."; "Tue./12." We have supplied missing information within brackets, thus: "Dec. 12. [1912]"; "Tue./12. [12 December 1912]." For conjectural dates we have added a question mark to the appropriate element. Closings are uniformly centered. Garland normally used an ornamental flourish beneath his signature, which we have omitted. For those few instances when he both typed and signed or initialed his name, we have ignored the duplication and/or retained the holograph signature. Postscripts or eccentrically placed postscripts (e.g., those scrawled at the top of a page) have been uniformly placed flush left after the signature. Marginalia have been placed after the signature, or following the postscript, when present, with a note explaining location.

Finally, we have silently omitted the following: typist's initials; signals—such as "(over)"—that the letter continues on the back of the paper; and Garland's record-keeping notations. For example, on holograph drafts and typed copies, Garland habitually marked "Not Sent" to differentiate drafts and copies from the original mailed letter, which he occasionally requested be returned to him. We have not transcribed these record-keeping marks.

Annotations

Garland kept most of the letters he received, which has, in many cases, enabled us to supply rather full annotations. Accordingly, unless otherwise indicated by library location abbreviation, all unpublished correspondence and manuscripts referred to in the notes are located in the Hamlin Garland Papers, Doheny Library. References to manuscripts appear with their cataloguing number. On occasion our annotations refer to Garland's diaries, held by the Huntington Library. Garland revised these diaries as he composed his memoirs, in many cases substantially altering his initial impression as time tempered his judgments. Although Donald Pizer has published a portion of these diaries as *Hamlin Garland's Diaries* (San Marino CA: Huntington Library Press, 1968), his transcriptions follow Garland's revisions. Since Garland's initial impressions have seemed more valuable for annotation, references in this edition are to the original entry in the manuscript diary. Finally, previously published letters have been re-edited for this edition and are acknowledged in the notes or the letter's header.

Principal Locations of Garland's Letters

In preparing this volume of Garland's letters, we have examined approximately 5,325 letters in some eighty-eight archives. What follows is a brief description of the contents of some of the more significant collections. We have deposited a copy of our inventory of Garland's letters in the Hamlin Garland Papers, Doheny Library, the University of Southern California.

The largest single collection of Garland's letters is at the Doheny Library. Some 8,500 letters deposited there consist of letters Garland received from almost 3,000 correspondents. An additional 1,587 are by Garland, most drafts or carbon copies, addressed to some 650 correspondents. Approximately 350 of this latter group are originals. Significant clusters of letters include those to members of the Vitagraph film company (James Blackton, Jasper Brady, William Wolbert); to his family—his parents, Richard and Isabelle, his wife, Zulime, and his brother, Franklin; to his brother-in-law Lorado Taft; and to his friends Alexander G. Beaman, Henry B. Fuller, Hermann Hagedorn, Katherine Herne, Vachel Lindsay, and Augustus Thomas. Others are to various publishers (George Acklom, George Brett, Frederick Duneka, Henry Hoyns, Harold Latham, John Macrae, Edward Marsh). A finding aid to the entire Garland collection (which lists correspondence alphabetically) has been published as *Hamlin Garland: Centennial Tributes and a Checklist of the Hamlin Garland Papers in the University of Southern California Library*, compiled by Lloyd A. Arvidson, USC Library Bulletin no. 9 (Los Angeles: University of Southern California Press, 1962).

The Henry E. Huntington Library, San Marino, holds approximately 660 letters, most of which are undated and are directed to Garland's wife, Zulime, and to his daughters, Mary Isabel Johnson Lord and Constance Harper Doyle. These letters chiefly concern his lecture trips, his visits to England and Europe in 1924 and 1925, business matters, and a large number are devoted to his activities concerning *The Mystery of the Buried Crosses.*

Garland's correspondence with his *Century* publishers is located at the New York Public Library. About 300 letters are addressed to Richard Watson Gilder, Robert Underwood Johnson, Albert Shaw, Robert Sterling Yard, *New York Times* editor John H. Finley, and others. The Butler Library of Columbia University holds 238 letters addressed principally to Brander Matthews, Paul Revere Reynolds, Edmund Clarence Stedman, and Arthur Stedman. Of the 511 letters housed in the archives of the National Institute and the American Academy of Art and Letters, the majority are about Academy business; a smaller portion concerns the composition of his literary logbooks.

Miami University, in Oxford, Ohio, holds some 365 letters, including 168 to Garland's first biographer, Eldon Hill, and clusters of others to the playwright Augustus Thomas, to Johnson Brigham, the editor of *Midland Monthly,* and to Albert Bigelow Paine, John Bradley, and Carl Van Doren. In addition, the library has a microfilm of about 100 letters to John H. Finley held at the New York Public Library. Alderman Library of the University of Virginia houses some 146 letters, 57 of which are addressed to William G. Chapman, the president of the International Press Bureau. The Library of Congress holds 138 letters to William Allen White, Theodore Roosevelt, Walt Whitman, Horace Traubel, and additional letters to others. Garland's correspondence with George Steele Seymour and Flora Warren Seymour, who formed the Bookfellows, amount to 197 letters at the Seymour Library, Knox College, in Galesburg, Illinois.

Smaller collections include 77 letters at Harvard's Houghton Library, addressed to William Dean Howells, Mildred Howells, Amy Lowell, Walter Hines Page, and William R. Thayer, among others. Yale's Beinecke Library has 71 letters addressed to various correspondents, among them Wilbur Cross, Herbert Stone, Thomas Lounsberry, and William Lyon Phelps. The Van Pelt Library at the University of Pennsylvania holds 40 letters to Van Wyck Brooks, and 12 others to Theodore Dreiser and Arthur Hobson Quinn, among others. Indiana University's Lilly Library has 65 letters, 36 of them to James Whitcomb Riley and 4 to Upton Sinclair. The Newberry Library holds 56 letters to 16 correspondents, among them Henry B. Fuller, Alice French, and Herbert Stone. Thirty letters to Stuart Pratt Sherman are at the University of Illinois Library; 28 to the poet Edwin Markham are held at the Horrmann Library of Wagner College, Staten Island; and 46 letters to Fred Lewis Pattee are at the Pattee Library, Pennsylvania State University. Finally, the following libraries have microfilmed their collections of Garland's letters: Doheny Library (University of Southern California), the New York Public Library, Butler Library (Columbia), Alderman Library (Virginia), and the Lilly Library (Indiana).

Chronology

ously referred to as the "Homestead" and "Mapleshade," and moves his parents to it. Moves to New York City in the fall to live with his brother. *Prairie Songs* (poetry) and *Prairie Folks* (fiction) are published.

1894   Settles in Chicago (474 Elm Street), making periodic lecture trips to the East, South, and West. *Crumbling Idols* published. Meets Henry B. Fuller, who becomes a close friend.

1895   *Rose of Dutcher's Coolly* published; travels to Colorado and New Mexico with Chicago artists Charles Francis Browne and Hermon Atkins MacNeil, gathering material on American Indians.

1897   Takes a trip through the West, living on several Indian reservations. Joins the Players Club (New York).

1898   Returns to Washington DC to complete Ulysses S. Grant biography; leaves for a trip to the Alaskan gold fields. Becomes a charter member of the National Institute of Arts and Letters. Publishes *Ulysses S. Grant: His Life and Character*.

1899   Takes first trip to England. Marries Zulime Taft, 18 November.

1901   Becomes involved in agitation for Indian rights. *Her Mountain Lover* published.

1902   *The Captain of the Gray-Horse Troop* published.

1903   Mary Isabel Garland born, 15 July. *Hesper* published.

1906   Takes second trip to England.

1907   Constance Garland born, 18 June. Forms the Cliff-Dwellers, a Chicago literary club modeled after the Players Club and named for the novel by Fuller. Moves to 6427 Greenwood Avenue, Chicago.

1909   *Miller of Boscobel*, Garland's first performed play, is presented in Wisconsin and Chicago. Ten-volume "Sunset Edition" issued by Harpers.

1910   *Cavanagh, Forest Ranger* published.

1911   Becomes Secretary of the Chicago Theater Society.

1912   The Garland Homestead, in West Salem, Wisconsin, burns.

1913   Organizes a Chicago meeting of the National Institute of Arts and Letters.

1914   Serializes "A Son of the Middle Border" in *Collier's*.

1916   Vitagraph Studios begins filming four of Garland's novels. Buys a summer cottage in Tannersville, New York, "Camp Neshonoc." Moves to 71 East 92nd Street, New York City, to be closer to his publishers and literary life.

1917   Organizes a dinner to commemorate Howells's eightieth birthday on 21 March. Goes to Battle Creek Sanitarium in April for treatment of sciatica. Attempts to get women elected into the National Institute. *A Son of the Middle Border* published.

1918   Elected to the American Academy of Arts and Letters. Becomes a member of the Century Club. Begins service on Pulitzer Prize juries.

1919   Theodore Roosevelt dies, 6 January. Begins work for the Roosevelt Memorial Association.

1920   William Dean Howells dies, 11 May.

1921   Chair of Pulitzer Prize juries for both the novel and the drama. *A Daughter of the Middle Border* published.

1922   Twelve-volume "Border Edition" issued by Harper's. Receives Pulitzer Prize for *Daughter*. Takes family to England for six weeks.

1923   *The Book of the American Indian* published. Agitates for a more active role for the American Academy.

1924   Spends summer alone in England. Meets Edith Wharton.

1925   Begins correspondence with Van Wyck Brooks. Moves to 507 Cathedral Parkway, New York. Buys a summer house, "Grey Ledge," in the club community of Onteora, New York.

1926   Mary Isabel Garland marries Hardesty Johnson, a singer. Presents the American Academy's Howells Medal for Fiction to Mary Wilkins Freeman. *Trail-Makers of the Middle Border* published.

1927   Constance Garland marries Joseph Harper, of the publishing firm.

1928   *Back-Trailers from the Middle Border* published.

1929   Begins an annual "Medal for Good Diction over the Radio," sponsored by the American Academy. Moves to Hollywood, California, in August. Henry B. Fuller dies, 28 July.

1930   *Roadside Meetings* published. Begins to sell his collection of autographed books. Builds a house at 2045 DeMille Drive, Hollywood.

1931   *Companions on the Trail* published. Receives the Roosevelt Memorial Medal of Honor.

1932   *My Friendly Contemporaries* published.

1934   *Afternoon Neighbors* published.

1936   *Forty Years of Psychic Research* published. An exhibit of Garland's books, manuscripts, and memorabilia begins a four-year tour. Lorado Taft dies, 30 October. Zulime becomes seriously ill with Parkinson's disease.

1937   Guy D. Haselton makes a two-reel biographical film of Garland. Garland becomes obsessively involved in psychic investigation of buried objects.

1939   Garland's last book, *The Mystery of the Buried Crosses*, is published. Garland worries about the disposition of his papers after his death.

1940   Garland dies, on 4 March, of a cerebral hemorrhage.

Abbreviations

DESCRIPTION OF LETTERS

al	autograph letter
alc	autograph letter, carbon (from Garland's Letterbook, 1901–04, USC)
ald	autograph letter, draft
als	autograph letter, signed
tl	typed letter
tlc	typed letter, copy
tls	typed letter, signed
trl	transcribed letter

LOCATION OF LETTERS

Am Acad	American Academy of Arts and Letters, New York City
Bancroft	Bancroft Library, University of California, Berkeley
Boston PL	Boston Public Library
Brigham Young	Brigham Young University, Provo, Utah
Columbia	Columbia University, New York City
Congress	Manuscript Division, Library of Congress, Washington DC
Duke	Duke University, Durham, North Carolina
Harvard	Houghton Library, Harvard University, Cambridge, Massachussets
Hunt	Henry E. Huntington Library, San Marino, California
In HS	Indiana Historical Society, Indianapolis
Indiana U	Lilly Library, Indiana University, Bloomington
Knox	Knox College Archives, Galesburg, Illinois
Miami U	Miami University, Oxford, Ohio

Middlebury	Middlebury College, Middlebury, Vermont
Morgan	Pierpont Morgan Library, New York City
Nat'l Arch	National Archives, Washington DC
Newberry	Newberry Library, Chicago
Northwestern	Northwestern University, Evanston, Illinois
NYPL	New York Public Library, New York City
Ohio St	Ohio State University, Columbus
Penn HS	Historical Society of Pennsylvania, Philadelphia
Penn St	Pennsylvania State University, University Park
Players	Hampden-Booth Theater Collection and Library, The Players Club, New York City
Princeton	Princeton University, Princeton, New Jersey
Pulitzer	Pulitzer Archives, Columbia University, New York City
Southwest	Southwest Museum Library, Los Angeles
Syracuse	Syracuse University, Syracuse, New York
Tulane	Tulane University, New Orleans
U Cal-Davis	University of California, Davis
U Chicago	University of Chicago
U of Del	University of Delaware, Newark
U of Ill-Ar	University of Illinois Library, Archives, Urbana
U of Ill-R	University of Illinois Library, Rare Book Room, Urbana
U of Iowa	University of Iowa, Iowa City
U of OK	University of Oklahoma, Norman
U Penn	University of Pennsylvania, Philadelphia
U Texas	Harry Ransom Humanities Research Center, University of Texas, Austin
USC	University of Southern California, Los Angeles
USC LB	Garland's Letterbook (1901–4), University of Southern California, Los Angeles
Virginia	University of Virginia, Charlottesville
Wagner	Wagner College, Staten Island, New York

Wis HS   State Historical Society of Wisconsin, Madison

Yale   Beinecke Library, Yale University, New Haven

SHORT TITLES

Afternoon — *Afternoon Neighbors*. New York: Macmillan, 1934.

Back-Trailers — *Back-Trailers from the Middle Border*. New York: Macmillan, 1928.

BAI — *The Book of the American Indian*. New York: Harper, 1923.

BET — *Boston Evening Transcript*.

Companions — *Companions on the Trail*. New York: Macmillan, 1931.

Contemporaries — *My Friendly Contemporaries*. New York: Macmillan, 1932.

Daughter — *A Daughter of the Middle Border*. New York: Macmillan, 1921.

Flanagan — John T. Flanagan. "Hamlin Garland Writes to His Chicago Publisher." *American Literature* 23 (1952): 447–57.

Holloway — Jean Holloway, *Hamlin Garland*. Freeport NY: Books for Libraries Press, 1960.

McCullough — Joseph B. McCullough. "Hamlin Garland's Letters to James Whitcomb Riley." *American Literary Realism* 9 (1976): 249–60.

Roadside — *Roadside Meetings*. New York: Macmillan, 1931.

Son — *A Son of the Middle Border*. New York: Macmillan, 1917.

"Uncollected" — Kenneth M. Price and Robert C. Leitz III. "The Uncollected Letters of Hamlin Garland to Walt Whitman." *Walt Whitman Quarterly Review* 5 (1988): 1–13.

Wertheim — *The Correspondence of Stephen Crane*. 2 vols. Ed. Stanley Wertheim and Paul Sorrentino. New York: Columbia University Press, 1988.

Selected Letters of Hamlin Garland

The Tyro: 1885–1899

Introduction

B Y THE TIME Garland had arrived in Boston from South Dakota in October 1884, he was already familiar with the works of the French historian Hippolyte Taine and the influential agnostic Robert Ingersoll. He immediately immersed himself in the writings of Charles Darwin, Herbert Spencer, John Fiske, Hermann Helmholtz, and Ernest Heinrich Haeckel in an effort to understand how evolutionary and biological processes in nature led from simple to complex forms, as well as how these processes could be applied to society. He eagerly read Walt Whitman's poetry, absorbing the poet's view of the spiritual brotherhood of workers, as well as his nationalistic feeling. His reading of Henry George's *Progress and Poverty* (1879) in early 1884 confirmed his own experiences of farm life and quickly converted him into an advocate of the single tax, which sought to correct the injustice of the unearned increment (profits made from the increased value of land) that favored property owners at the expense of the laboring farmer. In short, Garland feverishly became involved with the intellectual, artistic, and philosophical currents of the time, but although he desired to participate in them, he had only a vague idea about where such involvement would take him.

Shortly after his arrival in Boston, Garland visited the Boston School of Oratory, where he heard a lecture by Moses True Brown on "The Philosophy of Expression." Brown, the school's principal, was impressed with Garland's eagerness to learn and, learning of his poverty, offered him free tuition in exchange for proofreading a manuscript. In May, Garland became an instructor of literature for the summer term, and he assumed a full-time teaching position for the 1885–86 school year (*Son*, pp. 333–40). Late in 1885, Garland began work on a project based on his lectures in which he intended to deal with American literature in a manner based on scientific principles. In 1886, he outlined its contents, calling it "The Evolution of American Thought," and in early 1887 he worked on rewriting nearly the whole thing.[1] Although never published, Garland's research led him to a near-militant advocacy of the value of local color in literature, and his efforts to turn his lectures into a book led him to launch a series of letters to the leading writers of the day, at times adopting a "professorial" tone as he sought to clarify his ideas.

One of Garland's preoccupations before 1895 was with advancing the cause of Western literature. His earliest surviving letter, to the poet and editor Edmund Clarence Stedman (16 December 1885), reveals the youthful aspirant lecturing his more famous correspondent about his failure to include a poet in his *Poets of America* (2 vols., 1885). Such chutzpah would soon flavor his letters as he began a lifelong habit of initiating correspondence with authors whom he admired, notably E. W. Howe, George W. Cable, Walt Whitman, James Whitcomb Riley, Mark Twain, Louise Chandler Moulton, William Dean Howells, Stephen Crane, Henry B. Fuller, Alice French, and Mary E. Wilkins Freeman.

Through numerous addresses and articles Garland expressed local-color theories and called upon Western writers and critics to abandon their allegiance to the standards of the past and of the East and to produce and evaluate an indigenous literature. He felt that the West could only grow to literary maturity when it freed itself from the cultural domination of the East. He believed that the dialect poems of James Whitcomb Riley, whose works he first discovered in the summer of 1886, not only attempted to break with obsolete literary traditions, but exemplified some of the best tendencies in American literature. Garland and Riley's extensive correspondence from 1887 until 1915 manifests a mutual interest for the other's works, particularly with respect to the regional elements contained in those works. Garland's letters also reflect the concern that he shared with many other young writers of the time regarding the local-color movement and the question of the use of dialect in poetry.[2] Similarly, Garland's letters to E. W. Howe are full of praise for the indigenous quality of the novelist's works and again show Garland's militant advocacy of the local-color movement and Western literature, as do his letters to Francis F. Browne, editor of *The Dial.*

One of Garland's most important literary relationships was with Walt Whitman. Garland's letters to the poet continually reveal an unabashed admiration from a youthful disciple, as for example in Garland's first letter to the poet: "I am an enthusiastic reader of your books; both volumes of which I have within reach of hand. I am everywhere in my teaching and writing making your claims felt and shall continue to do so" (24 November 1886, letter 8). But as Kenneth Price and Robert Leitz point out, these letters demonstrate more than Garland's adulation:

Perhaps most intriguingly, they clarify how Whitman's followers turned defeat in Boston into a major victory. For Whitman to gain a sympathetic hearing in Boston was no small local matter. . . . The poet must have been gratified to read Garland's reports of his growing following in Boston, a city whose district attorney in 1882 had declared his poetry to be obscene literature, banning *Leaves of Grass* from the mails. . . . Garland's letters—accurate although slightly overstated because of his desire to bolster Whitman in his declining years—provide an important record of how New England journalists, students, and lecture audiences responded to Whitman.[3]

Furthermore, Garland believed that his own fictional work was influenced and inspired by Whitman.[4] Writing to Horace Traubel on 13 January 1892 shortly after the publication of *Main-Travelled Roads* (1891), Garland remarked that "The best part of my success is that it has come while I am doing a work whose spirit is in part Whitman's and thoroughly reformatory. I am a reformer—a radical—a promoter of Democracy and yet the people sustain me in it. I wish Whitman could realize that. I tell you the whole temper of the republic in letters as in politics is changing" (letter 64).

Another of Garland's chief literary acquaintances in Boston was William Dean Howells, the reigning dean of American letters. Garland met Howells sometime in mid-1887 in Boston. Although he had been critical of Howells in his lectures prior to 1886, by 1887 he was converted to an avid disciple. Their meeting set the stage for a lifelong friendship which proved profitable both personally and artistically for Garland. Only twelve of Garland's letters to Howells survive—enough, however, to indicate the centrality of Howells in Garland's life and the importance he placed upon Howells's judgment.

Garland was early attracted to the stage, and particularly to the acting of the noted tragedian Edwin Booth. "I observe you use a low, strained dispirited tone, a little tremulous, as if constraint were laid upon it—as if the mind of the speaker wavered between two emotions or more. (How clumsy and inadequate words are in attempting to describe these subtleties of the voice!)," he observed about Booth's impersonation of Macbeth in a 21 February 1889 letter to the actor (letter 28). His painstaking observations of Booth's gestures, facial expressions, and vocal delivery would soon inform the depiction of character in his fiction and would become the basis for four lectures about the actor that he would deliver periodically for the next twenty years.[5]

In January 1889 Garland saw James A. Herne's *Drifting Apart*, and his interest and ambition was again directed toward the drama. His meeting with Herne and his wife, the actress Katharine Corcoran Herne, in May led to a close friendship and to a renewed interest in playwriting. Only two letters to Herne survive (out of twenty-seven received), and both are unusual in Garland's correspondence. A January 1889 letter reveals the depth of Garland's admiration for the Hernes' acting and suggests the influence of acting techniques upon his fiction; and a 21 November 1890 letter reveals a rare, boyish exuberance (letters 25, 54). He drafted several plays, publishing *Under the Wheel* in June 1890 and giving an "Author's Reading" of another, *A Member of the Third House*, four months later. In numerous letters Garland rallied Boston's literati to support Herne's plays, writing to the noted critic Brander Matthews on 29 December 1889 to promote Herne's *Drifting Apart*: "My idea is that if we have an American drama we must encourage what is good and true and condemn what is bad in every play—not condemn or praise a play indiscriminately. In this way a standard of taste for a new play is created" (letter 43). With the Hernes he also formed the Boston Independent Theater Association in 1891, America's first art theater, to provide a venue for Herne's Ibsenesque *Margaret Fleming* after commercial managers refused to produce it.

Garland's dramatic ambitions would never leave him, and he would return to dramatic criticism and theatrical promotion at various times in his life. But he was eager to get published, and fiction and poetry seemed a more promising basis upon which to launch a career. Once Garland had resolved to write fiction, intending to interpret his section of the country to those readers who had no personal knowledge of life on the middle border, his associations with Richard Watson Gilder, editor of the prestigious *Century*, and Benjamin Orange Flower, editor of the radical *Arena*, gave impetus to his publishing career. Between 1888 and 1890, Garland was having difficulties getting his realistic stories of the middle border into print. Garland wrote to Gilder in September 1889 as a local-color writer, hoping to get a sympathetic reading of one of his stories: "The only favor I ask for the enclosed stories is: that they be read with a due regard for the aims of the author. First I aim to be true to the life I am depicting and to deal not with abnormal phases so much as with representative phases. I am western born and the dialect and descriptive matter can be relied upon." (letter 35).

He was elated when Gilder accepted "A Spring Romance" and paid Garland seventy-five dollars—more money than he had yet received for a story. But though Gilder would continue to accept his stories, Garland grew increasingly dissatisfied with the *Century* because of long delays between the acceptance and the appearance of his stories and of the rejection of a major portion of his work. He had much better success placing his stories, however, with Flower, who encouraged Garland to produce political and economic material. During 1890–93, Garland contributed more than half of his short stories, articles, and reviews to the *Arena*.

Unfortunately, none of Garland's letters to Flower survive. However, Garland's extensive and important correspondence with Gilder does, and a consideration of it is critical to assessing Garland's development as a writer in the 1890s. A marked preoccupation in Garland criticism has been the degree to which Garland "declined from realism" and the effect of Gilder's editorial suggestions upon Garland's fictional practices.[6] While it is true that Gilder rejected most of Garland's polemical writings that were submitted to him, most of Garland's letters are not attempts to appease Gilder, but rather explanations and arguments in response to questions Gilder raised. The letters do, however, show the extent to which Garland took Gilder's criticisms seriously and how he tried to produce good art while at the same time producing fiction with strong social messages.

Although Garland was appearing often in print by 1892, his work was not selling as well as he had hoped, and much of his middle border material was being criticized in both the East and the West. By 1894, tired of the controversy surrounding his middle border fiction, he announced in a letter to his publisher, Herbert Stone, that *Crumbling Idols* would be his last controversial work and that he intended to look elsewhere for his material: "I shall not repeat either my economic writing or this literary and art reform. Having said my say I shall proceed on other things" (18 January 1894, letter 76). But while Garland's turn to the Mountain West for his material signaled a change in those subjects with which he had been occupied in his middle border fiction, the change was not nearly as abrupt as it seemed. Garland's interest in the problems facing the American Indian, for example, can be found as early as 1890, with his publication of "Drifting Crane" (*Harper's Weekly* 32 [31 May 1890]: 421–22), written even before Garland had experienced Indian problems firsthand. This was followed by a long series of stories written over the next twenty years and later collected in *The Book of the American Indian* (1923). From the beginning, Garland considered himself a Western writer and had an emotional, though romantic, attachment to the West.

In fact, Garland had decided to move on to other things somewhat earlier. In late 1892 Garland made an extended trip to the Pacific Coast with his parents. When he returned to Boston in January 1893, he had not only decided to cease writing economic and social fiction, but he had also decided to move to Chicago, though it would be more than a year before he made the move permanent. In the spring of 1893 he spent several weeks in the mountains of Colorado. Finally, two more trips to Colorado in the summers of 1894 and 1895 confirmed his desire to begin a career as a writer of Mountain West fiction. Donald Pizer suggests several reasons why Garland resolved to settle in Chicago:

> He was firmly convinced of the need for each locality to express itself in literature, and he was equally certain that local literary centers would arise to aid this expression. As a Midwesterner, he felt that Chicago was his literary center and that the time had come to assist its growth. Moreover, as a local colorist who believed it was necessary to verify his impressions and recollections, he realized that Chicago was within easy distance of his material. . . . Lastly, Garland hoped to settle his parents in West Salem, the Wisconsin coulee town near which he had been born. And West Salem was only six or seven hours from Chicago.[7]

Another effect of resolving to move to Chicago was his decision to allow the recently established publishing firm of Stone and Kimball to reissue *Main-Travelled Roads* in 1893. Within two years, the Chicago-based firm became the publishers of five of Garland's books. While Garland was impressed with the quality and attractiveness of the books, his many letters to Herbert S. Stone and Hannibal I. Kimball Jr. are often contentious, for Garland was frequently dissatisfied with the marketing, promotion, and sales of his books. As he now was largely dependent upon their sales for his income, Garland intended to be actively involved in all aspects of his literary properties. His irritation would also extend to his literary agent Paul Reynolds, whom he angrily and repeatedly instructed in how to sell his books.

Garland went to London in April 1899 to arrange for the publication of his books in England and to meet some of his English literary acquaintances. Before returning to the United States, he decided to visit France, arriving in Paris on 30 May and staying until 12 June. His three letters to his parents, who were then living in West Salem, record his European activities, as well as capture his moods and interests far removed from his literary and domestic concerns at home. Upon his return he renewed his protracted courtship of Zulime Taft, an artist and sister of the noted sculptor Lorado Taft, whom he married on 18 November 1899.

NOTES

1. *See* Kenneth M. Price, "Hamlin Garland's 'The Evolution of American Thought': A Missing Link in the History of Whitman Criticism," *Walt Whitman Quarterly Review* 3 (fall 1985): 1–20. An incomplete MS of the book exists in the Garland Papers (item #465).

2. Particularly helpful in understanding Garland's views about the use of dialect in poetry are three unpublished, undated manuscripts located in the Garland Papers: "James Whitcomb Riley," "Riley and the Question of Dialect," and "Vernacular in Verse" (item #524).

3. Price and Leitz, "The Uncollected Letters of Hamlin Garland to Walt Whitman," 1–2.

4. For Garland's relationship with Whitman, see Bruce McElderry, "Hamlin Garland's View of Whitman," *Personalist* 36 (1955): 369–78; Nancy Bunge, "Walt Whitman's Influence on Hamlin Garland," *Walt Whitman Review* 23 (1977): 45–50; and Thomas Bucknell, "Hamlin Garland's Response to Whitman," *The Old Northwest* 7 (1981): 217–35.

5. Garland's Booth lectures are extant in the Garland Papers: "Edwin Booth as a Master of Expression," "The Critical Problem: Action," "Edwin Booth as Hamlet," and "Edwin Booth as MacBeth" (item #584).

6. See, for example, Claude M. Simpson Jr., "Hamlin Garland's Decline," *Southwest Review* 26 (winter 1941): 223–34; Bernard I. Duffey, "Hamlin Garland's Decline from Realism," *American Literature* 25 (1953): 69–74; James D. Koerner, "Comment on 'Hamlin Garland's Decline from Realism,'" *American Literature* 26 (1954): 427–32; Bernard I. Duffey, "Mr. Koerner's Reply Considered," *American Literature* 26 (1954): 432–35; and McCullough, "Hamlin Garland's Romantic Fiction," pp. 349–62.

7. Pizer, *Hamlin Garland's Early Work and Career*, p. 112.

1. to Edmund Clarence Stedman   als, Columbia

Jamaica Plain.
Boston.

12/16/85

Mr. E. C. Stedman:[1]

Dear Sir: Holding you as the most authoritative of our critics I write on a matter which will at once concern you, and ask your consideration. I enclose a few poems by an author who is a stranger to me but one which I do not think you can afford longer to remain ignorant of.

I ask your careful attention to these poems. They were published in the "Providence Sunday Journal" and attracted my attention and finally affected me so power fully that I sought to know more of the author. I found Mr. Burleigh to be one of the well-known Burleigh family of Connecticut.[2] His hair has grown white in literary work. For forty years he has been writing and has published but a mere tithe of his work. Latterly he has sent out some extracts from his longer poems. By the merest chance I met him here in the city, and as we talked together he opened up the plan of his works which are prodigious. I do not conceive that you could have left him unmentioned in your late work had you known of his writings. I ask you to read the "Song of Beauty"[3] and the "Song of the Architect" with this plan in your brain:—

The scene opens on a high wooded height, at still noon. The poet lies gazing into the sky. Suddenly a light, brighter than the noonday sun, announces the approach of a lovely female figure floating at will, without wings. Upon the fillet on her head a single star blazes still more brightly. Behind her an innumerable train floats, till lost in the upper deeps. It is *Alèthè* and her attendant spirits.

> —"The glorious company who keep
> The worlds in rhythmic march."

As the dreamer questions concerning life and its mysteries, Alèthè and her spirits of Wisdom, Beauty, Love, etc answer.—The slips sent contain two of these songs which will *faintly* indicate the splendid character of the rhythm and music, and grandeur of the thought. I have no hesitancy in saying that I believe this poetry to bear the characteristics of the poetry which shall spring "like an Alpine torrent from the glacial facts of science." Mr. Burleigh strikes me as an *Evolutionistic Hugo*. However my opinion is of no consequence—what do you think of it? It is probable that you will wonder why he has not published more and all I could reply is, he seems a very retiring man and—is poor. Friends are now urging him to print and "Alethe" is the particular poem, we urge. It seems to me that our literature can ill afford to lose work of the character of "Song of the Architect" and "Silence of the Stars" which are mere fragments. His range is enormous: running from poems for the "Nursery" and "St. Nicholas" up to the poems enclosed. Are we deceived or is this a remarkable genius? Is that "Silence of the Stars" a mighty hymn of a soul filled with the glory of science or is it rhymed dissertation? It pleases me so well that I dare not say whether it is poetry to Smith or Hobbes. What shall we say of a man who catches and swings the "Nebular Hypothesis" thus.

> "The fine mist of primeval time
> My breath condensed like summer rain
> Swept on as by a hurricane
> *Each drop a burning world sublime*"

Or this:

> "I sunk the glooming gulfs of space
> Down which the stellar maelstrom whirls;
> That for its *seething foam-crest, hurls*
> *The pallid nebulae in heaven's face.*"

Observe the contrast of the great and small in each stanza.—But nothing I can say will add to them, they will speak to you in their own fashion. Believing that you will feel an interest much greater than my own I have written thus freely. I should be very glad to hear from you, or a letter directed to Mr. Burleigh at this point would be pleasant. Any questions from you would be gladly answered.

Mr. Burleigh is here for a few days. As I indicated he is in no way connected with me except as a congenial mind.

Most respectfully
Hamlin Garland

Will you please return slips. They are all I have and are valuable to me.

1. Edmund Clarence Stedman (1833–1908), genteel poet, editor, and stockbroker, whose *Poets of America* (2 vols., 1885) Garland refers to. This is apparently the earliest surviving letter by Garland.

2. George Shepard Burleigh (1821–1903) published poems chiefly in magazines and newspapers.

3. Full title: "A Song of Beauty in her Winter Realm."

2. to Edmund Clarence Stedman   als, Columbia

Jamaica Plain.

Dec 22/85

Mr. E.C. Stedman:

Dear Sir. I write to thank you for evident kindliness and to beg pardon for troubling you.[1] I did not know of your ill health and considered that as student of our social life and literature you would be interested in such a character as Mr. Burleigh. I will also say that Mr. Burleigh *knew nothing* of the letter till some time after it was written. He is the last man to seek a vehicle in someone else.

With deep regret I read your words giving up criticism. Hoping you may yet be able to do much to reform that much abused department of our literature I am

With great respect
Yours sincerely
Hamlin Garland.

1. Stedman had written on 20 December that he was receiving a dozen letters like Garland's each day, and that he seldom deigned to respond, and then curtly concluded: "In the present case I send these few lines to say that I know something of Mr. Burleigh's family, of his last work, etc., & then the earnestness of his life & its eloquent expression command my highest sympathy & respect. But it would be impossible for me, even if I were under the slightest obligation to do so, to enter into any discussion of his lines with you or with him. My critical labors are forever ended." Stedman's letter is pasted at the front of Garland's copy of Stedman's *Poems, Now First Collected* (1897).

Jamaica Plain.

Jan 22/86

Mr. Edwin Booth.[1]

Dear Sir: You may possibly, be interested in the work I am doing or trying to do upon a subject which touches you nearly. I enclose a very scanty and incoherent synopsis of a lecture which I have been delivering.[2] The lecture is itself a synopsis of a larger work which may grow into a book.

I was led to take up the study of expression in connection with my work in literature, by the idea that all writers are sooner or later dependent upon an artist of expression, whether they get complete hearing or not. That is: *voice* and *action* can not be written, they are only indicated, and upon the degree of their expressiveness are the authors ranked. The matter of expression has, however, been for the most part in the hands of "professors of Elocution" till Darwin in 1872 put it upon a universal basis; and Spencer, Bain[,] Mantegazza and many others have since pushed it into the region of science and into the splendid domain of causes.[3] What I began as an aid to teaching literature I now recognize as a branch of psychology (scientifically) and a great art in the realm of esthetics.

My aim has been to treat of your work in a general way as indicated in the enclosed slip. Giving the broadest principles known to me. Then to consider each of your characterizations as a whole. Giving your conception of each *as it appears to me through your expression*, believing that for the most part you make your idea discoverable if we are quick to see and hear.

Then lastly I intend treating of particular passages, analyzing the voice, the cadences, rate, force etc. And of action in accordance with the generalizations of Darwin, Spencer[,] Mantegazza, etc. All this I have sketched out. Iago, Hamlet, Macbeth I am at work upon.

It certainly remains to be seen whether I have improved on the methods of the average critic. I should like to fix in some degree the meaning of your work upon paper both for my own pleasure and the pleasure of others. Whether it will interest you, remains to be seen. Of course, you are wearied and busy and not in a condition to think on the matter but at any time, if you are interested, I should be pleased to put into your hand sketches of my work and methods of study. In closing I would say, it has

been a pleasant labor thus far, to pay some slight tribute to one who has
done so much to embody the sublime dramas of Shakespeare.

Sincerely yours.
Hamlin Garland

1. Edwin Booth (1833–93), a noted American actor, often cast in the role of the tragic
leading man (Hamlet, Othello, Lear), became known as "The Prince of Tragedy."

2. Garland's lecture, "Edwin Booth as a Master of Expression" (ca. 1885–86), together with copies of three related unpublished lectures, "The Critical Problem: Action," "Edwin Booth as Hamlet," and "Edwin Booth as MacBeth," are in the Garland
Papers (item #584).

3. The British philosopher Herbert Spencer (1820–1903) anticipated many of Darwin's theories and was the first to use the phrase "survival of the fittest." His *First
Principles* (1862) was a tremendous influence upon Garland and other writers, and his
application of evolutionary theory to ethics, politics, sociology, and even aesthetics to
many seemed to provide a "synthetic philosophy" that unified all knowledge. Alexander Bain (1818–1903) was a Scottish psychologist who wrote several philosophical
works, including *Moral Philosophy* (1852), *Senses and the Intellect* (1855), and *The Emotions and Will* (1859), as well as English grammar and composition and rhetoric texts.
Paolo Mantegazza (1831–1910) was an Italian physiologist and anthropologist who
founded the Museum of Anthropology and Ethnology at Florence.

4. to E. W. Howe als, usc

Jamaica Plain

July 2/86.

E. W. Howe.

Dear Sir: I have just finished reading the "Moonlight Boy"; and having
seen your face and after careful attention to your first works, I feel almost
as though I knew you.[1]

As for myself I am a critic in a small way, lecture some and teach
slightly more, and what is more significant still am western born. I know
several "Davy's Bends",[2] and "Country Towns."[3] I was born in Wisconsin
and grew up in a troublesome manner on the great Iowan prairies.

All this for saying I like your stories. Your strong true delineation, of
the monotonous and provincial life of the rural west compels my admiration, though it grieves me to think how unavoidable the most of its life
is. Has it not seemed to you a terrible waste of talent many times, when

you have met men and women of fine powers, musical maybe, who were hedged in by circumstances, walking a dull routine of petty duties, compelled to forget the outside world? I have met many such and it has been a question whether I did them good by rousing them from their lethargy.

I have just been thinking of "Annie Benton"[4] whose case presents very nearly, the situation of several young women I have met—I mean the musical talent and latent aspirations for a nobler life. This leads me to what I had started to say: you speak of these people not as one who coldly looks on them as "picturesque" but in an earnest sincere tone *as from among them.* Your work has an *indigenous* quality which appeals to me very strongly, perhaps more strongly than to most critics. I can value your strong, idiomatic, western prose, I think, better than one who has not heard it spoken.

I suppose you will be wondering what reason I can possibly have for troubling you with my opinions, and rightly too, for there is no especial reason for such conduct. To come at the matter briefly: the circular within gives the synopsis of a volume upon the "Evolution of American Thought" which I deliver in the form of lectures at the B.S.O.[5]

Therein I design to treat of yourself and work in the 9th chapter. There are representative names standing for "local, scene and character painting"; in which category you stand in solitary grandeur, in the midst of the great west (myself your only rival, not having published yet).

Now if you could think of giving me a few points concerning your life, such as you would like published, they would be of use to me and I think to you. I would undertake to have a magazine publish that part relating to you. I would try at any rate and if I failed I can use the Transcript whose literary editor is an intimate friend, and who is moreover much interested in you.[6] Please do not look for any ulterior motive here. I admire your work which so finely voices the middle west, that and the fact that I am western born explain my willingness to do you any good which lies in my power to do. In the midst of my press of study and writing upon critical lives, I am myself striving to express some of the unuttered thought of the western prairies.

Pray do not think I ask for a biography or anything approaching it but if you saw fit to give me some sketches of your boyhood, residence, schooling etc, I could at the least give you a column in the Transcript, which would be something; and possibly some magazine might be captured by a taking article.

I shall have some hand in the review of the "Moonlight Boy" which by the way is puzzling all—myself included. It is realism with a vengeance. It strikes me as an avowed departure, is it so? "All the conventional novelist would have done he has avoided" is one of the notes I sent in when I returned the book to Mr. Hurd of the Transcript.

It is not so tragic, so powerful, of course, as the other two but it has a charm of its own. I like it for its truthful treatment of homely, prosaic people in their restricted lives.

Hoping you will understand me rightly and value at least the good will of my letter. I remain

Most sincerely your friend.
Hamlin Garland

1. Edgar Watson Howe (1853–1937), editor of the Atchinson, Kansas, *Daily Globe* (1877–1911), whose pioneering realistic novel *The Story of a Country Town* (1883) traces life in a Midwestern community. Garland reviewed Howe's novel *A Moonlight Boy* in the *Boston Evening Transcript* on 16 July 1886.

2. The decaying river town in Howe's second novel, *The Mystery of the Locks* (1885), modeled after the town of Brownville, Nebraska.

3. Garland refers to Twain Mounds, the setting of Howe's first novel, *The Story of a Country Town*.

4. Church organist for Davy's Bend.

5. The Boston School of Oratory. For a discussion of Garland's lectures, see Price, "Hamlin Garland's 'The Evolution of American Thought.'"

6. Charles E. Hurd (1833–1910) was the literary editor of the *Boston Evening Transcript*. Howe replied on 7 July 1886, saying that "I will give you the facts requested, with the understanding that you do not quote me." He then provided a number of biographical details, before confessing that while he did not enjoy journalistic and editorial work, he could not risk living on his writings alone.

5. to E. W. Howe

al, usc

Jamaica Plain.

July 15/86.

E. W. Howe.

Dear Sir: I have pondered much upon the singular life which you outlined to me in your letter and am more than ever convinced that the author of the "Country Town" is the strongest writer the west owns—and more than that: from him is yet to come work greater then the *best* of anything he has now written. Only, he must not work upon that paper till he sears his sensibilities and loses the power of receiving new subtle and enduring impressions. His three books are in large measure the results of reminiscences, he must move on to a wider field and (still using the past) make a deliberate and exhaustive study of the middle west and its mental horizon.

Great mental revolutions are going on around him, social and religious, that should be portrayed. The empty shell of Christianity is dropping from every sane thinker in the east as well as the west. A newer and broader idea of morality is taking its place. The mental struggle, the change from the old to the new has many profound and striking aspects —They should be recorded.

Then again there are human souls blossoming under the eye of the author of "The Locks." Swedes, Danes, Germans, with the seal of "divinely appointed" despotism on their dulled and weary faces debauch into the prairies of Kansas like great seivers. They set to work. The sod turns under their feet; houses are built; food broadens their faces; freedom adds to their stature and lightens their eyes.

Their children—ah! Their children are a new race under the sun! They are born of the sun and winds and grain of Kansas. They speak two, often four languages. They go to school, mayhap college—now look at the strong, clean free young men and women one generation only removed from the men and women herded like cattle in the depots of Chicago, stupid, dazed, ill smelling; punched and pushed and ticketed like baggage—Here is a picture which the author of "The Locks" will one day give the world.—To speak direct, Mr. Howe the west is not known as yet. All that vast seething transfiguring mass of men in the Mississippi valley, because they have not produced their own writers are, unknown.

Travellers go through and write a few lines as observers. Here and there some one writes of material or semi-material things in prose, *none* have given the deep, unseen *true* life of the people. Do not think I am "lecturing," on the contrary this is downright *talk*, just as I would look you in the face and say if I had the chance.

All the time I fear you are thinking: "What sort of an axe does the fellow want to grind." Confound it! I've *no* axe to grind. I simply want to say that I believe in you and I want to see you enthrone the office cat in that editorial chair while you sit down to write that "best book." We are not rich enough in genius to allow a man to "boss" a daily paper who can write "The Story of a Country Town."

I do not presume to offer advice being fully (?) three years younger than your self, but it does seem as though you could risk the relinquishment of that editorial chair.

[omission] [1]

these writers as Howells find it amusing and frivolous. — See the *comedy* element, in short. Others say the present is solemn, momentous and grand beyond any past. This is the belief of Walt Whitman our greatest poet.

I do not know how you feel as regards your work, (I should like to meet and talk with you upon the matter) but judging *from* your work as published, I think you find something more than comedy in your world.

You go deeper than Howells. You have not his exquisite art for you lack his leisure and his temperament but you have what moves me more, the ability to perceive and to voice the passions that shake the soul.

1. Apparently, page(s) which precede and follow the next section have been lost.

6. to George Washington Cable

als, Tulane

Jamaica Plain

July 29/86.

G. W. Cable: [1]

Dear Sir: In treating of your work, in which I am greatly interested, I have tried in vain to remember where I have seen an article of yours upon the negros of New Orleans or vicinity. The article was a short one and treated of them in their picturesque dances or something similar. One point which attracted my attention was the *races* named and distinguished. As you know we of the north think a negro is a negro and do not know that striking mental as well as physical differences exist; and that under an observant eye they become as individual (I suspect) as the Indian races.

I do not mean the articles in the *Century* upon some songs but the one in which you have described the dress and race characteristics of each member of the company as they come in. [2] I have no doubt you will know at once the one I mean. I wish you would give me notes of these article[s] and I will look them up in the library here.

I am familiar with all your published books but felt that those articles were of special value. I hope you will give us more of the same sort. Since yourself and Harris[3] began to write the conventional "Darkie" is seen to be an absurdity. I enclose a little slip containing a view of my work which I am using in Professor Brown's Summer School.

Hoping you will find time to jot down the date and name of paper containing the articles indicated (very vaguely I am afraid) I am

Very respec'fly'
Hamlin Garland

1. George Washington Cable (1844–1925), author of local-color stories set in New Orleans, whose works include *Old Creole Days* (1879) and *The Grandissimes* (1880).

2. The specific article to which Garland refers is not clear. The articles in the *Century* that he mentions include the following: "The Freedman's Case in Equity," *Century* 29 (January 1885): 409–18; "The Silent South," *Century* 30 (September 1885): 674–91; "Creole Slave Songs," *Century* 31 (April 1886): 807–28; and "'A Reply' to John W. Johnston's 'The True South Vs. the Silent South,'" *Century* 32 (May 1886): 166–70.

3. Joel Chandler Harris (1848–1908), Georgia writer of plantation tales which appeared in several collections beginning with *Uncle Remus: His Songs and His Sayings* (1881).

7. to George Washington Cable   als, Tulane

Jamaica Plain.

Aug 7/86.

Geo. W. Cable:

Dear Sir: I thought I had read all your articles in the Century but I find upon looking up the February number that I had read about half the article on the Congo Dance.[1] The part which was copied in some obscure magazine, is the part I did not read. It was a single paragraph describing them as they came in and naming the parts from which they came. Seeing it alone gave me a strong impression and I wondered whether a whole article had been devoted to that phase of the subject. This explanation I feel is due me, with the further word that at that time I was at work upon the "Rise of the Landscape School" which was alien to the article.

I aim to keep informed upon what fills the leading magazines though I am not able to read them all. All articles previous to 1880 Poole's Index helps me find; it is not so easy if the articles are since that date.—

Your work is of great interest to me and I want to be able to understand you, and your themes as well as one can who has seen neither the
Creole nor the negro. To me that article brought up the wonderful truth
that inherited aptitudes and race ideas, appearing thus in the negro, give
a swift realization of the dark place out of which he has just emerged.
Some of Spencers great laws flashed upon my mind.—

Hoping you will excuse a seeming lack of enterprise and attribute my
bad memory to my preoccupation—I sign

Yours sincerely
Hamlin Garland

1. "The Dance in Place Congo," *Century* 31 (February 1886): 517–32.

8. to Walt Whitman

als, Congress
publ.: "Uncollected"

Jamaica Plain
Boston.
Mass.

11/24/86.

Mr. Walt Whitman.

It is with profound sorrow that I read in the papers the news that you
are again suffering from your old trouble.[1] I trust it is not so serious as
reported. My regard for you is so great that I am very sorry not to be able
to buy more copies of your books and thus give a more substantial token
of sympathy.

I am an enthusiastic reader of your books; both volumes of which I
have within reach of hand.[2] I am everywhere in my teaching and writing
making your claims felt and shall continue to do so.[3] I have demonstrated
(what of course you know) that there is no veil—no impediment—between your mind and your audience, when your writings are *voiced*. The
formlessness is only seeming not real.

I have never read a page of your poetry, or quoted a line, that has not
commanded admiration. The music is there and the grandeur of thought
is there, if the reader reads, guided by the sense and not by the external
lining or paragraphing. Even very young pupils feel the thrill of the deep
rolling music though the thought may be too profound for them to grasp.

In a course of lectures before the Boston School of Oratory last summer I made a test of the matter. I do not think a single pupil held out against my arguments supplemented by readings from your work. The trouble is they get at your work through the daily press or through the defenders of Longfellow or Tennyson (whom it is supposed you utterly antagonize).[4] When it is brought to them by one who appreciates and measurably understands your methods and ideals I do not think there is any doubt of the favorable result. I have found much opposition but it was mostly ignorant or misled.

I am a young man of very ordinary attainments and do not presume to do more than to give you a glimpse of the temper of the public which would not do you wrong, deliberately, but who by reason of the causes hinted at above, fail to get at the transcendent power of "Leaves of Grass."

If I have given you the impression that I believe in you and strive to interpret you, you will not feel that I have over-stepped the privileges of a pupil in the presence of a great teacher.

The enclosed slip is a meagre out-line of a volume which I am writing and which I hope to get out this coming spring. As the motto-page of this volume I have used a paragraph from your "Collect" which is entitled "Foundation Stages—then Others."[5] While it is not strictly essential to the book, yet I should esteem it a favor if you would consent to its use. One sentence, "*In nothing is there more evolution than in the American mind*," I have also used in company with Spencer's great law of progress upon my title page.[6] It helped to decide the title, which is: *The Evolution of American Thought*: an outline study of the leading phases of American Literature, etc. In the latter part of the volume I have treated of the Age of Democracy and its thought, taking as foundation the splendid utterances of M. Taine upon the modern age. It is in this chapter that I place your work.[7] I quote from you quite largely both in treating of your writings and in treating the general theme of present and future democratic ideals. I hope to be able to please you with my treatment of your great work. Beside this I am preparing special lectures upon the same subject.

Have you any objection to the quotations which I find it nescessary to use? In conclusion let me say that without any bias in your favor, (rather the opposite from newspapers) your poems thrilled me, reversed many of my ideas, confirmed me in others, helped to make me what I am. I am a border man; born in Wisconsin and raised on the prairie frontier. I am a disciple of Mr. Spencer and therefore strive at comparative methods of criticism. That your poems should thus convert me is to me a revelation of their power, especially when I can convince others in the same manner.

And now revered friend (for I feel you are a friend) think of me as one who radiates the principles of the modern age, and who will in his best manner (poor at best) strive to make his hearers and readers better aware of the goodness and grandeur of the "Good Grey Poet" and his elemental lines.

Your readers are increasing, and may you live to see the circle infinitely extended, is my fervent hope. I do not expect a reply to this other than the signification whether I may quote you or not. I wish I might see and talk with you but that is not possible—except through your volumes.

I am most sincerely yours,
Hamlin Garland

1. The "old trouble" is Whitman's paralytic stroke. On 19 November 1886 Whitman wrote William Douglas O'Conner, "I go out by my own volition not at all, as my power of walking &c. is quite gone" (*Walt Whitman: The Correspondence*, ed. Edwin Haviland Miller [New York: New York University Press, 1969], 4:54).

2. Garland owned at this time both *Leaves of Grass* and *Specimen Days*. Garland's marked copy of *Leaves of Grass* (Boston: Osgood, 1881) is in the Garland Papers (USC).

3. Garland refers to his teaching at the Boston School of Oratory and, probably, to his unpublished history of American literature entitled "The Evolution of American Thought." For the text of the chapter dealing with Whitman, see Price, "Hamlin Garland's 'The Evolution of American Thought,'" pp. 5–18.

4. For Garland's comments on Longfellow and his poetic contemporaries, see Price, p. 10. Early in his career Whitman was, for the most part, sharply critical of his poetic contemporaries. As he asked in "Democratic Vistas": "Do you call those genteel little creatures American poets? Do you term that perpetual, pistareen, paste-pot work, American art?" (*Prose Works 1892*, ed. Floyd Stovall [New York: New York University Press, 1964], 2:388–89). Following the deaths of Bryant in 1878 and Emerson and Longfellow in 1882, Whitman became more conciliatory in such pieces as "My Tribute to Four Poets," a chapter of *Specimen Days*.

5. The "enclosed slip" is not extant. "Foundation Stages—then Others" first appeared as paragraph ten of "Thoughts for the Centennial" in Whitman's *Two Rivulets* (1876). The piece was reprinted in *Specimen Days & Collect* (1882).

6. Garland is probably referring to Herbert Spencer's belief that mankind was slowly but inexorably moving toward social perfection.

7. Garland read Hippolyte Taine's *History of English Literature* during the winter of 1883–84 and was much impressed by his theories regarding race, milieu, and epoch.

9. to James Whitcomb Riley

als, Indiana U
publ.: McCullough

Jamaica Plain

Oct. 25/87.

James Whitcomb Riley:

Dear Friend:

I was very glad to receive a letter from you saying your new book was forthcoming and Mr. Hurd rejoiced with me.[1] Send me a copy as soon as convenient as I shall use it in my lectures and shall give you a good notice in *Transcript*, be sure of that.

I *hope* the poems are down among the clover blooms and among the corn-shucks. Your fantastical work has very little value to me as compared with "William Leachman" "Old Fashioned Roses" etc. And above that profoundly touching and splendidly true poem in the *Century*, "Nothin' at all to Say." So simple, so true and so full of unutterable pathos. That is great work, friend Riley. To express what thousands feel and can not express, that's what makes the true poet. The throb of a thousand hearts is in the rhythm of his lines.

Mr. Hurd tells me that there are times when you feel that success has been slow, and if any words of mine can assure you that you have not failed, I would gladly give them. I meant what I said in a previous letter. You are true to the horizon of the farmer, and voice his emotions better than any American who has yet written. I am perfectly aware however that such fidelity to truth has not been rewarded, and that the people are but beginning to enjoy the art-setting of their every-day lives, but the change is coming and you will find each year your circle of friends widening. I was much gratified to hear that you were in demand for lectures. I suppose you read the poems which are in these books—some of them at least. Are they not well received everywhere? Is not the interest growing therein? Your letter indicated that you were in good health and spirits, for which I am glad. Your lectures can but awaken the people to the beauties and art-capabilities of their humble lives. Would it be asking too much, to request that Mr. Riley send his photograph—if the books have not a frontispiece? I like to have the face of my friends in their books if possible.

I hope our acquaintance may continue and that I may meet you veritably, in the flesh.

Yours most sincerely,
Hamlin Garland

1. James Whitcomb Riley (1849–1916), Indiana poet best known for the series of dialect poems by "Benjamin F. Johnson," originally published in the *Indianapolis Journal.* His collections include *The Old Swimmin'-Hole and 'Leven More Poems* (1883), *Old Fashioned Roses* (1888), and *Rhymes of Childhood* (1890). Riley's "new book" is *Afterwhiles* (1887).

10. to James Whitcomb Riley

als, Indiana U
publ.: McCullough

Jamaica Plain.

Dec. 17/87.

Dear Friend Riley:

Your beautiful little book[1] came to me two or three days ago and to say I am delighted is to say nothing. I dare not say how touching many of these poems are to me. — If Mr. Hurd and I do not give your horn a *toot* in the ears of the Bostonians it will be because we've lost the little influence we had with the press. — But why didnt you bind all previously published poems into this volume? All the "Old Swimming Hole" and the lyrics in "Boss Girl" *ought* to have been in this volume sure[2] — however we are thankful to get so much.

I am writing a special article for the *Transcript* to be published early next week.[3] I take the greatest pleasure in writing an article on your work, it is so genuine, so faithful to the lives and loves of the humble folk. It does not attempt to soar the Empyrean it walks in the dewy clover-blooms, it tells aloud what many humble folk think but can not put into words.

— I will send a copy of the article to you as soon as it is published and if it is of the slightest use to you, you are welcome and any thing I can do for you at any time I will gladly do. — I must be candid and say that I do not take the same interest in your tendency to the fantastic. The first part of the book I do not so much care for. "Old Aunt Mary's" is a good text to use in my criticism. Now dialect could have aided that but still the thought, the conception is after all the secret. I mean: that a conception can be conventional and continue even under the most perfect dialect while the reverse can also be true. Your power lies in voicing the emotions of the farmer and other humble people. All that you write is exquisitely true, your other work is by no means lacking in power and originality, yet it is not so distinctive. Note well I do not say you could not be successful without dialect, you certainly could, but dialect gives you an opportunity for those curious felicities of thought, abrupt changes of emotion etc, which makes the rest of us despair of equalling it. — We were glad to hear that you captured the audience at New York.[4] — If my advice is worth anything use it and welcome. I say stick to the dialect, in at least homely themes. Try always to give such reality of emotion as is in "Afterwhiles" and your place will be high.

With the utmost faith in the "Hooser-poet"

I am yours fraternally
Hamlin Garland.

1. *Afterwhiles.*

2. *The Old Swimmin'-Hole and 'Leven More Poems* (1883), Riley's first book; *The Boss Girl, A Christmas Story and Other Sketches* (1885) consisted of prose sketches.

3. In "James Whitcomb Riley," BET, 12 December 1887, Garland noted the weaknesses in *The Boss Girl* and favorably reviewed *The Old Swimmin'-Hole* and *Afterwhiles.* Garland emphasized that Riley was unprecedented, arguing that "previous to that little volume (*Afterwhiles*) the Western farmer had not found his poet"; that farmers to whom he had read these poems "felt as though their most silent emotions had been expressed by this little book of dialect poems"; and that Riley's characteristic genius was to be found in his dialect poems.

4. In November 1887 Riley made his initial appearance in New York City at Chickering Hall, under the auspices of the International Copyright League. After his first day's success before a distinguished audience which included Mark Twain, James Russell Lowell introduced Riley for a second day's reading and concluded: "I can say to you of my own knowledge, that you are to have the pleasure of listening to the voice of a true poet" (quoted in Marius Dickey, *The Maturity of James Whitcomb Riley* [Indianapolis: Bobbs-Merrill, 1922], p. 221).

11. to James Whitcomb Riley

als, Indiana U
publ.: McCullough

Jamaica Plain.

Dec. 21/87.

My Dear Riley:

A merry Christmas to you and yours. I hope you are not snow-bound at some "Prairie Junction," "Merry Christmas" is a mockery in such cases. —

I send a notice written hastily.[1] I hope to do more for you at some other time. The article is rendered a little obscure at points owing to the fact that Mr. Hurd could not read my terrible hand-writing. — I can only say that all this and more I could say with perfect sincerity of your work. I believe you can and will make yourself one of the greatest realistic farmer's poets voicing feelings common to all. I read your poems to farmers in the west, Wisconsin and Dakota and they had such an appreciation for them as was beyond their expression.—Go on give us more. Give us a volume of collected works.

Yours fraternally
Hamlin Garland

P.S. My poems take this direction: see enclosure "Lost in the Norther." [2]

    1. Garland refers to his review in the 12 December BET.

    2. "Lost in the Norther" was first published in *Harper's Weekly* 31 (3 December 1887): 883; it was reprinted in *Prairie Songs* (1893) and *Boy Life on the Prairie* (1899).

12. to James Whitcomb Riley

als, Indiana U
publ.: McCullough

Jamaica Plain.

Feb. 11/88.

My Dear Riley:

Your breezy note made up for any tardiness, by being so unconventional and so characteristic. As for your kind appreciation of my occasional verse—I thank you, but I fear I am too heavily weighted with philosophy to be very much of a poet.[1] I have the desire to put that life into art-form but it will probably be in form of the novel. I know my own limitations too well to get very much inspirited over my future. I am better in such work as my prose description of "Holding Down a Claim" printed in Harpers Weekly for Jan. 28. You saw it no doubt. There is no discount on some of those paragraphs. I will have a second article in *American* for March. "The Thrashin' Season" which I know you will enjoy.—[2]

I write today principally to say that I must voice my judgment concerning your sonnets and other poems not in dialect. I hate a sonnet God knows! but such work as "Silence" and especially "When She Comes Home" is magnificently done. The last is beyond all praise—so human, so full of genuine passion. Those of "Time"[,] "Death" etc are good but not so strong. My Dear Riley you have a great career before you. I said to a company of ladies the other day where I was lecturing—that James Whitcomb R. was the most promising young poet in America. I do not say this to flatter for a moment, I want it to make a profound impression. You seem fitted to express the longing, the tenderness, the unaltered desires and fears of the Western farmer and his poor hard-working wife. Set yourself to it earnestly. Put what you know and feel of those western folk into song "Tell of the things just like they were." "They don't need no excuse." I know about it but I can not compress it into verse as you do. Did I tell you I am western-born? Born in LaCrosse Co. Wisconsin. You've been there no doubt—then I went out on the prairies of Iowa. I know all about it. Sometime I will tell you about it—but in fiction.—I am very glad to see that you are getting hold of the public—I can only say dont write too fast—though I think there is no danger of that in your case.—Did I send you my new circular? My kind of lecturing goes off rather slowly.—In conclusion I can only say that the more I study your writing the closer it stands to me. Dont fail to write when you can find time and send copies of your contributions to western papers.

Hamlin Garland

1. Garland is referring specifically to Riley's letter of 17 January 1888, in which he employs dialect and other characteristics while talking about Garland's poetry: "Long before I had your pen-and-ink self before me I knew you by name and poem; and I've riz up, more'n once, straight on my haunkers at the things you've said in rhymes! You've got the voice of the storm in that, and the zipp and the whirr, and the muscle and brown of the darlin' Old Tempest himself its so good to know and to hear—and to be buffeted by, and to have one's hair tossed with, and one's Death whipt into gasps of the praise of it all. Keep up that lick and I'll love you as long as I last."

2. "Holding Down a Claim in a Blizzard" appeared in *Harper's Weekly* 32 (28 January 1888): 66–67. "The Thrashin'" appeared in the *American* 7 (March 1888): 570–77. The second of six articles which Garland published in the *American* between January and October 1888 about his experience growing up on the prairie, the series eventually formed the heart of *Boy Life on the Prairie* (1899).

13. to Walt Whitman

als, Congress
publ.: "Uncollected"

Jamaica Plain.

April 19/88

Walt Whitman:

Dear Sir: It is probable that my friend Kennedy[1] has told you something of me and the work I am trying to do for you and for American literature. I have not written to you for the reason that you are sufficiently plagued with letters but now I feel that I have reached the point where I can presume on your interest. Mr. Kennedy I know writes to you in a depressed mood many times, saying that he finds a "solid line of enemies" (I think those were his words). This is not true of my experience. I am often astonished at finding so many friends and sympathizers in your work and cause. In my teaching and lecturing I find no difficulty in getting converts to the new doctrine and find your poems nearly irresistible in effect. True they do not always agree that they *are* "poems" though acknowledging their power and beauty. I do not care what they call them (I say to them) and receive their allegiance just the same. I hope to do much in the way of reading and lecturing to bring your work before the people and it would give me pleasure to know you consider my work valuable. I am just now delivering a course of lectures in the city on "The Literature of Democracy" concerning which I enclose a couple of slips.[2]

In these I am trying to analyze certain tendencies of American life somewhat in accordance with the principles you have taught. How successful I may be remains to be seen.—

I have not seen Mr. Kennedy for some months, he is so busy these days, but I had a characteristic letter from him a few days ago.

I have the greatest hope of seeing you some day and to talk with you upon these matters face to face. Let me assure you again that there is everywhere a growing respect and love for you and a growing appreciation of your poems. The papers no longer ridicule or even condemn unreservedly. An acquaintance among the younger literary editors of the city warrants me in saying that there is much more sympathy and appreciation among *them* than our friend Kennedy realizes. There is great gain.

It would give me great pleasure to hear from you if you are able to write.

With greatest love and esteem.
Hamlin Garland.

1. At this time William Sloane Kennedy (1850–1929), another Whitman admirer from the Midwest, was at work on a study entitled "Walt Whitman, Poet of Humanity." Kennedy later wrote *Reminiscences of Walt Whitman* (1896), and *A Companion Volume to Leaves of Grass* (1926), and edited *Walt Whitman's Diary in Canada* (1904). In "A Backward Glance O'er Travell'd Roads" Whitman chose to quote Kennedy's negative account of the reception of *Leaves of Grass*—"I find a solid line of enemies everywhere"—rather than the more positive account Garland offers in this letter. The evi-

dence about Whitman's reception was in fact mixed; the poet's own preference for Kennedy's bleaker and more melodramatic account is one of the many indications that Whitman cultivated his role as a misunderstood genius. See *Leaves of Grass*, Comprehensive Reader's Edition (New York: New York University Press, 1965), p. 562.

2. Garland may have included with his letter either notices from Boston papers about his lectures on "The Literature of Democracy" (a chapter from "The Evolution of American Thought") or an advertising brochure such as the one reproduced by Lars Ahnebrink in *The Beginnings of Naturalism in American Thought* (Cambridge: Harvard University Press, 1950), pp. 440–41.

14. to William Morton Fullerton

als, Virginia

Jamaica Plain.

May 2/88.

My Dear Fullerton:[1]

I have been expecting to see you every day since the appearance of your very just and able article on my work, but for fear you may think I am ungrateful I drop you this note.[2] Come up and see me at 7 Beacon St. on Thursday at four o'clock. I mean come if you can conveniently, I have a class from three to four. Or on Friday at 4 pm after symphony. I would like to have you meet Mr. Pellew.[3]—I saw your first editorial in the "Public Opinion"—I am glad they know a good thing when they see it. It would be glorious if the *Advertiser* could be something of an exponent of these new ideas in Literature.

Yours sincerely
Hamlin Garland

1. William Morton Fullerton (1865–1952?) was one of the founders of the *Harvard Monthly* and a staff writer for the *Boston Daily Advertiser*.

2. The *Advertiser* praised Garland's speech, "Literature of Democracy," as "a singularly penetrating and just exposition of the great principle which, we believe, is always recognized by the Zeet Geist as dominant in the progress of literature . . . the sovereign necessity of truth and sincerity in literary expression." See "Democracy in Literature," *Boston Daily Advertiser*, 12 April 1888, p. 4. Since Fullerton was in London, he did not comply with Garland's request for a meeting at this time. He cordially acknowledged his note, however, on 19 November 1888 and indicated that he hoped to see Garland "soon in the manner that you suggest to talk things over a little in a way we have not yet done."

3. George Pellew (1859–92), author and journalist for the *New York Sun*.

15. to James Whitcomb Riley

als, Indiana U
publ.: McCullough

Brown Co.
Ordway—Dakota.

[31 July 1888]

Dear Riley:

Before sending off the enclosed poem I send it to you to read and criticise.[1] Your judgement is valuable because we are agreed on the matter of free verse-form. I am free to say I like this, but the point is to get the opinion of someone else as to whether it is complete enough and whether the story is a detraction from its value. It has value because of its pictures rather than the story. Has it got the swing and trample and rush of halterless herds and the prairie? I wish you would read and return to me as soon as possible. Did you see my story in Belfords?—[2]

I am writing away on a little article concerning your work. Expect to complete first rough sketch in a few days.—I remember with the keenest pleasure my visit with you—I wish it could have lasted longer though I am not so sure of your feeling.—

Dont fail to let me know when your poem on the Miller is out "What's it a-talking of?"[3]

Yours sincerely
Hamlin Garland

1. Garland enclosed "Ladrone the Wind and the Prairie." This poem was later included, in revised form, in *Prairie Songs* (1893) and *Boy Life on the Prairie* (1899). On Garland's 1898 sojourn to Alaska, an expedition which is detailed in *The Trail of the Goldseekers* (1899), Garland purchased a Canadian-born Arabian horse, which he named Ladrone, and, through much difficulty, brought him back by rail to the family homestead in West Salem.

2. "A Common Case," *Belford's* 1 (July 1888): 188–99; reprinted as "Before the Low Green Door" in *Wayside Courtships* (1897).

3. Garland refers to "That-Air Young-Un," first published in *Northwestern Miller* (Christmas 1888), a poem about the young-un who spent his days sitting beside the creek above the dam near the mill. He was becoming acquainted with the meaning of "what the snake-feeders thought . . . and knowed Turtle talk." His father used to watch him from the mill and wonder at him. The young-un couldn't figure out "jes' what the wet Warter is a-talkin' of!" During a storm the dam breaks and the child is drowned; the miller wonders "Now what's it-a-talkin' of?"

16. to James Whitcomb Riley

als, Indiana U
publ.: McCullough

Ordway.

Aug. 5/88.

My Dear Riley:

I send herewith a skeleton of what I design finally to be a lecture and magazine article concerning your work.[1] I wish you would run through it and see how many objections you may have to offer why said out-line should not be filled up. Remember this is a first draft written at odd moments and must not be judged as final finished literary form.

I wish you would say frankly what you think of the design and whether I have misrepresented you or not. As for my judgements concerning your work that can not [be] changed of course except in detail, because right or wrong it represents *my* judgements.

I hope however that on general lines I have approached your own distribution of values.

I shall lecture this winter on "Dialect and Dialect Poets" wherein I hope to adequately set forth the claims of divers and sundry writers of the new school who aim above all things at truth.

Please read and return as early as convenient. — I send a photo in exchange for yours. If you dont want it dont keep it. I shall begin harvesting tomorrow. Already look brown and still "*Browning*" —

Hamlin Garland

1. Garland never published an article about Riley's work, but he may refer to "Riley and the Question of Dialect," an unpublished MS extant in the Garland Papers (item #524).

17. to James Whitcomb Riley

als, Indiana U

Ordway.

Aug 28/88.

Dear Riley:

What in the world have you done with that article of mine of J.W.R.?[1] I am a little concerned for that scrawl. There are some good things in it — (quotations I mean) and I hope it has reached you. I want to "lick it into shape" and do something with it. Dont fail to let me know just how much it worries you. —

I expect to start home soon.[2] May possibly speak again in Indianapolis. I hear from Kirkland[3] occasionally also from Mr. Howells and other Boston friends. Do you plan a trip to Boston this fall?

In our humble way we'll strew palm branches. — How would it do for you and I to write a play? Did I speak of this before? I have a good plan of a new one. "The McTurgs." Scene: Bank of Miss. near Lake Pipin. Need a Hoosier such as Riley could do. I'll act "David McTurg" young Hunter. Riley (inimitable comedian.) "Samuel Tunstall." Stunning combination! Prodigious success!!!$$$. *rolling* in Fame with capital F. —

Yours in haste.
Hamlin Garland

Seriously. I'm going to write a play that will be true and it will go. My brother is an actor and we will bring it out. I have written two already. Shall present one this winter (I think) to manager.

1. Riley responded on 1 September 1888: "I' b'en away from home. — 'ats why! *Now* tell me where to send it — so's it'll be *shore* an' reach ye."

2. Garland travelled west during the summer of 1888 to gather additional material for his fiction and to lecture on the single tax in various cities en route.

3. Joseph Kirkland (1830 – 94), novelist, was the author of *Zury: The Meanest Man in Spring County* (1887) and its sequel *The McVeys* (1888), whose realistic depiction of dreary midwestern life Garland much admired.

18. to James Whitcomb Riley

als, Indiana U
publ.: McCullough

Ordway.

Sept. 4/88.

Dear Friend:

If by "too good" you mean too full of praise of Riley *I'*d be willing to risk it, still I dont think I'd like to have *any* of my listeners think me a "fool friend" of Riley. I am aware of the high praise I give but it is not indiscriminate. I praise you for your fidelity to the types you attempt to portray. I do not compare you with Swinburne or Browning nor with our own Lanier and Whitman. I simply say you make an advance in *genre* lines. You and I know that Burns had a lot of conventional stuff mixed up with his genuine passion. We know that Whittier in his best gives *his own* reminiscences of farm-life, that he never really speaks from the poor soul of the farmer or mechanic as centre. He is not dramatic. He glazes the bare realities—we know it and by the eternal I'm going to say what I think. See with what a splendid coverage Mr. Howells stands up and says what he thinks about conventionalisms in fiction and poetry. They cuff him but—what's the odds?—he'll win in the long run and so'll I. But if you think it'll do you harm I'll kinda lick it into shape so't it'll slip down slicker'n grease—see if I dont!—You didnt say nothin' about "Ladrone." Whaddy ye think of *it*? Belford's bring out another sketch of mine soon that I think will please you.[1] When shall I see you again? I shall be in Chicago about the twentieth, perhaps in Indianapolis. Has "What's the Warter Talkin' Of?" been printed yet? Dont fail to send it.—Was it comparison to Burns and Whittier that shocked you so? Specify.—I am making studies here. Expect to see the magazines full o' me—later.

Yours f'r deep plowin'
Hamlin Garland

Minneapolis. Minn.

I expect to speak twice in Minneapolis on reform.—Enclose "Ladrone" please.

---

1. Although "Daddy Deering," the story to which Garland refers, was accepted by *Belford's* in October 1888, it did not appear until the April 1892 issue of the magazine.

19. to James Whitcomb Riley

als, Indiana U
publ.: McCullough

Jamaica Plain

Oct. 11/88.

Dear Riley:

I wonder if you sent the M.S. as per my order to Minneapolis. If you did I dont know what has become of the bundle.[1] I have written to all point[s] where it is likely to be but it has not yet been heard from.

I sent you my poem "Ladrone" also, did you enclose that with the essay on Riley?—I am back at my desk here in Jamaica Plain and shall be for the next nine months so you will know where to find me.—I meet everywhere admirers of J.W.R.'s poems. The latest one was Mrs. W. D. Howells, though I do not think she realizes the breadth of your work.

By the way I received a letter from Edgar Fawcett[2] the other day which was an absolute surprise to me. He has been helping my work on and believing in me for the last year and writes most flatteringly of my writings more particularly verse. He was almost the last man I expected to get such a letter from. My work is mainly open, objective, full of sun and air while his is full of the delineation of the abnormal types, voicings of elusive psychological moods.[3]—I am as full of business these days as a bug on a hot platter and can only scrawl a few lines today. Dont fail to send me a copy of the Miller's story. I want to read it bad.—I suppose you are jest humpin' y'rself these days—"Good lack," as the sailor says it.

Hamlin Garland

1. In a letter to Garland on 13 October 1888, which accompanied Garland's manuscript on "Riley," Riley explained that he sent the manuscript at top speed; that it was just returned to him two days ago.

2. Edgar Fawcett (1847–1904) was a reader for the *American* magazine and the author of several satirical novels and plays about New York society, including the novel *Purple and Fine Linen* (1873) and such plays as *The False Friend* (1880), *Our First Families* (1880), and *Americans Abroad* (1881).

3. In an undated reply, Riley expressed his confidence in Garland's poetry and the naturalness of Fawcett's admiration for it: "I don't wonder at all that Edgar Fawcett finds in it, and all your work, such marrowfat for praise. Don't you be other than reposeful as to your worth. Keep always to that, and no fear then of anything" (quoted in Florence French, "Dear Man!: Bluff Letters of Literary Friendship from James Whitcomb Riley to Hamlin Garland," *Ball State University Forum* 20 [Spring 1979]: 39).

20. to Walt Whitman

als, Congress
publ.: "Uncollected"

Jamaica Plain.

Oct. 18/88.

Dear Mr. Whitman:

I began a course of twelve class lectures in Waltham yesterday in which I take up "Walt Whitman's Message."[1] I never have any difficulty in obtaining respectful listeners upon that theme. I hope to speak many times upon it. I had a very friendly letter from Mr. Burroughs[2]—I am sorry I did not see him as I came through.[3] I want to say also that I did not write that little notice of your book in Transcript.[4] I am waiting till you send that autograph copy—then I will write a goodly review for Transcript or elsewhere.[5]—I have not seen Kennedy since returning—nor Baxter.[6] Hope to do so soon. At earliest possible moment I intend to get that article into shape concerning your work as a landscapist.[7]

I do hope you'll keep gaining in strength—as Burroughs wrote me you were.

With greatest esteem,
Hamlin Garland

1. Little is known about Garland's lectures in Waltham, though he probably based his talks either on his teaching notes from the Boston School of Oratory or on his writings about the poet in "The Evolution of American Thought."

2. The naturalist John Burroughs (1837–1921), author of *Notes on Walt Whitman as Poet and Person* (1867), had written to Garland on 16 October 1888: "I am very glad to see the rising men like you espousing Whitman's career. I congratulate you. It is a battle for the young to win. When I was younger & the odds were much greater than they are now I took a hand in, but I look upon the matter more dispassionately now, I feel more inclined to let things take their own course, which means I suppose that I am getting old."

3. Garland had visited Whitman in Camden on 26 September 1888, and had stayed for half an hour after being instructed by Whitman's doctor to stay only two minutes. For Whitman's account of this visit, see Traubel, *With Walt Whitman in Camden* (New York: Appleton, 1908), 2:383–84.

4. On 7 October 1888, Whitman sent William Sloane Kennedy a pre-publication copy of *November Boughs*, which David McKay would bring out the following week (*Correspondence*, 4:220). Kennedy reviewed *November Boughs* in "Whitman's New Volume," BET, 17 October 1888, p. 5. He noted that some of the poems reveal Whitman's "full power" but others "show marks of the advancing lethargy of age."

5. On 15 November 1888—less than a month after Kennedy reviewed *November Boughs*—Garland also reviewed this book for the BET in "Whitman's 'November Boughs'" (p. 6), praising the poet's gift for titles and his calm, patient, and philosophical outlook. He concluded his review with both praise and a call for material assistance for the poet: "We should hasten to do him honor while he is with us. Praise too often builds monuments when it should buy bread; furnishes tombstones when it should warm houses."

6. Sylvester Baxter (1850–1927), a publicist and author of *The Cruise of a Land-Yacht* (1891), *Old Marblehead* (1906), and *The Unseen House* (1917), met Garland probably in 1887 at the home of Joseph Edgar Chamberlin of the *Boston Evening Transcript*. Baxter, a friend and correspondent of Whitman's, also wrote articles about Whitman and reviewed *Leaves of Grass* and *Complete Works*. In December 1886, Baxter had proposed to Whitman plans to secure a pension for the poet and to form with other supporters a "Whitman Society."

7. In the late 1880s Garland frequently gave what he called "Lecture Studies in American Literature and Art" (advertising brochure in the Feinburg-Whitman Collection, Congress). These lectures were working drafts of chapters Garland intended to include in "The Evolution of American Thought." In the 1888–90 season, Garland advertised a lecture entitled "The Literature of Democracy: The Genre and Landscape

Poetry of Whitman." The Garland Papers (usc) contain what appears to be a later version of this piece—entitled simply "The Literature of Democracy"—but this version has virtually nothing to say about Whitman as a landscapist.

21. to Walt Whitman

als, Congress
publ.: "Uncollected"

Jamaica Plain.

Oct 24/88.

Dear Mr. Whitman:

I am over-joyed to receive your volume and autograph be sure it will be read and heralded to the world. I saw Mr. Howells yesterday spent the afternoon with him in discussing reforms, literary progress, etc[1]—He spoke of you again with a good deal of feeling. I think it of very great importance that you send him an autograph copy of "November Boughs".[2] If it has not been done dont fail to do it at once. If you send it immediately upon receipt of this letter address

W.D. Howells
Little Nahant
(near Lynn) Mass.

If you do not send till next week address

W.D. Howells
330 East 17th St.
New York City.[3]

And I will write him again about it. He is more than friendly to you and all progressive movements.

With deepest regard—
Hamlin Garland

1. Garland had written "Lemuel Barker," a very positive review of William Dean Howells's novel *The Minister's Charge* in the bet, 31 January 1887, p. 6. He was anxious to meet "the Dean of American Letters," and, after receiving a letter of introduction from Edward Clement, the editor of the *Transcript*, he made the short trip to Lee's Hotel in Auburndale, Massachusetts, to visit Howells. In a letter of 2 May 1887, to Whitelaw Reid, Howells noted: "A Mr. Hamlin Garland has called upon me, and has greatly interested and impressed me by his view of literature" (*Selected Letters of W. D. Howells*, ed. Robert Leitz III [Boston: Twayne, 1980], 3:187).

2. Howells reviewed *November Boughs* in the "Editor's Study," *Harper's Monthly* 78 (February 1889): 488. While Howells objected to Whitman's "gospel of nudity," he was otherwise favorably impressed by Whitman's volume.

3. Howells resided in Little Nahant during the summer of 1888; in November he returned to New York.

22. to Walt Whitman

als, Congress
publ.: "Uncollected"

Jamaica Plain.

Nov. 9/88.

Dear Mr. Whitman:

I talked last night to my Waltham class (of forty ladies) about your work and read to them. I wish you could have seen how deeply attentive they were and how moved by "Out of the Cradle" "To Think of Time" "Sparkles from the Wheel" and others. Many of them will now read your works carefully and understandingly. I told them to come at you through "Specimen Days". I always advise my pupils so. After reading your prose they are better prepared to sympathize with your poetic views. I am much pleased with "November Boughs" and expect to do quite a good review soon. Mr. Clement[1] of the *Transcript* is a personal friend and is quite kindly disposed toward your work. Indeed, all the leading men on the *Transcript* are.—Baxter is away—Kennedy I have not seen. Chamberlain[2] is in the library as usual. I think I told you of the good letter I had from Burroughs.

I hope Mr. Howells will succeed in doing something for "November Boughs" in December number it is such a great number usually—

It rejoices me to think you are gaining. I hope the winter will not be too severe for you—though I believe you stand the cold better than the heat. I hope to hear a word from you occasionally.

Very sincerely—
Hamlin Garland

1. Edward H. Clement (1843–1920) was assistant editor (1875–81) and editor-in-chief (1881–1906) of the *Boston Evening Transcript*. Garland met Clement shortly after he had his review of Howells's *The Minister's Charge* accepted for publication in the *Transcript*.

2. Joseph Edgar Chamberlin (1861–1935) was a member of the editorial staff of the *Transcript* and author of *The Listener in the Country* (1896), *The Listener in the Town* (1896), *The Ifs of History* (1907), and *The Boston Transcript: A History of Its First Hundred Years* (1930).

23. to Walt Whitman

als, Congress
publ.: "Uncollected"

Jamaica Plain.

Nov. 16/88.

Dear Mr. Whitman:

I send copy of the Transcript containing a notice of your work. It is not intended to be a study or an elaborate review simply a good word which will allay if possible some of the antagonism which still exists toward your work. I shall do more of course but this little notice has its work to do. I send copies to Mr. Howells and to Mr. Burroughs. I hope you are feeling as well as when you last wrote. — I saw Judge Chamberlain and other of our friends today.[1] Called on O'Reilly but he was out.[2] Hope to see him soon. I hope to do something specially useful for you by and by. — Baxter has returned from Europe. I shall see him in a day or two at his home.

Steadfastly.
Hamlin Garland

1. Mellen Chamberlain (1844–1900) served as judge and chief justice of the Boston municipal court from 1866 until 1878; from 1878 until 1890 he was librarian-in-chief of the Boston Public Library.

2. John Boyle O'Reilly (1844–90), an Irish-born editor of the *Boston Pilot* (1876–90) and poet (*Songs from the Southern Seas* [1873], *In Bohemia* [1886], and other books of poetry), was one of the original members of the "Whitman Society" and treasurer of the "Cottage Fund," organized to purchase a summer cottage for Whitman.

24. to James Whitcomb Riley

als, Indiana U

Jamaica Plain

Dec 19/88.

My Dear Riley:

Have just read "Pipes o' Pan"[1] It aint *my* copy tho! But I look for it daily. With Riley's hand-write on it. I send tickets to "Song and Story" be on hand early or you wont get a seat. —[2]

There is some talk here of your going abroad as a consul — but dont y' do it. Dont y' Darst! You've got a bigger mission than t' go to any dam ol' forin port. You'll be like Bret Harte git fat an' forget what y'r country looks like — an you'll fergit the "County Ditch" an' Kingry's Mill an' all them thare things we like t' hear about.

The Tyro: 1885–1899 37

Now to business. What is the name of your agent I talked with him while I was there about sometime handling my work—always provided I dont interfere with his service to you. Our work is so essentially different I dont see as it would. I will send press notices soon and if he can serve Mr. Clark and myself in the west we shall be glad to treat with him. I shall try Staylar afterward.[3] Everybody is enthusiastic over "Song and Story." And I wish we could get into our native west. Mr. Clark was born at Beloit—but he has lived in Germany sixteen years. He is a marvelous man and a magnificent pianist.

Dont forget "Pipes o' Pan."

Yours sincerely
Hamlin Garland

1. *Pipes o' Pan at Zekesbury* (1888).

2. "Song and Story" is the title of an "intellectual entertainment" given by Frederick Clark and Garland at the Clark-Steiniger Pianoforte School in Cambridge. See "Theatres and Concerts," bet, 22 December 1888.

3. "Staylar" has not been identified.

25. to James A. Herne

trl, Am Acad[1]

[before 6 January 1889]

Dear Mr. Herne:[2]

I want to write and thank you for the very great pleasure I took in your play, "Drifting Apart." It was at once a surprise and an inspiration. A surprise to find such work done by a man whose very name was unfamiliar to me; an inspiration, because I said he is a product of the new spirit of truth. Perhaps, without knowing it, you are linked with the new school of genuine realists; not the realists of the tank-drama and the fire-engine, but the school of artists who are trying to depict the essentials of the life common to us all of to-day. There are, of course, minor things which I might criticise; but the entire play is so good, I am disposed to pass over them in silence, especially as they do not obscure the beauty of the whole. I want specially to say how much I admire *Katharine C. Herne* as *Mary Miller*. The character of Mary Miller is a peculiarly sweet and lovable one, and Mrs. Herne's characterization of it has all the charm, the elusiveness, and the moving power of life itself. Critics can feel it, but find it difficult of analysis or description. I do not hesitate to call it one of the most remarkable pieces of acting I have ever seen.[3]

In the first act we have presented the *girl* Mary Miller. Sweet and innately refined, loving Jack Hepburne, who had been at once her elder brother and lover. Her irresistible, gleeful laugh at Seward shows how little the deeper parts of her nature have been stirred. Her world is narrow, but it is true and good, and the thought of breaking her promise to Jack had never entered her mind. There is one beautiful touch of doubt expressed; as she leaves the handsome young fellow, her face saddens and her innocent eyes are filled with a momentary shadow as if she felt an indefinable loss. This exquisite touch is but one of the many which the careful observer may see in the first act.

The second act, — unapproached for its sweet, homely realism, — shows us Mary Miller the *wife*. The action here of Mr. and Mrs. Herne for tenderness and truth in representing the early married life of an American working man has never been equalled, and the by-play of Mrs. Herne is subtle and exquisite beyond description. The little caressing tones and gestures, the action of the house-wife, sewing or moving about the room, the tones of mock indignation, the fond admiration of Jack's jokes and actions, these and a hundred other indescribable things make this act so real that many are deceived into saying, "that's not acting at all; its just what any woman would do in her place," and yet it is the perfection of art. These little things that look so spontaneous are so, because they are carefully studied. This technique is perfection, and comes from comprehension of aims and ends. The means are subtle and multiple, but directed to an end.

One of the most marvellous things in the act, is the incident of the baby-garment, that holiest of confidences between wife and husband. The first time I saw it, when the first burst of laughter came I was shocked, and I wondered how the actress could command silence. Her method was as simple as it was thrillingly sweet, and as she took the little garment, and with the majesty of maternity already on her face, kissed it and folded it on her bosom, the effect was electric, — the vast audience hardly breathed; this is genius. She seemed at that moment the type of all tender womanhood, seeking only to be true. She commanded her audience as if by a spell.

In the third act her reading became absolutely marvellous for its intensity and suppression. That low, halting, quivering voice is the utterance of Mary Miller, but Mary with her life broadened and deepened by sorrow and besetting perplexities. The fair face and great, luminous dark eyes reflect every change in her thought and feeling, as she defends herself before Jack. Pathos could go no farther without becoming tragedy, and that is what follows in the fourth act. Everywhere here means are few, but they are so true and intimate that they appeal with irresistible power; it is a terrible test of the actress, that fourth act, and only a woman with genius can meet its requirements. A mother who had given up home and comfort to go back with her husband into the great city to starve, and who now sits with her dying child in her arms waiting for her husband's return. What a sinister situation! What chances for conventional raving and contortions! But there was nothing of that here. I felt as if sitting before a great picture by Millet,[4] so dumb, interior and voiceless was that sorrow. The great eyes looking out of the gray-white face, were filled with the awful sorrow of a mother; the sensitive spectator shrivelled under it, while his throat filled.

The grief of the mother was too deep for tears or cries; it had only negative expression. Definite lines would have weakened or defeated expression, and yet so accustomed is the public to exaggerated forms of expression, that while it feels this marvellous art it does not estimate it.

Nothing that I have ever seen surpasses the infinite pathos of that slow, fascinated, unwilling, *furtive*, side-long glance at the dead child, a glance that tells she hopes it is asleep, yet fears the worst.

And then the deep sigh of relief which follows, and the faint smile around the sad mouth, as she looks at the placid face and thinks it asleep. What action!

And what poignancy of fear and despair was put into that single, low, thrilling cry, "Margaret!" And what meaning in the relaxation which lets the body fall, while the face was uplifted as if to follow the little soul in its flight, and as she rose at length, and staggered to the door, a desperate resolution on her set and rigid face, I felt that the mother was charging her baby's death to the world. How significant to me was the covering up of the little form on the cot, the caressing touch with the doll, and the final sinking upon her knees, and burying her face on the little feet that could never move again.

All these, and many other almost equally true expressions, made this one of the most piercingly and truly great pieces of acting I have ever seen. It is the work of an intellectual and gifted woman, as well as an actress; of a wife and mother, whose imagination leads her art, and whose art expresses her intellectual powers, and her fervent emotional apprehension of life.

In such a moment we feel what Valdes meant when he said, "There are no trivial things, absolutely. Values are relative; that which is trivial to one, is a great fact to another; the death of a child, for example." [5] Such scenes will teach us sympathy with fathers and mothers of those babies dying, murdered, rather, in the crowded tenement houses. Never again will the death of a child be a trivial fact with me.

The last act, opening with the sound of sleigh-bells, bringing back the sweet and wholesome life of Gloucester, was a splendid effect. Life flows on, though the individual suffers and dies. While tragedy is dwelling with Mary Hepburn, sleighing parties, with laugh and song, pass the door in the bright winter sunshine.

Mrs. Herne, in this act, gives us again the tender, and naturally refined wife. Subdued, and anxious, but bravely facing the uncertain future. The same undefinable flavor, charm, which captivated me in the second act, is here; but made more rich and admirable by contrast with the grand simplicity and reserve of the fourth act.

And so this remarkable conception closes, with their future uncertain, but with a developed love and strength which seems prepared to meet anything. To how many a wife and mother must this drama carry hope, to how many men a warning?

My dear Mr. Herne, I join one of the greatest critics of the day, and one of the greatest painters of the day, in saying, "This is a great achievement." You have done a service to American drama, and your wife has done a service to the new methods in acting, by demonstrating that by leaving effectism out of account, the greatest results follow. If I can serve you in any way, command me. I cannot give my service in a better art cause. [6]

Sincerely,
Hamlin Garland.

1. The copy-text for this letter is a circular issued to promote a revival of *Drifting Apart* in January 1890; besides Garland's letter, the circular includes reviews excerpted from the *Boston Evening Transcript*, the *Boston Times*, and the *Home Journal*.

2. The actor and playwright James A. Herne (1839–1901), with his wife, the actress Katharine Corcoran Herne (1856–1943), were among Garland's closest friends after they met in May 1889. On 4 July 1890 Herne's *Margaret Fleming*, the first Ibsen-inspired drama to appear in America, opened in Lynn, Massachusetts. In 1891 Garland and Herne founded the Boston Independent Theater Association, modeled after the independent theaters of Europe, to produce experimental realistic drama on a subscription basis without the worry of turning a profit, after they failed to interest commercial managers in their plays.

3. *Drifting Apart* is a melodramatic temperance play without the traditional didactic sermons preaching the evils of drink.

4. Jean François Millet (1814–75), French painter.

5. Armando Palacio Valdés (1853–1938), Spanish novelist whose comments about "'*effectism*,' or the itch of awakening at all cost in the reader vivid and violent emotions," would shortly influence Garland's critical theory. See Donald Pizer, *Hamlin Garland's Early Work and Career* (Berkeley: University of California Press, 1960), p. 124.

6. Herne responded on 6 January 1889: "Your kindly concieved and earnestly written letter lies before me — I have read and reread it, and each perusal has added strength to the already firm conviction I had in the ultimate success of my play — By success, I mean that by which the managers measure — "financial" for be the play or players never so fine, where there is no *show* — there are no open doors — Your letter demonstrates the fact that as you saw my work, — others will see it also, not so readily, nor so clearly — but they will see it. . . . The opinions and convictions of a man like you carry great weight. They are repeated. One says, 'Well if Mr. Garland endorses such and such a thing, it must be meritorious. I will look into it' he does so — prejudiced in its favor — he repeats your opinion to another — he to another and so on until all find themselves interested in something they are the better for having known." Subsequent letters reveal that Garland influenced Herne's revision of the play.

26. to Walt Whitman

als, NYPL

publ.: "Uncollected"

[10 or 11 January 1889]

Dear Mr. Whitman,

I have words occasionally from you and it gives me great pleasure to know you are so comfortable. — I get a card from Kennedy semi-occasionally, he seems to be very busy. I passed a pleasant evening with Mrs. Louise Chandler Moulton,[1] the present week, and we had some considerable talk of you. She is an appreciative admirer of your work and prizes the chat she had with you last year. She writes a literary letter to the *Herald* each Sunday and gets in a telling touch once in a while on your work. She is a very charming and able woman. Your stalwart supporter Judge Chamberlain of the Public Library, I see frequently, a very thoughtful and fearlessly out-spoken man. He does some valuable historical lecturing and often says some inspiringly good things about our artificiality on poetry and the drama.

I wonder if it ever occurred to you that our novel and drama is *now* slowly changing base, coming around to the "idealization of the real." The whole out-look to me is full of hope. I think I see in what our aristocratic friends are pleased to call "vulgarity in fiction and the drama," the sure sign of the native indigenous literature we have waited for. If I could ever get to you to see you I should take pleasure in enlarging upon this. It forms the staple for a number of my lectures on the Literature of Democracy—

Our friend Baxter had an extended notice of "Complete Works" in *Herald*, you saw it of course.[2]

filially yours
Hamlin Garland

1. Ellen Louise Chandler Moulton (1835–1908), an editor, poet, and short story writer, had corresponded with Whitman since 1876 and had visited him in Camden on 23 April 1888. For several years Moulton was Boston literary correspondent for the *New York Tribune*, and from 1876 to 1892 she contributed a weekly letter on books to the *Boston Sunday Herald*. She also held a Friday Salon in Boston, which included such guests as Whittier, Longfellow, Holmes, and Lowell. In all likelihood Garland met Moulton in his Boston literary circles.

2. Sylvester Baxter's review, "Whitman's Complete Works," appeared in the *Boston Herald*, 3 January 1889, p. 4. He was lavish in his praise for the volume, remarking that this edition is "monumental in our literature."

27. to James Whitcomb Riley
als, Indiana U

[17 February 1889]

Dear Riley:

I see by the papers that you are coming to the city of bean-pots and I am glad. I write in haste to ask whether you would care to appear with me at the New England Conservatory of Music say on Friday night at eight. I am at present lecturing there and have a sort of connection with the institution—likely to be one of its faculty and I would like to introduce you, have you read a few pieces, alternately with me. Do as little or as much as you please. The institution is a huge one and has a strong pull on the city and the whole country. We will send invitations to the literary people of the city and if you can spare the time, hold a reception in the parlors after the hour of readings. I shall be proud to occupy the platform with you. I would read "Ladrone" and one or two other similar pieces, leaving to you the humor and pathos.

I write hurriedly and cant out-line the matter but detachedly but I think it will do you good and Brutus[1] good to thus meet the Conservatory people. I wish you would write me, saying how much time you can spend in the city, and what you think of the plan.

My connection with the Conservatory is teacher of American literature and I shall make *our* principles of art, shake the circumjacent atmosphere. And getting you there is part of my scheme. I hope to have Howells and other modern realists and Americans.

Yours sincerely
Hamlin Garland

1. "Brutus" has not been identified.

28. to Edwin Booth alc, usc

Jamaica Plain
Boston Mass.

Feb 21/89.

Dear Mr. Booth:

I saw your magnificent presentation of "Macbeth" on last Saturday eve and it was one of the greatest artistic successes any body ever made. It was absolutely above criticism.

I saw you during the week in Hamlet and Brutus, in which you played easily. I take it you could not stand the strain of playing each time as you did Saturday evening. I shall have little to change in my study of your Macbeth. It seems to me I got at its core but I would like to ask you what you conceive Macbeth's motive of passion to be when he returns from the chamber of the king with Lenox, saying:

"Had I but died an hour"—etc

I observe you use a low, strained dispirited tone, a little tremulous, as if constraint were laid upon it—as if the mind of the speaker wavered between two emotions or more. (How clumsy and inadequate words are in attempting to describe these subtleties of the voice!) I can not get firm hold upon that reading.

Again what do you conceive the attitude of Iago's mind toward Desdemona's self to be when he leans over her in illy-assumed sympathy during the long speech of the stricken woman? I note you stand with calm countenance, expressing little — the habitual non-committed face of Iago, but with a keen watchful eye fixed a trifle obliquely down upon her. —

You may remember my somewhat elaborate study of your Iago. I think I caught the leading phases of the presentations but one or two places like that I am not decided upon. Whether Iago really loved (in his measure) Desdemona, or whether he readily acceded to Othello's determinations to kill her as well as Cassio — are still debatable with me. I am not quite sure how much genuine entreaty you mean to express in the line "Let her live I beseech you." "But let her live" is the exact line but if my memory serve, you use the additional words "I beseech you." —

If you can find time I should like to have you write me of these points. I make all reference to your impersonations in teaching Shakespeare and I should like to be mainly correct.[1]

Yours gratefully
Hamlin Garland

1. Garland quotes Booth's response in *Roadside*, pp. 48–51.

29. to Samuel Clemens

als, Bancroft

Jamaica Plain
Boston Mass.

[21 March 1889]

Dear Mr. Clemens:

When Whitcomb Riley was here he wanted me to meet you and it would have been brought about to my great pleasure, had you not been delayed in reaching the city but his name and the name of Mr. Howells will no doubt put me on proper footing with you.

I have an axe to grind — we all have — but I trust it will appeal to you as worth a whirl of the crank. Mr. Howells and many others of my literary friends think so. I wish you would glance over my subjects for lectures on American literature and see how you like 'em.[1] You will see that I am a literary democrat, believing in the present, exploiting the present in my own work as well as in my critical studies. Of course my work does not appeal to Harvard College but I believe it would appeal to the people — Mr. Butterworth[2] heard me on "the new South" and assures me there is a field for me — Now I'd like to get into that field. But how, that's the question.

The Conservatory have made arrangements for me to teach these revolutionary American ideas of literature for the coming year and have also taken me into their bureau, so far so good; but now we've got to get the public aware of me and interested in my matters. I assault you because I want you to know I'm in the field as the champion of the first group of American writers who are not afraid of their surroundings. But the special object in writing to you is to ask advice as regards getting hold of the Southern people. This later group of novelists have large space in my book of lectures and I am enthusiastic over their future. I wish I could help them at the same time I help my-self.

Mr. Butterworth thinks there is a great field for me in the South and gave me some names to send to, but it occurred to me that you and Mr. Warner[3] knew the South thoroughly and could render me assistance if my work appealed to you as worthy. I wish you would satisfy yourself upon that score and give me some advice as to procedure. I am (of course) poor as the traditional Job's turkey, or I would go forth into the country hiring halls and proclaiming the gospel. I have worked away in my garret for years getting my guns shotted, and now the time has come to open fire. Could you give me names of people likely to be interested. Either as managers of my tour or otherwise. Americanism must be proclaimed.

I suppose it seems like asking a good deal of a busy man but—the cause, the cause! This cause appeals to me *almost* as strongly as the need of bread and butter.—

If you should by any chance come to Boston this spring send me a card, please, that I may run in on you. We have mutual friends in Howells, Whitman, Riley and others, and I have wanted to meet you for a long time but had no good opportunity.[4]

Yours sincerely
Hamlin Garland

1. Enclosed with the letter are Garland's lecture circulars, 1888–89.

2. Hezekiah Butterworth (1839–1905), journalist, author, and assistant editor (1870–1904) of the *Youth's Companion*, a prominent weekly magazine for children published in Boston. Garland published two poems in the *Youth's Companion* in 1889: "A Dakota Wheat Field" 62 (18 July): 366; and "By the River" 52 (15 August): 410.

3. Charles Dudley Warner (1827–1900), contributing editor to *Harper's New Monthly Magazine* (1884–98) and collaborator with Clemens on the novel *The Gilded Age* (1873).

4. In pencil in Clemens's hand on the envelope, postmarked 21 March 1889, are the words: "Please tell him / Gone away to / finish a book, / & left no address. / slc."

30. to Walt Whitman

als, Congress
publ.: "Uncollected"

[3? April 1889]

Dear Mr. Whitman:

I saw lately that you were not so well—but hope it is a newspaper report merely and that you are continuing to gain. I saw Mrs. Dr. Spaulding recently.[1] She is doing all she can for the acceptance of L. of G.—By the way I found a lover where I least expected it, in Mr. Hezekiah Butterworth of the "Youths Companion" who said when I invited him to hear me lecture upon your work—"I shall come by all means. I think Whitman one of the greatest if not the greatest of our American poets." He is not afraid of your work but wishes some of it were left out of it, for a popular volume. He would think it all right in itself I presume—Mrs Moulton has gone south for a month. Returns in May. I hope she may be able to see you before she sails for England in June.—Kennedy I never see now. Dont know what he is doing. I should like to see him very much. I am digging away in a fair way to earn a living. I gave two evenings to your work before my class at New England Conservatory. My class is composed of about fifty bright young girls studying music. You see I am not afraid to carry your word to anyone. To me there is not a line that has a downward tendency. Still I recognize the fact that to many people "A woman waits for me" is wholly inadmissible, and I know that the rest of the book is a sealed book to them—perhaps it would be anyway—there's consolation there.[2] I shall have "Specimen Days" in my class during spring term.

With greatest esteem
Hamlin Garland

1. Mrs. A. H. Spaulding, of Boston, was an admirer of Whitman who praised him publicly. On 17 March 1889 she visited Whitman in Camden; upon her return to Boston she wrote to thank him for the visit and, on 28 March, she sent Whitman flowers.

2. In 1882, "A Woman Waits for Me" and "To a Common Prostitute" were two of the poems regarded as most offensive when the Boston district attorney officially classified *Leaves of Grass* as obscene literature.

31. to Walt Whitman

als, Congress
publ.: "Uncollected"

Jamaica Plain.

May 28/89

Dear Mr. Whitman:

I shall be with you on your seventieth birthday nothing intervening.[1]
Kennedy cant come. I dont know whether Mr. Butterworth will or not
but he was much interested in the project and hoped the results would be
satisfactory. I speak in Philadelphia in the evening but that will not interfere with my attendance at the dinner. I hope Mr. Howells can go down.

Sincerely
Hamlin Garland

1. Garland attended Whitman's seventieth birthday celebration at Morgan's Hall in
Camden on 31 May and gave a brief address praising Whitman's themes of "Optimism
and Altruism—Hope for the Future and Sympathy Toward Men." Howells did not
attend the celebration, but he did send a letter of tribute.

32. to Walt Whitman

als, Congress
publ.: "Uncollected"

[June 1889]

Dear Mr. Whitman:

I send you a few pages of notes which I intend printing if you do not
object.[1] I want the authority to say some of these things. They will do you
good. The first few pages will be taken up with a bit of description of the
Banquet and so on. The rest of the letter is a free report of what we talked
about in my visit to you. If any part of this displeases you, or misrepre-
sents you—mark it—or indicate it to Mr. Traubel[2] and return it to me.

Hartman and others have done so much to misrepresent you in the
papers that I wish to present something counter which shall help men to
understand you.[3] I wish you would read Mr. Howells later books—and
essays, he is taking fearlessly high grounds.

If you dont feel like writing, ask Traubel to reply.

Everybody hear sends well-wishes—Baxter—Chamberlain—Clement
etc—

With greatest esteem—
Hamlin Garland.

1. Garland sent Whitman a typescript entitled "Whitman at Seventy" (item #532c), which was later published in the *New York Herald*, 30 June 1889, p. 7. Whitman, as was his practice, carefully revised Garland's essay, changing it in subtle but important ways. For example, Garland's typescript quotes Whitman as saying that most American writing lacks a distinctive national twang: "Most of it might have been written in England or on the continent." Whitman allowed this passage to stand but added a conciliatory remark: "I myself like Cooper, Bryant, Emerson, and Whittier."

2. Horace L. Traubel (1858–1919) had known Whitman since 1873, when the poet had first moved to Camden. Beginning in 1888, Traubel made almost daily visits to Whitman, engaging in conversations that led to Traubel's five-volume *With Walt Whitman in Camden.*

3. Carl Sadakichi Hartmann (1869–1944) published "Walt Whitman. Notes of a Conversation with the Good Gray Poet by a German Poet and Traveller" in the *New York Herald*, 14 April 1889, p. 10. Whitman felt that Hartmann had done him a disservice and complained in a letter to William Sloane Kennedy about "That infernal farrago of my *opinions!!* in the Herald" (*Correspondence*, 4:331).

33. to Walt Whitman

als, Congress
publ.: "Uncollected"

[June 1889]

Dear friend:

I sent my article on you to Walsh some weeks ago—have not heard from him but assume he will use it soon.[1] I will write him again if I do not hear this week. I thought it but fair that he should print an authentic report he has printed so many that were not true.

I am very busy lecturing and writing now. I want to get out a volume of stories this fall—stories illustrative of the west and of social injustice. I am now bargaining with Roberts bros. thereto.—[2]

I am also writing dramas. My fourth and last is praised highly by practical managers and by literary critics.[3] I shall try to bring that out next spring—

I send you my photo—it may be of interest to you—I had just been lecturing upon your prose and the book in my hand is "Specimen Days."

With deepest wishes for your good health.
Hamlin Garland.

1. William S. Walsh (1854–1919) was editor of *Lippincott's Magazine* (1885–89) and literary editor of the *New York Herald.* He published Garland's article on Whitman's birthday dinner.

2. Garland's *Main-Travelled Roads* was not published until 1891 by the Arena Publishing Company.

3. Garland likely refers to his play "Under the Wheel: A Modern Play in Six Scenes," which appeared in Benjamin Orange Flower's muckraking magazine *Arena* 2 (July 1890): 182–228; it was published in book form as *Under the Wheel* (1890). The other three plays he refers to are probably "Love or the Law," "The Rise of Boomtown," and "The McTurgs," none of which were published or produced and exist in fragments in the Garland Papers (USC).

34. to Horace Traubel   als, Congress

[8 July 1889]

My Dear Traubel:

I can help you in getting subscriptions for Whitman but it must be by your being very candid with me. There have been so many conflicting reports concerning Whitman's condition and so many untoward things done that it handicaps us—My own impression is that Whitman is *very* poor. That he lacks the necessities of life. I dont mean meat and potatoes but a clean and wholesome room in a clean and wholesome street. I couldnt exist where he does and yet Dr Bucke[1] and Burroughs both replied that W. lived there out of choice, that he did not need etc—It is only the natural pride and sublime endurance of a great soul that keeps Whitman silent. It *is* a terrible thing for a man of his vast powers to be forced to make his needs known but when the fact is recalled that for his services he ought to be pensioned by the government as one of its war-heroes— his poverty is seen in a different light. If he were not a great poet or thinker it is monstrous injustice that keeps him where he is.

Now you must tell me if possible whether Whitman would not if he were able, live elsewhere. Is it not poverty that keeps him where he is? Would he not like to go back to Long Island to spend his last years. What was the reason that the money which Baxter raised for a cottage was never applied to that purpose?[2]

This letter is a private letter. Dont trouble Whitman with it, but these are a few of the things which embarrass us here. If I could state publicly that he was poor that he *did* need money for running expenses (as I think he does) and that his relatives and neighbors can not or do not help him —then I could do something for him.

This is a very frank statement my dear Traubel, and I want an equally frank letter from you. Tell me as far as you can why Baxter's fund was not applied as it was designed—and why so little was ever said about it by Whitman through his Camden and Philadelphia friends. I suppose it went to pay Doctor's bills and nurse's bills—etc.—

I dont know whether you can answer these questions but I think as you are on the ground you can throw *some* light on the matter.

I enclose a list of names which will be of use to you. If you were to send to each of these your little Banquet pamphlet together with a letter explaining the need of the guarantee fund most of them would respond. You could also send to many leading politicians like Gov. Long, Gov. Ames,[3] etc—all of whom would be interested in W's war-record—

Please answer at once and *without laying the matter before Whitman* at all. It makes me hot with indignation to think of the grand old man in that hot little room in that festering street—It must be dreadful in summer.

Yours fraternally
Hamlin Garland

1. Richard Maurice Bucke (1837–1902), a physician specializing in psychiatry, was the author of *Walt Whitman* (1883) and *Walt Whitman, Man and Poet* (1897). As literary executor of Whitman's estate, he joined Traubel and Thomas B. Harned in compiling a collection of essays by Whitman's followers entitled *In Re Walt Whitman* (1893) and in editing *The Complete Writings of Walt Whitman* (1902).

2. Traubel did not respond to Garland's question in detail, but mentioned in a reply on 23 August 1889: "All is right here. . . . If you were here I could talk with you more fully about the affair of the nurse. But let it pass. It is not a great sum of money I am soliciting, and I can no doubt raise it." In *Walt Whitman in Camden*, Traubel expanded on the incident: "Although not reading him [Garland's] letter there were a couple of points I referred to W. I told W. that in soliciting contributions to the nurse fund I had never put it on the ground of poverty but of necessity that a nurse should be kept and of the grace it would do W.'s friends in these last days to make it their own voluntary offering. W. said at once—'That was right—I approve that myself!' To Garland's statement—'If I could state publicly . . . then I could do something for him,' W. quickly replied—'Horace—write to Garland—tell him it would not please me to have him make any statement in the public prints. Tell him I don't want him to discuss my Philadelphia and Camden friends.' And as to Garland's question, what had become of the cottage money, etc., W. was equally quick to retort—'That was fixed—understood—fully settled—long and long ago—it is a closed book—it is a question not again to be reopened.' On the point of Garland's description of the hot and festering street and all that, W. only smiled, and without a word, pointed to the fine northern skies, and the trees swaying almost boisterously in the wind. It seemed like enough comment. By and by he said: 'Hamlin does not understand.' Then we let it drop" (5:355).

3. John Davis Long (1838–1915) served as governor of Massachussetts from 1880 to 1883 and later became the secretary of the Navy (1897–1902). He was the author of several books, the most important of which is *The Republican Party, Its History, Principles, and Policies* (1888). Oliver Ames (1831–95), the governor of Massachussetts from 1887 to 1890, was also the president of the Boston Art Club.

35. to Richard Watson Gilder als, NYPL

[before September 1889]

R. W. Gilder:[1]

Dear Sir: The only favor I ask for the enclosed stories is: that they be read with a due regard for the aims of the author. First I aim to be true to the life I am depicting and to deal not with abnormal phases so much as with representative phases. I am western born and the dialect and descriptive matter can be relied upon.

Pardon me for bombarding you at wholesale.

Sincerely
Hamlin Garland

1. Richard Watson Gilder (1844–1909) joined *Scribner's Monthly* as an assistant editor in 1870; he became editor-in-chief in 1881 when it was succeeded by the *Century* and remained as editor until his death. Gilder accepted one of the submitted stories, "A Spring Romance" and paid Garland seventy-five dollars for it, the most he had received up to this point for a story. Garland discusses the importance of this event in *Son*, p. 412.

36. to Richard Watson Gilder als, NYPL

Jamaica Plain.
Boston.

Sept. 7/89.

R. W. Gilder:

Dear Sir: I enclose a couple of western stories which I hope are suitable for your use.[1] The longer story would be excellent for the two mid-winter months—it seems to me. Will you kindly look them over at your earliest and if any changes will make them more acceptable be sure I will do all that is in reason. There may be some objection to the strong language—

if so it can be easily softened down. I hope to see you soon as I shall probably be in New York on the 16th.—I aim at stating things just as they appear to me and as I lived that Dakota life it will be evident that I state it with considerable fidelity.—

Sincerely
Hamlin Garland

1. Of the two stories submitted, Gilder accepted "Ol' Pap's Flaxen," but rejected "A Prairie Heroine."

37. to Edmund Clarence Stedmanals, Penn HS

Jamaica Plain
Boston. Mass.

Sept. 23/89.

Dear Mr. Stedman:

Mr. Herne writes me that he called upon you. I am glad he did for I think you must have liked him and his wife also. With the time you have given him he will be able to give you just the right sort of selections.

As for myself I am ambitious to represent the middle prairie west in verse and fiction and though I do not know that I am admissible as such a representative yet—I'd like to have you read some of the enclosed. Most of them have been published in papers and magazines, *Harpers Weekly*[,] *American, America* etc. I don't know that you are using such matter as mine but if you are here is a taste of my quality.[1]

Sincerely.
Hamlin Garland

1. Stedman was the co-editor, with Ellen M. Hutchinson, of *A Library of American Literature* (11 vols., 1888–90). He declined Garland's submissions in a letter of 25 September, and explained: "If these poems had come to me a year ago, it is probable that we should have been grateful for the privilege of using some of them. Our work is near its close, among the very youngest men, & is all planned & almost completely edited. We have to exclude *scores* of writers equal to many that are included, & we take no poems, except from *books*, unless they are so well-known as to be necessary for purposes of reference, & in everyone's life. We already have freely represented the prairie &

frontier life, & I don't see how we can find space for a line more; & we shall have to add to the size of our next vol. in order to get in Mr. Herne's Dramatic matter (a kind of literature which we wish especially to represent.)" Stedman's letter is pasted at the front of Garland's copy of Stedman's *Poets of America* (1885).

38. to Richard Watson Gilder   als, NYPL

Jamaica Plain.

                                                                          Oct 10/89.

Dear Mr. Gilder:

All you say is very true—"Prairie Heroine" in some phases is a little too obviously preaching.[1] My tendency is to present things concretely and let others find the preaching, I know when I did that final section that it was a falling off, from the artistic stand-point—but I wanted to "let the light in" as Walt Whitman asked me to do.[2] I wanted to give hope, somehow.—

But as far as the two first sections go they are artistic—they exalt me with pity, and resolution to help these toiling men and women. I aimed to show (not that free-trade was right, not that the single-tax[3] was a panacea and right—) but to show that the whole condition of the average American farmer was *wrong*. Had I stopped there your criticisms would only have referred to minor points. As it is you are right.

"Ol' Pap" I like.[4] In the main it satisfied me. I can read it again and again and enjoy it as if it were written by someone else. (Mrs Herne read it and was delighted especially with it—never tires of speaking of the men—"great simple types")

Of course I will submit to any reasonable change—and I feel that you would require *nothing* unreasonable. I feel your appreciation very deeply.

I thank you sincerely for your frankness as well as for your appreciation of the work I am trying to do.—

Sincerely yours
Hamlin Garland

I have planned a drama on "Flaxen"—Do you think the public would receive such a drama from me—with the same emotional comment and the same sincerity? H.G.

1. "A Prairie Heroine," a bitter depiction of the degradations of farm life, was criticized in detail by Gilder in his response to Garland's letter of 7 September 1889. Omitted from *Main-Travelled Roads* (1891), the story was published in the *Arena* 4 (July 1891): 223–46. It was later included in *Prairie Folks* (1893) under the title "Sim Burns' Wife" and in *Other Main-Travelled Roads* (1910) as "Lucretia Burns."

2. In *Son*, Garland recalls an early meeting in which Whitman "spoke of one of my stories to which Traubel had called his attention, and reproved me gently for not 'letting in the light'" (p. 409). Garland also discusses his first meeting with Whitman in October 1888 at length in *Roadside*, pp. 131–43. He initially recorded this meeting in Camden in a revised typescript which he entitled "Let the Sunshine In" (item #469), and which he later published in a revised form as "Whitman at Seventy. How the Good Gray Poet Looks and Talks," *New York Herald*, 30 June 1889, p. 7, by slightly altering the significant phrase: "And finally, I repeat Whitman's word to the young writer, 'Don't depict evil for its own sake. Don't let evil overshadow your books. Make it a foil, as Shakespeare did. Somewhere in your play or novel, let the sunshine in.'"

3. The single tax was the fundamental idea behind Henry George's *Progress and Poverty* (1879) and was strongly supported by Garland. George proposed that a single tax be levied on land, and that unused land should be confiscated. He urged all rent to be appropriated by taxation in order to reduce the profit to landlords through increased rents when their properties rose in value as a result of "progress," therefore leading to an increase in poverty of the tenants.

4. *Ol' Pap's Flaxen*, a short novel written in 1888, but not published until 1892 in the *Century* issues of March, April, and May. Garland wanted to publish it as a Century book, but he was angered by Gilder's delay and gave the rights to Appleton, who published the novel under a new title, *A Little Norsk*, in June 1892. See Garland to Gilder, before March 1892, letter 65.

39. to Richard Watson Gilder

als, NYPL

[October 1889]

Dear Mr Gilder:

I have gone over this *carefully*. I have taken out fully four pages. I dont see very well how more could go without cutting into essentials but if you think there can be and *must* be others I'll do it. It is *essential* to know a little more of Kendalls character, and of the position he leaves Flaxen in, etc—However I have taken out several pages. I suppose you will return the whole to me (to be proof-read) in type-writing. I am as anxious as you are to have this story in perfect form (so far as I can make it).

I enclose a poem which I have read with great success during the last year.[1] I dont suppose it possible but if it *could* be used with illustrations by Remington it ought to please your readers.[2] Please give me your opinion thereon.

Sincerely

Hamlin Garland

I've marked a few places, (which can be taken out), by a pencil mark. They seem quite nescessary and if I have brought it together sufficiently— I would like to have them remain.—

Another plan of mine is to ask Remington to go in with me and make a little book of the prairie west to be called "On the Prairies" or something like it—He to furnish drawings and I to furnish poems of that life— I'd like to meet him sometime and *sound* him.

H.G.

1. The enclosure has not survived, but it was likely the poem "Ladrone."

2. Frederick Remington (1861–1909), sculptor, illustrator, and painter, who chose for his subjects soldiers, Indians, and cowboys, was the illustrator for Garland's *The Book of the American Indian* (1923). Although Garland wanted Remington to illustrate his early books, he became disenchanted with Remington's work and did not like the illustrations done for BAI. See *Roadside*, p. 394, and *Contemporaries*, pp. 409–10, for Garland's assessment of Remington's work.

40. to Richard Watson Gilder

als, NYPL

[October 1889]

Dear Mr. Gilder:

I am as wax in the hands of the potter—I mean clay! I wish we might retain page 99 but if you *must,* take it out. The places I have drawn a light line across are intended to remain (with your consent.) Your other points and markings are well taken. As for final line speaking of his death wouldnt that read like a—wouldnt it be like doing as the old Greeks did? When they got through with a character they had a derrick which caught the unhappy actor behind and tossed him over the wall out of sight. Death is worse than divorce in this case. I like also the characteristic and altogether chivalrous position of Gearheart in the house. Of course everybody considers Anson her father and there is no serious scandal involved.

Page 102 I like very much but if it must go I wont complain. It has a mellow warmth which seems nescessary. *At that point.*

You didnt say anything of "Ladrone." I hoped you'd like it. Perhaps you did. Please let me know exactly how I've suited you with latest revision.

Sincerely
Hamlin Garland

41. to Richard Watson Gilder

als, NYPL

Jamaica Plain.
Mass.

Oct. 30/89.

R W Gilder:

Dear friend: In considering that "addenda"—please remember that I will revise it carefully—filling it out in detail—but the plan will remain the same. I dont want you to misunderstand me. *I like it,* but it is a question whether it detracts from the value of the whole as a work of art. I dont know why the preceding part is not just as strong and artistic with this added—but if it does not appeal to you strongly dont use it. I wanted among other things to insist on the majesty and mystery of maternity—as Whitman does. To do a little toward *de-vulgarizing* it. Is it not worthy [of] my art?—

By the way for illustrations of such work Remington is the only man I know. I wish you could bring out "Flaxen and Other Prairie Waifs" in book form during the year, with proper selling and illustrations.—I am busy on another prairie story which promises well after much labor.—

I was in despair and rapture over "The Doll Home." Rapture over the astounding power—despair over the future of my own dramatic work.[1]

Sincerely
Hamlin Garland

1. Henrik Ibsen's *A Doll's House* opened at Boston's Globe Theater on the afternoon of 30 October 1889, with Beatrice Cameron in the role of Nora. The date on the holograph letter is partially corrected and obscured by an ink blot, but the context suggests that Garland wrote the letter on 30 October 1889 immediately after seeing the play.

42. to Elizabeth Porter Gould

als, Boston PL

Jam. Plain

Nov. 11 1889.

Dear Miss Gould:[1]

I *was* glad to know your little book was out[2]—Have advised several friends to buy it and think it will do good especially among women. I hope you are in good health and spirits. I am a little jubilant over a victory at the *Century*. They are much pleased with my work. Did you see my Ibsen letter?[3]

Yours cordially
Hamlin Garland

1. Elizabeth Porter Gould (1848–1906), poet and author of essays on education, great statesmen, and women's issues. Author of *Gems of Walt Whitman* (1889), followed by *Anne Gilcrest and Walt Whitman* (1900).

2. Gould appended a note: "Reference is made to my 'Gems from Whitman.'"

3. "An Ibsen Club," *BET*, 9 November 1889, p. 5.

43. to Brander Matthews

als, Columbia

Dec 29/89.

Dear Mr. Matthews:[1]

I want to say how much I liked your candid and progressive essay in recent *Mirror*.[2] It is almost the same plea which I made not long since in *Literary World* and in *Transcript*. I want also to call attention to a play soon to be seen in New York that has many admirable qualities—I enclose a circular concerning it.[3]

I saw the play quite by accident knowing nothing of it or of Mr. and Mrs. Herne. It made a profound impression upon me. Such an impression that I got Mr. Gilder, Mr. Howells, Roman Zuboff[4] and other of my literary friends to go to see it. They were all delighted not only with the play but with the sincerity, delicacy and naturalness of the acting of the principals. Mr. Chamberlain of the *Transcript* one of the most thoughtful of critics wrote of it at length—as you will see. Because it had so much that was fine and strong we have all given our aid freely and I ask you to go and see it and write of it if it impresses you as I am confident it will. My idea is that if we have an American drama we must encourage what is good and true and condemn what is bad in every play—not condemn or praise a play indiscriminately. In this way a standard of taste for a new play is created. Your article ought to do good. And you have my entire support on those lines. I had not thought we were so nearly in line—

Mr. Howells, Mr. Zuboff, Mrs. Moulton and many others declared Mr. Herne's Impersonation to be flawless and those who saw Mrs. Herne at her best early in the week said the same of her. They are, personally, very fine people and deserve their success to its full measure, and more.

I should much like to meet you if you should come to Boston, and talk dramatic principles with you. There are so few of us that we should know each other and be able to work together for "Americanism in Art"—If that phrase be less offensive than "realism."

Sincerely
Hamlin Garland.

1. [James] Brander Matthews (1852–1929), professor at Columbia University from 1892 to 1924, playwright, prolific author of works on literary history, drama, fiction. President (1910) of the Modern Language Association, he was a founding member and president (1913–14) of the National Institute of Arts and Letters.

2. "The Dramatic Author and the Theatrical Event," *New York Dramatic Mirror*, 28 December 1889, p. 1.

3. Garland refers to two letters he published praising Herne's *Drifting Apart*: "Truth in the Drama," *Literary World* 20 (16 September 1889): 6; and "Another American Play," *BET*, 12 January 1889, p. 10. For the "circular," see Garland to Herne, 6 January 1889, letter 25.

4. Roman I. Zubof (misspelled by Garland) (1866–96) claimed to be a Russian nobleman when he arrived in Boston in 1889 amid the Tolstoi craze. He gained the support of W. D. Howells and was lionized by the literati. He published several novels, among them *Mrs. Henry St. John* (1892), in which he depicted a number of prominent Bostonians, before committing suicide in New York in 1896 after his arrest for non-payment of a hotel bill.

44. to James Whitcomb Riley   als, Indiana U

[5 January 1890]

My Dear Riley:

Mr. Herne has written me that he has offered you a box at the Windsor.[1] Dont fail to go if he has or does. These people are with us perfectly.

So free from effectism is their playing that people are deceived into under-
estimating it—you will not. Go and see the play and see Mr. and Mrs.
Herne and my brother.[2] They admire your work so much. They'll be delighted to see you.

All goes well with me. Did you see my latest story in the *Harpers Weekly*
for 24th (last).[3]

Prayerfully yours,
Hamlin Garland

1. Herne reopened *Drifting Apart* for a short run from 6 January through 11 January
1890; his next play at the Windsor theater was *Hearts of Oak*, which ran from 28 April
through 3 May 1890.

2. Franklin Garland (1863-?), an actor who had a small part in *Hearts of Oak* and
toured with Herne's company.

3. "Old Sid's Christmas," *Harper's Weekly* 33 (28 December 1889): 1038–40, not the
24th, as Garland indicates.

45. to Louise Chandler Moulton als, Congress

[10 January 1890]

Dear Mrs. Moulton:

I like the "Strength of the Hills" and the last two lines in "Old Jones"
are superb! So is "At Sea." So the last lines of "Mid Ocean." "A Cry"[,]
"Voices on the Wind" and the others we have talked about I need not
speak of—you know what I think of them. In "At Sea"[,] "Their Candles
are All Out"[,] "My Mother's Picture"[,] "Shall I Look Back?" and
"Straight on to Port" you are at your very best, and that best is very good
indeed. It is difficult to conceive of better expression for these moods.
Splendid research of words. Straight-forward genuine *sure* expression.[1]

But read continuously the book suffers. In certain moods to read in
this little volume would be to find splendid expression of common doubts
and fears. It is not to be read as a *business* as the reviewers must needs do,
it must be read at night by the fire, when the apparently secure knowledge
gives place to the real insecurity of all things—then one gets the thrill
which the poet felt as she wrote. It is an injustice all such purely subjective
poetry is liable to.

The main criticism therefore is not lack of originality but monotony of
key—too largely minor—and still in this minor strain there are many

subtle variations so that the monotony is only relative after all. I like most of your "French Tunes" too. You ought to do more in that lighter vein, it would throw into greater relief your deeper and stronger utterances. I liked the "Funeral Piece" with its stark realism. I wish the mood to try these realities would come to you oftener. You are so good in what you choose to utter, as a friend I would have you disarm criticism by widening the range of your subjects. I'm not sure but your very best work is when you give us your impression of the sea—of winds of space or some realities with the emotional comment. In saying this I do not forget "Paolo to Francesca" or "A Parable."

I have said enough however to show you that I have read discriminatingly most of the poems in this book. I have written frankly as I think our friendship warrants, but please don't take this as final. I shall have more to say when I see you again—

Sincerely
Hamlin Garland

Thanks indeed for your words of appreciation of "Old Sid." Old age to the poor *is* better.

1. Garland probably refers to *In the Garden of Dreams*, which appeared in the fall of 1889. Although Moulton published only two volumes of poetry, her first being *Swallow-Flights* (1878), she considered her poems her most important work.

46. to Richard Watson Gilder

als, NYPL

Jan. 10/90.

Dear Mr Gilder:

I send you my play which I'd like *you* to read with a view to publication.[1] I dont much expect it could be used by you but the *print* is *so* clear and easy to read that I'd like to try. Mr. Howells calls it a great play and Mr. Herne agrees from the actors standpoint. These opinions make me courageous enough to send it to you. We hope to produce it perhaps in May. I have the story or "Book o' the Play" which I'll send if you are interested. The publication of either book or play would help the production and the production would help the sale of the publication. It's worth bringing to your notice any how. Please take the thing home on Sunday and spoil your only day of leisure by looking at it.

Sincerely

Hamlin Garland

P.S. The third act I *know* will please you. And in the story the descriptive matter is in my best vein.

1. *Under the Wheel: A Modern Play in Six Scenes*, *Arena* 2 (July 1890): 182–229. The play was republished by the Barta Press of Boston later that year, using the *Arena* plates. It then appeared as the novel *Jason Edwards* (Arena Co., 1892) before being republished by Appleton in 1897. *Under the Wheel* was never produced.

47. to Richard Watson Gilder

als, NYPL

[ca. January 1890]

Dear Mr. Gilder:

I'm praying like a Dervish that "Jason Edwards" may win your sympathies to the point at least of giving me a chance to make his story suitable for your use. You couldnt do me more good than by the publication of my drama—which is at least an *American* drama. It would please me more than anything else I have written.—

Mr. Herne and I address the Actors Order of Friendship on next Sunday at 8 ᴾᵐ. Wouldnt you like to come? There'll be about a hundred actors and actresses present with some few literary fellows. We advocate the single-tax and show its effect on Art.

That was a beautiful little verse on Robert Browning, a *genuine* thing.[1] I wish you found time to write more.—

—I made an attack on *St Nicholas* with some Boy life articles and hope to hit their long-felt want.[2]

I'd like to see you but I speak Sat. night in New Haven and dont get into New York till Sunday morning. I may be able to run in Monday morning a moment.

Sincerely

Hamlin Garland

1. Gilder's poem has not been identified.

2. Garland may refer to "A Pioneer Christmas," *Ladies Home Journal* 11 (December 1893): 11.

48. to Richard Watson Gilder

als, NYPL

[after 31 March 1890]

My Dear Gilder:

My story is a "chunk o' life."[1] I dont know why he cant go to Congress—except that when love came to him it weakened him. He wasnt strong enough anyway to fight for such leading positions as the west offered.

But the aim of the story is to set forth a common case of western ambition. A river lost in the sands. Out of twenty five fellows who started with me, fellows of equal or greater powers of grappling and holding, seventeen are settled as Albert Lohr[2] is settled in those dead an[d] alive western villages, as pettifoging lawyers, principals of schools, or shopkeepers. I saw fifty bright fellows (at the very least fifty) during my six years of seminary life drop out and down as Albert did. Growing at length indifferent and in a way content with husks to fill their bellies. In a general way the story is a comment upon the all-pervading poverty and barrenness of western life. Specifically it is a presentation, (in the best manner of the writer), of a bit of real life—of Albert Lohr a typical case.

Now I am ready to listen to suggestions. Can it be made fit for your uses by changes here and there? If you are free to say I shall be very very glad to consider. I know it must appeal to you. There are certain subtleties of treatment which I felt sure would reach you. Notably the handling of the boy in the last chapter. And the character of Hartley—which my brother counts one of my best.

In re-reading your letter I see one or two questions more. Why cant he become a congress man etc—He *may* but the chances are "agin him." Why didnt he postpone the marriage? Well for one thing—he was acting under the impulse that makes run-a-way marriages sometime. And second he saw that if he were to begin married life within a year, it would be worse than folly to leave the girl to struggle there alone, while [he] spent all the money he had and wasted a year in study which should be used in earning money.—

I'm afraid you dont know the drear hopelessness of a small country town—especially in the west, as well as I do. What he would be most likely to do would be to *go west.* Almost never would such a man look east.

Let me have a word further with you.

Sincerely
Hamlin Garland.

I can easily put the ideas I have written you into the story in explanation. Oblige me with an early note, wont you. H.G.

1. "A Girl of Modern Tyre" was finally published by Gilder in *Century* 58 (January 1897): 401–23; it was reprinted as "A Stop-Over at Tyre" in *Wayside Courtships* (1897). Here Garland is responding to a number of questions about the story raised in a letter from Gilder to Garland on 31 March 1890.

2. Albert Lohr is the protagonist of the story. Hartley, mentioned later in the letter, is a secondary character in the same story.

49. to Richard Watson Gilder
als, NYPL

12 Moreland St.
Roxbury
Boston.

[after 5 April 1890]

Dear Mr. Gilder:

There is this saving clause about dialect (though parents may never think of it). It is *usually* spoken by one whom the child reading feels is illiterate and not to be copied. I believe in general that *dialect* does not corrupt a child so much as "high-falutin language." The child says to itself, "This man talks funny—the writer knows he talks funny—I mustnt talk as he does."

Practically any one capable of reading my work would feel precisely this way. The only possible danger of corruption of language which could come from good dialect writing is in occasionally letting a really fine thoughtful fellow like Albert Lohr say "Yup" for yes. But this I think you and I realize is not at all a great danger.

Our great trouble today—over "corrupting" of the language of youth as you indicated in your note[1] springs more from the infernal conglomerate, stilted, vulgar conventional "newspaper English" which is not

graphic, dignified nor characteristic. I think the language of the common people is beautiful, pictorial and splendidly dramatic beside it.

I feel that we are not far apart on these things. I *love* the language of
the farmer and the mechanic so swift sure and direct, but I loathe the
reporters diction and the diction of the country newspaper. I intend using
it but in the way of ridicule, to help drive it out. However I feel the pressure which is brought to bear upon you on these lines, and I am perfectly
willing to make compromises to make your predicament less vexatious. I
feel that you would not ask me to sacrifice unnescessarily and I think you
must know me well enough to know that everything I do has *lift* in it—
that I want to bring beauty and comfort and intelligence into the common
American home. All I write or do has that underlying purpose.—

I shall therefore soften down the lingual sins of Albert. I dont think
there is danger from the dialect of Hartley—because they will see that *he*
is not the principal personage, not the one having the authors complete
sympathy. The other suggestions I will carry out and return the M.S. soon.

Sincerely
Hamlin Garland

1. In his letter of 5 April 1890, Gilder criticized Garland's manuscript of "A Girl of
Modern Tyre" for its use of vulgar dialect: "Here is really a predicament, and feeling
that predicament, we at least think a dialect story,—especially of this kind, where 'yup'
is used for yes, for instance, and where all sorts of vulgarisms occur—should very
strongly recommend itself before being sent into almost every cultivated household in
the United States! Had you thought of the matter in this connection? I am very far from
wishing to go to extreme in the other direction—lords and ladies—but I think we
should not go to an extreme in this direction." A revised version of Gilder's letter appears in *Roadside*, p. 183.

50. to Walt Whitman

als, Congress
publ.: "Uncollected"

12 Moreland St
Roxbury, Boston.

April 15/90.

Dear Walt Whitman:

I have seen reports that you were not so well just now, as well all hoped
you'd be at opening of spring. Let me send as a spring message (as I sent
a year ago) I find everywhere a growing respect and even tenderness for

you. I have spoken several times during the year upon your work and have made converts always. The mere reading from some of your pages serving to open the eyes of my hearers. I am perfectly certain that this will be my spring message as long as you stay here with us. — As for myself I am hard at work and beginning to succeed with the *Century, Harpers, Arena* etc.[1] I am still too poor to do what I'd like in the way of having a copy of each edition of your works. I hope to be able to so soon. Please give my regards to Traubel and other friends. Ask him to send me a line if you do not feel like writing.

With deepest regards.

Hamlin Garland

1. Garland had published two stories in *Harper's Weekly* in 1889, "Under the Lion's Paw," 33 (7 September): 726–27, and "Old Sid's Christmas," 33 (28 December): 1038–40; and he had two more awaiting publication in that magazine: "Drifting Crane," 34 (31 May 1890): 421–22, and "Among the Corn-Rows," 34 (28 June 1890): 506–8. In addition to publishing "Under the Wheel," in 1890 the *Arena* also brought out a critical article, "Ibsen as a Dramatist," 2 (June): 72–82; and a short story, "The Return of a Private," 3 (December): 97–113.

51. to Richard Watson Gilder   als, NYPL

12 Moreland St.
Roxbury, Boston

[after 7 May 1890]

Dear Gilder:

Your letter at hand. Glad the tale needs so little cutting.[1] Criticisms accepted. "Horrible little lamp" meant its *odor*. "Horribly smelling" should be the words. Blaine's book seems nescessary for the fun — or at least it ought to be *partisan*. We can use any name we please. "Thompson" or "Smith's fifty-years in Congress". I didnt mean to be exact. There's such a delicious bit — Hartley's giving such a book to Mrs. Welsh — and proposing a morocco copy of same for Maud! It wants to be a book that *some* people wouldnt touch with tongs. I think we can get around that all right by some other name.

Yes I believe in the single-tax and "the single-tax" with me means international copyright, the sermon on the mount and summer vacations for everybody — but why didnt you send your photo. I want to have a presentment of the Editor who first measured my work. I didnt send mine because I thought you'd care for it so much as to get yours.

Sincerely yours
Hamlin Garland

1. Garland's letter is in reply to a 7 May 1890 letter from Gilder, in which he had requested further revisions of "A Girl of Modern Tyre," among them dropping the name of "Blaine" because of its "violent and disagreeable controversies" and the substitution of "Vanderbilt" for "Jay Gould" who "is a live thief whom we would rather not honor, even in that way."

52. to William Dean Howells   als, Harvard

9 Talman Pl.
Roxbury.

Oct 29/90

Dear Mr. Howells:

Will you still hold to promise of inviting Mr. Seymour and Mr. Childs to the play?[1] Do it by letter if it will be better.—I enclose some more tickets to use in this way. I don't want you to pay for the invitation of such people—I mean where it is a matter of business to me.—I have changed three acts already but it takes the vim out of the dialogue because making it so much vaguer. The tug of war comes on the fourth act.

Mr. Herne send regards. He's doing well but misses us all. Will be glad to turn face eastward.

Sincerely,
Hamlin Garland

If you don't want to use these tickets return to me at once. H.G.

1. Seymour is perhaps Silas Seymour (1817–90), an eminent engineer and friend of Howells. Childs is probably George William Childs (1829–94), American publisher (Childs and Peterson, 1854–60), co-owner of the *Philadelphia Public Ledger* from 1864, and the author of *Recollections of General Grant* (1885). Garland offered an "Author's reading" of "A Member of the Third House" at Boston's Chickering Hall on 30 October 1890. Although he was unsuccessful in getting the play produced, it appeared as a novel under the same title in 1892.

53. to Richard Watson Gilder

als, NYPL

9 Talman Pl.
Roxbury.

Nov. 1/90.

Dear Mr Gilder:

I've been looking with more (or less) than anxiety for the appearance of my stories a beginning of which was promised for October. I *hope* you havent put me off another year for I've got some other things I want to send you.—I'm to be in New York on the 16th and I'll try again to see you. I've just read a new play "A Member of the Third House" which has stirred 'em up a little. Would you like to read that with a view to publishing it? I havent decided what to do with it yet—may publish it myself—may let the "Development Bureau" have it.

Are you going to let me see the proof of "Flaxen" before it appears—

The *Arena* prints next month a story I would have sent to you only you have two or three of my stories now.[1] The next story, one I'm writing for you is called "Up the Coulé" and is laid in the La Crosse region of Wisconsin.[2]

Very sincerely
Hamlin Garland

1. "The Return of the Private," *Arena* 3 (December 1890): 97–113.

2. "Up the Coulé" was not published by Gilder, but made its first appearance in *Main-Travelled Roads* (1891).

54. to James A. Herne

als, USC

Nov. 21./90

Dear Herne:

Things is boomin' here. These Flowers are "Corkers."[1] I enclose a slip that explains itself.[2] I've accepted the editorial management of a "Single-tax Department."—and so it goes! It means a lot of work for me but we must keep up our end of the whipple-tree. Gads! Aint we livin' in great days? This election has simply turned people loose. Wait till you come east again and you'll *feel* it. The farmers are *wild*. The Democrats are getting bold as kittens and the devil's to pay—from the conservative standpoint.[3]

B. O. Flower and I are getting chums. He's one o' my kind. Dont smoke, chew, drink n'r fool away his time. He's indefatigable. A tremendous worker. His last editorials (*December Arena*) are the most electrifying editorials ever printed as editorials of a magazine in America.[4] He's concentrated moral purpose—

And behind him stands that brother of his pouring out money wherever needed. By the great horn-spoons! I wish we had a few more such —You see his Roman hand in the enclosed of course—.[5]

I'm going to go west to listen mainly to get my father to tell yarns with my hunter uncles. O I'll make it pay never fear.[6]

People seem all well out at Dorchester. I go out once or twice a week and discipline them for not doing some writing on single-tax.

Mark my words these Flower bros. are going to be one of the great forces of the age. The *Arena* will print 30,000 copies as the first ed. this month. Nearly three times the circulation of the N. American Review— and twice the circulation of *Forum* and N. Am. Review put together— and all inside a year. Do you wonder I'm enthusiastic?

Must go to work—

As ever

Garland.

1. Benjamin Orange Flower (1858–1918), editor of the reformist monthly *Arena*, and his brother, Dr. Richard G. Flower, who ran a prosperous sanitarium in Boston. From 1890 to 1893, the *Arena* provided Garland with the principal outlet for over half of his fiction, essays, and reviews.

2. The enclosure has not survived.

3. In the election of 1890 the Farmers' Alliance sent several candidates to Congress.

4. See "A Transition Period," "Fronting the Future," and "Conservatism and Sensualism an Unhallowed Alliance," *Arena* 2 (1890): 124–28, all of which advocate a visionary populism.

5. The enclosure has not survived.

6. Garland's deep interest in the Populist revolt led Flower to commission him to investigate the movement and write a serial novel for the *Arena*. *A Spoil of Office* ran from January to May 1892 before being published in book form in September of that year.

55. to William Dean Howells   als, Harvard

9 Talman Pl.
Roxbury.

[ca. 1890]

Dear Friend:

I have just finished reading "The Career of a Nihilist" and am filled with emotion by the reading.[1] It has the lift the breadth of a great and devoted man's thought. It is moreover dramatic and powerful, as a novel. It leaves me stirred and in a way exalted as few books have left me. It is a great book full of delicacy as well as power and the gift of seeing and stating.

I want to meet this man. I can understand and appreciate though I would not join in such work. The simple solution with me would be to emigrate and leave the accursed land to the Tzar and his police.

I wish you'd forward this word of appreciation to Stepniak and arrange a meeting if you can. I shall read his other books also, at my earliest opportunity.

Sincerely
Hamlin Garland

1. *The Career of a Nihilist* (1889), by Sergei Stepniak (1852–95), pseudonym of Sergei M. Kravchinski, a Russian revolutionary and author, who evidently met Howells in late December 1890.

56. to Richard Watson Gilder   als, NYPL

9 Talman Pl.
Rox. Boston.

2/6/91.

Dear Mr. Gilder:

Cant you give me just a hint of your opinion of "The Widow at Alleys." I like it so much myself that I'd like to know *how* it really strikes you. Is it *hopelessly* unsuited to your purposes? I could write a second part at a pinch though I think it more suggestive as it stands.[1]

I shall send you a story of Wisconsin soon[2]—but if I could make this story suitable I'd try it.

Yours
Hamlin Garland.

1. Garland apparently never published this story. A revised typescript of the incomplete piece can be found in the Garland Papers (item #194).

2. Probably "Up the Coulé" or "A Branch Road."

57. to James Whitcomb Riley

als, Indiana U
publ.: McCullough

9 Talman Place
Rox. Boston.

April 15/91

Dear Riley:

I wonder if you saw my little note of your last book in the *Transcript*? I enclose it.[1] It dont carry much weight but it will show that we're alive to all you do. I told my class of you and they went and bought all the books they could find bearing your name. It is a "Back Bay" class. You wouldnt think they'd like your things but they did. It shows the power of sincerity and truth.

I'm going to issue a story soon, a vol. of 200 pages. The *Century* are also to begin to publish my stuff. They've got six or eight hundred dollars worth on hand. The Arena Co. pub. my book.

Cant you let me hear from you occasionally? What have you on the stocks at present?

I'm just the same Single-Tax crank as ever.

Yours for truth and freedom. And the Single-Tax as a road to both—

Hamlin Garland

1. Garland enclosed his (unsigned) review of *Rhymes of Childhood* (1890), which appeared in the *Boston Evening Transcript* on 12 February 1891.

58. to Lillian Woodman Aldrich

als, Harvard

[May 1891]

Dear Mrs. Aldrich:[1]

Mrs. Herne told me about your generous appreciation of "Margaret Fleming", which was pleasing to us all.[2] I'm sorry Mr. Herne and I should have been walking when you and the Richardson's called.[3] We need all the help we can get in the fight for a better art. I have given three weeks of my time to make "Margaret Fleming" known to the Boston public and I would give as much more if I could, because it all seems to me very vital to American drama. This entitles me to ask you or any one interested to lend a hand.

Mr. and Mrs. Herne are people who deserve the highest praise and generous reward and I wish literary Boston might become alive to their splendid work. That is a work it seems to me you could help in. It would not take much interest—only a few hundred of the right sort of people to make "Margaret Fleming" a financial as well as an artistic success—and it is the financial success which counts with the managers.

I wanted to see you today to see if we could not do something at once to encourage these noble artists. I know them so intimately that I can say no one better deserves the highest success. It is depressing to them to work years in devotion to an art which brings them small honor and no profit.

I think Mrs. Herne told me you had asked her to lunch. This is good but something better would be the formation of theatre parties for Thursday and Friday night. It ought to be easy for a few well known women to get the hearty co-operation of the thinking women of Boston in aid of a great play and a great artist.

I hope you'll understand Mr. Flower's position and my own. We dont want to push matters unduly and yet we want to use every proper means to further what seems to us a most important and far-reaching movement in literature and the drama. Let my zeal in the cause excuse special pleading.

I shall try to call tomorrow morning as your maid suggested and I'd like to meet Mr. Richardson also if you'll kindly give his address.

Very sincerely
Hamlin Garland

1. Lillian Woodman Aldrich (?–1927), wife of the influential critic Thomas Bailey Aldrich, was an active advocate for the arts and the author of a book of reminiscences, *Crowding Memories* (1920).

2. Herne's realistic play *Margaret Fleming* received its second performance at Boston's Chickering Hall on 4 May 1891. For discussion of Garland's involvement in attempting to reform the theater, see Donald Pizer, *Hamlin Garland's Early Work and Career*, pp. 78–90.

3. Garland may refer either to Francis Henry Richardson (1859–1934), a Boston artist, or to George Tilton Richardson (1863–1938), city editor of the *Boston Advertiser and Record*.

59. to Horace Traubel als, Congress

[24 May 1891]

My Dear Traubel:

I'm very sorry I live so far away that I can be at your dinner to Walt Whitman only in ink and paper. I dont know what I can add to express my regard and admiration for a man who has dared to be himself native and unaffected. In these days of apparent drift toward centralization of power, his doctrine of the Individual, comes to have majesty like that of Ibsen's surpassing it indeed for with equal weight of unswerving resolution Whitman has a more fervent humanity. He is a natural lover of men and does not forget the wounded and crippled even in this moment of hottest warfare.

I need only add that prejudice against our most American of poets is rapidly passing away in Boston. There is very little of it remaining among our most thoughtful critics. Our papers deal kindly and with regard, with his great name and were it possible for him to come to Boston once more the truth of what I write would be made manifest by deeds and words of greeting, by clasp of hands and by smiling lips. Men (and women too) begin to understand that he stands for the strength of wisdom and not the weakness of ignorant innocence. That he stands for self-government, for individual development, for liberty[,] love and justice.

The free and individual *form* of his verse is reaching wide circles of readers each year. It will have incalculable effect upon future verse form not by way of imitation but by its power to educate the ear to freer forms and subtler rhythms.

Once more I make salutation to a great personality, a powerful poet and a serene prophet of a glorious America and faithful American literature to come.

Hamlin Garland

60. to Louise Chandler Moulton als, Congress

[1 June 1891]

Dear Mrs. Moulton:

I don't need to say how well that review reads.[1] Everybody speaks of it as being a very strong article irrespective of the subject. My only fear is that I cant "live up to it" as the fellow said when his fellow-townsmen presented him with a "plug" hat.

I got the *Century* this morning with my "Spring Romance" in it.[2] I hope they'll push some of the novelettes to the front this summer and fall. I'm full of plans for work how many of them I'll get done I dont know.

Accept my thanks—as you know they come—from deeps where silence is the better expression.

I am pleased in an impersonal way more than you realize perhaps. It is such a victory for my theory—which is that the mystery and significance of high heaven falls like the sun-light on the far Iowan prairie as well as upon the Rhine—the Rhine and the Right.

I shall come to see you a moment before Sat.

Yours sincerely
Hamlin Garland

1. Moulton's unsigned review of *Main-Travelled Roads* appeared as "A Drama of the West," *Boston Herald*, 31 May 1891, p. 22. Moulton began her lengthy review by stating, "I have never before felt the desperate unspeakable pathos of the prairie farmer's struggle with life as I have felt it while reading the proof-sheets of [*Main-Travelled Roads*]." Moulton praised Garland's realism, noted the influence of Ibsen, and devoted most of her comments to summarizing "A Branch Road," with some reservations about its treatment of adultery: "It is, I confess, far too minutely and baldly real to please my own taste. . . . However, this grim realism is Mr. Garland's theory of art; and I must confess he uses it as the setting of a story as strong and as inevitable as a Greek tragedy."

2. "A Spring Romance" appeared in the *Century* 42 (June 1891): 276–302, and later appeared in *Prairie Folks* as "William Bacon's Hired Man."

61. to Charles E. N. Wingate

als, Virginia

Roxbury.

July/23/91

Dear Mr. Wingate:

The kindly intention of your letter in *The Critic* merits my acknowledgements.[1] It seems to me that when one comes to see what "realists" are really driving at that *violent* opposition ceases—for however mistaken we may be, our intentions are of the best. I wish we had a new word to

express what Mr. Howells really means by realism—"The Truthful Treatment of Material" is good but it is a phrase and a word is needed. I have
suggested *Veritist.* Is it worth being set going? I have a story commencing
next month in *Century* which I think will please you.[2]—Thanking you for
kindly notice.

Sincerely

Hamlin Garland

1. Charles E. N. Wingate's "Boston Letter" appeared in the *Critic,* n.s. 16 (18 July
1891): 32. In it Wingate praised Garland as "the leading spirit" behind the Boston Independent Theater, which had earlier staged James A. Herne's *Margaret Fleming* on 4
May, and which was making plans to revive the play in the fall.

2. "A Spring Romance."

62. to Barrett Wendell

als, Knox

The Arena

Dec 12/91

Dear Mr. Wendell:[1]

Your words of commendation are all the more valuable because you do
not believe in my reform ideas and because we are at variance upon so
many other points. I take pleasure in such tributes not because of any
personal vanity but because as dear almost as life are my ideas of progress
in art and society. When I am praised for my work it is as if something
impersonal were being praised. I think you will understand. I am soon to
bring out another book "Jason Edwards" whose reform motive I hope to
keep properly subordinated to the art motive. My serial in the *Arena* is
likely to be the most important attempt at delineation I have yet published.[2]

Believe me I am trying to be true. I toil to be true. I toil to reflect the
infinite subtlety and abounding interest of life. It gives me real pleasure
to get an earnest word of commendation from you—

Sincerely,

Hamlin Garland

1. Barrett Wendell (1855–1921), professor of English at Harvard University, and author of *Cotton Mather, A Puritan Priest* (1891) and *William Shakespeare, A Study in
Elizabethan Literature* (1894).

2. "A Spoil of Office."

63. to Horace Traubel

als, Congress

211 North Capital St
Washington. D.C.

Jan 13/92

My Dear Traubel:

Infinitely touching is that little inscription "from the sick-bed". Did he really think of me? If he did he has paid me the greatest tribute of my life. Does he realize the work I am trying to do? The best part of my success is that it has come while I am doing a work whose spirit is in part Whitman's and thoroughly reformatory. I am a reformer—a radical—a promoter of Democracy and yet the people sustain me in it. I wish Whitman could realize that. I tell you the whole temper of the republic in letters as in politics is changing. Whitman's prophecies are be[ing] realized. Not in the exact form in which he seemed to expect them but in spirit and interior purpose they are coming. Convey that assurance to him if he can listen.

His enemies are almost gone. Those who know him admire and love him. My extended travel and study of literature make me capable of speaking decisively here.

Once again Hail and may it not be fare-well.

Hamlin Garland

64. to William Dean Howells

als, Brigham Young

211 North Capital St
Washington D.C.

[ca. January 1892]

Dear Mr. Howells:

I enclose the Salt Water sketch.[1] Hope it will please you. Let me know about the other matter as soon as may be—

Yours as ever
Hamlin Garland

P.S. Your note just at hand. I think a better expression of the idea would be "the force of circumstance." It was not habit but the things[,] thoughts and duties around the man that killed off his romance. The more one thinks about that story the more it means. When I have revised the proof it will be worthy of us both.[2]

Whenever you are at all in doubt of my address send to *Arena.*—

My mother is gaining and I feel very happy over it. I shall go on about May 1st.

H.G.

1. "Salt Water Day," *Cosmopolitan* 13 (August 1892): 387–94. In a letter of 25 June 1892 Howells said of the article, "Salt Water Day is a bit of true and broad observation, a real 'impression'" (*Selected Letters, 1892–1901*, vol. 4, ed. Thomas Wortham et al. [Boston: Twayne, 1981], p. 21).

2. Garland refers to *A Spoil of Office.*

65. to Richard Watson Gilder

als, NYPL

No. 15 E. 11th St
City.

[before March 1892]

Dear Mr. Gilder:

I have decided to let Mr. Appleton bring out my little story.[1] I do this because he does it at once and because he is to give me place of honor in his summer series of American novels. I'm getting *old* and I must make hay while the sun shines.

I wish you'd send me advance sheets of the May Century and indeed the April number as I shall want to revise it at once. I hope that your people will see that my extreme age and poverty makes it nescessary for me to get things moving.

Yours truly
Hamlin Garland

1. "Ol' Pap's Flaxen" appeared in the *Century* 43 (March–April 1892) and 44 (May 1892), before being published by Appleton as *A Little Norsk* (1892). Holloway dates this letter as "November 15, 1899" (p. 164), but evidently misreads the address on the letter for the date.

66. to William Dean Howells
als, Wagner

F. J. Schulte & Company,
Publishers,
298 Dearborn Street,
Chicago

[ca. July 1893]

Dear Mr. Howells:

I want to let Mr. Markham shake hands with you.[1] He's a product of the soil of California and Oregon and I look to see him do something exceedingly good. Indeed he already has done good work but he is coming to his own.

Yours sincerely
Hamlin Garland

1. The poet Edwin Markham (1852–1940), author of *The Man with the Hoe and Other Poems* (1899). Garland met Markham in June at the office of F. J. Schulte, where the poet had gone to seek a publisher. Their shared convictions led them to form a friendship. For Garland's influence on the development of Markham's poetry, see Jesse Sidney Goldstein, "Two Literary Radicals: Garland and Markham in Chicago, 1893," *American Literature* 17 (1945): 152–60.

67. to Francis F. Browne
als, Middlebury

Wood's Hotel
West Salem, Wis.

Oct 12 1893.

Dear Mr Brown:[1]

You will find me generally at 550, Caxton Bg. Schulte's office when I am in city. I shall be down again next week and shall be glad to see you.

My objection to the *Dial* is here stated seriously. I dont think it can ever be much use to the west so far as its critical judgements go, until it leaves off its long-sight glasses. The common criticism being "It cant see anything this side of England and the 17th century."

I confess I do not read it though I think it the best *printed* journal in the country. It does not represent me in any way and its opposition is more largely made up of covert personalities than befits a critical journal. I dont mind how much your editors pound away at my theories but hard words are not argument. This weakness extends to every conservative journal in the country, and in my judgement displays profound inherent weakness of cause. My attention was called some weeks ago to an editorial in the *Dial* wherein was a covert allusion apparently to Riley, Field and myself, which was pitiable in a western journal.[2] You did not write it of course but you should not have allowed such stuff to go in. You cant afford it.

I write this in entire friendliness to you personally and I do not purpose making any reply in kind either to the *Dial* or other journals. I would not write this except as a personal letter to you for whom I have respect and liking.

A journal that will call Riley's work "doggerel" is not a critical journal it is a conservative rear-guard. If you can help it, you cant afford to keep *The Dial* in that track.

Yours sincerely
Hamlin Garland

1. Francis Fisher Browne (1843–1913), poet and founder and editor of *The Dial* (1880–1913).

2. Garland had published "Literary Emancipation of the West," *Forum* 16 (October 1893): 156–66 (reprinted in *Crumbling Idols*), his most controversial tract to date. In it he argued that the West could only grow to literary maturity when it freed itself from the cultural domination of the East. His article met with an onslaught of criticism, including the unsigned editorial he refers to here, "The Literary West," *Dial* 15 (1 October 1893): 173–75, which attacked the writers he names above and described Garland as a writer who "recounts the monotonous routine of life on the farm or in the country town, and is straightway hailed as the apostle of the newest and consequently the best realism." For discussion of the context of this and the following letter, see Joseph B. McCullough, "Hamlin Garland's Quarrel with *The Dial*," *American Literary Realism* 9 (winter 1976): 77–80.

68. to Francis F. Browne

als, Middlebury

Stone & Kimball
Publishers
Cambridge & Chicago.

Oct 21./93.

Dear Mr. Brown:

I can return the compliment without straining moral fibre, I like you and I dont think you are far wrong—but you are not the *Dial* and did not write the article or articles in question. As to my personalities—observe this difference. Mine were used in a friendly *private letter* to *you*. I have never said a word in public print reflecting upon anybody. This takes what little force is left out of your recrimination. As for Mrs. Wooley's article— I have nothing to say in reply.[1] As for the larger question let me say to you I am young and shall probably live to make a part of my prophecy good —and I say—this question of the liberation of creative art from the benumbing domination of the past is just beginning to be fought out. We'll win, for death is mercifully on our side.

I hope to see you some time and *talk* what I have no time—nor inclination—to write. Careful reading of my *Forum* article will show that I am fair.[2]

Yours sincerely
Hamlin Garland

1. In "The East and the West Once More," *Dial* 15 (16 October 1893): 216–17, Cecilia Parker Woolley, in response to Garland's article in the *Forum*, argues that "Garland's advocacy of the merits of one geographical section is colored by suspicion and hostility toward another." Her article is also a response to the unsigned editorial, "The Literary West."

2. Brown pencilled on Garland's letter, "'Ephraim is joined to his idols; let him alone.'"

69. to Louise Chandler Moulton

als, Congress

Hamlin Garland,
Care Arena Pub. Co., Boston.

Nov. 17/93.

Dear Mrs. Moulton:

Your kind note was the first to come in about the Chants.[1] Some of the poems are *my* way of writing verse. Others are little things written during the last ten years at odd times. I dont rank them with my prose at all, but I like them for their memories of the great land which I love and which I must know more of. I dont care for Europe but the untracked plain is a mad delight. Dont put my prose down.[2] Somebody has prophesied (after reading those songs of mine) that the public will not accept me in any other work hereafter but that was the enthusiasm of a friend. They are really only moods, reminiscent.

I thank you for your kind words all the same.

Yours sincerely
Hamlin Garland.

1. *Prairie Songs* (1893).

2. On 16 November 1893, Moulton wrote to Garland, "I am not inclined to agree with you that your prose is 'larger' work — for these poems delight me. They have a note of their own. The wind sighs through them — the wild bird's cry is in their music. They make me see and feel the very life of the prairie."

70. to Johnson Brighamals, Miami U

Office of the
Arena Publishing Company,
Copley Square
Boston, Mass.

Nov. 19 1893

Dear Mr Brigham:[1]

I seize the first unhurried moment to tell you how deeply interested I am in your venture. It is very fine and brave and I believe the Iowa people are ready for it. I am anxious to see our western people uttering themselves freely without subserviency to conventional criticism. I think you can do much to bring our Iowa people in touch with the latest thought in art and literature. Dont be afraid of the new thing. The creative mind is always a dissenter. Art comes down to that, a personal statement of the relation of a human soul to its environment.

I hope to make many circuits in the west preaching the doctrine of freedom in art. I hope "The Midland Monthly" will not confine its pages to amusing fiction but take bold stand for native high-class thinking as well. A magazine edited to high aims can do more than any university in developing the love of truth and beauty in its readers.

Of course I think Chicago must be the center of production for a really great magazine but that does not prevent you from doing a splendid work for Iowa. As you say, my prices on fiction are too high for you to use much of my work now but I enclose a little "Boy-life sketch" for which I will take $35 in cash and a page of advertising of my books in Jan. and Feb. I have another little sketch called "Under Winter Stars" which you can have for $25. It is very short — only 800 words.

I will send the cut in a day or two. It is all electrotyped.

Sincerely

Hamlin Garland

1. Johnson Brigham (1846–1936) published the *Midland Monthly* out of Des Moines from its inception in January 1894 until he resigned to become the Iowa State Librarian in 1898; the magazine survived only until June 1899. Brigham published three of Garland's articles in the *Midland Monthly*: "Boy Life in the West — Winter," 1 (February 1894): 113–22; "Mount Shasta," 2 (December 1894): 481–83; and "A Night Landing on the Mississippi River," 3 (February 1895): 142–43.

71. to Herbert S. Stone

als, Newberry/Yale [1]

Hamlin Garland

Care Arena Pub. Co., Boston.

Dec. 16/93.

Dear Mr. Stone: [2]

The reason why I do not care to promise another book, just now, is because I feel your facilities are inadequate for doing the work of distributing the books. This delay has been very disastrous to me. It has cut me off from any proper attention from the critics and has made the success of the whole enterprise doubtful.

Had I published the book according to my original plan it would have been out by the 1ˢᵗ of October and would have been handled by both Schulte and the *Arena Co.* The injury caused by such a delay can not be repaired by a years subsequent work. The book must now go into the ruck of Christmas books and will not get ten lines of notice. [3]

Then again you have no means of advertising except at great expense, and your time is divided between your studies and your business, this is a great objection.

I am very sorry, but you can see that at this stage of my publishing experience I cant afford to take any chances on successful publication. I have two good facilities of my own for publishing. You need experienced help, you need a regular office and you need to give your whole time to the matter. In view of the fact that these things are not possible with you now I cant see my way clear to letting you have so important a book as my essays. I dont think you can blame me — under the circumstances. I gave the M.S. of "Prairie Song" into your hands last August. I have not a copy of it yet. This is terrible delinquency.

I want to aid you to build up a fine publishing house in Chicago but until you get settled and know what you are going to do and how to do it, I dont feel safe in letting you have my essays. I have been deeply worried and chagrined by this delay and to take on myself more such distress would not be just to myself.

Yours very sincerely
Hamlin Garland

1. The first leaf of this letter is at Newberry; the second and third leaves are held at Yale.

2. Garland's relationship with Herbert S. Stone (1871–1915) and Hannibal I. Kimball Jr. (1887–1933) began when Stone and Kimball were Harvard undergraduate students in 1893. After leaving school, the two established the firm of Stone and Kimball in Chicago, where Stone's father, Melville E. Stone, published the *Chicago Daily News*. After 1896, when Kimball sold his interest and moved to New York, Stone operated his own publishing firm, Herbert S. Stone and Company, until 1906. Stone and Kimball published three of Garland's works — *Prairie Songs* (1893), *Crumbling Idols* (1894), and *Rose of Dutcher's Coolly* (1895) — and republished *Main-Travelled Roads* in 1893 and *Prairie Folks* in 1895.

3. Garland was decidedly unhappy that *Prairie Songs* and a new edition of *Main-Travelled Roads*, which was promised for the fall of 1893, were delayed. He also wanted Stone and Kimball to reissue *Prairie Folks*, since its original publisher, F. J. Schulte, had temporarily failed shortly after the book's publication in 1893, causing the book to receive virtually no attention.

72. to Herbert S. Stone als, Yale

Jan 3/94.

Dear Mr. Stone:

I dont want you to feel that you must take "Prairie Folks." Our ideas and tastes on book-making differ so widely that I doubt if we are to find co-operation possible. You are putting too much time and expense in the *making* of the book whereas the *distribution* is of paramount importance.

With regard to "Prairie Folks" I have involved myself with Mr. Carpenter—because at that time I had planned to publish the book myself.[1] Under these circumstances I dont feel like shutting Carpenter out entirely. At the same time I dont feel like asking you to pay for what you dont want. My reply is simply this, if you dont really want to handle the book dont do it under any sentiment of doing me a favor. You know your own mind, so act as you see fit in the matter. I can put the book into the *Arena* series, and proceed as before. I only thought it would make a good companion piece to M.T.R.

I have seen no notices of the books except those which came from my friends. I hope we shall not fail to get the press notices because that seems all that we can get this year. There will be no sale with times as hard as flint. Write me concerning P.F. at once.

Yours Sincerely
Hamlin Garland

1. Horace T. Carpenter (1857–1947), an artist and illustrator, did the decorations for the Stone and Kimball edition of *Main-Travelled Roads*, contributing a frontispiece, six headpieces, and an endpiece.

73. to Samuel S. McClure

als, Virginia
Jan 8/94

Dear McClure: [1]

I send here by Mr. Crane the M.S.S. you let me read. They are good but nothing like what I looked for. If you have any work for Mr. Crane talk things over with him and for Mercy Sake! Dont keep him *standing* for an hour, as he did before, out in your pen for culprits.

Yours sincerely
Hamlin Garland

1. After the success of his newspaper syndicate, Samuel Sidney McClure (1857–1949) in 1893 founded *McClure's Magazine*, which emphasized profiles of personalities and would soon become a major muckraking periodical. Garland supplied McClure with a number of articles, including a contribution to its first volume, "Real Conversations— II. A Dialogue Between Eugene Field and Hamlin Garland," 1 (August 1893): 195–204; and, in the following month, "Real Conversations—IV. A Dialogue Between James Whitcomb Riley and Hamlin Garland," 2 (February 1894): 219–34. For a time Stephen Crane believed the McClure's syndicate had accepted *The Red Badge of Courage*, which he completed early in 1894; tired of McClure's delay, Crane took the manuscript to the Bacheller syndicate, which serialized a condensed version in a number of newspapers in December.

74. to Herbert S. Stone

als, U of Ill-R

publ.: Flanagan

Jan 16./94

Dear Mr Stone:

It was never a loss of confidence in you but in your *situation*. You had so many distracting interests. You are making yourself felt but it will take a year for you to get settled. I think you're going to build up a great publishing house but you need the machinery of a publishing house in Chicago. I'm interested in you. I want to see you dwarf M^c^Clurg.[1] I believe also in the co-operative plan we talked over but I'm afraid your books are costing too much to ever pay a profit to you or to me.

Now with regard to "Prairie Folks." All would be simple if I had not become involved with Mr. Carpenter. The matter would stand thus. I would put in plates and share equally with you which is, of course, a thing I would not do on a new book. As the matter seems to stand you want

me to put in plates.	$75.
settle with Carpenter.	50.
	$125.

and share equally. Which is a little hard.

It seems to me the way out might be this.

1st   pay Carpenter $50. and use any or none of his drawings.
2nd   I'd put in the plates.
3rd   Make the book at not more than $300. Uniform with M.T.R. Same cloth dies etc. and sell at $1.25
4th   Push the book quite like a new book.
5th   Pay me 1/2 of all profits.

The drawings from Carpenter have arrived and I have written him that only six of them meet my approval. These are endpieces and they could be set in at a very small cost either on the bastard-title page or at the end of the stories or not used at all.

Of course there is an advantage in having the book uniform with the other books and if I give you "Crumbling Idols" that should also bear substantially if not exactly the same device of corn. That should be kept *my* trade-mark and where-ever possible use Carpenter for designs.[2]

Now we come to the essays. You say you can assure me of a profit on the first edition—well now *can* you. As we figured on the other books they were to pay me $187.00 on each book the first edition exclusive of the special edition. That would be 75%. Can you assure me of that?

Unless something definite is arrived at about cost, I am helpless. If the books cost $650. instead of $500. my profit is wiped out. This wont do for one who has made his start. This arrangement makes me to a certain extent (nescessarily) a partner and I must know how things are going. If I let you have these books you have four of my best books and it is very important that the whole matter be carefully canvassed.

Your books are costing too much. No one but an expert can tell the value of a book like Miller's.[3] "Crumbling Idols" should not cost above $360. It is a small book. There are not above 40,000 words and I think about 36000. Say 180 PP at 80 c and good paper and press work should not bring it above 36 c per copy. 40 c at out-side.

I dont mind saying that I have been approached by several old firms here for a book and that they are willing to pay unusual royalties and make unusual concessions — but I am interested in your work and I have not offered the book of essays and shall not do so until it becomes certain that we can not agree on terms. It is a very important venture and I cant afford to run any risks on "Crumbling Idols."

1 st   Can you assure me a profit of 15% or $187.50 on first edition.
2 nd   Can you sell a limited edition.
3 rd   Do you intend to make it uniform with the other books.
4 th   Do you expect to make head-quarters in Chicago during the year.

These questions are important and I hope they will not seem out of place. I think you can not blame me for taking great care about this book. I confess to being very much distracted about the matter just when I am swamped with demands for stories and essays.

Carpenter is making a frontispiece. I wrote him to hold on until I had reached a decision as to "Prairie Folks." If you could put into his hands any designing or other work he would feel resigned to the matter with the $50. which would pay for the absolute trouble to which I have put him. He would make a fine office man if you need any such work — or a salesman.

Send me any special reviews you receive. I'll return them at once. I had a nice letter from Gilder who likes the whole. I'm going to give Stedman[4] a copy — unless you sent him one.

Yours sincerely
Hamlin Garland

Send me 10 copies of Prairie Songs. They are likely to all go to "press people" but charge me with five of them. Miss Dromgoole wrote me a very appreciative note.[5] She is to review it for *The World*—I saw Arthur Stedman[6], he is very much interested. He writes to the *Dial* I believe and other out of town papers.

PRAIRIE FOLKS[7]

A companion volume to Main Travelled Roads.
Containing Studies of men and women in the Great North
West by Hamlin Garland, Native Westerner.

1894

1. A. C. McClurg and Company was a major trade book publisher in Chicago in the 1890s.

2. *Crumbling Idols: Twelve Essays on Art* appeared in 1894 and contained similar cornstalk designs that were used for *Prairie Songs* and *Main-Travelled Roads*.

3. Stone and Kimball published Joaquin Miller's utopian romance, *The Building of the City Beautiful*, in 1893.

4. Edmund Clarence Stedman.

5. Miss Will Allen Dromgoole (1860–1934), journalist and author of local-color stories of the Tennessee mountains.

6. Arthur G. Stedman (1859–1908), the son of Edmund Clarence Stedman, was an editor and literary agent who wrote the biographical sketches for his father's anthology, *A Library of American Literature*, co-edited with Ellen M. Hutchinson (11 vols., 1888–90).

7. Garland enclosed this in a box.

75. to Henry Blake Fuller

als, Newberry

107. W. 105. St
New York City.

Jan. 17/94.

Dear Mr. Fuller:[1]

I have just read your "Cliff-Dwellers." It interests me profoundly to see you doing such a book. It shows great power. It is a brave thing to grapple with the life of a great city like Chicago, and while I'm not entirely satisfied with your point of view—which is essentially unsympathetic—I recognize it as a fine forceful out-put.

I hope when I come to Chicago we may meet and find common ground. Mr. Howells' wonderful tribute to your work has had a vast influence.[2] He has never praised a book more unreservedly. I am very glad he has done so if it will add to your courage to deal with the vital realities of our modern west.

I do not intend to write herein my criticisms upon the book, I want to close my letter as I began with praise. It looks as though in you Chicago had found her first indigenous novelist.

I am to be in Chicago in Feb. and shall hope to meet you.

Sincerely yours.
Hamlin Garland

1. Henry Blake Fuller (1857–1929), Chicago novelist who was to become one of Garland's intimate friends. Garland much admired *The Cliff-Dwellers*, which appeared in 1893, and which supplied the name of the Chicago Literary club he founded in 1907. Fuller satirized Garland in "The Downfall of Abner Joyce," a story in *Under the Sky-lights* (1901).

2. Howells reviewed the novel in *Harper's Bazar* 26 (28 October 1893): 883.

76. to Herbert S. Stone

als, U of Ill-R
publ.: Flanagan

Jan 18/94

Dear Mr. Stone:

Your strong enthusiastic letter pleased me very much. There is a chance to do great and fine things in Chicago and I'm glad you see it. You will take rank as the only house in the city where original work is put into artistic dress. You cant do a better thing than to establish a snug little office and salesroom and *make Carpenter your gentell salesman and representative.* I think he would accept a position of salesman and sort of "reception committee" in such a high-art establishment as you will make. You could call him your designer or anything, but he could be present to receive people and to sell books when other[s] of the firm were not present. He is such a lively fellow. I can see him doing some work of that sort which would give him time to work hard on his figures. He is excellent on landscape and flowers but he needs hard study on figures.

Now I think you may go ahead on both books. I didnt mean to restrict you particularly, as to the *exact* plans but approximately. I dont agree with you entirely concerning the effect of my "Crumbling Idols." The effect of "Prairie Song" is going to be very great in way of correcting any narrow view of my work. Making "Crumbling Idols" date 1st of April, and the effect of the verse will have been very wide. Moreover I find Stedman, Janvier[1] and many others in full sympathy with me in my attempt to break the bonds.

Then again I am ready to send out purely literary books hereafter. I shall not repeat either my economic writing or this literary and art reform. Having said my say I shall proceed on other things.

I have nearly ready a book to be called "Western Landscapes" (like those in Atlantic) on which you can lavish all your book-making skill. Also a book of purely dramatic and artistic stories called "Glimpses of Women." Also a number of novelettes. One especially called "Tregurtha."[2] If things move forward so that you become practically my publisher you need not fear repetitious or monotonous work. You dont know my plans and resources. I dont feel piqued at all over your frank suggestions. I read them to my brother and he smiled. He knows me better.

The book of essays I should make somewhat like Miller's book but with a little longer page and larger type—with similar plain cover with corn design smaller. Using same die for back that you now have. However your taste in book-making I can trust. Have you seen the essays of Richard Le Gallienne?[3] You might get some ideas from that. I mean the make-up, the book itself dont amount to very much I fancy.

I will send Carpenters endpieces but the others are quite out of the question as I have written him. I will write at once to Mr. Schulte to send the plates to you.—Did you see the Christmas *Californian*? They review "Prairie Folks" there. I understand the Jan. number has some personal matter. The *World* will review my verse next Sunday so Miss Dromgoole wrote me.[4] Of course the letters I sent you are *private* though I've no doubt they would permit you to use them. I shall hear from Mr Stedman very soon about the verse. I sent him an autograph copy yesterday. I shall send one to Brander Matthews also. Mr. Janvier is to send one to Mistral the great Provençal.—[5]

Did you mean that you could not dispose of an autograph edition of the essays?

Yours sincerely

Hamlin Garland

1. Thomas Allibone Janvier (1849–1913), author of several works of short fiction, including *Color Stories* (1885), *The Aztec Treasure-House* (1890), *The Uncle of an Angel* (1891), and *The Passing of Thomas* (1901).

2. "Western Landscapes" appeared in the *Atlantic Monthly* 72 (December 1893): 805–9. Garland did not publish any of the works mentioned with Stone and Kimball. "Glimpses of Women" eventually evolved into *Wayside Courtships* (1897); "Tregurtha" appeared serially as "The Doctor" in the *Ladies' Home Journal* from March 1897 to March 1898.

3. Richard Le Gallienne (1866–1947), English poet and essayist, published the first series of his *Prose Fancies* in 1894; the second series was published by Herbert S. Stone and Company in 1896.

4. See George Hamlin Fitch, "Is the West in Literary Bondage," *Californian Illustrated Magazine* 5 (January 1894): 235–44. The review of *Songs* appeared in the *Literary World* 25 (27 January 1894): 26–27.

5. Frédéric Mistral (1830–1914), Provençal poet and Nobel Prize winner (1904).

77. to Johnson Brigham

als, Miami U

Jan 26/94.

Dear Mr Brigham:

You need not be troubled about conventional opposition to my verse.[1] It was a fore-gone conclusion that certain critics should say ironical things. You will soon find—if you have not already done so, that there is a literary war in progress—the same old war between the new and the old—and critics of the traditional school read the new to condemn. This does not disturb the new.

The west should be on the side of the radical in art—but it isnt that's the discouraging thing. Often it out-herods Herod. I should like to see *The Midland* stand for the fresh and vivid comment of Americans upon life.

You saw poetry in "Prairie Songs" because you know the life. Why should you be troubled by the conventional judgement of any man. You are the court of last resort in the matter. If you are moved by a work of art you have the right to say so against the world.

I dont care what the *Tribune* says of my work[2] but I dont like to see you hedge on what I felt was an honest expression of feeling. The west must stand on its own legs, and in so far as possible the *Midland* should steady it.

Again I hope you'll give the preference to home themes. I dont care for two of the stories in the February number. Ask for home themes. Encourage your young writers to write of things they know all about. Keep close to homely things. These are my words of advice which you may think are impertinent.

Yours sincerely
Hamlin Garland

Personal.

1. The *Midland Monthly* printed eleven poems from the advance sheets of *Prairie Songs* in its first issue: "Massasauga" (in MS facsimile), "Horses Chawin' Hay," "A Winter Brook," "April Days," "The Wind's Voice," "A Summer Mood," "In the Autumn Grass," "Dreams of the Grass," "The Herald Crane," and "Boyish Sleep" (1 [January 1894]: 22–27). Most reviewers dismissed *Prairie Songs* as derivative of Whitman.

2. In an editorial in the February issue of *Midland Monthly* (1 [February 1894]: 196), Brigham quoted the *New York Tribune*'s review of *Prairie Songs,* which asked, "Must we call it poetry?" Brigham declared that "there *is* poetry to be found in the unconventional verse of 'Prairie Songs'" and then cited the *Critic*'s praise of Garland's "'intimate knowledge of [the prairies]'" by way of answer.

78. to Julius Chambers

als, Virginia

107. W. 105.

Feb. 2/94

Dear Mr. Chambers:[1]

Let me introduce Mr. Stephen Crane whom Mr. Flower and I both think a most original and powerful young man. He ought to be able to do some very striking work for the *Recorder.* Mr. Howells is also deeply interested in the young fellow.

Yours sincerely
Hamlin Garland

1. Julius Chambers (1850–1920), managing editor of the *New York World* until 1891, when he resigned to write for a number of publications, among them the *New York Recorder.*

79. to Edmund Clarence Stedman   als, Columbia

#2 Banks St
Chicago. Ill.

                                                          Feb. 5/94.
Dear Mr Stedman:

Your kind letter was none too long. It was like you, frank and appreciative. Your only mistake is in thinking I consider the verse my real work,
and in thinking I am likely to repeat it (the book) in some form. I do not
think of doing so. I had a peculiar emotion to express—"Prairie Songs"
does it and that probably ends it.

I have vast schemes for fiction and drama which I shall turn my attention to now that the verse is out of the way together with the essays. I'm
glad you sympathize with my *convictions* to the point of not seeing any
real damage in them.

It is my aim to keep my economic convictions from any obvious or
direct showing in my fiction. The point of danger—if there ever *was* a
point of danger—has certainly passed. I have written two books to describe two phases of the matter and I shall not repeat them.

I go to Chicago to lecture and I am going up among the snow and
pines and choppers of my native state.

I am sorry I could not have come to your house again but I shall try to
do so when I come back. I am to lead the discussion of "Veritism" at the
March meeting of the 19 th Century Club so I *must* get back by March 13 th.

                              Yours sincerely
                              Hamlin Garland
Care F. H. Head [1]

   1. Franklin H. Head, a Chicago banker and patron of the arts who became treasurer
of the Central Art Association.

80. to Herbert S. Stone   als, U of Ill-R
                                                   publ.: Flanagan

Chicago. Ill.

                                                     [ca. March 1894]
Dear Mr. Stone:

It occurs to me that it is imperative that we have a page of the essays
give the names of my other books and also some of the critical opinions

for this reason. It will provide controversy and will be read by people who do not know the names of my books, and weight will be added to these essays by the evidence of my successful work. It could be a very handsome page with lines of comment from Mr. Howells, Mr. Stedman[,] Prof. Boyesen [1] etc. using only names of that sort. I know it looks better not to have these things in and yet it seems to me best in this case.

This will close my controversial work for the present. My next book can be two very strong and artistic novelettes or a vol. of short stories of my very best, but it seems to me necessary just now to see what can be done by a smart discussion of the question of a real American literature.

We must also look carefully after the English rights.

Yours sincerely
Hamlin Garland

1. Hjalmar Hjorth Boyesen (1848–95), Norwegian-born author and educator. A professor of German at Cornell and Columbia, he wrote fiction for adults and children, as well as several scholarly works.

81. to Stephen Crane

als, Columbia
publ.: Wertheim

April 22/94.

Dear Mr Crane:

I saw your study in the *Press* today.[1] It reads amazingly well. If you'll come to the stage door tomorrow night and ask for my brother he will hand you the $15. and also a pass for "Margaret Fleming."[2]

Dont trouble yourself about the borrowing, we all have to do that sometime. You'll soon be able to pay it back and more too. You're going to get on your feet mighty soon.

Yours sincerely
Hamlin Garland

1. "An Experiment in Misery," *New York Press*, 22 April 1894, sec. 3, p. 2.
2. Crane used the loan from Garland to redeem the second half of the manuscript of *The Red Badge of Courage* from his typist. Crane lacked the money to pay for the typing of the novel, though the typist agreed to let him claim half of the typed manuscript. She would relinquish the other half on payment of a $15 fee. Garland's younger

brother, Franklin, was appearing in Herne's *Shore Acres* at the Daly Theatre. Herne was also producing a revival of *Margaret Fleming* at the Fifth Avenue Theatre.

82. to Horace Traubel

als, Congress

West Salem
Wis.

Sept 2/94

Dear Traubel:

I did not see the copies of the Conservator, you mention.[1] It probably went to the Arena office and was not forwarded to me. I want to see your event go forward but I think it ought to be something more than a mere fellowship club. There is a fight nescessary to get rid of benumbing traditions and the Walt Whitman Fellowship should mean business. Just now as you know I am being made the scape-goat of the fellows who *believe they believe* in the past. Of course its all in the evolution of things and I so consider it—but the radicals should have a fellowship and stand together. The traditions have all the organizations and colleges and institutions with which to over awe youth. I dont quite see the value of the Fellowship unless it is to stand for the spread of Walts central idea of Democracy, individuality in art, and freedom from the out-worn.

This is in friendly criticism. I'm a born proselytor as you know, and *must* be candid in the matter. I may have not understood your full purpose, however.

I hear most comfortingly from Burroughs once in a while. He perceives my purpose and agrees with it as expressed in "Crumbling Idols."

I am getting every dollar together to make a payment on my fruit farm here and so find myself pinching things very close. Things will be easier with me a little later in the year.

With best wishes.

Hamlin Garland

1. Horace Traubel founded the *Conservator* (1890–1919), a monthly magazine which attempted to popularize Marxist socialism and the ethical culture movement. In 1894 the magazine altered its emphasis to the promotion of Whitman and his work. Garland contributed three minor pieces to the journal: "Sprigs of Lilac for Walt Whitman," 3 (June 1892): 26; "Realism and Romanticism in Literature," 5 (April 1894): 30; and "Whitman and Chicago University," 6 (June 1895): 60–61.

Sept. 9/94

Dear Miss French:[1]

Your letter came to me in a rain-storm. Think of it — 100 days without rain here, where rain is so heavy most seasons. The summer wore upon us all but not so much as one would suppose. The hills and coulés were lovely through it all — but it was dusty — dusty.

My summer was profitable however. I had two weeks of the Rocky Mountains — a weeks ride in the trails of the White River plateau country far beyond the wagon track. It was glorious! It brought back all the old joy of horse-back riding on the wild prairies. I wonder if women ever feel that marvelous exaltation in the face of the absolute wilderness? — I'm back now with my mother who is not strong. I am writing principally things which wont sell of course.

Mr Page (of *The Forum*) writes me that "the traditional brethren" are much excited over my essay.[2] He sends me cards of editorial assaults. I dont read them. What's the use. I try to be true to my best convictions. That is my care — not to square my opinions with traditions.

Speaking of working — I'm the most disreputable looking tramp-hand you ever saw. There's no fun in digging in the garden with a linen collar on. I take off layer after layer till I get down to a shirt thin enough to let the sun soak into me — the blessed sun — and then I begin to enjoy it. I've got four acres here and a comfortable farmer-like house and barn and I'm going in for black-berries, straw-berries, potatoes[,] onions and sweet-corn. I wish you and your Harvard bro. could come up on some stray steamer sometime and aid me in my war on "Pussley."[3] We aint [illeg.] a bit. I suppose my critics think I'm a terrible dude livin' in a baronial mansion but I aint, I'm a farmer lad always was. I served a year at the carpenters trade but that dont make me any less a farmer. Thats why I fight so. I want to see the farmers life made stable, easy — beautiful. It's the basis of all — but it should not be the foot-stool of all.

Theres a whole ever-lasting lot of things we ought to talk over somewhere where we could shriek and pound the chair-arm and arrive at an understanding. I dont believe you've begun to use your splendid art. I dont mean in way of didacticism — obvious preaching is bad art (and I've *had* to preach a few times but the work I've done for the last five years has been *indirectly* suggestive —) There is not enough of struggle in your books. I dont mean that you should be gloomy, the thing I miss is subtle as all real personal qualities in art are. There is just a little too much fore-shortening. You look at them all from too secure a height—but there, good heavens! I didnt go for to criticise. I believe in personal art. I believe in the evidence of individual temperament in art—only—Well I give it up—till I see you.

I write reams of fiction—my very best work which the editors return with deprecating shake of the head. Do you do so? I imagine not. Burlin-game wont have a line I write.[4] I dont blame him any. Sometime I'll send you one of the M.S.S. which they return, just to see how it strikes you.

I hope you'll be in Chicago during the winter. My hand to you.

Your friend
Hamlin Garland

1. Alice French (1850–1934), local-color writer who published under the pseudonym Octave Thanet. Although she wrote several novels, she is better known for her short stories, which were collected as *Stories of a Western Town* (1893), *A Captured Dream, and Other Stories* (1897), and *Stories that End Well* (1911).

2. Walter Hines Page (1855–1915) was the editor of *The Forum* until the summer of 1895, when he left to become the associate editor of *The Atlantic.* Garland's essay is "Productive Conditions of American Literature," *Forum* 17 (August 1894): 690–98.

3. "Pussley" is a variant of "pursley," short for "purslane"—a fleshy-leaved trailing plant with tiny yellow flowers that is a common troublesome weed.

4. Edward L. Burlingame (1848–1922), the editor of *Scribner's Magazine.* Garland never did publish in *Scribner's.*

84. to Hannibal Ingalls Kimball

als, U of Ill-R
publ.: Flanagan

Sept 16/94

Dear Mr. Kimball:

I defer discussion of the disputed matter till I come down. I wish you would co-operate with me on the lecture business.[1] We'll feel its effects very soon after. I wish you could secure a list of the colleges in the Middle West and send our circular out to them and charge the postage to me. If I had a manager to actively take hold of my lecturing I could make it profitable for us both. Being without a manager I must be content with

what comes in of itself. If however you would allow your clerk to send out
the circular to such lecture committees and other persons as we could
reach I am satisfied good results would follow for us all. In case of all
lecture com. etc. I would pay the postage.

I'd like you to see that sketch of me and tell me how it would do reproduced (as a zinc etching) about 8x10, to be used as a lithograph. Please
let me know if you have had it brought to the office.

If it seems to you and Mr. Stone to be suitable have Richmond go
ahead on it either as a 7x9 or 8x10 zinc engraving at 7^c per each.

I hope to be down on the 27th and we'll have a long delayed understanding.

Very Sincerely

Hamlin Garland

1. Garland was looking for someone to manage a lecture tour for him. He also wrote
to Melville Stone on 18 September 1894 (Newberry) about the same issue: "The boys
wrote me a very discouraging letter. I dont know whether its the general stagnation in
trade or their lack of experience or my failure to reach the people. I want to see you at
our leisure for important matters to be decided./ If I had a manager with bright energetic methods I could do well in the lecture field. I wish Eugene Field would join teams
with me." However, both Stone and Kimball were too busy with the publishing company to offer Garland any encouragement.

85. to Herbert S. Stone

als, U of Iowa

Sat. [January] 26/95.

Dear Mr Stone:

I think you go too far in your attempt at justification. I wrote *repeatedly*
for a contract concerning the essays and also for the quarterly statement.
As the year [illeg.] on, I wrote two or three times before I could get an
answer with the yearly statement. I did not require "bulletins"—I required the quarterly statement which I did not get. As for the publication
of "Prairie Folks" and the essays together that was the inducement. I had
an offer for the essays alone from a New York firm, as I told you, and it
was your talk at 107 W. 105st that decided me to let you have the essays. I
hold your letter showing this.

However the experience with the serial has been more unpleasant.[1] The
payment was to be cash. I told you why—it was to meet a payment, and

it was only by humiliating demands repeated several times that I received part of it when I needed it. Now if you had said candidly "we are hard-pushed" I would have felt better over the matter but you treated me as if I were a borrower. I couldnt understand this. Either my M.S. is worth something or it isnt. There is no compulsion about the matter of price—and after you have fixed a price you should stand to it.

With regard to your hot declaration to refer the matter to your father, I beg to say there is more relevancy in my suggestion than you seem to know. I came into this firm through him.[2] He was the man I knew and it was on his word alone that I finally let you have the books.

I dont like to be at cross-purposes with a man I am to meet socially and I have been very sorry over the whole matter but it simply came to a time when it was nescessary [to] make a protest. I dont understand your attitude in this matter and I havent for six months. I put off writing again and again in the hope that you would feel it worth while to attend to the matters in suspense on your own motion.

It would have been an easy thing to write me saying "Dont you think we had better defer pub. of "Prairie Folks" or to say at the end of March—"we have only sold 200 books and there is nothing due you." In your attempt to put a good face on the matter you deceived me—probably you thought for my good—but it wasnt. I want to know exactly the way things stand. Its a hard year and I accept the low sales as inevitable.

I do not say you broke the broad terms of your contract but you ignored or neglected the details and in the case of the serial you troubled me very much. I sold you one of my strongest stories at a very low rate and you afterward treated me as if I had small claim on your consideration!

However we have reached a certain understanding of the case so much is gain.

Very Sincerely
Hamlin Garland

1. Garland's "The Land of the Straddle Bug" appeared serially in the *Chap-Book*, 2 (15 November 1894–15 February 1895); it later appeared under the title *Moccasin Ranch: A Story of Dakota* (1909).

2. In early 1893 Garland had written to Melville E. Stone, publisher of the *Chicago Daily News*, about his publishing difficulties with the failed firm of F. J. Schulte and his desire to acquire a respectable publisher. Stone passed on the letter to his son, Herbert,

then an undergraduate student at Harvard, who replied that he wanted to publish Garland's works.

86. to Richard Watson Gilder als, NYPL

474 Elm St
Chicago.

April 19/95.

Dear Mr. Gilder:

If possible I wish you would let me see the M.S. of "A Good Fellow's Wife." I would like to make a few changes of names in it. It is one of the few stories I have written upon a basis of actual occurrence and while it is not a serious complication, the delay in using its story makes it a little bit complicated—for I have bought a summer place in the little town in which the scene is laid.[1]

I hope to send you something else one of these days though I fear you've lost interest in my work. I'll try you with something more at any rate.

With grateful memories
Hamlin Garland

1. The central incident of "A 'Good Fellow's' Wife" concerns a banker's embezzlement, the subsequent failure of the bank, and his wife's efforts to restore the lost money and her husband's reputation. The story appeared in the *Century* 55 (April 1898): 937–52; it was reprinted in the 1922 edition of *Main-Travelled Roads*.

87. to Henry Blake Fuller als, Newberry

May 8/95.

Dear Fuller:

Page 86. I must stop to say this is one of the biggest, brainiest, most suggestive works ever written in America.[1] It is *the* book of Chicago. It is broad simple tender. If it holds up to the end I'll want to dance old Dan Tucker with you. Why man alive this is wonderful work! No wonder you pitched into my poor stuff.

I havent been so excited about a book in five years. All the other fellows in Chicago shall go to school to you or they'll suffer be-heading.

Dont let yourself have another gloomy moment and let me see you to shout and swear praises at when I come down next Tuesday.

Yours excitedly
Hamlin Garland

1. *With the Procession* (1895).

88. to Henry Blake Fuller   als, Newberry

Mapleshade.

May 9/95

Dear Fuller:

Book winds up all right. Severe but just and in epic proportions. Only one part where I skipped a word—I shall go back and read it all over again.

Chicago has found its novelist. No outsider could write that book or anything touching it. I think I will be believed when I say as I soon shall somewhere that it is the greatest book yet written in the west.

Here's my hand! [1]
Garland

1. Garland here drew a hand. In *Roadside* Garland amplifies his praise: "Masterly in the precision of its phrase, its characterization, and its humor, 'With the Procession,' in my judgment, ranks with Howells' 'A Modern Instance' and 'Silas Lapham.' Cosmopolitan in its technique, it made all other stories of Chicago seem raw and crude" (p. 267).

89. to Robert Underwood Johnson   als, NYPL

474 Elm St
Chicago.

May 13/95

Dear Mr Johnson: [1]

When I wrote the "Good Fellows Wife" I was a mere tourist in Salem and the incident which was real appealed to me strongly—I have not used characters because I dont know the man—his wife I dont remember even to have seen. But I *live* in Salem now and the appearance of the story this summer will look like a deliberate study of my neighbors. I would suggest you publish the other novelette which you hold, first and use this one in the winter. Not earlier than December. I will be away then and can watch the effect from a safer distance.

I wish I could do some more work for you but you've held these off so long I concluded you had all of my work you cared for. I am writing another long story, the intimate history of [a] girl, but it is hopeless to expect to print it serially, I imagine, so I've secretly plodded away at it and shall try to get it into book shape by October.[2]

I shall be in New York soon and shall look in on you if I can find slightest excuse. With regards to Mr Gilder.

Very sincerely
Hamlin Garland

1. Robert Underwood Johnson (1852–1937), editor, poet, and U.S. ambassador to Italy (1920–21). A lifelong friend of Garland, Johnson served as an associate editor at the *Century* from 1881 to Gilder's death in 1909, whereupon he became editor until he resigned in 1913.

2. *Rose of Dutcher's Coolly* (1895).

90. to Harry Thurston Peck

als, Virginia

The Alamo Hotel
Colorado Springs, Colo.

July 11 1895

Dear Mr Peck.[1]

Allow me to compliment you upon the admirable appearance of *The Bookman*. I think it one of the most inclusive of our literary news journals and its criticisms are pleasingly free from personal prejudices. There has never seemed to me to be good reason for saying ill things of a writers personality because his work was not admirable to me. The vicarious assaults—incessant assaults upon Mr. Howells in some quarters seems to me to be the smallest sort of meanness for he is not only one of our foremost figures but one of the kindliest and most generous natures I have ever known.

I am glad to see you give a page to Stephen Crane. He's a very remarkable boy. He used to come up to my flat in Harlem with those "Lines" fresh from his pen. He was a little bewildered over it all but I saw or felt rather, his power from the first. I met him in Avon New Jersey when he was nineteen and a year later he brought "Maggie" to me.[2] He has a marvelous hold on words — They are always precise and unworn with him.

With best wishes.
Hamlin Garland

West Salem
Wis.

1. Harry Thurston Peck (1856–1914), professor of Latin at Columbia University and the first editor of the *Bookman*. In "Stephen Crane" (*Bookman* 1 [May 1895]: 229–30), Peck briefly sketched Crane's career.

2. Garland first met Crane in August 1891; Crane showed him the manuscript of *Maggie* in August 1892.

91. to Mary Wilkins Freeman

als, Knox

474 Elm St

Jan 19/96.

Dear Miss Wilkins:[1]

There are certainly signs of overwork in your handwriting and I advise you to stop short off for a time and rest. Go out and farm with the Chamberlins. They are a good hearty tonic.

I am profoundly interested in your new book and shall watch for it eagerly.[2] If you have not already secured my new book I will send it to you asking you to autograph either "Pembroke" or "A Humble Romance" for me. I think I prefer "A Humble Romance —" No I have that also. Make it "Jane Field" or "Pembroke" as the new book.

I am to be East again and I hope to see you then and find you quite yourself again. We cant afford to have you work when work is a weariness.

Very sincerely
Hamlin Garland

1. Mary E. Wilkins Freeman (1852–1930) was best known for her local-color stories of New England rural life. Her first two collections of tales, *A Humble Romance* (1887) and *A New England Nun* (1891), established her reputation and contain her best work; her novels *Jane Field* (1893) and *Pembroke* (1894) are also well regarded.

2. Garland probably refers to *Madelon: A Novel* (1896).

92. to Victor Lawson

als, Brigham Young

West Salem. Wis.

[ca. 6 June 1896]

Dear Mr. Lawson:[1]

Your representative in La Crosse needs to be "called down." In reporting the Old Settlers Meeting in your Sat. issue he makes false report and
in trying to do me harm maligned the Old Settlers who listened courte-
ously and cheered me heartily at the close of my little talk. I don't think
you can afford to keep a man with so remarkable imagination. His field is
in the tin-sword romance. This letter is for your private eye as I do not
care to break my rule of not replying to malignancies of this character.
You should know the character of your reporter however.

Very sincerely
Hamlin Garland

Personal[2]

1. Victor Lawson (1850–1925) was the editor and publisher of the *Chicago Daily
News*. Garland had read a newspaper account of a lecture he gave at La Crosse, Wisconsin, entitled "Hisses for Hamlin Garland/Occasioned by the Author's Praise of Chief
Black Hawk" (clipping, Brigham Young), which reported that he had "declared the
Indians in the Black Hawk war entirely right and the whites entirely wrong. He said the
name of Black Hawk should ever be revered and remembered. He was greeted by hisses
from hundreds, who gave a tremendous demonstration of disapproval. Judge Brindley
replied vigorously and was cheered for several minutes. Mr. Garland left in disgust."
Lawson wrote at the top of Garland's letter, "Mr Geo Bush, Plse investigate, & return
this letter to me. Lawson." Bush duly investigated and reported to Lawson that the
account was accurate.

2. Written in top left corner.

93. to Brander Matthews

als, Columbia

New Amsterdam Hotel
4th Avenue & 21st St.
New York

Oct 14 1896

Dear Mr Matthews:

I was very glad to get your book with your hand-write therein.[1] We are
quite agreed. You improve the plea by the use of "Colonialism." What we

want is Americanism. Posnett[2] made a strong plea along these lines: A national literature must rise from the nations midst. All great literatures of the past were the expression of certain definite characteristic conceptions of life. The Greeks, the Skandinavians, the Egyptians—each found the life of their own people sufficient theme. The Roman literature was weak *because* it looked away from the Roman life—copied a fact, etc.— The point is a literature should be local in its subject and universal in its appeal. However, enough of discussion at this point.

I wish to have you accept in exchange something of mine. Have you my "Rose"? or my "Songs"? I shall be glad to let you choose from my list. Also I hope you and I may become better acquainted this winter.

Very sincerely
Hamlin Garland

1. Garland probably refers to *An Introduction to the Study of American Literature* (1896), among the earliest textbooks devoted to American literature, in which Matthews mounts a nationalist argument for a distinctive native literature.

2. Hutcheson Macaulay Posnett, an evolutionary critic whose *Comparative Literature* (1886) was influential in the development of Garland's critical theories.

94. to Hannibal Ingalls Kimball tls, NYPL

Stone & Kimball
139 Fifth Avenue
New York

October 15, 1896.

Dear Mr. Kimball:

It seems to be very difficult to find you in so I indite this note. I want to know definitely about the "Spoil of Office" and about the English edition of "Rose" before I leave town which will be within a few days. I want to know if we have the right to dictate terms on the edition of "Rose" and if so, I want a larger royalty in case the book sells above a certain number, say two thousand copies. I want to provide against any extraordinary sale which might arise. I thoroughly believe that within a very short time the sale on my books is going to be considerable and if it is, I want a large share of the profits. I wish you would go over this matter and explain to me just when your two per cent on the transaction is to end and whether

ten per cent is all that we can get. I have had letters from England concerning any future book I may bring out and concerning "Rose" and
"Prairie Songs". I feel that together with the Grant matter and the English
edition of "Rose" that there will be a demand for my work in England
and I want to know what you think is the best we can do in the matter.
However, I think you had better write me a letter stating the arrangement
which holds with "A Spoil of Office", "Prairie Folks" and "Crumbling
Idols" as you probably remember there has been no contract in regard to
these books and they must be settled before I leave town this coming
week. Now please let us get down to accurate business.[1] I am at the New
Amsterdam Hotel and can be seen at any time either there or at McClure's
office.[2]

Very sincerely yours,
H. Garland

1. As Holloway points out, "Garland must have overlooked the fact that his contract
signed the previous year on November 1, 1895, on *Rose of Dutcher's Coolly*, contained a
paragraph extending for a period of five years the original one-year agreements covering *Main-Travelled Roads* and *Prairie Songs*, and containing standard clauses as to foreign rights." Nevertheless, within two weeks of Garland's demands, "Kimball signed a
two-year contract for publication rights on *Prairie Folks* and *Crumbling Idols*, agreeing
to pay the author one-half of the net profits after publication expenses, a gesture of little
significance in view of both the firm's and the books' obvious lack of prospects"
(pp. 132–33).

2. Garland signed another contract with S. S. McClure Company within the same
week that he signed the new contract with Kimball, for a monthly serialization for
McClure's of his biography of Ulysses S. Grant, a project on which he had worked for
a year.

95. to Walter Hines Page

als, Harvard

474 Elm St

Nov. 24/96.

Dear Mr Page:[1]

You mustn't get cranky in your old age. If I were to do many such
stories as "The Healer"[2] it would be abnormal in me. To do a certain
proportion of such stories is presenting phases of life that I touch from
time to time. I deny on my part that there is an indecent suggestion in it.
What's the matter of you fellows there in the East? The upshot of that

story is the mystery cropping out of apparently normal conditions—and here you are crying indecency!

I'm sorry you did not return the story before I left New York. I had a place to put it. I don't think you'll want the one you have "The Widow at Alleys."[3] My work don't "mesh in" with the *Atlantic.* Please decide on the thing at once and let me have it. The other two that I spoke of are worse than any of those you have so the case is hopeless, as I told you when we first talked of it. I never sell the copy-rights of my stories anyway.

Ever yours sincerely
Hamlin Garland

No offense taken only I know youre wrong about the yarn.

1. Page was the assistant editor of the *Atlantic Monthly* (editor, 1898–99), then editor of the *World's Work* (1900–1913) before leaving to serve as ambassador to Great Britain (1913–18).
2. The story was eventually published as "The Healer of Mogalyon," *Circle* 3 (March 1908): 140–45.
3. See Garland to Gilder, 6 February 1891, letter 56.

96. to Doane Robinson

als, U of Iowa

The Regent
Washington, D.C.

Feb 2. [1897]

Doane Robinson
Yankton. Dakota.

Dear Mr Robinson:[1] The *Century* has forwarded to me your notes concerning my story. Privately, you've come pretty near the mark. I live in the coulé country summers—West Salem Wis. The colloquialism of the boys, I'm told is troubling the west but the story represents the boys of fifteen years ago—and you know that even now the college boys of the west drop into that jocular free and easy style when talking among themselves. I never pay attention to the squeamish people of the west who would like to have all its fictional characters talk in Johnsonian English or blank-verse.

Why dont you write more are you buried in newspaper work? I see your name but seldom these days.

You have my best wishes.
Hamlin Garland

1. Doane Robinson (1856–1946) established the *Monthly South Dakotan* in 1898, a magazine devoted to South Dakota history, became the secretary and superintendent of the South Dakota Department of History, and was the author of many books about South Dakota history and culture. Robinson's letter has not survived, but it referred to Garland's "A Girl of Modern Tyre," *Century* 58 (January 1897): 401–23; reprinted as "A Stop-Over at Tyre" in *Wayside Courtships*.

97. to Richard Watson Gilder

als, NYPL

The Regent
Washington.

Feb. 2/97.

Dear Mr Gilder:

I have an article upon "The Corn Dance at Acoma" the wonderful desert pueblo.[1] It is capable of superb illustration. Lungren knows it thoroughly. Is it anywhere near your plans for the next few months?

The objections to the colloquialisms of my college students, troubles me not at all. If they had talked like "Chemmie Fadden"[2] as I have heard Yale and Harvard students do, it would have been considered reasonable. That they should fall back into the familiar idioms of their farm-life native dialect appears to me quite in line with the tendency of the Scotchman to drop into his brogue in his unbraced moments. I hope you're not troubled by it—if you are I'll write a paragraph of back-talk which will put an end to any criticism of you.

Very sincerely
Hamlin Garland

1. Published as "The Dance at Acoma," Albert Bigelow Paine Syndicate, 1896.

2. Chimmie Fadden, the tough Bowery hero of various stories and sketches by Edward W. Townsend (1855–1942), which were originally published in the *New York Sun*, and later were collected in a series of volumes beginning with *Chimmie Fadden, Major Max, and Other Stories* (1895).

98. to Franklin Garland als, Hunt

Washington.

Feb. 3/97.

Dear Old Man:[1]

This is hard and I dont know what I can say to comfort you. You and I have talked these things over before and you know my thought. It is only a space between her going and the going of us all. We are both of an age when Death must be an expected visitor.

I would only say: go back to work. Thats the best case for the heartache and no doubt if she could communicate with you *she would* agree with me. If I were in your place I should take her body to Salem or put it somewhere in Chicago—and then go back to work.

But what ever you do, old man; count on my aid and deepest sympathy.

Let me know your plans. If you must come to New York come this way and see me, but if you can do so go back to work—the habits and associations of the theater will aid you. I wired you yesterday to send for mother if you needed her. I thought it might be a comfort to her and to you. Dont sit down—dont brood over it—go on reading, acting. It seems cruel to say this but your philosophy will help you see the virtue of it.

Whatever you do, call on me. Taft or Brown will aid you in any way and you can draw on McClure for $100^{00}. Aunt Susan will aid also, draw on her in my name.[2]

Your brother
Hamlin

1. Garland had received word that Stella Esther Burkhart, whom Franklin had married in 1895, had died.

2. Lorado Taft (1860–1936) was a Chicago sculptor known for his large public compositions; Charles Francis Browne (1859–1920) was a Chicago artist; Susan Bailey Garland was the Garlands' paternal aunt.

99. to James Harrison Wilson

als, Congress

The Regent.
Washington, D.C.

Feb. 11 1897

Gen J. H. Wilson:[1]

Dear Sir:

Please let me say that the articles appearing in McClure's do not fully represent me. They are much trimmed.[2] I feel as you do, that Grant is big enough to have the human side of him brought out—and no real biography of any man can be written without due recognition of his weaknesses as well as the delineation of his strength.

It is my aim to put in book form my own conception of Grant and not some editor's idea of what it is politic to say.

I know you have much to tell but I felt delicate about approaching you for I had been told you were preparing something for publication yourself. My idea is to show the things Grant contended with. Among other things was that question of "sincerity of rank"—and also the powerful feeling of jealousy which not even a great war for a great nation could root out of the minds of certain officers.

I am going to do this work not as a soldier or a politician but as a literary man and I'm going to tell the truth as I see it. I cant do it in the magazine but I can in the book.

If agreeable to you I will see you Saturday or Sunday as I am going to New York soon.

My friend and colleague Thomas Nelson Page offered to write a letter of introduction to you.[3] He knows my place in literary affairs and feels that I am on the right track. He assures me that I will enjoy a visit with you. I sincerely hope that I may not prove a troublesome interviewer.

Very sincerely.
Hamlin Garland

1. James Harrison Wilson (1837–1925), author of *The Life of Ulysses S. Grant* (1868). Garland was at work on his own biography of Grant, *Ulysses S. Grant: His Life and Character*, published by Doubleday in 1898 after appearing as a serial in *McClure's*.

2. In all, Garland published ten articles on Ulysses S. Grant in *McClure's* from December 1896 to May 1898. At this point, three had appeared: "The Early Life of Ulysses S. Grant," 8 (December 1896): 125–39; "Grant at West Point," 8 (January 1897): 195–210; and "Grant in the Mexican War," 8 (February 1897): 366–80. Garland became

increasingly dissatisfied with the drastic cutting that the manuscript received from *McClure's* editors, not only because he felt that his depiction of Grant was being distorted, but also because he suspected that *McClure's* was attempting to save money, since Garland's agreement stipulated that he be paid according to the number of words accepted. See Holloway, pp. 135–41, for the history of Garland's dealings with *McClure's*.

3. Thomas Nelson Page (1853–1922), Virginia local-color writer whose best-known collection is *In Ole Virginia* (1887).

100. to James Harrison Wilson   als, Congress

The Regent.
Washington, D.C.

March. 8 1897

Dear General Wilson:

I am to be in Washington during the next few weeks probably I shall room here. Referring back to your letter and my own which called it forth perhaps I should have said your theory did not explain *all* the facts in my possession. The matter stands thus. You have a body of facts in your hold—so have I. *All* the facts in the case are known only to God. I cant write from your standpoint. I take your evidence and put it in corroboration (or opposition) of my facts and forge ahead. Manifestly if I should write to please any member of the family or take any view not arising from the totality of the evidence I question whether I would be writing from some other man's point of view and not my own. Every biography at the last analysis is colored by the writer. Facts are infinite in number— the biographer selects. This selection colors his narrative of course.

Very sincerely
Hamlin Garland

101. to Hannibal Ingalls Kimball   als, Duke

The Regent.
Washington, D.C.

March. 12 1897

Dear Mr Kimball:

I handed in those revised sheets last fall before going west and you promised me you would send them at once to the printer's. If it had been done the new edition and the Eng. Ed would have had these corrections.

I have no assurance now that they will go other than the same promise you made before.

Now the edition of "Prairie Songs" is out. Render me a negligence to put it mildly.[1]

"Rose" has had very little advertising and yet it might have been packed with Frederic's book at slight expense.[2] I suggested this last fall and you agreed. At the time I supposed you intended to carry out the suggestion.

If Mr. Beeman has done nothing on the book you are justified in breaking the contract.[3] I have another firm that will take it—at least they said so when the book was new. They were about to communicate with me when they saw a notice that Beeman had it.[4] That's the only word that Beeman put into the press concerning it. It knocked us out of a good publisher. I have written him myself for news.

Very sincerely
Hamlin Garland

1. There may be a leaf missing from this letter. The page break appears between "Render me a" and "negligence."

2. Harold Frederic's *The Damnation of Theron Ware* (1896) was a large success for Stone and Kimball, immediately selling over twenty thousand copies and going into additional reprintings. By contrast, sales of the equally shocking *Rose of Dutcher's Coolly* were disappointing.

3. The British edition of *Rose* (and, in 1898, of *Wayside Courtships*) was published as a result of Stone and Kimball's arrangement with Neville Beeman, but Beeman seems to have done little to advertise the book.

4. Garland probably refers to D. Appleton and Company, which had published *A Little Norsk* in 1892 and was now ready to reissue any new titles that Garland could deliver. Holloway explains that "In February of 1897 Garland signed a contract with D. Appleton & Company, providing for a straight 15 per cent royalty on *A Spoil of Office* (which had evidently been released to him by Stone & Kimball before the debacle) and on a new volume of short stories to be entitled *Wayside Courtships*" (pp. 138–39).

102. to Augustus Thomas — als, Miami U

1342 New York Ave

Friday. April 23/97

Dear Mr Thomas:

I want to thank you for a most delightful evening spent with "The Hoosier Doctor."[1] There is nothing more homely true on our stage and some of it was so fresh and new it startled me. I sat on the edge of my seat the entire evening. "Harriet" and "Fred" and "Alviry" are new types on the stage and so indeed is "Gran-ma."

I feel the novelist in you—which is to say you study human kind, not other peoples plays. Please consider me one of your champions. I liked "In Mizzoura" but in some regards "The Hoosier Doctor" is better—in others not so good.

Very sincerely
Hamlin Garland

1. Augustus Thomas (1857–1934), author of over 60 plays, was noted for his depiction of American background in such works as *Alabama* (1891), *In Mizzoura* (1893), *The Capital* (1895), and *Arizona* (1899). *The Hoosier Doctor* opened at the New National Theatre in Washington DC, on 22 April 1897. Thomas later became one of Garland's close friends.

103. to Brander Matthews   als, Columbia

United States Indian Service,
Crow Agency,
Montana.

July 12/97

Dear Mr Matthews:

Whenever you feel able to properly move in the matter you may present the names of Franklin and Hamlin Garland to be voted on at the Players Club.[1] We shall both join this fall if the Club thinks proper to admit us. We are in the mountains and will be for a long time therefore I write now at my first good chance since leaving home. The memberships are to be non-resident memberships of course. My brother is one of the actors in "Shore Acres". I think you have met him. We both would particularly like to have you present our names and to have them presented together.

If you should wish to drop me a note address West Salem Wisconsin and it will be forwarded.

Very sincerely
Hamlin Garland

1. The Players Club, at 16 Gramercy Park, New York City, was founded in 1888 by Edwin Booth as a meeting place for actors, writers, painters, sculptors, and musicians. Garland became fond of the club and its patrons and would regularly stay there during his visits to the city.

104. to Thomas Wentworth Higginson   als, Virginia

The Players
16 Gramercy Park

Oct 16/97.

Dr T. W. Higginson

Dear Mr Higginson:[1]

I have been intending to write to you for some time to thank you for the kind words you say of me and my trials in literature. Some of them I hear of, more of them no doubt do not reach me. I hope you will take my words at their full meaning when I say I thank you.

I am so constituted that "Art for Art's Sake" does not appeal to me with the power that is in the newer phrase "Art for Truth's Sake"[2] and yet it is not my intention to preach or throw morals at the heads of my readers. At bottom I want my work to *mean* something and unless it does it seems comparatively unimportant.

Sometime I wish you would send me an autograph copy of some one of your books and I will return anything of mine you care to designate.

Very sincerely
Hamlin Garland

1. Thomas Wentworth Higginson (1823–1911), reformer, soldier, frequent contributor to the *Atlantic Monthly*, and author of many works, including *An Afternoon Landscape* (1889), *American Sonnets* (1890), *Cheerful Yesterdays* (1898), and *Old Cambridge* (1899).

2. See James A. Herne, "Art for Truth's Sake," *Arena* 17 (1897): 361–70, for a relevant discussion of this debate.

105. to James Harrison Wilson

als, Congress

23 Grammercy Park.

Oct 21/97.

Dear General Wilson:

I hope we are not to be drawn into any controversy over statements for or against Gen. Grant. You told me *with great emphasis* that I was at liberty to quote anything you said. "I want you to distinctly understand, Mr Garland that I am not talking in confidence." Those were your words. I am quoting you therefore wherever it seems like to draw out contrary evidence. I am after the facts. I am not writing this history in the interest of any special factions. I regard you as the chief critic—I may say detractor of General Grant and I feel under great obligation to you for your frank talk and under the circumstances considered myself perfectly free to quote you.

If you feel differently now your wishes shall be respected. Please let me know your present attitude at your earliest convenience. You remember my words as we parted after your long and very distinctive analysis of Grants character. "General you have made his character more mysterious than ever." You could not expect me to take your way of thinking any more than the Grant family can expect me to write a life in conformity to their wishes.

Very sincerely
Hamlin Garland

106. to Stephen Crane

als, Columbia
publ.: Wertheim

23 Grammercy Park

Nov. 29/97.

Dear Mr Crane:

I was very glad to hear from you and from Mr Conrad.[1] I wish you had written another page to tell me how you were getting on and what you intended to do. I heard you were to make your home in England but this I take to be somebody's lie. I shall not believe it till you write and tell me so.

Mr Conrad's work is not known to me, I am sorry to say, but I shall be all the more delighted to have a copy of the book you speak of. Beeman now has some five of my books. What do you hear of him there? Is he considered a good publisher?

Dont let yourself lie fallow. I do not see much of you lately—This is good if you are working on some larger thing. With best word.

Yours sincerely
Hamlin Garland

1. Joseph Conrad (1857–1924), a Pole who emigrated to England in 1874 and became one of England's leading novelists. Crane had settled in Ravensbrook, Surrey, in June 1897 and had met Conrad in October. Crane had likely mentioned Conrad's *The Nigger of the "Narcissus,"* which appeared as a serial in the *New Review* from August through December 1897, and in book form in December.

107. to Annie Nathan Meyer

als, NYPL

The Regent

Jan. 13/98.

Dear Mrs Meyer:[1]

Your letter was not too long. It interested me very much. Any author—no matter how exciting—would feel touched and gratified by your generous enthusiasm. Please consider that I am trying to do all things to the glory of America and to the furtherance of human happiness on earth. That sounds like a large claim—I only mean it to be the statement of a resolve.

I could not find time to ask Carman about the verses.[2] I saw him, but only for a moment at the club. I am sorry. I would write him if I were you, care Copeland and Day.

With regard to your friend[3] I am very much interested and would willingly give her my aid and advice but as you see I am in Washington and shall not be in Chicago for many weeks. If I can be of the slightest service in the matter either here or there command me. I can trust your sense of the fit and helpful.

I am pushing my Grant to my full limit and hope to finish it by the 1st of March. If I do I may return to New York to read proof. If I am in New York bring me to know your friend and then I can judge better of what she can do in the world. I sympathize very deeply with the peculiar injustices which a woman in her position must suffer.

Let me repeat that I am very glad to know you like "Rose."

Hamlin Garland

1. Annie Nathan Meyer (1867–1951), author, dramatist, and worker for the advancement of women. One of the first women to enter Columbia College, she later helped found Barnard College. She was the editor of *Women's Work in America* (1891), a volume of medical essays written by women physicians, and the author of *Women's Assumption of Sex Superiority* (1903), as well as several plays.

2. The poet [William] Bliss Carman (1861–1929), who edited *The Chap-Book* and whose books include *Low Tide on Grand Pré: A Book of Lyrics* (1893) and *Songs from Vagabondia* (with Richard Hovey, 1894).

3. Probably Dr. Mary Putnam Jacobi (1842–1906), daughter of publisher George Putnam, the first woman to graduate from the New York College of Pharmacy. The author of many articles for medical journals, she practiced medicine in New York.

108. to Franklin Garland

trl, USC

Glenora, B.C.

July 22/98.

Dear Junior:

I have made 1000 miles of hell's own trail.[1] No danger, but discomforts many. I am as hard as nails. I walked and led my horse 150 miles, wallowing in the river, going to bed with wet feet for twenty days. No sun, no game, no flowers, no fruit, no dry land. I lost one of my six horses. He got lame and I had to kill him. We are now comfortably housed in our tent, waiting for our horses to recuperate. I don't know exactly what I shall do next. I may go to Leslie Lake with Burton and start him down the river, and then return to the Coast, visit Skagway and go home, arriving about September 13. If I don't go with Burton to Leslie, I will go down the Yukon as far as I can and get back and then go home. If it does not cost too much I will bring Prince home with me. He hadn't a mark on him when I pulled in here, but he was thin. He is a wonder in all ways. He is on grass here now and will soon be sound and fat again.

I am sending some pictures of Burton and myself as we looked after a thousand miles of trail. See Mariner and when they are developed send all the pictures that are not of Burton and myself on to the Magazine.[2] Burton will not have so much time to prospect as we had hoped, but will be able to put in Sept., Oct. and Nov. probably. He may join forces with a couple of Manchester boys who are camped near us,—good, clean fellows.

Everything is dead here. The wagon road has been temporarily abandoned by reason of some political wrangle. It rains every day here but is dryer at Leslie so I am told. If I go to Leslie you will not be able to hear from me often for I shall be obliged to depend on chance comers to send letters out. If I go the other way it will be easy to connect with mails.

I am glad to hear you are all well at home. Burton and I had a short-cake today, the third and last. There are a few red raspberries on the hills. We may find time to pick some. I am writing of the trail a sort of story,—hope to make an acceptable thing of it. It was a tremendous experience. I had only one pair of shoes and one pair [of] trousers hanging to me when I reached telegraph, but I could swing 50# sacks like dumb-bells. Love to all.

Your bro.
H.G.

1. On 3 May 1898 Garland, with boyhood chum Burton Babcock, set out from Ashcroft, British Columbia, to the Yukon, where Garland was more interested in experiencing and writing about the excitement of wilderness adventure than he was in seeking gold. After fifty-nine arduous days along the Telegraph Trail, they arrived at the Stikeen River, where they floated down to Wrangell. Learning of his mother's ill health, however, Garland decided to turn over the remaining supplies to Babcock and return home but, hearing about a gold strike near Skagway, he instead booked passage by steamer up the coast, then went overland to Atlin Lake, where he panned gold for a few days. Eventually, he returned to Wrangell and, after some difficulty with securing passage for himself and his horse (which he later named "Ladrone" after the subject of his favorite poem), he returned to West Salem on 22 September 1898. See Holloway, pp. 145–50; and *Daughter*, chapter 5: "The Telegraph Trail."

2. Before he set out for the Yukon, Garland published an article detailing the various routes to the gold fields and the needed supplies, "Ho for the Klondike," *McClure's* 10 (March 1898): 443–54. Accounts of his adventures appeared as "The Prairie Route to the Golden River," *Independent* 51 (20 January 1899): 245–51; "Trampers on the Trail," *Cosmopolitan* 26 (March 1899): 515–22; and *The Trail of the Goldseekers* (1899).

109. to Paul Revere Reynolds   als, Columbia

474 Elm St

[before 25 November 1898]

Dear Mr. Reynolds:[1]

My letter to you was meant to be entirely friendly. It is your fault if you take it otherwise. I wanted you to understand the kind of mess you were getting into. You are quite wise in getting out of the matter. Those plates are worthless without the "leave to print" and the leave to print is not transferable without my consent.

Another thing. You say you have just got the poems back from *Harpers*. I am disappointed at that because I sent the poems to you thinking it an advantage. I thought you could save time and get more money out of them. If you merely send them to one publisher after another of what advantage is that to me? I can do the same? I supposed you were able to get m.s.s. before editors at once, get bids and off to another. If you merely take them round at my own prices leaving them to be read in the ordinary course where is the advantage to me?

Now I should like to employ a literary agent but I want to know how it advantages a man in my position. I have a long serial to sell. How could you do me good unless you secured bids for it? If I fix a price and you merely send it round you are of no advantage to me for I can do the same. I am disposed to use an agent but I want to know that he earns his commission the same as any other salesman. This is business on your part as well as mine. *Harpers* have had those verses two weeks. If each editor takes an equal amount of time, I shall gain nothing whatever by using you. Please let me know exactly what you can do both in this matter and in respect to a long serial.

Yours
Hamlin Garland

1. Paul Revere Reynolds (1864–1944) established the firm of Paul Reynolds and Son, America's first literary agency, in 1893. He handled a number of important writers, including Garland, Frank Norris, and Stephen Crane.

110. to Richard Garland and Isabelle Garland als, USC

Hotel Chatham
Paris

May 30 — 1899.

Dear Father and Mother: I have had a busy day in this great city.[1] It is like New York only greater. It is quite unlike London and in many respects I like it better. It is not so dull and conventional. Men dress more as they please and dress well[,] in England they dress as they think they ought to. I got tired of the high hat and the one eye-glass. The women dress better

here and are almost as handsome as American women and that is saying
a good deal. I took a long walk today out to the great church of *Notre
Dame* and past the Palace of Justice and the great Palace of the Tuilleries.
All around the Palace of Justice a cordon of police was drawn, resolute
looking fellows in blue uniforms. Things are getting warm again in the
Dreyfus case[2] and the authorities are alert. There is not a particle of danger of any trouble but they want to be on the safe side.

This is a great city and the French are a great people. It changes a man's
opinion to come here and see the people face to face. The place they call
"The Place of Concorde" is the greatest square I have ever seen. It made
me think of the Worlds Fair as I looked at it tonight.[3] It was lit with
hundreds of lamps and there were towering shafts all about—the Eiffel
tower away to the west and the Egyptian monolith close by. Paris has little
smoke but some dust today which made it seem like the World's Fair too.
I came back by the way of the Madeline one of the greatest buildings in
the world—a Catholic Church now. I went in and listened to the service
which was absurd to me—all but the music that was superb. I am just
back to my room which is very tasteful and bright. I am comfortable for
the first time since I left Chicago.

Thursday night [1 June]. I have just come in from the street which is
filled with people shouting cheers at Major Marchand, the African explorer.[4] It was worth while. The crowd was immense, goodnatured and
very happy. For hours they waited cheering on every pretext. They made
a sound unlike any cheering by our people. It was high-keyed and continuous. A shrill roar which never intermitted. This was re-enforced at
times by a rhythmic clapping of hands and cries of *rat-a-plan, rat-a-plan,*
in imitation of a drum, and at the last some one started the *Marsaillaise.*
It was a thrilling thing to hear these people sing that wild and splendid
hymn. It made my blood leap. The people were all or most all well-
dressed and cries of "Vive-l'armee" brought Marchand out. He is a fine-
looking fellow with a black beard and a pleasant cast of face. He bowed
again and again but the crowd could not get enough of it. They were still
there in immense numbers when I came in. I wish I could be here when
Dreyfus is brought back. Excitement will be dangerously high—but these
people can take care of themselves. They are more like Americans than
the English. I must say I like the Frenchman on his own ground. He's
quite a different man from the one who travels.

I met Landau today—the La Crosse artist you remember.[5] Also

MacNeill the man who went to the snake dance with me.[6] Mr Zangwill is coming over next week and I'm going to have the best time of my trip.[7] I went up the Eiffel tower today. It is a wonder. Nearly a thousand feet high. It was like going up in a balloon. I really went on fathers account. I knew he'd want to know all about it. I dont believe the fair is going to be a fine as the Chicago fair.[8] The buildings will not be as fine that I know—but Paris itself is a splendid city—the best I have ever seen.

Well I am thinking about home now. I shall leave here on Monday the 12th for London. After being there a few days I go to Liverpool to take the *Lucania* which sails on the 17[th][,] in New York on the 24th where I shall stop a few days to attend to some business then home. Frank will still be playing in Chicago I hope and we can look at the Chicago property together.

Mother, I'm glad to hear you continue to improve. Keep up the diet. Dont eat too much straw-berry short-cake. *That* will take courage to refuse.

Your son

Hamlin Garland

1. On 27 April Garland arrived in London to arrange for the English publication of his books. After visits with English writers, including a weekend stay with the dramatist George Bernard Shaw, Garland went to France for two weeks before sailing home. Garland records his impressions of his French visit in *Roadside*, chapter 37 ("A Glass of Old French Wine"), which reprints portions of this letter; and in "Paris in Times of Turmoil," *Outlook* 63 (1899): 968–73. Letters 110, 111, and 112 have been published by Lars Ahnebrink as "Paris in Times of Turmoil: Three Letters of Hamlin Garland to His Parents in 1899," *Études Anglaises* 9 (1956): 246–51, to which we are indebted for our annotations.

2. Alfred Dreyfus (1859–1935), a French army officer convicted of treason and imprisoned in 1895, was pardoned in 1899 after leading intellectuals took up his cause. Dreyfus returned to France on 1 July, at which time Garland was back in America.

3. The World's Columbian Exposition, held in Chicago in 1893.

4. At the time of Garland's visit, Jean Baptiste Marchand (1863–1934), a French officer and African explorer, was one of the most notable figures in France. In 1898 Marchand established a French post at Fashoda (Kodok) on the White Nile and resisted Dervish attacks until Lord Kitchener, commanding a British force, arrived. Marchand later withdrew and a clash between England and France was avoided.

5. Sandor Landeau, Hungarian-born portrait and landscape painter, lived and painted in La Crosse, Wisconsin, and was a member of the American Art Association in Paris, whose Wanamaker Prize he won.

6. Hermon Atkins MacNeil (1866–1947) was an American sculptor who studied art

in Paris and afterward taught at Chicago's Art Institute. MacNeil received the silver medal at the Paris Exposition of 1900, where he exhibited the "Last Act of the Moqui Snake Dance."

7. The English author Israel Zangwill (1824–1926), whose works include *Children of the Ghetto* (1892) and *Dreamers of the Ghetto* (1898), became Garland's close friend during Garland's stay in London and served as his guide and advisor. See Garland, "I. Zangwill," *Conservative Review* 2 (November 1899): 402–12.

8. The Paris Exposition of 1900.

111. to Richard Garland and Isabelle Garland   als, usc

Hotel Chatham

Paris

June 4. 1899.

Dear Folks: I have just returned from a visit to Madame Blanc down in the country.[1] It was beautiful June weather and the country was very fine. The rye was waist high and potatoes in bloom in some of the gardens, so you see the season is something like ours. The town was very old some of it a thousand years old. Madame Blanc and her brother took me all about the town and made me very much at home. They both spoke fairly good English. Madame is going to write an article about me for the Review here.[2] I was much interested in this French home and came away today feeling that it was a profitable trip.

I had a note from Frank saying he was at work again—so you may enclose my letter to him to keep for me. I am going to go to see Napoleon's tomb tomorrow and the Palace of Luxemborg where they have a great collection of pictures. This afternoon I went out on the principal drive here which was swarming with people and all kinds of carriages. It is wonderful to see so many automobiles.—

Monday [5 June]. The weather continues very fine. The city goes about its business quietly notwithstanding the assault on the President yesterday.[3] Files of soldiers come and go and today I heard the movement of cavalry on the hard street—a peculiar sound. The government does not intend to have any nonsense about this thing now. The court has decided in Dreyfus favor and it must stand.—I visited Napoleon's tomb today. It is a most impressive tomb. More splendid than Grants in some respects but I dont know that it is any more appropriate.

I have many a curious time going about among the people. My French is very limited and they cant speak a word of English. However I manage to eat and to get where I want to go. They grin and I grin and we part good friends. There is very little drunkenness here although they all drink wine at their meals as if it were milk. It isnt very strong I use it to flavor water with. It tastes a good deal like vinegar but "squinches" thirst when mixed with water. They have no ice and the water is very warm and not very good.

I enclose a photo taken by the dramatist Geo. Bernard Shaw at whose house I stayed. It is very good it seems to me.

I havent much more to write. I will enclose the photo and let it go.

Your loving son,
Hamlin

June 5/99.

1. Marie Thérèse Blanc (1840–1907), a French novelist and critic who wrote under the pseudonym Th. Bentzon, introduced Mark Twain, Henry James, and Walt Whitman to the French public in such works as *Les nouveaus romanciers américains* (1885) and *Les américains chez elles* (1896).

2. Blanc's extended interview with Garland and an essay upon his work appeared under her pseudonym as "Un Radical de la Prairie," in *Revue Des Deux Mondes* 157 (1900): 139–80.

3. President Loubet was assaulted at the Auteuil races on Sunday, 4 June.

112. to Richard Garland and Isabelle Garland   als, usc

Hotel Chatham
Paris

June 10. 1899.

Dear Parents: I am nearly ready to take the back trail. On Monday I return to London. A week from tomorrow I sail by the best boat for America.— I have just received a copy of my new book.[1] It looks very well but I dont think it will interest very many people. I hope it may. The weather continues glorious here but I am eager to get away. I'd rather be in the wild mountains than here. As I read my new book I feel again the charm of it. I get tired of looking at things here—and then, I feel I ought to be at work.

I received a thousand dollar check from MacMillans, one of three which are due before Nov.

I have not heard from you for a week now but that is because Frank is away. I'll find a letter in London when I reach there. I may meet Henry James after all. He is coming to Paris soon. Mr. Jacacci the director of the Art Dept on *McClures* is here now and is going to call on Zola the great novelist who stood up for Dreyfus, and I may go to see him also.[2] This afternoon I am going to call on Madame De Vaulse who has translated some of my stories into French.[3] Madame Blanc is going to write an article about me for one of the great magazines here. They all seem very interested in my work. I hope it will continue.

I am figuring all the time now on how to secure that place near Chicago. I wish we could manage that farm. Then the next best place is the one in Geneva. I have written to Frank to look up the places in Elmhurst which is very near Chicago and is very nice and grassy with good trees. Thomas Bryan the big land-owner of the place is anxious to have me settle there and make it very easy for me. I shall see him at once when I land in Chicago.[4]

We can rent for a year and see how we like it then if we buy we can have the rent apply on the purchase price. Meanwhile I hope Junior bantered [illeg.] about buying part of the lower end of the old lot. We could leave everything just as it is in the old house and buy new down there—at least till we find out how you like it. You'd like it winters I feel sure.

My next letter will be from London probably.

Your son,
Hamlin

June. 9/99.

1. *The Trail of the Goldseekers: A Record of Travel in Prose and Verse*, about Garland's trip to the Klondike in 1898, was published by Macmillan.

2. Émile Zola (1840–1902), the French novelist and supporter of Dreyfus, had been living as a fugitive in England since July 1898 before he returned to Paris on 5 June 1899.

3. Alice Foulon de Vaulx had translated *A Member of the Third House* in 1897.

4. Thomas Barbour Bryan (1828–1906), a Chicago lawyer and businessman, was one of the vice presidents of the World's Columbian Exposition. Garland was unable to find a suitable property in which to house his parents, so he remodeled the family home in West Salem, Wisconsin, instead.

113. to Walter Hines Page

als, Harvard

West Salem. Wis.

Aug. 27/99.

Dear Mr Page:

I hear you are to form the *Mᶜ Clure-Harper* staff. I am very glad to hear this. It will give you wider scope.—Mr. Finley wrote me that he had spoken to you about my novel "The Eagle's Heart."[1] It will reach *Mᶜ Clures* office on Friday of this week and I should like you to see it. It is a rough draft. I am going out into the Cattle Country this fall to make verification—I intend it to be the epic of the prairie people merging into mountaineers—I mean so far as my powers can make it an epic. It is just what the new combination needs—or will be when I can turn to it for the finishing touches.

Yours sincerely
Hamlin Garland

1. John Huston Finley (1863–1940), educator, author, and civic leader. He was president of Knox College (1892–99), editor of *Harper's Weekly* (1899), professor of history at Princeton University (1900–1903), president of College of City of New York (1903–13), and editor of the *New York Times* (1921–38). *The Eagle's Heart* was published by D. Appleton & Company in November 1900, after appearing as a serial in the *Saturday Evening Post* 172–73 (16 June–8 September 1900).

114. to Augustus Thomas

als, Miami U

West Salem

Aug. 29/99.

Dear Mr Thomas:

My brother told me he had handed to you "Business" and "Love or the Law."[1] A word of explanation is due me. "Business" is hardly more than a rough draft and is a valuable subject for a novel if not for a play. I did not take time to write in stage business to any extent nor to eliminate waste material for I saw I had become too radical in spite of my notion to make arbitration the great plea. Please let me know how it strikes you and be careful of it for it is valuable to me as subject for fiction. If you see a chance of re-writing have it re-copied so that my copy can come back to me as it stands.

"Love or the Law" is also a scheme for a story as well as a drama and was planned twelve or thirteen years ago. Please keep my copy as it stands and make another if you think it worthwhile to join hands on it. I can make better dramas of either or both of them but I cant afford the time or the chance of it while my fiction pays me so well.

I am pushing the Institute but it's a long pole from here to New York. Run in and see Miss Knight Mabies secretary.[2]

Yours as ever
Hamlin Garland

1. Garland refers to the working title of the play "Miller of Boscobel," which exists in manuscript in the Garland Papers (item #209). The Prologue and Act I of "Love or the Law" (dated 1887) is extant (item #203), as are ten holograph leaves of the novel version (dated 1888, item #135). See Garland to Robertson, 6 February 1909, letter 169.

2. Garland was a charter member of the National Institute of Arts and Letters, which was founded in 1898. With membership limited to two hundred fifty, the Institute was formed to promote and to recognize excellence in literature, music, and the fine arts. Garland became a vice president in 1907. Hamilton Wright Mabie (1846–1916), associate editor of the *Outlook*, was the secretary of the National Institute.

115. to Franklin Garland

als, Hunt

474 Elm St

Tuesday [24 October 1899]

Dear Junior:

Zuliema has yielded to my plans and on Mothers account will come into our family home Thanksgiving week. At present we plan to be married very quietly at her home in Kansas early in Nov.[1] Then I want to take her to see Ouray and the mountains. We will then return to West Salem about Nov. 25th to stay a week. On Dec. 5th I am to lecture in Boston and she goes with me for that trip. We will stay till Jan 15 in the east if Mother keeps well returning to Chicago and West Salem for the rest of the winter. Of course all these plans are contingent on Mother's health. Please do not mention the matter outside of our family. We are both averse to publicity. I am very glad to find that she cares nothing about a public wedding or the use of the church and minister. She is a mighty fine liberal girl. She is as free from the usual prejudices as any woman I know. You'll like her better and better as you come to know her. She is yielding a great deal to me but does it most graciously. I make no demands I merely stated the case and she concedes because she knows Mothers hold on life is insecure. Mother was radiant when I told her. It gives her something new to brood over.

Write soon

Your bro.

H.G.

1. Zulime Taft (1870–1942), a fin-de-siècle artist whom Garland had met in 1894 through her brother, the sculptor Larado Taft, and with whom he had a protracted courtship. He occasionally spelled her name "Zuliema" according to its pronunciation. Garland and Zulime were married by a district court judge at St. Joseph, Missouri, on 18 November 1899. They then departed for a brief tour of the Colorado mountains before spending Thanksgiving at the Garland family homestead in West Salem, Wisconsin.

116. to Franklin Garland als, Hunt

474 Elm St.

Wed. [25 October 1899]

Dear Junior: Mother wants to know where her pillow-sham holders are. I enclose her pathetic scrawl. She is decidedly gaining. If I can get Mary Nelson I will feel quite easy.—We are planning our campaign Zuliema and I and we are very busy. She is a great girl. I have discovered that she plays the piano very well and reads music with ease. She is a superb house-keeper and *likes* it. She paints landscapes with modern touch and may be able to illustrate my work. I want to go west at once but may not be able to do so without a trip home.

Write to Mother often.

Senior.

Bank of Hanover.
Private Bank.
Taft & Son.
Hanover, Kansas.

Nov. 15—99

Dear Taft:

I am at home with Zuliema and your quaint old Father is beaming. He is delighted to find I am a handy man with saw and hammer, that I am an early riser and that I am economical. We sit and talk by the hour—he does most of the talking except when he is drawing on my biography. He is pleased to know I make a good income but happier to know I have no debts. On the whole I think I have made a good impression. Zuliema is blooming. She made a few magic passes over a bundle of red and black ribbons yesterday—and behold a Paris hat. Her necromancy today concerns a gown. She is cutting out trouble for herself for I shall ask her to conjure me a hat or a shirt or something.—We leave here Saturday—after a very brief legal ceremony conducted we hope by Judge Sturges—to spend a week in my mountain country. She is eager to see the country of which I am writing so much. Nothing troubles us now but the thought of my own mother impatiently waiting to welcome her fine new daughter.— I hear there has been a great deal of fuss over us in the press. I have seen nothing of it—but friends write me about it. Please consider my letter very private except to Brown and Turbie.[1] You are so careless about letters I must ask you to always keep securely or destroy mine.

With greetings to your little wife and all the triumvirate circle.

Yours fraternally
Hamlin Garland

1. Turbie is Zulime's younger sister, Turbulance, who was first married to the painter Charles Francis Browne, and later to Angus Roy Shannon.

The Activist: 1900–1918

Introduction

A S HE SETTLED into married life, Garland began to quell the restlessness that had marked the last ten years of his life. At first, Zulime accompanied her husband on his lecture tours, but she soon became pregnant and remained at home. The baby was stillborn—a calamity that Garland never addressed in his memoirs or his letters and only alluded to cryptically in his diary (26 June 1901). In 1903, Mary Isabel was born, followed, in 1907, by another daughter, Constance.

Garland's voluminous output of the previous decade, coupled with a steady stream of lecture engagements, had enabled him to achieve a small measure of financial independence. By 1900 he had published seventeen books and over forty-five short stories, as well as articles, notes, and other ephemera of a man of letters. He had achieved a confidence in his writing that enabled him to adopt, at times, a querulous tone with his agent, Paul Revere Reynolds (see letter 148), and with publishers (see letters 150 and 171). But as he approached his fortieth birthday, he began to weary of the constant negotiating of each contract with capricious publishers.

Theodore Roosevelt's ascension to the presidency in September 1901, upon the assassination of William McKinley, was of signal importance to Garland. He felt much affinity with Roosevelt—a fellow writer, outdoorsman, and lover of the wilderness, whom he had first met in 1896 when Roosevelt was the New York City police commissioner. Garland had followed Roosevelt's career closely as he moved through the political ranks, meeting with him occasionally as their paths crossed. Soon after Roosevelt was sworn in as the twenty-sixth president, Garland wrote to congratulate him and to offer his support: "It is strange and very appealing to think of having a man president who has written books and whose vocabulary is not made up from the briefs of country lawyers and stump orators. The whole situation appeals to my literary imagination with great power" (24 September 1901, letter 123). Garland's letters to Roosevelt reveal his near adoration of Roosevelt's energy, prestige, and accomplishments. Before their 1896 meeting, Roosevelt had read Garland's frequent pronouncements on behalf of "Americanism" in literature and at first regarded Garland as excessively polemical, as he wrote to Brander Matthews on 21 May

1894, upon the publication of *Crumbling Idols*: "I saw a review in the *Tribune* of Hamlin Garland's new book of Essays. He is a man with some power and with half an idea, but he is such a hopeless crank that nothing can be done with him, I fear. He is one of the very men who give us most trouble in producing a spirit of sane Americanism, because his excessive foolishness creates a reaction against us." [1] But as Garland's youthful radicalism mellowed with age, the two became warm friends, with Garland dining occasionally with the president in the White House.

Garland saw in Roosevelt an opportunity to enact changes in government policies regarding two of his abiding interests: the impoverished reservation life of the Indians and the conservation of the wilderness. During his western trips of the 1890s Garland had visited reservations in New Mexico, Arizona, Montana, Colorado, Oklahoma, and the Dakotas. He was fascinated by the "primitive" condition of the Indians and the spectacle their customs presented to his literary imagination; moreover, the Indians also appealed to his evolutionary conception of racial and social progress, confirming his study of Taine and Spencer. As he explained in a letter to Estelle Reel, the Superintendent of Indian Schools,

> "I am an evolutionist as regards the question of what to do for our red brethren. They can not be transmuted into something other than they are by any fervor of religious experience nor by any painful attempt to acquire the higher education. They must grow into something different by pressure of their changed conditions. This is not my dogmatism—it is the teaching of science and the fruit of my study of races. . . . Our work should be that of a friendly race who having passed the first stages of our adaptation turn with sympathy and insight to assist those who are coming up behind us" (15 June 1903, letter 149).

But Garland was appalled by the harsh and often uninformed treatment of the Indians by inept Indian agents and punitive governmental policies. Soon after Roosevelt attained the presidency, Garland began an intensive campaign to alter official government policy by lobbying for a shuffling of government officials and by undertaking, through an unofficial appointment by Roosevelt, a project to regularize the "renaming" of the Indians according to white patrilineal custom.

The General Allotment Act (also known as the Dawes Severalty Act) of 1887 had given the president discretionary powers to assign reservation lands to individual Indians, 160 acres to heads of families and lesser amounts to others. The intent of the Act was to encourage the assimilation of Indians into the dominant culture by making them farmers, with citizenship conferred along with title to the land. "Excess" land would then be opened up to white settlement, once the allotments were distributed. But because inheritance laws assumed a record of descent through the surname, the potential for fraud, confusion, and litigation existed, since the nature of Indian naming practices was incompatible with Anglo customs. In addition, Garland's aesthetic sense was offended by the incongruous, inconsistent, and occasionally insulting names given by whites to the Indians, a people whom he had grown to respect during his annual visits to the reservations. He therefore welcomed the opportunity to head a committee charged with "renaming" Indians in accord with white customs. "My ideas are these, in general," he wrote on 3 November 1902 to William A. Jones, the Commissioner of Indian Affairs. "To start every allottee with a decent and reasonable name and to group the allottees on the rolls according to family relation so far as possible and to allow each child at school to retain his family name or as near it as practicable" (letter 143). In essence, Garland wanted to treat Indians as new immigrants were treated: to retain Indian names whenever they were easily pronounceable; to use clan names as surnames and to conventionalize the spelling; to get rid of insulting or foolish names (such as Tail Feathers Coming or Ghost-faced Woman); and to use common English names as first names.

As Daniel F. Littlefield and Lonnie E. Underhill point out, Garland's humanitarian attempts to rename the Indians may have done more harm than good, for although Garland acted to protect the Indians' rights to their land and culture, his efforts to assimilate them into the dominant culture "unfortunately struck at the Indian's very identity—his name."[2] Garland seems to have been unaware that his effort to avoid what sounded "ugly" in a name led him to an overzealous application of Anglo-American standards. Name changes in his handwriting on the Cheyenne-Arapaho census of 1901, for instance, reveal that he changed the name American Horse to A. Horss, Albert Spotted Horse to Albert Spotted, Brave Bear to Bravber, and Black Owl to Blackall.[3] Garland's efforts to protect the Indians' property and culture through standardizing names ultimately had little effect on government and school practice, due to lack of support by officials in the field. As Littlefield and Underhill point out, "It is probably of little credit to reformers that the American Indian today follows the European system of naming. Acceptance came with time and education."[4] There is also considerable irony in the fact that, as he was campaigning on behalf of Indians' rights to their land, Garland himself was buying parcels of land near Colony, Oklahoma, amounting to one thousand acres. As he explained to his father, "'Like Henry George we both understand the value of unearned increment.'"[5]

Garland's literary efforts on behalf of the American Indian culminated in 1902 with the publication of *The Captain of the Gray-Horse Troop*, a novel based on his visits to the Cheyenne reservation at Darlington, Oklahoma, where Major George Stouch, the agent in charge, and John Homer Seger, the founder of the Indian school at Colony, provided him with material for the novel, which pits cattlemen against the Indians. Upon its publication the novel garnered good reviews and sold more copies than any of Garland's previous novels. Garland entered into negotiations for its dramatization, which fell through, but the novel appeared as a Vitagraph film in 1917 (see Garland to William Wolbert, 31 January 1917, letter 221).

Garland's brush with Washington politicians seems to have whetted his appetite for political organization, and he began to be drawn more deeply into cultural affairs as he found his success and contacts opened doors. He was a charter member of the National Institute of Arts and Letters, founded in 1898 to recognize and promote distinction in literature, music, and the fine arts. Formed as an offshoot of the American Social Science Association, its membership eventually numbered 250. At the direction of the Institute's first president, Charles Dudley Warner, Garland and playwright Augustus Thomas drafted the organization's constitution. Although his active participation in the Institute was limited because of his Chicago residence, Garland was an enthusiastic proponent and became a vice president in 1907, and in 1912 proposed that the 1913 meeting be held in Chicago to demonstrate the national scope of the organization. He was made chairman of the committee on arrangements and embarked on a letter-writing campaign to publicize the meeting.[6]

Never one to take a back seat where organizations were concerned, Garland was, with Robert Underwood Johnson, a prime advocate for the formation of the American Academy of Arts and Letters, an inner, elect body of thirty (later increased to fifty) formed in 1904 from the most distinguished members of the National Institute. Garland was elected to the Academy in 1918 after the success of *A Son of the Middle Border* and soon became a member of its board of directors.

In 1907 he formed the Cliff-Dwellers, a Chicago club modelled after New York's Player's Club and named for the novel by Henry B. Fuller, which Garland hoped would become the center of Chicago cultural life. In 1911 he helped form the Chicago Theater Society, an organization dedicated to promoting non-commercial theater. As its secretary, Garland hoped it would become a means to foster his dream of an innovative American drama, but relentless infighting over goals and methods soon left him dispirited.

By 1910 Garland was feeling the ennui of middle age. His most recent novel, *Cavanagh, Forest Ranger* (1910), had received mediocre reviews. Even Howells, his long-time friend and mentor, had written to chide him for abandoning his early promise. "I'm running low on motives," Garland replied on 29 March 1910. "I don't care to write love-stories or stories of adventure and I can not revert to the prairie life without falling into the reminiscent sadness of the man of fifty. . . . My own belief is that my work is pretty well done but as I remember the cordial endorsement of men like yourself and Gilder I have no reason to complain. I have had in way of honor (and pay) all I deserve — probably. I am dissatisfied only on the artistic side" (letter 172). Club activities and Chicago social life began to consume more and more of his interest, but even that failed to satisfy. In his diary entry for 30 December 1911 he summed up his year's work: "1911 has been a rather futile and disheartening year. I have done many things but nothing that seems important except the work on 'The Middle Border.' All this club and Theater Business is disturbing work which does not add to my life work. My distaste for Chicago increases."

Garland had recently taken up "The Story of Grant McLane," a biographical memoir he had dictated to a secretary in Washington before leaving on his Klondike expedition. After a series of revisions, Garland queried Howells on 29 June 1912 about the advisability of publishing it, for Harpers, his publishers, were balking:

"Major Leigh is afraid that the publication of this book will [be] taken to be my 'swan song' as a novelist, and he is therefore reluctant to bring it out. On the other hand, the book interests me very much, and as I have been just a quarter of a century a writer of fiction, it seems to me that I could, with perfect propriety, bring out a book of this character. As I tell the Major, it is all a question of whether the book is worth while in itself. I think it highly probable that I shall never write another novel, for the reason that love stories no longer seem to me worth while" (letter 185).

Howells was encouraging, and six months later Garland sent the manuscript to Edward Bok of the *Ladies' Home Journal*, who rejected it. Bok believed that its realism was too intimate, and Garland embarked on another round of revisions.[7] The narrative continued to garner rejections: the *Century*, the *Saturday Evening Post*, the *Yale Review*, and *Harper's*, among others, turned it down. Finally, in January 1914, Mark Sullivan, the editor of *Collier's*, accepted six chapters for publication. "We owe a debt of gratitude to Mark Sullivan," Garland wrote to Zulime, "which we can never repay. He has given me a chance to 'come back,' as they say of a temporarily defeated prize-fighter" (*Companions*, p. 537).

The five sketches that appeared in *Collier's* in the early months of 1914, under the title "A Son of the Middle Border: A Personal History," were purportedly based on an abandoned autobiographical manuscript by Lincoln Stewart (the hero of *Boy Life on the Prairie*). Alternating between first-person accounts by Lincoln Stewart and third-person editorial comments by Garland, the five published sketches bring Garland to his early years at Cedar Valley Seminary and, unlike *Boy Life*, stress the drudgery of farm labor and Garland's growing rebellion against farm life rather than the more romantic local-color sketches of the earlier book. In 1914, Garland began yet another revision, this time putting his tale back into first person in preparation for book publication.

The final revised version of *A Son of the Middle Border* was published by Macmillan in August 1917 to nearly universal acclaim. Howells followed his initial, private estimation (letter 227) with a long, enthusiastic review in the *New York Times Review of Books*. "In all the region of autobiography," Howells began, "so far as I know it, I do not know quite the like of Mr. Garland's story of his life, and I should rank it with the very greatest of that kind in literature."[8] Theodore Roosevelt contributed a laudatory review to be used for promotional purposes (see letters 226 and 227). Other honors soon followed. He was elected to the American Academy in January 1918, and then to the prestigious Century Club. "This is the top," Garland jubilantly wrote to Fuller on 6 November 1918 (letter 237). "I cant get any higher until I seek the Gates of Pearl. I went in with Howells in my nominating paper. I am a 'Senator' now!—"

NOTES

1. *The Letters of Theodore Roosevelt,* vol. 1, selected and edited by Elting E. Morison (Cambridge: Harvard University Press, 1951), p. 379.

2. Daniel F. Littlefield and Lonnie E. Underhill, "Renaming the American Indian: 1890–1913," *American Studies* 12 (fall 1971): 34. For an extended discussion of Garland's interest in and reprintings of his writings about the American Indian, see Underhill and Littlefield, *Hamlin Garland's Observations on the American Indian* (Tucson: University of Arizona Press, 1976).

3. Littlefield and Underhill, "Renaming the American Indian," 42.

4. Littlefield and Underhill, "Renaming the American Indian," 42.

5. See *Daughter,* pp. 226, 249–50.

6. For Garland's published comment on this meeting, see *Companions,* pp. 504–5, 509–10, 520–24.

7. See Holloway, pp. 216–24 for a discussion of *Son's* publication trials.

8. "A Son of the Middle Border, by Hamlin Garland: An Appreciation," *New York Times Review of Books,* 26 August 1917, pp. 309, 315.

118. to Zulime Garland   als, Hunt

West Salem

> Thursday. Morn. [7 June 1900]

Dearest Girl:

Dont think of coming home till the end of the gayeties. The weather is perfect. You are among just the right people and it would be shameful to run away. We are all right as a trivet. Mother was out riding yesterday and is quite smart in her mind. The weather is most glorious. I've sold another story and so we eat short-cake and play tennis—and are as happy as we can be with the queen of our hearts away.

I've found a wondrous little trail which I'm eager to show you. It has wonderful opportunity for sketches.—We have Old Settlers today and Frank is going to read. I may talk a little.—Now my dear, I would suggest your remaining till Friday night—Then take the night train and save the wearisome ride. Or if you come in the day time take the parlor car.—I'm glad you met Mrs Judah and Miss French. They are two of my best friends—good discerning fearless souls. I didnt think Mrs Judah would be there bring her home with you—please. Dr. Burton went by without calling.[1] Couldnt make a "go" of his visit.—I am writing just now a reminiscence of poor Stephen Crane—but intend to continue on "The Red Pioneer."[2] Of course we miss you—I find you have come to fill a big place in my life and it isnt so much fun being a bachelor as it was in 1885. Be happy you good thing, and dont hurry home.

Yours

H.G

1. Mary Jameson Judah and John Judah were friends of Garland in Indianapolis. Richard Burton (1859–1940), professor of English literature at the University of Minnesota, author, and drama critic, later served with Garland on several Pulitzer Prize juries. See Garland to Moses, 10 January 1919, letter 240.

2. "Stephen Crane: A Soldier of Fortune" was published in the *Saturday Evening Post* 183 (28 July 1900): 16–17. "The Red Pioneer" was the projected title of a volume of

stories about the American Indian that wouldn't be published until 1923 as *The Book of the American Indian.*

119. to Robert Underwood Johnson   als, NYPL

Fort Yates—N. Dak—

July 10 [1900]

Dear Mr Johnson: As you see I am already out of your reach—I wish we could be at home and entertain you. It would give us pleasure. I want to say also that you have an ally in Mrs Garland who advises me to accept your offer and this I will do with some changes.[1] I dont think there is any likelihood of a difference in the editing—I merely meant that I wanted your suggestions first—no doubt most of the changes are such as I would make myself on final revision. The main point of difference is in the royalty. I am offered 20% from the start by several firms but I am sensible of the advantage of your advertising channels and I will make a concession. I will accept the $500 advance but the 20% royalty should begin after the first 3500 copies have been sold. This will clear you and will leave everything favorable for the big sale which we all think is in the book. Another point needs statement. Would you make it a regular $1.50 book or less? Would you estimate? My own idea would be to make it a handsome book and sell at $1.50. If it is not too much cut it will make a very fair sized novel. I do not feel that I have written too much taking the story as a whole. The date of publication might be next June or October. I thought it a good summer book. Appleton pub. my "Eagles Heart" this fall and Harpers have a little book,[2] so if you wish the book to go over it could do so—only I think it unwise to let it go later than mid-summer 1901. A long strong pull just now might get my books going in a little boom. I am willing to wait till 1901 if you think best but not later. I have a feeling that the coming year is to deal kindly with me and that I must not wish anything—as Jim would say. Your letter gave us pleasure and we are glad that Mr Gilder is to have a "look in" on the m.s. Remember us to him. Address me at West Salem my brother will forward your letter.

Hamlin Garland

Of course the $1500 would be due on delivery of corrected m.s. The $500 on pub. of book.

1. Negotiations are over "Jim Matteson of Wagon Wheel Gap," which appeared serially in the *Century* 61 (November 1900–April 1901) before being published in book form by The Century Company under the title *Her Mountain Lover* in 1901.

2. It is not clear which book Garland refers to. Harper became Garland's publisher in 1902 with *The Captain of the Gray-Horse Troop*.

120. to Richard Watson Gilder

als, NYPL

474 Elm St

[before 29 August 1900]

Dear Mr Gilder:

We are but just this moment returned from a circuit of five thousand miles in the west and I hasten to write in answer to your letters. We are, naturally, much gratified to know that "The Mountain Lover" is acceptable to you and in the main your criticisms fall in with my notions of the revision. It seems to me however that you lost sight of the fact that I am not giving my idea of English society but Jim's. The note of disgust in Mary I know to be true but possibly I over-emphasize it—though I state somewhere (or she acknowledges rather) that it was a mood and likely to pass in a moment. My wife is willing to stand between us in this matter and she is a very reasonable person. I think I may call her in as the party of the third part. Anyhow we will not fall out so long as the essentials of the story are looked after. About the proposition. I confess I can get a better thing for the book considered alone and I consent only in the hope that the serial and the magazine advertising may lead to larger results than could come otherwise. As I wired you last night you can go ahead on the announcement and God be on our side!—I am now in reach of you either at my Chicago home or here. For a few days write me at 474 Elm St Chicago.

Yours sincerely
Hamlin Garland.

121. to Horace Traubel

als, Congress

474 Elm St

May [24] 1901

My Dear Traubel:

Your letter finds me in the Southwest—but I take time even in transit to send greeting to all the Whitman brotherhood.[1] The value of the message he uttered is increasingly admitted. It is hard to find these days a thoughtful man who does not have at least a dim notice that Whitman was a sort of prophet. His influence radiates like sun-shine and the blooming of his philosophy in unexpected places and in curious forms can after all be traced to his influence. I find myself quoting his thought if not his words, many times—and I know very well that he has been to me a great force in ways difficult to trace. I wish I might meet with you, but I am of the west and the trail is long between my teepee and your council chamber. Lift your palms my way and my thought will be with you. Keep the peace. Be brave.*

> —Yours most sincerely
> Hamlin Garland

*written at Oklahoma City Friday the 24.

1. The Walt Whitman Fellowship held a celebration for Whitman on 31 May, the anniversary of the poet's birth, and several newspapers and periodicals reviewed it. Garland's letter was read at the annual meeting of the Fellowship, then reprinted, along with comments from others, in the July issue of the *Conservator*.

122. to Katharine Herne   als, USC

West Salem.

June. 3.ʳᵈ [1901]

Dear Mrs Herne, and dear children:

I have just this moment read the announcement of James A's death in the paper, and it makes my throat fill with pity for you all.[1] I wish I could help you but I am thirteen hundred miles away and before I could reach you you would have passed the worst of it. Julie's letter was so encouraging I had made up my mind the crisis was past. I can write nothing to comfort you beyond saying that you made him happy. He was proud of you all and he had you all with him at the last. I rejoice to think he lived long enough to educate his girls and put them where they can earn a living.

I hope they will keep at their work for it will help them to bear the loss—On you will fall the heavy burden—and dear friend, remember that he would not have you falter at this moment or sorrow over him. He did a good work—and had reached a time when he could go without a sense of failure. Had he died in 1890 how much sadder it would have been! He had put himself among the first of our dramatists—and you will see his fame suddenly bloom now. During the last year I have seen words of praise for him from pens hitherto given to criticisms only. His work has counted heavily in his favor this last year and he has left a noble legacy to his children.

Julie said he was perfectly calm and mentally clear. I am glad of this for it will help you to carry out his plans and his wishes. If there is anything I can do let me know. If there is anything he wished me to do, tell me. I suppose you will go to Herne Oaks as soon as possible—Nature helps us to bear burdens like this. The trees and good crisp wind will clear away the air of the sick room. Be brave and philosophic. These events are a part of life. They are coming thick to me these later years. In the old Ashmont days they seemed far in the future. When you can find time and feel the impulse to do so, write me. Zulime deeply sympathizes with you—but of course can not know as I do the terrible wrench it gives you to give up so powerful a personality as James was. Our Single Tax cause will miss him— What a power he was in that. I know it was a comfort to him to feel he had done noble work for humanity. I wish I could be with you at the funeral but that is impossible. You will be surrounded with friends and will not need me perhaps but I wish to be remembered by you all as a faithful friend.

Hamlin Garland

1. James A. Herne died on 2 June 1901, after a lengthy illness at his home, Herne Oaks, in Long Island, New York. The Herne children were Julie (1881–1955) and Chrystal (1882–1950), who both went on to become accomplished actresses, Dorothy (1885–?), and John (1894–?).

123. to Theodore Roosevelt   als, Congress

474 Elm St. Chicago.

Sept. 24. [1901]

Dear Friend Roosevelt:

I wonder if you recall the prophetic note I wrote you after your election as Governor of New York State? I hinted there at your present great office

but of course no premonition of this dark tragedy came to me.[1] I knew
your power and that you were in line—now here you are in the most
difficult of positions under almost crushing conditions. I can enter imagi-
nably into a few of your resolutions but of the terrible welter and weight
of confusing forces, interests and cares I can not even faintly conceive.
You have my sincerest sympathy and my confidence. Mrs Garland and I
go about saying what we believe that you are more than equal to the great
demands now being made upon you. We remember your superb health
with pleasure. You will need all the stored up vitality of your vacation in
Colorado to carry you through the winter. It is needless to say to you how
great your opportunity is—and no advice I can offer would be of value. I
am writing only to express my deep, very deep interest in your career. It
is strange and very appealing to think of having a man president who has
written books and whose vocabulary is not made up from the briefs of
country lawyers and stump orators. The whole situation appeals to my
literary imagination with great power. I think of you as at the lunch at the
Antler—with the broken-eared veteran on your left and the sky guide on
your right, and I can scarcely realize where you now sit. We are but just
returned from Colo. and Arizona and our distance from printing offices
and the like, during the time of greatest excitement, adds to our present
bewilderment. Our hearts are sincerely with you in this great crisis and I
felt that I must write to say so even at the risk of finding you too busied
to read the message.

With deepest respect—and confidence—
Hamlin Garland.

I saw Snyman the Boer in Colo. Springs.[2] A grand good fellow. I was quite
drawn to him and we learned much of you.

---

1. Vice President Theodore Roosevelt (1858–1919) assumed the office of President
upon the assassination of William McKinley (1843–1901) at the Pan-American Exposition in Buffalo, New York, on 7 September 1901.

2. General W. D. Snyman (?–1897), a commander in the Boer army, fled to Mexico
shortly before the end of the war.

124. to Charles F. Lummis
als, Southwest

Hotel Jefferson
102–106 East 15th St.
New York City

Dec. 24 [1901]

Dear Mr Lummis:[1]

In talk with Thompson-Seton and Grinnell I have pushed the notion of a new League in aid of the Indian to a point where we would like to submit a plan to you and other good friends.[2] I have suggested the name "The Tipi League"—or "The Teepee League"—and both Grinnell and Seton think it good. It symbolizes much of the charm of the old life and lends itself to campfire meetings—to ornamental letter heads—etc. It could be taken as a trade-mark on goods manufactured—and so on. I am going to help Grinnell draft a trial constitution which we will send to you. My ideas as to objects are these.

1. To promote the welfare of the red man. To defend him against aggression. To foster legislation in his behalf.
2. To instruct him in ways of living. To teach him to be self-supporting along the lines of his natural aptitudes. To revive and perfect his native industries.
3. To secure a market for his products.
4. To educate and ennoble him as a red man preserving all that is fine and picturesque in him, so that his progress will be an unbroken evolution from his past as a hunter to his future as a craftsman and industrialist.
5. To unite in a non-partisan, non-sectarian league all those who have the redmans happiness and good cheer at heart.

This is a very brief and crude out-line of the scheme. I wish you would give it thought and if it seems to you worth while write me your notion of it—suggesting modification, lists of names, etc. The president should be a very well known man. The secretary should be a worker and his services paid for—all the rest should serve for the joy of doing good. It could have its fine artistic side by meeting all the men and women of art[,] literature and philanthropy in a pleasant informal organization with local "camps," etc. There could be a Los Angeles Camp, a Chicago Camp (or Teepee) and these local clans or sub-tribes might be made most charming

The Activist: 1900–1918 143

to their members as well as helpful to the Indian. They could serve as sales-rooms or exhibition rooms for the red craftsmen.

There are great possibilities in the matter and I hope it will appeal to you as practicable. I shall see Mrs Doubleday and her friends as soon as the plan matures—she has already approved of its vague out line.[3]

As soon as you reply (I hope you will suggest a list of names) we will privately secure forty or fifty well-known signatures and then make our statement to the public. Please let me hear from you soon.

Very sincerely
Hamlin Garland

1. Charles F. Lummis (1859–1928) became editor of the regional magazine *Land of Sunshine* in 1895, retitling it *Out West Magazine* in January 1902. In the editorial section "In the Lion's Den," Lummis crusaded for the various causes that concerned him, founding in 1902 the Sequoya League for Indian Rights, which addressed the issues of land allotment and the corruption of the Indian school system. In a ten-page letter of 2 January 1902 (misdated 1901), Lummis detailed his thoughts on an Indian Rights Association. He explained that while Garland's suggested name "The Tipi League" had some merit, the word did not precisely signify what was needed. He indicated also that he wanted to have Garland on the first year's National Advisory Board, but cautioned him that plans must not move too quickly.

2. Ernest Thompson Seton (1860–1946), originally named Ernest Seton Thompson, English-born author, artist, and naturalist, wrote several books on wildlife, including *Wild Animals I have Known* (1898), *The Biography of a Grizzly* (1900), and *Lives of the Hunted* (1901). George Bird Grinnell (1849–1938) was an ethnologist and the editor of *Forest and Stream*. In 1895 he was appointed commissioner to the Blackfeet and Belknap Indians, and interceded in a bitter land controversy among the Sioux on the Standing Rock Reservation. He was the author of several books, including *Blackfoot Lodge Tales* (1892), *The Fighting Cheyennes* (1915), and *By Cheyenne Campfires* (1926).

3. Neltje De Graff Doubleday (1865–1918), wife of the publisher Frank N. Doubleday, wrote *The Piegan Indians* (1889), as well as several volumes on birds and wildflowers. In *Companions*, Garland records a diary entry of 22 February: "A letter from Mrs. Frank Doubleday concerning the recent order of the Indian Department instructing its teachers to foster aboriginal art, led me to spend the forenoon writing letters to her and to the commissioner, endorsing and commending the order" (p. 65).

125. to George P. Brett

alc, USC LB

Hotel Jefferson.

Dec 3[0, 1901]

Dear Mr Brett: [1]

Unless you feel a genuine enthusiasm for my novel and feel sure of making it a great success—dont give any further time to it.[2] You publish a great many books and unless I feel that mine appeals to you with unusual power I cant afford to put it into your hands. In these days of black-letter advertising a book no matter how good is lost unless it has the publishers personal care. What I would like you to determine is this. Is the book of great personal interest to you—and do you consider it worth putting the whole power of your house behind it. If you do not then a smaller firm would serve me better. The reading of the ms. of course does not commit either you or me to anything further.

Hamlin Garland.

1. George Platt Brett (1859–1936) was the editor-in-chief of The Macmillan Company and was Garland's publisher from 1899 to 1902.

2. Garland refers to *The Captain of the Gray-Horse Troop*, which was appearing as a serial in the *Saturday Evening Post* 174 (14 December 1901–29 March 1902). After sounding out various firms, Garland eventually settled upon a newly reorganized Harper and Brothers as his publisher, which brought out his most successful novel in March 1902.

126. to Albert Shaw

als, NYPL

The Players
16 Gramercy Park

Jan. 24. [1902]

Dear Dr. Shaw: [1]

Have you seen the reports relating to the recent "order" by Com. Jones [2] requiring that the Indian shall forthwith cease to sing, dance, wear native costume etc? I have had a note from Grinnell about it.[3] It is too atrocious to be credible. I wish you would look into the matter and editorially oppose such an idea—if it is given out. The Indian question is in a critical stage just now—rations are being cut down in places where the people cant endure it—and trouble will come. Some of the reservations as you know are barren and unable to support the people—they need help until some system of irrigation is in operation.

The Activist: 1900–1918 145

If you want any further information write to Grinnell—as I will give you a talk. We can not afford to kill the redman by legislation no matter what our excuse.

Sincerely

Hamlin Garland

1. Albert Shaw (1857–1947), editor of the American edition of *Review of Reviews* from 1891 to 1937, each month devoted some sixty to eighty paragraphs to an editorial feature entitled "The Progress of the World."

2. William A. Jones (1844–?), U.S. Indian Commissioner from 1897 to 1905.

3. In a 7 February 1902 letter to Charles F. Lummis (Southwest), George Grinnell explained that "newspaper despatches about Jones' order were fakes. I . . . asked him about it, and he told me that his letter merely urged agents to discourage the growing of long hair and the painting of faces by returned students."

127. to Albert Shaw

als, NYPL

Hotel Jefferson

102–106 East 15th St.

New York City

[31 January 1902]

Dear Dr. Shaw:

My brother and I are going into Mexican land. We have a chance to get some choice acres at one dollar per acre provided we can handle 50000 acres. I wish you'd talk with my brother. We are keeping the subscriptions among the "literary chaps." This land sells in small parcels at four and six dollars per acre—hence our wish to unite with some one else. Any suggestion you make will be welcomed.[1]

Yours sincerely

Hamlin Garland

1. Holloway points out that "Although for a year or more Hamlin wrote constantly to Shaw and other 'literary chaps' about this proposal, it seems never to have attained much substance. Garland's dreams of becoming a landed proprietor had to be satisfied by the acquisition of additional small tracts in Oklahoma near his original half-section. John Homer Seger, and after him his children Jesse and Neatha, acted as Garland's agents in these enterprises" (p. 179).

128. to Charles F. Lummis

als, Southwest

The Players,
16 Gramercy Park.

Feb. 1 [1902]

Dear Mr Lummis:

I think our new Society should stand for this general principle as regards the Indians of the Northwest: They should be aided to stock their ranges with cattle and to irrigate (wherever possible) their lowlands for gardens. It will not do to cut off their rations too quickly for if they are hungry they will eat their cattle and so defeat the purpose of the Gov. The reservations in Dakota and Montana are dry and bleak, and crops are very uncertain—on most of the land—impossible. To make allotments in dry lands will result in suffering and vagabondage. In my new book[1] I am out-lining a policy which I have seen partly worked out by men of my acquaintance. I will send an advance copy of the book to you soon. Of course it is a novel but incidentally I hope it will give you a picture of conditions on the northwest reservations. I am anxious to have you push the organization of the New League to a working condition—for just now Congress is disposed to do something and might be induced to do the right thing. Grinnell and I are both urging the giving of a couple of thousand cattle to the Cheyennes of Lame Deer. They can be made self-supporting in a few years by right management. Please keep us posted as to the League and call upon us for any work which comes in our scope.

Very sincerely
Hamlin Garland

1. *The Captain of the Gray-Horse Troop.*

129. to Charles F. Lummis

als, Southwest

Hotel Jefferson
102–106 East 15th St.
New York City

Feb. 5. [1902]

Dear Mr Lummis:

Your constitution is all right in its general intent—big enough to turn round in. Grinnell and I vote for Calumet League.[1] It's trite but everybody knows what it means. I held a long talk today with Albert Shaw of *The Review of Reviews*—he is a very close friend of the president and has already talked to him along our lines. We are going to make a point of seeing President Roosevelt together. He doesn't know the field as we do but he's all right in feeling and theory and is a strong man. The president has him down of a Sunday every little while and talks to him most intimately. He should be on your advisory board. If he is not already on I would suggest your putting him on. If you haven't time to write wire him and I'll see and explain the matter. In fact I did explain yesterday. I got in some licks with Dr. Lyman Abbott the other day at lunch and he sees one or two things quite differently.[2] You are right on many counts and yes I feel that men like Shaw and Abbott are most important. I hope you'll get organized before I leave New York so that I can help Grinnell organize the local council here. I wish we could use the picturesque nomenclature of the red man all through our constitution.

I may organize a special artistic movement to preserve the artistic and picturesque side of the Indian's life but this would work alongside your bigger scheme.[3]

Very sincerely

Hamlin Garland

1. Despite Garland's suggestion, a consensus eventually emerged in favor of Sequoya League, as indicated in a letter to Garland from Lummis dated 4 March 1902.

2. Lyman Abbott (1835–1922) was the editor of the *Outlook*.

3. In his reply of 13 February, Lummis argued vehemently against Garland's suggestion, pointing out "we have to save our Indians first; afterward we can decide about their tailoring . . . you can alienate a great majority by keeping the Indian picturesque."

130. to George B. M. Harvey

als, In HS

Hotel Jefferson

102–106 East 15th St.

New York City

Feb. 5 [1902]

Dear Col. Harvey:

I've been thinking of doing a rather careful and extended article on "The Present Needs of the Indian" or "The Present Status of the Indian" or some such topic.[1] Would such an article interest you? It would fit into the North American Review and coming just now might arouse discussion and do great good.

Very sincerely
Hamlin Garland

1. George B. M. Harvey (1864–1928) edited the *North American Review* from 1899 to 1926; the article appeared under the title "The Redman's Present Needs" in the *North American Review* 174 (April 1902): 476–88.

131. to Albert Shaw

als, NYPL

Hotel Jefferson.

Feb. 19. [1902]

Dear Dr. Shaw:

I want to see you as soon as possible about the Mexican Land Scheme and also about the Indian Dept. The tribes of the northwest are having a hard time—the government with its usual fatuous brutality has cut the rations at the beginning of winter. I am writing an article for the N.A. Review on the matter—I wish you could get Grinnell to treat same subject. Let me know when you are at liberty—Can you lunch with me tomorrow? I am at the Jefferson again—Mrs Garland is in Chicago returns next week—

Give my regards to Mrs Shaw and the boy. Are the Severances in town? [1]

Yours sincerely
Hamlin Garland

1. Cordenio Severance, a St. Paul, Minnesota, lawyer, and his wife Maidie.

132. to Theodore Roosevelt

als, USC

Hotel Gordon
Washington, D.C.

April 1ˢᵗ [1902]

Dear President Roosevelt:

I met Gifford Pinchot this afternoon for the first time—and was deeply impressed with him. [1] I wish we had a Commissioner of Ind. Affairs of his stamp—If you are thinking of changing your Sec. of the Interior why wouldnt Pinchot do? He is your kind of a man clean, vigorous, broad-minded and of independent living. Senator Beveridge and Prof McGhee both speak of him in highest words of praise.[2] If he moved up, Capt Aherne would make a good Chief of the Forestry.[3] I know Aherne, he is a fine able fellow.—With regard to Commissioner Jones I feel he is not a strong man—he seems a nice man, gentle and (so far as I know) honest, but I dont feel that he dominates his forces—Grinnell and Lummis and Shaw feel much the same way. There was no special reason for his selection in the first place—he was I believe merely a banker in a small town in Wisconsin. Why he, out of some other millions should have been made Com. of Ind. Affairs I never understood. I wish the whole department could get some infusion of your vigor. A merely negatively good man is not our need there—we should have a vigorous, up-to-date young man—or at least one in confident use of his powers who would dominate the affairs of his office and have the fullest command of his field service. I should like to see men who represent your ideas of thoroughness and modernity of methods at the head of the Indian Dept. One or two men of this stamp can "jack up" a thousand lesser office-holders and enormously increase the efficiency of the service by example. I suspect we need a new Commissioner—and a new Assistant Commissioner—as well. Miss Reel[4] seems to be very active though then again we need not merely the one who is doing well but one who is doing the best possible.

The chief work with the Indians from this time on is to be *instruction*, using that word in its broadest sense, and agents I have met (for the most part) had very little interest in the practical field work of the "farmer"—in fact the agent seldom goes out over his reservation. I wish you could inaugurate a deep-plowing reform along the lines of better service from Commissioner down to "Black-Smith-Helper."

Our Sequoya League is formed to help you. Any information I can give is at your service. I go at once to the Cheyenne and Arapahoe Reservation and if you would like a perfectly accurate report of what is being done I will send it.

Most sincerely yours
Hamlin Garland

1. On 1 April Garland met with Theodore Roosevelt to discuss a plan to standardize procedures for naming Native Americans to assimilate them more quickly into Anglo-American culture. Roosevelt appointed Garland to head a committee to oversee the

allotment rolls, and he devoted much of his energy to the project for the next two years. For discussion of the project and Garland's role in it, see Littlefield and Underhill, "Renaming the American Indian," 33–45. Gifford Pinchot (1865–1946), chief of the Forest Service from 1898 to 1910, instituted charges against U.S. Secretary of the Interior Richard Ballinger, maintaining that Ballinger had revised the Roosevelt conservation policy. Ballinger was upheld by Taft and Pinchot was dismissed in 1910. See related note in Garland to Howells, 29 March 1910, letter 172.

2. Albert Jeremiah Beveridge (1862–1927), Republican senator from Indiana (1899–1911), was an organizer of the Progressive Party. He won a Pulitzer Prize for his four-volume work, *The Life of John Marshall* (1916–19). W. J. McGhee (1853–1912) established the Geological Society of America in 1888 and headed the Bureau of Ethnology from 1893–1903.

3. Lt. George P. Aherne served as Garland's guide when he and his brother Franklin visited the Tongue River Reservation, near Fort Custer, Montana, in 1897. Garland accompanied Aherne on his rounds at the Crow Agency, where he told Garland stories, one of which was worked into *The Captain of the Gray-Horse Troop* (1902), along with other Cheyenne materials.

4. Estelle Reel (1866–?), U.S. Department of the Interior Superintendent of Indian Schools.

133. to Charles F. Lummis   als, Southwest

474 Elm St

[after 1 April 1902]

Dear Lummis:

Great things are really doing. The president was very frank and intimate in his talk with Merriam and myself.[1] He is all right. He has just asked Grinnell to go to Standing Rock and look into that leasing matter. Isn't that good work? Now I am to see Grinnell when he comes through and post him a little—if he asks it—I will go with him although I am very busy. This will lead to a long talk and out of it a possible understanding. I am afraid to open the subject and will not do so unless he should mention it—I mean unless the president or someone else has spoken to him—in which case I shall urge him to accept. With the president and the Sequoya League behind him Grinnell could set in operation plans that would carry the redmen far on their road to self-support. This I will urge as strongly as possible.

The League being believed Grinnell will make him a strong candidate in the presidents eyes.

The president may need to get a new Sec. of the Int. also. He should be a western man in perfect sympathy with us. There are one or two men here in Chicago whom I would support. Sec. Hitchcock[2] with Grinnell for Com. would be fairly effective although he is old and slow.—Did you get "The Captain of the Gray Horse Troop?" I hope you will like it on both counts as a story and as a plea for "the small peoples" of the earth.—

There is another scheme. How would it do to have the president make Grinnell "Inspector General" with power to represent the Executive—reporting only to the Executive—or something like that. My plan is, however, to make Grinnell Com. and a man like Capt. Aherne (now head of Forestry Dept. of Philippines) Asst. Com. to work *in the field.* Major Jesse Lee is also a good man, and so is Col. Scott.[3] McGhee is a good man for second or third choice—Merriam a fine man. But Grinnell by all the laws of honorable warfare is the man for Com.

Yours hastily

Hamlin Garland

1. Clinton Hart Merriam (1855–1942) headed the Division of Ornithology and Mammalogy of the U.S. Department of Agriculture from 1885 to 1904.

2. Ethan Alan Hitchcock (1835–1909), a wealthy businessman from St. Louis, was appointed ambassador to Russia in 1897. He served as Secretary of the Interior from 1898–1907.

3. Jesse Matlock Lee (1843–1926) served for twenty-two years on the Indian frontier and, through his mastery of sign language and reputation for fair treatment, became respected by the Indians and successfully negotiated the surrender of four thousand Indians at Wounded Knee in 1891. Hugh Lennox Scott (1853–1934) spent the majority of his professional career in the Indian service, where he was in charge of investigating the Ghost Dance disturbance (1890–91) before taking charge of Geronimo's Chiricahua Apaches (1894–97). After duty with the Bureau of Ethnology, where he was at work on a volume on sign language, he became adjutant general of Cuba (1898–1903).

134. to Charles F. Lummis als, Southwest

474 Elm St. Chicago

April 15/02

My Dear Lummis:

I am writing this from the Seger Indian School at Colony Oklahoma but return home soon so in writing me address me at my old address as above.[1] I hope you found my N. A. *Review* article one that you can agree with. I tried to keep it within bounds so that the League could generally endorse it rather than make war upon it. I hope you found the novel worth while also. I had a great deal of talk with the president—he made me free for a week of the Executive Chamber in order to have as much talk as possible. Naturally we talked the Sequoya League and its work. He liked my article in the *Review* so well that he said, "I'm going to send that out among the agents in the field." He was more than open to conviction—he was convicted on several points. He was particularly struck by the two points "grouping in small villages," and in "instructing the red people along the line of their inherited aptitudes." I think we are quite revolutionizing the ideals of field workers and missionaries.—I saw Jones and Hitchcock. They both seemed worried and tired. Kennan has made Jones uncomfortable.[2] He must clear himself of suspicion or he will have to go. *If* he goes—we must have a good man ready to suggest. Grinnell is the man if he will take it but I fear he would not consider it. McGhee might take it—or Merriam. Whom would you suggest? I would like to see Grinnell Commissioner and Captain Aherne Asst. Commissioner with one of them in the field all the time. No matter what comes to pass we must have a program and be ready to carry it out. I saw many of the chief friends of the Indian while in Washington but they were rather weary. The president was not—he touched me deeply by his cordial welcome of my ideas and his instant declaration to do all that lay within his power to aid the Indian.

Let me hear from you. This letter is for your private ear alone.

Sincerely
Hamlin Garland

1. John H. Seger (1846–1928) served as superintendent in charge of the Arapaho Mission School at Darlington, Indian Territory, in 1872. In 1886 he took 152 Cheyennes and Arapahoes and formed Seger's Colony, a manual boarding school on a twelve-hundred-acre farm, fifty miles from Darlington, where he was superintendent. He became a valuable source of information about these tribes for Garland.

2. George Kennan (1845–1924), American journalist and assistant manager of the Associated Press, Washington DC (1877–85); correspondent in Cuba for the *Outlook* (1898); and the author of several books, including *Campaigning in Cuba* (1899).

135. to David A. Munro

als, Virginia

474 Elm St

[ca. April 1902]

Dear Mr. Munroe:[1]

I am getting a great many letters concerning the *Review* article.[2] I laid it before the president one day asking him to read it sometime. When I saw him next day he said, "I've read your article and I like it. I like it so much I'm going to send it out—with a few omissions—among the employees of the Dept in the field." He was especially struck he said with my ideas of grouping the people and with the contention that they should be educated along the lines of those inherited aptitudes. He also read the novel and liked it even better—so I feel that the objects of both novel and article are partly attained even now. I should like to know from you what response the article serves to get.

Very sincerely
Hamlin Garland

1. After emigrating from Scotland in 1872, David Alexander Munro (1848–1910) joined the literary department at Harper and Brothers, where he remained for most of his life. He edited the *North American Review* from 1896 to 1899, before rejoining Harpers after its reorganization under George B. M. Harvey in 1900.

2. "The Redman's Present Needs." The novel Garland refers to later in this letter is *The Captain of the Gray-Horse Troop.*

136. to Louise Morgan Sill

alc, USC LB

Eagle's Nest Camp. Oregon. Ill

May 12—[1902]

Dear Mrs Sill:[1]

I am quite willing to write out the notes you ask for although I do not see why any one should be interested.

1st: I make copious notes while on the trail and among the Indians. I take down the actual (translated) conversation of the red people. I sit with them around the fire in their teepees—and have their songs and prayers interpreted to me as they go on. I do not trust to my memory so far as the basic facts are concerned. These notes however I do not use literally I seldom refer to them—but the mere effort of writing them down seems to organize them in my mind.

Often I strike out a paragraph which takes form in my mind and set it down in my note-book as a key-note—or color-note which is to [be] given a chapter. Sometimes as in making studies for "The Gray Horse" I plan a chapter or set down a scrap of conversation. My aim is to write only when my material is colored by my own emotional relation to it—that is only when I find it worth while. When I get back to West Salem where I have a big low-ceiled study or to Chicago where I have a "den" papered with a Navajoe pattern of wall paper, I sit down to serious and consecutive work. My practice is then to rise at 7 or 7^{30} break-fast lightly and go to my study to write till 12^{00} when I take my heartiest meal at 12^{30} or a little later. In the afternoon I do some hard manual labor if possible or ride my good gray Ladrone. Sometimes when work is pressing I get to work again at 4^{pm}—but usually I write letters, read the newspaper and take it easy till next morning.

Of course I do not always feel like working—but when I live regularly and nothing distracts me I find myself keen for work each morning and have no trouble in taking up the work where I left off. I generally read what was written the day before—This gives me a running start so to say and keeps the work revised to date. I do all the first writing with a pen— on paper of pocket note size—and my writing is damnable. When it is in a vicious tangle I send it to the typist and get it back clean and clear. This is the most joyous period. I now *enjoy* the product. I revise and revise from this time on and all joy goes out of the work. It is drudgery then of the most unrelieved sort. I get no further joy out of it till about six months after it is published.

The teepee is now up and the sun-light on it—you shall have a picture of it as soon as it can be made.

By the way a note could be made of this. I went with Captain (then Lieut) Aherne from his quarters at Fort Austin to see him inspect a drove of cattle brought into the Crow Agency. He rejected the herd and the cattlemen were furious. This incident set me to thinking[,] suppose I had the power and could appoint Aherne agent. What would he do. Here was the germ of the story, this was in 1897. Aherne is now the head of the Forestry Dept in the Philippines. He is not Curtis—to tell the truth he is not at all like Curtis but he suggested the situation to me. My idea in Curtis was to take a man of action and few words and put him in a re-sponsible position.

The sign-talking is absolutely true—you might make a note of that. John Seger—the Superintendent of the Seger School in Oklahoma uses the sign-language for all his daily communication with his Indian workmen. I have visited him three times and spent many hours with him while he conversed with the old men on the traditions of the tribe. This last trip gave me several beautiful new examples of its power to convey emotion. We spent all one rainy afternoon in the teepee of an old medicine man while he told us of the brave days of old. In this way I have got at the human side of these people. I could have delineated their bad side but it would have necessitated search—they have always shown their good side to me.

I am satisfied that there is "pull" in the Indian side of this book. I have written Major Leigh to that effect.[2] People are ready to receive the human side of this perishing race. Please consider that I am ready to cooperate in any way possible.

With thanks for your continued interest—

Very sincerely

Hamlin Garland

1. Louise Morgan Sill (1868–1961) adapted, with Rachel Crothers, Garland's novel *The Captain of the Gray-Horse Troop* in 1903 for the stage, though the play was never performed. A member of the editorial staff of Harper and Co., she was also the author of a number of works, including *In Sun or Shade* (1906), as well as a translator of volumes from French.

2. Frederick T. Leigh, vice president of Harper and Co.

137. to Louise Morgan Sill

alc, USC LB

West Salem. Wis

May 29. [1902]

Dear Mrs Sill:

If any one is disposed to question the case of communication in sign-talk revealed in The Captain. You can say that I have a friend and interpreter—John H. Seger of Seger's School Colony Oklo—who transacts all his business in the sign language. His people are both Cheyenne and Arapahoe and to save the trouble of learning both languages he fell back on their common means of communicating thought—the "sign talk." One rainy day I sat in the teepee of one of the head men and *watched* Seger and the chief while they signed stories, traditions and history. Communication was instantaneous and almost without hitch or pact. I have kept well within the probabilities in the case of Curtis.

I received a clipping not long ago speaking of a reproduction of the cut of myself and home in the Tribune. I hope it comes out well.

Thanks for your continued encouragement. I have had the teepee photos taken and am waiting for them to be finished. They will be sent soon I hope.

Sincerely
Hamlin Garland

138. to Theodore Roosevelt als, Nat'l Arch

West Salem Wis.

[about 29 July 1902]

Dear President Roosevelt:

I have just received a letter from Grinnell telling me of his trip to Standing Rock and the work done there. I am very glad to know that he brought the lease into satisfactory shape and that he hopes to protect the Grand River settlement from serious injury. It is rather curious but one of my friends here in La Crosse was a partner in one of the first companies to try for a lease and refused to have anything to do with it when he understood what it involved.—I want to thank you for sending Grinnell on this mission. He was the man for it. There is one other matter which I wish you would ask him to take up and that is the naming of the red men as they become citizens. It is imperative that family names should be reasonable and according to some system. The whole list is an inextricable tangle. For example practically only one man can straighten out the family ramifications among the Southern Cheyennes.—I dont want to burden you with this matter during vacation but I wish you would make Grinnell[,] Merriam and Lummis a committee to take the matter up. It isnt fair to start a decent red fellow off with a name like "Tail-feathers-coming"—especially as that may not be even a literal translation of his name. Many of these names can be made to conform rather closely to our own—so that the red children will not be forever under a cloud of ridicule. I dont believe in naming them "Robert Burns" and "Grant Jones" either. They must be named according to their family relation in order to

prevent endless legal complication. I experimented a little with the list of
the Cheyennes and found it rather easy to soften their own names and yet
retain enough of their original sound to identify them. This is a crying
necessity and yet the department has not gone about it as systematically
and as sympathetically as it should have done. The work should be done
by a central committee and not by the various clerks of the agencies. I
make this suggestion hoping it may fall in with your own view, and that
of the Department.[1]

Very sincerely yours
Hamlin Garland.

1. Roosevelt forwarded Garland's suggestion to William A. Jones, the Commissioner
of Indian Affairs. See Garland to Jones, 3 November 1902, letter 143.

139. to George Bird Grinnell

tlc, Southwest

West Salem, Wis.

July 29th. [1902]

Dear Grinnell:—[1]

Your letter found me here attending my father who is in bad health.
I am glad to know you were able to do the people good up there. I am
particularly glad to know you came through all right, because I urged the
president to use you.

I am writing here at the present moment about the naming of Indian
families. As you know, the present state of affairs is deplorable. Family
connections in the So. Cheyennes for example are known only to "Robert
Burns"[2] and a few other Indians. Schools are allowed to give "fancy
names" to the pupils, and the cow-boys name the old people "Guts"
and "Tail-feathers", as you know. Now the Department has never really
taken hold of this, and these people need to have their own names preserved. It is not difficult. Many names can be retained in Indian form like
To-re-ach, which is easily spoken, or Chonoh. Others will need slight
modification only, e.g. Black Bull could be changed to Blackbill or Black-
bell, and Standing Bull could be Stanbull. Robert Burns and I went over
the list and I am satisfied a system could be devised that would preserve
family names and clear the way for inheritance. The whole matter should
be taken up by a commission and handled with care. To name the people

"Bobby Burns" and "Cyrus Field" is foolish and belongs to the Col. Pratt era.[3] These people now have property. They are landed proprietors, and "Robert Burns" is the head of a family. His real name should be restored to him. I wish you would write Lummis about this, and send my letter to Merriam for his consideration. This is really an important matter. A man is handicapped sadly who enters citizenship with a name like "Drunkard" or "Buffalo Dung". And this can be remedied without going to the opposite extreme of naming children after famous Americans.

Let me hear from you on the subject.

Hamlin Garland

We go to Colorado soon.

1. From a copy of the original letter made by Grinnell and sent to Lummis.

2. Garland met Robert Burns Whiteleaf, a young, educated Cheyenne, during his trip to the Darlington Agency in 1900 where Burns worked as a clerk under Major George Stouch. In *Companions* Garland recalls his talk with Burns, who gave him insight into "red psychology" and strengthened his determination "to do a book of Indian stories" (pp. 35–36).

3. Richard H. Pratt (1840–1924) organized the first nonreservation Indian school at Carlisle, Pennsylvania, in 1879, and was its superintendent until 1904.

140. to George B. M. Harvey

alc, USC LB

West Salem Wis—

Oct 7 [1902]

Dear Col. Harvey:

I have just sent to Major Leigh a mss. called "My Chief the Sitting Bull." I wish you would consider it in two ways as a possible serial for the N. A. *Review*—(or weekly) and also as a book to follow "The Captain."[1] I hope you will find this story as much worth while as it seems to me. I have thought of going up to Standing Rock and reading it through my friend Primeau[2] to a group of the old men in order to test its truth. Let me know what your people think of the M.S. as soon as you conveniently can. I may be addressed for a couple of weeks at West Salem Wis—

Hamlin Garland

1. Garland refers to his epic about Sitting Bull, told from the perspective of Iapi, one of the Silent Eaters, Sitting Bull's personal bodyguards. After its composition in 1900, Garland submitted the piece to *Century*, on 27 March 1901, where it was rejected. It was eventually published under the title "The Silent Eaters" in *The Book of the American Indian* (1923).

2. Louis Primeau, a half-Sioux trader who interpreted for Garland. See Underhill and Littlefield, *Hamlin Garland's Observations on the American Indian*, 37–40, for discussion of this story.

141. to James MacArthur alc, USC LB

West Salem Wis—

Oct 19. [1902]

Dear Mr McArthur:[1] I have read your scenario—and understand your point of view—but I do not think it nescessary to make so many concessions to the Litt audience—I dont believe it nescessary to have Sennett so palpably the villain of melodrama—Before going into so thorough-going a piece of melodrama lets try to construct a pretty good play.

Your opening scene is good—but I would bring in Maynard there as bearer of the order transferring Curtis to Int. Dept—He could also bring comedy element—he and Calver and Jennie a lively trio.—Why not have young Sennett the clerk leaving the old man agent as before—Young Sennett could be developed into a reckless young lover of Elsie—rival of Curtis. The killing of a cattleman can be brought about more naturally than in your sketch—It could come in a row over beef contracts or some illegal business—The cattleman could be the man Cut-Finger deserved to kill— The killing could be done actually by young Sennett or by Cut-Finger in self-defense. The Cow-boys could come after him as before—These instances will show what I mean by saying it is too melodramatic. I wouldnt want to go on along these lines—but if you want to put it through on these lines let me know—address me at 474 Elm St—Chicago—I am starting on a lecture trip—

Hamlin Garland—

1. James MacArthur (1866–1909), former joint editor of the *Bookman* (1894–1900), reader, and general literary advisor for Harper and Brothers. MacArthur wrote several

play adaptations of novels, among them Ian MacLaren's *Beside the Bonnie Brier Bush* (1895), Rex Beach's *The Spoilers* (co-authored with Beach, 1906), and Bunyan's *Pilgrim's Progress*. MacArthur's adaptation of *Captain* does not seem to have gone beyond producing a scenario.

142. to James MacArthur alc, USC LB

West Salem — Wis —

[20 – 27 October 1902]

Dear Mr McArthur: I am very sorry but I dont believe I can write along these melodramatic lines — Do you think that we must work in the wronged husband and the villain of the bowery? My book doesnt lend itself to that kind of thing and I cant write along those lines. Harpers have written me that Wallaces Ben Hur contract will out-line their arrangement with me [1] — This eliminates me as a dramatist anyway — but as I gave you permission to go ahead I shall remain faithful but I really must beg off from doing any writing. I will help you verbally all I can when I come on in Dec — I believe you are mistaken in thinking that we have to write the conventional melodrama — please dont mistake me — I am not complaining because the scenario departs from the book — I expected it to do that — but it is too conventional a plan. How would it do for you to go ahead on your own plan and I will keep to my own. I gave you leave to go ahead and of course shall keep my word but I do not feel that I can do more than assist you verbally when I come on. It is nescessary also that all the business details be settled as regards Harpers and myself — and then between you and me before the actual writing begins. I had not anticipated anything but a fair scenario. I sincerely hope you will not be offended by my candor in the matter — and that you may see your way to a less conventional form.

Sincerely
Hamlin Garland.

1. Harper's published Lew Wallace's popular novel *Ben Hur* in 1880, and it became a sensational hit in 1899 when William Young dramatized it for the stage.

The Activist: 1900 – 1918 161

474 Elm St. Chicago

Nov. 3. [1902]

To the Com. Ind. Affairs:

In reply to M. 57 972/1902—

Dear Sir: I am to be in Washington about the 25th of the month and will be glad to lend you any assistance in my power. If Mr Grinnell can come on he and Dr. Hart Merriam and I will confer with you on the matter. My ideas are these, in general. To start every allottee with a decent and reasonable name and to group the allottees on the rolls according to family relation so far as possible and to allow each child at school to retain his family name or as near it as practicable. As to the exact methods of doing this I can only make a few very rough suggestions—on paper. When I see Grinnell and can give my reasons at length they will be less likely to seem impracticable to you.

1st   Whenever an Indian's real name is easily vocable—as say "Ki-as" or "To-nah" he should retain it. In many cases a long name can be abbreviated to a pleasant word.

2nd   As a large number of each tribe are named after animals as "Wolf," "Black Wolf," "Antelope," "Bear" etc—I would retain such names in translation—conventionalizing them perhaps as "Robert Blackwolf," or "John Black-bear."

3rd   I would wipe out all foolish or cumbersome names like "Ghost-faced Woman" "Tail-feathers Coming" etc. Many of the interpretations of Indian names were originally made by cow-boys and ignorant guides and interpreters and some Indians are called "Guts" and "Drunkard"—names that are a serious handicap. "Dog-turning-around" is an example of clumsy translation—it might better be Turningdog—or Whirlingdog.

4th   In using English Christian names I would always employ plain simple names like John, Robert[,] Peter, Stephen, Louis etc. and in the case of women would take especial care to keep away from "fancy" names.

—In short as the redman is now half-way between his old life and the new his name must nescessarily indicate it. He must not be cut off from his family connection for legal reasons—as well as to prevent intermarrying.
—To give school-boys and girls fancy names is not only a wrong to them

but leads to great confusion. Endless litigation will spring from a short-sighted policy of this kind.

I would take a pay-roll say that of the Southern Cheyennes and Arapahoes as a basis and with the aid of men like Robert Burns Whiteleaf indicate in the names as far as possible the present family relations—by use of middle names on the part of married women.—Wherever possible I would secure the consent of the parents to the naming of their children—giving the reasons for it.[1] John Seger would be valuable in such a work but Burns is the one man who can straighten out family relations among the Cheyenne. I went over the list with him and with Major Stouch[2] and it will not be difficult to put matters in fairly comprehensible form—except so far as the allotments are concerned. This work should have been done when the allotments were made. As you know these quarter-sections are now marked on the map as belonging to "Scabby Bull" "Bull Looking Around" and other names quite as impossible. I would urge you to correct this where other lands are being allotted.—I will not go further in the matter now and of course can not take time to argue the need of some system—but as soon as I reach Washington I will be very glad to give you my ideas in full—and with the aid of Dr Merriam, Prof. McGhee and Dr Grinnell we can surely bring some sort of order into Indian nomenclature in these various rolls. If you can not wait—and I feel that the circular ought to go out at once—write me again and I will dictate a fuller exposition of my plan—[3]

Sincerely yours
Hamlin Garland

1. In his letter of 16 December 1902, Jones indicated to Garland that the copy of the Cheyenne and Arapaho roll would be made as Garland suggested, and that authority was granted to bring Whiteleaf to Washington from the Cheyenne and Arapaho Agency at government expense.

2. Major George Stouch first met Garland in 1887 when he was Indian agent at Lame Deer, Montana. He later became Indian agent at Darlington, Oklahoma, renewing his acquaintance with Garland and becoming one of his principal sources of Indian lore.

3. The circular, which Garland wrote detailing a specific plan regarding Indian renaming, was issued to all agents, allotting agents, school superintendents, and teachers from Jones's office on 1 December 1902. It "amplified and reissued" a circular that had been put out from the commissioner's office on 19 March 1890. A copy exists in the Charles F. Lummis Papers (Southwest).

144. to Charles F. Lummis tls, Southwest

The Players Club.
New York City.

November 26, 1902.

Dear Mr Lummis: This letter is a copy of one sent to my friend Seger.[1] It follows up my suggestion to the President.

Dear Mr. Seger:

Some time since, I made the suggestion to the President that our Indians should be entirely renamed, according to some general system. I made the plea that unless this was done, a great deal of litigation would result when the Indians came to the point of transmitting or inheriting property which must soon happen. He asked me [to] make the suggestion to the Commissioner of Indian Affairs. I have done so, and after some conversations with him and members of the Bureau of Ethnology, I have made the following six or seven suggestions:

First—To retain the Indians' own name wherever possible, shortening or modifying it so that it can be easily spoken by the red man's white neighbor.

Second—To name all children after their father, or after their mother, taking either the father's name or a name chosen by the mother.

Third—Wherever a man is willing and has a name generally known, and where the name is plain and simple, like Eagle, or White Shield, to retain it in its translated form.

Fourth—To strip out of the rolls all ridiculous or vulgar sounding names, like Bull-Coming-Up; Scabby Bull; Big Belly, &c.

Fifth—To add the name of the father to the school name of every child, dropping out the middle name, as for example, a child now on the school rolls as Walter Scott, would be named Walter Kias, thus indicating his father and at the same time preserving his identity among the school children and teachers.

Sixth—It is the intention of the Department to secure the co-operation of the red people in this matter. The necessity of a family name should be explained to them, and the transmission of property be made the basis of a plea for them to adopt the white man's way of naming. I think they could be made to understand this and to co-operate. Wherever possible, the actual names of the children in the native tongue might be retained, or the parents could be asked to give each child a name which could be easily written and pronounced by the white teachers.

What we are after, you will see, is a system which will show family relations, which will meet the wishes of the red people, and be comprehensible to the white people. In this way, for the first time, the Department hopes to systematize the naming of all the Indians on the various reservations, and especially to assist the teachers of the schools in naming the immense number of children coming to them each year.

I wish you would go over this carefully in your mind, and let me know if you see any decided objection to it. I believe all objections can be met, but from your long experience in the field, and your knowledge of the Indians, I hope to gain some new light on the subject. We intend to make a trial with the Cheyenne and Arapahoe lists, and at once. I wish you would also talk with some of the old men, explaining the matter to them, and get their opinion of it. Please do this at once, and write me or the Indian Office at your earliest possible convenience.

Sincerely yours

Grinnell and I are at work on a model list. We are taking the Cheyenne and Arapahoe. It looks to me like a very important and far-reaching job. What do you think of it?

Hamlin Garland

1. Garland added the prescript and postscript to a carbon of the letter he sent to Seger; another carbon of the Seger letter is in the Garland Papers (usc).

Washington

December 2, 1902.

Miss Estelle Reel,
Superintendent of Indian Schools.

Dear Miss Reel:

Our circular is probably on its way to the various schools and agencies, and I hope it will be effective at once. It so happens that Mr. Mooney,[1] who is now studying among the Kiowas, furnishes an exceedingly pleasant example of native naming, and I think you ought to know about it. It seems that a very intelligent Kiowa objected to having his children named Betsy Kahn, Labonia, Burt Heidsick, and asked his friend Mooney if he would not see the Agent and get him to allow his children to retain their own names. Mr. Mooney did so, the Agent gave written order, and the children were named in accordance with his wishes. Here we have a typical family:

The father,	——	Gunaoi
The mother,	Deon	"
First daughter,	Halli	"
Second "	Aisima	"
Third "	Imguna	"
First son	Inali	"
Second "	Zepko	"

To repeat, here is a typical family, all well named, with names which the father himself desires. There is only one weak point in it, as you will see, and that is, the names do not indicate the sex of the children. Aside from this, there is not the slightest objection to it. For if any teacher objects to these names as seeming a little difficult at first, she can be reminded of the exceeding difficulty experienced in Chicago when dealing with the Poles and Hungarians. It occurred to me that an instance of this kind might be valuable to you in talking about the new system as you go into the field, and for that reason I have taken the trouble to send it to you — quite unofficially, of course.

Mr. Mooney will be of great value to us in handling the Wichitas and Kiowas, who have just been allotted, and we can straighten matters out there with very little labor.

Hoping you have entirely recovered from your indisposition, I am,

Very sincerely yours,

Sex could be indicated Kiowas by ending. It is so indicated among most.

1. James Mooney (1861–1921), an American ethnologist, served on the staff of the Bureau of Ethnology and was specially employed as an investigator of Indians of the South and West. He was also co-author of *Handbook of American Indians* (2 vols., 1907–10).

146. to Charles F. Lummis   tls, Southwest

Washington, D.C.

Mr. Chas F. Lummis,
Editor, Out West,
Los Angeles, Cal.

December 3, 1902

My dear Lummis:

I think I wrote to you sometime ago concerning my plan for renaming the Indians in conformity with our own system of maintaining the line of descent.

My letter of suggestion to the President was handed over with endorsement that it be acted upon, to the Commissioner. The Commissioner invited further suggestion. Accordingly, I have taken the matter in hand and by consultation with Merriam, Hodge, Mooney, and Grinnell, and the Department have devised a system which is to be applied to the Indians of Oklahoma and the Northwest.[1]

Now, of course, in handling the Pueblo Indians where the clan is the important division or unit, it will be necessary to make some modifications. It has been suggested by Hodge that we take the *clan name* among the Zuni and the others of the Pueblo tribe as the surname, retaining for first names those which the parents have already given their children, and thus cut off the foolish and fancy names being given by the school teachers. In other words, a boy's name would be Titsa Ainshi, instead of Walter Scott or Burt Heidsieck; Ainshi being the name of the Bear clan. As there are some twelve or fifteen distinct clans, and as the lands allotted according to clans, and the number of people to be named small, Mr. Hodge's suggestions seem to be reasonable, but I would like to have your opinion.

You can see what we are driving at. The present system takes no account of the line of descent. It supposes that each child stands alone in the world; that all relationship is of not account; brothers are named "Claude Melnott," and "Daniel Webster;" no hint is given of the father or the mother. This is in full accordance, of course, with Col. Pratt's idea that each Indian child is himself the beginning of a new race, or a new line, and should be cut off entirely from all his red relations—but we do not agree with him.

Among the Cheyennes and Arapahoes and the Kiowas and Wichitas, for example, a new system has become imperative. Lands are now held in severalty, valuable lands, and in a few years, the question of inheritance will not only be an important one to individual Indians, but it will be a responsibility to the government. Already a bill is formulating to sell the lands of dead Indians, and distribute the money to the heirs. Immediately, the question of relationship will assume legal importance. Therefore, the President and the Commissioner have expressed a profound interest in my suggestion, and have invited me to proceed in formulating a working hypothesis.

I write this in order that you may understand it; and also to invite suggestion from you with regard to the Indians you have lived with, and whom you know better than we. Write me care of the Players' Club, New York city.

This matter is one that the Sequoya League can take up a little later with exceeding great propriety, but at present perhaps you would better not deal with it publicly. I wish to get the matter pretty thoroughly in motion before making any public announcement of it, because we can confidently expect opposition on the part of Col. Pratt and his party.

I hope your Warner ranch matter has come out to your complete satisfaction. I shall be very glad to hear from you if you can find time to write.[2]

Very sincerely,
Hamlin Garland

The Players Club
New York.

1. Frederick W. Hodge and James Mooney were ethnologists with the Bureau of Ethnology who advised Garland about the allottees.

1. Frontispiece from *A Member of the Third House*
(Chicago: F. J. Schulte, 1892). (Courtesy Miami U)

2. Above: James Whitcomb Riley and Garland at
Greenfield, Indiana, 1893. (Courtesy USC)

3. Right: Letter to August Thomas, 23 April 1897
(letter 102). (Courtesy Miami U)

1342 New York Av

Dear Mr Thomas:

I want to thank you for a most delightful evening spent with "The Hoosier Doctor". There is nothing more homely true on our stage and some of it was so fresh and new it startled me. I sat on the edge of my seat the entire evening. "Harriet" and "Jud" and "Alviry" are new types on the stage and so indeed is "Ma-ma!"

I feel the novelist in you — which is to say you study human kind, not other peoples plays. Please consider me one of your champions. I liked "In Mizzoura" but in some regards "The Hoosier Doctor" is better, in others not so good.

Very sincerely
Hamlin Garland.

Friday.
April 23/97

4. Above: Garland taking notes in camp along the
Klondike Trail, 1898. (Courtesy Miami U)

5. Right: Zulime Garland, ca. 1900. (Courtesy USC)

6. Top left: Garland at his West Salem, Wisconsin, home, 1906. (Courtesy USC)

7. Bottom left: Garland and Mary Isabel, 1907. (Courtesy USC)

8. Top right: Mary Isabel *(left)* and Constance Garland, ca. 1910s. (Courtesy USC)

9. Bottom right: William Dean Howells. (Courtesy USC)

10. Top left: Garland impersonating Nathaniel Hawthorne at a costume party, 1918. (Courtesy Miami U)

11. Bottom left: Members present at the opening of the American Academy of Arts and Letters building, 22 February 1923. Front row: Augustus Thomas, William M. Sloan, Robert Underwood Johnson, Garland, Arthur F. Hadley, and Cass Gilbert. Center row: William C. Brownell, Edwin H. Blashfield, Lorado Taft, Frederick MacMonnies, Daniel Chester French, William Gillette, and Charles Dana Gibson. Top row: Childe Hassam, Joseph Pennell, Maurice F. Egan, Owen Wister, Paul Shorey, Paul Elmer More, and Nicholas Murray Butler. (Courtesy USC)

12. Above: Garland the lecturer, ca. 1934. (Courtesy Miami U)

13. Above: Garland in his Hollywood study,
1936. (Courtesy Miami U)

14. Right: Letter to Eldon Hill, 25 January
1938 (letter 371). (Courtesy Miami U)

2045 DeMille Drive
HOLLYWOOD, CALIFORNIA
MORNINGSIDE 12733

Jan.25.

My Dear Young Critic:

I do not remember hearing Melvilles name mentioned by any-
one in my youth. I knew of him by reason of Hawthorne's ~~mention~~ *disciplen* of him as
a neighbor in the Berkshires. Very slight mention of him was made when he
died. I didnt even know that he was *still* alive when I was studying in Boston.

I greatly admired passages in MOBY DICK but felt bored by the lumbering
apostrophes. They were absurdly out of character in the book. I felt that
it greatly needed blue-pencilling. I feel ~~more than~~ *that now more* than ever ~~now~~. I
did not read ~~the~~ *two* other books. I think him greatly over-rated by a *the* claque
which arose a few years ago. I am bored by Mufford's book. I find even
"Benito Cereno" hard reading.   He had no sense of proportion. I find him
worth reading only in spots. When he is walking on the deck of a boat or on
the earth he is often vigorous and direct but at other times he just does
not get clear of his cloud of pseudo philosophy. I can imagine that he
bored Hawthorne by his vaporings. The man had power and insight but ~~had~~
never acquired the art of writing a sustained narrative or essay.

All the *#* hullabaloo *by* ~~of~~ the men in New York was just one of those sudden
~~enthusiasms~~ *enthusiasms* which arise for no solid reason whatever. It has all died away
and will not be renewed.   Melville was an extremely interesting character
but he was not a great writer. He was best when he dealt with what he had seen
and heard.

H.G.

P.S. It may be that "Typee" and "Omoo" are
simpler and more direct in expression. I'll try them out sometime.

15. Eldon Hill, ca. 1930s. (Courtesy Miami U)

16. Above: Garland and his psychic, Sophia Williams, gathering evidence for *The Mystery of the Buried Crosses*, 1939. The caption reads "Hamlin Garland unearthing a cross." The photo was taken by George Palmer Putnam, Amelia Earhart's husband (see letter 365). (Courtesy USC)

17. Below: One of Garland's mysterious crosses, from *The Mystery of the Buried Crosses* (New York: Dutton, 1939). (Courtesy Miami U)

18. Van Wyck Brooks,
Westport, Connecticut,
1934. (Courtesy USC)

2. Lummis replied on 7 January 1903: "The general line of your suggestion seems to me sensible. There is no question that the present fashion of pasting absurd names on the Indians, 'without the consent of any other nation' (nor of their parents or themselves) is an absurdity and an outrage, and should be stopped. And where there is nothing else to go on but clan names, they are certainly far preferable to any other basis that I can think of./ Don't forget, however, that all the Pueblo Indians practically have Spanish baptismal family names; and where this is the case it would be an absurdity and an outrage to change them." Lummis also mentioned that the Warner Ranch matter, evidently a private matter involving disputed title to land that Lummis was attempting to get, was not yet completed, as the "red tape factory in Washington has not yet concluded its examination of the titles." In a letter of 9 May 1903 (Southwest), Garland informed Lummis that Commissioner Jones agreed with his suggestion regarding the retention of Pueblo Indian baptismal names.

147. to Hamilton Wright Mabie

als, Am Acad

West Salem.

Jan 25 [1903]

Dear Mr Mabie:

I regret very much my inability to be present at the annual meeting of the Institute.[1] I hope some one will give expression to my feeling that the Institute should take immediate action as an organization along the lines suggested by some of our members vis — that it should be our duty as an organization to emphasize the need of the higher life in America. Our ideals are not those of business policies or religion and they are to my mind higher than those of commerce or politics and more liberal and fruitful than those of the churchman because including the highest achievements in science and the liberal arts. It should be the work of the Institute to dignify art — to insist upon the importance of poetry — of beauty in American life. We have a right to insist that there are other things better worth while than acquiring millions or being elected senator of a state. The young people of America are in danger of thinking there are only two ideals — the commercial success — and the social success. Would it not be a source of power to the Institute if it would take for its motive the exaltation of other and nobler ideals for the aid and direction of the young men and women of today and tomorrow? Art and literature are no longer disposable in America — and our organization is right and proper. The American Institute of Arts and Letters need not hide in a corner. A national association seems not merely a natural but a nescessary thing now that artists and book-makers are become so numerous and so important to our life.

Whether the Institute should enter upon practical reforms like the copy-right bill, the relations of author and publisher[,] tariffs—in art, etc —I am not so sure. I am inclined to think that committees might properly be appointed to consider those matters. As soon as practicable we should have a secretary at a salary with an office to serve as a nominal center at least of the organization. The monthly dinners I think an excellent idea provided they are kept as simple and informal as not to be a burden on any member. The members should make it a point to keep informed of the good work being done in other lines of endeavors than their own and a committee might be appointed for this specific work of bringing before the Institute candidates for special honor each annual meeting. These are of course merely the suggestions which occur to me as I write. I cannot close my letter without saying that I knew Chas. Dudley Warner and have many pleasant memories of his kindly appreciation of my trials at being a novelist. He and Howells and Stedman (after Lowells death) came naturally to be the chief men in American letters to whom the young men looked for encouragement and advice. Was there ever a kindlier group? In this connection will you please vote for me when the question of retaining Howells as head of the Institute comes up.[2] Don't allow him to resign or take a back-seat. He belongs just where he is in the chair. He needn't speak and he needn't stand—he can and might be the Chairman at all meetings of our organization. Character and achievement both combine to fit him for the place.

I am to be in New York in Feb. and hope to be able to sit down at the first of the monthly dinners.

Very sincerely

Hamlin Garland

1. The National Institute of Arts and Letters.

2. Howells had succeeded Warner as president of the Institute upon Warner's death in 1900.

148. to Paul Revere Reynolds   als, Columbia

West Salem

March. 1ˢᵗ [1903?]

Dear Mr Reynolds: [1]

I shall be glad to entertain any bids for these two stories — but as people
are writing me each week for stories I hope you will use your best efforts
to dispose of them at once or return to me. "Howling Wolf" is of course
more salable than "The Red Pioneer" but it is not a pleasant story and is
a little long therefore I will consider a reasonable offer on that. [2] Your
system has always repelled me. You are no more value to me than a mailing agent unless you can find out my highest market value and sell my
goods at that price. Moreover I can get prompter consideration of my
m.s.s. I do not say this in way of complaint but to explain why I do not
patronize you. If I send you a crate of berries to sell I expect you to find
out the highest bidder by offering the berries — not at my price which may
be above or below the market — but at the highest you can obtain on the
open market. I have a new novel to sell. I don't know what I can get for
it. One man has offered me $3000. Another man may say: I'll give $4000.
There may be a third man who will say I can sell it at $5000. If I thought
it would pay me to put it into your hands I would do so. But if I fix a price
say at $3000 and you send it round at that price you are doing no more
than I can do sitting here. And I'd be out $300. There is nothing in it for
me unless you can get $350 more than I could possibly do. You may serve
a firm like Heineman or McClure but at present I see no way in which
you can benefit me.

Very sincerely

Hamlin Garland

1. Garland had placed several of his Indian stories into Reynolds's hands. In other
letters (Columbia) Garland reiterated his exasperation with Reynolds's failure to place
his work more efficiently.

2. "Howling Wolf" appeared as "The Outlaw" in *Harper's Weekly* 47 (13 June 1903):
972–73, and (20 June 1903): 1036–38. It was later revised and published as "The Story
of Howling Wolf" in *The Book of the American Indian* (1923). Although Garland elsewhere calls "The Red Pioneer" his working title for a projected volume of Indian stories, here the title appears to refer to a single story.

149. to Estelle Reel   alc, usc lb

West Salem. Wis—

                                                        June 15. [1903]

Dear Miss Reel:

I am sending to you herewith a letter which I would like you to read at
the Ed. Congress if you think it will advance the cause of tolerance—
and help to an understanding of the red-brother's peculiar place in our
civilization—

Let me know how it strikes you—

                        Yours sincerely
                        Hamlin Garland

Dear Miss Reel:

I have not forgotten my promise to write you a letter concerning Indian Education but pressing literary engagements make it impossible for
me to write at length. I hope you will put the re-naming of the allottees
(as out-lined by the Dept) clearly before the convention and ask their co-
operation. As you know I have enlisted the good services of Dr. Grinnell,
Mr Mooney, Mr Lummis, Mr Hodge and many other of the good friends
in the field and the work seems to go on satisfactorily to the Commissioner. Dr. Eastman Ohiyesa has been detailed at my request to assist
among the Sioux tribes and is at work on the Sissila Reservation.[1] I hope
he will make so good a showing that he will be continued in the work. Dr.
Grinnell has promised to start the work on the Crow, Northern Cheyenne
and Black-foot reservations during the summer and this is a great help.
The agent on the Standing Rock Reservation reports the roll re-written in
accordance with the Dept's. Circular. The Indians tell Seger, Eastman and
other of our special agents that they are ready to carry out this plan—
They see its justice and its value. No great difficulties thus far have arisen.
It is a long and tedious work but it ought to be done.

I wish you would also speak a special word about retaining the pretty
girls' names. And if you and your teachers think a list made out (as among
us) for mothers and teachers would be useful I will try to have it done.
Eastman could do this work beautifully for the Sioux and Robert Whiteleaf could make a similar list of Algonquin names.

With regard to the general educational problem—I can only repeat my
published words. The redman can not be turned into a whiteman. My
sympathy and coöperation go out to all those teachers who are attempting

to make of the Indian a cleanly, happy, and peaceful redman. I am not concerned about his conversion to any special religious creed nor exultant over his ability to "acquire higher mathematics." It seems [to] me that we can learn of Booker Washington at this point.[2] The tooth-brush and the bath-tub are wondrous civilizers. The redman was once a cleanly man — much given to bathing and he will take kindly to the use of water when he can get it. We should be careful to give the redman the essentials of right living — the humanities of our civilization — not its fads and worn-out creeds. In saying this I know I am in opposition to many devoted teachers and missionaries but I believe the fundamental precepts of Christian civilization can be taught without any of its cant — with little of its bitter prejudices. The teacher who is at the same time a proselytor for some specific creed is in my judgement over-stepping his province and should be replaced by a man who is wholly concerned with teaching the red-children to be clean, honest[,] happy and reasonably ambitious. Right living is not dependent on the creed of any one denomination nor upon the faith of any organized church. Without doubt men are profoundly benefitted by their signature to a creed but back of the profession must be good blood — good breeding, good moral instruction.

I am an evolutionist as regards the question of what to do for our red brethren. They can not be transmuted into something other than they are by any fervor of religious experience nor by any painful attempt to acquire the higher education. They must grow into something different by pressure of their changed conditions. This is not my dogmatism — it is the teaching of science and the fruit of my study of races. Furthermore if I could in the twinkling of an eye convert the red men into white men I would not perform the conjuration — I am not eager to see all the peoples of the earth run into the anglo-saxon mould — If the suffering and sorrow of the redman's transition period could be averted every man would rejoice but such is not the history of past races. They must change — slowly — and suffer in the change — Our work should be that of a friendly race who having passed the first stages of our adaptation turn with sympathy and insight to assist those who are coming up behind us.

In certain phases the Indian question is like the Negro question — although the two races are very widely divergent in character. The extremists, the fanatical are losing their predominance in the Negro question and the reasonable, the human and the practical are in the ascendant. Booker Washington has replaced Wendell Phillips, Mrs Stowe and the Lovejoys who believed that the negro was a whiteman in a black-cuticle.[3] Does any

one think a habit of mind less persistent than the color of a race's skin?
It is time that the same reasonableness be applied to the education of
the red children. As they are inheriting the color of their race so they are
carrying forward the ways of thought peculiar to their people. These
ways can be modified and very rapidly but they can not be obliterated and
fine new anglo-saxon ways of living and thinking substituted. Permanent
modification is not so easily secured.

While the law of evolution is thus inexorable and discouraging from
our point of view—from another it is singularly satisfying. It is certain.
The adaptation will be made—or the organism will perish. And here
again we get another thought. Care of the body should be made absolutely the first consideration for unless the redman is taught how to take
care of himself under the new conditions he will die—he is dying. His
close, ill-ventilated dirty cabins are poisoning him. Inactivity and conse-
quent vice are corroding him. This is what he needs—instruction as to
his bodily welfare not on a religious basis—but on a purely hygienic basis.

He should be taught that bad air has no relation to the whitemans religion but that it is destructive. He should be taught that drunkenness is
despised by white people of all creeds. In short I would carry to them the
gospel of the tooth-brush and the corn-planter and leave the question of
their soul's salvation to a time when their security and peace here on earth
may be more confidently published to the world.

I want the red people to be happy—I want them to be more joyous
than even in the best of the olden time—The earth is a beautiful place in
which to live. The Lord God to my thinking is wondering why man has
taken so long to live at peace and in plenty in his shiny world. Why not
go to the redman as a friend and not as a school-master or doctrinarian?
They have much to give us—you who know them best know this—without them our history would be commonplace—They have a future if we
will but grant to them some rights, some privileges. Come let us make
them good and happy redmen and give over our austere attempt to make
all the world worship our idols, acknowledge our God. Surely the universe
is a large thing and our window a very narrow peep-hole—Has the high
Creator blundered? Very well who will hasten to set His laws aright.

President Roosevelt is fond of saying "let us get at the equities in the
case." I would say in conclusion—let us get at the equities in the Indian's
case. Let us be just. Let us try to get his point of view—and look at the
world and the whiteman and the whiteman's learning from that side—We
will begin to grow tolerant and patient—and understand this man bet-

ter if we remember that he is a product of his environment—and that he must adapt himself to new physical conditions before he will be able to take on the whitemans faith.

I intended to speak of the importance of recreation in this work—of civilizing the redmen. A people must have recreation quite aside from singing hymns and listening to sermons—and the way of approach to the young people is through their willingness to take on the whiteman's sports. I would encourage foot-ball, dancing picnics, brass-bands. The bicycle sets up a different train of thought from the pony. The brass-band is a fair out-let for the lungs of every a navajo. I have met missionaries who seemed eager to strip away every moment of pleasure—every amusement in order to reduce the redman to a sombre joyless religious fanatic. These people I am frankly in opposition to and I do not find in Christs teachings any sanction for such austerity.

The native sports were founded in the needs of the people and their needs will continue to perpetuate some form of recreation.—In short the time has come when these red people should be treated as we would treat any other people in our midst—Their rights should be respected. They should be taught not lectured and prayed at—As the president has said "Give the redman a fair chance." A fair chance at pleasure, at comfort as well as at Sunday schools and week-day toil. Our own religious prejudices should not prevent us from understanding the place other beliefs by necessity hold in the scheme of evolution. So long as the redman obeys the common law[,] is decent and peaceable he should be allowed to worship the great spirit as he wishes—the same as any other citizen.

Hamlin Garland.

1. Charles Alexander Eastman (Ohiyesa) (1858–1939), a Santee Sioux, served as government physician to the Pine Ridge Agency (1890–93) and the Crow Creek Agency (1900–1903) after receiving his M.D. degree from Boston University in 1890. He was the author of ten books on Indian life, including *Indian Boyhood* (1902), *Old Indian Days* (1907), and *The Soul of an Indian* (1911).

2. Booker T. Washington (1856–1915), son of a slave and a white man, founded Tuskegee Normal and Industrial Institute which emphasized industrial training. He was the author of *The Future of the American Negro* (1899), his autobiography *Up from Slavery* (1901), and *The Story of the American Negro* (1909).

3. Wendell Phillips (1811–84), an American reformer and abolitionist, joined the Anti-Slavery Society with William Lloyd Garrison, assuming its presidency in 1865. Har-

riet Beecher Stowe (1811–96) came to nationwide prominence with the publication of *Uncle Tom's Cabin* (1852). Elijah Parish Lovejoy (1802–37) became editor of the St. Louis abolitionist *Observer* (1833), but moved to Alton, Illinois, in 1836 when he was threatened with violence, and began publishing the Alton *Observer*. He was killed defending this paper, which was attacked several times. His brother, Owen Lovejoy (1811–64), carried on his cause, became a leading Illinois abolitionist, and served in Congress from 1856 to 1864.

150. to Frederick A. Duneka alc, USC LB

West Salem Wis.

June 29 [1903]

Dear Mr Duneka:[1]

I wrote you rather hurriedly last night about the novel.[2] I take time to write more leisurely today. 1ˢᵗ Neither Mrs Garland nor myself like the name of the book. "Rampart Ranger" is not alluring. It is harsh and not descriptive either. I find myself unable to think of it under that name.

2ⁿᵈ While we realize the force and courtesy of your letter we do not see how we can get along without that serial royalty—it seems to be the one absolutely certain thing about the business—and I have written to Reynolds telling him to hustle and sell it. I am also in touch with a good syndicate in Chicago.

3ʳᵈ I want to publish this fall. I will have been out of the field over eighteen months and it is time to reappear—but if I published direct and sold only five or six thousand I would be in bad temper and the Garland's would be shut out from the best circles for lack of new gowns and things.

4ᵗʰ If I am not of prime importance to Harpers I cant afford to publish with them. This is a disagreeable and low-minded business-like way of speaking and I ought to be ashamed of it—but I'm not. The fact is I have no other way of making a living. I've written the best book I could conceive at the time—it is now in printable form and I am going out as you would do to do the best I can for it and for myself. This necessitates a serial publication and if a serial publication can only be arranged by disposal of the book rights also you can not blame me for making such a trade. Of course you may be right that the book is not a good serial story —if that develops then I shall certainly want to publish this fall.

What I shall now do is this: I will give the revised M.S. into Reynolds' hands (as you do not care to bother with it) and let him feel of the market. If he finds it not a likely serial—or if he succeeds in placing it I will publish this fall—with you if we come to terms. If he finds a market for it dependent upon a little time to publish—or if he finds a suitable offer for both serial and book rights the one dependent on the other it will be my duty to wait I think—even at the risk of a lesser sale next year.[3]

I would like to publish direct—there is something fine and dignified in making ones appeal that way but hunger humbles the provident author—and I cant take the risk—unless as I wrote you yesterday the firm of *Harpers* is able to do even greater and more distinctive advertising for this book than for "The Captain."

I may say that Mrs Garland is on your side—To this extent she believes in you and Col. Harvey and wants me to publish with you if possible. And so do I. It is only this lately developed business sense in me that causes me to hesitate and makes me think that a smaller house might be less swamped with books and more likely to develop all that my book contains.—I am writing frankly as you requested. I am trying to apply the same set of principles to my side of the case that you so ably apply from yours.

With the hope that we can arrange the whole matter.

I am sincerely yours
Hamlin Garland.

1. After working as city editor of the *New York World*, Frederick A. Duneka (?–1919) became the general manager of Harper and Brothers when George B. M. Harvey reorganized the firm in 1900, and vice president in 1915. Harper's bought the book rights to *The Captain of the Gray-Horse Troop* on 15 January 1902 under Duneka's direction.

2. *Hesper*, published by Harper in 1903.

3. *Hesper* did not appear as a serial.

151. to Theodore Roosevelt als, Congress

West Salem Wis.

July 16. [1903]

Dear President Roosevelt:

We have a little daughter.[1] She came yesterday and Mrs Garland is in excellent condition this morning. She was much pleased by your hearty words and prizes them above rubies and will hand them down as an inheritance to her daughter. Every woman who passes through the maternity battle should be sainted. After seeing Zulime in her agony sweat—I am not prepared to follow you in your advocacy of large families. It really is a wonder that they live through it. I dont see how Mrs Wister did come through.[2]

However, it is over now and both mother and babe are peaceful. Please tell Mrs Roosevelt—we know she will sympathize.—While watching night before last I re-read "The Wilderness Hunter"[3] and enjoyed the nature side more than ever. Some of those pictures of river and forest are as good as anybody does—and the whole book was a tonic to me in my nerve-racked state.

Your instant word of hearty good cheer gratified me quite as much as it did my wife.

Yours with admiration—
Hamlin Garland

1. Garland's first daughter, Mary Isabel, born 15 July.

2. In 1898 the novelist Owen Wister married his second cousin, Mary ("Molly") Channing. By the winter of 1901–2, the Wisters had three children, with twins born on 21 September 1901. In July 1903, Molly Wister was again pregnant. In 1913 she died in childbirth, leaving Wister with six children.

3. Roosevelt's account of the sportsman's (hunter's) wilderness experience, published by G. P. Putnam's Sons in 1893.

152. to Theodore Roosevelt

als, Congress

West Salem Wis.

July 22. [1903]

Dear President Roosevelt:

Your letter impressed me profoundly in several ways—in no way more deeply than by its revelation of your attitude toward women.[1] The trait that always drew me to Grant was his purity of speech—he did not make a joke of maternity—and the characteristic which always repelled me in Lincoln was his obscenity—which I fear can not be explained away. Your attitude is Grant's rather than Lincoln's and it carried deep. It was another evidence of your many sided character—essentially the most manly that has ever reached your place.

With the latter part of your letter I am really in substantial agreement—I wrote that line while my dear girl was fresh from a really frightful struggle. The child was saved only by a powerful and skilled physician from La Crosse.[2] I recognize the perfect consistency of your male

argument—and theoretically admit the conclusion—temperamentally as
you know I am not the optimist that you are—I could not live a week
under the pressure of such a life as yours—I bow down before your marvelous endurance, your equanimity, your resolution. I congratulate the
States on having you president even though I am not an "Expansionist"
nor Militarist. You are consistent in what you say of women and the
family and of men and their duties as soldiers. I must admit you are right
as things now stand although from the quiet of my study I permit myself
to dream that battle-ships are an anachronism and the need of soldiers
imaginary.—Your letter increased our admiration of you—and so joyous
that point of view I do not regret the bitterly jocular remark which led
you to give so much care to its answer.

We have never happened to discuss this subject before and I am sincerely glad you opened your heart to me in this good letter.—Mrs. Garland slept last night for the first time in eight days—I mean to really
sleep—and she is much better today—entirely out of danger. She was in
superb health before this came on—and had the child not been so lusty—
with such fine cranial development, all would have been easier. I think a
good surgeon is one of God's messengers. Dr. Evans of La Crosse will live
in our memories as a master of his profession and a saver of man.

Most sincerely yours
Hamlin Garland.

1. In a 19 July 1903 letter to Garland (Congress), Roosevelt argued that women
have a duty to bear children and that they must breed large families; if not, the race
deserves to die out: "The woman who flinches from childbirth stands on par with the
soldier who drops his rifle and runs in battle. . . . If . . . a man or a woman refuses to do
his or her duty, why they are contemptible creatures and have no right in the
community."

2. Dr. Edward Evans, whom Garland recalls in some detail in *Daughter*, pp. 286–88.

153. to Edmund Clarence Stedman als, Columbia

247 Fifth Avenue.

Nov. 2 [1903]

Dear Mr Stedman:

Mrs Grossman is deeply pained over the publication of those Booth
letters to Stoddard—and is asking you and other friends to discounte-

nance their further use.[1] It seems to me a most unwarrantable use of the
very private correspondence of a great man whose daughter still lives—a
sensitive and shy soul—and suffers deeply over any word which in any
degree reflects upon her father. Who did this? And what can we do to
prevent further desecration of Booth's confidence? You of all men are the
one to protest and I hope you will do so—I dont know where to reach
you and so I send this to the *Century*.

Very sincerely yours
Hamlin Garland

1. Edwina Booth Grossman, the daughter of actor Edwin Booth, had written to Garland on 1 November 1903 to complain about the publication of her father's letters: "I
am quite frustrated this morning on seeing the publication in the Herald of my dear
father's Letters to the Stoddards. Material so sacred is not for the Public Eye—and as the
daughter of so noble & revered a father, I resent such a dastardly breach of confidence.
Had I only known of the existence of such Letters—I would have endeavored to have
had them confiscated in Mr Stoddard's life time." In "The Heart of Hamlet," *New York
Herald*, 1 November 1903, magazine sec., pp. 1–3, Dolores Marbourg Bacon contributed
a profusely illustrated article, with facsimiles and transcriptions of Booth's letters to
the novelist Elizabeth Drew Stoddard (1822–1902) and her husband, the poet Richard
Henry Stoddard (1825–1903). In these letters Booth provides an intimate glimpse into
his friendship with the Stoddards, as well as his guilt and pain over his belief that he
had contributed to the death of his wife, Mary Devlin, through "certain disturbing
stories" carried to her by misguided friends. Stoddard had given the letters to the Author's Club shortly before his death.

154. to Edmund Clarence Stedman   als, Columbia

The Players Club.

Nov. 7. [1903]

Dear Mr Stedman:

Mrs Grossman wrote to me *after* writing to you—and she did not ask
me to ask you to act on the matter. I thought of you at once—as the man
to act effectively. I am not a member of the Author's Club—and do not
know the management and can not direct my letter vaguely to the club
but I wish I could add something to the weight of remonstrance against
this kind of piracy. An Authors Club above all others ought to be as flint
against the use of unauthorized material.

Mrs Grossman was calling upon my wife (who was ill) and in this visit confessed the pain the published letters had brought her. She left a note to me merely asking me to do what I could to prevent the further dese-cration of her fathers confidence—Please do not think she put me before any of her long-tried friends—chief among whom is Edmund Clarence Stedman. I was so ignorant of the situation that I did not know Hitchcock was doing Stoddards "Memories."[1] You see I have been in the wilderness for six or eight months—and it was precisely because I knew you were the one man to give weight to the protest that I turned to you. Dr. Sea-man[2] one of Mrs Grossman's friends had not seen the article neither had Underwood Johnson—neither had I—but I saw the notices of the let-ter and remembered your talk about them the night we dined together. Therefore I was perfectly aware of the nature of the offence against copy-right law and good taste. If I seemed precipitate in the matter please lay it to my desire to serve Mrs Grossman who asked my aid just as she asked that of Dr. Seaman and others near to her—not out of a doubt of you but to help you in your protest against the outrage which we perfectly under-stood would touch you nearly.

With sincerest respect
Hamlin Garland

1. Stoddard's *Recollections, Personal and Literary*, ed. Ripley Hitchcock, introd. E. C. Stedman (New York: A. S. Barnes, 1903).

2. Frank Seaman was the proprietor of Yama Farms, a semiprivate inn near Ellen-ville, New York, and was the head of "an enormous advertising bureau" (*Back-Trailers*, pp. 131–32).

155. to William A. Jones

als, Nat'l Arch

16. Morningside Ave.

Dec. 7 [1903]

Com. Ind. Affairs.
Washington. D. C.

Dear Mr Jones: Dr. Eastman has just been here to talk over the work of re-enrolling the Sioux—a sort of informal report to me. He told me that you had directed him to return to the west—also that you had forbidden him to lecture during such time as he was in the employ of the Gov.

Now while I sympathize with you in your desire to have the Doctor's entire service I am afraid we cant demand it. His attitude in the matter is quite justifiable it seems to me. He is anxious to finish the work but so far as his own interests are concerned he is losing time and money. His literary fame is greatly on the increase and the demands on him for lectures are numerous and I fear that if he consults his own interests he will resign now.

The situation is this, Mr Commissioner, he has spent several months in tracing all the family relationships and in deciding on family names for about 5000 Sioux—These memoranda are pencilled on rough rolls (which he was forced to copy in his own hand—a most laborious task) and now must be copied again in type-writing. This work he can do as well here in the east as elsewhere and under my oversight. I regret that I could not have given more time to this matter last summer but the illness of my wife quite prevented.

For these various reasons I would suggest that you either continue Dr. Eastman on the rolls as at present—the simplest way—or put him on half-pay till the 1st of April when he will be ready to return to the west. This will give him time to go over these names with me and to copy them into their final position—The names themselves are decided upon by consultation with the Indians.

I sincerely and earnestly hope that so long as you can do so you will retain Eastman in this position. He can handle the Assiniboine, Crow, No. Cheyenne and possibly the Grosventre and Black-foot rolls. He is the one man to do it and I most respectfully suggest that so long as he is willing to continue in the position we ought to strain a point to retain him. It is cold and bleak and most unpleasant on the Dakota reservations during the winter months and so long as his task is confined to the shaping of these 5000 names I do not see why he can not do it to advantage here in the east. He is within easy reach of New York where he can consult with Dr. Grinnell and me and can also proceed to Washington at any time to consult with you.

We are getting the services of a skilled man very cheaply even at $1500 per annum and I very much hope that you will withdraw your restrictions as to his out-side work. He will do his official duty I am sure of that. Count on my services on his record and leave him free to go along with these rolls in which he is profoundly interested. Thus far he has had a great many disadvantages. He had no house on the reservation—and his wife and children had to be provided for. They are now in Mrs Eastman's old home and while Eastman has the re-enrollment much at heart I doubt whether he would be willing to return to the west during the winter months—

especially as he has this clerical work to do before he can take up another district.

I am in entire sympathy with you in your desire to get the best service from each government employee—and if I thought this work would really suffer by Eastmans residence here this winter I would certainly second your wish, but frankly I think the best interests of the work lie in his remaining where he is till April 1ˢᵗ. I am planning to go into the field with him in May and if my family is well will stay with him till the people are all acquainted with our plan. He says he finds no opposition on their part and though there are perplexities and barriers he is over-coming them. The need of the change is great.

I hope you will pardon this letter. My wish to have the re-naming go is its excuse—

Most sincerely yours
Hamlin Garland—

156. to William A. Jones
als, Nat'l Arch

16 Morningside Ave

Dec. 22—[1903]

Dear Mr Jones:

I have just gone over a long section of the roll on which Eastman is at work and so far as I can see he has done well with it. It is a very difficult job to do perfectly and though I made a few suggestions they were merely suggestions. I feel that he understands the situation perfectly and is doing as well as any one could. Naturally I would like to see more of the Indian names retained but no doubt he had been guided by considerations which only a verbal explanation could set forth. These rolls are now ready to be put upon your official rolls. I am profoundly in the hope that we may continue Eastman in this work and that we can start the new allottees right.[1]

I wish we could furnish to the teachers lists of native names easy of pronunciation to be used in place of the badly over-worked "Johns" "Mary's" "Roberts" and the like among us. I will assist in making lists of this kind if we can get them used. Can we bring any pressure to bear in that direction?

Very sincerely yours
Hamlin Garland

1. On 18 February 1903 Jones passed on Garland's recommendation to Ethan Alan Hitchcock, the secretary of the interior, that Eastman be granted a leave of absence from his position as physician at the Crow Creek Agency, and that he be employed temporarily in revising the Crook Creek allotment rolls and the rolls of other Sioux agencies. His recommendation was accepted and on 5 March 1903 (by letter from Jones to Eastman), Eastman was appointed a clerk at one hundred dollars a month for the remainder of the year to revise the names on the Sioux rolls. On 22 December 1903, Jones immediately answered the above letter from Garland, telling him that for some reason Hitchcock was not pleased with the work that was being done by Eastman, but that he (Jones) was trying to keep things quiet so that there would be no excuse for ordering him back to the Crow Creek Agency: "The Secretary does not know where the Doctor is now located, and unless his attention is especially called to the fact that he is East, I do not think there will be any trouble in keeping him there. Personally I am perfectly willing to have the Doctor continue his work in the East, as you say it can be done as well there as upon the Reservations."

157. to Ora V. Eddleman

als, U of Oklahoma

16 Morningside Ave

Dec. 29. — [1903]

Dear Miss Eddleman: [1]

Your letter interested me exceedingly and I should like very much to see your magazine. If you will send it to me I will try to write something for you though I fear it will not be fiction. I have so much work to do that is actually promised that I can not afford to send you a story but I will write something now and then of interest to your people.

I was particularly struck with your statement of your purpose. There is to my mind no good reason why the life and character of the redman should be condemned *in toto*—for there were many fine and beautiful things connected with his way of living. He should retain his traditions, his stories, his songs—whatever was picturesque without being harmful he has a right to carry forward into his new life. He ought to retain so far as possible his own names—As you may know I am unofficially helping to re-name many of the tribes—restoring their own proper nomenclature where possible—insisting only on a family name—and stripping away all senseless or vulgar translations. This work I think you will find yourself in full sympathy with when you come to understand it. Perhaps I will write about this if you care to have me do so. In general my practice is this: The redman must conform to our civilization but he has a right to remain a redman and to retain as many of his customs and tribal habits as do not conflict with the whitemans laws. I would not convert him to the Christian religion. That will take care of itself. Whatever appeals to him in our way of living he will adopt naturally. We can not club or shoot him into grace. For all these reasons I was glad to read in your letter a broad and catholic statement of faith.

With best wishes for the new year I am
Very sincerely yours,
Hamlin Garland

P.S. Write also to Geo. Bird Grinnell. 246 Broadway. N.Y. ^{Ed} *Forest and Stream* and also to Ernest T. Seton. #80 W. 40th St New York City. Mention my name. Send sample copies to them also.

1. Ora V. Eddleman began publishing *Twin Territories: The Indian Magazine* in 1899. As editor, she wrote to Garland on 19 December 1903, introducing him to the magazine, a copy of which she was sending under separate cover. She explained that "Twin Territories is distinctively an INDIAN Magazine," whose contributors were primarily prominent Indians. "The great object of Twin Territories," she continued, "is to preserve the old life of the Indians—their folklore, but at the same time to keep foremost in the minds of the people the fact that the Indians are entering into a new life and are developing into a new people." The magazine ceased publication after its May 1904 issue, without Garland ever publishing something in it.

158. to Theodore Dreiser   als, U Penn

16 Morningside Ave

Jan. 3—[1904]

Dear Mr Dreiser:

It may strike you as a very late day for me to come to a reading of "Sister Carrie" but in this case as in many others it is better late than never.[1] I was deeply impressed with the power and the verity of this book and I should like to know more about the author of it. I take it you are of the west and specifically of Chicago and I am going to be quite honest and say that my information concerning you is very scant. You can lay this to my bad memory and also to the absorption of a man trying to do things on his own account. I hope you will not feel my compliment wrongly when I say that in reading this book I was powerfully reminded of Norris' "McTeague" which I vastly admired. The way in which you

The Activist: 1900–1918 185

trace the disintegration of Hurstwood[2] is fairly of the same relentless sincerity of manner with which poor "McTeague" is set forth by Norris.

Here's hoping you will do more books as good as "Carrie."

Very sincerely yours
Hamlin Garland

1. Theodore Dreiser (1871–1945) published *Sister Carrie* in 1900.

2. Garland's spelling of "Hurstwood" is illegible. For a discussion of this letter in the context of Garland's friendship with Dreiser, see Lars Ahnebrink, "Garland and Dreiser: An Abortive Friendship," *Midwest Journal* 7 (1955–56): 285–92. Although Dreiser's reply is dated "January 8, 1903," Dreiser has misnumbered the year, for Garland's diary shows him finishing the novel on 9 November 1903.

159. to Zulime Garland als, Hunt

The American Club
City of Mexico

[19 April 1904]

Dear Girl:

The fellows are gone—left ten minutes ago.[1] They go by way of Laredo—I go by way of Aguas Calientes and El Paso. Tell Father that Frank and I will both be in Oklahoma—if he has not gone when you go up.— Well we all went in to see President Diaz today and we were profoundly impressed with him.[2] He is a small man much more amiable than his pictures show him, and of finer manner. His phrases were neatly turned and his compliments graceful. He was interested to know that I had written a life of Grant and seemed pleased when I asked him to accept a special copy of the book—He was interested in Bacheller and me as literary men, and seemed the least bit constrained—but not in the least presuming on his position. No northern gentleman could have been simpler in manner. He listened attentively almost eagerly to what we had to say through the interpreter Mr McCreery (Sec. to the Embass.) and leaned to catch every word. His Spanish was so simple and direct I could almost follow him.—He is seventy four years old but looks about sixty! He has the air of a sympathetic and powerful physician—a little sad in expression at times but very amiable and likable when he smiles. I told him I had heard Roosevelt speak of him pleasantly and he replied with a bow—

"Thank you senor. It is not the first time that I have heard of such words by President Roosevelt, and it gives me pleasure." He made no sign of dismissing us and when we rose he seemed still interested and shook hands again most cordially.

I liked him very much. He is a really wonderful man. He has done harsh things—probably unjust things—but his worst enemies say he loves Mexico and that he is working for good—

I shall leave here tomorrow morning and will be with Frank tomorrow night. How long I will stay there I dont know but probably two days. I will try to reach home by the 1ˢᵗ—I will let Frank go in my place to meet Father and show him about—I am anxious to see that little "toof" in baby's mouth.—You can write me at Weatherford Oklahoma but be sure and put a return on it. Use the government envelope and write in your name so that it will return if I do not get it—Preserve this note for its study of Diaz.—

Your husband and baby's Dada—
Hamlin

1. Garland had bought a mine near the village of Camacho in Mexico, which his brother Franklin was working. He decided to inspect the mine, accompanied by Archer Brown, a Chicago investor, and Irving Bacheller (1859–1950), a novelist, whose works include *Eben Holden* (1900), *D'ri and I* (1901), and *Silas Strong* (1906). Garland established a lifelong friendship with Bacheller, whom he had met in the 1890s through his dealings with Bacheller's newspaper syndicate, which distributed much of his early fiction to the nation's newspapers.

2. As Garland explains in *Companions*, pp. 225–32, when he stopped in Mexico City on his way back to Chicago, he met Frederick Guernsey, the editor of the Mexican *Herald*, who introduced him to a "Mr. McCreery," who in turn arranged a meeting with Mexico's president, Porfirio Díaz (1830–1915).

160. to Samuel Clemens

als, Bancroft

West Salem Wis.

July 7. [1905]

Dear Mr Clemens:

Your letter was a deeply felt gratification to me and goes far to compensate me for the work I put into that book.¹ In the nature of things it cant have a wide circulation but if I meet the commendation of men like yourself and Howells I shall feel repaid. I very much wish I could talk the book and the subject over with you and perhaps when we both get back to town we will be able to do so. I have tried in this book to be just to all sides. Spiritualism has its beautiful side and I have not intended to obscure that side. I should be very glad to believe that my mother and sister are still sentient personalities—and I dont *know* that they are not but I remain unconvinced. The scientific mind (unless it is a bigoted mind) is willing to follow the evidence.—But we will sometime talk this. It gives a man of my generation great comfort to get the praise of yours—in this sense I too am an "ancestor worshipper." Mrs Garland joins me in greetings to you all. Do you know MacDowell the musician? He must be near you. He is ill but expects to rally now that he is out of the roar and heat of the city.[2]

Most gratefully yours
Hamlin Garland

1. Garland refers to *The Tyranny of the Dark* (1905), a novel of psychic investigation.

2. Edward Alexander MacDowell (1861–1908), New York–born composer of many piano works. He was the head of Columbia University's department of music (1896–1904), but he resigned his position and suffered a nervous collapse in 1905. After his death in 1908 his widow, the pianist Marian Nevins MacDowell, established the Mac-Dowell Colony for composers, artists, and writers at the MacDowell farm in Peterborough, New Hampshire.

161. to Theodore Roosevelt

als, Congress

Chamber of Commerce
Colorado Springs, Colo.

[ca. 6 August 1905]

Dear President Roosevelt:

I enclose the copy of a letter which I sent to the Colorado papers concerning the plan which I presented to your consideration three years ago.[1] There is great interest in the matter here and I think something can be done—at any rate this article is a "feeler." Let me take this opportunity of saying that I rejoice over your efforts at peace-making.[2] It quite warms my blood to see so good a fighter so effective a referee.—I am very sorry Paul Morton ever went into your cabinet although I was very fond of his father and I believed in him. He has done you harm, I fear. Root is a

splendid fellow I think but I wish we didnt have to use so many corporation lawyers in our big positions.[3]

With highest esteem
Hamlin Garland

West Salem Wis.

1. Garland's letter was published as an interview, "Hamlin Garland Suggests for
Colorado New National Playground," *Rocky Mountain News*, 6 August 1905, sec. 1 (clipping, Congress). He proposed establishing a national park in Colorado, particularly
"making the crest of the Rocky mountains one vast forest preserve. Every mountain
crest from an altitude of 8,500 feet should be so reserved and held forever under the
jurisdiction of the national government."

2. Roosevelt's effort to mediate a peace in the Russo-Japanese War (1904–5) was
rewarded with the 1906 Nobel Peace Prize.

3. Paul Morton (1857–1911), a vice president of the Atchison, Topeka & Santa Fe
Railroad, was the sole railway manager willing to testify before Congress concerning
illegal rate rebates. His poise impressed Roosevelt, who appointed him secretary of the
navy in July 1904. In December 1904 a traffic controller of the Santa Fe Railroad admitted granting illegal rebates while Morton was his supervisor, and the resulting scandal
led to Morton's resignation in July 1905. Morton's father, Julius Sterling Morton, was
Grover Cleveland's secretary of agriculture and founded Arbor Day. Elihu Root (1845–
1947), known as one of the nation's foremost corporate lawyers, became secretary of war
(1899–1904) and then secretary of state (1905–9).

162. to Theodore Roosevelt

als, Congress

West Salem Wis.

Aug. 15 [1905]

Dear President Roosevelt:

I was very glad to get your letter. It has encouraged me to proceed. I
saw Gov. McDonald before I left Denver, and presented the matter to
him. He seemed much impressed and said he would take the question up
with the senators and congressmen.[1] On the matter of forest preservation
in general I have volunteered my services and on Sept. 1st I am the "Con-
vocation Orator" at the Chicago University and my subject "Vanishing
Trails" will be a plea for the arresting of all needless and wanton despoila-
tion of the wild.[2] — I am keeping in touch with the Indian Dept. also and
will do all I can to aid Mr. Leup.[3] — I realize the force of what you say
about Corporation lawyers. On certain sides the training they get is most

admirable and if they are willing to "cut loose" as Sec. Root has done, they ought to serve the whole people single-heartedly. Your unfaltering optimism has my highest admiration. I am struggling hard to maintain my own youthful ideals and enthusiasm — but time tells! —

If you should happen to read my latest book (which I sent to Mrs Roosevelt) don't think I have gone over to the dark. The fact is along about '91 I put in several years study of occult matters as a member of the executive board of the Am. Psychical Society, and this novel is the result. It was "in my system" and had to be worked off. I shall not carry it any further. Nothing could be more alien to you than this book and you wont like it but it is being translated into several European languages and has won praise from the most eminent of English men of science — that is my excuse for writing it. It expressed my student side. I think its outcome is wholesome. I intended it to express the sanity which every phase of life presents to the man who recognizes no such thing as the super-natural. —

Yours as ever, faithfully,
Hamlin Garland
Dont go down in that boat. Remember, we need you.[4]

1. In his reply of 9 August (Congress), Roosevelt noted: "I think you are performing a valuable service in agitating that plan for a national park in Western Colorado. Of course I will give the project any backing I can." Roosevelt went on to note that, appearances to the contrary, he was confident of both Morton's and Root's integrity.

2. Published as "Vanishing Trails," *University Record* [University of Chicago] 10 (1905): 53–61.

3. Francis E. Leupp (1849–1918), in charge of the *New York Evening Post*'s Washington bureau, became the commissioner of the Indian Bureau in 1905. He was the author of *The Man Roosevelt* (1904) and *The Indian and His Problems* (1910), among other books.

4. Roosevelt piloted a submarine off Oyster Bay on 25 August 1905.

163. to Richard Watson Gilder

als, NYPL

Nov. 12 [1905]

Dear Mr Gilder:

As you know Edward MacDowell is smitten with an incurable disease and will never do any more work. A few of us are forming a "MacDowell Club" with the purpose of spreading a knowledge of the fine arts and to make a special study of his theories of music and its relation to the fine arts. It has the usual arrangement of an advisory board on which St Gaudens, French, Seth Low, Sfonoff, Alexander, and many others have consented to serve.[1] We would like your name and what advice and assistance you may from time to time *volunteer*. I hope you'll consent to serve. This tragic removal of our greatest musical genius is a good time to call attention to the depth and breadth of his work and also to prepare to carry out the plans which he had so deeply at heart. Mr Johnson has taken an interest in the Society and may be able to talk the plan over with you. Let me know your feeling in the matter.

Very sincerely yours
Hamlin Garland

1. Augustus St. Gaudens (1848–1907), born in Dublin, studied sculpture in Paris and Rome, where he was influenced by the Italian Renaissance. Upon his return to America he became the foremost sculptor of his time. Daniel C. French (1850–1931) was a New Hampshire sculptor best known for his statue "The Minute Man." Seth Low (1850–1916), American merchant, politician, and educator, was mayor of Brooklyn (1882–86), president of Columbia University (1890–1901), and mayor of New York (1901–3). Vasili Safonov (1851–1918), a Russian conductor who was the first to dispense with the baton, was a guest conductor of the New York Philharmonic in March 1904 where he was a sensational success. John White Alexander (1856–1915), a painter who did wash-drawings for *Harper's* while still a boy, later became a member of the board of the Metropolitan Museum of Art. Garland served as the society's vicepresident. See M. H. Dunlop, "Unfinished Business: Hamlin Garland and Edward MacDowell," *Old Northwest* 10 (1985): 175–85.

164. to Theodore Roosevelt   als, Congress

Harper and Bros.
45 Albemarle St
London. W.

Saturday. 16. [16 June 1906]

Dear President Roosevelt:
    I am following your fight with the oil and beef men with intense interest. You are doing great work. You are reported as having withdrawn an

immense body of oil and coal lands from the market, with a plan to lease them on a royalty. *This is right.* That is the way to cripple the monopolies. To open to the highest bidder the coal and oil lands of Oklahoma and Ind. territory alone would check both oil and coal monopoly. It is of course the very thing we Grange men have been wanting but we wont say so—at least I hope no one will raise the cry—Your fame is very great over here. Bernard Shaw, Kipling, Zangwill all spoke of you with enthusiasm. And well they may. Personally I want you to remain in four years more notwithstanding I am a free-trader. It looks like Bryan again and I like Bryan, but I want to see you have a chance to carry out your magnificent reforms.[1] The price of building material is becoming almost prohibitive and the free-traders (or the tariff reformers) are going to be very strong next year. From my standpoint as an out-sider it looks as though the fight is to be a hot one.—I know a good deal about Sinclair's attempts to get into the limelight and I confess to a prejudice against him.[2] However he seems to have done some good in this case.—I was most kindly received here by Embassador Reid—to whom Howells gave me a letter, and attended the reception to your daughter on Wednesday last. It was a very splendid affair and your daughter seemed to enjoy it as well as one can who must smile and shake hands with a thousand people.—[3]

More power to your good right hand is my heart felt wish.

As ever your profound admirer—
Hamlin Garland

1. William Jennings Bryan (1860–1925), a free silver advocate, became a dominant figure in the Democratic Party and was defeated by McKinley in 1896. In 1908 he was again defeated for the presidency, this time by Taft, whose nomination was dictated by Roosevelt, who had already served two terms as president.

2. A pure food and drug bill was pending in Congress but had stalled in the House. The publication of Upton Sinclair's muckraking investigation of the meat industry, *The Jungle*, in March 1906 caused Roosevelt to form the Neill-Reynolds Commission to investigate the Agriculture Department. By threatening to release this report, Roosevelt forced the bill through Congress. In June Roosevelt signed both the Pure Food and Drug and the Meat Inspection acts.

3. Whitelaw Reid (1837–1912) had been appointed Ambassador to Great Britain in May 1905. While in England, Garland attended a reception for Roosevelt's daughter, Alice Roosevelt Longsworth, and her husband, Nicholas Longsworth, a Republican congressman from Ohio, at Dorchester House in London, on 13 June 1906. The reception was attended by 1,500 guests, including Great Britain's King Edward.

165. to Hugo Münsterberg

Harper & Brothers
Franklin Square, New York

November twenty-third,
Nineteen hundred and eight

Professor Hugo Münsterberg,
Harvard University,
Cambridge, Massachusetts.

Dear Professor Münsterberg:[1]

I have read your letter with pleasure, and with care. It is a good letter,—just the kind I had hoped to get from you. I would not have been surprised nor hurt had you neglected to open the book, and yet one of the main purposes of the book has been from the start to interest scientific men in this problem.[2]

I am going to ask you to do something which I have never asked anyone to do for a work of fiction from my pen. I am going to ask you to let me use your letter, or at least, such part of it as will state fairly and fully your position. I need not say how highly I value your personality and your point of view; indeed, it is precisely the kind of view which appeals most to me, and yet I assure you that with my eyes fully open to the possibility of trickery, I have during all these years been more and more mystified by the phenomena hitherto called "spiritualistic," but which modern Italians have re-named "unexplored human biology." I am getting a little balled up here because I am dictating, but you understand what I mean.

Now, my publishers feel as I do the value of your opinion, and if you have no objection—and please be perfectly free to object—we would like to have the privilege of using at least the salient lines out of your communication to me. In order that you may not be surprised into consenting to something of which you have not retained a copy, I am enclosing a copy of your letter.

I don't know exactly how this is to be used, but it may be that they will ask me to comment upon the position; at any rate, it is well to be perfectly frank in the matter, and say that they will undoubtedly use it to stimulate interest in "The Shadow World" and the argument which it contains.

With sincere respect and admiration, I am

Very sincerely yours,
Hamlin Garland

1. Hugo Münsterberg (1863–1916), German-born psychologist who was elected president of the American Psychological Association in 1898.

2. On 16 November 1908, Münsterberg began his letter to Garland: "Let me thank you for your 'Shadow World' and for your letter. I have read the book from cover to cover and do not hesitate to say that it is certainly the most winning presentation of the spiritualistic phenomenon which I ever saw. It is thoroughly fair and yet — and yet: less would be more. You see you yourself are carried away to more complex statements the further you proceed, from the mere overorganic limbs to whole new personalities and if we have reached such a point it is clear that all which we call knowledge has not only become insignificant but must be thrown overboard in the interest of a few rare phenomena."

166. to Harrison B. Hodges — als, Players

The Players
16 Gramercy Park

Nov. 24. [1908]

Dear Mr. Hodges:[1]

On Jan 2nd *The Cliff Dwellers* of Chicago light the first fire on their hearth. This club is modelled directly after *The Players* and *The Century Assoc.* of New York City — especially has the plan of Mr Booth (for a union of the various arts) been carried out. Two-fifths of the membership may be laymen, three-fifths must be professional or directly connected with the fine arts. We start with fairly proportionate representations of painting, sculptures, poetry[,] fiction, music and architecture. Our membership including laymen is fixed at 250.

In view of the close relationship between this club and *The Players*, I think it would be a highly appreciated act if the officers of The Players should send to us a greeting to be read (if possible) by a representative member of The Players on the night of our Hanging of the Crane. — As Mr Howells said to me yesterday we are establishing traditions.[2]

We feel that we are founding a club that is worthy of a place among the brotherhood of clubs of which *The Century* and *The Players* are such admirable examples. Hoping that this suggestion will meet with your approval I am

Very sincerely yours
Hamlin Garland

President
The Cliff Dwellers

1. Harrison B. Hodges was the Secretary of The Players Club.

2. Garland followed up with three other letters requesting a representative to speak. In a letter of 24 December (Players), Garland reminded Hodges that both San Francisco's Bohemian Club and New York's Tavern Club were to have poems read by a Players Club representative, so the Cliff Dwellers "must have *The Players'* greeting read by some distinguished member if possible." The actor Otis Skinner (1858–1942) read the Players' greeting during the 6 January ceremony.

167. to Thomas Wentworth Higginson   als, U of Iowa

The Players
Sixteen Gramercy Park

Dec. 15. [1908]

Dear Colonel Higginson:

I know you will be interested in the new club which I have helped to organize in Chicago. It is a kind of Century Club—a union of writers, painters, sculptors[,] musicians, actors, and architects in Chicago and vicinity. It is the first successful attempt at bringing these elements into one organization and as its president I am anxious to have it start off happily. On Jan. 6th we have a fire-lighting ceremony wherein our relation to the America of the past and the present will be shown. If the spirit moves you, wont you as a representative of the old New England send a few words of greeting to the new New England. Our fellows would highly appreciate it and would be delighted to have you accept honorary membership in the club.[1]

With greeting from the son of a "transplanted New Englander"

I am very sincerely yours
Hamlin Garland

1. In his reply of 19 December, Higginson declined Garland's offer of an honorary membership in The Cliff Dwellers. After reminiscing about his pleasant memories of

Chicago, he said: "I should feel honored by being an honorary member as you kindly suggest; but I am within three days of 85 and doubt if I ever see Chicago again."

168. to Harrison B. Hodges   als, Players

6427 Greenwood Ave.
Chicago

Dec. 20. [1908?]

Dear Mr Hodges: I do not know any of the men in this present list of candidates and so I vote against them on general principles. We can have the best in America and I see no reason why we should overcrowd our space with those who have no special claim upon us. I am not saying that these men are not eligible but in general I still feel that the board does not take high enough view of the possibilities of the club. It should be a meeting place of the fine arts and the most distinguished laymen. It is the best equipped club in America—I mean it has the mellow charm, the distinction that comes from Booth's founding and the association of great actors, writers and musicians. Why let down the bars to those who are merely tyros in the arts, journalists of untried powers, and others who are excellent men in themselves but who lend nothing to the interest and dignity of the club? *The Players* is a singular and splendid opportunity to build up and perpetuate a fellow-ship among the artists and actors and literary men of America and I for one am sorry to see any laxity in membership list. I should like to see it difficult for men like myself to get in. It ought to be a distinction to belong to *The Players*. We are not in need of members. Why not become each year more selective?—I do not mean to debar youth but I would scrutinize youth. I would inquire closely into fitness and I would demand some marked achievement. I dont mean to say that laymen should be shut out but they should be *distinguished* laymen. As a non-resident I make these suggestions with only mild emphasis knowing that what you do is really none of my business. Please take my remarks in the light of suggestion merely.

Hamlin Garland

169. to Donald Robertson   als, Northwestern

6427 Greenwood Avenue

Chicago

[6 February 1909]

Dear Robertson:[1]

The criticisms are generally unfavorable I think but that does not mean that the play is actually a failure. It interested the people right through to the end but it did not arouse enthusiasm. I am very grateful to you and to the whole company. Wont you thank them for me. Your hurried departure made it impossible for us to talk matters over—so I put into this letter my belief that we can make a moderate success with the play. I wish you could produce it at Peoria—and one or two other places.—The real test is—did it interest the people. I think it did. Of course they talk of its lack of this and that as they did of Moody's play[2] but that will not matter if the interest is warm enough and cumulative enough.—I am off for New York on the 10^{30} train. Will return whenever I am needed. Probably I will be here on the 16th of Feb.—

Yours hopefully

Hamlin Garland

1. Donald Robertson (1860–1926) headed the Donald Robertson Players (1907–9) and the Drama Players (1911–13), Chicago theater troupes dedicated to offering innovative Continental plays. As part of an effort to include American plays in his repertory, Robertson staged Garland's play *Miller of Boscobel* at Fullerton Hall of Chicago's Art Institute on 3 February after two tryouts in Madison and Appleton, Wisconsin (29 and 30 January). See Kathryn Whitford, "*Miller of Boscobel*: Hamlin Garland's Labor Play," *Midcontinent American Studies Journal* 8 (1967): 33–42.

2. William Vaughn Moody's *The Great Divide*, which had opened as *A Sabine Woman* to poor reviews in Chicago in April 1906 before going on, after revision, to become a major hit in New York in October 1906.

170. to William Dean Howells

als, Harvard

6427 Greenwood Ave.

April 6. [1909]

Dear Mr Howells:

I dont think you have done Herrick an injustice in your review. I *feel* his purpose in the book but as a matter of expression perhaps he left it a bit ambiguous.[1]

Yours as ever
Hamlin Garland

1. Garland apparently read an advance copy of Howells's "The Novels of Robert Herrick," *North American Review* 189 (June 1909): 812–20, in which Howells praised Herrick's work in general but expressed misgivings about his depiction of adultery in *Together.* "The question is whether a woman who despises the weakness or badness of her husband to the extreme of going off for several days and living with the man she has come to love, can be taken to have sufficiently expiated her sin by refusing, when left free, to marry the man she lawlessly loves" (p. 814).

171. to Frederick A. Duneka

als, Morgan

The Players
Sixteen Gramercy Park

Feb. 17. [1910]

Dear Duneka:

I hope this will find you at your desk for Major Leigh and I dont work well together. I dont like his attitude toward authors in general and myself in particular. There is no reason for violent speech or bullying gestures. Why is it that publishers lose their tempers when an author differs with them as to the value of a commodity? One would think an amicable trade might be made in M.S. as in bricks or cloth. To be loyal to a publishing house is one thing to bully an author is quite another thing. I am too old in the game to submit to this kind of treatment. Leigh becomes furious the moment my side of the case is stated. This is unpleasant and I dont care to put myself in the way of any more of this violent speech. I have a good book and so far from receding from the terms of my others I am disposed to advance.[1] If Harper and Bros want the book on my terms well and good if not I'll go elsewhere.

I intend to speak my mind quite freely at all times and if Major Leigh
cant put up with it I dont feel inclined to have any further business dealings with him. The old idea of the sovereignty of the publisher and the
meek suppliance of the author is out-lawed, for me at least.

In the hope that you will be at your post soon — I am

Very sincerely yours
Hamlin Garland

1. Garland refers to *Cavanagh, Forest Ranger*, which Harper published in 1910. On
23 February 1910 Duneka wrote to reassure Garland that *Cavanagh* was important to
the firm: "We shall push it with all our energy and we expect to advertise it liberally —
at least as proportionately liberally as we have ever advertised any one of your books."

172. to William Dean Howells   als, Harvard

6427 Greenwood Avenue
Chicago

Mar. 29. [1910]

Dear Mr Howells: Your letter came this morning and I gratefully acknowledge and welcome your criticism.[1] I have *not* measured up to my opportunity but perhaps waiting would have been of no avail. The plain truth
is I watched the Forestry Service develop for sixteen years and it was only
last summer that the motive to use it came. I'm running low on motives.
I don't care to write love-stories or stories of adventure and I can not
revert to the prairie life without falling into the reminiscent sadness of the
man of fifty.

My own belief is that my work is pretty well done but as I remember
the cordial endorsement of men like yourself and Gilder I have no reason
to complain. I have had in way of honor (and pay) all I deserve — probably. I am dissatisfied only on the artistic side. Why does not our literature
tally with the big things we do as a people? I had hopes of doing it once
but that was only the foolish egotism of youth. I find myself appalled by
the multitude of men all addressing themselves to the same theme, the
same scenes, the same characters. (It was not so in Hawthorne's day). I
start on a poem now — and suddenly recall that someone else has done it
— better. In the same way we say there is an infinite number of characters in

The Activist: 1900–1918   199

American life but we don't see them—we only see types handled by somebody else. Then the omnipresent press! The reporters wear every new subject to rags before creative men have a chance at it. Don't you see that this will happen to my Forest Ranger? I had to "beat them to it" or come in six months from now with a wornout theme and an indifferent or yawning public. I agonized over those points before consenting to the immediate publication of the book. For once in my life I anticipate the journalist and I take a malicious satisfaction in that.—In a sense the theme is all there. Shorthanded perhaps, but indicated pretty clearly so far as the ranger end of it is concerned—If only I had succeeded in making the reader feel a little plainer the epic side of the ranger's life I would not lament my haste. The mountains I hope and believe are really in the book as it stands. I wish I could take you really through some of those prodigious effects of cloud and peak—but it can only be seen from the back of a horse.

With sincere regards to Mrs Howells and with the hope that she is to recover her former health and spirits

I am as ever your disciple—
Hamlin Garland

P.S. If you write about me please speak your mind with the utmost plainness—H.G.

1. This is in response to Howells's criticisms of *Cavanagh* in his letter of 27 March 1910. Among other things, Howells argues that Garland "should have made more of it; you had most interesting people in hand and a prodigious scene, and I wish you had given us the drama of the epoch more deeply and largely than you have done. It was a pity to have cramped so noble a scheme to the measure of a contemporaneous incident. But I liked your people, and I followed them to the end, only wishing there were more of the tale, and more circumstance and detail both in respect to the dirty little cowtown and the sublime country. One day, I hope you will revert to the temper of your first work, and give us a picture of the wild life you know so well, on the lines of 'Main-Traveled Roads.'" The "contemporaneous incident" refers to the Ballinger-Pinchot controversy. See Garland to Roosevelt, 1 April 1902, letter 132, note 1. Garland later explained that the novel was hastily written in six weeks under pressure from Frederick A. Duneka, "who was (like most publishers) enslaved to a program" (*Daughter*, p. 347).

In a related letter of 9 March 1910, Gifford Pinchot wrote to Garland about an introduction that he was preparing for *Cavanagh*: "I have just finished your book and shall hope to get my introduction completed tomorrow . . . Now as to the book itself: you have struck in the center of the problem which the Forest Service had to handle in very many of the National Forests when it first took charge. You have, of course, made the cattle and sheepmen wickeder than you would have made them had you been writing a scientific discussion of the question, and I think you somewhat under-estimated the willingness of the West to accept the new order; but I have nowhere else seen a cleaner statement of the difficulties with which we were confronted. For the most part we have already gone by the point your story occupies, and it is the great merit of the Service that it has had a share in pushing the West past that point."

173. to William Dean Howells

als, Harvard

6427 Greenwood Avenue

Chicago

April 3 [1910]

Dear Mr. Howells:

No indeed—I did not resent in the least anything you said because its all true.[1] Your first letter is the truest—your second letter is too kind. The book has good spots in it but on the whole it is not worthy the time and place and the man—I mean the ranger. I do not see another book (even of this quality) when I look into my mind. Writing is coming to be a weariness and a plodding. What is the use when all the themes are old and one has grown old with them?—Certain forms and seasons of nature interest me still and yet I can't write of them with original power so I do not write of them at all—If you are ever moved to write of "Cavanagh" please "sweeten it good and plenty"—as they say out west. You need not fear—I know my own limitations too well to ever flinch when they are mentioned.

With regards to you and yours
believe me yours gratefully
Hamlin Garland

1. Howells's response to Garland on 30 March 1910 contained considerably more praise for the novel than did his first letter: "I am afraid I hurt you by my over-scrupled praise. There is not a falsely drawn figure in your book; the scene is nobly imagined and boldly set, under that mountain sky with the mountain breath blowing over it. The girl and the mother are both mighty well; and that awful flyblown hostelry; and those old beasts of men lusting round! What I felt was the hurry of the book where there ought to have been rest. / Dear boy, *don't* think you're written out—you're just at the beginning of your greatness. Don't be daunted by the vastness of our material achievements. It's more for Wisconsin that you and your literature have come out of it, than all the mines, and farms and railroads in the State amount to."

174. to Nicholas Vachel Lindsay

als, usc

The Cliff-Dwellers
168 Michigan Avenue
Chicago

Mar. 7. [1911]

Dear Mr Lindsay:[1]

I, too, am poor but I can help in your crusade—and I am sending you two dollars. I wish you would mail one copy of your magazine to the Librarian of the Cliff Dwellers, and one copy to Henry B. Fuller, care *The Record Herald,* and one more copy to me. I am quite as deeply moved by your out-burst as was my friend Wheeler of *Current Literature.*[2] You are a phenomenon. I wish I could be of service to you as a lecturer perhaps I can be—I greet you as a poet as well as a Village builder—and to build a town right requires poetic vision.

One thing more. Send me your portrait to paste in this book—and if there is any book of mine which you'd like to have please let me know. If you had written nothing but the lines about the acorns I should still continue to call you a poet.[3]

With hearty congratulations—
Hamlin Garland

1. Nicholas Vachel Lindsay (1879–1931), known as "the vagabond poet," blended a visionary populism with a "new" poetry based on strong rhythms and chant. His best-known works include *General William Booth Enters Into Heaven and Other Poems* (1913) and *The Congo and Other Poems* (1914).

2. Garland refers to "An Illinois Art Revivalist," *Current Literature* 50 (March 1911): 320–23, an unsigned review by the editor of the periodical, Edward J. Wheeler, of Lindsay's self-published *The Village Magazine* (1910). Wheeler praised Lindsay's fanciful blend of illustration and poetry and his aesthetic evangelism and reprinted an excerpt, "An Editorial for the Art Student Who Has Returned to the Village." Lindsay noted at the top of this letter, in response to Garland's later request to return his letters for use in his memoirs, "I cannot find your first letter. This is obviously the second one. Vachel Lindsay." See Garland to Lindsay, 18 May 1931, letter 332. Garland discusses Lindsay at length in *Companions*, pp. 462–71.

3. *The Village Magazine* was adorned with Lindsay's art work, some in the form of acorns scattered through the pages. Garland refers to a poem that begins, "'Great oaks from little acorns grow,' / Each acorn is a magazine / Of leaves and twigs in embryo; / The strongest forest ever seen / Was once a hickory nut or so, / A maple seed some bird let go, / A bitter acorn, brown and green."

175. to Upton Sinclair

als, Indiana U

6427 Greenwood Avenue
Chicago

Mar. 14 [1911]

Dear Mr Sinclair:

I have read your book with great interest,[1] and while I can not justify all you have put into type it seems to me to be a significant and sincere utterance. I can not tell how much of it is fact and how much fiction but it reads as if it were all fact—a real human document. There is a great deal of very plain speaking in the book and I assume you are prepared for war. I found the story too prolix and too didactic to hold my interest at every point but as a whole it is profoundly appealing. If it is based upon your own experience (as I assume it is) your persistence in the face of such discouragement is heroic and deserves success. Your chapter on the birth of the child is terribly true and very noble in its implications. If the men who make maternity a jest and woman a play thing could be brought to read this chapter there would be fewer libertines in the world. I do not care to enter into any defense of the exceedingly plain-spoken—or rather out-spoken—pages of this book but I will say that I do not find the sexual side of it unduly insisted upon. Your hero is interested in woman but he is even more profoundly interested in literature and in social betterment, and yet I've no doubt you will be accused of writing a salacious work. I dont know that you are seeking advice—probably not—but at the risk of seeming somewhat like the advisors of your hero, I suggest that you restate some of the passages in this book. It's the same old problem that confronted Whitman—and that confronts those of us who would like to press the reading of Whitman on the young. If only people *would* see the significance and high purpose in "Leaves of Grass" but they dont and they wont, and these democratic songs are still almost universally tabooed. I have followed your career (at a distance) since your first letter to me and I should be glad to see you make a success without any further sensational advertising. This book is worth it but in its present form it will be open to the charge of having been written to shock the reader. To me it seems a human document, sincere if rebellious, and I should be sorry to see its good points lost in a war over its extreme and self-revealing candor.

Very sincerely yours
Hamlin Garland

The Activist: 1900–1918 203

1. Upton Sinclair (1878–1968), prolific novelist whose works include *The Jungle* (1906), *King Coal* (1917), and *Oil* (1927). Sinclair had written to Garland, 8 March 1911, concerned about the publication potential of his autobiographical novel *Love's Pilgrimage*, which included discussion of the sexual limitations of his marriage; he enclosed a copy of the manuscript; and he requested "a letter which I can use in defence of the book, if need be." Garland evidently lobbied the publisher, Mitchell Kennerley, on behalf of the book, because a letter from Kennerley dated 21 March 1911 informs Garland that he will publish the book, despite earlier reservations. Garland found the book hard to lay down, as he wrote in his diary on 13 March: "I stayed at home and read Sinclair's new book and appallingly frank book—reflecting all the storms of his private—his most private life—It is the frankest book ever written in America. Franker than any German or French book I have any knowledge of—I read till mid-night to the hurt of my eyes."

176. to Nicholas Vachel Lindsay

als, usc

The Cliff-Dwellers
168 Michigan Avenue
Chicago

Mar. 30 [1911]

Dear Mr Lindsay:

To be perfectly candid I think you over-value the drawings and under-value your verse.[1] You are not an "artist" to me—you're a writer. I think the most of the men consider the drawings imaginative and quaint but not important. So go ahead with your writing. As to the publishing. If Small Maynard will take a book of verse let them have it. It will give you a start. I consider Kennerley a better publisher however. You shall have "Rose of Dutchers Coolly"—and I will return the tramp verses soon.[2]

Very sincerely yours
Hamlin Garland

1. In a letter of 26 March, Lindsay had asked Garland, "Can anything be done with my Village Improvement Parade? Do the Art Institute people like it? It is the best I have done, poor as it is, and I would like to put it somewhere where it will *stay* put." Lindsay's "Village Improvement Parade" consisted of a set of drawings which he gave away during his walks; Mitchell Kennerley published *General William Booth Enters Into Heaven and Other Poems* in 1913 and Lindsay's account of his walking tour, *Adventures While Preaching the Gospel of Beauty*, in 1914.

2. Lindsay had requested a copy of *Rose* in exchange for "a set of War Bulletins," an

irregularly issued collection of poetry and prose. Garland was also reading the manuscript of "A Handy Guide for Beggars."

177. to Alice Kauser als, Virginia

Mapleshade West Salem
Wisconsin

July 19 [1911]

Dear Miss Kauser: [1]

As secretary of the Chicago Theater Society I am on the look-out for
the new and unconventional American comedy. Can you suggest to me
any play of striking literary as well as dramatic merit which while not
fitted for the use of a star—and not sufficiently popular to tempt the
manager who seeks a long run, is after all of such appeal as would make
it suitable for a repertory company? If you can help me to any such piece
I shall be very glad. We want to give an opening to plays of the quality
(say) of Granville Barker and Synge [2]—plays that have the quality of a fine
piece of fiction but which act well when handled by a company where
there are no stars. Do such plays come to you? Is there a body of dramatic
writing of high quality which the ordinary manager does not consider
profitable?—

I shall be very glad to have you write me along these lines and when I
come to New York it will give me pleasure to talk the matter with you—I
feel that I know you through my friends the Hernes. Pardon my not
knowing your office address.

Very sincerely yours
Hamlin Garland

address
care The Cliff Dwellers.
Orchestra Hall
Chicago.

1. Alice Kauser (1872–1945), play broker and author's representative. Garland's brief
account of the founding of the Chicago Theater Society appears in *Companions*, p. 471.
His diaries reveal that he was intensely preoccupied with the society, so much so that
he neglected his own work. As it became clear that the society would not dedicate itself
to the promotion of American drama, his daily comments become increasingly bitter.
He resigned in November 1913. See Keith Newlin, "Uplifting the Stage: Hamlin Garland

and the Chicago Theater Society," *Journal of American Drama and Theatre* 8 (Winter 1996): 1–17.

2. Harley Granville Barker (1877–1946), British playwright. His *Voysey Inheritance* (1905) and *Madras House* (1910) explore the conflicts between an older and younger generation and were popular offerings of the noncommercial theaters. John Millington Synge (1871–1909), Irish playwright whose most important works include *Riders to the Sea* (1904) and *The Playboy of the Western World* (1907).

178. to Edith R. McCormick   tlc, usc

Greeley, Colorado

July 24, 1911.

Mrs. Harold F. McCormick
Lake Forest, Ill.

Dear Mrs. McCormick:—[1]

I am enclosing with this letter a letter to the Shuberts and a copy of our list of plays which you can forward to them, if the letter and the list meet your approval.[2] Of course in submitting this list to the Shuberts we must be very careful to make the list just what we want it. The only way we have of protecting ourselves, is not to put on it anything we do not want produced. I wish it could wait until we have all had opportunity to talk the matter over, but I will leave the matter in your hands. Mr. Bissell will be back in a few days and you can consult with Mr. Logan and Mr. Taylor concerning the predicament in which we find ourselves.[3]

I have had a letter from Mr. Robertson in which he seems to feel that I have in some way done him wrong by my criticisms but with full knowledge of the feelings of the newspapers in Chicago, I still hold to my belief that his policy is very short-sighted to say the least.[4]

Now Mrs. McCormick, have you not someone in mind who can take my place as Secretary of the Chicago Theater Society. I am afraid it is not going to work out along the lines I had hoped and if we begin our first season without a single American play, as we seem likely to be forced to do, my usefulness is ended. I should be very glad to be able to escape the responsibility and distraction that accompanies this position. I only went into it because I thought it might prove an inspiration to American dramatists, and if you have anyone who expresses your own feeling in the matter more freely than I, I hope you will be free to say so.[5]

Very sincerely yours,

1. Edith R. McCormick (1872–1932), the wife of a prominent millionaire and the daughter of John D. Rockefeller, was the president and principal benefactor of the Chicago Theater Society.

2. The Chicago Theater Society acted as a sponsoring agency, providing a guarantee fund for its productions. The Shubert Brothers, based in New York, handled the business of renting theaters and managing the details of the productions. As the chair of the Play Selection Committee, Garland was to provide a list of thirty plays to the Shuberts, who would then select eight for production by Donald Robertson's Drama Players.

3. Arthur Bissell, the Society's Business Secretary; Frank Logan, its Treasurer; and Bert L. Taylor, a columnist at the *Chicago Tribune* and probably a member of the Play Selection Committee.

4. In drawing up a tentative list of plays for consideration, Garland had leaned heavily toward American authors, and in particular plays by his good friends William Vaughn Moody (*The Faith Healer*, 1909), Augustus Thomas (*Arizona*, 1899), and James Herne (*Shore Acres*, 1892). Garland prematurely leaked his proposed list to the press before the society had made the final selection; in response, Robertson gave his list to James O'Donnell Bennett of the *Chicago Record-Herald* (Diaries, 18 July 1911). The resulting controversy nearly shattered the fledgling society. Robertson complained bitterly in a letter to Garland, 14 July 1911: "You not I gave out that list of plays—that has met with such a chorus of disapproval and by the number of letters I have received it would seem I am to [be] held responsible for their selection. As I told Mrs McCormick, if you finally decide you wish these plays I will loyally endeavour to produce them, but I think it would be little less than criminal in me not to point out to your committee the mistake they are making in my judgement." For Garland's public attempt to clarify matters, see "Starring the Play," *Nation* 93 (20 July 1911): 54.

5. McCormick replied, 4 August 1911, that she agreed the society should produce three American plays and pleaded with Garland not to resign: "Please do not think of leaving this house! It is so fine, and will be so far reaching and so developing to the Drama and to American Playwrights."

179. to Donald Robertson

tlc, usc

Greeley, Colorado

July 24, 1911.

Mr. Donald Robertson,
The Cliff Dwellers,
Chicago, Ill.

Dear Robertson:—

I am just writing Mrs. McCormick enclosing a list of the plays to be sent to the Shuberts upon her approval. If you are in town before I return you might talk this matter over with her. I have sent to her a very good drama based on Dombey and Son, written by H. P. Mosson and as the Dickens' Centenary comes on the Seventh of February, it has been suggested by some of our friends that the production of a Dickens play might be a very nice opening for our season.

The committee are agreed that there is no special reason for the production of the Fan which Taylor and Fuller consider not a worthy representation of Goldoni and hence have chosen the Coffee House and suggest to Shubert that Mr. Fuller be asked to translate it. Taylor has it partly translated but Fuller could do it better than anyone I know. The Committee is a unit in its desire that we shall have at least three representative American plays on our list and that so far as possible all morbid and gloomy plays should be avoided. I have just read both Lucifer and The Stronger and I find Butti's play much better technically than Giocoso's but its close is exceedingly painful and for that reason I am in doubt whether to advocate it or not. If we could find something equally good with a less tragic ending I think we should use it. I have Royle's Struggle Everlasting and I am asking Mrs. McCormick to read that.[1] I wish you would also read it for it is out of the common. A very strong and original morality play. I have sent to Mrs. McCormick several of these plays and the authors you will find either at Mr. Post's desk or at Mr. Bissells. I feel sure that before long we will secure a play that is genuinely worth while that we can add to our list and make the third play to represent America.[2]

The question at issue between us is merely this; the policy of making a confidant of one dramatic editor and ignoring the others, is sure to lead to very serious friction and the guarantors of the Society would suffer from their combined attack upon what we are trying to do. I hope when you get to the city you will get into touch with Mr. Chas. W. Collins. Mr. Post and Mr. Bissell can give you his telephone address, and that you will make all your announcements through him.[3]

I shall be here until Friday and next week my address will be Boulder, Colorado.

Sincerely yours,

1. The plays Garland refers to are Goldoni's *The Fan* (1763) and *The Coffee House* (1750), Butti's *Lucifer* (1900), Giacosa's *The Stronger* (1904), and Edwin Royle's *The Struggle Everlasting* (1907).

2. The plays by Continental authors that the society eventually settled upon were *The Learned Ladies* (Molière, 1672), *The Thunderbolt* (Pinero, 1908), *The Lady from the*

Sea (Ibsen, 1889), *The Stronger* (Giacosa), *The Passing of the Torch* (Hervieu, 1901), *The Coffee House* (Goldoni), and *The Voysey Inheritance* (Granville-Barker, 1905; subsequently dropped). The three plays by American authors were *Gold* (Ancilla Hunter, 1911), *June Madness* (Henry K. Webster, 1911) and *The Maternal Instinct* (Robert Herrick and Harrison Rhodes, 1911).

3. Charles W. Collins (1880–1964) had been the drama critic for the *Chicago Inter-Ocean* and was the Chicago Theater Society's press agent; Louis F. Post (1849–1928) was the editor of the liberal journal *The Public*, an advocate of the single tax, and was active in Chicago club life.

180. to Alice Kauser

als, Virginia

"Mapleshade"
West Salem, Wisconsin

Aug 29 [1911]

Dear Miss Kauser:

As I wrote you before we do not hope to get plays written for the millions but we do hope to get plays that are out of the race for instant acceptance by the masses or classes. There must be plays written as good books are written without regard for the *dollar*. These plays if they are really *written*—we would like to see. We dont want the conventional situations nor the characters that reappear in every "success." We will read the plays sent to us irrespective of their commercial appeal.—

I shall be glad to see Mr Oppenheim's plays.[1]

Sincerely yours
Hamlin Garland

Did you see Royle's "Struggle Everlasting"[2] when it was produced in New York? He seems to have gotten outside the rest in that play—

1. James Oppenheim (1882–1932), poet and novelist, became the editor of the avant-garde magazine *The Seven Arts* in 1916. His play *Night* was produced by the Provincetown Players in 1917.

2. Edwin Milton Royle (1862–1942) was best known for his romantic Indian play *The Squaw Man* (1905). In *The Struggle Everlasting* Royle attempted a modern morality play with the abstract characters Mind and Soul struggling for possession of Body, a courtesan.

181. to Alice Kauser

als, Virginia

"Mapleshade"
West Salem, Wisconsin

Sept. 8 [1911]

Dear Miss Kauser:

I have read the Oppenheim plays and find them all very interesting but "The Seventh Night" hits me hardest. I am returning "The Three" and "The Call of the Million." If we had our own theater ready to hand I would urge the production of Mr Oppenheim's little Jewish play.[1] It is admirable in all ways and has almost the best European finish to it. I am sending it to the other members of the committee. This play in a broad sense is what I am hoping to develop. I want to see our dramatists get out of the rut in both theme and treatment. This little play in it's way is sociologic as Barker's plays are, and is at the same time moving and very simple in its method. It seems like a bit out of life — the life we New Englanders know so little about. Please send to Mr Oppenheim my sincere regards.

Very sincerely yours
Hamlin Garland

1. We have been unable to discover any evidence of production of these plays.

182. to Alice Kauser

tls, usc

The Chicago Theater Society
"The Cliff Dwellers"
Orchestra Hall
220 South Michigan Avenue
Chicago

Oct. 7, 1911

Miss Alice Kauser,
1402 Broadway, N.Y.

Dear Miss Kauser:

I have read the play GOLD by Angela Hunter, and I quite agree with you. It is a very remarkable play. I don't believe we can consider this for our first season, but I should like to see it done. It is a play to be very

carefully considered. What can you tell me about the writer?[1] It is a sort
of grim, Arnold Bennett interpretation, and the writer is unquestionably
a person of power and discernment. I am very much obliged for your
kindness in letting me see this M.S. With your permission I am going to
ask one or two others of our Committee to read it.

Very sincerely yours,
Hamlin Garland

1. Hunter has not been identified. Her first name is variously spelled "Ancella," "Ancilla," and "Angela" in the press and in Garland's letters. In an extended review of the society's season, Robert Morss Lovett describes the play as being about the effects of inherited greed. A domineering father has passed on his greed to his three daughters: one has "inherited his sordid greed"; another "has an equally unintelligent desire for a social career and power"; the third "is the victim of an undiscriminating appetite for pleasure." The play concludes in a tangle of extortion, manipulation, and extramarital sex. See Lovett, "The Season of the Chicago Theatre Society," *Drama* no. 6 (May 1912): 238–59.

183. to Nicholas Vachel Lindsay

tlc, usc

Oct. 21, 1911.

Nicholas V. Lindsay
S. 5th St.,
Springfield, Ill.

Dear Mr. Lindsay:

I am returning your ms. herewith, because I really think you had better
work on it a little bit more.[1] It will not do to peril the success of the ms.
by being too hasty. What I would like to see you do is to carry your quaint
advice all the way through the ms. Wherever the fancy strikes you insert
some phrase that would act as a suggestion to the beggars who are supposed to be following your lead.

I think the Outlook people would be very apt to consider it favorably,
but I would be very glad to send it to any other publisher. It is very condensed, as you say, and it is extremely good as far as it goes, but you can
carry it farther.

With best wishes,
Very sincerely,

1. Garland refers to the manuscript of *A Handy Guide for Beggars*, a series of sketches concerning Lindsay's tramping adventures, many of which were published separately in the *Outlook* before appearing in book form in 1916.

184. to Nicholas Vachel Lindsay

tlc, USC

May 20, 1912.

Dear Mr. Lindsay:

Your proposed expedition interests me greatly and I hope you will keep us fully informed of your route, and if there is anything I can do for you, I hope you will let me know. Probably, you will not accept of a letter of introduction or any other help of that general nature.[1] The Cliff Dwellers ought to be posted with regard to this trip of yours, and I will be very glad to put a little bulletin on our Board if you will formulate it for me.

I am very glad to know that John Phillips[2] has taken you up. I expect great things of you.

Very sincerely yours,

1. Lindsay had announced in a letter to Garland, 18 May 1912, that he was embarking on a two-year tour of the West, by foot, to gather material for his poems. As he explained in *Adventures While Preaching the Gospel of Beauty*, his "rules of travel" "were to have nothing to do with cities, railroads, money, baggage or fellow tramps. I was to begin to ask for dinner about a quarter of eleven and for supper, lodging and breakfast about a quarter of five. . . . I was to preach the Gospel of Beauty." He would take only *Rhymes to Be Traded for Bread* and drawings from *The Village Improvement Parade* (quoted in *Adventures, Rhymes and Designs*, ed. Robert F. Sayre [New York: Eakins, 1968], p. 49.)

2. John Sandburn Phillips, editor of the *American Magazine*, which would publish Lindsay's "Rules of the Road" in its June 1912 issue.

185. to William Dean Howells

tlc, USC

June 29, 1912.

Dear Mr. Howells:

There is a question at issue between the Harper office and myself which you may be able to help settle. I have written a considerable volume, probably over a hundred thousand words, called A SON OF THE MIDDLE BOR-

DER,[1] which is a study of my own life and surroundings from the return of my father in 1865 to the establishment in West Salem. It is of course autobiography, but it is something more. It makes large account of my father and mother, who were always on the border, until my brother and I rescued them in 1893 and brought them back to Wisconsin.

Now the problem is this, Major Leigh is afraid that the publication of this book will [be] taken to be my "swan song" as a novelist, and he is therefore reluctant to bring it out. On the other hand, the book interests me very much, and as I have been just a quarter of a century a writer of fiction, it seems to me that I could, with perfect propriety, bring out a book of this character. As I tell the Major, it is all a question of whether the book is worth while in itself. I think it highly probable that I shall never write another novel, for the reason that love stories no longer seem to me worth while. However that may be, I see no good reason why I should not put a period in my career by the publication of this partial autobiography. What is your own feeling about it. I wish you would write me at your earliest convenience, for if the book is to be brought out, it will have to go into the mill very soon.

I don't think it is an egotistic book, because I have gone beyond that stage. It is rather an attempt to catch for my children some part of the beauty and significance of the life of the border during the forty years of my remembrance. You have been my constant advisor during these twenty-five later years, and I very much wish you would let me know precisely how the plan strikes you.[2]

Yours, as ever,

1. "A Son of the Middle Border, A Personal History," first appeared in *Colliers* 53, issues of 28 March, 18 April, 9 May, 7 June, and 8 September 1914. It was published in substantially revised book form by Macmillan and Company in August 1917.

2. Howells replied on 2 July 1912: "I understand why Major Leigh should have pause, but not why he should remain in it. It seems to me that such a book as you contemplate would be important and delightful, and would add to the interest in your other books. I for one should like to read it."

186. to Theodore Roosevelt

tls, Congress

The Cliff-Dwellers
220 South Michigan Avenue
Chicago

Aug 7, 1912.

Colonel Roosevelt
Oyster Bay, L. I.

Dear Colonel:

It was a thrilling Convention, and as I listened to you, I got historical perspective on the whole thing.[1] It stirred my fighting blood, and I am offering myself to the campaign committee in the hope that I can be of some real service in the movement. I saw Pinchot for a few moments, and secured from him a promise of help in getting together some inside facts concerning your administration. I did this because I want to make my talk very direct and personal. I want to be able to answer some of the mistaken statements which are very common in the mouths of your enemies. I shall not be East until November, unless I come to speak in the campaign. I should like to have a suggestion from you, if there is any special work in the campaign which you think I am fitted to do.[2] Everything seems to be working out for the best, and I am more than hopeful of the November results.

Yours, as ever
Hamlin Garland

1. During the first national convention of the Progressive Party, held in Chicago, 5–7 August 1912, Roosevelt became the party's presidental candidate.

2. In his reply of 14 August 1912, Roosevelt suggested Garland confer with Henry S. Cochems, chairman of the Progressive National Committee's speaker's bureau, and Joseph Medill McCormick, who headed the western division of the Progressive Party. Garland published an editorial entitled "Roosevelt Praised as Man and Leader by Hamlin Garland" in the *Chicago Evening Post*, 21 October 1912 (clipping, item #723) in which he explains why people should support Roosevelt and the Progressive Party.

187. to Harriet Monroe   als, U Chicago

Mapleshade West Salem
Wisconsin

Sept. 13. [1912]

Dear Miss Monroe: [1]

I gladly subscribe to the magazine and hope it may succeed beyond your present hope—which I know is high. I shall be very willing to shout for it although I am afraid the day for wide-spread appreciation of first-class verse is past. The newspapers with their easily apprehended lines seem to have killed off the reflective reader. I shall be in town again soon and may be able to discuss the matter with you verbally. A magazine such as this promises to be will be a credit to the city.

Very cordially yours
Hamlin Garland

1. Harriet Monroe (1860–1936) founded *Poetry: A Magazine of Verse* in 1912 and soon became renowned for her championing of the "new" poetry, including the work of Vachel Lindsay, Carl Sandburg, D. H. Lawrence, Ezra Pound, H. D., William Butler Yeats, and others. Garland himself published four poems in the November 1913 issue: "Magic," "A Gray Sunset," "To A Captive Crane," and "The Mountains Are a Lonely Folk."

188. to Lorado Taft   als, USC

West Salem. Wis.

Oct. 9. [1912]

Dear Lorado:

I am writing in the midst of desolation and creosote. [1] The old house is riddled from cellar to garret. Fire or water is over it all but the frame-work is standing and the inside can be restored. My M.S.S. were saved but many keep-sakes, mementoes and family portraits are gone. Father lost several that he prized. Our Enneking—the beautiful spring scene and the T. C. Steele that we loved and a pastel by Ault—are in ashes.—No it isnt funny but we're bearing it with as much humor as we can command. I was used up for one day so lame that I could hardly move but I'm tearing around today clearing up the mess. It *is* a mess. The girl is better and the children are quite recovered from the shock. The loss will exceed three thousand dollars. Part of it will come back to us—I hope. We cant tell till the adjuster comes.

We're all deeply obliged for your sympathy—

Yours
Hamlin

1. On 6 October 1912, the Garlands were awakened during the night by a calamitous fire. Although the Garlands escaped unharmed, their maid was burned and their home suffered significant damage. Garland recounts the effect of this fire, as well as his toil in rebuilding the homestead, in *Daughter*, pp. 355–68.

189. to Nicholas Vachel Lindsay

tlc, USC

The Cliff Dwellers
220 South Michigan Ave.
Chicago

Dec. 26, 1912.

Nicholas V. Lindsay
Springfield, Ill.

Dear Mr. Lindsay:

I fear I have bewildered you with advice.[1] The MS. as it now stands is nothing what I had hoped you would make it, and I fear I cannot tell you by letter exactly what I mean. It seems to me that you must put aside your "localism" and "Gospel of Beauty" and deal with this subject from the standpoint of literature pure and simple. The original preface was very taking and very promising, but I fear you are getting farther and farther from the notion I first had of it.

Perhaps it would be better for you to abandon this altogether, and take up a genuine connected and fluant,[2] leaving out all your preaching, and permitting yourself to tell a story. I am very sorry but I fear Mr. Kennerley would not take the MS. as it stands.

Very sincerely yours,

1. Lindsay had sent Garland a sheaf of sketches which would go into *A Handy Guide for Beggars*, published by Macmillan in 1916. Lindsay had ended his walking tour in

New Mexico, he explained in a letter dated 14 November 1912, because "I lost my
nerve."

2. A word is missing in the copy text.

190. to Wilbur L. Cross tls, Yale

The Cliff-Dwellers
220 South Michigan Avenue
Chicago

Jan 13, 1913.

Wilbur L. Cross
Yale Review
New Haven, Conn.

Dear Mr. Cross: [1]

Your communication interests me exceedingly, for the reason that I
have in my desk, as well as in my head, stories which are not precisely
suited for popular magazines, yet which are, in my judgment, the best
work I do.[2] There should be a magazine in this country hospitable to work
which is out of the ordinary in theme and treatment, and I shall be very
glad if I can be of any service to you, either by way of suggestion, or by
way of actual contribution. I cannot afford to absolutely present these
MSS. to you, but I will accept a price lower than that which I would get
for my stories of love and adventure. What could you pay per thousand
words, or, to put it another way, how large an honararian could you offer
for a story or article of four or five thousand words?

I have also in my desk a MS. upon which I have been at work for many
years, which I call A SON OF THE MIDDLE BORDER. It is based upon my
own experiences, but is almost as much a study of emigration and of the
movement of a family, as of a biography. All of my friends who have seen
it regard it as a very good example of my work, and two of them notably,
Henry B. Fuller, and John S. Phillips, consider it among the most important of my writings since MAIN TRAVELED ROADS. Would you like to see
this MS.? I should expect some pay for it, but nothing like the price which
I get for my popular fiction. One section of it deals with my migration
from Dakota to Boston, and the beginnings of my literary career in the
East. If you care to see this section of the MS., I shall be very glad to
forward it to you. In fact, you may see any of these special MSS., which

are not sufficiently wide in their appeal to make them available to magazines like the American, and McClures.

In the way of essays, I have four studies of Edwin Booth, which I have
used many times as lectures. It might be that these, which, by the way,
were read and approved by Mr. Booth himself, would come within the
scope of your review. However, I will know better after a study of the
January number, which I shall await with interest.

Very sincerely yours,
Hamlin Garland

1. Wilbur L. Cross (1862–1948), professor of English at Yale, founded the *Yale Review*
in 1911, and later became the governor of Connecticut (1930–39).

2. Cross's letter has not been located. Garland was desperate for money to rebuild
the West Salem Homestead. In later correspondence to Cross he suggested articles
about James A. Herne, Howells, and Henry James, among others.

191. to Theodore Roosevelt

als, Congress

The Cliff-Dwellers
220 South Michigan Avenue
Chicago

Jan. 22. [1913]

Dear Colonel:

I understand that you have been asked or are about to be asked to speak
in Chicago next Autumn at the Annual Meeting of the National Institute
of Arts and Letters.[1] I hope this is true *and that you will accept.* It would
make an enormous success of our meeting and it would mean much to
American Art and Letters—especially *Western* art and letters. I suggest
that you speak on the influence of the west on Literature or some such
topic—in fact I suggested it to the Committee.

Yours most faithfully
Hamlin Garland

1. During the 1912 National Institute meeting, Garland proposed that the 1913 meeting be held in Chicago to demonstrate the national scope of the organization. He was
made chairman of the committee on arrangements, gathered together the leaders of
Chicago's artistic clubs to promote the event, and embarked on a letter-writing cam-

paign to publicize the meeting. For Garland's published comment on this meeting, see
Companions, pp. 504–5, 509–10, 520–24.

192. to William Dean Howells

tlc, usc

Feb. 7, 1913

Wm. Dean Howells
Harper & Bros., Franklin Sq. N.Y.

Dear Mr. Howells:

I hope Johnson and Sedgwick[1] have told you about our great plan for
the next Annual Meeting of the Institute in Chicago. The Cliff Dwellers
will act as hosts, on this occassion, and intend to make the trip very pleasant for the Eastern members. It is my thought that the Club might properly furnish accommodations here, and also extend Pullman accommodations, as a kind of moving Club from New York to Chicago. I cannot
see that there would be any impropriety in doing this. It would leave to
the members the payment of their actual railroad fare, and their choice of
going to the Club here in Chicago.

What I am anxious for is a large attendance, and with the full co-
operation of the Thomas Orchestra and the Art Institute we can make it
the most important meeting ever held outside of New York City.

Let me know where I can address you hereafter.

Very sincerely yours,

1. Robert Underwood Johnson and Henry D. Sedgwick, the secretary of the National
Institute.

193. to Robert Underwood Johnson

tls, Am Acad

The Cliff-Dwellers
220 South Michigan Avenue
Chicago

Feb. 20, 1913

Dear Johnson:

The death of Joaquin Miller has started me writing an article on him.
As you may know, we were very good friends and when he was in Chicago

in 1898 I induced him to sit for Lorado Taft and Ralph Clarkson, and
during these sittings I kept tab pencil in hand and got a great deal out of
the old man. He was very much of the seer and mystic in his later life. Do
you want to use an article, and illustrations from these studies in an early
number of the Century? If you do please let me know.[1]

I have just had a perfectly splendid note from T.R. He is coming and
that secures the absolute success of our meeting. He does'nt want to be
pressed for an absolute promise, but indicates that I have him "hands in
the air." He's a "trump" sure enough. I think sometime in mid-summer
if we approach W. W. rightly, we can bring him into line, also.[2]

Yours sincerely,
Hamlin Garland

1. Garland's memoir of Miller appeared as "The Poet of the Sierras" in *Sunset* 30
(June 1913): 765–70. He had earlier published "An American Tolstoi: Hamlin Garland
Describes a Visit to Joaquin Miller's Farm," *Philadelphia Press*, 17 June 1894, p. 26. Ralph
Clarkson (1861–1942) was a Chicago artist active in promoting the arts.

2. President Woodrow Wilson (1856–1924), a member of both the National Institute
and the American Academy of Arts and Letters, was unable to attend but sent a letter
which was read during the ceremonies. See "West an Art Power, Immortals Find," *New
York Times*, 15 November 1913, p. 9, for the text of his message.

194. to Theodore Roosevelt

tls, Congress

The Cliff Dwellers
220 South Michigan Avenue
Chicago

March 4, 1913

Dear Colonel:

Johnson's idea is not in the least mine.[1] He represents the academic,
whilst I am a Progressive in literature as well as in politics. I am asking the
program Committee to put the arrangement of the dinner program, so
far as it relates to your place and subject, in my hands, and I think they
will do this, then you and I can discuss the matter and find out in what
way we can best serve the cause of Americanism in literature, for I would
like to see you take up some subject like THE INFLUENCE OF THE BORDER
ON AMERICAN LETTERS, or THE VALUE OF THE OPEN AIR SCHOOL OF FIC-
TION AND POETRY, or some subject which springs naturally from your

studies of THE WINNING OF THE WEST. I am saying that this meeting can be made and *must* be made the most important meeting the Institute ever held, and it must strengthen the national spirit in literature and art. I have long wanted to talk with you about the Institute and the work which it can do if we who beleive in progress take vital part in its organization. Please make no final decision until I have had time to work out a scheme which will utilize you to the highest possible advantage.

At the present moment, my thought is to ask you to be the cheif speaker for the Institute on the occassion of the official Chicago Banquet to be given by the Cliff Dwellers to the members of the Institute and Academy. I am certain our entire membership would be delighted to have you speak out of the fullness of your heart, and to place your own limit on your address.

The scheme at present involves—

First—An official banquet as a welcome to the members of the Institute, to be given by the Cliff Dwellers. Speakers Matthews, Roosevelt.
Second—A special concert by the Chicago Symphony Orchestra, made up of compositions by members of the Institute.
Third—A reception at the Art Institute, opening an immense exhibition of painting and sculpture by members of the Institute.
Fourth—A private dinner and business meeting of the Institute.
Fifth—Two regular sessions of the Institute and Academy.

The Cliff Dwellers will act as host, and I think a special train of Pullmans will be provided to bring the members on from the East. Thus, you will see it is the intention of the Committee to make this meeting national in its scope and importance. Would you consider the position which I have here outlined—I mean as cheif orator on the occassion of the banquet? I am perfectly sure that you and our Committee together can work out something that will be vital to the cause of American letters.

Hamlin Garland

1. Roosevelt had written, 26 February 1913, that Robert Underwood Johnson had asked him to speak for twenty minutes as part of a symposium. Roosevelt declined the invitation because he did not like the artificially imposed time limit and did not like sharing the podium. Garland received word in July that Roosevelt would not be able to attend the National Institute's 13–15 November meeting because he was sailing for Rio de Janeiro in October.

195. to Franklin Lane   tls, Nat'l Arch

The Cliff Dwellers
220 South Michigan Avenue
Chicago

March 21, 1913

Franklin K. Lane
Dept. of Interior
Washington, D.C.

Dear Mr. Lane:[1]

I was profoundly interested and gratified by your appointment of a man to serve as instructor in Indian music, and more especially, by the words of understanding with which you accompanied the order. I have been for many years actively interested in promoting the welfare of the red people on our various reservations, and have tried by means of novels and lectures to make my readers and hearers understand that Sioux and Cheyennes are folks like the rest of us, with very much the same parental feelings and love of nature. Under the Roosevelt administration an attempt was made, at my suggestion, to re-name the Indians using their own words, but grouping them into families as among ourselves. This work was never carried out as fully as it should have been, and the work of Dr. Eastman, who was made special feild worker for this very purpose, was never properly enforced among the schools and missions. I hope you will take this matter up and see if the young redmen cannot be saved from the handicap of ludicruous or vulgar names.

By reference to the work of Dr. Eastman, and the circular[2] (which I helped to write) you will see that there was no attempt at forcing upon these people *alien* names. Each head of a family was asked to choose the name which he would like to have as the family name. His children were then related to him by name precisely as among ourselves. Whether Dr. Eastman is still at work in this way I do not know, but I do know that the teachers and missionaries in the field have never properly and fully carried out this perfectly sensible and necessary change.

If I can be of any service in these or any other matters concerning your Department, I shall be very glad to co-operate.[3]

Very sincerely yours,
Hamlin Garland

1. Franklin K. Lane (1864–1921) became secretary of the interior under Woodrow Wilson on 5 March 1913. He instituted reform of the way in which Indian affairs were conducted and was largely responsible for the establishment of the National Park Service in 1916.

2. See Garland to Jones, 3 November 1902, letter 143.

3. Lane replied, 15 April 1913 (Nat'l Arch), that he had recently appointed Vincent Natalish, "an educated Apache," to continue the work among the Apaches, but that renaming could not "be done in the case of allottees, for the reason that their names have gone on record, and thus a legal status under that name has been given." Lane concluded that with a supervisor in the field, he expected "the work should receive an impetus."

196. to Frank A. Morgan

tlc, USC

April 15, 1913

Dear Mr. Morgan:[1]

In order that you may answer any questions concerning my lecture WITH THE FOREST RANGER, I here set down some of the facts concerning it.

It is illustrated with nearly one hundred and twenty slides, some of them colored by government experts, and many of them were taken by myself and represent phases of the ranger's life which have not been photographed even by the Department.

The lecture is given without MS., and is based on my own experiences in the mountains extending over a space of twenty years. It delineates the daily life, duties, dangers, and heroic and lonely deeds of the forest guard. I have ridden with the ranger, camped with them, helped build trail, and have watched them at many of their technical operations, such as cruising for lumber, laying out lines, studying the forest floor, and various other required duties.

As I have done my part in fiction to delineate the heroic side of the cowboys, the miner, and the Indian, so now I indicate the heroic side of "the man in moss green uniform."

The talk is not technical, and is intended to entertain an audience, while giving a broad conception of the forestry service. It deals with the enemies of the forest, with the fires, the winds, the faults, homesteaders, as well as with the defenders of the public lands. It has given schools, and clubs, a very clear idea of what the lonely forest ranger stands for, and has been acceptable to Womens Clubs, for the reason that it gives them precisely what they should have in way of knowledge of the organization of the Service. I enclose one or two letters which will give you further idea of this phase of my talk.

Very sincerely yours,

1. Frank A. Morgan, president of the Mutual Lyceum Bureau in Chicago. Morgan booked Garland for lectures in Illinois, Iowa, and South Dakota in December (Morgan to Garland, 23 May 1913).

197. to Theodore Roosevelt

als, Congress

6427 Greenwood Avenue
Chicago

April 22 [1913]

Dear Colonel:

Here is a fundamental reform — I have long held this to be but simple justice but never expected to see it even framed into an enactment.[1] Every child born into the world is legitimate and should not suffer a handi-cap — furthermore seducers will not be so free to take advantage of youth and ignorance — This is something for Progressives to take up.

Hamlin Garland

I have written about this and shall be glad to do so again.[2]

1. Garland probably enclosed "Bill to Help Babies," *Chicago Tribune*, 20 April 1913, sec. 1, p. 5. This news release announced plans to introduce a bill into the Illinois state legislature "legitimizing babies born to unwed mothers and making the birth constitute an act of civil marriage." One of the provisions of the bill would mandate imprisonment for an offense "politely mistermed 'disorderly conduct.'"

2. See Garland's letter to the editor, "Legitimize Every Child," *Chicago Tribune*, 23 April 1913, p. 8.

198. to Wilbur Cross

tls, Yale

The Cliff Dwellers
220 South Michigan Avenue
Chicago

April 25, 1913

Wilbur Cross
Yale Review.

Dear Mr. Cross:

I am very much pleased by your note concerning my article on Steven Crane. I shall be very glad to do the work you suggest. Can you give me an idea of what you will be able to pay for the work? It would give me pleasure to make the article as important as you have indicated, and of course, I do not expect anything like my fiction rates, but it will take considerable extra writing to make the changes you suggest.[1]

I have other chapters from my autobiography which I think are suited to your pages, and if you could use them, I should be very glad to submit them. I have a chapter dealing with my first years in Boston, which I think quite in line with your editorial policy. Also one which might be called HOW I CAME TO WRITE MAIN TRAVELED ROADS.—But first of all, we will come to an agreement on the Crane article. Please return it, and I will set to work on it at once.

Very sincerely yours,
Hamlin Garland

1. After some haggling over the amount he would pay (sixty dollars), Cross accepted "Stephen Crane As I Knew Him," *Yale Review* 3 (1 April 1914): 494–506.

199. to Theodore Roosevelt

als, Congress

6427 Greenwood Ave
Chicago.

[after 28 April 1913]

Dear Colonel: Your note rejoiced me.[1] The strongest phase of our movement is its humanitarian phase—and next—and a part of it of course—is the woman's phase. The bill I advocate is a woman's bill—a bill of rights for the poor little unwed mother and her nameless child. The married seducer of a girl should be treated as a *bigamist* not as a "disorderly person." All present laws relating to seduction favor the man. This bill favors the woman and child.—I have a chance to discuss this in nearly one hundred papers and I shall do so with great frankness—I should like to have your advice and co-operation in the matter. I want my skill and reputation—what little I have—to count for the good of the race.—I am the father of two little girls as you know and these wrongs will soon become *possible* to my children. I want to help the Progressive movement but feel I should have pay enough to keep the pot boiling while I am away—

As ever yours
Hamlin Garland

1. Roosevelt approved of the intent of the bill, but noted that it "would not reach the case of a married man who seduced an unmarried girl. . . . As regards the punishment of disorderly conduct, I think that it should be imprisonment for old offenders, but young girls who have been more sinned against than sinning should simply be put with probation officers or in some reform institution." See Roosevelt to Garland, 28 April 1913 (Congress).

200. to Theodore Roosevelt

tls, Congress

The Cliff Dwellers
220 South Michigan Avenue
Chicago

May 8, 1913

Colonel Theodore Roosevelt
C/o The Outlook
New York

Dear Colonel:

Your little note is tremendously important to me.[1] The way you are putting yourself behind these humanitarian movements is magnificent. Your power, your position, your security of fortune give you more transforming authority than any other reformer in America possesses. I am trying to do something myself to lessen the misery of the world. The Scripps-McRae syndicate is about to use three exceedingly candid articles by me, and that means an enormous and instantaneous reading. Mark Sullivan has also accepted an article "This is a Man's World" which is very plain spoken indeed.[2] — Two bills of somewhat similar character are about to be introduced into the Illinois legislature legitimizing children, and if they are properly drawn, I shall do all I can to aid them.[3] I shall take a hand in any other work of the same sort that comes under the head of true progress.

Very sincerely yours,
Hamlin Garland

1. Roosevelt had briefly noted, 6 May 1913, that treating the married seducer as a bigamist had resolved his objection.

2. Garland's three-part editorial appeared in the *Cleveland Press*: "Sin No More Against 'Nature Children,' Says Novelist: Let Us Make Them Legitimate," 2 June 1913, p. 5; "It's Full Time to End Our Pitiless Injustice Toward Unwed Mothers, Says Author," 3 June 1913, p. 6; and "Must Men Always Be Beasts, Trampling Women in the Mire?" 4 June 1913, p. 6. In 1913 Mark Sullivan (1874–1952) was editor of *Collier's Magazine*, which did not publish "This is a Man's World." A partial manuscript, heavily revised, is extant at the Huntington Library under the title "Paternity." For discussion of Garland's efforts, and a reprinting of his editorials, see Keith Newlin, "Hamlin Garland and the 'Illegitimacy Bill' of 1913," *American Literary Realism* 29, no. 1 (1996): 78–88.

3. Joseph A. Weber introduced a bill "to amend the statute of descent concerning the rights and powers of inheritance of children born out of statutory marriage" (H.B. 902, 3 June 1913). The bill was referred to the Committee on Judiciary, where it died.

201. to Robert Underwood Johnson   als, Am Acad

Mapleshade West Salem
Wisconsin

June 28. [1913]

Dear Johnson:

What can be done about the Drieser matter? Can we postpone his election? I feel as you do about these things and I do [not] wish to seem to sanction for a moment any such baseness as he seems engaged in.[1] I am willing to publicly withdraw my nomination if it seems nescessary but you would need to stand behind me as my source of information. I certainly shall oppose his election on the basis of your letter. Let me know what is being done.

Hamlin Garland

P.S. If we *knew* Thomas was to get the medal we would arrange to have one of his plays brought out during November. When can we know? — If

Gillette we would do the same thing and they *should both be here* in Chicago.[2]

1. Eager to include more writers from the Midwest in the National Institute, Garland had proposed Theodore Dreiser for membership in January 1913. On 16 June 1913 Johnson had written to Garland that he had resigned from the *Century*, in part because of an editorial dispute over the magazine's forthcoming publication of extracts from Dreiser's *A Traveller at Forty*. "I found it contained accounts of the author's illicit relations with five different women, with disgusting details," Johnson wrote. "More than this he told the cost of his adventures amorous in Venice, gave a list of the most notorious houses of ill-fame in Paris and made defense of his conduct from the moral point of view—the most unblushing and immoral thing I have ever read." Dreiser was not elected to the institute.

2. Augustus Thomas, a member of both the institute and the American Academy of Arts and Letters, received the institute's Gold Medal in 1913, awarded annually for "distinguished service to art or letters in the creation of original work." Playwright William Gillette (1855–1937) was much admired by Garland for his stage realism. Garland's intention to have the Chicago Theater Society stage one of Thomas's plays did not come about.

202. to Wilbur Cross   als, Yale

Mapleshade West Salem
Wisconsin

Aug. 8. [1913]

Dear Mr Cross:

I may, soon, send you the M.S.S. of "The Middle Border" my autobiographic story. If you could squeeze out a matter of twenty dollars per thousand and use say fifty thousand words it might pay you and be worth my while. I dont know that I could afford to let it go for so small a price but I'd like you to read it any way—It is full of reminiscences of Howells, Herne, Gilder, Stedman, Seton[,] Burroughs, Roosevelt—and many others—for I have had a very wide acquaintance.—It is a working man's story—also a story of the building of the prairie west—.

As soon as I get back to my office (and my secretary) I will set to work on the Howells and Herne subjects and see if I can detach them from the text of the narrative.

Very sincerely yours
Hamlin Garland

203. to Robert Sterling Yard als, NYPL

Mapleshade West Salem
Wisconsin

Aug 14. [1913]

Dear Mr Yard:

Would you advise me to write a love story into "The Middle Border?" [1] Pardon me for keeping at this subject but as you have read the M.S. with attention and are quite disinterested, I would like your opinion. Should I fetch up the sexual side of the subject by putting in Lincolns very remote and shy relationship with women? — Of course I could manufacture a continuous love-story but it would not be true — it would be introducing a fictional strand but my publishers (I mean *Harpers*) think it would help. My own feeling is against it. You come at the problem freshly and I shall be aided if you put down your candid judgment. I have a notion that the book is more distinguished as it is, but naturally as Riley says "Thats jist Because I'm prejudiced." —

I am coming to see you when I reach New York. You have a tremendous opportunity in your present position. In a very startling way your presence in that office means change — change in American letters and change in American readers.

I hope you will succeed in keeping the best and most vital in poetry and fiction.

Most sincerely yours
Hamlin Garland

1. Robert Sterling Yard (1861–1945), who had just become editor-in-chief of the *Century*, was a former newspaperman and co-founder of the publishers Moffat, Yard & Co. Yard wrote to Garland on 19 August 1913, advising him to "leave the book as it stands," for Garland's contemplated changes would introduce "a foreign element into a perfectly consistent and dignified work of art and literature." Yard then noted that "a lot of magazinists seem to have lost their heads" about the current "sex craze" afflicting magazines, assured Garland that the fad would be temporary, and enclosed a proof of his first editorial for the September *Century*.

204. to Robert Sterling Yard als, NYPL

Mapleshade West Salem
Wisconsin

Aug. 22. [1913]

Dear Mr Yard:

I am delighted with your letter and editorial and especially pleased to learn that the *Century* is *not* to even remotely "follow the lead" of those magazines whose editors trade on sexual passion in order to win circulation.[1] Every magazine and weekly now has a picture of a young girl on its cover—too often some man's idea of a young girl, a soulless figment of a lewd imagination and in many of the stories lies an open appeal to the flesh.—I am not precisely a prude and I've never lacked the man's animal side but when it comes to exploiting women and especially young girls in order to increase sales, I revolt.—I am looking forward with interest to meeting you in your office in October—and meanwhile I hope you'll find something in my fiction which will fit into the pages of the *Century*.— Thank you very sincerely for your candid words concerning "The Middle Border."—

Hamlin Garland

1. In his editorial, entitled "The Spirit of the Century" (*Century* 86 [September 1913]: 789–91), Yard affirmed that the magazine would continue the course set by Gilder, to define "what is noblest and forwardest in American life" (p. 789).

205. to Wilbur Cross tls, Yale

The Cliff Dwellers
220 South Michigan Avenue
Chicago

Oct 2, 1913

W. L. Cross
Editor—Yale Review
New Haven, Conn.

Dear Mr. Cross:

In looking over the Crane volume again I am not quite sure of the poem which Crane brought into Herne's dressing room. The lines on page 52, I think, are the ones.[1] I remember very well that it was a bitter study of some sociologic problem. Anyhow, it is quite safe to use this as the one in question.

Could you afford to pay $100 for an article on Howells, and the like amount for one upon Herne. If you can I will set to work upon them at once.

Very sincerely yours,
Hamlin Garland

You must help make the joint meeting of the National Inst in Chicago a success—

1. When Garland sent Cross the manuscript of "Stephen Crane As I Knew Him," he did not include any quotations from Crane's poetry because his copy of *The Black Riders and Other Lines* (Boston: Copeland and Day, 1895) had burned in the Homestead fire. Upon arriving in Chicago, he borrowed a copy of the volume and here refers to "I stood musing in a black world."

206. to Fred Lewis Pattee

als, Penn St

6427 Greenwood Avenue
Chicago

Dec. 30 [1914]

Dear Professor Pattee:

Your questions have let loose upon you a flood of material for it happens that I have given a great deal of thought to the very subject you have outlined.[1] I am to be in Philadelphia on the 13th and 14th of Jan. and if you should chance to be in the city at that time we could talk it all at the Franklin Inn Club. In case you cant, I will send to you a chapter out of my autobiography which will, I think, answer all your personal questions. I date my own fictional awakening from 1887—but I was at work on the problem you have in mind for two years. I disagree with Burroughs. I think our real American literature began after 1870. Ibsen, Kipling, Tolstoi, Hardy and Maupassant were the new influences. But write me at *The Players* and we'll talk the personal side of this—

With thanks for your interest.
Hamlin Garland

1. Fred Lewis Pattee (1863–1950), a professor of American literature at Pennsylvania State College, had written to Garland on 27 December 1914 to test the thesis of his *A History of American Literature Since 1870* (1915), then in progress, that "after the war a new spirit came over America, a new national spirit, and that it swept away the atmosphere through which the mid-century school viewed life and literature." Pattee noted that the naturalist John Burroughs disagreed with his thesis, arguing that "the war made no difference at all." Pattee also queried Garland about the writers who influenced his early years, suggesting as candidates Dickens, Harte, Eggleston, Cable, Maupassant, Flaubert, and Daudet. Garland describes his meeting with Pattee in *Contemporaries*, p. 36.

207. to Sinclair Lewis

als, usc

Oct. 5. [1915]

Dear Mr. Lewis:[1]

I hope you wont take my judgement too seriously when I say *The Hawk* lacks the quality which pleased me in "Mr Wrenn." This may be because I am grizzled—we'll let it go at that. The book is written and on its travels and there's no use saying things about its technic which cant be altered.

Lay my lack of interest to age—to ignorance anything you like (I'm only one) and go ahead on your next.

With best wishes
Hamlin Garland

P.S. Of course I realize the truth and humor of the western scenes and western character.

1. Sinclair Lewis (1885–1951), Nobel Prize–winning novelist and satirist of the middle class and author of *Our Mr. Wrenn* (1914), *The Trail of the Hawk* (1915), *Main Street* (1920), *Babbitt* (1922), and *Arrowsmith* (1925), which received a Pulitzer Prize (which Lewis declined). Garland's varied duties as a Pulitzer Prize juror and as a member of the National Institute and American Academy would bring him into increasing conflict with Lewis, whose novels were too risqué for the aging Garland's taste.

208. to Fred Lewis Pattee

als, Penn St

The Players
Sixteen Gramercy Park

Oct 29 [1915]

Dear Prof. Pattee:

I am reading your American Literature and find it very much to my liking.[1] Quite aside from your kindly notice of my work your judgements in the main are sound.—One point you must consider. After a certain work was done—as in Miss Wilkins' case—the writer cant go on doing it over and over. So in my stories after Middle Border—once having said my say I naturally passed on—as many of my characters did—to new scenes. Then too, the first taste of a writer is the one that has *tang*. Surprise is in this first reading—surprise and a sense of discovery. Later work can not of course continue or even bring up this flavor.—

I think you are in error about Riley.[2] As humorist he is a most remarkable figure.—However its a good book and a timely.

With sincerely prompt congratulations
Hamlin Garland

1. In his *A History of American Literature Since 1870* (New York: Century, 1915), Pattee had praised Garland's early work but noted that in his novels "there is a sense of dilution, a loss of effect" (pp. 373–77).

2. Pattee had dismissed Riley as "an entertainer, an actor, a mimicker," whose dialect "does not ring true," and who "must be dismissed as artificial and, on the whole, insincere" (pp. 326, 328).

209. to Zulime Garland

als, Hunt

Park Avenue Hotel
New York

Nov. 10. [1915]

Dear Zulime: Sullivan practically agreed to take four more sections of "The Middle Border" and then took my breath away by asking me if I would accept a certain position at one hundred dollars per week. I cant tell you what it is but if it comes to a head you wont have to worry about anything. It is not exactly an editorial position it is bigger than that. I'll let you know just as soon as it comes to a contract.[1] Even if this dont come thru, I have now several men nibbling for moving picture rights and any one of these will take care of us for a year. It looks as though you would have to pack up and come on to help me out with these schemes.

Charles and I had supper tonight and *he* said I didnt look a bit sick — and Barton Hepburn on whom I called said I didnt look a bit like an author — "You're too well-groomed" said he. Dr Barklay has cut me down to three small rolls of bread per day — and I feel better. He is to report finally on my diet tomorrow or next day. — I have not seen him since the ex-rays.

I shall probably take a nice seven room flat here — furnished and you can bring Alice with you if she wants to come and you can be moderately free to help me.

This new position will involve some travel but all expenses will be paid. I hope to know within a week — It interests me greatly as a "job" quite aside from the pay.

Gertrude is coming to take me for a ride — plan to stop at the Bok's. They want you.

Hamlin.

1. According to a diary entry of 9 November, Mark Sullivan wanted to issue a large set of American novels, with Garland in charge in Chicago. "If it comes off it is the most important event in my life," Garland recorded on 7 December. "He is confident that we can do it but it is not yet fully decided." Sullivan's plan, however, did not work out. Other persons referred to are Barton Hepburn, a Chicago financier, and Edward Bok, the editor of the *Ladies' Home Journal.*

210. to Fred Lewis Pattee

als, Penn St

The Players
Sixteen Gramercy Park

Dec 4 [1915]

Dear Prof. Pattee:

I am re-reading your book with minute care, and on the whole I agree with it. I think I see bits of "Crumbling Idols" scattered through it — so it is no wonder it suits me! — As you know, I correlated that "Local Color" movement in "Crumbling Idols" — not as completely as you have done but I saw it and wrote of it — I think in *The Forum* when Page had it.[1] My publishers told me that nearly a thousand Editorials were penned in opposition to my poor little book which was addressed to creative men—as you remember. It did not sell and its message was distorted into an opposition to culture! I hope your book gets adopted as a text book for on the whole it is just, and certainly it is American. If you had not spoken so well of me I could write an article in praise of it but as it is I can only commend it in private.

I still think that your Riley chapter is unjust and also that on Howells is not quite adequate. His work is so varied and of such a high general level that it must stand for the best of its period.—

I again express my sincere appreciation of your services to a true Americanism—

Hamlin Garland

1. Garland refers to "Productive Conditions of American Literature," *Forum* 17 (August 1894): 690–98. See also Garland to Alice French, 9 September 1894, letter 83.

211. to James Stuart Blackton

tlc, usc
April 4. [1916]

Dear Commodore Blackton:[1]

I am greatly troubled by the scenario and cast of the story of HESPER, and I am returning the M.S. with many suggestions. Unless we can give the play more distinction I can not afford to let it go out as the first of a series of my plays. It would be better to put out Money Magic or Cavanagh which do not lend themselves so readily to conventional treatment. I cant let a play go out with a lot of scenes involving a drunken girl. I dont want an actress to be called on to play such scenes. In the book there is only a glimpse of "Claire." But the trouble goes deeper than this. If we are to advertise my plays as "types of the higher photo-plays" they must have something distinctive in the setting[,] costumes and characterizations, otherwise we expose ourselves to the critics. Mr. North[2] should not begin the work of the camera til we have worked out the sets and costumes to the finest detail. I do not wish to be a nuisance but the very essence of our plan involves a more careful preparation.

Before any work on Money Magic is done the scenario shud be submitted to me and the whole play thot out. Part of the cast for Hesper is satisfactory to me. The man who is to play Kelly is admirable. Hesper is too small and the Raymond is too young. The set for Kellys cabin is without interest. I did not object the other day for the reason that I wanted to read the scenario and the book. Unless we lift this play to a higher plane it will only be another play of wild west bustle. We cant afford to start a campaign for the higher movy and repeat all the conventions of the wild west pistol play. It would be better to start with Money Magic. This scenario is so hurried that it has retained almost nothing of the charm of the book.

I am sorry to be so insistent but I've spent thirty years building up a reputation for true and clean fiction and I cant depart from my method now.[3]

1. James Stuart Blackton (1875–1941) formed the Vitagraph Company with Albert E. Smith in 1896. Blackton became a commodore of the Atlantic Yacht Club in the early 'teens and thereafter referred to himself as Commodore Blackton. Blackton resigned from Vitagraph in 1917 to form his own company, Blackton Productions. With studios located in Brooklyn, Vitagraph was the largest and most important of the early film companies and filmed four of Garland's novels in 1916 and 1917: *Hesper, Money Magic, The Captain of the Gray-Horse Troop*, and *Cavanagh, Forest Ranger.*

2. Wilfrid North (1863–1935) joined Vitagraph in 1912 and became its leading director.

3. In his reply of 5 April 1916, Blackton reassured Garland that "we will co-operate with you to the fullest extent of our ability," and noted, "You must not allow yourself to be misled by the literal wording of the scenario. It is the skill and technique and artistic and dramatic perception of the picture director which translates the thought and meaning of the author into the visualized picture." See *Contemporaries*, pp. 98–103, 106–13, and 119–24 for Garland's account of his experiences with Vitagraph.

212. to James Stuart Blackton

tlc, usc

June 29. [1916]

Dear Commodore Blackton:

I confess to a great discouragement after seeing Hesper.[1] All the romance and beauty of the mountain life is left entirely out of it and the general effect is drab and commonplace. As I said to you once before I have hesi[tated] about offering any criticism after the [pic]ture is made for I do not see how we can change it. I wish the ending could be changed. It is not one that will leave [a] fine picture in the minds of the specta[tors.]

There are many suggestions that I [would] make if it were possible to change the play but I suppose the only thing we can do is to shift the emphasis by cutting [and] restoring the film already made. At present there is too much that is mere busi[ness.]

I am hoping that in the plays [which] are to follow I shall have a chance to [go] over with you the scenario, the costuming and the general trend of the scenes be[fore] the picturing begins. Unless we can get [some] of my distinctive country into the film we will fail of the high mark we have [set] for ourselves. The painful consideration of the author is that once done the sto[ry] can not be done again.

Very sincerely yours,

1. The copy text of this letter is Garland's carbon copy. The typewriter ran over the right margin of the carbon, resulting in the loss of some letters and words. Reconstructions are in brackets. Garland had seen a pre-release version of the film, which was filmed at the Vitagraph studios in Brooklyn and at locations in New Jersey. The film was released on 31 July; Garland had still to supply the titles. In *Contemporaries*, p. 119, Garland recounts his reaction to seeing the film.

213. to Edmund Henry Eitel als, Indiana U

Canton
N.Y.

July 23 [1916]

Dear Mr. Eitel: [1]

The morning paper brings the news of Riley's passing and puts a chill into my heart. I have known him so long that it will be hard to think of the West as not still possessing him in the flesh as it will still possess his spirit—Please accept for the family the grateful homage of my two daughters, my wife and myself. I wish I could be at the memorial service to lay my wreath on his body but I am far away and the time too short. No doubt the Institute and Academy will be represented in an official message but that is at best but a formal impersonal word—I would like to write a little poem in praise of the work Riley did in sensitizing us to the homely phases of our common life. Perhaps I can do this later.

Very sincerely yours
Hamlin Garland

1. Edward Eitel was Riley's nephew and secretary who, along with Riley, supplied the material for Marcus Dickey's official biographies, *The Youth of James Whitcomb Riley* (1919) and *The Maturity of James Whitcomb Riley* (1922).

214. to Philip D. Sherman   als, Brown

Canton. N.Y.

July 23. [1916]

Dear Prof. Sherman:

I am afraid Crane's books have gone out of print.[1] Mrs Crane was at work on a story of her husband's life but that has not appeared. I am sorry not to be able to help you more than this. — Crane's marked individuality is, probably, his undoing. He was like some strongly flavored cake — when the taste changes that particular pastry loses value. His use of English was my high admiration.

Hamlin Garland.

1. Philip D. Sherman (1851–1957), an associate professor of English at Oberlin College, was teaching a summer course and wrote to Garland 14 July [1916] to ask whether Crane's *Red Badge of Courage* was still in print and whether a biography had appeared. He concluded, "Some of my colleagues hold that I am extravagant in feeling that by Crane's early death American literature lost a real genius." Cora Crane did not publish a biography of her husband.

215. to Theodore Roosevelt   ald, usc

71. East 92nd
New York City

Nov. 21. [1916]

Dear Colonel:

Colliers is beginning a new series of my "Middle Border" in December and Mark Sullivan wants to use your beautiful appreciation in the opening number as a kind of editorial introduction. — This seems a perfectly proper use of it and I told him that if you saw no objection I would be glad to have it so employed. It could appear in the book "The High Trails" afterward. My publishers are disposed to make larger use of it in connection with my Sun Set Edition. — [1]

I've reached chapter 10 of *The Holidays.*[2] Technically this is your best book. It is very vivid and clean-cut of phrase. What a world you cover! Each of these trips is material for a volume. The quality I miss is your humor. I should like to have more of those delightful characterizations which come out in your conversation. I particularly liked the chapter on your hunting companions.

Faithfully yours.
Hamlin Garland

1. Roosevelt drafted his laudatory evaluation on 10 November 1916 and sent it to Garland, who transcribed it and sent it to *Collier's* for use in promoting the serial version of *Son* (item #778). *Collier's* began the second series on 31 March 1917 and not, as Garland indicates, in December. Roosevelt's appreciation appeared later as "An Appreciation of Hamlin Garland" in *They of the High Trails* (1916).

2. *A Book-Lover's Holidays in the Open* (1916), essays and sketches that had for the most part previously appeared in periodicals.

216. to Theodore Roosevelt

als, Congress

Nov. 24 [1916]

Dear Wilderness Trailer:

I've finished the book. It is the best piece of writing you've ever done. It has a keener sense of the beauty and wonder of the Wilderness. It is as if your eyes being less occupied with game had borrowed time to study the trees, clouds and flowers. It is a handsome book in every way and I give thanks a second time for it. It covers an enormous field — too wide indeed, for you are forced to stop, as if at a signal, in Chile and leap to Quebec. You could easily have written a volume on South America alone. — There are paragraphs of pure description in this volume that I laugh over — I mean such a one as that in which you tell of the birds in the Gulf. Your description of the Man of War Bird made me think of Whitman's lines

"Them who hast slept all night upon the storm
Waking at morn on thy renewed pinions."[1]

There's a word missing there — no doubt you can supply it. — All the early part of the book made me homesick. I've been five times into the Southwest. I've heard the Navajo shepherd sing his quavering song at dawn—and I've seen the Hopi women toiling up the trail with water jars —Acoma, Laguna, Santa Clara, Isleta all come back to me as I read.—I have slept on the sand and have seen the sunrise from my blanket beside a bunch of greasewood just as you tell of it. Your appreciation of the beauty and mystery of that desert country gives these early chapters a quality which those in which the game-hunter's alertness is dominant, lack. They are less hurried also. The book closes well and my chief regret is that you did not, here and there, pop in one of your humorous characterizations.

What are you writing now?—I am sure you have some project in hand. Was it not fine that Burroughs should have the medal for *Belles Lettres?*—[2]

With the regards of us all
Hamlin Garland

1. Garland's quotation of the opening two lines of "To the Man-of-War-Bird" is slightly off: "Thou who hast slept all night upon the storm, / Waking renew'd on thy prodigious pinions."

2. John Burroughs had been nominated to receive the National Institute's Gold Medal and had tied for first place with William Cary Brownell. Those members present at the annual meeting in November voted the Medal to Burroughs.

217. to Theodore Roosevelt tls, Congress

6427 Greenwood Avenue
Chicago

Dec. 10. [1916]

Dear Trailer:

Did I tell you that Blackton of the VITAGRAPH CO. is to do four or more of my books? MONEY MAGIC is to be put on soon and in the early spring THE CAPTAIN OF THE GRAY HORSE TROOP will be done in So. California and Blackton has asked me to go out and help put the play into film. I'd like to talk with you sometime on the prelude which is a series of pictures of the Cheyennes from the early times up to the era of captivity where the story of "Curtis" begins. I want this done in a big way and if you should happen to meet Blackton he may speak to you about it. If he does, a word of encouragement from you may do him good. I am working on these scenario myself, and shall try to get some of the real west on the screen.

I've signed a five-year contract with Blackton and if he goes about it in the right spirit we'll do something that will be of service all around.

Blackton seems a fine fellow and our relationship is cordial. I really think he wants to do the right thing by me. He is to put CAVANAGH on in the early summer.

We are all talking of the delightful visit we had with you. You gave us just that side of you which the politicians do not get.

With sincere affection from us all.
Hamlin Garland

218. to Theodore Roosevelt

tls, Congress

The Joint Committee of the Literary Arts[1]
15 Gramercy Park

Dec. 20. [1916]

Dear Colonel:

I was greatly interested in your son's account in the *Bookman* of the writers of South America and I should like to get in touch with him.[2] Is he to be in the city this winter?

The above committee is planning a dinner to some S.A. writers to be given in Feb. and we want to have the most representative available novelists and poets and no doubt your son Kermit can give us some valuable hints.

The idea of the dinner is mine and its object is to bring about a wider interest and a better understanding in literary circles of what is being done in our Sister Republics. I am told that a school of local color fiction is at work in Brazil and that interests me. This is the time to show a friendly interest in our neighbors. We are keeping the dinner non-political and non-commercial and non-partisan. Any suggestion you can give me will be of the utmost service. I am told that one of the Ambassadors—Calderon—is a man of letters.

Faithfully yours,
Hamlin Garland

1. Printed on the letterhead are the names of the members of the Joint Committee of Literary Arts, with Garland as chairman and Edward J. Wheeler as secretary. They

include John G. Agar, president of The National Arts Club; Winston Churchill, president of The Author's League of America; Ernest Peixotto, president of The MacDowell Club of New York City; Ida M. Tarbell, president of The Pen and Brush Club; Augustus Thomas, president of The Author's Club; and Edward J. Wheeler, president of The Poetry Society of America. Garland formed the committee and sponsored the dinner, he notes in *Contemporaries*, pp. 141–43, to promote the arts during World War I.

2. Belle and Kermit Roosevelt, "Two Book Hunters in South America," *Bookman* 44 (October 1916): 137–45.

219. to William Dean Howells

tlc, Miami U

Dec. 22 [1916]

Dear Howells:

We were disappointed not to see you while you were in New York. I thought of you as being in Boston. It may be that the time has come for me to cut off all my other clubs and become a Centurion. Irving is sure of it.[1] I havent the money at this time but by the time the club admits me —which will not be for a year—I shall hope to have the fee.

My wife has just returned from a visit to a friends "cottage" at Hot Springs Virginia, where her living cost ten dollars per day. Luckily she was not required to pay it and her friend has an income of a thousand dollars every day so it didnt worry her—or us. Today Zulime is doing her own cooking and is quite resigned to it. She has abandoned any idea—as I have—of ever having any more than we have now, and so we are rich in friends.

Fuller writes quite cheerily. He is writing again but his writing is very cold and critical and the publishers are not very enthusiastic. I am trying to get him to visit me but he is harder to move than you are. He will not stir out of Chicago. We are very glad of our little home here and have no desire to go back—at least I have none.[2]

The children are well and very happy in their school. Mary Isabel is deep in dramatics which she loves. She is full of Lear and Hamlet just now. It amazes me to think that my little babe is now a student of Shakespeare. Time is agallop.

1. Garland refers to Irving Bacheller. Garland became a member of the prestigious Century Club in late 1918. See Garland to Fuller, 6 November 1918, letter 237.

2. The Garlands moved to New York City in late summer 1916, establishing a home at 71 East 92nd Street.

220. to James Stuart Blackton

tlc, usc

Jan. 10 [1917]

Dear Commodore:

I have just seen in the Review that the name of THE CAPTAIN has been changed to "The Long Fight." I wish you and I could have had a talk about this important matter. They have a way of doing as they please out there. My contract calls for the use of the name of the novel and the name of the author and I do not like the way in which the authors share in it is ignored. Thru all my talks with you and Col. Brady the use of the name of the book and the name of the author made a part of the general scheme.[1] No doubt there are good reasons for a change of name in the case of this play but I think I should have been consulted and that the name of my book should not be lost out of the advertising.

Is there not some one to whom you can delegate this campaign who can meet me and keep me posted as to what is going on? I know how busy you are and I don't like to put any more work on you but I would like to get a little closer to what is going on with this my most important venture.

I think we should make this an educational film. Make a point of its being clean and picturesque. It needs a special campaign. How can we organize it? It should be treated like the CRISIS. We should be planning for it now.

1. Jasper E. Brady, the manager of the manuscript department of Vitagraph, resigned from Vitagraph in February 1917 over artistic differences with Blackton and went to Universal Studios. Blackton replied on 15 February 1917 that while the sales department has "been suggesting alternative names for pictures which possessed long titles," he had never authorized a change of name and that "such *change will not occur*." The movie version was released on 7 May. Garland demanded that Vitagraph hold up production of *Captain* and work on *Cavanagh* instead to give the studio time to produce a competent film of his favorite novel. In other letters Garland stressed the necessity of using authentic locations and the Cheyenne Indians rather than California or Pueblo Indians.

221. to William Wolbert

tlc, usc

Jan. 31. [1917]

Dear Mr. Wolbert: I am very glad to hear that you are making use of Lummis. He can put you in touch with just what you want. As I wrote you yesterday I may come out yet. I sent a letter to the Commodore last night which may decide matters. In any event your letter shows the play is to be given careful attention.[1]

The most of the directions of the scenario are mine. The poetic lines were written in by the man in the office. Probably they will not reach the screen but they give a hint of the effect on the ordinary eastern mans mind and are valuable for that reason. I wish you could get the opening scenes of Curtis and his striker far back in the great peaks — on the shore of a lake. There should be wild charm in this.

If I knew just where you were at work in the play I could be of more service. The make up of the Blackfoot courier should be distinctive and his calm indifferent action as he delivers his message should not escape you.

If Moreno[2] plays the part he should make up as a man of thirty five. He must not look like a matinee hero. I wish I could have been there to help you get the costumes. Once you start on the work you will not be able to change. All the army uniforms were blue in those days. The saddles were dark as you know. Dont let your ranchers all wear chaps and neck-er-chiefs. As a matter of fact few of them wore chaps in the summer time — they were too hot. Some of the ranchers — many of them[—] should dress like farmers.

The Cheyennes are a proud war-like and ceremonious people and at all points in this play the chiefs should be dignified but they should not strut. I knew Four Horns, White Bull[,] Porcupine and American Horse and their action went on under my eyes from day to day. They were simple[,] dignified and never boastful.

As I have indicated in the notes their dances are ceremonies. They receive one another according to ancient ways. No matter how ragged and poor they are the chiefs retain a marked yet simple dignity.

In those days they wore their hair long and braided the two braids drawn over their shoulders. Most of them had cattlemens hats. All wore moccasins and some still wore the buck-skin trousers. If you have any Sioux, Crow, or any other plains Indians to draw on you will be able to approximate the character of the chiefs.

The scenery in and around Lame Deer was not so very unlike the foothills in and around Sierra Madra. You can easily get that. The agency ought to be carefully built and if Miss Storey[3] will surround herself with just the right properties she can give a fine contrasting picture. There was always a studio at these agencies in those days.

It was my idea, as I think I indicated in the notes, to make the Indian dances historic, and if it is not too late I suggest that you get George Bird Grinnells History of the Northern Cheyennes. If you could do the famous charge of Roman Nose, and represent a meeting of the chiefs with Miles it would be fine. It might be that we could take a scene out of Sitting Bulls life—his rejection of the treaty with the Gov. in the early eighties.

In general if we could give a sweeping picture of the plains people from the primitive times to the era of captivity and then pass to the story of Curtis and his attempts to teach them the white mans road we would have a film that would be at once authentic and interesting. This should be our ideal. You cant do it if you are hurried by the hard and fast events of a schedule.

The main criticism of Money Magic was in the matter of Berthas costumes. They were up to the minute while the carriages were back in the nineties. Miss Storey missed something by not having the costumes in the time of the mutton-leg sleeves. The same discrepancy will appear if she does not conform to the fashions of 1897. The manager of the Rialto was very severe on this. To have the army uniforms of twenty years ago and Miss Storeys gowns of today will be absurd. It is in these adjustments that you need time to think it all out.

Then too the lighting of Money Magic was too monotonous and I suggested the use of tints to indicate the change of time. I dont know whether they made use of my suggestion or not. In these days of intense competition, when every new film has some claim to novelty The Vitagraph cannot afford to lag behind.

In the play you have in hand there is abundant opportunity to make striking effects and I sincerely hope your photographer will take full advantage of them. Night effects at the camp-fire, sun-set effects. The passage of time between one event and another should all be indicated.

That "raw" effect of most films can be overcome and must be overcome if we are to hold our place with the other advancing men. Then too, the actors must be kept from doing the stereotyped head-shaking and mumbling. Miss Storey really acts and the man who plays Curtis must act. Audiences—the kind of audiences we wish to appeal to[—]will not tolerate all those conventions of the early stages of the art.

With sincere desire to help and hoping to be nearer you soon,

1. William Wolbert (1884–1918) was an actor and director whose career was cut short by his death in the 1918 influenza epidemic. Wolbert directed the film versions of

Captain, *Cavanagh, Forest Ranger*, and *Money Magic*. At Garland's suggestion, Charles Lummis had supplied Wolbert with details concerning the depiction of the Cheyenne and had recommended that Wolbert depict authentic sign language — a suggestion Wolbert adopted. Wolbert also informed Garland that since they were more than half finished with the film, no advantage would be gained by his coming to California (Wolbert to Garland, 24 January 1917). The film of *Captain* was released on 7 May 1917.

2. Antonio Moreno (1888–1967), Spanish-born actor who played Captain Curtis in *Captain*.

3. Edith Storey (1892–1967), a Vitagraph actress who starred in many of its early films, here playing the part of Elsie Brisbane, Curtis's love interest.

222. to William Dean Howells

ald, usc

[before 21 March 1917]

Dear Dean of us all:[1]

As I look back over the many years since first I dared to present my letter of introduction to you at Lee's Hotel in Auburndale — it seems but a short space — and I have no sense of having grown thirty years older. Nevertheless the kalendar is right — and you are also thirty years older — but as I read your latest novel[2] I am not conscious of any ageing in the pen that traces your visions on the paper — or is it a type-writer that is doing your work? — Any how from my fifty sixth milestone I hail you at your eightieth — hoping that I may be one-half as alert as keen of appreciation as you are this day. Alas! I fear my generation has not your staying power — your wholesome philosophy of life and work.

1. As Chairman of the Joint Committee of Literary Arts, Garland arranged a dinner to commemorate Howells's eightieth birthday on 21 March, held at the National Arts Club. As part of the program, letters of tribute were read and then bound into a book which was presented to Howells in September. Garland's letter of tribute is a formal statement of his gratitude and differs substantially from this more personal letter of greeting. Howells, who was in Augusta, Georgia, was not present at the dinner, but wrote, 7 April 1917, to thank Garland for arranging the testimonial: "Nothing, as I imagine it, could more gratify a departed spirit, and I fully realize what time you have spent and trouble you have taken for a rather ungracious ghost. I cannot love you more than ever, but I can thank you, and I do thank you. When the bound volume of obituary testimonials comes to me I will write a general acknowledgement which I will send to each of the friends; until then I suppose I can do nothing. I can never say how truly I feel and highly value the whole affair; I do not see how any man could have received greater honor or deserved it less."

2. *The Leatherwood God*, published in 1916.

223. to Brander Matthews

tls, Columbia

Mar. 21. [1917]

Dear Brander:

The reason why I have not been round to see you is simple. My damned sciatica has been getting worse and I have hardly felt like a walk even of a mile. I keep up my little round and am carrying on the Howells meeting but save myself all I can. My doctor is now talking of sending me to Battle Creek.[1] I dont want to go alone. Come on in—the dieting is fine! I shall go about the First of April. I am trying to get up a party of incapables.

They claim marvelous results from the regimen out there. I shall stick it out till I get relief. I feel pretty well while sitting still but I cant lift my left leg and bending down is a painful feat. A letter from Burroughs this morning confirms my doctor in his plan.[2] So I shall go soon.

The Howells meeting promises to be most successful. I shall have nearly 150 letters to go in the book.

I'm going to get round and see you soon.

Regards to you and yours.
H.G.

I enclose a suggested list of candidates—How would you vote on them?

1. Garland describes his treatment at the Battle Creek Sanitarium during April in *Contemporaries*, pp. 151–56. After enduring its bland food and "prison ship" atmosphere, he made ready to leave, but Dr. Kellogg talked him into staying another week. Thereafter he enjoyed smuggled coffee and slipped away to the home of a friend for an occasional dinner.

2. Burroughs had written on 20 March 1917 to praise his treatment at the Middletown, New York, Battle Creek facility and to advise that "the only effectual remedy [for sciatica] I found was heat and electricity, and a meatless diet."

224. to William Lyon Phelps

tlc, usc

Mar. 27. [1917]

Dear Phelps:[1]

Williams and I feel that we are about to the point where The Inst. must take account of the work of women and we are ready to attempt their entrance by getting them to stand for election. Thorndike is with us in this matter.[2] The names agreed upon are:

Mary E. Wilkins Freeman
Edith Wharton
Margaret Deland

to whom might be added

Ida Tarbell
Jane Addams
Cecilia Beaux.

Before even mentioning their names we would have to secure their full consent to enter the fight for it would be a fight.

Shall we as a nominating committee precipitate the fight?

Garland.

1. William Lyon Phelps (1865–1943), professor of English literature at Yale University, popularizer of the humanities through many books and his "As I Like It" column in *Scribner's*, and who, with Jesse Lynch Williams and Garland as chair, comprised the Literature Selection Committee on nominations for the National Institute in 1917.

2. Ashley Thorndike (1871–1933), a noted Elizabethan scholar who taught at Columbia from 1906 to his death, was the secretary of the National Institute.

225. to Ashley Thorndike   tls, Am Acad

Hamlin Garland
71 East Ninety-Second St.
New York City

Mar. 29. [1917]

Ashley Thorndike:
Sec. National Institute Arts and Letters:

Dear Sir: The Nominating Committee beg leave to report the following names as suitable candidates for Membership in the Institute:

Albert Bigelow Paine, novelist, historian and poet.
Irving Bacheller, novelist and poet.
Rupert Hughes, novelist.

Vachel Lindsay, poet.
Ray Stannard Baker (David Grayson) novelist and publicist.
Walter Pritchard Eaton, Essayist and critic.
Edward Sheldon, dramatist.

Also

Mary E. Wilkins Freeman, novelist,
Edith Wharton, novelist,
Margaret Deland, novelist.

The Committee advise an immediate vote on these names so that the members can be reached before they go to their summer homes. The autumn is not a good time to get a full vote.[1]

In presenting these names the Committee wish it to be understood that the writers named have not been approached on the subject of their candidacy and that it is especially nescessary to proceed with caution in the case of the women mentioned. If they can be induced to stand for election the Com. favors making a test of the sentiment of the Institute.

Respectfully submitted,
Hamlin Garland
Chairman.

1. Because the Institute had been embarrassed in the past by nominees' public refusal of election, a rather detailed nomination procedure was designed to prevent the Institute from a recurrence. Committees representing each art form selected the names of potential candidates to stand for election within their section, with each candidate requiring three nominations. Nominations were normally sent on 1 October to members of the section, who cast a preliminary vote, with three-fourths majority needed for a nomination to stand. The nominator then secured the consent of the nominee to stand for formal election and, with the candidate's consent, the name was formally presented and voted upon by the entire membership at the Institute's annual meeting. In a letter sent to the three women candidates in October 1917, Thorndike informed them of their nominations but noted: "Although there is no clause in our constitution limiting the membership to men, I believe that there has up to the present time been but one woman member, Mrs. Julia Ward Howe. . . . I imagine that our membership is divided on the advisability of admitting women, although I am sure that all would agree that, if women are to be admitted, the three nominated will certainly be selected" (copy enclosed in Thorndike to Garland, 24 October 1917). None of the women candidates were elected in 1917.

6427 Greenwood Avenue
Chicago

July 17. [1917]

Dear Wilderness Hunter:

I am asking my publishers to send advance sheets of my "Middle Border" to you. Dont bother to read it if you have other and more profitable business but I think you'll find in it some part of your vanished world as well as a world that is more recent—but also vanished.[1]

We've read with deep emotion of the sailing of your sons and our hearts are with Mrs Roosevelt.[2] We pray they may all come back to her and to you in added honor and good health.

I've been re-reading parts of "The Holidays"—and I am filled with longing to re-traverse the deserts and the high peaks we both know so well. I knew Ganado and Hubbell[3] and I knew the desert dawn and the clear song of the coyote—I spent a night in the Grand Cañon alone. The only human being in it from end to end—so far as I knew. The Snake Dance I saw in 1895—I studied the old cave dwellings west of Espinosa and climbed the Round Mesa—The Natural Bridge I did not see. Do you know I liked that trip of yours just *because* you did nothing but get there— look, and return! That's the way I go about.—

My gout or whatever it is continues to worry me so that my efficiency is impaired but I am doing what I can.

With sincere regards to you both,
Hamlin Garland

1. Roosevelt replied, 26 July 1917, that he was "immensely interested" in *Son* and enclosed a three-page, highly laudatory review of it for promotional purposes (item #778).

2. Sons Theodore Jr. and Archie received commissions in the American Expeditionary Forces, while Kermit enlisted in the British army. The youngest son, Quentin, had enrolled in flight training school.

3. Garland refers to the trading post of Lorenzo Hubbell, at Ganado, Arizona, to which he had a made a brief visit in November 1899 to buy Navajo art for wedding gifts for Zulime.

227. to Theodore Roosevelt   als, Congress

Onteora.
Tannersville.
N.Y.

Aug. 1ˢᵗ [1917]

Dear Rancher:

Your splendid letter came just as I was leaving New York City and this is my first opportunity to write. I am going into camp here with my children for a month or two.—I think my publishers will use parts of your letter[1] to put with Howells' and Burroughs' letters in their initial announcement of the book.[2] Meanwhile I return my grateful appreciation of your approval. It was like you to read it so promptly.

There is one point in your note which worries me. You mis-read my reference to my father.[3] I am proud of his action in volunteering.—I put it in that form as a contrast to the attitude of so many men of today. My "tone" in saying that would have made my meaning perfectly clear. It is because he believed—and I believe in a "silken rag"—that I put it just that way.

I shall take this up with my publishers. I dont want any one to misunderstand this expression.

Yours faithfully
Hamlin Garland

1. That is, the review of *Son* that Roosevelt had enclosed in his letter of 26 July.

2. Howells had written, 22 July 1917: "So far as I know your book is without its like in literature. It is perfectly true to life, and beautiful with right feeling, from first to last. I wish every American, every human being, might read it. Never before has any man told our mortal story so manfully so kindly. I would like it to go on forever." When Garland asked Howells for permission to use his letter to advertise the book, Howells replied, 4 August 1917: "I have most decidedly refused to let MacMillans quote from my letter to you. I hope to be your friendliest critic, not their advance agent. To let a publisher quote from such a letter as I like to write to a brother-writer would take all heart and trust out of friendship, and I *never* do it." Howells reviewed the book on the front page of the *New York Times Review of Books*, 26 August 1917, praising the autobiography as one of "the very greatest of that kind in literature."

3. In the first edition of *Son* Garland had intended to refer ironically to his father's joining Grant's army at Vicksburg: "What sacrifice—What folly! Like thousands of others he deserted his wife and children for an abstraction, a mere sentiment. For a

striped silken rag — he put his life in peril." In subsequent editions the passage is attrib-
uted to his father's "pacifist neighbors." See *Son*, pp. 6–7. Roosevelt had taken exception to this attribution in his letter of 26 July: "I very much wish you would make one
change in the book. You seem to slight your father's going to the war. This is not worthy
of you, and it is not doing justice to him. I regard your family as of the kind which,
when conditions become proper in this country, will stand for what is best in our nation's life; and it would not so stand if your father had not had it in him to render the
supreme service which patriotism demands."

228. to Peter J. Shields

als, U Cal-Davis

71 East 92nd St.
N.Y. City

Dec. 10. [1917]

Dear Judge Shields:[1]

Your very thoughtful and complimentary letter came to me a few days
ago and made me think as well and stirred in me a grateful sense of your
profound interest. In reply I can only say that I have put down the way in
which I felt *at the time* without attempting to justify it. In 1893 we were
all pretty "blue" and as it happened my personal out-look was colored by
the facts narrated in my story — I put down my feeling as it was at that
time and not my feeling now. My Main Travelled Roads describe a condition that is much ameliorated today — and my "Middle Border" is a
story of a vanished world — I am trying to recover the psychology of the
epoch I describe — as I go on, the psychology will change. My father and
mother lived in peace and comfort for many years in our Wisconsin
home. Both are gone now and they loom ever larger as I think of their
calm heroism — You will find more of my father in the second volume.
He became a serene and admirable old man. He died only three years ago
eighty-four years old.

I am grateful for your letter and shall file it away as one of the most
valuable of the many I am receiving.

Most cordially yours
Hamlin Garland

1. Peter J. Shields, a California State Superior Court judge in Sacramento, had written, 3 December 1917, a lengthy and detailed letter in appreciation of *Son*. After testify-

ing to the book's ability to loosen "a flood of memories which have moved me very deeply and filled me with a kind of anguished extacy," Shields gently chided Garland for emphasizing the "'futility' of your mother's life" and the sense of lost opportunities rather than the nobility of sacrifice and the heroism required to overcome privation.

229. to Brander Matthews   als, Columbia

71. East 92nd St.

Jan 27. 1918

Dear Brander:

You won!—The fellows turned down the women for another year. I bear no ill will. I am still a believer in the will of the majority and you had 29 to our 17. I hope you get home all right. I wanted to slide out, too, but I didnt. I stayed till the end. The fellows were all very well about my election to the Academy.[1]

Yours ever
Hamlin

1. The National Institute had its annual meeting on 26 January, during which, after much debate, candidates Edith Wharton, Mary Wilkins Freeman, and Margaret Deland were not elected. Garland had earlier received a telegram from Matthews on 11 January notifying him of his election to the American Academy of Arts and Letters that day.

230. to Robert Underwood Johnson   als, Am Acad

16 Gramercy Park
Manhattan

Jan 28. 1918.

Robert Underwood Johnson,
Sec. American Academy of Arts and Letters:

Dear Sir: I am in receipt of your letter notifying me of my election to membership in the Academy, and I hasten to express my deep sense of the honor and to say that I accept it with that keen pleasure which comes when a great good fortune falls unexpectedly into one's life.[1] No higher honor can come to me than to be thus called into comradeship by my seniors who represent the Allied Arts in this most influential organization. I am very humble and profoundly grateful in accepting a chair among them, and I hope that all I may do hereafter may be consistent with the high purposes of this the chief association of Arts and Letters in America.

Very faithfully yours
Hamlin Garland

1. Although Garland had known of his election for over two weeks, Johnson, the permanent secretary of the Academy, had requested a formal reply to his equally formal notification of 26 January 1918.

231. to Brander Matthews   als, Columbia

Jan 29. [1918]

Dear Brander:

You are right—if it is going to bring division serious division into the Institute. Mrs Garland says you are "extremely right" and she is a suffragist!—Anyhow I shall do no more in the campaign. We are going along so well that it seems a pity to bring any discord into the organization—Nothing shall bring lasting war between you and me—that's settled.—

Faithfully yours
Hamlin

232. to William Allen White   als, Congress

The Players
16 Gramercy Park

Feb. 14. [1918]

Dear White:

Your noble editorial came, a little delayed, to me today and I was deeply moved by it.[1] You know the west and you know me and your review of my career has the value of being at once authoritative and in good English. I wish I might see you and tell you by a grip of the hand how much this means to me.—Are we to see you east?—Dont fail to let me know.—The Inst. in spite of us all turned down the women—not some women but any women. They said it was unwise to bring the question into the Institute. We made a fight for it but were defeated. Thomas himself spoke strongly against the women—and so did Johnson.[2] I wish you had been present.

I shall write you again a little later—

Faithfully yours
Hamlin Garland

1. William Allen White (1868–1944), owner and editor of the *Emporia Gazette* (Kansas), fellow member of the National Institute, and author of many books on political and social events. His posthumously published *Autobiography of William Allen White* won the 1947 Pulitzer Prize. White had written to Garland on 8 February, enclosed his review of *Son* which had appeared in the *Emporia Gazette*, and asked Garland about the result of the Institute's proposition to admit women.

2. Augustus Thomas and Robert Underwood Johnson.

233. to Frank D. Fackenthal

tls, Pulitzer

71 East Ninety-Second Street
New York City

Mar. 25. [1918]

Dear Mr. Fackenthal:[1]

I have seen WHY MARRY by Jesse Lynch Williams and find it an admirable piece of comedy.[2] If the others are willing to vote the prize to it I will be glad to join them. There are some things in the piece which I do not like but on the whole it is the best piece of drama I have seen this year.

I have not gone out very much by reason of my lameness and I have not seen the plays you mentioned in a previous letter.

Very sincerely yours,
Hamlin Garland

1. Frank D. Fackenthal (1883–1968), secretary (1910–37), provost (1937–45), and acting president (1945–48) of Columbia University. Fackenthal was primarily responsible for the formation and administration of the Pulitzer juries and award system from the prizes' inception in 1915 to 1948. Garland served on the Pulitzer drama juries from 1917 to 1922, as chair in 1919 and 1920, and as chair of both the drama and fiction juries in

1921. *Why Marry?* was the first play to receive the Pulitzer, the jury having deemed no play produced during the 1916–17 season as worthy of the award.

2. In *Contemporaries*, Garland evaluates the play more fully: "Jesse is a neat workman. His piece is compact, clean cut, witty, and essentially fine. As a father and as a decent citizen, he resents the pornographic obsession of the day, and in 'Why Marry?' takes a whack at it. It is a highly diverting and well-written comedy, a little like Bernard Shaw, human as well as humorous, presenting a real problem without obvious preaching" (p. 178).

234. to Theodore Roosevelt   tls, Congress

71 East Ninety-Second Street
New York City

May. 8. [1918]

Dear Colonel:

It was good to see you looking so fit last night.[1] I wish I could step along as lithely as you did in crossing the platform! However I am not so lame and the warm weather is going to bring me around all to the good.

I am speaking and writing as occasion offers—that is about all I can do. I am going into the campaign for Universal Military Training, and I am writing in favor of the suspension of the alien press. Wisconsin would be a better state today if her German papers had been forbidden twenty years ago.

We all send affectionate greetings.

Faithfully yours,
Hamlin Garland

1. At a "Win the War" meeting at Carnegie Hall on 7 May, sponsored by the American Defense Society and American Rights League, Roosevelt denounced the Germans' sinking of the *Lusitania* and called for an army of ten thousand men to be sent to France.

235. to Theodore Roosevelt   als, Congress

Camp Neshonoc
Onteora Road
Tannersville
New York

July 22 [1918]

Dear Trailer:

I have been hoping hoping—but that report from a German commander seems final.[1] It brings a lump into my throat to think of that boy fighting like an eagle, and falling like an eagle. There is something magnificent in such a death and I can imagine that it must make it easier to bear. To have him go quickly, gallantly is better than to go lingeringly on the battle-field. —We think of you every day and our hearts are with you in your anxiety for the other boys. We pray they may be spared. There is a kind of comfort in the thought that thousands of other American fathers and mothers are watching and waiting too. All my friends are in constant dread. The war has come home to us—even to us who have no sons to give.

In my second volume of "The Middle Border" I find much of you. Only yesterday I was writing of the luncheon I took at the White House with you and Mrs. Roosevelt and the children. This was in 1903 or 4— and Quentin was a lad and Alice not married. How long ago it seems—at least to me—and now the boys are all soldiers! —

It brings to me a keen sense of the passing of the years—and of profound change. My lameness is less acute but I dare not volunteer for service in any way till I feel a little more secure. I shall go to France if possible but it would be foolish to go and be a burden instead of an aid.

With all love and loyalty
Hamlin Garland

1. Roosevelt's twenty-one-year-old son Quentin, one of four Roosevelt boys fighting in World War I and an aviator with the American army, was shot down over Château-Thierry, France, on 14 July 1918. After a week of conflicting reports, Quentin Roosevelt's death was confirmed in a note dropped by German aviators on 20 July.

236. to Theodore Roosevelt   tls, Congress

71 East Ninety-Second Street
New York City

Oct. 14 [1918]

Dear Colonel:

Rosebault told me yesterday that he was going to resign from his place in The Vigilantes.[1] I dont know just what this means but I have been giving a good deal of thought to the work of the Vigilantes and it seems to me that the organization should be maintained altho the particular work of rousing the country is accomplished. One of the needs of the time it seems to me is a campaign in favor of a closer alliance with England. I hear that there is a tendency on our army's side to belittle the part which England has taken in this war. Our men are said to fraternize with the French but not with the English.

I hope this is not true for the burden of this colossal war (as you have so often said) has fallen on England. Where would we be without her fleet? What would have happened to France if England had not thrown into line her army which we now know to have been a *little* army? It seems to me that you and those of us who realize these things should form ourselves into at least an irregular society to promote a closer friendship with England. When I think of the millions of men and the millions of money England has put into this monstrous war, my heart goes out to her. After all she is closer to us than any other nation. Do you feel that my suggestion is worth taking up at the Vigilantes?

I am in town for the winter and feeling better. I have been doing some speaking and I shall be glad to do more along the lines of this letter.

With greeting from us all
Hamlin Garland.

1. Charles Jerome Rosebault (1864–1944), managing editor of the newspaper and magazine services of the Vigilantes. As their letterhead explained, the Vigilantes was "A Non-Partisan Organization of Authors, Artists and Others for Patriotic Purposes." With an executive committee of seven, the Vigilantes comprised some ninety contributing members, including Roosevelt and Garland, who offered articles upon patriotic themes to the nation's newspapers through the Wheeler Syndicate and the American Press Association. Garland syndicated at least four articles from May to November 1918: "Our Alien Press," advocating the abolition of foreign-language newspapers in the

United States (16 May); "Universal Military Training" (31 May); "The Crime of Profi-
teering" (24 September); and "No Negotiated Peace" (2 November).

237. to Henry Blake Fuller
als, usc

Queen City Club

Nov. 6. [1918]

Dear Fuller:

Yesterday at Washington I lunched at the Congressional Library with Putnam[1] and his band of book experts—and one of them inquired with much interest about you—wanted to know if you were writing yet. I told him you were. He said he was accustomed to read the "Chevalier" at least once a year. Also liked the "Lines Long and Short" and altogether was agreeable.[2] I think his name was Ernot but I am not sure. Putnam also spoke of your work with respect. If you go to Washington—which you wont—make yourself known to these good friends. I found in Washington also a woman who has dramatized "Silas Lapham" and it is to be brought out soon. One of the Howells comedies is to be done in New York also and I think Howells will stay in the city to see them both.[3] He is at the *St. Hubert, 57th St.* if you want to write. He seems very well and I hope he can stay on for a month.—I am almost entirely well and speaking twice a day this week. Return to New York for the opening of the Annual Book Show Nov. 12.th—[4]

Write to Howells, he will be much interested to hear from you.

I have resigned from the Players and am now a member of the Century Club. This is the top. I cant get any higher until I seek the Gates of Pearl. I went in with Howells in my nominating paper. I am a "Senator" now!—

Yours
Hamlin Garland

1. Herbert Putnam (1861–1955), the Librarian of Congress.

2. Fuller's books *The Chevalier of Pensieri-Vani* (1892) and *Lines Long and Short: Biographical Sketches in Various Rhythms* (1917).

3. Lillian Sabine dramatized *The Rise of Silas Lapham*, which opened at the Garrick Theater in New York on 25 November 1919.

4. The Joint Committee of Literary Arts, from 1917 to 1919, sponsored an annual exhibit of the year's three hundred "most important" books. A jury of one hundred

editors and critics made the selections, which were exhibited at a dinner held during November at the National Arts Club. Because of the book shortage caused by the war, the 1918 exhibit showcased books "dealing directly or indirectly with the war" (Garland to Henry Holt, 15 October 1918, Princeton).

238. to Theodore Roosevelt

tlc, USC

Nov. 22. [1918]

Dear Colonel Roosevelt:

Your letter concerning the grave of your son Quentin and your statement that sometime you would build a simple monument over his body produced in me a desire to aid in the building [of] that memorial.[1] Without doubt his burial place will be one of the spots to which pilgrims will be directed after the war for he was not only a typical aviator but a representative American volunteer soldier. He responded like the minute man of '76 and in this action has the admiration of us all.

If you will permit it I will ask some of his friends and mine to serve as a committee to receive subscriptions to a fund to be used in buying a little plot of ground enclosing his grave and in erecting a memorial of stone or bronze. I am sure there are many who will feel as I do about this tribute and that it is possible that when you make your visit to the grave next summer you will find it planted to trees and surrounded by flowers.

My thought is to ask for a popular subscription, perhaps with a limit of one dollar so that a great many people can share in the enterprise. If there is any money left after the land is purchased and the stone erected it can be devoted to the care of other graves or it can be turned over to some good cause in the work of reconstruction.

In the hope that you will consent to this subscription

I am very faithfully yours,

1. In *Contemporaries* Garland records that he presented the proposal verbally to Roosevelt, who was in the hospital from 11 November to 25 December suffering from lumbago. Although touched by Garland's gesture, Roosevelt declined the memorial, preferring not to distinguish Quentin as a "hero" over the other soldiers who died (pp. 202–5).

The Advocate: 1919–1929

Introduction

FRESH FROM the success of *A Son of the Middle Border*, his estimation of his worth validated by election to the American Academy of Arts and Letters, Garland devoted much of his energies during this decade to promoting American literature and art while he continued work on his Middle Border volumes. In 1918, Frank D. Fackenthal, who was the secretary of Columbia University and who was responsible for the administration of the Pulitzer Prizes, asked Garland to serve on the drama jury for the 1917 prize. Garland was naturally gratified by the recognition such service conferred, and he went on to serve on the drama jury from 1917 to 1922, as the chair in 1919 and 1920, and as the chair of both the drama and fiction juries in 1921. In some ways, Garland was an odd choice for a drama juror: his frequent travels on the lecture circuit often made him unavailable to see the plays he was to judge, and he soon came to rely upon others to tell him which plays he should see. His credentials as a drama juror were also suspect: he had, after all, made his reputation in fiction, and his fellow jurors were established playwrights or drama critics. Nonetheless, he evidently saw his position as Pulitzer juror to be an opportunity to promote the realistic drama for which he had campaigned so vigorously in Boston in 1891, yet he soon found himself out of his depth because the plays being produced belonged, for the most part, to a generation far more liberal in its treatment of sex than even the author of *Rose of Dutcher's Coolly* could tolerate. Garland consistently lobbied against voting the prize to Eugene O'Neill's plays. Only reluctantly did he join in voting for *Beyond the Horizon*, which won the first of O'Neill's four Pulitzers, informing Columbia President Nicholas Murray Butler, "I can not regard O'Neill's play as 'Noble' or 'Uplifting' which are I believe the expressed terms of the bequest" (11 May 1920, letter 254). And for *Anna Christie*, the tale of a prostitute, he had nothing but scorn. "I do not see how we can vote a prize to the morbid kind of play that O'Neill writes," he noted in a 28 April 1922 letter to William Lyon Phelps. "He has had one prize on those lines and to give him another would be to emphasize a kind of thing which is essentially unwholesome. . . . It seems to me we have had too much pornographic literature this year. The Pulitzer

Prize should not add to its vogue. I hate the whole school which is essentially unAmerican" (letter 278).

His service as chair of the 1921 fiction jury was especially problematic. The leading candidate was Sinclair Lewis's *Main Street*, which posed problems for the increasingly conservative Garland. "I confess I am tired of all this pornographic fiction," he wrote to fellow juror Stuart Pratt Sherman, in what would become an incessant litany of complaint. After a fractious series of letters, Garland reluctantly joined in the decision for *Main Street*, only to have the decision overturned by Columbia's board of trustees in favor of Edith Wharton's *The Age of Innocence*, with the jurors then protesting the decision in print.[1]

Ironically, although Garland was a conservative voice on the Pulitzer juries, he was perceived as a radical in the staunchly conservative American Academy of Arts and Letters, where he campaigned vigorously for the institution to take a more active role in American cultural life, lest it be seen as superfluous. "The Academy should be a progressive force in American Arts and Letters," he wrote to Brander Matthews, the Academy's chancellor, on 7 October 1921. "We must not be senile. We are called 'an old man's Home'" (letter 272). As a member of the Academy's board of directors, Garland was in a position to set policy and chart its future. His letters of this period reveal the infighting that blocked his attempts to get the Academy to do more than serve as a gentleman's club. He was most concerned that the munificence of the Academy's principal benefactor, Archer M. Huntington, not be squandered, and he therefore worked tirelessly to safeguard Huntington's considerable investment in the institution. His attempt to publicize the Academy by bringing in nonmembers for "tea" was quashed by the board (see Garland to William M. Sloane, 7 October 1923, letter 286), but other efforts were more successful. He published an article in the London *Bookman* outlining the Academy's history and goals,[2] and he proposed and took charge of an Academy Medal for Good Diction over the Radio—an effort to counter what Garland perceived as the slipping standards of speech and an opportunity to encourage a national standard of "melodious speech."[3]

During these efforts to encourage a national literary culture, Garland was busy writing the volumes of his Middle Border saga. *A Daughter of the Middle Border* appeared in 1921. Disappointed with Macmillan's publicity campaign—and the lack of critical or popular interest—Garland lobbied the editors of leading magazines to review it as a continuation of the more successful *A Son of the Middle Border*. Even when he received word that *Daughter* had won the 1922 Pulitzer Prize for biography, he continued his lobbying. "In rendering your verdict on A DAUGHTER OF THE MIDDLE BORDER," he wrote to William Allen White, one of the jurors, "did you bear in mind that it was in fact the completion of the publication of A SON OF THE MIDDLE BORDER? I want to say that the prize is for the two volumes if I can. The official announcement has come to me but not for publication as yet. When my publishers announce it they want to make it cover both volumes. I requested them to so treat the two books" (20 May 1922 [Congress]).

The prize money of one thousand dollars enabled Garland and his family to go to England for the summer, for purposes of business and pleasure. He wanted to revisit England and his English friends to freshen his memory to revitalize his lectures; moreover, despite the lack of critical interest in *Daughter*, he began to plan another volume that would trace the family's fortunes along the "back trail." Finally, Mary Isabel, who had graduated from Finch Academy, had announced her desire to pursue a stage career. Garland, who had come to regard the stage as another manifestation of "pornography," promised her six months in Europe if she would reconsider her decision. Once he arrived in England Garland promptly renewed acquaintanceship with his old friends Kipling, Barrie, Shaw, and Zangwill, and he embarked on an ambitious round of dinners and calls. His notes of his meetings would provide him with fresh material for his lectures, and when he returned to America in October, his daughter Mary Isabel accompanied him on the lecture circuit, where she read from the Middle Border volumes dressed alternatively as her mother and grandmother.

The success of his lectures encouraged Garland to make return visits to England in 1923, 1924, and 1925, without his family. The notes of his literary encounters not only supplied him with fresh lecture material, but these recollections, together with his diaries (which he began keeping in 1898), would become the basis for his four volumes of literary "logbooks," which he began in 1929.

Garland prospered, both socially and financially. In 1925 he bought a summer home in the exclusive club community of Onteora, New York. The Middle Border books became a family project, with Mary Isabel typing the manuscripts and Constance providing illustrations. *Trail-Makers of the Middle Border* appeared in 1926, to good reviews; *Back-Trailers from the Middle Border* followed in 1928. He found himself to be the recipient of a wave of letters soliciting his advice on literary matters or requesting him to evaluate manuscripts.

Garland's comfort and security, however, was soon ruptured: Mary Isabel announced her marriage to Hardesty Johnson, a singer, in 1926; Constance followed the next year with her marriage to Joseph Harper, of the publishing firm. Both daughters moved to California and, realizing that the separation would be too painful to bear, the Garlands decided to follow them there in late 1929, purchasing a lot next door to Mary Isabel's home. "At sixty-nine years of age," Garland noted, "I found myself facing not only a future without my daughters but the still more disturbing realization that my wife was about to suffer a painful bereavement. That such separations had been the rule in our ancestral history is true, but in my case it was not absolutely necessary. I can write as well in California as in New York or Massachusetts" (*Afternoon*, p. 547).

NOTES

1. See Garland to Fackenthal, 11 May 1921 (letter 267). See also Robert Morse Lovett, "The Pulitzer Prize," *New Republic*, 22 June 1921, p. 114, for his public discussion of the board's decision; and "Pulitzer Prizes Picked to Pieces," *Literary Digest* 70 (16 July 1921): 26–7.

2. See "The American Academy of Arts and Letters," *Bookman* (London) 65 (November 1923): 89–92.

3. See "The Value of Melodious Speech," *Emerson Quarterly* 9 (November 1929): 5, 6, 22, 24.

239. to Edith Roosevelt

ald, usc

71 East Ninety-Second Street
New York City

Jan. 7. [1919]

Dear Mrs Roosevelt:

I feel so deeply the death of Theodore Roosevelt that I can not use my voice in speaking of him.[1] As you know we were friends for over a quarter of a century. He has been a vast and helpful presence in my world for so long that I can not believe that he is gone—and yet at the same time the pain in my throat testifies to such a belief.—It is a pleasure to me to think of the visits I made to him at the hospital—and the recollection of his voice and face as he took my hand and called me by my first name, comforts me now. We talked much of the days gone and I came away with a sense of having drawn closer to him than ever before.—I shall write of him—I have written of him—in the story I am writing of the west, for he seems a western man to me—he understood the west better than most western men.

If there is anything I can do now or hereafter to make his fame more entirely permanent, be sure that I will do it with a sincere joy.

Most faithfully yours
Hamlin Garland

1. Roosevelt died on 6 January. Garland recounts what his death meant to him in *Contemporaries*, pp. 213–15. Garland mailed another version of this letter, which is unlocated, and wrote in the top left corner of this draft: "Not sent. Another slightly different."

240. to Montrose J. Moses

tls, Duke

71 East Ninety-Second Street
New York City

Jan. 10 [1919]

Dear Mr. Moses:

As Chairman of The Pulitzer Prize Committee on Drama, I am trying to find a play which is worthy of that prize.[1] It must be an American play, not in any sense an adaptation, produced in New York during the calendar year of 1918. The only candidate thus far is the COPPERHEAD and I am not favorable to that for the reason that it was built round another man's short story and the cleavage shows. I would be greatly obliged for your opinion concerning the plays of the year as I know you have seen most of them.[2]

Very sincerely yours,
Hamlin Garland

1. Montrose J. Moses (1878–1934), drama critic and editor, whose works include *The American Dramatist* (1911) and *Clyde Fitch and His Letters* (with Virginia Gerson, 1924). Garland had received a 10 January 1919 letter from Frank D. Fackenthal naming him chair of the Pulitzer drama jury, with fellow judges Richard Burton and Clayton Hamilton (1881–1946), playwright, teacher, author of eleven books on drama and fiction, and drama critic for the *Forum*, the *Bookman*, *Everybody's Magazine*, and *Vogue*. Fackenthal noted that Augustus Thomas's *The Copperhead* had thus far received the only nomination.

2. In his reply of 16 January 1919, Moses suggested that, although they fell outside of the time limit, Robert Housum's *The Gipsy Trail* (opening 4 December 1917) and Edward Childs Carpenter's *The Pipes of Pan* (6 November 1917) were suitable candidates. He counseled that no play produced in 1918 revealed "any unique merit."

241. to William Dean Howells

tlc, Miami U

Jan. 12. [1919]

Dear Howells:

For the last three or four days I've been writing about Roosevelt. He has filled my mind so completely that I have been in the mood for no other work. I have known him so long that his going leaves a vacant place in my horizon. I am putting together my impressions of him not with any intention of publishing them but to get them down.[1]

There is a chance that I may come rikochaying down thru your land one of these days for I am asked to do some talking for the cantonments. Also I am talking on Howells and Mark Twain for two or three schools. If I will promise not to talk of Howells perhaps you will get me a chance to speak in Augusta. I am sorto specializing on this talk which is entirely off hand and has been very successful. I am so much improved in health that I am even coketting with the idea of going to France to speak for the YMCA over there. All depends on the verdict of my doctor.

Irving is at Winter Park Florida.[2] I shall get as far as his place and may stay there a little time. I dont like the cold myself and the thought of getting away for Feb. is attractive. It may be that I shall not get away till late in the month. We all send love and best influences against the influenza.

Faithfully,

1. Garland's recollections of Roosevelt appeared as "My Neighbor, Theodore Roosevelt," *Everybody's Magazine* 41 (October 1919): 9–16, 94; and "Theodore Roosevelt," *Mentor* 7 (2 February 1920): 1–12.

2. Garland refers to Irving Bacheller.

242. to Charles C. Baldwin tl, USC

Jan. 25. [1919]

Dear Mr. Baldwin:[1]

Some years ago I wrote an article for the North American Review on Howells.[2] I enclose part of it which may be of use to you. I can not find time to do a new article. In my MIDDLE BORDER there is a chapter about Howells and I think you can get permission to quote that if you write to Mr. Marsh of Macmillans. You may use the material I send herewith. I suggest that you quote it without giving my name as by "a writer in the North American Review" or better yet rewrite it into the body of your own chapter.

With regard to my own work: Main-Travelled Roads, Rose of Dutchers Coolly, The Captain of the Gray Horse Troop, and A Son of the Middle Border give a pretty good idea of what I have been doing for the last thirty years. A Son of the Middle Border not being fiction must be sharply differentiated from the others. My Colorado stories Hesper and Her Mountain Lover were among my most successful books but in some ways Money Magic is a better book.

It is probable that A Son of the Middle Border will outlast all of my stories except Main Travelled Roads for the very good reason that it is a social history, the story of a family during a time of National migration.

The reason why I prefer not to be quoted is obvious. If you use any of the material which Howells put into his comment on my work I can not be quoted about him. We can not appear to be praising each other in the same volume. Please be very careful about this.

I hope all this may be of some help to you.

Very sincerely yours,

1. Baldwin had contracted to write *The Men Who Make Our Novels* for Dodd, Mead & Co. He had written, 22 January 1919, to ask Garland if he would write 1500–2500 words on Howells, "the man, the friend, the critic and the novelist . . . what he has meant to you personally and to your literary day, your beginnings and Mark Twain's." He also asked Garland to rank his own books. The book was published under the pseudonym of "George Gordon" by Moffat and Yard in 1919.

2. Garland refers to "Sanity in Fiction," *North American Review* 176 (1903): 336–48.

243. to Hermann Hagedorn ald, usc

71. East 92nd St
New York City

[4 February 1919]

Dear Mr Hagedorn:[1]

The personnel and the plans of the Roosevelt Memorial Committee are inspiring and my daughters and I want to be among the early contributors. Please put us down for twenty dollars, ten on my own account and five dollars each for Mary Isabel Garland and Constance Garland.

My acquaintance with Theodore Roosevelt began in the early nineties when he was Police Commissioner and I have many vivid memories of him scattered all through the years of our long friendship. He meant much to me and I earnestly desire to assist in furthering the plans of your committee.

My first suggestion is that you issue a call for Roosevelt stories.[2] As in the case of Lincoln—tho in an entirely different vein—there are innumerable characteristic stories of Roosevelt lying in the minds of those who knew him. These stories are now being retold. Men are thinking about him—now is the time to gather them together. This, it appears to

me, would be a perfectly proper work for your committee to undertake.
Perhaps some sort of memorial volume to be called Stories of Theodore
Roosevelt could be issued by your committee or under its auspices, the ·
income of which could go to the memorial in some fashion. I shall be
very glad to contribute to such a volume.

Very sincerely yours
Hamlin Garland

1. Hermann Hagedorn (1882–1964), historian, biographer, novelist, poet, dramatist,
editor, and secretary of the Roosevelt Memorial Committee. An authority on Theodore
Roosevelt, his works include *The Boy's Life of Theodore Roosevelt* (1918), *Roosevelt in the
Bad Lands* (1921), *The Americanism of Theodore Roosevelt* (1923), *The Works of Theodore
Roosevelt* (1923–1926), and *The Bugle That Woke America* (1940).

2. Garland himself drafted a letter calling for stories of Roosevelt, which appeared as
"Wants Roosevelt Stories," *New York Times*, 6 February 1919, p. 10. He chaired the
committee gathering the "stories" and wrote to people who had known Roosevelt, soliciting their recollections. The memorial volume was eventually published as *Roosevelt
As We Knew Him*, ed. Frederick S. Wood (1927). Garland's "story" appears as "Recollections of Roosevelt." See *Contemporaries*, pp. 216–23, for Garland's participation in
the Roosevelt Memorial Association.

244. to Frank D. Fackenthal tls, Pulitzer

Hamlin Garland
71 East Ninety-Second Street
New York City

Mar. 22 [1919]

Secretary Columbia University:

In the judgement of your committee no play produced in New York
City within the calendar year 1918 is entirely worthy the prize of The Pulitzer Bequest. Whether by reason of the turmoil of war or from some
change in the temper of managers and audiences, most of the plays of the
year in question are either very light entertainment or so crudely melodramatic as to be of little literary value. No play by a native author stands
out commandingly and as your committee can not wholeheartedly commend any candidate, we advise that the award go over to another year.

Your committee further suggests that as the period of play production
is during the winter months, the theatrical and not the calendar year be

taken as the limit in which the competing plays shall be staged. Confusion results from splitting the theatrical season in half. Furthermore the author is less likely to be shut out of the year to which he naturally belongs if he has the entire theatrical year in which to bring his play to a New York stage.[1]

With sincere regret that our report must be negative we remain very sincerely yours,

Hamlin Garland

Richard Burton

Clayton Hamilton

1. The Pulitzer Advisory Board adopted this suggestion, beginning with the following year.

245. to Lorado Taft

tl, USC

May second. [1919]

Dear Lorado: Your highly diverting and moderately informing letters have reached us from time to time and make me thankful that I did not go over.[1] I fear I could not have stood the rain and the cold. The reason why we have not written is this; namely; to wit; it seems like firing a shot in the dark. We never know where you are to be and so we let it go till the next letter. However we have written several times. Your letters are amusing but do not raise any extravagant hopes about the future. The army is to be all out of France by Sept. and I dont see the point of building concrete houses. However that is the way the army has to work. It can only assume the status quo.

Just now I am also speaking with almost equal success. If the truth ever gets out it will be known that you and I are wonderful orators. I am getting more and more of a confirmed platform humorist. I am not yet as degraded and shameless as you have become—I never pun for example but I make people burst into laughter. They do not laugh their heads off or anything like that but they smile. I had a very successful visit to Colgate and Cornell last week. On the ninth I speak at a Walt Whitman meeting and also at the big reception at Columbia when a Roosevelt Memorial collection of things connected with him is formerly displayed.[2]

My roomatism is almost subdued. I can run up and down stairs and lead my children a merry race in the park. We shall walk all over the hills this summer. Yes we are expecting you and the whole darn family. I have built on a couple of rooms and have a little separate guest house besides. Things are going very well with me this year. My lectures and my farms have brought sunshine to our humble flat—also the fact that I am better of my aches helps some. We are going up to the place at the earliest moment. I am eager to get where I can set to work on some new material. I cant do it here the distractions are too great.

Maude Radford came in and told us a few things and we are hearing from you from other sources. They ought to make the fullest use of you and they would if they could keep you from telling of Oregon and Jessie Louise.[3] Of course the French need to hear of your Community Idea but the boys are likely to be made homesicker by it. If I were Erskine I would not permit any such talk.[4]

We gave a big dinner to Markham[5] the other night, his sixty-seventh birthday. Nearly five hundred sat down in the New Commodore Hotel. Augustus Thomas presided with his usual grace. The town is so full of people that there are no houses or flats for them. It is the greatest city in the world now. Nearly seven millions. I am content to have even a little coop like this. We are expecting you in June. We all enjoy your letter. Hope you get better weather soon.

Hamlin.

1. As part of a YMCA effort to provide recreation and educational opportunities for American troops in France, Taft served as a lecturer at the AEF University in Baune, France, from January through May 1919.

2. From 10 May to 4 June 1919, books, sculpture, trophies, portraits, and other objects celebrating Roosevelt's life were displayed in Avery Library at Columbia University.

3. Jessie Louise Taft, one of Taft's three daughters. Maude Radford has not been identified.

4. John Erskine (1879–1951), a Columbia University professor of English, was the educational director of the AEF University in Baune in 1919.

5. The poet Edwin Markham.

246. to William Roscoe Thayer

als, Harvard

Hamlin Garland
71 East Ninety-Second Street
New York City

Nov. 26. [1919]

Dear Mr Thayer:

I have just finished reading your Roosevelt and must tell you how fine I find it.[1] It comes very near my own estimate of the debated points of his career. I knew him nearly twenty five years—Not as you know him of course but in a very frank direct fashion. We met on the simplest neighborly grounds and many of those meetings are now historic. I was with him at lunch just before that tremendous last speech in Carnegie Hall— and yet he only alluded to it as we were parting—He was making a test of whether criticism of the Administration was treason or no—"I've run up the black flag" he said with a smile.

I am writing a short sketch for *Mentor*[2] and hope to give it a little of the remoteness of posterity's judgment.—

What I like about your book is its frank admission of bias. No one could know Roosevelt without bias—in his favor. It is a noble book.

Faithfully yours
Hamlin Garland.

1. William Roscoe Thayer (1859–1923), Boston author and editor, wrote *Theodore Roosevelt: An Intimate Biography* (1919).

2. See "Theodore Roosevelt," *Mentor* 7 (2 February 1920): 1–12.

247. to John Drinkwater

als, Yale

Hamlin Garland
71 East Ninety-Second Street
New York City

Dec. 27. [1919]

Dear Mr Drinkwater:[1]

My wife and daughters went with me to see your "Lincoln" and all write with me in praise of it. It is a profoundly moving play—especially moving to me for I was born in 1860 and "Grant" and "Lincoln" are among the epic words of my earliest memories. My father was a soldier under Grant and an early abolitionist.—I have written a life of Grant—a book which cost me two years of labor and thirty thousand miles of travel—so you see I have a reason for being interested in your play. Will you not take tea with us some afternoon at the MacDowell Club and let us tell you a little more in detail how significant we find this work to be?

Perhaps I can get Bacheller at the same time. His book on Lincoln you should have—[2]

With sincere regard
Hamlin Garland

1. John Drinkwater (1882–1937), British playwright and poet, and author of the play *Abraham Lincoln* (1919).

2. Garland refers to Irving Bacheller's *A Man for the Ages* (1919), a novel about Lincoln.

248. to Walter Pritchard Eaton tls, Virginia

Hamlin Garland
71 East Ninety-Second Street
New York City

Feb. 2. [1920]

Dear Eaton:[1]

Our committee on the Prize Drama is as badly off this year as last. I do not see any play to which we can give a prize unless it is Drinkwaters "Lincoln." It seems that this play is eligible altho the author is not American and perhaps we can emphasize the pettiness of our native output by giving a prize to this serious and noble work.[2] True, it is not a play in the conventional sense but it comes nearer to the ideal expressed in the terms of the bequest than "Clarence" or "Lightnin'" which are just amusing *shows*. I am going south and may not see "Mrs Fair" which is another candidate. I shall be glad of your opinion.

Thomas' play was good technically but not original enough in story and characterization.

Faithfully yours,
Hamlin Garland

1. Walter Pritchard Eaton (1878–1957), drama critic for the *New York Sun* and the *New York Tribune*, author of several books of the theater, among them *The American*

Stage of To-Day (1908) and *At the New Theatre and Others* (1910). Eaton, along with drama critic Richard Burton and Garland (as chair), were the Pulitzer Prize jury for drama in 1920.

2. Garland had written to Nicholas Murray Butler (1862–1947), the president of Columbia University and chair of the Pulitzer Advisory Board, about the eligibility of the British playwright's *Abraham Lincoln.* Butler replied on 23 January 1920 that the play "seemed to fulfill Mr. Pulitzer's ideals more completely than any play I have ever seen." He explained that the Advisory Board had decided that "if a book or play was on an American subject, it would not be disqualified in competition although the author was himself a foreigner." The Pulitzer Plan of Award called for awarding the drama prize to "the American play, performed in New York, which shall best represent the educational value and power of the stage in raising the standard of good morals, good taste and good manners." The other plays to which Garland refers are Booth Tarkington's *Clarence*, Frank Bacon and Winchell Smith's *Lightnin'*, James Forbes's *The Famous Mrs. Fair*, and Augustus Thomas's *The Copperhead.*

249. to Elbert Jay Benton

tlc, USC

Feb. 3. [1920?]

Dear Prof. Benton:[1]

By skipping a big reception here I can remain in Cleveland to give you the talk on the Middle Border and so you may count on it. It will be a more or less humorous informal discourse without manuscript concerning almanacks, cow milking, ballads—and any other subject which comes into my head. I may even break out in song. I may also read a little from the Middle Border book. Thus far people have not gone to sleep on it. I have two other off-hand talks about Shaw, Barrie[,] Kipling, Zangwill, Hardy and other of my English writer friends but I think perhaps the Middle Border talk will be most likely to please your audience.

I want to go to a hotel that is out of the noise and dirt of the city. Can you tell me of one?

Very sincerely yours,

1. Elbert J. Benton (1871–1946), a professor of history at Western Reserve University.

Feb. 11 [1920]

Dear Lane:

I had Max Ravage to lunch with me today and held much talk with him concerning the matter of Americanization. He is a man of insight and knows the Ghetto thoroly. He intends to devote himself to the work of delineating the "New American" as he calls these foreign-born or foreign-derived men and women.[1]

He made a suggestion as to A Roosevelt Memorial which has interested some of the Committee greatly. He said: Why not establish A Roosevelt Memorial National Scholarship whose effect should be to take certain picked men and women of Polish, Russian, Jewish, Italian or other European origin, and send them to State Universities in the Middle West, schools that are in small towns where the life is not only American but where the college dominates the town. In this way we would be educating advocates of the things which Roosevelt stood for. These men and women wd become the most powerful influence against any violence or bitterness. He went on to say that it should not be done by private subscription but by the government but that it should be a Roosevelt Foundation.

It seems to me it would be worth your while to send for him and make use of him in some way. He is poor, of course, and must be paid something for his work.

With regard to the National Scholarship idea I have already spoken to the editors of Current Opinion and the Literary Digest and I believe they will take it up with the heartiest enthusiasm. It is the kind of working Memorial which Roosevelt believed in. Let me know how it appeals to you and if you can give it out in some sort of interview as a part of your general plan of campaign that is the thing to do. The National Memorial Committee will assist in any way possible.

I shall want your assistance on The Roosevelt Stories volume to the extent at least of a good characteristic anecdote.

Ravage may be reached at 436 Fort Washington Ave. NY. City.

Very faithfully yours,
Hamlin Garland

1. Garland admired Marcus Eli Ravage's *The Making of an American: The Life Story of an Immigrant* (1917). Lane had written, 31 December 1919, that he had had "a resolu-

tion put through the Committees on Education of both the House and the Senate, asking the Moving Picture Industry to interest itself in Americanization." Lane had been appointed to head a committee to take charge and wanted to talk with Garland about "some schemes for this work."

251. to Jasper E. Brady

tlc, usc

Mar. 31. [1920]

Dear Col. Brady:

I have just learned from my brother that you are in New York and I am writing to say that I am almost entirely free from the Vitagraph contract which has not been profitable. As a matter of fact Smith[1] has not produced a play of mine for two years and more and according to the release clause in the contract all rights have reverted to me. Previously to this I had induced Smith to exempt from the contract all my short stories, The Tyranny of the Dark, The Eagles Heart, and several others of the novels so that I am free to negotiate for these. My brother who is in Los Angeles has the agency for my work there and I am hoping you will be able to use some of my work here. If you find yourself able to help my brother in his work as an actor I shall be glad.

If you have a moment to spare some day I will come in and ask how you are. Did the boy come back safely? I hope he did and that he is going on successfully in his work.[2]

With regards to you and yours,

Smith only produced four plays which you selected, and they paid me only three or four thousand dollars all told. Perhaps this was due to the war but I think it was due to the way in which they were produced.

1. Albert E. Smith (1875–1958), Vitagraph's treasurer and business manager.
2. Garland is enquiring about Brady's son's service during the war.

252. to Frank D. Fackenthal

tls, Pulitzer

Hamlin Garland
71 East Ninety-Second Street
New York City

April. 19. [1920]

Dear Mr. Fackenthal:

Did you see Mackayes Washington? I did not get back from the South in time but my wife saw it and thought it admirable. "Beyond the Horizon" is a powerful piece of work but I am not sure of the man's motive.[1] It seemed to me ruthless for the sake of ruthlessness. I did not feel just the quality a prize play should have. If the Com. can agree on Mackayes Washington I will vote for it for I have read the play and I know how high the work is.

I shall see the other men soon.

Very sincerely yours
Hamlin Garland.

1. Garland refers to Percy MacKaye's *Washington, the Man Who Made Us* and Eugene O'Neill's *Beyond the Horizon.*

253. to Montrose J. Moses

tls, Duke

Hamlin Garland
71 East Ninety-Second Street
New York City

April. 22 [1920]

Dear Mr. Moses:

If you were giving a prize for the best American play produced during this season, on whom would it fall? I am asking some of my friends this question because having been away I have seen only a few of the plays.

How are you and the wife and child?

Best wishes from us all
Hamlin Garland

Did you see MacKaye's play?[1]

1. Moses replied, 23 April 1920, that "there is no doubt in my mind that the outstanding play of the season by an American is Eugene O'Neill's BEYOND THE HORIZON"; *Washington* he did not think "noteworthy."

254. to Nicholas Murray Butler

tls, Pulitzer

Hamlin Garland
71 East Ninety-Second Street
New York City

May 11. [1920]

Dear Doctor Butler:

The Committee was deeply disturbed by my test query as to whether they would be willing to give the prize to Drinkwater, provided the terms of the Bequest permitted it.[1] The Committee said that such an award would be a rebuff of American authorship and act in a way directly opposite to the intention of the donor of the Endowment. The committee is almost a unit in favor of BEYOND THE HORIZON Eugene O'Neills play. Dr. Burton and Walter Eaton are very emphatic on the choice, and they are supported by Clayton Hamilton and Montrose Moses two of our very best informed men. So far as my own judgment is concerned I can not bring myself to vote for a prize to a mere entertainment such as most of the successful plays are, and yet I can not regard O'Neills play as "Noble" or "Uplifting" which are I believe the expressed terms of the bequest. Nevertheless as it is the outstanding play of the season, thus far, I will join in the award.

Hoping this will answer the inquiries of your Advisor, I am very sincerely yours,

Hamlin Garland

1. At the Advisory Board's request, Butler had written, on 10 May 1920, to ask "what consideration, if any, was given to Drinkwater's Lincoln" during the drama committee's deliberations. Butler subsequently informed Garland, 13 May 1920, that the committee's decision was "in flat antagonism to the principles laid down by the Advisory Board in interpreting Mr. Pulitzer's deed of gift." O'Neill's *Beyond the Horizon*, which had opened on 3 February, was the 1920 recipient of the Pulitzer Prize for drama.

255. to Harriet Monroe

tls, U Chicago

71 East Ninety-Second Street
New York City

[ca. 2 October 1920]

Dear Miss Monroe:

I am coming to Chicago to visit my friends and to lecture for the universities round about. I hope I shall be able to see you either at the Little Room or elsewhere altho I shall have only a few days in the city. Meanwhile I wish you would tell me whom you consider the chief poet of present day America. Would you say that Amy Lowell is the most vital and commanding figure? Are any of our poets doing work of sufficient breadth to be compared with—say Moody for example.[1]

Faithfully yours,
Hamlin Garland

1. Monroe noted at the bottom of this letter:

Sandburg ⎫
Masters ⎪
         ⎬ power + vitality
Robinson ⎪
Frost   ⎭

Pound   ⎫
        ⎬ about beauty
Stevens ⎭

256. to Stuart Pratt Sherman

tls, U of Ill-Ar

American Academy of Arts and Letters
Office of the Permanent Secretary
Room 1412, 347 Madison Avenue
New York

Dec. 17. [1920]

Dear Prof. Sherman:

I am informed by Columbia University that you, W. H. Bishop and I are to decide on the prize novel for the year, and that I am to act as chairman.[1] All I can do is to pull our various judgements together, and to that end I wish you would send to me, from time to time, the names of such novels as you think I should read. If you will do this it will save me a great deal of wear on my eyes. My only suggestion at the moment, is MAIN STREET by Lewis of which I hear good things. I knew some of Lewis's work and like it.

There is some hope of my getting to Urbana in April. William Allen White is arranging a series of lectures for me in Kansas, and in coming and going I may be able to fill the dates which we failed to arrange for in November. If you are in town meanwhile—I mean New York—I hope you will let me know.

With Holiday Greetings. I am

Very sincerely yours,
Hamlin Garland

1. William H. Bishop (1847–1928) had to resign from the jury in January because he would be in France during deliberation; Robert Morss Lovett (1870–1956), a professor of English at the University of Chicago and associate editor of the *New Republic*, took his place. Garland also served as chair of the drama jury for 1921, with fellow jurors William Lyon Phelps and Richard Burton, and soon found his dual chairmanships severely taxing his time, for he was also revising the manuscript of *A Daughter of the Middle Border*.

257. to Rudyard Kipling als, USC

The Century Club
7 West Forty-Third Street

Jan. 4. [1921]

Dear Kipling: [1]

We are all delighted to have your promise of a letter concerning Howells.[2] Anything you send us will be keenly appreciated. It is probable that I (as Acting Secretary) will read your letter and I hope you will write as fully as you feel minded to do. We are hoping to have a similar message from Valdés and from the French and Belgium Academies.[3] At your convenience, I shall be most happy to receive the M.S. which I hope will be in your own handwriting, for it will go into the Academy Archives. I do not ask this, however for I would not add to the work involved. On the contrary I am especially desirous of a full expression of the regard I know you had for Howells. I am asking William Allen White to take up Howells kindly interest in young writers and anything you could add to that side of his work as critic would be most welcome.

With deep personal affection

I am faithfully yours
Hamlin Garland

1. Rudyard Kipling (1865–1936), the immensely popular British author of such works as *The Light That Failed* (1891), *Many Inventions* (1893), *The Jungle Book* (1894), *Captains Courageous* (1897), *Kim* (1901), and *Just So Stories* (1902). Garland first met Kipling in 1892 when Kipling invited him to dinner in New York. See "A Dinner With Kipling," chapter 14 of *Roadside.*

2. On 1 March 1921 the American Academy and the National Institute held a joint William Dean Howells Memorial meeting at the Stuart Gallery of the New York Public Library. Garland outlined the history of the Academy and the plans for the celebration in an interview, "In Honor of Howells," *New York Times*, 27 February 1921, sec. 4, p. 6. Kipling's tribute letter was published as "Howells Eulogized as Man and Author," *New York Times*, 2 March 1921, p. 8.

3. Armando Palacio Valdés (1853–1938), Spanish novelist whose books Howells championed in his "Editor's Study" columns.

258. to James M. Barrie

als, usc

71. East 92nd St
New York City.

[8 January 1921]

Dear Barrie: [1]

I have just returned from seeing your "Mary Rose" and I have seldom been so moved—so filled with the all-pervading tragedy of life.[2] Whether my daughters felt the same pathos, the heart-break of its message, I can not say—I hope they didnt for at sixty we look at such visions with different eyes to those we owned in youth. Furthermore as a student of psychic phenomena I found myself responding to the suggestion of it all—I am at work on the second volume of my "Middle Border" and the question I ask at the end is that which I find in your play—What is the meaning of the dream we call life?—There was an intolerable pathos in your play. It was an exquisitely cruel conception—that of bringing the young wife back to a family which had grown old! It is hard to say just why it moved me so. I came away wearied with the tension it put upon my imagination.

The scene in the Hebrides brought back to me the curious fact that at our luncheon in London many years ago the other guest was an Inspector of Schools in the Hebrides Islands. Do you recall him—a black-bearded man he was then—and his talk? He invited me to make the rounds with him and now I wish I had accepted. Your play would have meant all the more to me.—Shall you ever come to America again? If you do I hope you will let me know for I would like to have you dine with me and my wife and daughters. In summer we are near neighbors to Maud Adams[3] in Onteora and the tradition is that you have been up there at least once—. I often speak of you and our pleasant meetings when we were still on the sunny side of forty. I see all your plays as they come and I read them when they are printed with wonder of your imaginative freshness. Sometimes I think you must have the help of the Invisible Ones.—

With sincerest admiration
Hamlin Garland.

1. James M. Barrie (1860–1937), British novelist and playwright, whose *Peter Pan* (1904) enjoyed great success.

2. Garland was so moved by this play that he quotes this letter in its entirety in his discussion of the drama in *Contemporaries*, pp. 331–33.

3. Maude Adams (1872–1953), British actress who played in Barrie's *The Little Minister* (1898) and, in the role of Peter, in *Peter Pan.*

259. to Mildred Howells

als, Harvard

71. East 92nd St.
New York City

Jan. 21 [1921]

Dear Mildred:[1]

Your letter delighted me with its news concerning your coming to the Garlands. I wish you would think of us as almost of the Howells family and call on us for aid at any time. I wonder if your father ever told you that he was the first to be told of Zulime's engagement to me? He chanced to be in Chicago during the very first week of my new state and I hastened to show him my bride and receive his blessing. Then, the last time he called on us here—as he was leaving he stooped and kissed each of my children, leaving his blessing on them. He filled so large a place in my life that his going left me with a sense of awe, as if my whole world were crumbling—which it is!—

You are right. A volume of his letters should be gotten out at once and I shall do everything I can for you.[2] His letters to Twain, Matthews, Fuller and dozens of others should be called in at once. Why don't you have a Literary Note sent out asking for letters?—I shall be most happy to advise or assist in any way. When you come let us go all over the matter. Perhaps John can come to dinner with you. I wish I saw more of John but I suppose he thinks of me as an old man (which I am) and of small concern in his world.

I am going to tell Mr Anderson that the material he wants is not accessible.[3] He will be disappointed, as I am, but we can not ask you to go to York Harbor to dig the material up. As I think I wrote you I am speaking on your father's work at several of the universities late in Jan. but I shall return here the 5th of Feb. Please reserve an evening for us early in your New York stay. Could we say Sunday evening, the 6th? I hope so. We will have no one else for we shall want to talk over your plans.

Very faithfully yours
Hamlin Garland

You will want some of the most interesting photographs in the book of letters. The house in Jefferson Ohio is the one I should like to see a picture of. Those seven years in his little den under the stairway were wonderful years to him—and to us.

1. Mildred Howells (1872–1966), the youngest of Howells's three children.

2. In her 19 January letter accepting Garland's dinner invitation, Mildred Howells announced her intention to collect and edit her father's letters, which were published in two volumes in 1928 as *The Life in Letters of William Dean Howells.*

3. As part of the Howells Memorial Meeting, Edwin H. Anderson (1861–1947), the director of the New York Public Library (1913–34), coordinated an exhibition of manuscripts, books, and portraits. Mildred Howells had noted that material desired for the exhibition was in storage and she did not have the time to retrieve it.

260. to Sinclair Lewis

als, Yale

71 East Ninety-Second Street
New York City

Feb. 5 [1921]

Dear Mr Lewis:

Are you in town? — Having read "Main Street" I would like to see you and talk with you about it. Perhaps you and Mrs Lewis can take tea with us some day this week.

With sincere pleasure in your latest success.[1]

Hamlin Garland

1. Garland's diary entry about the novel (31 January 1921) is strikingly adverse to the "sincere pleasure" mentioned here: "It was a disturbing and depressing book. It was true amazingly true up to a certain point but there it failed to convince simply because the man seemed not quite large enough and generous enough to fuse the spiteful, disturbing details together — The characters were too much like clay figures — types rather than individuals. In the more individualized figures like Will Kendall they failed to convince for the reason that they did not hold to character. — The same methods would yield the same results when applied to any section of humanity."

261. to Stuart Pratt Sherman

tls, U of Ill-Ar

71 East Ninety-Second Street
New York City

Feb. 8. [1921]

Dear Prof. Sherman:

Did the novels come to you? Fackenthal has sent five or six to me. None of them except possibly MAIN STREET has any claim on us. The AGE OF INNOCENCE I have not quite finished but it has not stirred me at all. It is well done of course but seems rather arid. Have you read any of the list? Have you any suggestions to make? Phelps suggested BOOK OF SUSAN. I confess I am tired of all this pornographic fiction. SUSAN may not be that but I have my fears. MOONCALF left me rather tired of unimportant details in the life of a youngster who represents Newspaper English and Small-town Radicalism.[1]

Any suggestion you can make at any time will be welcome. I want to save myself all the unavailing judgments possible for I am very busy on a book of my own.

Very sincerely yours,
Hamlin Garland

1. The novels Garland refers to are Edith Wharton's *The Age of Innocence*, Lee Wilson Dodd's *The Book of Susan*, and Floyd Dell's *Moon-Calf.*

262. to Stuart Pratt Sherman   tls, U of Ill-Ar

71 East Ninety-Second Street
New York City

Feb. 14. [1921]

Dear Prof. Sherman:

Your helpful note is at hand. Thanks for it. It will not be necessary for you to waste your time on that list of books for Fackenthal. I have read— or tried to read—them all. Only "Lulu Bett" and "Main Street" deeply interested me. One or two were short stories and not specially notable. Most of them are not only uninspired as to subject but plodding in method. What is the matter of our writers? Their English is the cheapest kind of Newspaper English. Dreary, dre[adful.][1] "Lulu Bett" is amazingly deft. A kind of *short-handing* of diction. It is better in that regard than "Main Street". Its content is not large but is juicy.

Phelps speaks highly of Risings "Helena Cass" and of Dodd[s] "Book of Susan." Have you read either?

"Mitch Miller" didnt interest me at all.[2]

Hamlin Garland

"Lulu Bett" makes a good play. I've seen it twice.[3]

1. Garland's typewriter has run over the edge of the page.

2. *Helena Cass*, by Lawrence Rising, and *Mitch Miller*, by Edgar Lee Masters.

3. Published in 1920, Zona Gale's novel *Miss Lulu Bett* examines the economic exploitation of women against a backdrop of small-town prejudice. Gale quickly dramatized her novel, and the play opened on 27 December 1920 at the Belmont Theater for 176 performances. As chair of both the fiction and drama juries for 1921, Garland was considering *Miss Lulu Bett* for both the fiction and drama prizes. According to the

Pulitzer Plan of Award, the drama prize was supposed to go to an "original American play," but the drama jury ignored the "original" stipulation and awarded *Miss Lulu Bett* the drama Pulitzer for 1921. Edith Wharton's *The Age of Innocence* won the 1921 fiction award.

263. to Stuart Pratt Sherman   tls, U of Ill-Ar

> 71 East Ninety-Second Street
> New York City
>
> Mar. 10 [1921]

Dear Prof. Sherman:

I have read ten or fifteen of the books submitted and I must say I have no high opinion of any of them. I tried to re-read MAIN STREET and failed. It gave me a curious disgust. One reads it the first time out of a kind of curiosity. Will any one re-read it? Is it not after all a piece of clever journalism which will be dead in six months?

LULU BETT will bear re-reading. We laugh about it and use it for illustration but it is a small book after all. I dont see anything to which we can whole-heartedly give a prize. The whole field of American drama and fiction seems to me rather undistinguished. How does it look to you?[1]

> Hamlin Garland

1. Sherman replied on 13 March 1921: "It sounds to me as if you had just been attending a meeting of the Academy, where elderly gentlemen had all agreed that the younger generation is going straight to the devil." Sherman went on to praise the "rather remarkable abundance of new life, crude, fermenting, but with juice and substance" of the year's candidates, arguing strongly for *Main Street,* and suggesting that *Miss Lulu Bett* was too "slight" and lacked "depth" to win the prize.

264. to Archer Huntington   tlc, Syracuse

> 71 East Ninety-Second Street
> New York City
>
> Mar. 10. [1921]

Dear Mr Huntington:[1]

We all knew that you didnt want any "fuss" yesterday but you made us all very happy.[2] I want to tell you that—I for one—appreciate this so deeply that I shall willingly give any amount of time possible to the work of making your magnificent gift a force in American Art and Letters. I believe in organization—it seems to me that in a republic like ours the need of some stabilizing Institution of taste—such as the Academy is, is almost as nescessary as a government. At present our American literary world is a welter. The only judgements that carry far are those of the cheap magazines and the moving pictures. The American Academy should not be merely reactionary but it should stand for the best in each craft.

I am coming up to see you soon in regard to the publication of the Howells Memorial addresses. This publication should be made this spring.

Very sincerely yours
Hamlin Garland

1. Archer Milton Huntington (1870–1955), adopted son of the millionaire railroad tycoon Collis P. Huntington, was a noted philanthropist and scholar of Spanish culture. He founded the Hispanic Society of America and established its library, museum, and educational institution for the study of Spanish art and literature, in addition to donating hundreds of paintings to museums. The author and editor of several works on Spanish literature, Huntington also published six volumes of poetry, gathered as *Collected Verse* in 1953. Elected to the Academy in 1919, Huntington was largely responsible for its financial solvency in its early years, donating some three million dollars in operating funds and land between 1913 and 1936.

2. On 9 March Huntington presented a check for $200,000 — and promised another $200,000 — to the Directors of the American Academy to construct a building for its use on the condition that the benefactor's name not be revealed. The Academy heretofore had an office at 347 Madison Avenue and borrowed rooms at the Century Club for its meetings. In April Huntington loaned the Academy the use of a building at 15 West 81st Street until its permanent home (on West 155th Street) could be built. See *Contemporaries*, pp. 343, 351–52.

265. to Stuart Pratt Sherman
als, U of Ill-Ar

71 East Ninety-Second Street
New York City

Mar. 16. [1921]

Dear Prof. Sherman:

I recognize the truth of all you say about the years crop of novels, but I still think them impermanent. I cant imagine myself re-reading "Moon-Calf" or "Main-Street" a year from now—and as for five years! "Poor

White" I have not read but I shall do so, soon. Poole's "Blind" is a tract. "Noon-Mark" by Watts is mellow and gracious.[1] "The Book of Susan"— I have still to read. What I feel in most of them is the raw quality you define in discussing "Moon-Calf." They write not as artists, with a background of experience and study but as hot-shot reporters. I admit all you say of their power and interest but do we want to give a prize to a book that will be dead as a last year political speech almost before our announcement is made?—"Lulu Bett" *is* slight and I dont intend to vote for it so long as there is a chance of another claimant. Its technical ease is a joy, however.—What about Gertrude Athertons book?—I have not read that.

I am greatly obliged by your good letter. If this committee work ends in making us acquainted I shall be the gainer. Do you know Henry B. Fuller of Chicago?—He is an old old friend whose judgement I value highly. He is in agreement with you on the books you analyze. So is Carl Van Doren.[2]

If you happen on any novel which arouses your enthusiasm let me know at once. I'll do the same for you. We shall be called upon to report in April or early May.

With deep appreciation of your interested service.
Hamlin Garland

1. The titles Garland mentions are Sherwood Anderson's *Poor White*, Ernest Poole's *Blind: A Story of The Times*, Mary Stanbery Watts's *Noon-Mark*, and Gertrude Atherton's *The Sister-in-Law: A Novel of Our Time*, which was published in January 1921 and so technically ineligible for the 1920 Pulitzer.

2. Carl Van Doren (1885–1950), literary editor of the *Nation* (1919–22) and the *Century* (1922–25), and editor of the Literary Guild (1926–34). Like Garland, Van Doren preferred *Miss Lulu Bett* over *Main Street*. See Garland to Van Doren, 16 February 1921 (Miami U), and Van Doren to Garland, 17 February 1921.

266. to Montrose J. Moses   tls, Duke

71 East Ninety-Second Street
New York City

March 18 [1921]

Dear Mr. Moses:

What are the best plays you have seen on the stage of New York this season? I mean American plays. I have only seen three or four. I cant afford the time to go to those which are merely entertainment. I am again on the Pulitzer Prize Committee but only in the way of helping out the general Committee. Thus far no plays seem to me of extraordinary merit. I liked THE FIRST YEAR,[1] and I liked LULU BETT but they are not great plays by any construction. Let me know if you have discovered any that are very much worth while.

With best wishes for the whole family,
Hamlin Garland

1. By Frank Craven.

267. to Frank D. Fackenthal   tlc, U of Ill-Ar

71 East Ninety-Second Street
New York City

May. 11 [1921]

Dear Mr. Fackenthal:

Did I make the final report on the Novel Prize? If not here it is.

Stuart P. Sherman is very strong for allotting the prize to MAIN STREET by Sinclair Lewis.

Dr. Robert M. Lovett joins him with reluctance. He is not wholehearted in his agreement but will vote for Lewis' book.

I will vote for MAIN STREET rather than see the prize go by but I feel that the book is essential[ly] journalistic and of short life. Its tone is not high and I find its method lacking in the elements of dignity and pity. It has power and a kind of truth but its general effect is curiously repellent. With a touch of pity for the people who are "snared by circumstance" and an admission that there are some redeeming features in village life, the book would have lived. I am of the opinion that few will ever re-read it.

LULU BETT is better technically but it is very slight hardly more than a short story. The AGE OF INNOCENCE* has dignity and a fine method but the story is without originality. The book lacks emotion, but it is technically high. Of the fifteen or twenty others which I have read THE NOON MARK stands out as a warm, wholesome piece of work but hardly worthy of the prize. No others are sufficiently strong in appeal to win the agreement of your committee.

Very sincerely yours
Hamlin Garland

The Advocate: 1919–1929   289

* It would be in a way a tribute to the magnificent work Mrs. Wharton
has done to vote the prize to her.[1]

1. Typed at the top center of the page, presumably by Garland, are the words, "Copy
for Prof. Sherman." Fritz H. Oehlschlaeger argues that Garland's lukewarm endorsement of *Main Street* persuaded the Advisory Board to award the 1921 Pulitzer to Wharton's *The Age of Innocence* in "Hamlin Garland and the Pulitzer Prize Controversy of
1921," *American Literature* 51 (1979): 409–14. See also Robert Morss Lovett, "The Pulitzer Prize," *New Republic,* 22 June 1921, p. 114, for his public discussion of the board's
decision.

268. to Frank D. Fackenthal tls, Pulitzer

71 East Ninety-Second Street
New York City

May 11 [1921]

Dear Mr. Fackenthal:

Dr. Burton is disposed to vote "No Prize" and as there is no outstanding play on which your committee can agree, I am making that recommendation.

With regard to the prize for the novel I have already written.

Very sincerely yours,
Hamlin Garland

269. to Frank D. Fackenthal tls, Pulitzer

71 East Ninety-Second Street
New York City

May. 22. [1921]

Dear Mr. Fackenthal:

Here is a wire from Phelps. The situation is now this. You and I are
inclined to give the prize to the FIRST YEAR. Burton would join us in this
award but Phelps will not listen to it.

Phelps and Burton will vote for NEMESIS[1] and I will join in this vote
rather than miss an award.

Feeling that it would be a handsome thing to give the prize to a woman
Burton will join Phelps and me in giving the award to LULU BETT.

LULU BETT is not a great play but it is original and interesting, and Miss

Gale is a woman to whom such an honor can go with justice. I know her intimately and I know her work in fiction as well as in the drama. As the award has not gone to a woman before perhaps it would be a graceful concession to give her this years prize. I leave the matter in the hands of your Advisory Committee.

Personally, I do not feel deep enthusiasm for any of the plays and novels of the year. Not one has in it the element of greatness. Not one really stands out in a commanding position.

Very sincerely yours,
Hamlin Garland

1. The play by Augustus Thomas opened at the Hudson Theater on 4 April 1921. Phelps had also proposed Eugene O'Neill's *The Emperor Jones* but favored *Miss Lulu Bett* as his first choice.

270. to Brander Matthews

tls, Columbia

The Century Association
7 West Forty-Third Street
New York

Sept. 15 [1921]

Dear Chancellor:[1]

At our last meeting of the Academy Butler told us that it would be possible for the Academy or the Institute to take over the administration of the Pulitzer Prize Funds. In my judgement it would be an added source of power and influence for good if the Academy should take over this work. If it went to the Institute the effect would be to divide and weaken the effect of both their prizes and ours. We should either take it over entirely or control it by means of a joint com. on which we should hold the chairmanship. I'd like to see it done with you as chairman of a com. of five. Of these it would be well to have say John Finley[2] and William Lyon Phelps. I am to start on our program for the House Warming just as soon as we can hear from Butler as to what part of the detail he will assume at his office.[3] If we could announce the taking over of this Pulitzer Fund it would be helpful.

With best wishes to you and yours,
Hamlin Garland

The Advocate: 1919–1929 291

1. Matthews was the chancellor of the American Academy from 1920 to 1924. The administration of the Pulitzer Prizes remained at Columbia University.

2. John Finley, the editor of the *New York Times*.

3. Garland refers to the dedication of the Academy's first building, financed by Arthur M. Huntington, in November. Nicholas Murray Butler, in addition to his duties as president of Columbia University, was a member of the Academy's board of directors and served as its chancellor (1924–28) and president (1928–41).

271. to Brander Matthews   als, Columbia

15 West Eighty First Street

Sept. 22 [1921]

Dear Brander:

Huntington told me yesterday that often when he mentions the Academy, people say "Oh, you mean that Johnson thing."—He spoke of this humorously but it only made it more imperative to my way of thinking—that no one man in the future should be identified with this organization in just that fashion. I feel very deeply my own responsibility, for Huntington and I are working together. The weakness of the Academy lies in the sad fact that we are all growing old—Johnson as well as the rest of us. We must strengthen ourselves with youth.—How *can* we relieve Johnson gracefully. To have him resume the work which caused people to speak of the Academy as "That Johnson thing" must not be permitted—and yet he got us part of our endowment. He did work hard and faithfully. He is a good sort and in certain ways very able but—well you know the situation. What is to be our line of action. I write this confidentially. I like Johnson but he bores me. I dont like to work with him. On the committee he is long-winded and prosy. I am hoping he will go to the Hall of Fame and leave us free.—What we need is a stenographer and type-writer. And the $1800 we have been paying Johnson would hire one.—Mrs Vanamee is a trump, a wonder but she can not do type-writing and the other things she does so well.[1] [illeg.] is busy with the Burroughs matter and so our office is lacking in just the secretarial mechanism we need.[2] I write nearly all my letters myself which takes so much of my time that I must absolutely quit when Johnson comes. I cant write fiction and be general Secretary and yet I feel a deep responsibility for the forward movement of the institution. Lets meet and talk this over soon.

Faithfully yours
H.G.

1. The New York University Hall of Fame, of which Johnson was the director. Grace D. Vanamee (1876–1946) was the administrative assistant to the president of the Academy from 1915 to 1940, and the assistant secretary and assistant treasurer of the National Institute from 1925 to 1940. A lecturer and author, Vanamee was active in promoting women's political rights as a founding member and board director of the Women's National Republican Club and as the editor of *The Guidon* (1927–30). Vanamee also served as acting director of the Hall of Fame when Johnson was the U.S. ambassador to Italy (1920–21), and Garland assumed his duties as secretary of the Academy.

2. The John Burroughs Memorial Meeting of the American Academy took place on 18 November 1921. Garland delivered the address, "Burroughs the Man."

272. to Brander Matthews   tls, Columbia

[ca. 7 October 1921]

Dear Brander:

I am grateful for your good opinion but I am just downright discouraged. The situation is this. Huntington gave Sloane ten thousand dollars on which to run the Academy from now to the entrance into the new building.[1] Sloane put this into a time lock deposit and we have no money on which to hold *any* meetings. Unless Butler's Conciliation Society can again help us out we can not have either a cornerstone ceremony of any dignity or a reception in the present building. We are at a blank wall. I was trying to put the Academy on the map and understood Butler to say that we were to go ahead on the Foch matter[2] in all ways except as to the exact date. It seem[s] now that Foch is a guest of the War Department and we have no hold on him at all till he is done with Weeks.[3] This being so we are without our International guest and can not ask Butler to finance our meetings. We are in a bag. It is all so distracting and worrying that I can not do any of my own work and I am going to quit. I must quit.[4]

The worst of the whole situation lies in the disability of yourself and Sloane. Neither of you are in physical condition to take a daily interest in the work of the office as I have been doing and which is increasingly nescessary. We cant sit down in any empty building and wait for a new one. We must function and to function means that some one must be on the job and also we must use the means which Huntington intended we should use. To go to him again after he has provided for the current expenses of the institution will, I fear, vex him. Sloane should get that money out and use it for the Academy now. NOW is the time to make the Academy known. If we let this chance pass we will be a passive Institution for the rest of the two years. The truth is we are a lot of "elderly old

parties" who dont care very much whether school keeps or not—we'd
rather not if it involves any janitor work on our part. I wouldnt mind if
Huntington hadnt outfitted us so magnificently. It seems to me that in
justice to him we ought to draw together and see what we can do to put
life into the thing. We need a young, vigorous managing secretary, a man
not a member, a man who will be in the office all the time, as Haskell
serves Columbia. We cant be run by a volunteer member seventy years
of age.

Remember this. We now have two buildings to care for. We are likely to
have (if we show life) a big endowment. We cant function under our present office arrangement. I am writing plainly to you for we are old friends
and I can afford to tell you what my conclusions are after a year of service.
We must have a head either Sloane or you must be in that office during
the next two to three months. These are the months to make our Academy known and respected. Personally I feel that unless we rise to the magnificent gift we have in hand we can be accused of getting money under
false pretences. I think Huntington intends to endow us handsomely but
he wont if he finds us making poor use of what he has already given.

These are the consideration[s] which have led me to sacrifice most of
my time for six months. I have come to admire Huntington and like him.
He says he likes to work with me and I shall continue to do all I can for
the Academy without letting my own writing go by the board. I can not
be worried over the money side of the thing, and I can not be a party to a
passive policy. I am for war. The Academy should be a progressive force
in American Arts and Letters. We must not be senile. We are called "an old
man's Home"—and "That Johnson Thing." We have a chance to be of national scope and dignity but we need money and the active co-operation
of our members to attain this standing.

Ever faithfully yours,
H.G.

1. William M. Sloane (1850–1928), the president of the American Academy from
1920 to 1928 and a professor of history at Columbia University.

2. Ferdinand Foch (1851–1929) was the commander-in-chief of the Allied armies on
the Western front during World War I. As a representative of the French Academy, he
was to lay the cornerstone of the American Academy's new building. The ceremony
took place on 19 November 1921; the building officially opened on 22 February 1923.
Garland describes the event in *Contemporaries*, pp. 373–74.

3. John Wingate Weeks (1860–1926), the secretary of war.

4. That is, quit as acting secretary of the Academy. According to Garland's diary
entry of 5 October 1921, Academy board members were displeased with Garland's having proofs of a pamphlet printed and distributed stating that Foch would lay the cornerstone: "Butler and Matthews and Sloane were inclined to accuse me of precipitance
but as we had commissioned Butler to secure Foch and as he had reported that he had
an acceptance in all but the exact date; and as Butler had told the secretary to proceed
with the printing I do not see how I or the presidents secretary could be blamed except
that perhaps I was a bit too specific in tone." Matthews replied on 9 October 1921 that
"it was an error of judgment" to send out the invitations, but that all were grateful "for
your devotion and your zeal."

273. to Walter Pritchard Eaton als, Virginia

71 East Ninety-Second Street
New York City

Nov. 17. [1921]

Dear Eaton:

Your good letter was forwarded to me from Macmillans and has made
the Garland family happy.[1] I value your judgement and to have you speak
out so frankly on the book is deeply reassuring. I have tried to keep in
mind the tone of the period so that the two books may be a unit. They are
really one book—perhaps sometime we will put them into one cover. To
have men like yourself and Henry B. Fuller—so wide apart in years and
environment—agree on the book enables me to breathe a sigh of relief. I
must admit I was nervous over the opinion of my contemporaries—

I hope to see you. Come up here and meet my wife and daughters. We
live in a small apartment high above New York. Let me know when next
you are in the city.

Most gratefully yours
Hamlin Garland.

1. Eaton had written on 15 November 1921 to praise an advance copy of *Daughter*:
"Without the romance of that epic pioneering era to help you, you've still managed to
make an absorbing book out of the simple chronicle of your life. I suppose the secret is
out that it *is* simple. So darn few people can be simple when they write, or even when
they talk. Anyhow, the book 'got' me, and the passage about your father's death I think
is absolutely classic, & might be read over & over & over by everybody who aspires to
write."

71 East Ninety-Second Street
New York City

Dec. 18 [1921]

Dear Mr Latham:

It is clearly evident to me that Macmillans do not consider my book of sufficient appeal to warrant featuring it in their advertising and so I wish you would come tomorrow prepared to tell me what it will cost to give the book a quick sharp campaign of advertising in the *Times*, the Boston Transcript, the Chicago Tribune and the Los Angeles Times.[1] I have put too many years of work into this book to allow it to fade out. I have two plans whereby I can assist in the campaign. — I want both books advertised together and in a way to convey their importance — to the author any how. I want to go over the matter with the greatest frankness. I want to co-operate.

1. Garland was distressed by the lack of critical interest in *Daughter*. Although it was published in early November, only three reviews, by friends, had appeared: Henry B. Fuller, "Three Generations," *Freeman* 4 (9 Nov. 1921): 210–11; Carl Van Doren, "The Garland-McClintock Saga," *Nation* 113 (23 Nov. 1921): 601–2; and Joseph E. Chamberlin, "*A Daughter of the Middle Border*," bet, 10 December 1921, sec. 4, p. 7. By 4 January 1922, Garland was quite demoralized, recording in his diary that "'A visit to *Macmillans* today revealed with disheartening completeness the fact that only six or seven reviews have come in, and these were in reality the work of friends. The book is hardly published even now and the whole outlook is humiliatingly dark. It seems as if all interest in me has suddenly ceased. All that I had won by thirty-five years' effort, all that *A Son of the Middle Border* had gained, has evaporated. The end of my career as a writer is at hand'" (quoted in *Back-Trailers*, p. 167). A similar entry appears in *Contemporaries*, pp. 381–82. Ironically, *Daughter* was awarded the 1921 Pulitzer Prize for biography.

71 East Ninety-Second Street
New York City

Dec. 26 [1921]

Dear Mr Latham:[1]

I am keen to be moving in the matter of the new advertising. I am enclosing a rough suggestion of the kind of display I would like to see in

The TIMES and The CHICAGO TRIBUNE. If you will make up an ad of this kind using the new material which has come in concerning the DAUGHTER and submit it to me with the cost of say five insertions in each paper I will consider the matter of paying for it by having it charged against my royalties in some way. The TIMES [the] greatest agency for publicity in America has done almost nothing for me this time and I want to use it. It reaches my friends, the people who would buy my book.

Please take up the matter of the one volume edition. Let me know how many of the SON you have on hand. Can it be made uniform with the DAUGHTER at once? How soon can we advertise a single volume edition?

I want to put an immediate ad in The TIMES. It can be of The Daughter alone with a statement of the fact that it is the concluding volume of the SON or it can advertise a two volume edition. Please have your Advertising dept work out a display for use in the Times at once. When I know the cost I can tell you how many insertions I can afford to stand sponsor for.

Also let us start immediately upon the making of a fine twelve or sixteen page circular. I am desperately impatient to get moving. I shall be glad to come in and talk with you at the office at any time when you are at liberty.[2]

1. Harold S. Latham (1887–1969), vice president in charge of trade at Macmillan Co., joined Macmillan in 1909 and was Garland's editor during his negotiations with that firm to publish his literary memoirs.

2. In a lengthy reply of 30 December 1921, Latham took pains to outline Macmillan's position. They had spent over one thousand dollars on advertising, and ads had appeared in the *Atlantic Monthly, Century, Scribner's, Harper's,* and the *Outlook.* It had been advertised five times in the *Chicago Post* and the *New York Post;* six times in the *Boston Evening Transcript,* the *New Republic,* and the *North American;* seven in the *New York Times;* and eight times in the *Independent,* as well as appearing in eleven other publications. Latham concluded that Macmillan had exhausted newspaper advertising potential and proceeded to educate the exasperated Garland about alternative means of promoting books. He explained that although he did not recommend that an author advertise a book at his own expense, Macmillan would "place the advertisements for you" and charge his account. Latham concluded that he did not feel the market was ready for a jointly bound and promoted set of the Middle Border books. Garland was dissatisfied with Latham's explanations and scrawled at various places on Latham's letter follow-up queries and points of contestation.

276. to Walter Pritchard Eaton   als, Virginia

71 East Second Street
New York City

Feb. 2. [1922]

Dear Eaton:

Harper and Bros are going to bring out a twelve volume set of my fiction and I wish you could find time to read this set and write of it as a whole for some one of your publications.[1] It's a dreadful thing to ask of an inoffensive country-man and I dont ask it I only hope.—Marsh who has the matter in hand will probably write you in due course. I intend to be quite shameless in asking the aid of my friends in making this venture a reasonable success. Its my little monument.

Let us see you if you come to the city—

Hamlin Garland

1. On 3 January Garland met with Edward Marsh and Henry Hoyns of Harpers to plan the "Border Edition" of his work. Garland was to accept a smaller royalty and write a new preface for each work, which included *Main-Travelled Roads, Other Main-Travelled Roads, Boy Life on the Prairie, Rose of Dutcher's Coolly, The Eagle's Heart, The Captain of the Gray-Horse Troop, Hesper, Cavanagh, Forest Ranger, The Long Trail, Money Magic, The Forester's Daughter,* and *They of the High Trails.* In addition, Marsh and Hoyns proposed another volume, which would collect Garland's writings on the American Indian, *The Book of the American Indian,* published in 1923. See *Contemporaries,* pp. 394–98.

277. to Wilbur Cross   tls, Yale

71 East Ninety-Second Street
New York City

Feb. 11 [1922]

Dear Prof. Cross:

Anything you can do to let people know that A DAUGHTER OF THE MIDDLE BORDER is the second and concluding volume of A SON OF THE MIDDLE BORDER will be highly grateful to me. As usual the publishers have passed on to other enthusiasms so that I am dependent now on the good-will of the readers of the first volume.

My other publishers Harper and Bros, have fixed upon May as the date

for the publication of the twelve volume set of my fiction and I am hoping
that a few critics will find it possible to read these stories in the order in
which they were written and apprise them for their bearing on the North-
West. I dont say that they are worth such heroic sacrifice of time but I am
foolish enough to hope that some one may make it.

I had another engagement which kept me from the meeting. I hear it
was lively.[1]

Let me see you if you come to town,
Hamlin Garland

P.S. Is there anything I can write for you?
P.S.S. I am having the other volume sent—

1. Garland refers to the annual meeting of the National Institute.

278. to William Lyon Phelps

tls, usc

71 East Ninety-Second Street
New York City

April. 28 [1922]

Dear William:

I am off in a few moments for my trip into the West and do not return
for over two weeks. I do not see how we can vote a prize to the morbid kind
of play that O'Neill writes. He has had one prize on those lines and to
give him another would be to emphasize a kind of thing which is essentially unwholesome. I would rather give it to "THE HERO" than to "Anna
Christie" which is the story of a prostitute. It seems to me we have had
too much pornographic literature this year. The Pulitzer Prize should not
add to its vogue. I hate the whole school which is essentially unAmerican.
Its writers are—in many cases—for revenue only.[1]

Its our duty to make this prize count and we should withhold it if no
play deserves it—unless we wish to emphasize a tendency. I certainly do
not wish to encourage an art which is in distinct opposition to the terms
of the bequest.

I shall return on the Fifteenth of May. Perhaps something else may
develop.

Very faithfully yours,
Hamlin Garland

The Advocate: 1919–1929 299

Excuse this hasty note. I'll write a more considered one before the report must go in. —

1. Drama jury members in 1922 included Phelps (as chair), Garland, and Jesse Lynch Williams. *The Hero* is by Gilbert Emery.

279. to Brander Matthews   als, Pulitzer

University Club of Chicago

May. 7. [1922]

Dear Brander:

Phelps and Williams are for voting the prize to O'Neill's "Anna Christie." I have just seen it for the first time and do not think it as good a play as "Beyond the Horizon"—and to give a second prize to a man for a play not so good as the first seems to me a trifle absurd—I do not see any play worthy the prize.

I think we cheapen the award by bestowing it on plays that are not entirely worthy of it. —I think I shall keep clear of the thing hereafter—but my report for this year is "no award." —I infer you are on the Committee of Awards hence I report to you.[1]

Very sincerely
Hamlin Garland

1. With this split decision from the drama jury, the Advisory Board awarded *Anna Christie* the 1922 Pulitzer Prize for drama, the second of O'Neill's four Pulitzers.

280. to Catharine Amy Dawson Scott   als, U Texas

18 Queensberry Place.

Saturday. [24 June 1922]

Dear Miss Scott:[1]

I am greatly obliged for the card to the dinner but I do not feel much like going. The truth is I am getting too old to fit into companies of young writers. They are not interested in me and I am a nuisance to the kind person who has me in mind as a guest. I very seldom go when at home. The hot bad air, the noise and confusion of voices are wearing on elderly folk. I like small dinner parties where I am known and where explanations really explain. There is nothing more trying than to have your host say "Mr. Blank this is the great American author Mr. Blink—of course you've read Mr. Blinks incomparable works"—only to be met by a blank and painful stare. If people only wouldnt introduce me that way! No one over here knows my work or has any interest in me—except a very few who have been to America or who happen to have had some American connection.

For these reasons and for several others I find the dinners rather trying. I am a believer in the idea which you are so heroically embodying but I fear I can not be of much active service.

Cant you come down to the Authors Club someday for tea and talk matters over with me? There is a place on the first floor to which ladies are admitted as no doubt you are aware. It was good of you to listen so patiently to the elderly folk last night—or perhaps I should not include Captain Stuart and your mother in that characterization.

Very sincerely yours,
Hamlin Garland

1. Catharine Amy Dawson Scott (1863–1934), British novelist, poet, and editor, founded the P.E.N. Club in 1921 and had invited Garland to a P.E.N. Club dinner on 4 July. Subsequent letters show that Garland accepted the invitation.

281. to Henry Blake Fuller tls, Newberry

60 Albert hall mansions.

July 3. [1922]

Dear Fuller:

We are so comfortable here that we hardly realize that we are in London. We are as much at home as we were in 92nd street. We continue to do things. On Thursday Lord Balfour gave us a charming lunch with many lords and ladies—the chief of which being Sir James Barrie. On Friday we all went down in the country to Kiplings farm.[1] It was a lovely day—barring one shower, and when Miss Kipling motored us to see a Norman castle—Bodiam—our thrills began. It was an amazing experience to some upon that gray old castle in the midst of a sheep pasture, its outer walls looking as if built ten years ago. Naturally the children were delighted altho they had just seen Warwick and Oxford. There was something in this old ruin that brought the past very near to us all.

Kiplings house is three hundred years old and one of the most complete I have ever seen. We had a delightful visit with him and his wife and daughter.—Yesterday we dined in a home in which there were four titled ladies. Titles are thick over here. Everywhere we go we are set down with a title on either side of us. (Kipling and Shaw both refused titles I believe.) I am lunching with William Archer today and I am hoping he will have in some of the younger dramatists like Milne. We all go to a party tonight and tomorrow is the Embassadorial Fourth of July Reception, and at night the P.E.N. Club dinner. On the 11th I speak for the English Speaking Union, and on the 12th the Galsworthys have the whole Garland family to dinner.—Beyond that—!—

Yesterday morning we were at St Pauls for the morning service and lo and behold you, as we came out here were the three state coaches of the Lord Mayor of London and we had the best possible chance to see him emerge and get into the purple one. Couriers, out-riders, footmen—all in scarlet and purple and gold made a picture that quite exalted my two Republican daughters. It was a noble sight! I wish our Mayors would dress the same. It lights up this old world.

You may pass this note along to Lorado and the other relatives and friends who may betray an interest. People are disposed to be very kind to us. I can see that if it were not near the end of the season we would be almost too busy.

It is cold here. We keep a fire going in our sitting room all the time. I am wearing my overcoat, most of each day.

Write all the news,
H.G.

1. Garland describes the visit with Kipling in some detail in *Contemporaries*, pp. 448–56.

282. to Stuart Pratt Sherman

tls, U of Ill-Ar

71 East Ninety-Second Street
New York City

Dec. 26. [1922]

Dear Prof. Sherman:

After the manner of the Foxy parent I bought your *Americans* for my daughter in the belief that I would find it a book much to my taste. I was not mistaken. It is admirable. I sympathize deeply with your judgement of the Menken-Lewisohn-Untermeyer-Hackett school of Anti-English critics. Didnt you have a review some months ago in the TIMES REVIEW which is not included in this book? I recall reading with delight that review and it is in my mind as not the one you here print. That one seemed longer and a bit more inclusive but I may be mistaken.[1]

My daughter and I are going west again—as far as to the Coast but I am not sure of getting to Urbana. I wish I might be dated in your town so that I could have a talk with you.[2] You have Pattee with you now I believe. He is an old friend and one I value.

I hope *Americans* has a wide reading. It is fine to have you feel like saying the plain word at just this time. My five months residence in London brought home to me very vitally the fact that my ties of blood and sentiment were closer to England than to any other country save my own.

Best wishes for the New Year.
Hamlin Garland

1. Sherman's *Americans* (New York: Scribner, 1922) includes a chapter entitled "Mr. Mencken, the Jeune Fille, and the New Spirit in Letters," in which Sherman derides H. L. Mencken, Francis Hackett, Louis Untermeyer, and Ludwig Lewisohn, among others, as representatives of "a new spirit" in literature who are "vulgar and selfish and good-humored and sensual and impudent" in their break with traditional literary culture (p. 2). The chapter had been previously published as a review of Mencken's *Prejudices* (1919) under the title "Mr. H. L. Mencken and the Jeune Fille" in the *New York Times Book Review*, 7 December 1919, sec. 8, p. 718. Garland, however, is referring to Sherman's "Charge of the Literary Light Brigade," *New York Times Book Review*, 29 January 1922, p. 12, a review of six collections of essays of which Garland had earlier written in praise (to Sherman, 31 January 1922, U of Ill-Ar).

2. Sherman replied, 2 January 1923, that there were no funds available except for a week-long series of lectures.

283. to Stuart Pratt Sherman   als, U of Ill-Ar

71 East Ninety-Second Street
New York City

Jan. 5 [1923]

Dear Prof. Sherman:

Please dont give any trouble to the question of my lecturing in Urbana. The only possible time now would be on my way back from California the first days of May. It is very kind of you to take the interest your letter makes evident.—Apropos of Menken, I was in Baltimore recently and Dr. Guth[1] of Goucher College gave me some curious information of H.L.M.—He is pleasing and rather shy in personal contact but a totally different individual when he takes his pen in hand. He is of German strain. His fathers name was August Menken. One of the teachers spoke of him as of "Ruddy German Type."—Everybody in Baltimore feared him at one time but he was "soft-pedaled" during the war.—I wish you could talk with Dr Guth. The gossip is that Menken was strongly pro-German and "some people think he went away with Koenig in the 'U.' Boat" which touched at Baltimore.[2] Menken was at the banquet given to Koenig.—All this is past history, of course, and probably known to you but it tends to explain his general attitude. I am with you and Matthews and Fuller—The Lewisohn-Menken-Hackett-combination does not appeal to me.

If you come to New York, let me know.

Best wishes—
Hamlin Garland

1. William Westley Guth (1871–1929), president of Gardner College (not "Goucher") from 1913 to his death.

2. On 2 July 1916 the German merchant submarine *Deutchland*, commanded by Captain Paul Koenig, arrived in Baltimore with a cargo of dyestuffs. Amid much controversy, the submarine was officially declared a merchant ship and Koenig announced plans to begin weekly merchant service to and from German ports.

Sept. 23. [1923]

Dear Sloane:

The Chancellor thinks we should not put up another man who is not a literary man or an artist and so I may not go any farther with my nomination.[1] The thing which worries me is this; so many of us are getting on in years and the future of the Academy as an institution needs safeguarding. We need a certain number of men of wide influence and with experience as administrative officers. I have in mind Huntingtons noble confidence in us. We must look to the future. It is not merely a question of continuance it is a question of continuing service.

Edwin Arlington Robinson is a man who has won the honor of being nominated for membership, in many ways is better qualified than the man I mentioned before, for he ranks high as a poet and man of letters but he is not the kind of man who would aid in any work of the Academy. John Van Dyke is a good man in all ways but he lives out of town and is not very well. We have several artists who are entirely qualified but it seems to me we should name a man who is allied to letters.[2]

We have a superb plant now all in perfect order—what can we do with it? We should be a force for good in all ways, an active progressive machine. I want to see you and tell you some of the things I have been doing and others which I think we should attempt next year. I may be going against Mr. Huntingtons wishes in my activities—if I am you must tell me so—but I feel that the Academy is needed to hold the qualities which we call American. With more than a third of all our citizens here in New York foreign by birth or sympathies, and with all our drama, fiction and criticism colored by this European influence the work of the Academy becomes increasingly important. I have written an article for the English BOOKMAN and the editor is to use several of the pictures.[3] I am having several of the editors of literary magazines meet me at the Academy in order to show them the plant and get their interest and aid in the matter of our program for the future. I hope in all this to have your approval. I am doing this not as an official but as a member of the Academy. I want to be of use and as I know all these young men it seems to me a good way to do a little extension work. When Whitlock comes back I hope you will enlist him in this work.[4]

Let me see you at your convenience.

1. The surviving correspondence does not indicate whom Garland nominated.

2. Robinson was elected to the Academy on 10 November 1927; the art historian John C. Van Dyke was elected on 6 December 1923.

3. See "The American Academy of Arts and Letters," *Bookman* [London] 65 (November 1923): 89–92.

4. The novelist Brand Whitlock. Sloane replied, 25 September 1923, that he agreed the Academy needed younger members "*But,* having considered how other Academies do it I seem to discern that membership cannot be based on executive willingness and that the organization in every case has a captain, i.e. an efficient executive man, paid well, and driving the machine through consultation with inactive older members, absorbed in completing their life work."

285. to William M. Sloane

tlc, usc

Sept. 26. [1923]

Dear Sloane:

I didnt make my meaning quite clear to you. I am not bringing prospective candidates to the Academy, I am merely trying to increase its influence on the younger writers by a guarded publicity. We should have the good-will and co-operation of editors like Van Doren, Farrar, Smythe and Canby.[1] Unless you object I shall permit them to call on me at the Academy and talk with them of our plans for education. We have a fine and expensive plant and it seems to me we should make use of it. To merely keep a place like that open is a very passive attitude. If you object to my use of the room as a place to write I wish you would be quite frank and tell me so. I am willing also to pay rent for the lockers and it may be that we could make that part of our outfit partly self supporting. As no one else ever comes to the Directors Room Mrs. Vanamee seemed to think it agreeable to you but I should like to have an expression from you. I am perfectly willing to pay for whatever service the Academy does for me. I have no intention of presuming on my official connection.

Your thought about a paid man of high type as captain or manager is one which I have had in mind for some time. I wish it were possible to procure one.

I hope we shall meet soon.

1. Garland refers to Carl Van Doren; John Chipman Farrar (1896–1974), editor of the *Bookman*; Clifford Smyth (1866–1943), former editor of the *New York Times Book Review* (1913–22) and editor of the *Literary Digest International Book Review*, and Henry Seidel Canby (1878–1961), editor of the *Saturday Review of Literature*.

286. to William M. Sloane

Oct. 7. [1923]

Dear Sloane:

I understand that my "zeal" was condemned in toto yesterday and that I am not to do anything that will lead to any further discussion of the Academy.[1] It will be easy for me to comply. I can do as the others do, come now and again to a directors meeting and give no further thought to the Academy—if that is your wish and the desire of Mr. Huntington. If the Board feel that the thing to do is to sit down with that noble plant isolated from the city, I am ready to leave it that way. You and I have all along believed it should be of educational value. Perhaps we are wrong.

Mr. Huntington has done a noble deed in establishing us in this building and I am only anxious to carry out his wishes. I am sorry I had to run yesterday but I was speaking over in Jersey and came near to missing my train as it turned out.

The fact which appalls me is our age. We are all old fellows and some of us are far from well. How can we safe-guard the Institution? I wish you and I could have a talk about these matters. There is never any time at the board meetings. If you think it best that I do as the others do and keep away from the building except when called there to act as director I am perfectly willing to do that. I have thus far been careful to get your authorization but if you feel that the sentiment of the board is against my pestiferous activity I will cheerfully subside. I hope to see Huntington soon and get his full mind in the matter.

Very sincerely yours,

1. During the board of directors' meeting on 5 October, Garland's motion to have the Academy take a more active role through publicizing its activities and by offering teas to nonmembers was voted down by the board (Academy Board Minutes, item #683). In his diary for 6 October 1923, Garland noted, "The action of the Directors yesterday was for 'passive action': to sit tight and do nothing. I suspect that this is a reflection of Huntington's mind. He is disposed to make the building a literary museum rather than an educational center of influence. To this I have no objection on the contrary it is a most valuable part of our program but I do not agree that it should be all of our program. However Huntington is paying all our bills and has provided this wonderful home for us. We can not do a handsomer deed than to fall in with his general notion for I suspect that he intends to do wonderful things for us."

287. to Archer M. Huntington

tlc, usc

Oct. 7 [1923]

Dear Mr. Huntington:

I take it that there was qualified endorsement of my work for the Academy but your wishes are of the greatest force to me and I wish to assure you once again that in what I write your name will not be used at any time without your consent. I keep carefully in mind your previous expressions. Even in private conversations I am careful to keep our donors anonymous.

The truth is I feel a deep responsibility to you. You have done a magnificent thing. Through you we have the machinery for functioning—now we should function. Some of our directors can only give a few moments thought to the problem on the occasion of our meetings, I feel it my duty to give a great deal of thought to the Academy every day. It is too vital a factor in American arts and letters to be held passive.

I may be wrong in this and I may be in opposition to your views. I wish you would let me have your full mind in the matter. I shall not be offended if you say "Dont do that." I think I read in your attitude a desire to let the directors determine the policy but I am also aware that for the most part you and the office force—and I if you will permit—must carry on the immediate work of the Academy. The absence of both the President and the Chancellor this winter will throw upon Butler, the office of Chancellor.[1] He is the man for the place. He has vigor and experience in that kind of administrative work. I can give some time to the Academy this winter if you wish me to do so. Lets have another talk.

Very faithfully yours,
Hamlin Garland.

1. Sloane, the president, was going to California because of ill health, and Matthews, the chancellor, was too ill to preside in his absence.

288. to Fred Lewis Pattee

tls, Penn St

Hamlin Garland
71 East Ninety-Second Street
New York City

November. 24. [1923]

Dear Prof. Pattee:

How is it all going? I thought of you yesterday as I came thru Penn. I was on my way East after two weeks of lecturing in the North West. Have you seen Beers book on Crane?[1] I havent but I had some talk with him while he was in the midst of the writing. I read Whitlocks book and was greatly disappointed in it. It seemed to me—like Willa Cather's latest—a concession to the people who want female libertines in their books.[2] For a man of Whitlocks position it seems a sad stooping to describe a hired girls seduction of a youth. I am disgusted with a throng of my friends who are lending their talents to this kind of thing and I have written about it in a coming TIMES REVIEW.[3]

Let me see you if you come to town. Let me know what you are doing.

Best Wishes.
H.G.

1. *Stephen Crane: A Study in American Letters*, by Thomas Beer (1923).

2. Garland refers to Brand Whitlock's *J. Hardin and Son* (1923) and Willa Cather's *A Lost Lady* (1923).

3. In "Current Fiction Heroes," *New York Times Book Review*, 23 December 1923, sec. 3, p. 23, Garland blames the decline of moral taste in literature on the influx of European immigrants and he advocates censorship as "the organized collective protest against debasing forms of art." In his reply of 1 December 1923, Pattee chided Garland for his loss of perspective, reminded him of his own youthful iconoclasm in *Crumbling Idols*, and suggested that rather than condemn outright the new literature, he should attempt to "understand the psychology" of the movement. "Something has come over America," he noted; "what is it? Don't damn the new creators." Pattee then published a rejoinder to "Current Fiction Heroes" entitled "Those Fiery Radicals of Yesteryear," *New York Times Book Review*, 24 February 1924, sec. 3, p. 12. For a discussion of this letter in terms of the Cather allusion, see A. C. Ravitz, "Willa Cather Under Fire: Hamlin Garland Misreads *A Lost Lady*," *Western Humanities Review* 9 (1955): 182–84.

The Advocate: 1919–1929 309

289. to Harold S. Latham

tlc, usc

Nov. 25 [1923]

Dear Mr. Latham:

I am coming in to see you soon but before I do so I think it well to candidly say that I was never satisfied with the way in which the second volume of the Middle Border was started out. You will recall that I was quite frank about it at the time. I thought the approach was a foozle at that time and I think so yet. That the book was worthy of better treatment was made evident by the Pulitzer award.

I am reluctant to sign any contract with any firm which will leave me helpless in such a situation. I'll quit publishing altogether rather than go through another such a period of disappointment. Before we come to grips on another book I must be completely insured against any such sudden reversal of enthusiasm as came to the firm in the case of that book. It was one of the bitterest disappointments I have ever experienced in my authorship. I am still suffering from it.

I will not suffer another routine publishing at any firms hands. My work must be treated with distinguished emphasis or remain unpublished. It may not be worthy of such honor but I shall put my best into what I publish and the publisher must put his best into the advertising and sale of the finished product. I dont say that The Pathfinder of the Middle Border is worthy [of] publication but it will be when I am finished with it and you must make it worth my while to come back to Macmillans.[1] If you see something worth while in the book write me a letter saying what you are willing to do by way of advertising as well as advance royalty.

It appears to me that if Macmillans take the right attitude in respect of all my Middle Border books, including the fourth volume, there is a certain cumulative value in having them all under one firm['s] name but this is true only if they are distinguished from the dead level of books forgotten or half-forgotten. Here again I repeat that this may not be in the bounds of the reasonable but that is the way I feel about it now.

It is probable that there are two or three books in my diaries but to secure my future work will require something more than the regulation contract. I am getting old and independent—almost as haughty as a publisher. You have three of my best books, whether you have more will depend on the way in which you are willing to obligate the firm.

Very sincerely yours,

1. Published as *Trail-Makers of the Middle Border* in October 1926. Although the book was the third published in the series, it was the first volume chronologically.

290. to Mary Isabel Garland

als, Hunt

Canadian Pacific
Mediterranean Cruise
S.S. Empress Of Scotland

June. 10. [1924]

Dear Daughtie:

Your steamer letter comforted me and made me feel that I still had my Mary Isabel with me. There were times last winter when it seemed that you were passing out of my life. You and I have been closer comrades than most fathers and daughters and to have you go out of my world will be a sad day for me. I am relieved to know that you are to wait and that you hope for my approval. I can not write much today for I am still somewhat sea-sick but I shall write again when I get to land. I must be honest with you and say that Bill was pretty nearly right in his interpretation of my attitude.[1] I have reared you for great things. All your education has been toward a broad intellectual life. I fear that any life less literary, less esthetic would prove a disappointment and lead to unhappiness. — Study hard and play hard this summer so that next fall you will be prepared for a success-ful season—

With unabated love from—
Daddy.

1. Garland was opposed to the twenty-year-old Mary Isabel's desire to marry "Bill," an underemployed actor whom she had met while acting with the Walter Hampden Company. Garland counseled delay while "Bill" went to California to prove his wage-earning potential. Mary Isabel called off the engagement when she discovered her fiancé was acting—rather than working—in California.

291. to Hubert E. Collins

tlc, usc

July. 2 [1924?]

Dear Mr. Collins:[1]

It is a great surprise to me to learn that Seger is talking in that way about me.[2] He has been friendly for twenty seven years and I have scores of letters from him in which he not only gives me full right to use any of his stories but expresses gratitude for the home I furnished him after he left the service. He had no home and wished to live near Colony. I bought a farm and put him on it telling him to pay rent whenever he could or to work it out in any way he pleased. He was my agent in attending to my other farm and I paid him anything he asked of me. I made all sorts of dickers to help him out and defended him as best I could at Washington. I can not believe the complaint comes from him. He is very old now and Jesse his son writes to me in his stead but there has been nothing but friendship expressed. The one thing we have an agreement on is his auto-biography. I felt that he had a fine historical story to tell and so I got a short-hand reporter to sit by and take down all his talk with me. I then turned one copy over to him to revise and shape up, and I took the copy home thinking I might be able to help him get a publisher for it. It is however in a very confused nonchronological shape, and when I tried to shape it up for him, I found it an almost hopeless task. Meanwhile for years he has kept saying that he would get at it, and then Neatha[3] said he would try to retype it under the old man's direction but he was too old and too unskilled to do it and I was disheartened by the bewildering mass. I'll let you see it sometime when you are in the city. There is a big story there but it is an enormous job and the returns would be small. If he could have gone halfway in putting it into shape I might have found time to do the rest but the war came on and everything receded. Now I fear it is too late.

1. Hubert Edwin Collins (1872-?) wrote many books about machinery and published *Warpath and Cattle Trail* (1928), to which Garland contributed a foreword.

2. Probably a reference to the publication of Seger's *Early Days Among the Cheyenne and Arapahoe Indians*, ed. by Walter Campbell under the pseudonym of Stanley Vestal (1924), in which Campbell suggests that Garland misused Seger's recollections in his own work. See Holloway, p. 272n.27. Garland's editorial work on Seger's manuscripts is extant in the Garland Papers (item #457).

3. John Seger's other son.

Hotel Balzac
4, Rue Balzac
Paris

July. 27. [1924] [1]

Dear Family: At last Edith Wharton and I have met!—After a number of mischances I got off on a train for Sarcelles which is her station. It is about twenty five minutes out and on the first high ground north of Paris. She met me—*on foot*—(as it was Sunday her chauffer was off duty) and she came toward me alertly and with hand extended—nothing of the reserve she is credited with—She is a handsome figure. She wore an exquisite white gown and a lovely hat. I wish I could tell you about the gown but I can only say it was like those exquisite ones Mrs. Easton used to wear. She shows her years but carries herself well and her voice is charming—without any accent—a beautiful voice. Her eyes are brown and clear and friendly, and her expression candid and humorous.—It is a long walk up to her door and I fear in my keen interest in our talk I almost walked her off her feet. She told me that she had lived here for ten years, that she owns the place and that she spends her summers here and her winters in Hyères.—She feels the "foreign element" in New York just as I do—and she resents the assumption of our Europeanized critics.—She is humorous about it—not bitter. We came at last to her door—one of those heavy blank, forbidding portals that the French affect—but when it was opened, we confronted a delightful hall—and beyond the hall a glorious garden and a low line of hills. The house is long and low and open to the South —blind to the North. She has an acre or two of land filled with fruit and flowers, and as it is walled on all sides it has the privacy which English like.—We had tea in the midst of this garden talking steadily for we had much to discuss. I asked her if she had abandoned America and she said "Oh—no, dont put it that way. I shall come back for a few months every year." Nevertheless I feel that New York of today is not congenial to her. She said "I have lost two or three of my closest friends over there and it is rather sad to me on that account"—She showed me her garden—pear trees trained flat along a trellis—"Some of these trees are over a hundred years old" she said—She showed me her house, a lonely place built a hundred years ago for a young actress named Colombo—hence it is called "Pavillon Colombo." [2] It is beautifully simple. Some paintings by Fragonard are built into the walls and ceilings.—She took me to her little study, a pleasant little room. "But it is so neat!" I exclaimed. "So neat and or-derly."—She laughed. "But I *am* a neat and orderly person" she replied. She took me to a curious little open summer house of lattice work, in which was a table and writing material. "Here is where I put my writing guests" she said. She explained that this was a stable opening into an alley. She closed the door to the alley and cut away the western wall, thus mak-ing a most alluring shed or arbor. We talked of many things, of Howells, James, Fuller. Of her new books, of her poems—for she has a small vol-ume, published many years ago. I bragged of Mary Isabel's reading of her Roosevelt poem and she said. "I hope I may hear her, someday."[3] She spoke several times of my "Son of the Middle Border" but confirmed that she did not know "The Daughter." "I'll send you one," I said. Instantly she said, "I'll send you my box of little New York stories."[4] Naturally I told her that she was over-paying me but she insisted on sending the whole box.—We had much to talk about but at 6[30] I had to leave to catch the boat train—it being Sunday. She walked down the street with me till we reached the direct road then we shook hands and I went off down the hill feeling that I knew Edith Wharton at last.—It interested me to see that all the villagers knew her and regard her as their patron. She had just been giving a number of prizes to the school children and we met one of them with a big red book. They all were given prizes. As she handsomely said "Even the ones who were poor in attendance were given prizes be-cause they were in attendance on this occasion. That is sufficiently Bol-shevik, isnt it?" she said. She is never funny but has a glowing, quiet hu-mor that is delightful. She is witty in a quiet unobtrusive way and keenly observant, of course. She likes physical America, the environment of New York, the Berkshires, the Catskills but she is out of key with the South-western European, Jewish, Schlavonic invasion and will probably never live in New York again. Her home is almost as lovely as Maurice Hewletts old home at Broad-Chalk, absolutely retired and yet within half-an-hour of Paris Opera House.[5] I can understand the charm of such a life. I said "And yet it is a kind of exile, isnt it?"—"No," she said "I know many of the literary folk in Paris, and then my English and American friends can come to see me—Besides, you must remember it is only a few hours to London."—

She is a wonderful woman. She must be nearly seventy and yet she is alert as a girl in mind and on her feet. She spoke of the change between the period of her girlhood when women were old and retired at forty. She said she had always smoked until a few years ago when the doctor advised against it. For a matter of six months she went without but then the doctor told her to try and see if smoking would affect the heart again. "I found I didnt like the taste of it" she said humorously. "This alarmed me. If all my vices should turn out to be like that I would be devastated. I decided that hereafter I would reform slowly."—She said it a great deal subtler than this but it was to this effect. We talked of her Roosevelt poem again—and of the new edition which she was requested to have a part. "They wanted me to write an introduction to the New York volume but I thought it should be done by a historian—like Miss Schyler."[6]—She showed me her grandfather Stevens a strongly handsome man in uniform of a general in Washington's army. His face was as fine as Poe's—She is a genuine aristocrat but being genuine she does not insist upon it. I liked her—as hoped to do. I *think* she liked me—I hope she did and that we shall meet again.

1. Garland habitually revised and had transcribed for use in his autobiographies those letters he considered especially important or particularly useful as *aides de memoire*. In the upper left corner appear these instructions: "*Copy this but regard it as private.*" The letter that follows does not record Garland's deletions and insertions but is, as best as can be determined, the original letter he sent. The letter is neither signed nor paragraphed. A typed transcription, slightly edited, appears as "A Meeting With Edith Wharton" in the Garland Papers (item #531). For Garland's use of this letter in *Afternoon Neighbors*, see pp. 204–7.

2. Wharton's estate Pavillon Colombo, in the village of St. Brice-sous-Forêt, a dozen miles north of Paris.

3. Wharton's poem "Within the Tide" (1919) commemorates the death of Theodore Roosevelt.

4. *Old New York*, a collection of the novellas *False Dawn*, *The Old Maid*, *The Park*, and *New Year's Day*, published in a boxed set by Appleton in May 1924.

5. Maurice Hewlett (1861–1945), British novelist, poet, essayist, and author of historical romances. Garland's daughter Mary Isabel was especially fond of Hewlett's *The Life of Richard Yea-and-Nay* (1900). Garland had visited Hewlett in July 1922.

6. Lydia Schuyler, pseudonym of Mariana Van Rensselaer (1851–1934), author and art critic, whose most important book was the *History of the City of New York in the Seventeenth Century*, 2 vols. (1909). In 1923 Van Rensselaer received the American Academy of Arts and Letters' Gold Medal for distinction in literature.

293. to Edith Wharton

als, USC

Customers Room
Guaranty Trust Company of New York
1 & 3, Rue des Italiens
Paris

July. 28 [1924]

Dear Mrs. Wharton:

It was a great pleasure for me to see you in your seventeenth century setting, and I shall count it among the justifications for my trip which (at times) has seemed rather futile. The older I grow the less I value "sights," but I can still react to meetings with friends and to lovely scenery. As soon as my books arrive I will autograph "The Daughter of the Middle Border" to you—and if you are so kind as to send the box of New York stories it would be a great addition to their value if you would write in one of them a few words to Mary Isabel Garland telling when the poem on Roosevelt was written. She could then use these words in preparing her audiences for its reception. It is reported that you wrote the poem immediately on the news of Roosevelt's death. I may stay on till Saturday and if my books come today—as they should—I will mail you a copy at once.

Very sincerely yours
Hamlin Garland

294. to Zulime Garland

al, Hunt

Hotel Balzac
4, Rue Balzac
Paris

July. 31. [1924]

Dear Zulime: Your brief note reached me this morning just before I return to London. I wrote you about seeing Angus and having much talk.[1] I came away the very next day however and shall not see him again till he gets to New York.

I've just come in from a busy afternoon. I went to the Art Museum and—as usual—soon got enough of it. Such affected, uneasy, writhing

sculpture, such obviously sex inspired painting, such huge canvases, such
straining for originality! I saw hardly a *noble* piece in the course of my
rambles. A storm does not suggest to my mind a writhing mass of nude
female forms but most anything will do that for the French sculptors — of
the otherdays. I feel a stranger in the Frenchman's art as well as in his life.
He too, is a subdued man. There are many fine, sober handsome fellows
in the streets, and there are fewer painted females. I have lost in my admiration for French art and architecture but I've gained in regard for the
French people. They are less "gay" than as I recalled them and M. Roz[2]
says a reaction against vile literature has set in. I hope he's right but the
windows are still full of it. — Why are so many French women whiskered?
— Certain types have a distinct mustache. Then there is a class who go
about bare-headed, rusty, tousled, weather-beaten and sad. They swarm
in certain streets. — Versailles which I have just visited is a bleak and ugly
place except in the gardens of the palace. The palace is also ugly, a great
barracks of a place with square ugly windows, I had forgotten it was so
huge and so uninteresting exteriorly. I didnt go inside this time. I felt —
as Fuller did — "If I see any more 'priceless tapestry' and gold chains and
Napoleon swords and jewels I shall lose my reason." — They bore me in
much that same fashion. So do these gilded rectangles and canopy beds
and tables on which Napoleon signed deeds and abdications — but I enjoyed the deep gloom, the quiet, the flowers and the time-worn statuary
of the gardens. I was also a good deal surprised to find that the St Cloud
and the Mindon regions were also ugly. Their square, crude, porch-less
houses are repellent. The new ones are worse than the old ones for they
are garish in color. England has them beaten to a sadness in domestic
architecture and we are beating the English in our most recent types. If
we could only clean up our garbage! — We are so unkempt — and so flimsy
in much of our ugliness. However in another twenty five years we will
have no superiors — not even English architects — I mean in domestic architecture. Paris is belted by a zone almost as distressing as Hoboken —
but they've the Place Concorde, the Tuilleries and the Saint Chappelle.
This last is a marvelous little building (did you take the children to see
it?) and the tomb of Napoleon is one of the most beautiful and stately
memorials in the world — no doubt of that. To think that this small Cor-
sican five feet and three inches in height should have so stamped his im-
press on France! Men rail at him as "That little bandit" — but it does no
good. He was a wizard and we worship wizardry. As I returned from Ver-

sailles today, I crossed the Alexander bridge and had a last look at the Hotel des Invalides, and as I walked up the Champs Elyseè there was Napo-
leons Arch against the sun-set sky. Cant get away from him.

I am all packed ready to leave.

This ridge once held several villages. Nothing remains of them but a
few stones. I saw one which had on it something in which the word "perpetual" appeared. We had two priests in the party and when they saw this
stone which belonged to a church they felt vengeful. — I got no disheartening effect from it all. The bouyant courage and the skill of those men
as shown in their building and planting is proof once again of the power
of training and the force of habit. They set to work at once to restore along
familiar lines — but in many cases they improved on the former structure.
The women have the sad, weather-beaten, sallow and bitter faces. The
men are so busy in remaking, in harvesting that they are cheerful and
healthy. — Oh, how good my dinner tasted at 8 ᵖᵐ when I got back. The
food here is *too* good — all but the meat. I am suspicious of the meat.
Horse meat is plentiful so I am told. — Anyhow I am cautious on that side
of the dish. Eggs, fish, salads, fruits are delicious and the people of the
house friendly. —

I wish you and the children could be with me at this little hotel. The
food is delicious and the place is so clean. Tonight I had soup, cold fish
with a wonderful sauce, roast chicken, a mysterious mixture of vegetables
which I had never tasted — a noble salad (a whole bowl of it) ice-cream
and wafers and grapes. Each day the menu is varied so that it never palls.
I am paying about twenty one dollars per week. You and I could live along
here for about twenty five dollars per day. Next year prices will be lower.
This is a crowded year. I go back for a week to my old place in London
which is not as good as this but it is quiet and wholesome. — This place is
managed by a man of thirty five and his wife and his wife's mother and
aside from the noise on the front it is a most comfortable place. I dont
know where we could find just the same kind of thing in New York City.
All the same I shall enjoy getting back to London where I can mail a letter
without putting on extra stamps and where I can make my wants known.
— "Everybody" is getting out of Paris just as "Everybody" has gone from
London, and there is nothing to do but look at sights and I am not eager
for sights. If you go to any point of interest you are one of a mob. I was
surprised to find Versailles so full of tourists. — It is curious how familiar
Paris has grown in two weeks. I come and go in it now quite readily. I
have been in almost every part of it. It is very compact and only about

half the size of London or New York. I doubt if I could learn to speak in a year my verbal memory is so poor. I am delighted to hear that Onteora is not boring the girls. I was afraid it would be entirely lacking in young men this year—

I dont know what I shall do in London—except preside at that luncheon, for all my friends are in the country now. I may go up to Stratford. Noyes[3] wrote asking if I were not coming down his way—and I may visit Conrad who is having a lot of trouble. His wife is still in the hospital. Doyle will be back I think and I may go down to see him. I had a card from Dr. Seaman who is in Scotland. I may take a run up there. August is a slow month in London but I'll pull through—I may set to work on some writing.—

9[pm] Back in London in my old room which feels comfortable—[4]

1. Angus Roy Shannon, Zulime's brother-in-law.

2. Dr. Firman Roz, who wanted the French firm Dunod to translate and publish *Captain* and others of Garland's works (*Afternoon*, pp. 173–74).

3. Alfred Noyes (1880–1958), British poet, whose works include *Poems* (1904), *Tales of the Mermaid Tavern* (1913), and the trilogy *The Torch-Bearers* (1922–30).

4. Written across the top of the first page.

295. to Frank D. Fackenthal

tls, Pulitzer

Hamlin Garland
71 East Ninety-Second Street
New York City

Nov. 11 [1924]

Dear Mr. Fackenthal:

I hardly know what to say in respect of your invitation to serve again on the Pulitzer Committee.[1] I am all out of key with the pornographic drama of our day and I could not vote an award to any such play no matter what its technical excellence might be. I hate the entire over-sexed fiction and poetry of today. I regard it as a passing phase of the corruption of war experiences.

Now if with this plain statement of my prejudices, you still think I should serve, I will do so. There is another point to be considered. It is easy for Hamilton and Thomas to see plays for they are in the midst of the theatrical world but for an outsider like myself it is expensive business.

The Advocate: 1919–1929 319

It takes about five dollars to see a play, and for this reason I can not afford
to merely experiment. I can only plan to see a few of those plays which
are adjudged in general terms to be candidates. I do not think we should
accept tickets to any of these plays except it be from those of our friends
who are sufficiently understanding to grant us the most perfect liberty of
judgement. I should like to be able to meet any aftermath of complaint.

Very sincerely yours,
Hamlin Garland

1. In his letter of invitation, 8 November 1924, Fackenthal had assured Garland that
the Advisory Board was "very anxious to accept and to follow as closely as possible the
recommendations of the advisory juries" and that if it decided to vary from that decision, it would confer with the chair before doing so. Although Augustus Thomas was
designated as chair, he had to withdraw due to other commitments. Jesse Lynch Williams replaced him as chair, but he departed for California on 10 January though he
had seen the nominated plays before he left. Clayton Hamilton was thus de facto chair.

296. to Frank D. Fackenthal

tls, Pulitzer

Hamlin Garland
71 East Ninety-Second Street
New York City

Mar. 9 [1925]

Dear Mr. Fackenthal:

I have just had a conference with Clayton Hamilton, the first of our
meetings. He had a letter from Jesse Williams in which he spoke of only two
possibilities "What Price Glory" and "They Knew What They Wanted." [1]
Mr. Hamilton is opposed to "Glory" and I am opposed to giving a medal
to any of the plays I have seen.

In view of the fact that an agreement is almost impossible in the case I
am writing to ask you to drop my name from the jury. I can not afford to
have my name published as voting for plays that I hold in contempt. [2] I
have not yet seen the Howard play but from Hamiltons statement of the
plot it does not "best represent the educational value and power of the
stage in raising the standard of good morals, good taste and good manners." I shall see the play but as I wrote you in an early letter I will not
vote for any pornographic drama.

As Mr. Augustus Thomas is still in the city I suggest that you ask him to take my place on the jury. It may be that he will come to an agreement with the other members during the week. I regret that my letter of resignation comes so late but I have only just this moment been able to confer with Mr. Hamilton.

Hoping you will be able to release me at once, and with a repeated protest against being made to seem in any degree favorable to plays of the kind under consideration, I am

Very sincerely yours,
Hamlin Garland

1. *What Price Glory?* by Laurence Stallings and Maxwell Anderson, and *They Knew What They Wanted,* by Sidney Howard, which won the award.

2. Fackenthal wrote, 11 March 1925, to urge Garland to reconsider, asked him to put in "a minority report" if he did not agree with the other members, and assured him that his dissent would be published, if indeed he did dissent. On 13 March Garland again wrote to Fackenthal, stating simply, "Please drop my name from the jury. I am too ill to serve and do not wish my name quoted in the controversy."

297. to Brander Matthews   tls, Columbia

Mar. 11. [1925]

Dear Brander:

As you may know I have been on the Drama Jury again. When Fackenthal wrote me saying that Thomas* was unable to serve, I replied by saying that I was a poor man to put on this jury for I would not vote for any of these pornographic plays. Fackenthal more or less insisted that I stay on. Now the snarl I anticipated has come up. As my name would be used as a member of the committee whether I approved of the play or not I have asked Fackenthal to drop me from the jury. I cant publish one thing over my name and have the Pulitzer Committee publish me in approval of the very thing I detest. I am sick of these prostitute plays. I dont believe any of them come under the Pulitzer conditions. They do not "make for good manners or morals." I fought the award to "Anna Christy", but was overborne by the other members of the jury. I could not bring in a minority report. It creates a bad impression to go against the plain wording of the conditions of the award.

In a paragraph in LIFE not long ago, I learned that if all the street-walkers delineated in the drama this year were to walk up Fifth Avenue they would make the longest procession since the visit of Foch. Apparently none of our dramatists—or very few—are interested in any other type of woman. This is Continental and not American art. As for "What Price Glory" it seems to me—and to Hamilton—a weak play with strong language. A journalistic "slam" at war, all well enough in its way but not making for good morals nor good manners.

I write this in order that you may know the situation. To my thinking it would be a stronger gesture to let the year pass without an award than to give it where it would be nescessary to apologize for the action.

Faithfully,
Hamlin.

#Augustus is in town, make him go on the committee again.

298. to John Jay Chapman   als, Harvard

71. East. 92nd St.

Monday. [ca. April 1925]

Dear Mr. Chapman:[1]

I read your *Forum* article with keen interest.[2] I am glad that you are in a position to state your mind on this most important subject. You are right in your implication that there is something real at the bottom of the Ku Klux agitation. I have found that many of them are patriots.—

More power to your pen—

Hamlin Garland

1. John Jay Chapman (1862–1933), literary critic, essayist, and Emersonian individualist. Among his books are *Emerson, and Other Essays* (1898), *William Lloyd Garrison* (1913, revised 1921), and *Letters and Religion* (1924).

2. In "American and Roman Catholicism, II—Strike at the Source," *Forum* 73 (April 1925): 449–57, Chapman argues that Catholicism is incompatible with basic American democratic principles. As part of his argument, he notes: "Quite recently, the Ku Klux Klan has taken up the cry against the Roman machine in terms more rational than is generally suspected" (p. 454).

299. to Van Wyck Brooks

als, U Penn

Hamlin Garland
Seventy One East Ninety Second St.
New York City

May. 24 [1925]

Dear Mr Brooks:

Will you permit me to say that I think you have made a thought-pro-voking book of Henry James?[1] Probably my opinion will have no value to you but as I knew James and Howells rather well, I venture to write you my interest in the book. I knew William James also and have heard him speak of Henry in the terms which you quote. I have read Henry James for forty years and his picture hangs over my desk. Middle-Westerner that I am I have found keen stimulation in James—especially in his novelettes. Sometime when you are in town I should like to meet you and talk of James.

Very sincerely yours
Hamlin Garland

1. Van Wyck Brooks (1886–1963), critic and interpreter of America's literary past, whose *The Wine of the Puritans* (1909) and *America's Coming of Age* (1915) developed the thesis that America's Puritan past stifled its creativity. Garland refers to Brooks's *The Pilgrimage of Henry James* (1925).

300. to Van Wyck Brooks

als, U Penn

Hamlin Garland
71 East 92nd Street
New York City

May. 28. [1925]

Dear Mr Brooks:

Your letter finds me in Onteora where I am at work with saw and hammer repairing our shack. However I shall be in town again next week and if by any chance you are also coming in, I want to have you for lunch at the Town Hall Club.[1] We can then discuss our many differences and, perhaps, find some agreement. I did not read your "Mark Twain" for the reason—probably a mistaken one—that it was someone said a brief for the suppressed obscenity and profanity which are the negligible sides of

Clemens' genius.[2] I shall read the book now and deal fairly with its thesis for I found the James' study amazingly close and fine in its texture. In these days of cheap and easy newspaper "stuff," such work as yours is most grateful to my ageing mind. You will be interested to know that I have spent three successive summers in London and expect to go again about the middle of June. I have actually spent four summers there but only three in close succession.—My English ancestor sailed from the south of England three hundred years ago—lacking two years—and as I grow in days if not in wisdom I find increasing charm in my ancestral home—not the precise thing James was seeking but the human, the moss-grown, the ivy-covered.—My pioneering is done. At sixty five I am disposed to leave to others the America of the rodeo and aeroplane.—I know America, every state and almost every city of it and the America I loved has almost vanished so—

But we'll talk of this and other things.

I shall probably go in town about the 3rd of June—

Very sincerely yours
Hamlin Garland

1. Garland was one of the founders of the Town Hall Club, intended to be a civic center for people interested in civics, art, and education. The club opened in January 1925.

2. *The Ordeal of Mark Twain* (1920).

301. to Stuart Pratt Sherman

als, U of Ill-Ar

Camp Neshonoc
Onteora Road
Tannersville, N. Y.

June. 8. [1925]

Dear Sherman:

Brownell and Matthews have signed and I am having the paper go on to Sloane and Van Dyke.[1] Important item! We must make it plain that Hergesheimer is *not* a Jew. Perhaps his parentage is indicated fully in "Who's Who." I called him a "Pennsylvania Dutchman" and that I believe is the fact. Can you add a line or two before the paper goes to print?—I am sailing Wednesday for England. My fourth successive summer!—

In September we should consider several literary projects for the Town Hall Club.

Best wishes —
Hamlin Garland

Authors Club.
3. Whitehall Court
London.

1. Sherman had nominated novelist Joseph Hergesheimer for election to the American Academy and had asked Garland to sign the nomination paper (Sherman to Garland, 24 May 1925). Hergesheimer was not elected.

302. to Mildred Howells   als, Harvard

Hamlin Garland
507 Cathedral Parkway
New York City

Nov. 22. [1925]

Dear Miss Howells:

You may say that I was a disciple of Henry George — and that as often as I dared, I tried to win your father to a belief in the single tax.[1] He gave it his allegiance to the point of saying, "It is good as far as it goes but reform should go further." In other words he was more socialistic than I. We never *argued*—we just stated our theories and convictions. He was most sympathetic, and occasionally the land-reform idea came out in his essays at that time. —

If I can be of any help at any time please write me. —

All send greeting
Hamlin Garland.

1. In a letter dated 15 January 1888, William Dean Howells had written of Garland's "land tenure idea." Mildred Howells queried Garland, 20 November 1925, about what her father meant by the phrase and whether Garland was a disciple of Henry George.

303. to Mildred Howells

tls, Harvard

Hamlin Garland
507 Cathedral Parkway
New York City

Dec. 2. [1925]

Dear Miss Howells:

Of course you can use my notation.[1] I wish I could be of more help. If it will add interest I will write you more of that time and temper. It was a day of much questioning. George had written and was speaking, Bellamy had just made his amazing success with LOOKING BACKWARD and we were all drawn into two camps, one socialistic, the other individualistic. I was a disciple of Henry George and Herbert Spencer, while your father leaned toward the socialistic side—as did Mark Twain. Bellamy followed George by ten years or more but he appealed to another type of mind entirely. I impressed your father sufficiently to enable him to put into THE HAZARD OF NEW FORTUNES occasional notes on the "unearned increment" and the like.

If I can be of any further help, please be quite free to call upon me.

Very sincerely yours,
Hamlin Garland

1. Mildred Howells had written, 25 November 1925, to ask whether she could quote from Garland's letter of 22 November as an explanation of "the land tenure idea" in her forthcoming *Life in Letters*. The passage she wished to use was "as often as I dared . . . theories and convictions."

304. to William Lyon Phelps

tls, Yale

Hamlin Garland
507 Cathedral Parkway
New York City

Dec. 12 [1925]

Dear William:

Zulime came back from your lecture today quite filled with delight in your frank judgments. She conveyed to me the most important facts of your agreement with me and your "fearless attitude," so that I must write and say "More power to ye, and long life firninst ye." You said what I have

said of our pornographic commercialized fiction and drama. I have gotten to such a state that I will not read novels or go to plays unless I *know*
they are decent and helpful. I am not shocked—it is a little difficult to
shock a man who has come up through border conditions—but I am
disgusted with this school of the road-house and brothel.

Some of them profess to find in my work some kinship but as you
know when I was pleading for a truer fiction I was not advocating a literature of illicit sexual passion, on the contrary I knew that the French had
specialized in that sort of work for a hundred years and that originality
did not lie in that direction. As Mr. Howells put it I was not pleading for
"an exchange of the convention of decency for the convention of indecency." In all that I wrote I kept not only clear of crime but of vice. Ibsen
was more to my mind than Zola.[1]

When you come to town next, I wish you would make it possible for
us to meet either at lunch at the club, or here at my home. My wife and
daughters would be delighted to see you at tea or at dinner.

Best wishes to you and yours,
Hamlin Garland

1. In his reply of 15 December 1925, Phelps noted he was "disgusted beyond words
with so much of our present-day literature and drama" and then elaborated his position
at length.

305. to Carl Van Doren tlc, usc

Hamlin Garland
507 Cathedral Parkway
New York City

Mar. 2. [1926]

Dear Carl Van Doren:

I appreciate the very great compliment involved in your mentioning
me in your lectures—as one on the side-lines I am grateful for any remembrance now—but I do not see how you can find any connection
between Dreiser and myself. I am an old fogy. I believe in marriage, the
home, prohibition, censorship, the single tax and many other isms that
are now discredited by the "young" writers of fifty. I have always hated
obscenity, tales of vice and crime, and jokes about the chastity or modesty
of women. I have never written about vice or crime. My stories are hard

and rude and sordid but not in the beastly sense. I have never held with
the pornographic school and my most advanced notions in CRUMBLING
IDOLS, as you know, had nothing to do with the glorification of sexual
promiscuity. I am an individualist but my notions of liberty do not include license.

The pornographic school of writing is as old as the Cromagnon Man—
or older. It is so old and so hackneyed in theme that I have no interest in
it. My attempt has been to treat of themes which are characteristic of my
age and of America. It is so easy to write stories of sexual "irregularities."
I have tried to keep close to the normal, decent hard-working folk of my
day. The other kind of thing pays better but I could never quite bring myself to it;[1]

1. The copy text is incomplete. Garland noted in the upper left corner, "This letter
was not sent," here meaning he sent another version of the letter, and "Please return.
H. G.," which is a notation directed at Eldon Hill, to whom he sent this draft. The
mailed letter, which exists as a transcription made by Hill (Miami U), omits everything
after the first sentence and adds a paragraph arranging a meeting time. See Garland to
Hill, 22 January 1939, letter 386. Van Doren, who had been lecturing about Garland to
a graduate class in contemporary American literature at Columbia University, replied
on 3 March 1926: "My reason for putting you with Dreiser—which I admit seems odd
at first glance—is that you both, in your different ways, have done something analo-
gous in your indication of overlooked individuals. You were the first to point out, if my
literary history is correct, that the frontier was not made up entirely of convinced fron-
tiersmen. It had its poets and its persons who looked elsewhere to a more spiritual
existence than the frontier usually thought. Dreiser has pointed out another kind of
individual in the midst of American society.—The individual who does not accept or
at least illustrate the standard notions of bourgeois conduct and who succeeds or fails
without much reference to that standard."

306. to Mary E. Wilkins Freeman

als, USC

Hamlin Garland
507 Cathedral Parkway
New York City

Mar. 31. [1926]

Dear Mary E. Wilkins:

The Directors of the American Academy have asked me to make a little
address in the ceremony of the Gold Medal on April 23rd and I have ac-

cepted with peculiar pleasure for I recall the good days when we used to
meet at Edgar Chamberlain's house and elsewhere, when we were both
so keen on our writing that we found much in common to talk about.[1] I
have not much time allotted to me but I hope to put on record the lasting
regard I have for you and your fiction.

I sincerely hope no "Influ bug" or any other cause will prevent your
coming on this day.

Very faithfully yours
Hamlin Garland

1. The Academy had awarded Freeman the first William Dean Howells Medal for
distinguished work in fiction on 19 November 1925. The public ceremony took place
on 23 April 1926, at which Garland presented the medal. Garland habitually misspelled
Joseph Edgar Chamberlin's name.

307. to Mary E. Wilkins Freeman als, Miami U

Hamlin Garland
507 Cathedral Parkway
New York City

April. 12. [1926]

Dear Mary Wilkins:

Please tell me if I have said the wrong word at any place in the little
address which the Academy has sent you.[1] If we look at this presentation
from the historical stand-point it is not lacking in significance. That I,
a grandson of New England, son of a man who went west to settle the
empty spaces, should be called upon to present to you, the social historian
of the New England left behind, a Medal, is a theme on which we could
each comment worthily—if we had time. Perhaps we can suggest it in a
few words. Anyhow it is a great pleasure for me to act as spokesman for
the Academy.

Very faithfully yours,
Hamlin Garland

1. Garland's holograph address, and Freeman's typewritten response, are extant in
the Garland Papers (items #598, 748).

Hamlin Garland
Onteora Road
Tannersville, N.Y.

June. 6. [1926]

Dear Mr Maxwell:

I wish I had Mr. Bok's confident hope but I have not.[1] I can not believe that any single peace plan, however brilliant, can become operative to the extent of insuring universal peace. I can not believe that any individual plan will measurably influence a nation when aflame with the war spirit. Nations like individual[s] fight for place, for power, for wealth and when they strongly feel restriction they will continue to challenge their rivals. Men have been at war for twenty five thousand years and I am certain that peoples as well as rulers will continue to war in the future. As nations press against one anothers boundaries competition for the good things of life sharpens and the war spirit develops. History is so long in its course and makes inherited passions so deep-seated and powerful that only a *diminution in the number* of wars can be predicted. In many ways I am an optimist but I am not sufficiently the optimist to expect any sudden change in the nature of man. Nevertheless it is my duty to advocate every form of arbitration, every court of appeal in the hope of increasing the space between present and future wars.—

Hamlin Garland

1. In 1923 the former editor of the *Ladies' Home Journal,* Edward Bok, had established an American Peace Award of one hundred thousand dollars for anyone who could devise a practicable plan for world peace. Perriton Maxwell (1868–1947), head of the Southern Newspaper Syndicate, had written to Garland on 29 May 1926 to seek his opinion of Bok's award for use in a newspaper article about the prize. Maxwell was soliciting opinions from "ten representative Americans" and hastened to explain that he was addressing Garland "as one of ten outstanding Americans whose ideas on peace proposals generally will be most valuable to intelligent readers." He went on to ask for Garland's "frank comment on the American Peace Award and its probable effect, if any, upon the action of nations with respect to the suppression of war."

309. to Grace Vanamee

als, Am Acad

[ca. 4 September 1926]

Dear Mrs Vanamee:

In spite of what Dr. Johnson says Van Dyke and I know very well that some of the men in the Institute are not only indifferent but contemptuous. To offer them higher honors would be to cheapen the Academy and lay it liable to another public attack. A man like MacNeil is fairly safe but some of these others are not. There is no telling what Henri's attitude would be or Cram's either. Eugene O'Neill has made a great name and is a man of imagination and power but I would not vote for him till I knew most definitely that he had accepted nomination. Albert Bigelow Paine is opposed to the Academy.[1] You are in a position to guard the Academy and I hope you will be quick to do so. The Institute should also be guarded against the Sinclair Lewis type.[2]

Hamlin Garland

Personal[3]

1. Garland wanted to nominate the sculptor Hermon A. MacNeil for Academy membership and had earlier written to Vanamee to express his concern about gaining the candidate's prior consent to avoid the embarrassment of any potential rejection (see Garland to Vanamee, 30 August 1926, Am Acad). MacNeil was elected 11 November 1926; architect Ralph Cram was elected in 1940, and O'Neill in 1933. The painter Robert Henri and Paine were not offered membership.

2. Garland had become wounded by Lewis's attacks against the literary establishment. He had proposed Lewis for membership in the National Institute in 1922, which Lewis declined. Lewis had also been awarded the 1926 Pulitzer Prize for fiction for *Arrowsmith* but had refused the prize in a public letter, which was widely reprinted.

3. Placed at top left corner.

310. to Archer M. Huntington

als, Syracuse

Hamlin Garland
507 Cathedral Parkway
New York City

Nov. 14 [1926]

Dear Huntington:

It is only fair to me to tell you that I signed those nominating blanks for Edith Wharton, Mary Wilkins and Margaret Deland nine years ago,

The Advocate: 1919–1929 331

as a member of a committee.[1] I had nothing to do with bringing the names up for a vote at the Institute meeting. I was not a member of the Academy in 1917—and hence was not troubled by the effect of the ballot for women members of the Institute. I am for the rights of women, as a general proposition but I do not advocate their admission to either the Institute or the Academy just now. I fear the effect of a dissension in the Institute as a result of this election. The meeting was small and weak, hardly representative.

I should like to talk of this with you—

Hamlin Garland

1. Wharton, Freeman, Deland, and Agnes Repplier were elected to the National Institute in 1926. Huntington replied on 17 November 1926: "My feeling in this matter is that if women wish to be elected to the Academy their final election is certain, as we have no sound argument against them. It seems to me that the entrance of four women into the Institute has closed the question permanently."

311. to Fred L. Black

ald, USC

Hamlin Garland
507 Cathedral Parkway
New York City

Dec. 20. [1926]

Dear Mr Black:[1]

I went to Dearborn with a vague notion of Henry Ford, I came away with an enthusiasm for his Americanism, his patriotism and his wistful love for the home of his boy-hood. His interest in the old school-books, in the homely interests of farm and village was a revelation to me of the essential idealism of the man. To see him dancing among his neighbors changed my whole conception of him. I should like to convey this impression to others—and I have written down my change of attitude and sometime I shall use it—perhaps in my new book.[2] Before I use it, however, I shall want you to see it and pass upon it. I think it would do something toward making the fine side of Ford known to the east. I shall not use it without his and Mrs. Ford's permission. It would be a breach of hospitality to do so but I wish they would consider letting me use it in one of the big magazines. In "Jew York" Ford is a bogey, a wild man. I would like to make record of that side of him which it was my privilege to see.

I shall rest upon your judgement.

Very sincerely
Hamlin Garland

1. Fred L. Black (1891–?) was the advertising manager of the Ford Motor Co. and was also the business manager of the Dearborn *Independent.*

2. Garland sent a draft and drawings in a 29 May 1927 letter to Black, intended as an article for the Dearborn *Independent.* For Garland's published commentary on Ford, see *Afternoon,* pp. 359–68, 503–11. See also "The Homely Side of Henry Ford" (item #499).

312. to Arthur Hobson Quinn

als, USC

Hamlin Garland
Grey Ledge
Onteora Park, N.Y.

July. 4. [1927]

Dear Prof. Quinn:

I think the play is to be given on the 16th but it may go over till the 23rd.[1] *It is a big job!* Dont make a special trip to see it, but if you are on your way to New England along about that time—or if you would enjoy a motor trip, I'd like to have you as my houseguest. If we had the funds I should like to engage you to come and say a few words concerning the play—but like all similar organizations, every man and woman contributes time and talent—If you could dictate a short statement concerning the play, its various forms and dates leading up to Jefferson's it would be helpful. Dont do it if it requires much time.[2]

Hamlin Garland

1. Arthur Hobson Quinn (1875–1960), a professor of English at the University of Pennsylvania, was one of the foremost scholars of American drama and had corresponded with Garland about James A. Herne. Garland refers to his play, *Rip Van Winkle.* Garland had written Quinn to ask about the various extant versions. Heeding Quinn's advice that he write his own version, Garland promptly did so, adapting a script by Charles Burke, and the play opened at the Onteora Theater on 16 July 1927, with his daughter Constance in the cast. The play exists in manuscript (item #210).

2. Quinn referred Garland to his *History of American Drama from the Beginning to the Civil War* (1923) and provided a brief summary of the play's history (Quinn to Garland, 8 July 1927).

313. to Flora Warren Seymour

tls, Knox

New York City

November 26, 1927.

Dear Mrs Seymour: [1]

Sometimes in my moods of doubt, I wonder whether books are not predestined to join the clay tablets of Babylon and the papyrus rolls of Egypt. That the radio machine is changing the character of the reader as well as methods of intercourse is indisputable. That it will continue to grow in power and influence is equally certain. No one can foretell what its effect on the reader of books may be but for some of us a good book is a grateful refuge from the jangle and jazz. The reading lamp is still a necessary equipment in my home and the fellowship which your organization represents has my sympathy and support.

As a writer I am, naturally, a believer in print. I am an advocate of the reader rather than of the listener-in, but I confess that many current novels are worse than moving pictures and that is saying a good deal. Part of this lack of sympathy for present-day books is due, no doubt, to my years, but more of it is due to my bringing up. I am the son of a transplanted New Englander and have no apology to make for my attitude. I am proud of my Scotch-Irish strain and my Puritan forebears. They were essentially a reading people, although they had few books. None of them were lacking in vigor of speech or readiness of action. They cannot be called effeminate or ascetic, but they respected the decencies of life and the decorums of speech. So far as I know they were never bitter or cynical.

Because of my derivation from such book-lovers, I find myself in accord with most of the purposes and many of the judgments which the STEP-LADDER represents. I accepted the Chairmanship of your Advisory Board because of this sympathy and I am willing to continue if you think I can be of any service. The word is not a warrant for performance, however, for it is increasingly difficult for me to carry on the duties which are elsewhere required of me. Probably what I am doing is not important but so long as my publishers think it is I must continue on, in low speed at least.

The chief intent of this letter is to send greetings to the Bookfellows and to express my wishes for a prosperous New Year. The STEP-LADDER, and all the Bookfellows who mount it, in order to take down an old book or to put away a new one, have my greeting in print.

Very Faithfully Yours,
Hamlin Garland

1. Flora Warren Seymour (?–1948) and her husband, George Steele Seymour (1878–
1945), founded the Order of the Bookfellows, a Chicago literary and publishing club.
The *Step Ladder* was its magazine. The Bookfellows published Garland's *A Pioneer
Mother* in 1922 and *Joys of the Trail* in 1935. This letter appeared without comment or
introduction in the *Step Ladder* 14 (January 1928): 1–2.

314. to Constance Garland Harper

tl, Hunt

Grey Ledge Cottage
Onteora Park
Tannersville, New York

July 17 [1928]

Dear Daughtie:

We have just wired you in reply to your pathetic letter. We have no
wish to worry you and will not do so. What I wish Joe would do is make
such a strike that he could come on and stay. It looks now as tho Hardy
would get into the radio thru a quartette.[1] They have offered him a chance
if he can get a quartette together. He is down town working at it. If he
gets into this he will not go to California.

The truth is Daughtie I am greatly worried and I am relying on you to
give charm to this book as you did to the other one.[2] It is a more difficult
book to do than the others. It is a climax—or should be—and I am using
all my powers. I am up at half-past four and putting in six or seven hours
each day. I am tired and irritable but there is no help for it. I must work
to my limit.

It wont matter if the pictures exactly fit or not provided they give the
charm of our life in the East and in England. I enclose the only picture I
can find of the Jones house. We need a lovely drawing of that. We must
have a better one of the reservoir, one that gives the dream-like quality we
used to find there. A snow scene such as we had one Christmas would be
fine. We can adjust them after you get here. I have sent chapter heads.

Yours with love
DADDY.

1. Constance Garland had married Joseph Wesley Harper, a grandson of the founder
of the publishing firm, in September 1927. "Hardy" is Hardesty Johnson, a singer who
had married Mary Isabel in 1926. Both daughters had moved to California.

2. Constance was a talented artist and supplied illustrations for many of her father's
books, including the one referred to here, *Back-Trailers from the Middle Border*, which
was published by Macmillan in October 1928.

The Advocate: 1919–1929 335

315. to Grace Vanamee
tls, Am Acad

Hamlin Garland
507 Cathedral Parkway
New York City

September thirtieth. [1928]

Dear Mrs Vanamee,

You may count on me for October ninth but I fear I shall not be able to make satisfactory report of the radio matter. After finishing my book, which took all my time and energy, I found myself unable to use my eyes and so let everything "slide". Furthermore, I doubt if this is good time to push the radio prize program, for the political speakers have the floor. However, we will confer on the matter soon. I shall write Mr Elwood and get his reaction.[1]

I am enclosing a letter from W. L. Cross touching on Robert Frost's eligibility. I hear that he has a fine new work just out. If it is really fine I think his chances for election would be very good. I liked him personally very much and I will go on his nomination papers if it seems advisable. I dont want to go on too many nominating papers. With regard to Dr Richard Burton, I have much the same feeling. He is a fine man and a powerful influence for good in literature. He travels constantly and will be a noble representative of the Academy. He is widely known and could probably be elected.[2]

In the department of Architecture I should like to see Cram nominated. I think that however should go up to Cass Gilbert.[3] All these matters we should have ample time to discuss at our luncheon on the ninth.

With regard to the nominations for the Institute, it seems to me that something could be done to stir up nominations. With only three nominations and some twelve or fourteen vacancies, there is a fine opportunity to put in some of the younger and more important men. It might be well also to take up the suggestion of nominating Van der Stucken for the Academy. I do not know his work but apparently he is highly regarded by his fellow musicians.[4]

I hope to see you before the Tuesday meeting.

Faithfully yours,
Hamlin Garland

1. The Academy had instituted a Medal for Good Diction on the Stage, awarded annually beginning in 1925. In 1928 the Academy established a Medal for Good Diction over the Radio, with its first award to Milton J. Cross in 1929. For Garland's account of the importance of this award, see "The Value of Melodious Speech," *Emerson Quarterly* 9 (November 1929): 5–6, 22, 24. John W. Elwood was the assistant to the president, and later vice president, of the National Broadcasting Company.

2. Robert Frost was elected to the Academy in 1930; Richard Burton was not offered membership.

3. The architect Cass Gilbert, who designed the Academy's building on West 155th Street, was in charge of nominations for the Architecture section.

4. The musician Frank V. van der Stucken was elected to the Academy in 1929.

316. to Mildred Howells

als, Harvard

Hamlin Garland
507 Cathedral Parkway
New York City

Dec. 4 [1928]

Dear Mildred:

I have read both volumes of the Life, and last night I re-read, aloud, some of the choice lines for Zulime. She was as deeply moved as I by the later letters. Old age, at its best, is tragic business. I am appalled at times to realize that I am nearing seventy. This is a book to be studied and quoted. I am considering what I can best do for it. Perhaps Mr. Adams would print a letter in the *Times Review*.[1] The fact that the great novelist speaks of me so affectionately will cause some readers to discount my praise but that does not much matter. I tried to get Adams to use Fuller for a review but my suggestion came too late.

Let us see you if you come to New York. We all unite in best wishes for the book.

Faithfully
Hamlin Garland

1. J. Donald Adams (1891–1968) was the editor of the *New York Times Book Review*. Garland did write a letter concerning the *Life in Letters of William Dean Howells* (to "Editor, Times," n.d., USC), but the newspaper did not publish it.

Hamlin Garland
507 Cathedral Parkway
New York City

Dec. 18 [1928]

Dear Mr. Edgett:

I have just received your very generous comment on my work and I most gratefully thank you for it.[1] I wish also to thank you for the noble tribute you pay Edward Eggleston.[2] He was a grand old pioneer. He broke new ground in a most unpromising field. He meant much to me in 1871 when I read him first, on an Iowa farm. In a sense he is the father of all of us who are writing of the Mid-West.

There is nothing strange in turning East toward the places where my ancestors have dwelt for three hundred years. The older I grow the deeper the stir which ancient roofs and ingle-nooks produce in me. As I ride through New England I am made aware of my derivation by the poetic appeal of gray old houses, broad chimneys and lofty elm trees. My pioneering is done. Henceforth I shall toast my knees at the ancestral fireplace and *talk* of the plains and their blizzards. If this is old why—it is old age that's all! My wife and I dream of sometime owning a colonial farm house—not too far from New York—to which we can hasten whenever the city gets too noisy and too dangerous.

With The Best of Holiday Good Wishes,
Hamlin Garland

1. Edwin F. Edgett (1867–1948) reviewed Garland's work on the occasion of the publication of *Back-Trailers* in "About Books and Authors," BET, 15 December 1928, book sec., p. 8.

2. Edward Eggleston (1837–1902), Indiana novelist, whose *The Hoosier Schoolmaster* (1871) and *The Circuit Rider* (1874) were early exponents of literary realism.

318. to Constance Garland Harper   tl, Hunt

Hamlin Garland
507 Cathedral Parkway
New York City

Dec. 20 [1928]

Dear Conniekins:

I have just come from another talk with Mr. Latham. His plan is to re-issue the DAUGHTER as a newly and fully illustrated book, making much of the illustrations.[1] He would like at least twelve full page illustrations and I told him you would do it. They cant make any money on this edition, they are doing it to please me and I would like you to do your best on it and bring it up to the others. We like the drawings you have sent in but I want you to go on with the job and make the book as attractive as possible. We will try to bring with us some more photos which will help. The jacket might be the Mississippi River and hills, "poichence."

Joe's letter has just come and we are in a state of wonder why you didnt both plan to come on and spend Christmas here and take us home with you. We can do it yet if you tell us to—or do you want us to be out there while Joe is East?—If you change the plan wire us instructions. If plans are to remain as they are, do *not* wire. An air mail letter would reach us before we start. I have bought our tickets and we are about ready to pack but we can exchange for a later date if it seems pleasanter to do so. Whatever happens keep up the work on THE DAUGHTER. They want to have the drawings in by the first of February. NOTE THAT. THE FIRST of February. The new edition is announced for April.

Did you listen in on my speech last Sunday night?[2] It went all over the mid. west and reached the coast I think. Twas a great occasion. Fine reviews are coming in about the Back-Trailers. It is just beginning to be known to the public. So is the Middle Border Programs which the HIS-TRIES are giving over W.A.B.C.[3] They give two more. Next Sunday and the Sunday after. 2.30 here. Would that be ten thirty or such out there?

Yours with much love
Daddy.

---

1. Macmillan issued a new edition of *Daughter*, with illustrations by Constance Garland, in 1929.

2. In a radio address on 16 December, the American Academy announced the estab-

lishment of a Medal for Good Diction over the Radio. Garland spoke on behalf of the
award.

3. On three consecutive Sundays, a program entitled "Macmillan's Middle Border"
aired, presumably excerpts from Garland's books.

319. to Archer M. Huntington tls, Syracuse

Hamlin Garland
507 Cathedral Parkway
New York City

June. 4. [1929]

Dear Huntington:

Your munificence to the Academy is glorious and I want you to know
how deeply I appreciate it. We would have only a small office in a commonplace building but for you. I know you dislike being thanked but now
and again it seems that we must express our feeling toward you.[1]

Mrs. Vanamee assures me that you approve of the radio campaign and
that is highly gratifying to me for I have had to do most of the work. The
effect of the award on the press has been great beyond my expectation. We
have two large books filled with clippings, many of them editorials. Nothing the Academy has ever done has appealed so directly to the American
public. Many of the papers expressed satisfaction in having an "authoritative body like the Academy," take hold of this most important question.

We are in position to influence the schools and teachers all over the
nation, and we should not let our present prestige in the matter decline.
We are a nation of bad speakers of English, and the Academy by taking
the problem in hand has demonstrated that it has a present work to do,
something which is at once scholarly yet democratic. The French Academy concerns itself with the written word but we are engaged in a more
vital program, the betterment of spoken English.

The members cheered my oral report and voted unanimously to go on
for another year, in the same course, confining the award to the regular
announcers. After that we can make the award to "guest announcers" or
any other speaker on the microphone. I outlined my plan to interest professors of spoken English in the schools and Colleges, and the various
dramatic teachers and their pupils in the audition. I have some of best
men in the field acting with us now and more can be secured by correspondence. Both of the big broadcasting chains are co-operating on the
side of their stations. The N.B.C. has organized a school for the instruc-

tion of announcers. They are ready to put on a program of Academy addresses next year dealing with phases of this speech campaign and also in other of the five arts.

The cost of all this can be kept small but there will be some expense in way of correspondence and travel. Dr. Butler warned us not to go to much expense till we found out how the Academy would feel about the award. I am sure the directors are ready to endorse a reasonable expense for the next years campaign.

There is another still larger problem before us. The Talking film is a still bigger factor in the spread of spoken English. It is about to possess the world. I talked with Douglas Fairbanks about the effect of an award for good diction on the Talking Film and he expressed the opinion that the giving of such an award would have enormous effect. I believe he would raise the money for it if we would agree to administer it. What do you think of this? Shall we divert the present award to the screen? Or shall we found another award? Is there anything more vital for us to do than to influence the speech of the Nation?[2]

I would like to see you. Can you let me come in tomorrow or some other day this week? If you have time to spare let me know and I will come down. I have been lame but am gaining ability to walk.

Hamlin Garland

1. Huntington had provided funds sufficient to erect a second Academy building, containing an auditorium, pipe organ, and art gallery, at 632 West 156th Street. The ceremonial opening occurred 13–14 November 1930.

2. The Academy did not establish a medal for good diction in film.

320. to Harold Latham

tlc, USC

June 24. [1929]

Dear Mr. Latham:

You will soon have in your hands a clean carbon copy of the Ms. and we can then proceed with some degree of knowledge of what the book will ultimately turn out to be.[1]

First: The titles which are most satisfactory to my friend and to my wife and daughters are LITERARY TRADE*WINDS AND ROAD*SIDE MEETINGS. Wayside Meetings they all feel is too small in significance. If you talked with Mrs. Vanamee you will know that she feels a sweep in the ms which the idea of a series of meetings does not fully express. She is right but on the other hand we must not make it seem like a text book. Let me know what you think of LITERARY TRADE·WINDS.

Second: I am having qualms over the question of the portraits of my friends. Will their use make an attractive page? Or to put it more strongly will they spoil a handsome printed page? Shall we have only one for each chapter? Shall we have a box for the portrait and under it another for the name of the author? I believe this would add to the appearance of the page.

Third: If we have fewer portraits we could have more full page illustrations which would also be portraits. Constance will do whatever we decide will add to the beauty of the book.

Fourth: Some of my artist friends say: "Make it a handsome book and charge handsomely for it." They are for a five dollar book, one that will be a valued volume in the library. They suggest setting it in type and printing an edition from the type and then later a larger and more popular edition. In any case, they urge a beautiful book at a good price. I give this for what it is worth.

Fifth: The question of reproductions of letters bothers me. As I see the volume, it is too handsome to have the miscellaneous included. I am including all letters in the same type as the text. I dont like the choppy effect of a smaller type for quoted letters. If the letter is worth printing, it should be a part of the text and not a footnote or insertion.[2]

Sixth: In the copy which will come to you there will be a few discrepancies. Places where I have not had the time or the material to complete the text. There are also one or two mistakes of inclusion. As soon as I can I will indicate these so that your readers will not go wrong.

Finally, let your readers understand that this carbon copy is only a working version of the story and that there will be many changes before the book goes to press. I think we could make that galley proof version any time you can get at it. Certainly we can get at it during July before I go to California. Mrs. Vanamee has aided me enormously in having her most intelligent girls type the ms for me. It has saved us a month or more.

We hope to see you soon.

Hamlin Garland.

1. Garland was at work on *Roadside Meetings*, which would be published as the serial "Roadside Meetings of a Literary Nomad" in the *Bookman* 70–71 (October 1929–July

1930), before appearing in book form in September 1930. Garland wrote much of the manuscript at the American Academy, where many of his papers were stored, and where Grace Vanamee and her secretarial staff assisted him.

2. The book was published with sketches of Garland's acquaintances printed on the endpapers and with the text and letters in uniform type.

321. to Lorado Taft als, Hunt

2018 North Hobart Boulevard
Hollywood, California

Aug. 14 [1929]

Dear Lorado:

Here is the new family address. File it for reference. We shall be coming back by way of Chicago in Oct. probably about the 10th — We want to know a little more about Fuller's death. Did it come suddenly? — Did he leave a will? Did he name me as literary executer? Some one reported that he had done so. — His publisher wired for a portrait but I was on the way and could not help out. I have a fine portrait of Henry at about forty years of age and Connie is going to make drawing of it. I shall write an entire chapter on Fuller in the first volume of my *Roadside Meetings*—By the way how do you like that for a title? — We are perfectly comfortable here. I have a room which over looks gardens and a hill of trees. Zulime is happy to be with her girls. We're in for it! We shall be here half of each year.

Sit down and dictate a newsy bulletin. Did you see my letter in the *Times* about Henry? I was hoping Chicago papers would copy it.[1]

Faithfully
H.G.

1. Henry Blake Fuller died on 28 July 1929. Garland's chapter on Fuller appears in *Roadside*, pp. 262–75; his letter was published as "The Late Henry Fuller," *New York Times*, 1 August 1929, p. 26.

The Memoirist: 1930–1940

Introduction

GARLAND'S RELOCATION to Hollywood proved to be more wrenching than he expected: he left at the moment when his fame and influence were at their peak; he had a wide circle of friends and acquaintances; he was deeply involved—and had been for some time—in the promotion of American literary culture. He left with regrets, but he was determined to push along the trail. From Hollywood he turned even more to letter writing, and correspondence became the substitute for the "literary talk" to which he had become accustomed. More letters survive from the last ten years of his life than from any other, in part because of the sheer number he wrote, but also because he turned to the habitual use of the typewriter—and kept carbons. For other than routine correspondence, his practice was to draft the letter in longhand, and then type it—or have it typed—retaining a carbon.

His letters (as well as his diaries) show the emotional cost of his separation from New York and its literary culture. Letters to his close friends reveal his loneliness, his deepening sense of the futility of his life, and his despair over the declining heath of Zulime, who was suffering from Parkinson's disease. He also became disappointed with his daughters, both of whom obtained divorces in the mid-1930s. For Garland, who became even more conservative in his seventies, his beloved daughters' marriage troubles only confirmed his sense that he was a man out of his time. "I have given up reading fiction," he wrote to August Derleth on 16 April 1938 (letter 375). "I find it so pre-occupied with the animal side of sex life that I do not venture to open any modern novel. It would seem that virtuous women no longer interest novelists or dramatists. I am bored by the glorified prostitute and the girl libertine—bored and saddened."

Since the present was proving so distasteful to the aging writer, he began to dwell increasingly on the past—primarily his own triumphs. Aware that he was out of step with the contemporary literary scene, he devoted his remaining years to constructing a place in history for himself in four volumes of literary reminiscences. His letters portray Garland alternately despairing and encouraged as the volumes appeared; as his own health waned, and as he wrestled with the care of an invalid wife and what he regarded as "wild" daughters, he felt the need to ensure that his legacy would not be forgotten. Accordingly, in 1936 he mounted a traveling exhibit of his literary mementos, which consisted of his books, excerpts from his manuscripts, letters received from famous writers, and photographs. As the exhibit toured state and university libraries in California, Ohio, Illinois, Indiana, Iowa, and Wisconsin, Garland was gratified by the interest his "literary treasures" received, and especially so when a filmmaker, Guy D. Haselton, arranged to make a fifteen-minute biographical study of him.[1] Garland soon arranged for copies of the film to accompany his traveling exhibit.

The publication of his logbooks and the touring exhibit had their effect: increasingly, Garland was bemused and pleased to find that he was suddenly the subject of critical studies. Graduate students embarked on theses concerning his life, works, and people he had known; letters addressed to what he fondly termed his "young advocates" show his awareness that he was quickly becoming a "literary treasure," of value for his memories of the great and near-great he had known. But even this belated attention was not enough to dispel his growing sense of futility, of having been bypassed by time. To Floyd Logan, one of his "young advocates," he wrote on 5 February 1934 (letter 343): "[Your praise] reminds me of the first time Howells spoke to me of his waning fame. 'I have outlived my vogue' he said and it was a sad moment for me. He had a vogue, I have never enjoyed a boom much less a vogue, but I am in the midst of finding out that I am an old fellow of seventy four and that people are no longer interested in what I say or do or write."

But in 1936 Garland embarked on a project that was to fill his time for his remaining years. In 1932 Garland had received a letter from Gregory Parent which stated, "I wish to bring to your attention some very strange happenings in the life of my wife. She has discovered many hidden objects and she has taken many spirit photographs which I would like you to see."[2] Garland met with Parent and surveyed his collection of "ectoplasmic" photographs of spirits, taken years before, as well as a collection of archaic crosses which the Parents had found with the guidance of spirits. Although intrigued with Parent's tantalizing account of his wife's psychic communications, Garland's involvement with his memoirs caused him to forego further investigation.

When Garland returned to "the problem of the crosses," as he was fond of calling it, he discovered that Parent had since died. When he succeeded in locating Parent's papers and collection of objects, Garland embarked on one of the oddest events of his long and varied career: an attempt to verify the legitimacy of the Parent collection of crosses, an investigation that was to culminate in his last, and certainly strangest, book — *The Mystery of the Buried Crosses* (1939) — and was to become an obsession that consumed his final years. With the aid of the psychic Sophia Williams, Garland conducted séance after séance, guided by the spirit of his good friend the novelist Henry B. Fuller (who had died in 1929). Garland conversed with the spirits of his former literary acquaintances and devised a series of experiments to test his medium's validity, as well as recording and photographing the visitations in an attempt to gather scientific evidence of man's continued survival. As part of his investigation, Garland discovered buried objects at the direction of his spirits and tried to authenticate them through consultation with scientists and museums. These crosses, Garland believed, were pre-Christian ceremonial objects fabricated by Indians from Central America and southern California, who buried them to conceal them from Spanish missionaries, who viewed the objects as remnants of pagan religious rites.

His letters from 1936 onward reveal the obsessive nature of his quest as the problem — as well as his own declining health and growing sense of the futility of his career — began to dominate his thoughts. Obviously, Garland was drawn to this psychic investigation both as a means of validation of his career and for reassurance as he became increasingly aware of his own mortality. As he remarked in a letter to the *Saturday Review of Literature*, in response to a generally favorable review of his book, "If [the crosses] can be validated, they will not only indicate a very ancient migration of people from the south, but they will bear directly on the problem of continuing personality after death."[3]

The Mystery of the Buried Crosses was better received than one might suppose, although Garland had great difficulty finding a publisher willing to risk the venture. He mounted five touring exhibits of his discoveries, consisting primarily of the objects he had discovered, with mounted placards describing the evidence he had gathered and the "Mechanical Evidences of Human Survival," to over twenty-four libraries and museums across the country. He made a radio broadcast on his seventy-ninth birthday concerning the book, a dramatization with an interview, as part of cbs's "Strange As It Seems" series, and he contracted with the North American Film Corp. to do an educational film about his investigation.[4]

Throughout his work on this book he maintained a steady flow of letters. To Van Wyck Brooks, with whom he formed a close friendship and who was busily engaged in composing a series of literary histories, he wrote his memories of American writers and lent his collection of Howells letters. He patiently answered questions from students and professors; and he began to wrestle with the problem of the eventual disposition of his papers, at one point throwing up his hands in despair and writing to a horrified Brooks, "I have come to the conclusion that all my records except letters to me should be burned while I am alive to superintend it" (31 August 1939, letter 394).

NOTES

1. Copies of the 625-foot, silent, black and white film are extant in the Garland Papers at the Doheny, Huntington, and Miami University libraries, as well as the archives of the American Academy of Arts and Letters.

2. Quoted in Garland, *The Mystery of the Buried Crosses* (New York: Dutton, 1939), p. 15.

3. Garland, "Mystery of the Buried Crosses," *Saturday Review of Literature* 20 (29 July 1939): 9.

4. See Garland to Harold Latham, 7 September 1939 (Hunt); a clipping concerning the radio program (item #723, USC); and Garland to Alexander Gaylord Beaman, 10 May 1939 (USC).

322. to Barrett H. Clark   ald, USC

2166 East Live Oak Drive
Hollywood, California

Feb. 22 [1930]

Dear Barrett Clark:

You have written a thoughtful, candid and fair exposition of O'Neill.[1] I dont agree with some of your judgements but then I'm just an old fogy who believes that civilization is built on "inhibitions." All this talk of "sex repression" is poppy cock. Of course we have learned control—some of us—thats what life and social obligations mean. I have no patience with Freudianism or talk about the awful effect of "puritanism."

I dont like O'Neills violent and turgid plays. And I am willing to be quoted as saying that ten years from now he will be—or these plays will be, in the discord. He may pull out of the fog and muck of his present method—he is young enough to do so. I value your book because it does not praise the wrong side of this powerful, crude and struggling genius. The worst side of O'Neills plays is their *news value*. I doubt the lasting quality of a play which is startling as news.—But then I belong to a school which believes in certain laws of construction and simple writing. There is force, passages of creative characterization but no beauty as I see and feel beauty. There is something yellow and false running through everything I have seen or read of his.

1. Barrett H. Clark (1890–1953), actor, director, and critic, was Eugene O'Neill's first biographer. Clark had sent a copy of his *Eugene O'Neill: The Man and His Plays* (1929), which was a much-revised version of the original monograph, *Eugene O'Neill* (1926), with the inscription: "To Hamlin Garland with the hope that he will agree with *some* of my enthusiasm. Cordially, Barrett H. Clark. New York, February 13, 1930" (USC).

323. to George Ulizio   tls, Ohio St

2166 East Live Oak Drive
Hollywood, California

March. 10. [1930]

Dear Mr. Ulizio:

Your second wire has just come but as I am sure you had not received my air-mail letter I shall wait til tomorrow before sending a reply. I have on my desk the copy of the paper bound MAGGIE in which Crane had written "To my friend Franklin Garland," but with no signature.[1] It is in Cranes fine hand-writing on the title page. My own copy has in addition several lines written obliquely across the cover all in Crane's unmistakable script but without signature. If you will tell me just how you would like to have me put in the page of my own script I will do it before I send it on. The cover is in fair shape but a bit soiled and broken at the edges. Every page is present and clean. The outside shows a bit of wear. My own copy in New York is cleaner, and by reason of the superscription more valuable. I hesitate about letting this copy go altho it was not directly inscribed to me. I have in addition a copy of THE BLACK RIDERS which he dedicated to me and a holograph letter asking if I minded it. I'll include that if you think the added cost worth while. I will include a brief letter to my brother, or mentioning my brother, if I can find it.—We can arrive at terms now and when we get together in New York, I will show you all I have. There is not much point in my bringing these things out here and your plan about giving them to Princeton seems appropriate. I will not sell all I have but I will let such things go as you need to make your collection more complete. As I wrote you I have a good many other fine pieces. For example I have "The Ole Swimmin Hole" by Riley in the little parchment book he brought out himself. It is not autographed to me and I would sell it if assured of its full value.

If you wish the MAGGIE inscribed and sent at once let me know.

Hamlin Garland

1. B. George Ulizio (1889–1969) was the president of the New Jersey Investment Realty Corp. and a book collector who had purchased several of Garland's autographed books with the understanding they that would eventually be given to the Princeton University library. His second telegram (10 March 1930) informed Garland that he was mailing a check for five hundred dollars for Franklin Garland's inscribed copy of *Mag-*

gie and wanted to purchase Garland's copy as well. In a series of letters from 11 to 21 March, Ulizio confirmed that he wanted to purchase Garland's inscribed copy for four hundred dollars, with an additional one hundred dollars in payment for "writing a statement of the conditions under which Crane gave the book" (11 March 1930). This statement is inserted in Franklin's copy, held by the New York Public Library, and is reprinted in Wertheim, p. 67 n.1.

324. to Julian Hawthorne   als, Bancroft

2166 East Live Oak Drive
Hollywood, California

Mar. 31. [1930]

Dear Julian Hawthorne:[1]

I have just learned your correct address from Mr. Clemens.[2] Did I reach you at 26th St? I find that address in my notebook. I have written to several of the universities suggesting that they engage you for a talk on your father. I hope something will come from these letters but one never can tell. If by any chance you get down here, let me know and we'll have you to dinner. I want my wife and daughters to know you—and I want to talk with you. I doubt if I get north again till autumn but when I do I shall certainly look you up. —Can I be of any service in arranging for the publication of your reminiscences? —You should publish every line you have written about the Concord men. I am merely tie-ing on to your period. The Concord group was entirely gone when I went East in 1882—Holmes and Whittier were still living but very old. Let me know if I can aid in finding the right publisher. I am returning to New York in late April.—

With sincerest well-wishes to you both—
Hamlin Garland

1. The son of Nathaniel Hawthorne, Julian Hawthorne (1846–1934), published novels and memoirs of his family, including *Nathaniel Hawthorne and His Wife* (1884), *Hawthorne and His Circle* (1903), *Shapes that Pass: Memories of Old Days* (1928), and *The Memoirs of Julian Hawthorne* (1938).

2. Cyril Clemens (1902–?), a distant cousin to Samuel Clemens, became president of the Mark Twain Society (1927) in Kirkwood, Missouri, soon transforming this informal body into the International Mark Twain Society. He also founded the *Mark Twain Quarterly* (1936), which later became the *Mark Twain Journal.*

325. to William Lyon Phelps

tlc, usc

2166 East Live Oak Drive

Hollywood, California

Mar. 31 [1930]

Dear Phelps:

Julian Hawthorne old and poor is living in San Francisco, 1223 Eighth Street, and when I was in the city last fall I lunched with him. He is a fine, dignified gentleman. I had not seen him for thirty five years and could hardly recognize anything familiar about him. I always liked him and I found him delightful in his old age and poverty. He is married to an elderly artist, an intelligent woman who is very helpful to him.

Now this is my suggestion; Let us nominate him for election to the Institute? It would be a fine gesture. After all he is the distinguished son of a very great man, and I have never believed that he meant to defraud. Like Elwyn Barron he fell into bad company.[1] If we could offer him some such recognition now when he is nearing the end it would, I believe, afford him deep satisfaction. He is writing all that he can recall of the Concord Group and his work will have great value. I am offering to aid in getting this work published by the right publisher. I think a letter asking permission to put him in nomination would please him, even if he could not accept. I'll write such a letter if you think there is a possibility of his being elected.[2]

I am returning to New York in early May. Lets meet. Zulime has been in Egypt with Lorado, returns this week.

Faithfully,

1. In March 1913 Hawthorne was convicted of mail fraud in connection with some fraudulent Canadian mining investments. Upon his release from prison in October, he wrote *The Subterranean Brotherhood* (1914), an account of prison life in which he argued for the abolition of prison confinement. In April 1914 Elwyn Barron, an officer of the Sterling Debenture Corp., was convicted of mail fraud and sentenced to three years in prison.

2. Phelps replied, 3 April 1930, that because Hawthorne had served a prison term for mail fraud, his election would be difficult: "I agree with you that he is a gentleman and certainly not a bad man, but would it not drag the whole thing into publicity if we made such a nomination?" Garland also sounded out other National Institute members, among them William Allen White, Stewart Edward White, and Cyril Clemens. Hawthorne was not elected to the Institute.

326. to Mary Isabel Garland Johnson   tl, Hunt

May. 24 [1930]

Dear Daughtie:

I am enclosing some lines from Mr. Latham which seem to me most encouraging. To have him say that "the story is beautifully written, better than most mystery stories," is a real triumph for a first book.[1] No doubt he is right about the length and so on. Think them over carefully and see if you cant better the story. It is true that it more or less conforms to type. You can make it more original by taking care and swinging out into your own field. What I hope for is a verdict that with certain changes it will be possible for Macmillans. If they do not want it we shall try Duttons who specialize in mystery stories, or I'll try young Farrar. Also I shall try Brandt and Brandt as agents, and see if serialization can not be arranged for.

I get pretty lonesome for my family at times. I hope you wont miss us all too much this summer. You'll have two dogs to keep you busy! I am anxiously waiting to know Joe's decision. On Tuesday I shall go up to Yama Farms for a short stay. I can take my big bundle of proof and work on it up there. Mr. Latham says that all the young men about the office are interested in my book—which is encouraging. The publication day is to be Sept. 16, my seventieth birthday.[2]

I am having a rather exciting time with a firm of bookdealers who are interested in seeing all my Crane, Whitman, and other autograph material. They are to make me some sort of offer today. They want to go up to the Academy with me and go over the mass of stuff which is doing no one any good and which I am disposed to sell. If I do sell I'll put the proceeds into the house. Yesterday was a very disheartening day. It was 88 in the shade and the streets full of hot gas from the cars, and the air so filled with soot that I wore my glasses to shield my eyes. It took me an hour to go down on the bus and I thought of our clean sweet hillside with longing. I shall go up to Onteora next week and get it ready for Joe and Connie—in case they come. I am hoping for news of you all this morning.

Daddy.

1. Mary Isabel shared her father's writing aspirations and drafted a number of mystery novels and short stories. Her first published novel was the mystery *Abandon Hope* (Mystery House, 1941), followed by four others in collaboration with her second husband, Mindret Lord, under the name "Garland Lord." Garland enclosed one leaf from Latham's letter, which read in part: "I have finished Mrs. Johnson's novel. To be per-

fectly frank, I am a bit disappointed in it. It does not seem to me quite to fulfill the promise which the early chapters held out. It is a bit long, and some of it a bit obvious, and these facts seem to make the action drag. It is excellently written, the style being far superior to most mystery fiction."

2. Garland refers to *Roadside Meetings*. For some years Garland was not sure whether he was born on 14 or 16 September. The subsequent discovery of a family Bible with the date 14 September in his mother's hand settled the matter. See Garland to George Seymour, 26 February 1940, letter 404.

327. to George Ulizio

tls, Ohio St

Hamlin Garland
507 Cathedral Parkway
New York City

Sunday. 25 [25 May 1930]

Dear Mr. Ulizio:

Since coming to New York City I have been seeing a few experts in rare books in the effort to know what the market is. That sale of MAGGIE for twenty one hundred dollars was an astonishment to me as I imagine it was to you. It establishes a new price for this very rare book. I am told also that the OLE SWIMMIN HOLE is worth one hundred and fifty dollars. All these matters I should have secured advice upon before but I did not. It was a line of trade I had never entered upon. I am having my whole collection looked into for I have hundreds of autograph letters in the vaults of [the] American Academy and many first editions autographed to me. Some of these are duplicates and I would sell them. Some advise me to auction my collection but others say, show them to individuals who might want to bid for the lot.

If by chance you are in the city, I should be glad to talk the situation over.

Very Sincerely Yours,
Hamlin Garland

1. Garland was incensed by what he considered Ulizio's sharp trading practice. In an undated letter to Zulime, Garland wrote, "That man Ulizio is a crook. He took advantage of my ignorance of the [Crane] boom and 'chouselled' me." And on 5 July 1930 (Ohio St), he wrote to Ulizio to request that he "add to my brothers payment" to reflect the market price. Ulizio wrote several letters in 1932 asking for other books but Garland ignored his letters.

328. to Josiah Kirby Lilly

tls, Indiana U

Hamlin Garland
507 Cathedral Parkway
New York City

May. 28 [1930]

Dear Mr. Lilly:[1]

Mr. Chambers of Bobbs Merrill[2] suggests that you might be interested in a copy of Riley['s] first book, the little parchment covered volume which he brought out himself in 1883, the one he used to wrap and mail himself. I have owned it since 1886 when it was given to me by Chas. E. Hurd of the Boston Transcript. I am told that it is now very valuable. It is listed in some places at four hundred dollars, and one dealer told me it had sold sometime ago for six hundred dollars. I am not a collector and will sell this and other Riley items several of which were presented to me by Riley with an inscription. I am breaking up my library here and turning it over to my daughters in California. I have many items gathered in the natural course of my life and work as a writer.

Very Sincerely Yours,
Hamlin Garland

1. Josiah Kirby Lilly (1893–1966), a grandson of Eli Lilly, the founder of the Indiana pharmaceutical company Eli Lilly & Co. A noted collector, in 1956 Lilly donated some twenty thousand volumes to Indiana University, where the Lilly Rare Book Library was built to house the collection. The Lilly contains a substantial Riley collection.

2. David Laurence Chambers (1879–?), president of Bobbs-Merrill Co.

329. to Mary Isabel Garland Johnson

tls, Hunt

Grey Ledge Cottage
Onteora Park
Tannersville, New York

July. 3 [1930]

Dear Daughtie:

We have not had a line from you for over a week. We want to know whether the furniture has arrived and how it looks if it has arrived and how Hardesty's work goes on and what you are doing. We hear of J.W. more frequently. Yesterday, I went all over your taxi story again and made many slight changes which I should like you to study. You neednt adopt

The Memoirist: 1930–1940 355

them all but I would like to have you *affected* by them all. They will keep
your mss from betraying youth and inexperience. Rewrite the whole M.S.
incorporating any of my suggestions you like—but keeping your own
view. The ms is interesting and is—as I wrote you—"a good start" but it
is only a sketch after all. You must buckle right down to it in deadly earnest. Dig a little deeper into the psychology of the plot. Why did the third
man make no outcry as he got into the cab? Was he a part of the plot or
did he happen along? If he was in the plot how did he aid it? Why was he
on the road a mile or more from the house?

You should define Lane's character a little more fully. If he is to be the
center of the story, he must be deeply studied. His talk should be racy,
more like Will Rogers. Ward is too much the boy. Bring him up a bit. The
girls are both good. Bear down a little harder on the annoyance and possible harm to Patty's being implicated in the murder. Keep the talk between the men strictly to the mystery. Dont try to have the story entirely
local. Reach out to New York. Get at the back-ground of Hobart either
Chicago or New York.

If you are going to write you must set aside a certain part of your day
for CONCENTRATION. There is skill in this work, and it is interesting up to
a certain point then it fails of the higher or deeper interest. It shows haste
and a lack of CONCENTRATED THOUGHT. You can do it but you cant do it
and be running a car, tending a baby, answering the telephone and the
like. Set aside your morning and WORK!—

Daddy

I am remailing the M.S. Hope you'll not resent my changes!—I think you
should work on "The Stain" now and take up the taxi year later. That is
why I have held back on this.

330. to Mary Isabel Garland Johnson   als, Hunt

Grey Ledge Cottage
Onteora Park
Tannersville, New York

Sept. 3. [1930]

Dear Mebbsie:

I guess here is the place to say that I will finance you through the production of a little Mary Isabel—or Hardesty Garland as the case may be.

I suppose such a composition is more important than a novel. Dont let a few dollars stand in the way of such an achievement.

Mother is gaining but she needs the help of her daughters and John Wesley *and* her sons-in-law—not forgetting Blinkie.[1] I am not much good for her case. I'm too old and inert my self. If Dr. Sherman will order it I'll bring her out *before* Dr. Turck[2] arrives.—Mrs Sarris mother is at the point of death and so I have suggested calling off the dinner.—We are going into town today and I shall see Mr. Latham—Friday morning.

Your old *Daddy.*

1. Zulime's illness was diagnosed as Parkinson's disease. Garland also refers to John Wesley Harper, Constance's son, and the family dog, a Maltese poodle.

2. Fenton B. Turck (1857–1932), biologist and physician, won acclaim for his research in cell biology. Garland, who had been suffering increasingly from arthritis, found Turck's treatment to be miraculous and championed Turck frequently among his friends.

331. to William Lyon Phelps

als, Yale

Nov. 3. [1930]

Dear William:

Your enthusiastic word heartens me.[1] My book, as you see, is a quiet book. I had no malice to discharge and no enemies to scourge—hence "Roadside Meetings" has no "news value." If it lives it will be by reason of its method and the historical value of its content. It is going into college libraries, I'm happy to learn, and may be read by an occasional youngster who is curious about the men and women who wrote during his grandfather's day.—If you ever have a moment to spare when in town lunch with me at the Century Club—or at the Town Hall and we'll have Zulime there. We leave for Calif. immediately after the Institute meeting.

Gratefully yours,
Hamlin Garland

1. Phelps had written, 2 November 1930, that *Roadside* "is continuously, unflaggingly interesting!" and promised to review it in *Scribner's,* where he did so in his "As I Like It" column, *Scribner's* 89 (January 1931): 90–98.

332. to Nicholas Vachel Lindsay

tls, USC

The Century Association
7 West Forty-Third Street
New York

May. 18 [1931]

Dear Nicholas Lindsay:

In my second volume of Roadside Meetings, I touch upon our first contact in Chicago, making much of your fine evangel to the artists of the Middle West. I wonder if you kept my letters to you at that critical time?[1] If so I should like to have the one in which I sympathized with your opposition to the centralization of art and literature in the city to the neglect of the small town. We neither of us had much effect on the movement but there was logic on our side. I surrendered, ultimately, but you have been more or less consistent. New York knows you but you have never been a resident there—as I understand it. If by any chance you are here this spring let me see you.

Very Sincerely Yours,
Hamlin Garland

My winter home is Hollywood with my daughters.

1. See Garland to Lindsay, 7 March 1911, letter 174.

333. to Julian Hawthorne

als, Bancroft

7. W. 43rd St
New York City

June 10 [1931]

Dear Julian Hawthorne:

I am grateful to Mr. Carew for an opportunity to "sit in" at the dinner in celebration of your eighty fifth birth-day, for this letter will carry my ectoplasmic hand-clasp and etheric spoken word.[1] I deeply regret that I can not be present in a more substantial old-fashioned way.

As I think of your span of life I am stirred by the events it covers. Reaching from your illustrious father in his Concord home to Pasadena with its new school of physics and astronomy, it covers more of change, of scientific discovery than any other age in history. Some call this change advance and I am willing to grant that claim but I am not so sure that we who write have gone very far beyond that group of men in Concord who from their cottages under the elms sent out great books to a smaller world. Of all men living you are best fitted to speak of them and for them. The long list of your own books is evidence of a brave and busy life, and among them none are more lasting than those which record your own experiences in Concord and your association with the men of that group—and especially with your noble father who has been my literary hero for nearly sixty years. I have known you for nearly forty years and I am looking forward to seeing you in November when I return to California. I hope you are still recording your recollections, for at your age and mine there is nothing more valuable for us to do. You can tie the generations together more completely than any man I know and my sincerest wish is that your marvelous vitality may still urge you on to this work.

Accept my congratulations on your magnificent resistance to the elemental forces and my wishes for another and still more successful book.

Hamlin Garland

1. Harold D. Carew, literary editor of the *Pasadena Star-News*, arranged a dinner to celebrate Hawthorne's eighty-fifth birthday on 22 June 1931 and requested this letter, which was read at the celebration.

334. to Julian Hawthorne

als, Bancroft

Hamlin Garland
Grey Ledge
Onteora Park, N.Y.

Aug. 20 [1931]

Dear Hawthorne:

I am delighted to hear that you are busy on another autobiographic M.S. for there are literary jewels in your mine which no one else can dig out. I sometimes marvel at the good health which permits you to span the years between your illustrious father and the student of today, bringing to him a vivid concept of Concord and its amazing group of writers. Every scrap of information you can give us of Nathaniel Hawthorne and his neighbors is most valuable. Dont fail to put it *all* down. Anything which lingers in your mind should be put to paper. I wish I could be of service in getting this work done, and perhaps I can help by an expression of my eager interest. If I can aid in getting the right publisher or by writing of the book after it is published I hope you will call upon me.—My own literary log is going on into the third volume. The second volume "Companions on the Trail" is in press.—I hope we shall meet when I come north to San Francisco late in November.

My best word to you both
Hamlin Garland

335. to Nicholas Vachel Lindsay   als, usc

The Century Association
7 West Forty-Third Street
New York

Oct. 26. [1931]

Dear Nicholas Lindsay:

My wife and I rejoiced over your fine frank letter. I was a little apprehensive about your reception of my critical judgements of your "Congo" —but your letter makes it evident that you hold nothing against me.[1] I wouldn't give your poem on Poe for all your "Chants."[2] I regarded you as a miracle in those early days and put that feeling into the pages dealing with you—in later paragraphs I shall touch upon your platform work which I regarded as a kind of pot-boiling device—like my own. Most of us are obliged to do something of this sort of public performance. I am to do a few "talks" on my way to California Nov. 16—If you get to Calif. again this winter, call me up on the phone I am to be with my daughter—

Mrs. Hardesty Johnson.
2045 De Mille Dr.
Hollywood.

(In telephone book)

I am firmly of the belief that if you now write in the spirit of your letter you will win back the discriminating readers who delighted in your exquisitely lyrical poems—the ones which *were* miracles!—

Accept my very best wishes for your future work—

Your ancient monitor
Hamlin Garland

1. Garland refers to a chapter entitled "The Village Magazine" in *Companions*, pp. 462–71, where he concludes a generally laudatory discussion by noting: "He has disappointed my expectations. Influenced by the free-verse advocates and possibly from necessity, he has gone off into bizarre posturings and experimentation" (p. 470).

2. Lindsay's "The Wizard in the Street," which Garland touts as having "in it something of the quality which Stephen Crane had possessed" (*Companions*, p. 467).

336. to Mary Isabel Garland Johnson and Constance Garland Harper als, Hunt

The Century Association
7 West Forty-Third Street
New York

Tuesday 27 [27 October 1931]

Dear Daughties:

Today is the day of the Roosevelt Memorial Medal and I shall soon dress to go down to receive it.[1] I am to make a short speech but it's not to be radioed so you will only get a line or two of it. On the twelfth I am to present the Medal to a radio announcer and that you can hear probably between nine and ten—out there—altho your stations may not [care] enough about the work to give it place.[2] We got our tickets today and Mother may go to Chicago on Monday to visit Lorado while I lecture along the way. I'd like to go right now but I must earn some money to pay for windows and things. On Sunday I am guest at a Pen and Brush reception and at night Aunt Juliet has a dinner.[3] I think Mother may start on the 2nd but she may linger on till the 5th. Anyhow we are getting into action. It wont be long now till we will be with you!—We dare not think too much about the babies and our daughters, it makes us uneasy—and sad. It will be a joy to get back to our olive trees and our home circle. People are all the time thinking up reasons for keeping us here, but we refuse to be tied.

—*Later*—Wed. Morning. The Medal was presented last night and it is a very beautiful thing. We shall have it on the parlor table—under glass! —and padlocked!!—I made only a short address. It was well received. Many asked about my daughters. Mother did not go. She is feeling very well these days but avoids crowds—

Daddy.

1. Garland received a gold Medal of Honor from the Roosevelt Memorial Association for "distinguished service in the field of American historical literature." See "Roosevelt Medals Awarded to Three," *New York Times*, 24 June 1931, p. 7.

2. Garland presented the American Academy's Medal for Good Diction over the Radio to John Holbrook on 12 November.

3. Garland refers to the novelist Juliet Wilbur Tompkins (1871–1956), who was a close friend of the Garland family but not a relative.

337. to Harold Latham

tlc, usc

April 11 [1932]

Dear Mr. Latham:

If any radical change of form is to be made in the ms of MY FRIENDLY CONTEMPORARIES, the book will have to go over to another season.[1] It is essentially a diary form and cant be done in any other way without entirely rewriting it. As it is I cant turn it in before the Fifteenth of July. The nearer I come down to the present the more delicate the job becomes.

Furthermore it is the diary note which gives it authenticity and value. Its individual character arises from the fact that the characters come and go like characters in a novel. In this connection what would you say to printing a page or two saying; "The following persons appear in the narrative from time to time." I am [en]closing a partial list. This page should precede the text just as a dramatist announces his characters. Think of this and get your editors to think of it.

With regard to judgments; I am nearly seventy two years of age and have been a writer for nearly forty seven years, and this book is supposed to give my candid reactions to books and authors. It would be weak and sugary if it no where expressed an adverse opinion, or an individual judgment. I have no intention of expressing dislike but my judgments of books and men should have a certain value to my readers. Think of this also.

You read and approved the first half of the ms, and on this line I have proceeded. Date heads can be camouflaged a bit but it must remain a narrative diary. I cant rewrite it without immense labor.

1. Latham had written, 4 April 1932, that he believed the diary format would "scare off readers," and he urged Garland to eliminate "the dates as paragraph headings."

Moreover, he thought Garland's comments about "men and affairs" were more overtly critical than the earlier logbooks had been, and in particular he cited Garland's judgment of Nicholas Murray Butler and William M. Sloane, as candidates for the presidency of the American Academy in October 1920, as needlessly belittling. See *Contemporaries*, p. 315, for the disputed passage as it was published.

338. to M. A. DeWolfe Howe   tls, Harvard

2045 DeMille Drive
Hollywood, California

May. 19. [1932]

Dear Howe:[1]

That item about Miss Dickinson was taken from my diary just as I set it down.[2] I have a dim notion that the poet I met was a friend of Richard Burton and that I took her to be a niece of Emily Dickinson. One or two others have written me about it. Burton said nothing about it when he reviewed the book so I think there must have been a poet of that name at that time.

I am grateful for the lines you write concerning my Vol. II. They encourage me to hope for a kindly reception for Vol. III.

I am coming East in late June.

Faithfully Yours,
Hamlin Garland

1. Mark Antony DeWolfe Howe (1864–1960), editor, poet, and New England scholar, whose books include *Boston, the Place and People* (1903), *The Atlantic Monthly and Its Makers* (1917), and *Barrett Wendell and His Letters* (1924; Pulitzer Prize).

2. In *Companions* Garland had written, "To-day at Stedman's I met Emily Dickinson, a tall, slender, graceful creature in a very smart gown. She turned out to be a long-time acquaintance of Richard Burton, and on the basis of this mutual friendship we reached an almost instant understanding" (p. 121). Howe had written, 10 May 1932, to query whether Garland's memory was faulty, since Emily Dickinson had died in 1886. Garland's recollection in *Companions* was indeed faulty; he had met Dickinson's niece, Martha Gilbert Dickinson (1866–1943), a poet and novelist. See Dorys C. Grover, "Garland's 'Emily Dickinson'—A Case of Mistaken Identity," *American Literature* 46 (1974): 219–20; and George Monteiro and Barton L. St. Armand, "Garland's 'Emily' Dickinson—Identified," *American Literature* 47 (1976): 632–33.

[ca. September 1932]

Dear Will Rogers: [1]

After seeing you play the part of "Pike Peters"—I said to my wife, "that play is not worthy of Rogers. He should have a part that is at once big and humorous—a typical South-Western man—like Davy Crockett—for example—or a powerful individual and humorous old Cattle King in an epic story of the Southwest."

The more I think about it the more I dislike to see you going into a farcical play or even into a nice little character play. I think "The Yankee at the Court of King Arthur" is worth your while but that chicken man fills me with doubt. I'd like to see you swing out into something larger. You have won a tremendously important place by your wise and humorous comment and you are in a position to demand a proper medium of expression. You should have a play by the best American writer not a flimsy story by an unknown man. Your own story is so characteristically American that it can be made the basis of an epic story of the South-West. In fact I think you should have a large hand in building your next character part—especially in writing the dialogue.

There is another suggestion I would like to make: you should write your own life-story soon. Dont wait too long in this matter. You have an immensely interesting life story and you must write it yourself in your own fashion. So far as I know you have only one book—and in order to build a permanent place for yourself in American humor you must write not one book but several. [2]

Mark Twain was a marvelous orator and conversationalist but he also wrote letters and stories of ever-lasting value. I mention Mark for the reason that critics often speak of you in relation to him.

I have followed your amazing career for many years and now that I have met you and Mrs Rogers I feel a personal interest in your future work. [3] I hope you will think of me as an old neighbor from Iowa and meet me at the line fence now and again. If I can be of any service in the matter of a publisher just say the word. I know the most of them personally.

Mrs. Garland and I are coming back about Christmas time and we hope to see you and Mrs. Rogers in our home.—

Very sincerely yours
Hamlin Garland

1. Will Rogers (1879–1935), the popular humorist and actor, was a star of the Ziegfeld Follies from 1916 through 1925, where he dazzled audiences with rope tricks and home-spun humor. Rogers gained acclaim through his syndicated columns in some 350 newspapers, where he combined folk humor and political comment. His many films include *A Connecticut Yankee* (1931), *Down to Earth* (1932), where he played the role of Pike Peters, and *State Fair* (1933).

2. Rogers was the author of seven books, beginning with *The Cowboy Philosopher on the Peace Conference* (1919). His *Autobiography*, ed. by Donald Day, was posthumously published in 1949.

3. Garland describes his initial meeting with Rogers in *Afternoon*, pp. 552–57, where he recounts his own comic reply to Rogers's humorous toast to him at his seventy-third birthday celebration.

340. to Edward Foster   tld, usc

2045 DeMille Drive
Hollywood, California

Oct. 1. [1932]

Dear Prof. Foster:

Your letter has found me at my winter home in California and I hasten to reply.[1]

I have a good many notes from Miss Wilkins but they are short and personal and without special literary significance. I have put into ROAD-SIDE MEETINGS I think all that I can contribute to the biography you are writing.

I am delighted to know that such a book is being written for I hold Miss Wilkins to be one of the most original and skilfull short story writers of her time. Her early stories deal with what I consider characteristic New World material. They are not concerned with murder, suicide, seduction, adultery or any other of the stock themes of fiction. To write fifty or sixty stories of the elderly men and women of New England with sympathy and insight is to make a very real contribution to American literature as well as to our social history.

No doubt I was an influence on Miss Wilkins thought for we frequently discussed the subjects with which I dealt in "Crumbling Idols" and I several times wrote to her in praise of her work.

Just before her death the American Academy voted her the Howells Medal for Fiction, and designated me as the one to present the Medal. I took occasion to say once again in the few minutes allotted me how important her work seemed to me to be.

If I could talk with you it might be that I could add some interesting details but I can not take time to write them. I am to be in Syracuse university for four or five days next April. Perhaps Rochester would like to arrange a similar visit. Let me know when the book is to appear. Success to it.

1. Edward Foster (1902–?), a doctoral candidate at the University of Rochester, had written, 21 September 1932, that he was engaged in writing a study of Mary Wilkins Freeman and wanted to know when Garland had met with her. He asked for a copy of the letter from Freeman that Garland quotes in *Roadside* (p. 34); whether Wilkins was indebted to *Crumbling Idols* for her view of realism as expressed in her 1913 article, "The Girl Who Wants to Write" (*Harper's Bazaar* 47 [June 1913]); and whether Garland had contributed to "her development in realism." Foster's *Mary E. Wilkins Freeman: A Biographical and Critical Study* was published in 1956.

341. to Mary Isabel Garland Johnson   tl, Hunt

2045 DeMille Drive
Hollywood, California

Wednesday. [26 April 1933]

Dear Daughtie:

I have read "First Novel" and find it by all odds the best work you have done. I find a real achievement in it. You have got quite outside your customary self in it. It is not amateur in any way. I can see, however, why Macmillans debated it and finally decided against it. First of all it is very evidently suggested by what Mrs. Carroll[1] told us of her experience, and has been enhanced and made more colorful—which is legitimate enough but when you go further and satire the publicity stunts of the firm, I am inclined to say with Hamlet "All this is true but I hold it not policy to have it thus set down." It is the kind of thing Farrar [or] some other firms would do but it is not the kind of thing Latham would authorize. I didnt like your heroines philandering with those men while her fine serious husband was doing his duty in Kansas—and this I think is the main objection to your novel. Your heroine is too casual about that marriage. Was she just that kind of woman after all? I dont say she was not. I am asking. Your Hollywood episode which is the experience not only of Mrs. Carroll and Homer Croy[2] but of a dozen others, is admirably done. You might have gone a little further in this matter.

My final criticism is that the heroine too easily makes another success in a new field. It doesnt come as easy as that. Macmillan probably said, "This is too arranged." Sympathy for Phil as a final restorative emotion is natural but some of the details which accompany it do not ring quite true.—Summing it all up, I have the feeling that you can make a successful manuscript of this. It should find a place in a woman's magazine. I shall talk of it to Latham when he arrives. You could easily change the description of the firms personnel which now is too near the Macmillan set-up. Mr. Brett is by no means "senile" and young Mr. Brett is no longer "the college boy." Your "heavy set man" with the hard glance, is in Latham's chair but isnt a bit like him. You'd better make your firm a trifle more imaginative. The bit about the Friends of Literature Dinner is delicious but it wont endear you to the ladies who pay their dollars to hear those speeches—I made two or three of them myself.—Daughtie it is a good piece of work, speaking generally, and needs only a little care and taste in the revision. The case of the professor should have a more sympathetic treatment.

Mother is reading it now and may have some comment to make. I am really amazed at your progress. You have moved out of the amateur class. Your weak point as Mr Latham said is a looseness of plot.

Your critical but admiring

DADDY.

Write or wire Uncle Lorado. He is seventy five on Saturday.[3] 6016 Ingleside Ave.

1. Gladys Hasty Carroll published *As the Earth Turns* (Macmillan, 1933), a regional novel of Maine.

2. Homer Croy was a novelist and screenwriter whose *They Had to See Paris* (1920) was a popular novel and film.

3. Garland apparently errs in his recollection of Taft's age. Born on 29 April 1860, Taft celebrated his seventy-third birthday in 1933, when the 29th fell on a Saturday.

342. to Rudyard Kipling

2045 DeMille Drive
Hollywood, California

Sept. 16. [1933]

Dear Kipling:

Mr. Beaman[,] toastmaster at the dinner to me, on my birth-day, read your letter to the guests—and it is among the first which I am gratefully acknowledging.[1] I am now past seventy three and fully conscious of it—at times. When I think of our first meeting in New York a thousand light years ago, I see Howells and Matthews and Riley and all the other of our joyous friends of those confident and peaceful days. William Allen White in a recent letter wrote—apropos of the death of a mutual friend—"They are calling in the sentinels,"—and in all that I do now, I work in the hush of afternoon—a day deepening hurrying toward sun-set. My picture (like yours in a recent review) reveals the fact that I am living on borrowed time. A few men like Root[2] and Hawthorne can go on toward ninety but I do not expect that or even eighty. I tried to keep the speeches on the 14th to other subjects than myself, but I valued your noble letter more than I dare to say or write. When I think of your world-wide fame and my small achievement I am disposed to be very humble. The only rulers in whose presence I sing small are the Kings of Creative Art—I am entirely willing to be counted as seated below the salt in such company—I am appalled by the number of deaths among my English friends, Hardy, Zangwill, Conrad, Galsworthy, Doyle, Hawkins, Hewlett—all gone since my last visit to London. You and Shaw and Barrie are all that are left of my long-time associates and though I hear from you but seldom I permit myself to think that you now and again remember me when you are calling the roll of those who neighbored you in the [illeg.], and that you do not resent the brief records I have made of our infrequent meetings. My wife and daughters join in affectionate greeting—

Hamlin Garland

1. Alexander Gaylord Beaman, a Los Angeles businessman and close friend, arranged a dinner to commemorate Garland's seventy-third birthday. As part of the festivities, Beaman read over fifty letters of tribute, which were later bound (as the "Noble Book") and presented to Garland.

2. Elihu Root, former secretary of state under Theodore Roosevelt and chairman of the board of the Carnegie Corporation.

343. to Floyd Logan

tlc, usc

Feb. 5 34

My Dear Young Advocate: [1]

Your very frank good letter is on my desk and I feel that I must acknowledge it while its glow is still with me. It reminds me of the first time
Howells spoke to me of his waning fame. "I have outlived my vogue" he
said and it was a sad moment for me. He had a vogue, I have never enjoyed a boom much less a vogue, but I am in the midst of finding out that
I am an old fellow of seventy four and that people are no longer interested
in what I say or do or write.

This is not a complaint. I have had readers and listeners enough to
furnish me with a lovely home, and to allow me to live in a certain dignified publicity. It is probable that I have all the success I deserve but I
do resent the success of those who play upon the animal side of life.
Books that would not sell ten thousand copies without their pornographic scenes, are bought in hundreds of thousands. Only now and
then does a good decent study of life like "As The Earth Turns" find a
success. Nearly all the men and women in the spotlight today are playing
with the most cynical intent, upon the sensual "love" affairs of their
characters. They know that the American public is insatiable in these ap-
petites and so each one goes a little farther in the office of pandering. In
a recent success two pages are given to the experiences and sensations of
a man when a naked woman comes into his room and gets into his bed!
What the next one will do I can not conceive. No doubt the moving picture people will SHOW the woman getting into his bed. The awful thing
to me is that this and other similar incidents caused the book to sell by
the car load.

I say this is an awful thing for the reason that such a success will lead
other writers—young writers—to set down their bodily sensations and
call it literature. Mae West with her "smutty" plays, Sally Rand with her
naked dance are both a part of this hunger for the fleshly joys which now
fills public halls and sells millions of books. Our puritan traditions are
now anathema. Our moving pictures have made our children familiar
with men clutching naked women in what is technically known as the
"clinch"—and no producer will leave this out. We are sex-mad—from
my point of view—but I am aware that these incidents are considered
nescessary in an advanced literature. To me—as an evolutionist—they are
a return to the life of the animals who are supposed to be lower on the
scale of life.

The Memoirist: 1930–1940 369

My sadness comes not from a sense of my own failure but from the fear that my life will go out in an age of chaos and debasement. It may be that I am all wrong and that women will be happier passing from man to man as men have passed from woman to woman but it is revolting to me. Every book[,] every paper, every play is filled with this argument. "Fornication is natural why shouldnt it go into art?" There is no answer to that except to say that it seems like a return to a lower level of living. Perhaps it isnt. The home, children and sexual propriety are to vanish with all the other traditions which have been dear to me in the past and to which I hold. If it will make the world happier to have such freedom of intercourse I have no right to enter a demurrer but I am too old to attain that point of view.

Let us not deceive ourselves. The new deal extends to a shift in social customs. Religion has lost its power to control sexual relations. Divorces almost equal marriages in number. Soon a coupon will be issued with every marriage so that it can be snipped off at will. This is the system in Russia. It remains to say that we may become satiated with pornography —which as you know springs from a word meaning harlot—and that we shall in very weariness turn to something else. That is our only hope.

All this is for your private eye. It is possible to succeed as Mrs. Carroll did with a fine theme but the quick and sure success I am sorry to say comes with stories of libertines—men or women. It is astounding to find that the books and plays which the censor would ban are supported almost entirely by women. Mae West does not live by exciting men but by exciting and delighting women! My doctor told me of going to a play in New York that was viler than anything put on in Paris during the war and that three quarters of all the seats were filled by women—married women.

You and your young wife must take account of all these social currents and make your choice. It may be that pandering is just as honorable as any other catering to the public. It may be that sexual desire should be fed the same as any other hunger but I am too old to take that point of view. I can not even advise you, I can only applaud you if you go on in the fine traditions of Emerson, Howells and Hawthorne. I write at this unusual length because I would not have you take me as an example of success or self-satisfaction. Something of this disgust for animalism will go into my AFTER'NOON neighbors but to put much of it in would defeat my purpose. To you as one of my valued young advocates I must be honest and say, I do not expect anything but the library sale of this volume. It is a tale of dead men and dead issues. It is an old man's book, I could not blame you if you consider it a most excellent example to avoid.

With something of paternal regard, I am your sincere well-wisher.

1. Floyd Logan was with the Fort Wayne, Indiana, *News Sentinel* and was one of Garland's avid fans, writing some twenty-nine letters in their six-year acquaintanceship. In the letter to which Garland refers (29 January 1934), Logan noted that he and his wife were attempting to follow Garland's "wholesome, decent style" and that he, like Garland, deplored the sexual frankness of contemporary books.

344. to Barrett H. Clark   tlc, usc

Mar. 7. 34.

Dear Mr. Clark:

As you will see by this note-head, I am a long way from New York City. Hence the delay.[1] "Under the Wheel" was my first work in book form and was published by a young printer who was a fellow radical and willing to take a chance on the expense of the printing. It was not really published but an edition of a thousand was printed and I sold or gave away most of them. The booklet is now a very rare "item" as the collectors say. I have the only copies in existence and I am guarding them as a gold mine for my daughters.

It may interest you to know how I came to have these copies. My brother had it in mind to produce the play in Dakota where he was living and so I sent to him at that time several copies for the use of his fellow players. One or two have the suggested cast pencilled in. These lines add, I am told, to their curio value. I doubt if you can find in all the second hand bookshop world a single copy of this immortal work. It is fierce propaganda—or so it was considered at the time. It is very mild now.

I am coming to New York in May. I shall be very pleased to see you. I shall be at the Century Club.

1. Clark was cataloguing his collection of published plays by American authors and had written, 28 February 1934, to inquire about the publication history of *Under the Wheel* and whether it was possible to obtain a copy. Garland's carbon is typed on the back of Clark's letter.

345. to Van Wyck Brooks

als, U Penn

2045 DeMille Drive
Hollywood, California

Nov. 5. 34

Dear Mr Brooks:

I have been re-reading your Emerson for the third time, and I am moved to say again how much I find in it.[1] It consoles me for the cheapness and sleaziness of so much of our "literature." I thank you once again for packing so much significance into so small a space. It is superbly done. —

What are you doing now? — I wish you would do Hawthorne. There is a grand figure. I read and read his travel notes. They have the abstract authority of a literary Pope—yet assume nothing. — Let me have a line from you.[2]

Hamlin Garland.

1. *Emerson and Others* (1927).

2. Brooks replied, 11 November 1934, that he was grateful for Garland's interest, noted his next project would be a history of American literature, and then informed Garland that "your work has very largely helped to form my view of various parts of the subject."

346. to Eldon Hill

tls, Miami U

Dec. 3. 34.

Dear Young Advocate:[1]

First of all, you must bear in mind that I have done a great many poems since PRAIRIE SONGS appeared. I think I indicated where most of them are to be found. The Trail of the Goldseekers, has some of my best. I like "The End of the Trail." I think I will bundle up some of those which have not been printed in book form.

Riley used to call me "The poet of the winds" and in truth my life on the prairies and the plains where the wind is a never resting force, led me to write many poems in which its effect on the land or on me is a leading motive. I dont know of any one who has done just this sort of verse. In many of my other verses the birds, beasts, and other denizens of the plains are depicted. Yes, Lanier influenced me to some degree, and so did Whitman and Joaquin Miller but not to any marked degree. I had a theory that the subject should have its own dress, a garment which would take its shape from the inner urge. In some cases pure lyric was demanded, in others free or intricate rhythms. I did not believe in adopting a fixed form for the expression of all my poetic concepts. I used verse only when prose fell short.

I am sending in this mail some poems which were published in THE TRAIL OF THE GOLDSEEKERS or in magazines. Some of them may be new to you. I am interested to have you write of my verse which has dribbled from my pen from time to time for fifty years.

I have not catalogued what I am sending, and must trust you to keep them all together and to return them when you have read and after they have served your purpose.

H.G.

1. Eldon Hill (1906–1987) was preparing his doctoral dissertation, a study of Garland's life and works, which he had begun in 1931, and would write over 175 letters to Garland, as well as visit him, over a span of nine years. Garland was pleased by Hill's interest but was dismayed by the length of time it would take him to complete his study, "A Biographical Study of Hamlin Garland from 1860 to 1895," Ohio State University, 1940.

347. to Harry Carr   tld, usc

2045 DeMille Drive
Hollywood, California

Dec. 30. 34.

Dear Harry Carr:

In your kind note concerning my "literary log" you quote the paragraph which has been somewhat adversely commented upon.[1] The point which I intended to make is this; California is a land apart from the states east of the Continental divide. I felt this and so wrote of it forty-two years ago. I even dared to prophesy a new and distinctive literature for I believed with Taine that a distinctive literature springs from environment acting upon character. I had no prevision of course of the intrusion of a colony of motion picture scenarists who are not concerned with literature and who are utterly alien to the California scene.

I had in mind these facts: There are fewer violent contrasts in Southern California life. It is gorgeously colorful, suave, yet immensely picturesque. Its weather changes are subtler than those I lived through in Wisconsin and Iowa. Its winters have an utterly different quality even in the north where the snow falls. Its springs have their own peculiar loveliness. It should produce a subtler, less bitterly contrasted art and literature.

For example; My two grandchildren will grow to majority with no knowledge of blizzards such as I faced, with no feeling of frozen mud on their boots, no sting of sleet in their faces. Their springs will be those which come early and with fine gradations following the rains and not the calendar. Sunshine will be wholly natural, something to be expected every day. We wonder and exclaim over these conditions, but our grandsons consider them natural, just as mud, cold, snow, sleighing, skating, April Seeding and July harvest were natural factors in our thinking. My grandson or some one of his generation, will be the California author I had in mind in 1892 when I prophesied a literature of the Coast.

Merely writing a motion picture scenario of a divorce case or some other sexual complication in Hollywood does not contribute to a California literature, neither does reporting the vice and crime of our cities do so. A literature must have the reflective quality and it must use fitting words. Perhaps it will come by not taking thought about it. I like to think the best of it will come without consideration of pay but this is too much to ask. Probably it will combine the two motives, love of California life and respect for the judgments of the Eastern editors. When all is said, we shall still remain a colony of the East. We must still be one of the United States.

I honor, Harte, Miller, Norris, Markham, White and others who have made so fine a beginning but something more subtly characteristic is certain to come. What it will be I can not predict except that it will spring from race and environment, and be expressed with precision and grace.

As to the four volumes of my "literary log," they are based on the actual moods and judgments of my diaries. My moments of sickness and depression as well as my moments of elation and joy have their place. My friends protest against these paragraphs but they are there in the interest of truth like the judgments I record. My main theme throughout has been the presentation of the other fellow, meetings with the men and women who have made the art and literature of the last forty-five years. These books are pictures and impressions not biographies.

My home is in Southern California but I know the other six Californias. I have motored seven thousand miles to discover them. My only question is have I the right to so much beauty and comfort?

Hamlin Garland

Laughlin Park.

1. Harry Carr (1877–1936) contributed the column "The Lancer" to the *Los Angeles Times.* Carr had reviewed *Afternoon* (30 December 1934) and had criticized a paragraph in which Garland notes that "The Coast is only just beginning to produce a native school of writers, but they are writing for Eastern editors" (p. 587; clipping, item #723).

348. to Eldon Hill   als, Miami U

2045 DeMille Drive
Hollywood, California

Sunday. Nov. 3. [1935]

My Dear Young Advocate:

Your continued interest in my career deserves reward but I fear you'll never get it — certainly not a compensating reward. — I am sending an envelope filled with all sorts of odds and ends of clippings[,] essays, interviews and the like. As for the birth-day notices — Alas! I pasted them in "The Noble Book" and can only send duplicates. — I have sixteen letter files filled with letters from my friends dating from 1885 to the present time. I am trying to have them sorted and arranged in chronological order. When this is done, they will be available for study. They should all be copied, of course, and yet I dont like to have them go out of my hands. I am so tired after my five hours writing that I can not "tackle" this other most difficult job.

Hamlin Garland

349. to George Steele Seymour   tls, Knox

2045 DeMille Drive
Hollywood, California

Mar. 16. 36.

Dear Bookfellows:

I am so sick of lewd writing, lewd pictures and lewd women that I have stopped reading fiction and poetry and only occasionally go to a theater. You may say that I am all wrong about this and that sexual licence is just freedom and that pimps[,] prostitutes and adulterers are proper subjects for the poet and the novelist but as an evolutionist I am of the opinion that the monkey stage of human life should fall behind us.

Now in view of a possible difference of opinion on this vital question,

I think it well to give you permission to quietly forget to print my name at the head of your advisory council. Nothing need be said about it—just drop my name. I dont intend to be in any sense a drag on your wheels. You are younger and have a closer contact with the men and women who are finding adventure in writing of "sexual freedom" and all that the phrase connotes. Several times lately I have caught this feeling in your reviews. I have no intention of censoring what you write or print but I dont enjoy sponsoring it in any way. I am an old man and tired of road-house literature, that is all.

You have done a fine work, devoted and aspiring, and you have been a most loyal friend to me and I must not be a hindrance to you—in the slightest degree.

Most Sincerely Your Aged Friend.
Hamlin Garland

Personal and Private.[1]

1. Written at top left corner. Seymour replied, 19 March 1936, to plead with Garland to reconsider, reminding him that he'd been a member for seventeen years and that his name was inscribed in stone on their building.

350. to Harvey C. Minnich

tld, usc

2045 DeMille Drive
Hollywood, California

April. 2. 36

Dear Mr. Minnich:

I am returning the mimeographed volume of selections from Mc-Guffey's Readers, with a turned leaf to indicate the poems and stories which meant most to me when I was a boy on an Iowa farm in the early seventies.[1] That these selections had a very great educative influence on me is confirmed as I turn the leaves of the collection. Henry Ford and I once had a contest (in a review of these books) to see who could remember most of the poems and name most of the titles of the prose pieces. His memory was better than mine or else he had lately reread them. Up to a certain point our experiences had been similar. From a farm house near Dearborn he began his education in a district school where Mc-Guffey's Readers gave almost the only outlook on the world of fiction[,] poetry and the drama. He is grateful, as I am for that esthetic enrichment.

It is easy to laugh at some of these selections now but as I run over them I feel again something of the thrill of discovery which I then experienced as I came upon prose pieces by Dickens or Hawthorne, or poems by Poe, Tennyson, Whittier and Bryant. We had no books on the Border in those days, and our school readers were of inestimable value for that reason. McGuffey realized the literary poverty of our country schools and poured into them the material which his wide reading enabled him to select and assemble. With most of his judgments I still agree. They were the best that the time afforded.

I have marked the selections (as I have indicated above) not on their agreement with present standards but on their value to me in my youth.

Hamlin Garland

1. Harvey C. Minnich (1861–1952) was chair of the William Holmes McGuffey Memorial Association and had asked Garland to serve as an associate editor for a McGuffey memorial volume to celebrate the McGuffey centennial. Minnich had requested twenty-one McGuffey societies to submit lists of their favorite lessons. Garland would be one of the twelve board members responsible for selecting one hundred fifty "old favorites" from the lists. The volume appeared as *Old Favorites from the McGuffey Readers*, ed. Harvey C. Minnich (1936). Garland's copy of the reader (Miami U) has an earlier, holograph version of this letter pasted on the flyleaf.

351. to Alfred C. Howell

als, usc

2045 DeMille Drive
Hollywood, California

April. 15 [1936]

Dear Mr Howell:

My new book will soon be published and I shall see that you get a copy.[1] I do not expect much from this book but it has its value as a record of observation.—Since I saw you last a very great change has come into my family—My daughter Isabel has separated from her husband Hardesty Johnson whom I liked, and is planning to marry another man whom I do not like.[2] The separation was entirely amicable. She and Hardesty remain on friendly terms—in the modern way—but I am hit hard by it. It shows me the folly of saving up money for a possible son-in-law of whom I know nothing. In view of these changes, my wife and I are disposed to use what we have and let our sons-in-law provide for their wives. All this leads down to this: we are no longer bent on increasing my income but on making what I have carry us comfortably along for a few years more. I am in receipt of letters informing me that this or that issue of bonds is called in, or that they are not paying interest. These uncertainties lead me to ask what is going to happen to the Insurance companies? If they go, we are sunk!—Shall I take out another annuity? Or shall I take the safest government bonds and hold them against an emergency?

My daughters both say "Have what you and mother need—never mind us"—and this you will see has led to my changed attitude. Mrs. Garland remains about the same. She can walk and does walk several miles each day but she can not use her hands for writing or sewing. And I am disposed to give her some of the luxuries of life. You have been so kind that I venture to ask your advice once more. If you can spare the time to go over the list of my securities I shall be grateful.

It may interest you to know that the University Library here is arranging an exhibit of my books and M.S.S.—[3]

Hamlin Garland

Personal[4]

1. Alfred C. Howell (1884–1961) was the vice president of Guaranty Trust Company of New York. Garland refers to *Forty Years of Psychic Research.*

2. Mary Isabel married Mindret Lord on 21 December 1936.

3. The exhibit, "Hamlin Garland and His Literary Friends," later entitled "The Makers of American Literature," opened at the Doheny Library of the University of Southern California on 2 April and lasted through the summer. After that, it went on tour as "The Makers of American Literature" to at least eleven libraries, among them the state libraries of California, Iowa, Ohio, and Wisconsin, as well as to university libraries in Indiana, Chicago, and Ohio. See Garland to Vanamee, 14, 16, 19, 21 March 1936 (Am Acad).

4. Written at top left corner.

352. to Alexander Gaylord Beaman   tl, usc

2045 DeMille Drive
Hollywood, California

Sept. 18. 36.

Dear Friend Beaman:

Anytime you have some one you'd like me to meet invite them to the club at my expense and I will come down. I dont want *you* to go to the slightest expense in such an invitation. Or I'll come down with you and pay both our shots.

Cant we make another attempt to dig up those spook photographs of the man Parent?[1] Lets drive out and look the matter up. It may be that I shall make a little story of the meeting with Parent. Go to your files and see what you can find. You wrote me the sisters name and address but I dont think I have it. Those pictures are too singular to let rot.

It may be that I could put it into the shape of an interview. Think the Psychical Review would print it, perhaps the New York TIMES.[2]

I think I'll put in another ad. in the TIMES in a week or two. Using a photo like the enclosed Carrell ads.[3] What do you think of it?

H.G.

1. In 1932 Garland had been contacted by Gregory Parent, who wanted him to write about the psychic discoveries of his wife, Violet, who had died five years before. Violet Parent had found buried objects, some in the form of crosses, and had taken "ecto-plasmic photographs" of spirits. Garland was intrigued but was too busy with the com-position of his literary logbooks to investigate. Gregory Parent had since died, and Garland in this letter is enlisting the aid of Beaman to contact Parent's sister, Louise Stack, to recover the Parents' collection of objects, photographs, and diaries, some of which are now housed in the Garland Papers (item #556). Garland's obsessive interest in the problem of the crosses would culminate in 1939 with his final book, *The Mystery of the Buried Crosses.*

2. Garland published "Gregory Parent's Diary," in the *Journal of the American Society for Psychical Research* 33 (1939): 257–69.

3. The enclosure has not survived.

353. to Mary Isabel Garland Johnsonals, Hunt

Hotel Geneva
7A, De Londres 130
Mexico City
Mexico

Tuesday. [3 November 1936]

Dear Daughtie:

We are going home tomorrow. We both had a bad night and I suddenly realized how Uncle Lorado's death had destroyed your mothers interest in things here. She has stayed on, I fear on my account. She sleeps badly

The Memoirist: 1930–1940 379

and her eyes do not permit her to read much and so I think it wise to take her home—I am too old to be a cheerful companion to her in a time like this.—

We reach home Saturday.

Your Father.

1. After learning of Lorado Taft's death on 30 October 1936, the Garlands had originally planned to continue with their itinerary.

354. to Van Wyck Brooks

als, U Penn

2045 DeMille Drive
Hollywood, California

Nov. 8—36.

Dear Mr Brooks:

I am reading and re-reading your "Flowering of New England" as I have re-read and scandalously marked your "Emerson."[1] It fills me with a sense of my own short-comings, however. I once hoped to be a largish figure in American literature but alas! the need of supporting a wife and two daughters led to hasty and relatively unimportant work. I will not say that I deliberately cheapened my work by any trick for I did not but I was for some years unable to take time to work out my theme. I allowed my publishers to push me into a new book before the mood for writing was fully on me. I make no apology for "The Captain of the Gray Horse Troop"—it was good work then and it is good work now. It remains vital after thirty five years, for the reason that it was history as well as fiction. There are passages in all my books—even the poorest of them—which I wish could be somehow preserved.—I am led to speak of these things because men like Quinn and Van Doren are inclined to ignore these stories of the mountaineer—like "Mart Haney" and "Hesper." Howells liked "Haney" and so did Fuller. Fuller also liked my "Silent-Eaters" which none of the critics appear to have read.—

Later. Your photo. has just come, and I have put it into your New England book. I do hope you will come out. You may have the free range of my files. If our big guest room is not occupied, we will have you here with us for a few days. We find this is a heavenly place for old people to live but our daughters feel that it does not offer wide scope for literary or artistic talent—which is true. My brilliant friend John Bradley who was almost like a son to me, felt this and has gone to Lowell to be near his *alma mater*—Harvard. You should know him. He is an amazing young fellow. I want you to meet him. Another of my enthusiasms is Donald Peattie.[2] You three young men are after my own concept of what American literature should be.

The Academy has asked me to give the address on Howells, March 10 — but I can not take the risk of an Eastern trip at that time—and besides, my wife needs my care. She was much broken by her brother's death. I dont know what the Institute is to do but I have suggested that you be invited to speak as representing the Institute. I hope my suggestion does not come too late.

I do hope you'll come out this winter and settle near me so that we can discuss all these problems face to face. Howells is now the social historian of his time. He is at once fictionist and historian and when our people have satiated themselves with tales of pimps, prostitutes and panderers he will come back. He is so wise, so humorous and so wholly the artist in every line.

Hamlin Garland

1. *The Flowering of New England,* the first of a five-volume series of the "history of the writer in America," was published in 1936 and won a Pulitzer Prize.

2. John Bradley (1898–1962) was a professor of geology at the University of Southern California and the author of *Parade of the Living* (1930) and *Patterns of Survival: An Anatomy of Life* (1938), both of which Garland admired. Donald Culcross Peattie (1898–1964) was a naturalist whose works include *A Salute to John James Audubon* (1935) and *The Lives and Achievements of the Great Naturalists* (1937).

355. to Mary Isabel Garland Johnson als, Hunt

2045 DeMille Drive
Hollywood, California

Nov. 24—36.

Dear Mary Isabel:

In the middle of the night I heard cries for help as if in my dream. I awoke and hurried to your mother's room. She was on the floor unable to rise. I got her into her bed and gave her a sleeping powder—She slept till seven and is up this noon but she looks white and haggard—She could not get out of her bath yesterday morning and I did not hear her call for help—The fact is worry over her daughters, the death of her brother and her persistent influenza have brought her to a condition where she must be watched all the time—I have been writing you guarded reports of her condition but the time has come for plain-speaking. She and I are two disheartened old people with no one to whom we can turn for aid. Connie is fine but as she is in the midst of her legal complications—she can not find much time for us—At an age when your mother needs serenity and the care of her daughters she is called upon to face a most disturbing situation. I did not realize until Connie told me what you had done.[1] It was incredible even then. Now the question is—if your mother needs you will you come home? I'll send the money but *you must come alone.* Your mother may pull up but last night scared me. We may try Dr. Sausum again—but today she is to see Connie's doctor—It would be a comfort to her if you should come home for the holidays. Think it over and let me know.

Your Daddy.

1. According to a diary entry of 9 November 1936, Garland learned that Constance and her husband, Joseph Harper, had agreed to a separation; he had also recently learned that Mary Isabel had arranged for an absentee Mexican divorce so that she and Mindret Lord could marry (on 21 December 1936). His 10 November diary entry is singularly poignant: "If I ever have a biographer, he can take this as one of my darkest weeks. Both my daughters separated from their husbands, my wife an invalid, myself threatened with pneumonia and unable to see even the few friends I have left. I wonder if these young people who allow 'love' to lead them into strange places look back as I do on the joys of the past. Probably not. But have they not some obligation to spare their old father and mother?" Garland also recorded (23 November) that he had hitherto not disclosed to Mary Isabel the true state of Zulime's health.

356. to August Derleth
tls, Wis HS

2045 DeMille Drive
Hollywood, California

Dec. 4. 36.

Dear Mr. Derleth:[1]

I had no intention of questioning your ability as writer or critic but I have seen so many of these volumes published locally which are not only filled with feeble amateur verse but badly printed and bound, that I wished to be assured that your Wisconsin Poets had a real backing by a reputable publisher.[2] I felt that your enthusiasm and your state pride might have led you to accept material which was not up to standard, and to sign a contract with a publisher who was not metropolitan in scope.

There may be a high-class volume of poetry in Wisconsin mss but I can not believe it can possibly be large or important. I may be wrong, I hope I am. To conclude; You may use the poems which you named in your first letter[3] on the same terms as those you made with Ellery Leonard and Zona Gale. Trusting this will be satisfactory to you I remain

Very Sincerely Yours,
Hamlin Garland

The Publishers of my IOWA POEMS were connected with The State University. My correspondent was Frank L Mott. A smaller volume of Wisconsin poems could be made.

1. August Derleth (1909–71), prolific Wisconsin poet, novelist, and essayist, whose works include *Still is the Summer Night* (1937), *Bright Journey* (1940), and *The Wisconsin: River of a Thousand Isles* (1942).

2. Derleth wanted to include some of Garland's poems in *Poetry Out of Wisconsin*, which he co-edited with Raymond E. P. Larrson and which was published by Henry Harrison in 1937. Garland had not heard of the publisher and was unfamiliar with Derleth's work, writing on 25 November 1936 (Wis HS), "As I do not know you and as it seems rather out of the line of professional or academic editing, I must wait until I know more about your plan." Derleth replied on 30 November 1936: "Your letter of 25 November shocked and surprised me, and it brought home to me the fact that compared to yourself I am of course virtually a literary nobody," and he proceeded to detail his many magazine publications, his books, the critics who praised his work, his listings in *Who's Who*, and other references, and he assured Garland that the publisher was indeed reputable and that the anthology would be "a strictly royalty affair."

3. On 9 November 1936 Derleth had requested permission to include "The Cool Gray Jug," "November," "A Summer Mood," "Prairie Pioneers," "Plowing," and "The End of the Trail." Garland has misremembered the sequence of letters; Derleth's first letter requesting publication rights is dated 27 April 1936.

357. to Van Wyck Brooks

als, U Penn

2045 DeMille Drive
Hollywood, California

Dec. 21. [1936]

Dear Van Wyck Brooks:

It was most kind of you to take time out of your working day to write with your own hand to an old exile like me. Howells once said to me sadly "I have outlived my vogue"—I never had a vogue to outlive but I am feeling what every man of my years must feel—the fall of the dark month.

I read aloud to my wife and daughter your chapter "Hawthorne in Salem"—and so discovered new beauty and significance in it.[1] It is the most revealing chapter on Hawthorne ever written. It makes me wish to have you write a book on Hawthorne, one to place beside your Emerson. Hawthorne has been my admiration for sixty years. I have read most of the worth-while studies of him but they are all wooden compared to your chapter. I have just one fear—you are in danger of overloading yourself. You have undertaken a colossal job. I dont want you to fail of sustaining the high quality which your two latest books have carried to the end. If you feel yourself wavering, take a rest. I shall be greatly disappointed if you don't come out here. Am I right in thinking of you as a Californian?—Were you at Stanford?—Have you a family?—I know so little of you as a citizen. I did urge you as the Howells' speaker and I still hope you'll do it.[2] I've become extravagant in speaking of your work. No one is doing just that flexible, vital critical prose which comes—seemingly—so naturally to you. It is true, I am fitted to talk of Howells but I no longer enjoy lecturing. I did it for fifty years, now—I avoid it. It delights me to have you appreciate Howells.[3] He is so subtly humorous and so deft! It was not nescessary for him to deal with fornication and incest. He could make the normal woman and average man worth while. The taste of today is all for the naked woman, the prostitute[,] the gangster, the libertine. Every resounding success of the last twenty years has been by means of these subjects. Howells dealt with the human not the animal side of men and women. He was not journalistic in the sense of always exploiting the exceptional, the illicit—But what is the use of my telling *you* these things? You not only know them more completely than I but you can state them with far greater skill and tact. I hope you will reconsider and do the How-ells' address.—As I wrote you, I am not only closely confined to my home by the helplessness of my wife but sadly disheartened by her condition. I can not plan to leave her and she may not be able to travel—certainly not in March or April.

If you were here I would tell you of a singular psychical discovery which is absorbing my leisure hours. It involves the finding of a thousand buried crosses hidden by the Mission Indians something like one hundred and fifty years ago. The burial places were located by a clairvoyant.—I shall continue to read you to my wife. I like to read such prose as yours—

Hamlin Garland

Dont hesitate to use a typewriter in your letters to me.

1. Chapter 11 of *The Flowering of New England* (1936).

2. Garland had deferred presenting the keynote address at the Howells Centenary meeting of the National Institute because of his residence in California and had suggested that Brooks speak instead. Brooks had explained, in a letter of 14 December 1936, that although he was on the Centenary committee, he found public speaking exhausting and too interruptive of his writing.

3. Brooks, who was at work on *New England: Indian Summer, 1865–1915*, had written that he was reading Howells "all through this year . . . with the greatest joy and interest."

358. to Mary Isabel Garland Lord tl, Hunt

2045 DeMille Drive
Hollywood, California

Dec. 25. [1936]

Dear Daughter:

If you ever expect to hear your mother's voice again you'd better to arrange to come on soon. She is failing steadily. She may not be able to talk to you at all. She has moments when I can not understand her but for the most part I can only guess at what she says. We keep hoping but at times I am in despair and I think you should know it. I dont like to break into your plans or shadow your life but after all you owe something to your mother. I need your help. It is not a pleasure trip, it will be a very sad trip but it is your duty to make it. I cant keep a cheerful face in the circumstances. Nothing that we can do helps her much. She can walk when on her feet but she must be watched every moment. If she loses the power of speech it will be a tragic situation.

Come as soon as you can arrange your affairs,[1]

Your Father.

1. According to Garland's diary, Mary Isabel arrived on 11 January 1937.

359. to George Steele Seymour and Flora Warren Seymour

tls, Knox

2045 DeMille Drive
Hollywood, California

Thursday. [11 February 1937]

Dear Mr. and Mrs Seymour:

Mr. Haselton came yesterday and secured some motion picture scenes in which Zulime was an actor. This brings all of the family into the film. I know you will rejoice with me in this happy conclusion of a most able and patient attempt on Haseltons part. So far as I know only John Burroughs has been recorded in this way and in justice to Haselton I am going to help him sell or rent the film. It is a pure venture on his part. One print of the complete film will go to the Academy Archives, and I have one for my daughters which will remain here. I am saying to Eldon Hill that I will see that he gets a print for rent to any of the colleges interested. The cost of a film 400 feet is twenty five dollars and the rental could be fixed at five dollars or less.[1]

It is a satisfaction to me that in this film are my daughters, my grandchildren, my brother and now at last my wife. So far as I know these films are practically indestructible so that here is a record for my grandchildren. If you can suggest any plan of distribution to Mr. Haselton I shall be indebted for he has been most skilfull and persistent in the work. The idea was his. He didnt even know that Burroughs had been done. His address is Hotel Christie[,] Hollywood.

With greetings to you both.
Hamlin Garland

1. Guy D. Haselton made a silent, black and white biographical film of Garland in his Hollywood home. The film exists in two states in the Garland Papers: a 625-foot version, including stills of his books; and a 400-foot version, without the stills. See Haselton to Garland, 26 April 1938. Eldon Hill acted as Garland's midwestern agent in placing the exhibit of his papers. He lectured on Garland, accompanied by working versions of the film, at Indiana University and several clubs.

360. to Fred B. Millett tls, Yale

2045 DeMille Drive
Hollywood, California

March 1 37.

Dear Mr. Millett:

I appreciate your interest and shall do all I can to make your task easy—so far as I am concerned.[1] I am sending you a booklet which has much of what you need, but I hope you will call upon me for anything further at any time. I may be coming through Chicago about May first and I shall be glad to talk with you on any points which remain to be cleared up. Meanwhile ask me any questions you feel like putting to me. Yes, I had four silent pictures made of my novels. The Vita-Graph Co. brought out my novel THE CAPTAIN OF THE GRAY HORSE TROOP under the title "The Long Fight." I think they brought out HESPER under its own title, and CAVANAGH·FOREST RANGER under some such title as "The Forest Trail." They also used my novel MONEY MAGIC which I afterward re-named MART HANEY'S MATE.[2]

A re-issue was made of CAVANAGH but with no great success. In fact the four pictures came out during the Great War and suffered for that reason. They are now being considered again as "talkies."

Do you know my CRUMBLING IDOLS? If not, I am of the opinion that it would present some of the notions I once held and some of which I still hold. It is not as I would write it now but it has meat in it. In general I have tried to present life as I have seen it and lived it but I have deliberately cut out pornography for the reason that it is the most hackneyed of all themes. My aim was to present the average men and women in their normal modern relationships. It would have been easier to pick out the occasional murder, seduction or adulterous episode but I preferred to write drab or dull books of the ordinary well-meaning folks with whom my life was associated. Even in my stories of the mountains and the plains I kept away from the customary saloon and dance hall characters. The formulated pandering which had become so successful did not interest me. As I hate jazz music—or rather jazz tom-tomming—and the obscene whine of the crooner so I avoid the adulterous cabaret play.

In short I am an evolutionist and I do not enjoy seeing men and women returning to the morality of monkeys. The morals of the barnyard are not something to enter upon but to leave behind. The Great War brought as its aftermath a period of licentiousness like that which followed the Napoleonic wars and we are still in it but slowly emerging. That

The Memoirist: 1930–1940 387

is the way it appears to me. Nearly all the popular successes of the last twenty years have been the result of pandering to this taste for the illicit. Stories which used to be confined to saloons and brothels are now printed in regular book form and brought into the drawing room.

All this may be very old-fashioned in me but I can not endure pornography. It bores me and saddens me. When I see you we can discuss it at greater length than I can afford to take in writing a letter.

With thanks for your interest,
Hamlin Garland

I am mailing a booklet which you may find helpful—, today.[3]
I was painted by

Louis Bells of Chicago
Orlando Rouland New York (twice)
Henry Hubbell   "
Wayman Adams   "
Ralph Clarkson Chicago.

1. Fred B. Millett, an associate professor of English at the University of Chicago, was writing his *Contemporary American Literature* (1940) and wrote to Garland to request information for a biographical sketch and bibliography, as well as to ask whether any of his novels had been made into films.

2. The films were released under the following titles: *Hesper of the Mountains* (directed by Wilfrid North, 1916), *Money Magic* (directed by William Wolbert, 1917), *The Captain of the Gray Horse Troop* (directed by William Wolbert, 1917), and *Cavanaugh of the Forest Rangers* (directed by William Wolbert, 1918).

3. The "booklet" is a revised 1937 edition of a Macmillan publicity brochure, entitled "Hamlin Garland, a Son of the Middle Border."

361. to George Steele Seymour tls, Knox

2045 DeMille Drive
Hollywood, California

March. 22. 37.

Dear Seymour:

Have you some copies of JOYS OF THE TRAIL which are just ordinary copies which you can sell me at a modest price? I should have a few for occasional gifts.[1] I hope you succeeded in selling enough to pay for the edition. I intend to do something for your library when you get it built. I have an immense amount of ms, from which I can select something for you. It will not be pretty but it will be characteristic.

Haselton has sent you the film which is still incomplete on the biographical side but I thought it best to let you have it in its present state. I am going to go over the introductory part with Haselton and Hess, and when they are finished it will be the most complete biographic film ever made of a man of letters — if I may venture to call myself that. I want you to have it in its completed form and I shall do what I can to keep the cost down and to insure a complete record.

What would you like me to do for the STEP-LADDER, I will do an occasional paragraph for you if you think such contributions would help. Bits out of my diary might have interest.

Very Sincerely Your Debtor.
Hamlin Garland

1. The Bookfellows had published Garland's *Joys of the Trail* in 1935, a much-expanded revision of "Hitting the Trail," *McClure's* 12 (1899): 298–304, which was itself later reworked into a lecture and published as "Vanishing Trails," *University Record* [University of Chicago] 10 (1905): 53–61.

362. to Constance Garland Harper tl, Hunt

2045 DeMille Drive
Hollywood, California

Wednesday. [28 July 1937]

Dear Daughter:

By this time you have had your great success.[1] I know it was a success — you never fail in such things. You must write all about it. This letter is for you and Mary Isabel both. I am too tired to write separate letters. One of my eyes is failing me and I must begin to deal gently with it. I am waiting with great anxiety to hear from Latham.[2] When you see him tell him, that I have a great idea for novel advertising. We might quote William James, Theodore Roosevelt, Conan Doyle and other of my invisible critics precisely as if they were live. Col. Roosevelt said "Garland your work is revolutionary. It over-turns all the conventional concepts." James was equally emphatic in his praise. We could [quote] Sir William Crookes and

Dr. Geley[3]—any number of the great pioneers in this work. Wouldnt that astonish—and disgust—the critics? Another phase with which we are to win much publicity is the co-operation of the Padres in the work of making these crosses known to the Catholic world. What I think Macmillans should do is to bring me and Mrs. Williams on in October and demonstrate to the editors and critics. Five hundred dollars would do it and it would pay. You may talk this with Latham if you like. Chesterton who is a great Catholic has called once and I shall have a talk with him. I had a long talk with Coronado and also with Cortez' lieutenant Alvarado the other day. They told me who made the crosses and how they came to be brought here. Tell this ONLY to Latham. People will think I am quite mad. Alvarado had more accent than any of the others. I made Martinez laugh in the book by saying "You were not by any chance an Irishman?" His laugh was huffhuff huff. Perfectly plain. I am going to call up Houdini and Edison. Apparently Fuller can get any one I wish to speak to. Tis a great game!

I cant write any more this morning. Mother will dictate something.

Love to you all,
Mother and Daddy.

1. Constance had a role in a play.

2. At this time Garland had embarked on one of his oddest projects: the completion of a manuscript, eventually published in 1939 by E. P. Dutton & Co. as *The Mystery of the Buried Crosses*, recording his discovery of crude crosses, apparently long-buried, which no museum could identify. Inspired by the papers and objects discovered by Gregory and Violet Parent, Garland was led to these crosses through a series of séances conducted by the medium Sophia Williams. Garland made "ectoplasmic photographs," recorded spirit conversations under a variety of conditions with the shades of his literary friends, and through it all was guided by his friend Henry Blake Fuller, who had died in 1929.

3. Sir William Crookes (1832–1919) and Gustave Geley (1868–1924) were influential scientists in the study of psychic phenomena.

363. to Harold Latham

tls, usc

[5 August 1937]

Dear Mr. Latham: We got this from Williams' voices in day-light—partly in my study and partly in Constances studio.[1]

Mr. Fuller said, "I have been in communication with Miss Earhart and have the following facts to give you: They were off their course by reason of faulty navigation. They came down at a point far to the north and west of Howland Island. They came down from lack of fuel. They transferred the radio from the nose of the ship to its tail in order to have more time for messages. They knew the nose would sink first. It was in the early evening, and they could see a very small island. It is an uncharted island with a few trees. They started swimming toward it. It was cold, quite cold, and a high sea was running. They landed, wet and without food, and without extra clothing.[2]

"They lived on the island for twelve or fourteen days. They had a fire, so that there must have been some fuel on the island. They had very little food and very little water — rain water. Many storms swept over them. They were in the storm belt.

"Mr. Noonan died first. They had launched their rubber boat before the ship submerged. In this boat they put a message in a sealed package, hoping that it would be observed and picked up at sea or that it would land on some coast. Miss Earhart died of exposure, as we assume Noonan did.

"Mrs. Putnam said she wanted me to send a message to her husband, George Putnam, and to 'Freddie's wife' and added 'I went out in a blaze of glory, in the way I wanted to go.'"

Fuller says that he will have them both at our sitting tomorrow morning and that we will get full information from them direct. He approves of my plan to write a careful description of the way in which this message came and of its transmission direct to Mr. Putnam who knows me and who will undoubtedly be willing to credit it.

I'll write you again tomorrow. I have not heard from your office yet.

H.G.

1. The opening and concluding paragraphs are handwritten at the top and bottom of a typed page reporting the results of a séance. A second copy exists in the Garland Papers, dated "Aug. 5.," without the underlining, and with the addition of the following marginalia at the top of the page: "*Personal and confidential* / Received partly at the end of a 250 foot wire — and partly in my study."

2. Amelia Earhart and her navigator, Fred Noonan, were last heard from by radio on 2 July 1937, bound for Howland Island after departing from New Guinea on 1 July.

364. to Mary Isabel Garland Lord
and Constance Garland Harper   tls, Hunt

2045 DeMille Drive
Hollywood, California

Friday. [6 August 1937]

Dear Daughters:

We are having an exciting time just now. Fuller came yesterday and said he had talked with Amelia Earhart. She told him what had happened and she is coming this morning to talk with me. She wants me to write to her husband. She feels that he will believe a message coming through me. We got part of her message in the studio at a distance of two hundred feet but today I am keeping it all within the house in order to have a wire without any joints in it. I shall write more after our sitting this morning.

ALL THIS TO BE A DEAD SECRET. We dont want to be troubled by reporters.

We have lost our second chance at the silver. That dratted prospector turns out to be a psychic and Fuller told us yesterday that he was digging in the very spot where we were to dig. We still have two chances to get ahead of that fellow.

If Macmillans declines the book I want you to take an active part in placing it with Dutton or Harpers or Doubleday. I feel very helpless at this distance. As soon as this book is on the press we shall start in on another devoted wholly to personalities.

We like to hear of the childrens development. You sound very sane and happy also. We begin to say, "Another month and she will be starting for home."

I hope you have satisfied my tenant. He is holding up the final check until you finish those repairs.

DADDY.

P.S. We have done it! A padre has appeared on the same film with me!—Saturday—

The story of Amelia Earhart seems so important that I shall follow it out. If we do not get it, no one else is likely to tell it in anything like the detail which she can use in speaking to me for we can talk almost as freely

as by telephone. If the story of our talks should get out we would be
mobbed by reporters and friends of Miss Earhart and so we are proceed-
ing with great caution.

We are going to rush the photos as rapidly as possible. I believe we have
made the start now and that they will come along rapidly. I awoke several
times last night, pondering on the effect of another clear picture of a
padre on the same film with me. Guess we'll have to change our whole
attitude toward Mrs. Parent. "She was the goods".

Mother is deeply interested in Amelia Earhart and lies on the couch in
absorbed attention to the whispers which she hears much better than I
can. I have been writing since four on Chapter Twenty Four, The Problem
of the Photographs all from the new angle.

I shall get this off to you on the morning ship so that you will get it
Monday morning.

All well and weather gorgeous.

DADDY.

Confidential[1]

1. Written at top left corner of the first page.

365. to George P. Putnam tlc, usc

[6 August 1937]

Dear Mr. Putnam:[1]

I am quite certain that you have had many messages from mediums
giving information concerning the fate of your wife, but I hope that my
name and the fact that I am a fellow-member of the Century Club and
well acquainted with several members of your family will carry enough
weight to make my communication somewhat more authentic than the
usual dark-sitting utterances.

For some months I have been at work on a book supplemental to my
recent volume "Forty Years of Psychic Research" and I have been using
the very latest scientific methods and inventions. Before reporting what
happened today, I think it well to describe the method through which the
message was received.

It is my custom to place the psychic in my study in the light while I at the end of a wire nearly two hundred feel long sit in my daughter's studio with an amplifier before me. At the other end of the wire the psychic sits holding a microphone. The wire is a one-way telephone, and the psychic has no means of knowing, normally, what I am doing or the questions I am asking. I mention these conditions that you may understand how all deception is eliminated from whatever the messages may be.

My assistant in this work is my friend, Henry B. Fuller, who died about five years ago. No doubt you knew him or know of him. He is a keen, witty and widely read mind. He acts as "guide" or "gate-keeper."

Like many other similar experimenters, we have occasionally asked Fuller for news of Amelia Earhart, but up to within a few days ago, he has regularly answered, "She is still in the body." Last Monday, he said, "She is over here." And yesterday, Thursday, the 5th, he whispered in an excited tone, "I have information about her. She will speak to you tomorrow, Friday morning."

This morning I placed the psychic as usual in an easy chair in my study with the microphone in her hands. I then laid a wire running from this microphone under a closed door across a hall under another closed door into a room on the extreme end of the house where I had installed the amplifier. The cord connecting the microphone in the psychic's hand and the amplifier on the table where I was seated is nearly a hundred feet long. I changed from the studio to this room because in this way I could use a wire solid throughout its length. I am enclosing the results of the two sittings.

Very sincerely yours,

1. George Palmer Putnam II (1887–1950), Earhart's husband, formerly a member of the family firm G. P. Putnam's Sons, at the time vice president of Brewer & Warren Publ. Co., and author of several books, among them *The Last Flight of Amelia Earhart* (1937). Garland enclosed a five-page, double-spaced typewritten transcript of the séance with Earhart, dated 6 August 1937. In this séance, "Earhart" notes that her plane ran out of fuel and she and her navigator, Fred Noonan, crashed on a reef located "186° E. 15°." Howland Island is located at 0.48N 176.38W. Scrawled at the top are the words, struck out, "Duplicate" and "Not Sent"; and finally, "Letter returned." Putnam evidently took Garland's report seriously; in a letter to Mary Isabel dated "Tuesday" (Hunt), Garland noted that Putnam accompanied him on a cross-hunting expedition.

2045 DeMille Drive
Hollywood, California

August 7, 1937

Dear Mr. Latham:

I was greatly disappointed this morning by reason of a failure to receive any reply from you or from the office.[1] I am particularly anxious to close this matter at once for a very strange and exciting thing has happened to us, and this you must *treat with the utmost secrecy and care.* It has dynamite in it.

Day before yesterday, Fuller came to us and excitedly said, "Amelia Earhart is here, and will speak to you." I had the receiver in the guest room at the end of fifty feet of wire with the psychic in her usual place in the corner of my study. She was absolutely out of sight and hearing of what went on. She had nothing to do with it normally. Nevertheless, Miss Earhart spoke to me and expressed her wish to have her husband notified of her communication to me. After a few minutes the power weakened and at Fuller's suggestion we moved the receiver back into the room adjoining my study. There I was able to hear her perfectly and she told us very briefly but clearly exactly what happened. She wanted her husband and her mother informed of her story, and I have sent a transcript of what happened to Mr. George Palmer Putnam in care of the Century Club. If you think it of sufficient importance you might see him and talk the whole matter over with him. It has nothing to do with our book necessarily, but it might go into a chapter which I call "Talks with the Invisibles."[2]

What Mrs. Williams and I are anxious to avoid at this stage of our work is newspaper publicity, and I hope you will consider this absolutely confidential, letting no one know what has happened. Undoubtedly we shall have further statements from Miss Earhart and perhaps definite confirmation of the latitude of the island on which she died. (Also longitude) It may be that Mr. Putnam will talk the matter over with you and that you will advise us just how to proceed.

The book could go to the printers now if necessary, but we should have all the illustrations returned to us by air mail so that we can fit them into the text. In case you decline the book I hope you will be good enough to send the manuscript over to Dutton or to Harpers.

Very sincerely yours,
Hamlin Garland

The Memoirist: 1930–1940 395

1. Latham declined *The Mystery of the Buried Crosses* in a letter dated 6 August 1937. Although he thought the story was "exciting" and "absorbing," he wrote, "we simply don't believe in it. We do not know what the explanation is, but that you have really established communication with the departed, we gravely question. We think the book would be greeted in two ways—respectful skepticism from those who know and love you and your work, and entirely disrespectful guffaws from those who are no respectors of persons, however distinguished. It is our honest conviction that the publication of the book will do you no good."

2. Garland's account of the Earhart séance does not appear in the book.

3. Written in the upper left corner.

367. to Constance Garland Harper   tls, Hunt

2045 DeMille Drive
Hollywood, California

Wednesday. [11 August 1937]

Dear Connie:

Your anxious letter is here and I like to have you worried about me but I dont think you need to be. I am too old to care very much for what happens to me now. I can see that I made a mistake in the title and the foreword. It CAN be made a mystery story, taking out of it any direct argument for the theory of survival. *It might be that in this form Latham would reconsider.* The title THE MYSTERY OF THE BURIED CROSSES would give the key to the whole book. It could remain an attempt on my part to solve a mystery and leave it at the point where I am convinced as to the crosses and where they came from. Why not see Mr. Latham again and talk it over with him. Get his advice about whom to see next. FIRST OF ALL change that title and cut out that foreword. Tell him that I am going over the ms with the new thought in mind. I can shape it up so that he will not object to its fantastic character. Try to salvage the book for Macmillans. We should not go elsewhere if we can meet their objections.

Ask him about Edward Martin who still reads for Scribner I believe. He would understand it and be helpful in case we decide to offer it to Macmillans. Ask him about McCrae of Duttons also. I shall write him my self today or tomorrow, addressing it to Onteora.[1]

Your lawyer called up and we are wondering if he is a bit anxious about your overstaying your leave of absence.

I shall ask Latham to bring the ms up to O. with him and you can then
talk it over with Mebbs. Better be very careful about who sees it.

Christine fell on your staircase and is injured but the policy covers it.

Daddy.

1. John Macrae, the president of E. P. Dutton & Co., accepted the book for publication in a letter dated 14 June 1938. Latham, like Garland, maintained a home in Onteora.

368. to Robert Underwood Johnson   als, Am Acad

2045 DeMille Drive
Hollywood, California

Sept. 7. [1937]

Dear Johnson:

The news of Hadley's death deepens my disheartenment over the making of the Academy.[1] With a dozen vacant chairs to be filled and the pornographic group crowding to be nominated, I see the character of the Academy entirely changed. I am too old and too far away to do anything, in this critical time, except vote against the men I distrust. Why should we elect Lewis after his contemptuous public references to the Academy?[2] Why should any of those men without respect for training and tradition be welcomed into an institution which stands for just these ideals? Merely because a man wins wide acclaim and much money by pornographic fiction, I see no reason for his nomination to membership in an organization dedicated to good art and scholarship. They have ridiculed the Academy for ten years—why nominate them to a membership which they despise?—It merely gives them a chance to repeat their slurs—I sent in a list of those I am willing to vote for.

Faithfully,
Hamlin Garland

Personal[3]

1. Henry K. Hadley (1871–1937), composer and conductor.

2. Sinclair Lewis had received the Nobel Prize for literature in 1930. During his acceptance speech he had pointedly derided the National Institute and the American Academy and named twenty-one writers he thought more deserving of membership than those who currently occupied chairs. "While most of our few giants are excluded,"

he remarked, "the Academy does have room to include three extraordinarily bad poets, two very melodramatic and insignificant playwrights, two gentlemen who are known only because they are university presidents, a man who was thirty years ago known as a rather clever humorous draughtsman, and several gentlemen of whom—I sadly confess my ignorance—I have never heard" (quoted in *Portraits from the American Academy and Institute of Arts and Letters*, ed. Lillian B. Miller and Nancy Johnson [Washington: National Portrait Gallery, 1987], p. 78). In 1935 Lewis accepted membership in the Institute and, in December 1937, election to the Academy.

3. Written in the upper left corner.

369. to Van Wyck Brooks

als, U Penn

2045 DeMille Drive
Hollywood, California

Dec. 5. 37.

My Dear Critic:

To have you pause in the midst of your colossal job and write a letter by your own hand, is the finest compliment I have had in the last ten years. I can not see how you find time to read or provide gray matter for remembering the books required by your job. To vitalize and condense these books of the past as you must do is an almost superhuman task—and yet you talk of reading something more of my writing!—I wish I could talk with you of Howells—and Mrs. Howells. No one knows Howells who does not know of his loyal devotion to his wife. She was a lovely blue-eyed fair girl but after the birth of Mildred she became an invalid. When I knew her first she was a tiny figure, almost always with a shawl or scarf over her shoulders, very pale, with a piquant wrinkled face. She was a wraith physically but with gay, humorous outlook on life and literature. For some strange reason she liked me, and once Howells said, "Mrs. Howells sees very few people—but she always wants to see you." Her invalidism prevented Howells from entertaining or being entertained. She had an acute intelligence and loved to have him read to her. He read to her every day or discussed with her the books they had both read. She was eager to know all that was going on in the world she had renounced—and this aided him in his work for he was called upon to report what he had seen and to describe the people he had met.

He was infinitely patient with her. She was always asking him to close the window or to open it. One moment the room was chilly the next moment it was too warm but he rose each time to her wish without vexation. She was always social in her proclivities and loved to discuss social leaders and aspiring debutantes but she was also a lover of all forms of art and could talk of painters and sculptors as well as of authors and she wandered about galleries with her husband so long as her health would permit—avoiding the crowds always. She filled a large part of his thought. She was always his care. These facts are essential to an understanding of him. Her wit, her disconnected intuitive flashes of wisdom aided him in some degree but she kept him from mingling with men during her later years.—I can understand this better now that my own wife has been an invalid for seven years.

Wister made a good job of the address but he didnt quite state Howells point against the school of writers who made of fornication the road to success.[1] He turned away from that subject because it was banal, worn-out. He felt that in writing of illicit sexual affairs—he would be merely re-writing French or English fiction and drama. He was interested in themes characteristic of the new world. Seduction, arson, murder did not interest him as themes. He admired Mary Wilkins because she did not use these age-old themes. His humor was not concerned with subjects "below the belt" for the reason that they were cheap and commonplace—"monkey business" which as evolutionists we should leave behind—or below. Henry James in *his* way put those themes aside.—

Sometime I hope we shall be able to talk of Howells. I wrote an article on it once for the *Forum* or some other review while Howells was alive to read it[2]—I think I sent you a copy—It is true that Howells and James influenced me but I think the evolutionists are more responsible for my "puritanism" as some people call it. I admit that we stem from the monkeys but I dont believe in going back to them—or to goats and dogs.

Howells is our social historian for the period between 1865 and 1905— He cant be left out even by the pornographic advocates. No answer to this letter is required or expected.

With ever growing admiration
Hamlin Garland.

1. Owen Wister spoke at the Howells Centenary Meeting of the National Institute on 10 March 1937. In a letter dated 18 November 1937, Brooks had expressed a wish to hear a "longer account" of Garland's friendship with Howells than was offered in Garland's tributory letter read at the Institute meeting.

2. Garland may refer to one of the following: "Mr. Howells's Latest Novels," *New England Magazine* 2 (1890): 243–50; "Sanity in Fiction," *North American Review* 176

(1903): 336–48; or "William Dean Howells: Master Craftsman," *Art World* 1 (1917): 411–12.

370. to Eldon Hill

tls, Miami U

2045 DeMille Drive
Hollywood, California

Dec. 18. 37.

Dear Mr. Hill:

It is not easy to trace the influences which formed my method. I think Eugene Véron's book on Esthetics and Max Nordau's "Conventional Lies" influenced me more than any book of James.[1] Véron was especially in line with Howells' thought. I was influenced without doubt by the introduction to Olive Schreiner's "African Farm."[2] Whitman also instructed me in some ways. James influenced me in a *negative* way. His internationalism irritated me and rather appalled me and I became still more convinced that I should continue to do my work as a writer specifically of the New World.

I think of my readers as small circles of friendly but critical elderly folk. Although badly scattered they are in a sense neighbors. I must assume this personal interest in me and mine or I could not go on with my quiet books which have no news value whatsoever.—When it comes to technical matters however, I fear I do not take anybody into my workshop. I work very largely to please myself. I *enjoy* the hours I lavish on revision. I am like a piano player who practices six hours a day in order to bring his performance up to his own ideal. I do not try for the "precious" but for the lucid and the pictorial.

I hope these answers will help you.

H.G.

Ask any questions you would like to have answered.

1. Garland's copy of Eugène Véron's *Aesthetics* (1879) is heavily annotated and was, Donald Pizer suggests, the "most significant" contemporary critical work upon Garland's developing synthesis of impressionism and local color. Max Nordau's critique of marriage made for economic reasons in *The Conventional Lies of Our Civilization* (1887) influenced Garland's portrayal of marriage in "The Land of the Straddle-Bug" (1894) and *Rose of Dutcher's Coolly* (1895). See Pizer, *Hamlin Garland's Early Work and Career*, pp. 21–23, 151–52.

2. Olive Schreiner (1855–1920) was a South African novelist and essayist whose first book, *The Story of an African Farm* (1883), won acclaim for its depiction of the "New Woman." In the preface, Schreiner critiques the traditional romance plot, advocating instead "the method of life we all lead" in which "nothing can be prophesied" and in which conclusions develop from "the players."

371. to Eldon Hill   tls, Miami U

2045 DeMille Drive
Hollywood, California

Jan. 25. [1938]

My Dear Young Critic:

I do not remember hearing Melvilles name mentioned by anyone in my youth. I knew of him by reason of Hawthorne's description of him as a neighbor in the Berkshires. Very slight mention of him was made when he died. I didnt even know that he was still alive when I was studying in Boston.

I greatly admired passages in MOBY DICK but felt bored by the lumbering apostrophes. They were absurdly out of character in the book. I felt that it greatly needed blue-pencilling. I feel that now more than ever. I did not read his other books. I think him greatly over-rated by the *claque* which arose a few years ago. I am bored by Mumford's book.[1] I find even "Benito Cereno" hard reading. He had no sense of proportion. I find him worth reading only in spots. When he is walking on the deck of a boat or on the earth he is often vigorous and direct but at other times he just does not get clear of his cloud of pseudo philosophy. I can imagine that he bored Hawthorne by his vaporings. The man had power and insight but he never acquired the art of writing a sustained narrative or essay.

All the hullabaloo by the men in New York was just one of those sudden enthusiasms which arise for no solid reason whatsoever. It has all died away and will not be renewed. Melville was an extremely interesting character but he was not a great writer. He was best when he dealt with what he had seen and heard.

H.G.

P.S. It may be that "Typee" and "Omoo" are simpler and more direct in expression. I'll try them out sometime.

1. Lewis Mumford's critical biography *Herman Melville* (1929).

372. to F. Carleton Mabee Jr.tlc, USC

Mar. 19. 38

Dear Mr. Mabee:[1]

I am highly sympathetic to your work in reference to B.O. Flower and his ARENA for I considered THE ARENA and its editor of very great influence at the date you mention. It is true that it later fell into other hands and suffered a decline. I have many letters from Flower and I have very vivid memories of his kindness and sympathy with my work. I have the wish to aid you and perhaps I can. You may ask me any question you wish and I will reply to them as best I can.

The backer of the ARENA was a noble woman of elderly appearance when I saw her. Her name was Reed and she lived in Jamaica Plain, a suburb in Boston. The chief cause of Flowers financial worries was a young woman in his office who mis-appropriated funds. She was a very smart Irish girl whom he trusted with the entire management at the time when I knew him. Later several others came in as partners and all were of doubtful value. Flower himself was of no business ability. He was an idealist. He lived for the good of the world. I never knew a man of higher altruistic aims. He made the ARENA a very real arena for debate on all serious phases of life and literature. I hope you will call upon me if you think I can aid.

Very Sincerely Yours,

1. A graduate student working with Henry Steele Commager at Columbia University, Mabee had written Garland, 12 March 1938, for information about the organization of the *Arena* and its change in editorship in 1896. Garland's carbon is typed on the back of Mabee's letter.

373. to Eldon Hilltls, Miami U

March 28, 1938

Dear Mr. Hill:

I am glad you raised the question about my GRANT.[1] So far as I knew at the time and so far as I know now, it is a new form. Being a novelist, I said to McClure "I want full leave to write this biography as if Grant were the character in a novel. He had no prevision of what was coming to him any more than the character in a novel has. To say as so many biographers do 'You never would suspect that this man chopping cordwood in the suburbs of St Louis would in less than three years command a million men' is to give away your climax. I shall write of Grant as he felt and acted at each significant period of his life."

The firm gave a reluctant consent to this and I carried on my plan with most of the narrative. Furthermore, I decided to go to living sources. I say in my preface, that I travelled thousands of miles and interviewed hundreds of people who knew Grant. Refer to this preface and confirm this. I found that all the other biographies had used the same material over and over. They cribbed from one another. None of them told the continuous story of his life from boyhood to his death. — I read contemporary newspapers also, two from the East, two from New York, two from Chicago and two from the south. In short I acted as judge and jury over the material which I thus gained, so putting one biased opinion over against the other. I found that the closer I got to Grant, the simpler the problem. He was a very plain, unassuming man with an enormous sub-conscious endowment.

You may say that no one influenced me except in a negative way. I carefully avoided all the conventional biographic forms. You are right in saying that I did not get the credit due me for the novel form in which I cast my material. It is not fictionalized in any way except in its form. It is the story of Grant.

H.G.

P.S. I can illustrate what I mean by saying that several people wrote in to the magazine saying, "O why did you end the installment at such a sad point." I replied, of course by saying, "That is the way Grant felt at that time. He didnt know that he was to be Commander of all the Union Armies. He was concerned with making a living for his wife and babies."

I also tried to strip out all the evidence which had its origin after the fact. All prophecy by his neighbors I disallowed. It is easy to predict that he was to be a great man after he had proved it, and much of the comment was of that sort. Nevertheless, the comment of his neighbors at St. Louis, at Galena and at Detroit had great value. In the same way I made allowances for the political enemies he made, and for those writers who love to smirch a great man just to show his kinship to them. Out of it all I think I made a very real Grant.

Ask any questions you like—H.G.

1. In a letter of 22 March 1938, Hill had asked whether Garland, in preparation for writing his *Ulysses S. Grant*, had read other biographies, of Grant or of others, for "'inspiration' and guidance." Garland's extensive notes and records of interviews, comprising hundreds of pages in addition to fourteen notebooks, are extant in the Garland Papers (USC).

374. to August Derleth   tls, Wis HS

2045 DeMille Drive
Hollywood, California

April 8. 38.

Dear Mr. Derleth:

Your publisher has sent to me a copy of your book of poems but I am of the opinion that it came by your order and I write to acknowledge its receipt. I must be honest with you and say that they do not seem poems to me but poetic *thoughts*. I am too old and too old-fashioned in my tastes to welcome these bizarre forms. You may call me any hard names you feel like doing but I wish your printer had at least put your lines in a less "arty" fashion.[1] I appreciate your thinking of me and regret that I am not able to write of the book as I suppose you hoped I would be able to do.

Hamlin Garland

1. The "'arty' fashion" to which Garland objected in *Hawk on the Wind* (1938) was the irregular indentation and spacing of lines.

375. to August Derleth   tls, Wis HS

2045 DeMille Drive
Hollywood, California

April. 16. [1938]

Dear Mr. Derleth:

Your letter and its enclosure, carried me back to the time when I, too, had vast dreams of literary attainment and I hope you will achieve at least a part of what you have definitely announced.[1] I recall spreading out before Howells a scheme for a novel of most ambitious scope and of his quiet remark, "Dont be surprised if you lose interest in it." He was a wise old head! I did lose interest in it and never even seriously began it. Other

more pressing themes came into my thinking. I mention this as a warning. It does not do to lay out too big a program. Frank Norris never quite
realized *his* dream.

I have given up reading fiction. I find it so pre-occupied with the animal side of sex life that I do not venture to open any modern novel. It
would seem that virtuous women no longer interest novelists or dramatists. I am bored by the glorified prostitute and the girl libertine—bored
and saddened. I hope you can achieve a measure of success without "going Hollywood."

I am touched by your evident respect for me and I thank you for its
expression but I am now but an old fellow just ready to step off into
the Fourth Dimension, not worth your consideration. My judgments no
longer count for anything. My books are fading chronicles of a simpler
time. I am wholly out of key with this jazz age and its shameless women.
The radio and the moving picture depress as well as irritate me. I turn
these agencies over to those who find joy in them.

Once in a while I find something in the motion picture to rejoice in.
MAY-TIME, SEQUOIA, CONQUEST, PASTEUR, give me hope for this art for at
its best it is an art—They restore my faith in human nature.[2]

With Sincere Best Wishes,
Hamlin Garland

1. Derleth's letter and enclosure have not survived.

2. The films Garland refers to are *Maytime* (directed by Robert Z. Leonard, MGM,
1937), *Sequoia* (directed by Chester M. Franklin, MGM, 1934), *Conquest* (directed by
Clarence Brown, MGM, 1937), and *The Story of Louis Pasteur* (directed by William Die-
terle, Warner, 1935).

376. to George Steele Seymour and Flora Warren Seymour

tls, Knox

2045 DeMille Drive
Hollywood, California

April 22.38.

Dear Seymours:

My daughter and I have been over-hauling a mass of my mss and find
them in confusion worse confounded by reason of having been moved
two or three times. I cant offer a clean and complete ms of any kind but
if you would like a handful of this "mess" I will send it on to you. I have

two or three type-written copies with a million scrawled corrections in or on them. They may interest a few enthusiasts who like to see how an ineffective writer works. I shall send these mss to various of my friends and to certain libraries. By the way, they are talking in Wisconsin of making my old West Salem home a kind of memorial to me and my father's generation of Pioneers.[1] They will want some of my mss no doubt. I shall of course co-operate with them as far as propriety will allow. The State Historical Society has taken it up.

Let me know just what kind of ms you would like best—if you had your druthers, as Riley's characters used to say.

We are still talking of driving on to Chicago. If we do we may invade your peaceful home for a day or two but it is all so uncertain that you need not count on it.

Very Sincerely Yours,
Hamlin Garland

P.S. My daughter has also been copying all my poems old and new. Macmillans are disposed to publish them. Would you and Flora like to read them? They might amuse you because of their difference!

1. The Garland Homestead, now restored and maintained by the West Salem Historical Society, became a National Historic Landmark in 1973.

377. to George Steele Seymour and Flora Warren Seymour

tls, Knox

2045 DeMille Drive
Hollywood, California

May. 22nd. [1938]

Dear Seymours:

Duttons postponement of the date of publication has changed my whole summer. I shall remain here and put more work on the MS. It is probable that they will want me in the east early in September but I welcome the extra time on the book. It is to be made an important sequel to my FORTY YEARS and I want to add to its scope.

Macrae is in Canada just now and I must await his return for further instructions. This may be my last published book and I want to make it as scientific as possible. I am sorry not to have a visit with old friends in Chicago but that will come later.

A good friend of mine[1] has volunteered to sort out my MSS and there will be some for you when the time comes for distribution.

My Best Wishes to you both,
H.G.

1. Eldon Hill.

378. to Clarence Brown

als, usc

2045 DeMille Drive
Hollywood, California

May. 27—38.

Dear Mr. Brown:

My wife and I are moved to express to you our high admiration of "Conquest" which we have seen five or six times.[1] We regard it as one of the best motion picture plays we have ever seen. We quite agree with the committee which gave you honorable distinction for this work. We found it quite perfect in every detail of scene, costume and sequence of events. We wonder if you selected Miss Garbo for the part of Marie Walewesca? She gave a most beautiful and subtle characterization of this woman of whose life I have made especial study. I have never seen a more intuitive performance. Boyer was entirely satisfactory as Napoleon but Miss Garbo's Marie is unforgettable. My daughters also join in applauding this great picture.

Very sincerely yours
Hamlin Garland

1. Clarence Brown's film of Napoleon, starring Charles Boyer as Napoleon and Greta Garbo as the Polish countess, appeared in 1937. Among Brown's (1890–1987) other films are *Anna Christie* (1930), *Ah, Wilderness* (1935), *The Human Comedy* (1943), and *National Velvet* (1944).

379. to Howard Mumford Jones

als, usc

2045 DeMille Drive
Hollywood, California

June 28—38.

Dear Howard Mulford Jones:

I must applaud your out-spoken article in the *Atlantic.*[1] It is very much the kind of article I would write if I were younger. It is of no value for an old man to say the things you so vigorously express. I am appalled and saddened by the nudity, crudity and lewdity of the novels and plays of today. You put the case when you say this is not America—it is only some youngster's notion of shocking the public into buying his book or seeing his play. More power to your type-writer!

It is amusing to find *you*—a man of half my age—reading detective fiction as a relief from prostitutes and fornicators for that is precisely what I have been doing for twenty years.

My best wishes for your future.

Your ancient friend—
Hamlin Garland.

1. Howard Mumford Jones (1892–1980), Garland's former secretary during the composition of *Son*, became a professor of comparative literature at the University of Texas (1919–25), of English at North Carolina (1925–30) and at Michigan (1930–36), and of humanities at Harvard (1936–1960); and was the author of more than twenty books, including *Life of Moses Coit Tyler* (1933) and *Theory of American Literature* (1948). In "Relief from Murder" (*Atlantic Monthly* 162 [July 1938]: 79–85), Jones rails against the trend of sensationalizing murder, rape, and violence in recent novels.

380. to Grace Vanamee

tls, Am Acad

2045 DeMille Drive
Hollywood, California

July. 22. 38.

And now Wister is gone! I hope I shall live long enough to have one more meeting with my fellows at the Academy, and strength enough to read my paper. I am giving much thought to its general character. How would it do to make it somewhat reminiscent? I could call it "Past and Present Fashions In American Literature" or something to suggest the effect of the newspapers, the radio and the screen on our fiction and drama.[1] If my brain holds out I want to write something that will hit hard. I could begin on the reminiscent vein picturing the conditions of 1885 as a contrast to those of fifty years later. I could then pass to a very frank confession of my dislike of jazzed biography, pornographic fiction and moronic radio programs, all in relation to the purposes of the Foundation, as I under stand them. As I am about to pass into the Fourth Dimension it does not matter what the panderers of today think of me.

I shall write the address, at least in outline, in the next two weeks in order to make sure of it before any sickness or trouble makes it difficult for me to think. If you can suggest a better title or line of argument I shall be glad to have you write me about it.

Very Sincerely Yours,
Hamlin Garland

1. Owen Wister had died on 21 July 1938. In a letter of 14 July 1938, Vanamee had conveyed to Garland the invitation to deliver the Edwin Blashfield Foundation Paper at the Academy's annual meeting on 10 November. The purpose of the foundation, Vanamee reminded Garland, was "'to assist the Academy in an effort to determine its duty regarding both the preservation of the English language in its beauty and integrity, and its cautious enrichment by such terms as grow out of modern conditions.'" Vanamee then suggested a topic, "'Sanity in Literature,' or if you wish to make it more startling, 'Insanity in Literature.'" The address was published as "Literary Fashions Old and New," *Think* 4 (March 1939): 14, 24, 27.

381. to Eldon Hill tls, Miami U

2045 DeMille Drive
Hollywood, California

Aug. 2. 38.

Dear Young Advocate:

I do not object to your notifying the Colleges that I am going east for the first time in four years, and that I may be induced to appear at some of these schools but you and they should bear in mind my years and the uncertainties involved. Furthermore I should like to have you tell them about the film which will divide the time with me. The spectators like my humorous running comment on the pictures and it makes my program rather more attractive and easier for me.

One other point; I think I shall agree to stop only on my route. I could do one or two, possibly, near Chicago. The Northwestern, or Illinois. All must be *easy* for me.

I am grateful for your interest and hope you may be rewarded in some way. If I should stop at any point on my way back, I might be permitted to use the ms of my address to the Academy but what the committees really want is a last view of the Old Trailer. They will not expect much of me. I may read something as Frost[1] does and let it go at that. I shall ask a considerable fee, however.

Those studies which I sent to you, are not of much value.[2] They sound to me like the re-echoes of Van Doren and other New York critics, who read only one or two of my books.

Very Sincerely Yours,
Hamlin Garland

Your wife's piece was neatly done and delightfully humorous.[3]

1. The poet Robert Frost.

2. Garland probably sent to Hill two master's theses, one of which was Jean Hill Parker's "Hamlin Garland, The Pioneer," University of Southern California, 1938.

3. Mary Hill's "piece" has not been identified.

382. to Louise Ranney

als, Newberry

The Century Association
7 West Forty-Third Street
New York

Nov. 3. [1938]

Dear Miss Ranney:

My publishers feel that to find that box of letters would be the most conclusive test of my psychic.[1] I hope you will spare no effort to discover it—I shall arrive in Chicago on Sat. the 12th and if you chance to be coming to the city—I would be delighted to have you take tea with me and report—If I can aid by going up to your home on Sunday fore-noon I will do that.—

I enclose an envelope for reply—

Hamlin Garland.

I have found many letters from your uncle here—in the Academy.

1. Garland refers to the letters he wrote to Henry B. Fuller, Ranney's uncle, which had become misplaced. Garland recounts the psychic aid which led to the discovery of the letters in *The Mystery of the Buried Crosses*, pp. 295–96.

> 2045 DeMille Drive,
> Hollywood, California.
>
> December 6, 1938.

Dear Putnam,

My wife and daughters are inclined to consider sending to you the larger part of my collection of letters, autographed books and manuscripts. The Academy wants them, of course, but I fear few would ever see them there. Furthermore, it has no nooks in which students could work. Now, how would it do to send all my autographed books to the Academy and all my letters and other material for a possible biographer to you?

As I told you, I have here nearly one hundred notebooks, some forty diaries, and two thousand letters. Some of these letters are salable—letters from Barrie, Kipling, Shaw, Conrad and others are in demand. In addition, I have nearly one hundred letters from Howells, seventy from Burroughs, eight or ten from Frank Norris, Stephen Crane and others of that period. In fact, I have letters from nearly all of the leading writers of the nineties and the early part of the century.

I wish I could go over the whole problem with you in Washington, and it is possible that I may come on again in April. If I do, you can then show me the alcove in which you would store "Hamlin Garland's Papers".

I am wondering how permanent such an alcove would be. Is there not danger that some future librarian would split it up and scatter the material among other alcoves?

Question Number Two: Would you like to have me include my autographed books? Many of these are by men and women partly or wholly forgotten now, but they have historic value nevertheless.

Question Number Three: What about photographs? Would they have a place in such an alcove?

Question Number Four: IMPORTANT. Must I list and arrange this material before I ship it, or does your force do this kind of work for this kind of a transfer?

If I am to turn my material over to your organization, I feel that it should be done while you are there. Shall we take a chance on our both being alive on March twenty-fifth, and defer decision till then?

In the meantime, I wish you would tell me a little more definitely what you consider most appropriate for your alcove. I will then make as complete a list as I can and send it on.

Finally, will you not as a friend and not as a government official, advise me what to do with all this material? I have failed to mention that I have some tons of first, second and third draft manuscript. Shall I send some part of this material—I mean these manuscripts—to Chicago, to New York, and some to the Academy? The University here would like something out of my collection and so would the Huntington Library.

This is very serious business for me. It means emptying my shelves and cabinets of all the material which is a part of my life and which is, in a sense, a legacy for my daughters. It is so puzzling that I shrink from a decision.

You are very good to give thought to my small problem and I am presuming on it a little farther. It will soon be April and then a decision can be made.

Most sincerely yours,

1. Putnam was eager to see Garland donate his papers to the Library of Congress and advised him on 13 December 1938 that while the Library was eager to have his letters, notebooks, diaries, photographs, and selected manuscripts, he thought the autographed books should go to the American Academy of Arts and Letters. Putnam evaded Garland's question about the permanence of a "Garland Alcove," and suggested they talk the matter over when Garland got to Washington. A later letter suggests that Garland was more interested in selling his collection than donating it, for Putnam informed him, 19 January 1940, that the library lacked the funds to purchase his papers and he advised him to sell if there were buyers who wanted his material.

384. to Van Wyck Brooks
als, U Penn

2045 DeMille Drive
Hollywood, California

Dec. 27—38.

Dear Brooks:

I early recognized Mary Wilkins' quality 1885.[1] Her two volumes of stories are the most original character sketches in our literature. They are, in a sense, miraculous. It is easy to write stories of copulation, any one can do that and most young writers do—but Mary Wilkins presented elderly people or young people in new and puzzling relationships. She kept clear of all the cheap stuff. She never repeats herself. Her characters while typical are also individual. Her stories are humorous but never comic or malicious. She understood her characters so well that she had no need to pity

them or laugh at them. They just were! I read and re-read these amazing
sketches, appreciating them all the more now in this age of nudity and
jazz. I knew Mary well (as you know) and have some letters from her
although I saw her so often in the nineties that letters were not nescessary. I was delighted to be chosen to present to her, at the Academy—the
Howells Medal for fiction, and I was glad of the opportunity to make a
short statement of her claims to an enduring place in our fiction. I sat
beside her at lunch and while she was old and infirm, an occasional flash
of quaint humor came into her eyes. She was over-whelmed by the honor
we all joined in giving her, and appeared a bit dazed. Why did we wait so
long before presenting this medal? She died soon after—.

My "Mystery of the Buried Crosses" has gone to the printer and will
be out in March. I confess that this M.S. so absorbed my attention for two
years I have at the moment a sense of emptiness and futility. I have gone
back to my "Fortunate Exiles"—Vol. V. of the Literary Log-book series,[2]
but I can not say I have regained "the drive" I once had with it.—I am
boasting of your visit to me and saying that you are coming to California
within the year. I hope you do. There is a room here for you and your
delightful wife—

Take care of those eyes!—You have an enormous job to finish. Send
me a better photo than the one in your garden. I have bragged of your
good looks!—

Hamlin Garland.

1. Brooks had noted, in a letter of 14 December 1938, that he was at work on a section
about Freeman for his *New England: Indian Summer, 1865–1915* (1940).

2. Garland never published this final volume, and it remains in manuscript in the
Garland Papers (item #5).

385. to Van Wyck Brooks als, U Penn

2045 DeMille Drive
Hollywood, California

Jan. 20. 39.

Dear Brooks:

It would be grand to have you and your delightful wife in our guest
room and we shall definitely hope for it. Another of my enthusiasms John
Bradley will return at some time during the summer. His "Parade of the

Living" and "Patterns of Survival" are great books—great in their relentless logic and grace of style. They are books I'd like you to taste—I cant ask you to *read* any thing outside your required reading. He is nominally a geologist but he is much more than an ologist of any sort. You'll be called upon to meet him if you come to visit us.

By this time the Howells material is in your hands[1]—I hope it may give you a hint of something worthy of being added to your wide and deep knowledge of him—I forget whether I told you the story of my "Mystery of the Buried Crosses"—but it is in process of being published by Dutton. Acklom has it in hand.[2] He read the M.S. three times—and went over it a fourth time with me. He believes it to be essentially true at most points. I do not pretend to solve the problem—I merely present it. My chief "guide" was our friend Fuller whose whisper I caught on microphone (in full day-light) and with whom I conversed as if over the 'phone. It is the doggonedest yarn you ever heard but it happened!—It may be a sensation or a dud. John Macrae likes it and will give it a show.—I appreciate your advice about my "papers"—and I have just had a third letter from Putnam concerning them. Meantime a part of them are a peripatetic exhibit among the libraries of the mid-west universities. They are doing some good in this way. Did I tell you that my daughter and I are doing some work for the *Rotarian*? I have written of Whitman and Howells and she has made some capital drawings to accompany them. Case the editor—a fine fellow—is in Tucson for his lung's sake and in almost daily touch with us. I met him in Santá Fé—His home and office is in Chicago but he cant stand the winters there—.[3] I await your chapter on Howells with the greatest interest.

H.G.

1. Garland had sent Brooks his collection of some 130 letters from Howells as well as offprints of his various articles about Howells. Brooks devoured the material and was so fascinated that he interrupted his work on Sarah Orne Jewett to return to the Howells chapters of *New England: Indian Summer*, which he had put aside due to the complexity of the subject. As he explained to Garland in his reply of 27 January 1939, "The letters and your articles brought the whole subject to life in my mind and made me feel again how much I love that man."

2. George Moreby Acklom, Garland's editor at E. P. Dutton & Co.

3. "Let the Sunshine In," *Rotarian* 55 (October 1939): 8–11. Leland Case, the editor, had solicited the article and suggested the topic.

386. to Eldon Hill

tls, Miami U

Jan. 22. 39.

Dear Mr. Hill:

No, I did not discuss the play THE GREAT DIVIDE with Moody but in our trip into the mountains we talked much of the material which the High Country offered.[1] I was certain that it would come out later — he was so moved by it all. He was in truth exalted by the grandeur of the mountain landscape.

With regard to my work in promoting the native drama, it is worthy of note, I think, that I drew up the first suggestion for an "Independent Theater" in Boston, and that for nearly twenty years I worked with Howells, Herne and Brander Matthews along these lines. By way of articles[,] lectures and letters to the *Transcript* and other papers I clamored for a drama that should be true to our way of life and be filled by characters of our place and time. That I had some effect on the progress of the playwright is probable. — I think I sent you a copy of that first leaflet concerning the Independent Theater movement in Boston.

I enclose the copy of a letter which I wrote to Van Doren (but which I decided not to send), which expresses something which is rather vital. Return it to me.

Very Sincerely Yours,

H.G.

If you have time look up the *Circle Magazine* for a story of Oklahoma — about 1907–8 (never in book) and Belford's Magazine — 1888 for very early article on Wisconsin River life.[2]

1. Hill had been inspired by a talk by Arthur Hobson Quinn and was at work on an article concerning Garland's efforts to promote American drama. He had asked specifically if Garland had discussed William Vaughn Moody's *The Great Divide* with the playwright while Moody was drafting the play (Hill to Garland, 16 January 1939).

2. Garland may refer to "In That Far Land," *Circle* 2 (October-November 1907): 204–5, 298–300, or to "The Healer of Mogalyon," *Circle* 3 (March 1908): 140–45. "A Common Case" appeared in *Belford's* 1 (July 1888): 188–99, and was reprinted as "Before the Low Green Door" in *Wayside Courtships* (1898).

The Memoirist: 1930–1940 415

387. to Van Wyck Brooks

als, U Penn

2045 DeMille Drive
Hollywood, California

Jan 31—39

Dear Critic:

The Howells' papers came safely today and I was greatly pleased by your letter concerning them. I was not at all sure that they would prove of value to you. I was apprehensive that they might prove repetitious. To have you say that they made Howells "come alive" to you is highly gratifying. I *was* astonished to have them come back so soon. I expected you to keep them for a month at least.

I never met Sarah Orne Jewett but I had some correspondence with her. I liked her work and admired her at a distance. She was a handsome woman—I believe—Mary Wilkins was a shy little blonde girl when I knew her first. She was delightfully humorous but I think of her as always sitting when talking with me. She kept in the corner—or in the background watching with keen eyes what went on around her. Her companion, a spinster slightly older than she, told a group of us one night that she often "pushed Mary Ellen into her study and locked the door. Mary composed her story in her head—writing it out was just a chore."—I recall this very clearly for it was directly opposed to my way. I had only a vague notion of what I wanted to do—the pen running over the paper put my imagination into action. There was a mysterious quality in Mary. There is the unexpectedness of life in her stories—I hope you do manage to come out this summer. We'd like to show you about. We have a new Pontiac car and the best driver in the county—my daughter Isabel. You'll want to see the Fair but we shall want a very real visit with you here.

Very faithfully yours
Hamlin Garland

388. to Eldon Hill

tlc, USC

Feb. 14. 39.

Dear Mr. Hill:

You ask about my use of the word VERITIST. I began to use it in the late nineties. Not being at that time a realist in the sense in which the followers of Zola use it, I hit upon the word veritist which I may have derived from Veron. In truth I was an impressionist in that I presented life and landscape as I personally perceived them but I sought a deeper significance in the use of the word, I added a word which subtended verification. I sought to verify my impressions by comparing impressions separated [by] an interval of time. I sought to get away from the use of the word realism which implied predominant use of sexual vice and crime in the manner of Zola and certain of the German novelists. For the most part, the men and women I had known in my youth were normal, hardworking and decent in word and action. Their lives were hard and unlovely, sometimes drab and bitter but they were not sexual perverts.

As a veritist, I argued that one could be as real and as true in presenting the average man and woman as in describing cases of incest, adultery and murder. I found as Whitman told me he had found in the life of the average American, a certain decorum and normality. As a veritist I recorded my perceptions.

389. to Charles Bull

tls, usc

2045 DeMille Drive
Hollywood, California

Mar. 21. 39.

My Dear Mr. Bull:

I am interested, naturally, in your enterprise altho I do not encourage attempts to make something out of my life and deeds.[1] They are too unimportant to serve such purpose as you have in mind. Two or three other men are attempting the same thing, substantially. One of the earliest is Prof. Eldon C. Hill of Miami University, Oxford Ohio. To him I have sent much material which he has promised to return to me. Much other material is in a travelling exhibit of my literary records. I am mailing you two booklets which may be of some service to you. If it seems proper and helpful you might write to Hill.

The way to do the work you have undertaken is to read all my Middle Border books, and my four volumes of literary comment. The booklet I send will give you a fairly complete roster of my titles.

With very best wishes for your thesis — irrespective of my share in it.

Hamlin Garland

1. Bull was writing his master's thesis, entitled "Hamlin Garland; A Son of the Middle Border" (Boston University, 1939). He had written to ask Garland what made him "turn to realism . . . I know that your eyes were opened to all the cruel realities of Middle Border life as you had lived it, but why would you have seen it when so many had failed to see it?" (17 March 1939, Hunt).

390. to Alexander Gaylord Beaman

tls, usc

2045 DeMille Drive
Hollywood, California

April. 17. 39.

Dear Neighbor Beaman:

The time has come for me to say that if the MYSTERY OF THE BURIED CROSSES makes any money, I will attempt to pay a part of what I owe you for your many services. Furthermore as I have no son, and no sons-in-law to aid me and as my daughters are totally unfitted to the task, I would like to have you go over my records and plan what to do with them when I check out. For this also I expect to pay for your time and advice. I have days when I feel entirely helpless. My eyes will no longer permit the strain involved in reading over and classifying this material. The time is come also for making those loans to the libraries of the Middle West and I need your practical advice in this matter.

It is disheartening to find myself in this position but Constance's lack of interest and Mary Isabel's lack of time leaves me without the help which a man of my years has a right to claim. My brother is feeble and not fitted for such work and so I turn to you for such aid as you can afford to give me for a modest rate of payment, payment which I can increase as royalty comes in.

Some day when you have the time, come over and I'll show you where my records are to be found. I am inclined to ask Greever to advise with us.[1]

I am feeling my years — all of them — this morning.
Hamlin Garland

1. Garland Greever, a professor of English at the University of Southern California, was a close friend.

2045 DeMille Drive
Hollywood, California

June. 16—39.

Dear Brooks:

I would not interest you in my mystery book if I could. You cant afford distraction from your job—not that kind of distraction. If you should come to visit us we could talk it a bit.—We are interested in seeing your son. Tell him to 'phone us so that we can have him and his wife to dinner.

I confess that I am losing interest in fiction, politics and many other matters which once engaged me. I find that seventy-nine brings a keener interest in "The Fourth Dimension." These records of Mrs. Parent's discoveries absorb a great deal of my thought—I am even talking in public on them.[1] Even if the whole business of the crosses is a hoax, it is so prolonged, so subtly carried out, so substantiated that is has something of the quality of a detective problem. On the other side lies its clairvoyant evidence which I myself have tested—and finally, if these amulets were located by the help of the ancient padres and other neophytes—we have continuing memory and character after death. I dont know why this is not a legitimate subject of inquiry. I began to study it as a young man of thirty one. I have continued its investigation during the forty eight intervening years and I am deeper in it than ever. As I let go of one interest after another I find myself concerned more deeply than ever with this ultimate mystery. It is not with me a question of religion but of biology. Life patiently builds up a body, a brain a nervous system—then comes the change called death. In the decay of the body and brain—what happens to the *me?* If an invisible identity can direct me to the exact spot where he buried a metal amulet two hundred years ago, I have a physical argument for continuing memory.—This is what I have put into my latest book without argument, leaving the verdict with the reader.—Sometime when you can afford the distraction I'd like to have you read it—or come out and I'll go all over the problem with you.

I detest the man who brags of his youth at eighty! My business is to *be* old. I admit that my world is vanishing, that I am a man forgotten, that the age has no time for oldsters. To pretend to an interest I do not feel is foolish. Like old Walt, I have not only begun to "think of time" but of my physical dissolution. That is a part of my job—All join in prayers for your continued good health—

H.G.

1. Garland contracted with the North American Film Corporation to do two educational films, each one hour or less, which would be in effect lectures. One was to be entitled "Settlers of the Middle Border," the other "The Mystery of the Buried Crosses" (Garland to Beaman, 10 May 1939).

392. to Henry Ford

tlc, Hunt

[27 June 1939]

Dear Mr. Ford:

I am in my seventy-ninth year and as I near the end of the trail, the problem of what to do with my records becomes pressing. Several libraries including the Congressional Library have invited me to donate the whole or a part of my letters and manuscripts and I have already begun their distribution. As I think of your wonderful collection of work-worn and deeply significant tools, utensils and furnishings of pioneer times, I feel that a part of my letters and manuscripts would interest the many visitors who pass through your museum. I may be mistaken about this. It may be that among so many interesting objects my exhibit would be lost. Mr. Black suggests that we might try it for a time, as a loan.

I have in mind to send M.S.S. of certain chapters in manuscript from "A Son of the Middle Border" and "Back-Trailers of the Middle Border" which deal with the pioneer life of Iowa, and with the Wayside Inn, also autographed poems relating with those pioneer days. I am to see Mr. Black some time this autumn and get his judgement as to a list of items which I shall make out. If he thinks the items of sufficient interest, he can then take the matter up with you. In this list I shall include some letters and manuscripts dealing with John Burroughs.

From newspaper reports I learn that you keep your health. I hope Mrs. Ford is equally fortunate. Mrs. Garland and I both retain a fair degree of health and strength. We walk a mile or two every day. There is a possibility that I may be able to visit Dearborn in October. I want to see the final arrangement of your collection. It was being installed when I saw it last.

Most sincerely yours,

393. to August Derleth

tls, Wis HS

2045 DeMille Drive
Hollywood, California

July. 2. 39.

Dear Mr. Derleth:

I am pleased by the commission you announce.[1] Zona Gale was my neighbor and friend for many years and I have many letters from her. I shall ask my daughter to go over my material and select those letters which have most significance and will mail them to you or copy out the lines which may aid you. We all loved that sweet and wonderfully able little woman.

I appreciate your continued interest in my book. I regret the high price of my MYSTERY OF THE BURIED CROSSES for I should like to have all my friends read it. It follows directly on my FORTY YEARS OF PSYCHIC RE-SEARCH. I tried to have Duttons issue it [at] a lesser price but they refused to consider it.[2]

If you are to begin your work on the biography in August you will need what I have soon and I shall do my best to aid you promptly.

With keen interest in your commission.
Hamlin Garland

1. Derleth had contracted to write *Still Small Voice: The Biography of Zona Gale* (1940), and had written, 29 June 1939 (Hunt), to request any letters Garland had received from Gale.

2. *The Mystery of the Buried Crosses* sold for $3.75.

394. to Van Wyck Brooks

tls, U Penn

Los Angeles

Aug 31—39

Dear Van Wyck Brooks:

A young professor is here mousing through my records on the theory that he can write a publishable thesis or biography about me—notwithstanding my warnings that he is wasting his time. I cant forbid him to go on but I have reached the point in my life where its futility weighs upon me—if futility can have weight—and I dont enjoy the thought of a young fellow spending time and money trying to make a book about me. The fact is, I have come to the conclusion that all my records except letters to me should be burned while I am alive to superintend it.

I am writing this for the reason that I value your judgement. I wish you would tell me—not as a friend but as a critic and historian—what to do about this young enthusiast, and what to do about destroying all this mass of old mss. Relatives and injudicious admirers all say "preserve every scrap of it." But why preserve a manuscript which merely presents my blunders? If I were a very successful writer or even a significant figure, the argument for preserving these records would have slight weight.

Without intent to burden you, I would like your judgement on these points. I have tons of such mss but why expose my revisions and re-revisions? There are people who collect such stuff as others collect stamps or candle-sticks but why should I furnish them with specimens? I have gone beyond any illusions about my career. Few are interested in me now and no one will be interested in me tomorrow—as Hill will find out when he tries to find a publisher for his study of me. He has been at this job for six years or more. He is a nice studious youth but with no power as a writer. He has been at this job for six years or more. He has a foolish notion that anything pertaining to me has value. Shall I burn all this material?[1]

Hamlin Garland

We are all fairly well.

1. In his reply of 10 September 1939, Brooks carefully and encouragingly replied to each of Garland's worries. After noting that he "entirely agreed with the relatives who say 'Preserve every scrap,'" Brooks pointed out the limitations of contemporary judgments of value, that Garland could not "escape a biography" because his life would soon "stand for a whole phase of American history," and that even a writer with "no power" could help to arrange the papers. Finally, addressing Garland's increasing perception that his career had been futile, that "few readers are interested in you," Brooks objected, "how can you believe this when every book about American literature has a chapter about you?"

2045 DeMille Drive
Hollywood, California

Tuesday the 12th [12 September 1939]

Dear John:[1]

I shall be seventy nine on Thursday of this week, and the Columbia Broadcasting Company is putting me on the air "in person." I am to tell the story of my "Mystery of the Buried Crosses." Unfortunately the program "Strange as it Seems" comes at 11[30] in New York and I fear none of my friends will stay awake to hear it.—I am sending a short letter to Adams which I hope he can find space for.[2] It is a condensation of my protesting letter. I confess it hurt me to have the *Times* slur my record of over fifty years of honorable service to American Literature, and it pleased me to have another sober and intelligent estimate of the book printed in the *Review* this week.[3] I sincerely believe the subject is worthy an illustrated article. I am to present it to the State Historical Society—and the State Library has made an exhibit of the book and the artifacts. The *Psychical Journal* is taking it very seriously. They feel that if a man who buried something a century ago, can come back in some way, and lead me to the place where he hid it, we have proof of continuing memory.[4] This makes these crosses, worthless in themselves, of enormous value. I can not say that I am converted to "spiritualism" but I am inclined to believe in certain unacknowledged powers of the human brain. That is why I quoted Dr. Carrell on my title-page.[5]

I should like to write an article for the *Times* along these lines.—

I am deeply interested in this problem not only because I am old but because this second great war has so depressed me that I am ready to step off into the 4th Dimension!

Your old friend
Hamlin Garland

We are going to have another wave of interest in spirit return.

1. Before becoming the editor of the *New York Times* in 1921, John Huston Finley (1863–1940) was president of Knox College in Galesburg, Illinois (1892–99), president of the College of the City of New York (1903–13), and commissioner of education for New York State and president of New York University (1913–21).

The Memoirist: 1930–1940 423

2. Garland made his address on Thursday, his seventy-ninth birthday. J. Donald Adams (1891–1968) was the editor of the *New York Times Book Review*.

3. *The Mystery of the Buried Crosses* was reviewed twice in the *New York Times Book Review*. In the first (17 May 1939, p. 27), Ralph Thompson was decidedly flippant in tone, which prompted Garland to direct a "protesting" letter to Thompson in which Garland noted that "nearly all the reviews which have since reached me have shown careful study." He went on to note that the Doheny Library, the Los Angeles Public Library, the Mission Inn in Riverside, and the State Library in Sacramento took his discoveries seriously enough to mount an exhibit of them, and he concluded by enclosing a list of "Arguments for the Authenticity of the Parent Collection of Antique Tablets and Crosses" (Garland to Thompson, 7 August 1939, NYPL). Garland also sent a letter to Finley coincident in date with the letter to Thompson (n.d., Miami U) arguing that he had been treated unfairly, and he followed up on 5 September 1939 with yet another protest to Finley (Miami U). Garland's ire prompted a second, more objective, review, which appeared as "The Buried Crosses," *New York Times Book Review*, 10 September 1939, p. 11; as well as an unsigned editorial by Finley which quoted part of this (12 September) letter and noted, "Mr. Garland's eminence in letters and unquestioned integrity will not allow any one to doubt the accuracy of his statements as to what he heard and saw" ("Hamlin Garland's Byway," *New York Times*, 20 September 1939, p. 26). In the "short letter to Adams," Garland thanks him for the thoughtfulness and fairness of the review and recounts the arguments for the crosses' authenticity (Garland to Adams, n.d., Hunt).

4. The *Journal of the American Society for Psychical Research* published a laudatory review of *Crosses* in its July issue (33 [1939]: 219–22) and "Gregory Parent's Diary" in its September issue (33 [1939]: 257–69), consisting of an account of Garland's odyssey to validate Violet and Gregory Parent's discovery of the buried crosses and excerpts from Parent's diary, contributed by Garland.

5. The quotation reads: "'We know that clairvoyants may detect hidden things at great distances.'—Dr. Alexis Carrel: *Man, the Unknown*." Carrel (1873–1944) was a Nobel Prize–winning surgeon whose widely acclaimed book, *Man, the Unknown* (1935) explained to lay readers how science would improve human life and enable people to attain a higher spiritual level.

396. to George Steele Seymour   tls, Knox

2045 DeMille Drive
Hollywood, California

December 3, 1939

Dear Mr. Seymour,

As I recall it, Barta, the printer of this first edition of "Under the Wheel," was a young commercial printer. The edition may have been only five hundred copies. It was never copyrighted and hence is not on file at the Congressional Library. I copyrighted only the titles, which was then permissible.

This play afterwards became the novel "Jason Edwards", of which a paper edition was also published. On the cover of this paper edition was the picture of an elderly man reading an advertisement of free land. This drawing was made by Miss Laura Lee, a young artist in Boston.

The Arena Press brought out an edition of five thousand paper bound copies of "Main Travelled Roads". It is probable that an edition of five hundred copies was bound in cloth, partly grey and partly blue, small twelve mo. It contained only six stories; later it was taken over by Stone and Kimball, and later still by Macmillans. In its final form, published by Harpers, it is much larger.

"The Westward March of Men" was originally printed in MCCLURES MAGAZINE under the title "Joys of the Trail". Later, with the title "Vanishing Trails", I rewrote it as a commencement address for the University of Chicago. It was first published in this form by the University Journal. Later still, under the title "The Westward March of Men", it was published by an eastern educational press, upon the recommendation, as I remember it, of Miss Stella Center, and finally, it was printed under its original title by yourself.[1]

I think this answers your questions. If there is anything else you would like to know about, write me again.

Very sincerely yours,
Hamlin Garland

1. Garland's titles are slightly inaccurate. He refers, in order, to "Hitting the Trail," *McClure's* 12 (1899): 298–304; "Vanishing Trails," *University Record* (University of Chicago) 10 (1905): 53–61; *The Westward March of American Settlement* (Chicago: American Library Association, 1927); and *Joys of the Trail* (Chicago: Bookfellows, 1935). *The Westard March of American Settlement* differs significantly from the other works in that it is a tract on pioneering with suggested readings. See also Garland to Seymour, 22 March 1937, letter 361.

397. to August Derleth

als, Wis HS

2045 DeMille Drive
Hollywood, California

Jan. 9 — 40.

Dear Mr. Derleth:

Your letter reached me too late to allow of sending my grateful appreciation of your will to lecture on my work but I am sending you something which may answer your questions and provide material for another address if you decide to make one.[1] As I approach my 80th year I find myself in the favor of so many young people that I am a bit bewildered by their letters. I infer that this is due to the realization that I am not long for residence in the Third Dimension. Whatever the cause of this change of feeling toward me, it is a pleasure to perceive it and a duty to acknowledge it.

I am sending you that "Memorial" gotten out in Aberdeen Dakota.[2] Its title sounds like the title of a funeral address but it is in fact an authentic statement — in brief — of my career which is far less significant than I once intended it to be. Two or three young men are trying to make something out of it as a theme for a doctors degree, and I have not been able to refuse them such material as they have requested from me — and I am more than willing to lend my hand to your plan. I still call myself a Wisconsin man and I am interested in all that is developing in the state. — If you feel like letting me see one of your Wisconsin books — I shall be grateful for it.

I think I sent you the booklet gotten out by Macmillans. If I did not I hope you'll let me know. It is packed with information and if you'll overlook its commercial purpose, it may be of aid to you. Some time later I shall jot down something which will partly answer the queries you included in your letter —

Very sincerely yours
Hamlin Garland

1. Derleth had noted in a letter of 6 January 1940 that he was lecturing on Garland's work to his class and that he was preparing a book on regionalism in American literature. Derleth published his study in two articles, not a book: "America in Today's Fiction," *Publisher's Weekly* 3 May 1941: 1120–25, and "American Regional Literature," *Phi Kappa Phi Journal* 22 (March 1942): 26–28. Derleth also offered to send Garland his *Wind Over Wisconsin* (1938) and *Man Track Here: Poems* (1939).

2. Garland refers to the "Hamlin Garland Memorial," part of the American Guide Series published by the Federal Writers Project (item #745).

398. to August Derleth

als, Wis HS

2045 DeMille Drive
Hollywood, California

Jan. 16 — 40

Dear Mr. Derleth:

I was touched by your finely expressed letter and am moved not only to reply to it in my own hand-writing but to send it under an air-mail stamp in order to let you know at the earliest moment, my appreciation of your lecture upon my work. It is always a surprise to me when a young man discovers something in my books worth talking about. At eighty one realizes the gulf between youth and age. It is hard to even realize that Hamlin Garland is an old man. I was "That young radical Garland" so long that my name still retains something of youth in it but alas! When I look in the glass I can make no attempt to even think young. I have been writing for over half a century and I am sending you that booklet which will prove it — if any proof is nescessary. — I shall be very pleased indeed to read the two books you name — and in partial payment for them, I am mailing you my "Roadside Meetings" which will at least have the value of answering some of your questions. There are three other volumes of this literary-log but this is the one nearest your theme — I wish I might have the opportunity of serving you coffee on my patio this summer.

Very sincerely your ancient well-wisher —
Hamlin Garland

399. to Irving Bacheller

als, USC

[after 16 January 1940]

Dear Irving:

My attitude toward age is not the conventional one. I dont believe in assuming to be younger than I am. I *believe* in being old. It's my job to be old. Growing toward eighty is a natural and inevitable process. Why mourn over it or brag about it? I will confess that having been "That young radical Hamlin Garland" so long I am shocked into a realization of my years when I am showing myself before a glass. It does not help when people say, with polite interest, "You dont [look] more than seventy" for I know I look like ninety—and feel it at times.

Why fool myself? I know that I am headed straight for the 4th Dimension and my business now is to put my house in order so that my heirs will be able to find *some* of my deeds and contracts. I am content to run parallel to nature's path. I get irritated and depressed by small things but with regard to the inevitable and cosmic, I pretend to submission.

When I was a boy on the Iowa prairie, I found much amusement as well as literature in McGuffeys school reader, and one of the poems which pleased me was called "The Three Warnings."[1] It concerned an elderly English farmer who was greatly surprised by a caller named Death. The old fellow protested that he was not old enough for the journey which Death wanted him to make.

"Im not prepared. I have a lot to do," etc.

"Very well" said Death. "You shall be warned three times—before I come again."

The old farmer settled back comfortably in his routine. He smiled, read the newspaper, tended his stock and crops—forgetting his warning altogether. So passed some fifty years. Then suddenly Death again appeared. Again the farmer begged for delay. He had not been warned. Death disputed this. He forced the old man to [acknowledge] his dimming eyesight, his gray hair, his deafness, then sternly concluded "Youve had your three sufficient warnings. So come my friend no more we'll part"—he said, and touched the farmer with his dart.

I recite this poem now with somewhat different mood. It means more to me now than it did then. I can still smile at the old fellow's admission that he "was not able to stump about his house and stable" but my amusement is tempered by the fact that I have had my three sufficient warnings. I too possess gray hair, wrinkles, and stiffened knees. I too admit failing eye-sight and recognize several other superfluous warnings—so many indeed that Death can not take me by surprise.

I have no complaint to make, no fear of the going but I confess that I feel a pang at thought [of] leaving the good old earth and the friends and relatives still surrounding me. Man is vile but the earth—despite its wars and earth-quakes is alluring. I have no religious faith and not much in way of philosophy but I still trust the majestic "frame of things."

"Standing by deaths river deep and broad—I take my chances, ignorant but un-awed!"

Hamlin Garland

1. "The Three Warnings," by Hester Lynch Thrale, was included in the memorial
edition of *McGuffey's Reader* that Garland helped edit. Garland's references to the poem
are close paraphrases. In a letter of 16 January 1940, Bacheller had noted he was planning to write a book about "keeping well and strong and happy" when one grows old,
and he had asked Garland for recollections of what people had told him. Bacheller did
not publish this book.

400. to Grace Vanamee   als, Am Acad

2045 DeMille Drive
Hollywood, California

Feb. 3—40

Dear Mrs. Vanamee:

I am very sorry indeed to learn of your accident and of your resignation from the Secretary's (Institute) desk—but as you say this may be a
good movement.[1] You were over-worked as it was. I think I wrote you of
Zulime's terrifying back-set. We thought she had left us. For two days, she
lay in a coma and could not be roused. She came out of it however and is
again able to walk and to do a little house-work—but we are two melan-
choly old people. What with the war news, our tax increases and our
burden of years we feel ready to step off into the Fourth Dimension.

I am building a house for Mary Isabel so that she will, at least, have
shelter after I am gone. She and her husband are quite helpless in a business way. I am trying also to put my affairs in order so that some of my
books and papers can be located and disposed of. We do not feel it to be
the duty of our daughters to bear our burdens and fortunately we have a
good house, a new car and money to keep them going.

You and I have worked along together for many years and I regret that
I can not be of more aid now but as I near eighty I find my usefullness to
any cause or organization almost nothing. I am quite alone out here but
the beauty of the land and climate are so gracious to me that I cant think
of going back to New York. Zulime would not survive a month of New
York winter.

My young biographer after nine years of gathering material says that he
is now writing his story. As no one else has offered to do it, I cant refuse

to let him have the material he asks for. He has not referred to a shipment
from the Academy but Ive no doubt it was made. I am still meditating
what to do with the mass of stuff I have here. I may send it to the Huntington Library—where it would be accessible to my daughters. That
Grant MS. should go to the Congressional Library, I suppose. What more
would you like to have for my record there.

Faithfully—
Hamlin Garland

1. Vanamee had written, 29 January 1940, that she had broken her foot and that she
had resigned as the assistant secretary-treasurer of the Institute due to a suggested
amendment governing elections to the Academy.

401. to Hermann Hagedorn ald, usc

2045 DeMille Drive
Hollywood, California

Feb. 21—40

Dear Hermann Hagedorn:

I have read your book of poems and find it very disturbing. It is so true,
so powerful and so poignant that I can hardly go on with it—That passage
which pictures a despairing man with his two trusting children in his
arms is intolerably piteous—His sense of their trust in "Daddy" and his
fear of failure to meet that trust, wrung my heart.[1] My daughters have
leaned on me for thirty years—"Daddy" was at hand in every time of
need, now they are losing confidence in my ability to live out the present
storm. They are women but they still keep their childish faith in me. I am
still the wonder-worker to them in much larger degree than I can justify.
I have not your faith in man or God, and so your book fills me with
despair—even of America. I am inclined to agree with Mark Twains estimate of "the damned human race." On occasion he embroidered the
phrase. You try to add a hopeful note to your savage indictment but I find
it hard to follow you in that mood. We have come a long way from my
pioneer father and my uncles. When I see the raid on Uncle Sam's pocket
book, extracting billions upon billions of dollars wrung from enterprise
in mounting taxes I am appalled. I know that my children and my grand-

children will be called upon to pay these debts so gayly piled up by our new dealers. You have put into verse this doubt, this anguish and this hopelessness. What can I do?—Nothing, except to die out of this world into "the Fourth Dimension" in hope of leaving some of this senseless confusion behind. I admire your faith but I can not share it!

Hamlin Garland

1. Garland refers to the poem "Want" in Hagedorn's *Combat at Midnight* (1940).

402. to George Steele Seymour als, Knox

2045 DeMille Drive
Hollywood, California

February—21—40

Dear Seymour:

Do not misunderstand me. I deeply appreciate your loyalty to me and I shall do my best to remain on this plane till Sept. 14—but when I consider the work and the expense involved, I am appalled.—Beaman came in a few days ago and I made my meaning clear to him. I am deeply touched by the plan and it would be possible to attend two "parties" one here on the 14th and another on the 15th in Chicago.[1] The air-ships make such things possible. I hear talk of some sort of celebration in New York but nothing definite. All depends on my vitality and Zulime's condition. That my life force is ebbing is certain. I can no longer work the whole fore-noon at my desk. Three hours is all I can stand. Do you remember the poem "The Three Warnings" by Mrs. Thrale, where death came to visit an old farmer at thirty-six—and was induced to stay his hand? As he retired he promised three definite warnings. The farmer much relieved, went about his work some forty years—forgetting all about the warnings, when death suddenly stood beside him. The old farmer looked up aghast —"So soon!"

Death replied, "So soon ye call it!" and questions Dodson who admits he's lame, and blind and deaf but still is able to stump about his farm and stable. Death strongly says, "You've had your three sufficient warnings so come my friend no more we'll part" and touched old Dodson with his dart.

I've had my warnings but I still am able to stump about my house and lot—and Death may hold his hand till Spt. 14—but I'm not betting on his clemency!

Hamlin Garland

When do you want the article?

1. Seymour was planning an eightieth birthday celebration for Garland, to be hosted by the Bookfellows in Chicago. In a letter dated 5 February 1940, Seymour asked Garland to "write something for us," presumably to be read at the celebration.

403. to Arthur E. Morgan

tls, Harvard

2045 DeMille Drive
Hollywood, California

Feb. 26. 40.

Dear Mr. Morgan: [1]

Yes, I knew Edward Bellamy and liked him but being a Henry George apostle and a Herbert Spencer individualist, I did not attend any of the Bellamy meetings. I recall him as a gentle and kindly man of most unassuming manner. I heard much of him from my great and good friend William Dean Howells and from many others of my associates. His book had an immense influence with artists and literary men and women. Mark Twain was profoundly touched by LOOKING BACKWARD.

I dont remember to have had any personal discussions with Bellamy. I fear he considered me an unregenerate anarch. I acknowledged his nobility of character but I did not believe in his methods of reform. To me he was a poet, a dreamer with a very vague emotional plan of the world's redemption.

Very Sincerely Yours,
Hamlin Garland

1. Arthur Ernest Morgan (1878–1975) published a biography, *Edward Bellamy*, in 1944, and *The Philosophy of Edward Bellamy* in 1945. At the bottom of the letter, Morgan drafted his reply to Garland: "Dear Mr Garland—May I trouble you once again? You say that 'Mark Twain was profoundly touched by Looking Backward.' Can you tell me definitely what you know on that point? I have searched every where in an effort to get some evidence that Mark Twain and Edward Bellamy were acquainted, & that Mark Twain cared for L.B. Do you know anything of their acquaintance?"

404. to George Steele Seymour and Flora Warren Seymour

tl, Knox

2045 DeMille Drive
Hollywood, California

Monday. [26 February 1940]

Dear Seymours:

Beaman is wrong. The family bible sets forth the date of my birth in my mother's hand writing as Sept. 14. If I am well enough to do fly it would be possible for me to have two celebrations, one here on the 14th and the other on the 16th in Chicago. In WHOS WHO the date is stated to be the 16th, and for a number of years I was uncertain about it. The discovery of the little old bible settled the matter.

I have the warmest wish for the success of the new book. I read LaSalle with keen interest.[1]

I am feeling pretty rocky this morning. A severe attack of indigestion has given me a touch of dizziness which is another of those warnings I wrote you about. I very seldom have any trouble with my "Little Mary" as the British call it.[2] If any publicity is given my Chicago "Show" send me a clipping. Miss Mason has just written to thank me for an extension of the exhibit.[3]

H.G.

1. Garland refers to Flora Warren Seymour's *La Salle, Explorer of Our Midland Empire* (1939).

2. "Little Mary" is British slang, now obsolete, for "stomach."

3. Rosalind Mason was a librarian at the Chicago Public Library, which exhibited a collection of Garland's buried crosses and related manuscripts. Garland had five touring exhibits of his discoveries, which appeared at over twenty-four libraries and museums across the country.

405. to Eldon Hill

al, Miami U

[ca. March 1940]

Dear Mr. Hill:

When you reach a discussion of my psychic work, I want you to understand that I regard it as a legitimate subject for literary treatment. It is not a religious subject with me nor a wholly scientific pursuit—it is an extension of my work as a writer. Put out of your mind all the religious prejudices which color so much of the psychic poetry, drama[,] fiction and history and write of my books on the subject as you would deal with a book by me on a new continent or a new school organization. For nearly fifty years it has been a part of my work as a writer and now it becomes even more important as an exploration into unexplored biology. As a man of eighty I now ask naturally without awe or sorrow "where do I go from here?"

You are free to express your own feeling on this phase of my work but it is well for you to understand that I had no sense of abandoning my skill or sincerity of purpose when I took up this subject in "The Tyranny of the Dark" and "The Shadow World"—and in 1936, I entered to write as historian and fictioneer not as a convert to a new religion or as an opponent. In truth it had become [one] of the most important subjects of my world. Even now at eighty I am neither awed nor rebellious—I am curious, just as I used to be when crossing a range into an unknown valley. Each year lessens my regret at leaving the third dimension behind for my friends and relatives are now mainly in the unknown valley—and my work is less and less valuable to the public.

If you can honestly follow me into this final exploration of mine, do so—If not I shall not complain.[1]

---

1. According to a letter from Constance Garland Harper to Eldon Hill (15 March 1940, Miami U), Garland was apparently at work on this letter but died, on 4 March, of a cerebral hemorrhage, before he was able to complete it.

Pulitzer Office, Columbia University

Braun Research Library, Southwest Museum (Charles F. Lummis Manuscript Collection, MS.1.1.1603b)

Department of Special Collections, Syracuse University Library (Archer Milton Huntington Papers)

Howard-Tilton Memorial Library, Tulane University (George W. Cable Papers, Manuscript Collection 2)

Bancroft Library, University of California, Berkeley (MTP MS 44446-A, MTP MS 34530, Banc MS 782/236 z, Box 4)

Department of Special Collections, Shields Library, University of California, Davis (Peter J. Shields Papers)

Department of Special Collections, University of Chicago Library

Special Collections Department, University of Delaware Library

Archives of the University of Illinois at Champaign-Urbana (Stuart Sherman Papers [Box 2, Records Series 15/7/21])

Rare Book Room, University of Illinois Library at Champaign-Urbana

Special Collections and Manuscripts, University of Iowa Libraries

Western History Collections, University of Oklahoma (Walter D. Grisso Collection, Box 29)

Special Collections, University of Pennsylvania (Van Wyck Brooks Papers and Theodore Dreiser Papers)

Special Collections, Doheny Library, University of Southern California

Henry Ransom Humanities Research Center, The University of Texas at Austin

Clifton Waller Barrett Library, Special Collections Department, University of Virginia (Hamlin Garland Collection, #6324)

Wagner College Library (Markham Manuscripts Collection)

State Historical Society of Wisconsin (August Derleth Collection)

Beinecke Rare Book and Manuscript Library, Yale University (Yale Collection of American Literature)

GENERAL INDEX

Page numbers in **boldface** refer to the first identification of a correspondent. Annotations are not indexed (except when titles of Garland's works appear in annotations).

summer homes, 263; buys West Salem home, 99; on Christianity, 16; on comments about his work, 75, 80, 92, 106, 113, 115, 251, 252, 254, 295, 357; and conservation, xvi, 199; death of, xviii; on dialect, 2, 23–24, 64–65, 106, 107; on disposition of manuscripts, 406, 411, 414, 418, 420, 422, 429–30; on drama, 4, 58; evaluates career, xvii, 113, 115, 267, 345–46, 369–70, 374, 380, 426; exhibit of memorabilia, 346, 347, 378, 414, 417, 433; film of, 346, 386, 389; on film adaptations, 235–36, 236–37, 240–41, 243–45, 276; on habits of writing, 154–55; on his health, 247, 250, 255, 259, 271; on inherited traits, 19, 130, 173–75; on the Ku Klux Klan, 322; on licentiousness in literature, 203, 230, 262, 263, 299, 309, 317, 319, 320, 321–22, 327–28, 349, 369–70, 375–76, 384, 387–88, 399, 405, 408; literary ambitions of, 53, 63, 89, 92, 93, 199–200, 201, 213, 217, 225, 228, 229, 233, 327–28, 404–5; literary influences of, 231, 327, 372–73, 400, 401, 403 (*see also under individual authors*); on local color, 104, 234; marriage of, 6, 125, 126, 127, 129, 282; on Midwest life, 13, 16, 95; moves to Boston, xiv; moves to California, 264, 345; moves to Chicago, 6; moves to New York, 242; and 1912 presidential campaign, 214; on peace, 330; on poetry, 372–73; on psychic matters, 188, 190, 193, 281, 346–47, 379, 384, 389–90, 390–91, 392–93, 394, 395, 410, 419, 433–34; on race, 18, 17, 173, 275, 305, 313, 314, 332; on realism, 53, 59; on reform, 68, 76, 224, 225–27; on reviews of his work, 73, 74, 89, 90, 95, 234–35, 338, 373; sells autographed books, 350, 353, 354, 355; on the single tax, 1, 54, 62, 66, 68–69, 71, 141, 325; trip to England (1899), 6, xviii; trip to England (1922), 263, 301–2, 303; trip to England (1925), 324; trip to France (1899), 6, 118–23; trip to France (1924), 313–15, 316–19; trip west (1894), 95; on veritism, 75, 416–17; and Western fiction, xiv, 5, 6; on World War I, 250, 256, 257, 258, 270, 387; on World War II, 423; on writing about Indians, 154–57; and the Yukon, 116. *See also* Garland, Hamlin, lectures given by; Garland, Hamlin, works by

Garland, Hamlin, lectures given by, xviii, xiv, 1, 3, 96–97, 129, 270, 409; to the Actors Order of Friendship, 62; on American literature, 45; in Boston, 125; "Burroughs the Man," 293 n.2; in Chicago, 92; on conservation, 189; "Dialect and Dialect Poets," 30; on the Forest Ranger, 223–24; in Kansas, 280; in LaCrosse wi, 103; "Lecture Studies in American Literature and Art," 34 n.7; "Literature of Democracy," 27, 34 n.7, 43; with Mary Isabel, 263, 303, 304; on the Middle Border, 274; at the New England Conservatory of Music, 43, 46, 47; in Philadelphia, 48; on the radio, 339, 347, 419, 423; "Song and Story," 37; on veritism, 92; in Waltham, 33, 36. *See also under individual authors*

Garland, Hamlin, works by: *Afternoon Neighbors*, xviii, 370; "The American Academy of Arts and Letters," 306 n.3; "Among the Corn Rows," 66 n.1; "Another American Play," 59 n.3; *Back-Trailers from the Middle Border*, xvii, 263–64, 335, 339, 420; *The Book of the American Indian*, xv, 5; Border edition, 298, 299; "Boy Life in the West—Winter," 82 n.1; "A Branch Road," 71 n.2; "Business" (*see* "Miller of Boscobel"); *The Captain of the Gray-Horse Troop*, xv, 132, 145 n.2, 147 n.1, 152, 154 n.2, 155, 156–57, 159, 177, 267, 380; *The Captain of the Gray-Horse Troop* (film), 240, 243, 244–45, 387; *The Captain of the Gray-Horse Troop* (play), 160, 161; *Cavanagh*, xvi, 133, 198, 199, 201; *Cavanagh* (film), 235, 241, 387; "A Common Case," 29, 415 n.2; *Companions on the Trail*, xviii, 358, 360, 363; "The Critical Problem: Action" (ms), 7 n.5, 13 n.2; *Crumbling Idols*, xii–xiii, 5, 85–86, 89, 92–93, 94, 97, 105, 130, 234, 328, 365,